NATIVE TREES, SHRUBS, AND VINES

NATIVE TREES, SHRUBS, & VINES

*A Guide to Using, Growing, and Propagating
North American Woody Plants*

WILLIAM CULLINA

of the New England Wild Flower Society

A FRANCES TENENBAUM BOOK

HOUGHTON MIFFLIN COMPANY

BOSTON   NEW YORK

2002

For information about permission to reproduce selections from this book, write to Permissions, Houghton Mifflin Company, 215 Park Avenue South, New York, New York, 10003.

Library of Congress Cataloging-in-Publication Data is available.

ISBN 0-618-09858-5

The New England Wild Flower Society and Garden in the Woods are registered trademarks of The New England Wild Flower Society.

Disclaimer
A number of the plants covered in this work have long and rich histories as medicinals. Any information about medicinal uses is provided for historical purposes only. The author, the New England Wild Flower Society, and the publisher do not in any way recommend or endorse the use of any plants here described for medicinal, culinary, or herbal use.

Book design by Anne Chalmers
Typefaces: Minion, Univers, News Gothic

Printed in the United States of America.

WCT 10 9 8 7 6 5 4 3 2 1

With love to Melissa,
my partner, friend, and
bestest plant buddy

CONTENTS

PREFACE

Lists and categories can be seductive. They organize the chaotic, myriad splinters and pieces of our world into manageable segments, understandable generalizations. In a certain sense, this is a book of lists: this plant has fingered leaves, red bark, and plum-shaped, bloomy blue fruit; that one has a stumbling, wandering habit and leaves that smell like aftershave when rolled between your fingers. But lists and categories are dangerous, too. Their neat lines and rigid boundaries let the poetry of life drip through, like sweet tupelo honey from a sandwich held too long in the hand. In the end there is something remarkable, unknowable, and infinitely grand about life that will escape every well-meaning attempt to contain it. The same toe-tingling sense of wonder that courses through all children when they see a butterfly or a dinosaur skeleton for the first time is there still in all of us.

Before I noticed ferns, before I became interested in wildflowers, I came to know trees. I spent countless hours staggering around local forests (it's hard not to stumble when you are continually craning your neck to look up) trying to learn their personalities and preferences or attempting to identify them by silhouette as we sped by on the highway. I gravi-

tated toward trees, then shrubs and vines, in part because they are so big and noticeable. You can crush a small wildflower with one misplaced boot step, but you cannot miss a big oak or pine. Trees are big, and that takes a little getting used to. When we host children from the inner core of Boston at Garden in the Woods, one of the most striking things many of them learn is that trees are *alive*. In an environment of concrete and steel, it is easy to see how children could come to believe that big things—nonhuman, non-moving things—are inanimate. But in fact I think that most of us living in early-twenty-first-century America share their tendency to view trees as less "alive" than animals. Plants don't have eyes, and they don't move around like a porpoise or a panda, but they are absolutely, genuinely, vitally alive. They have blood and veins and they move and grow, and all it takes is a few strokes of the saw blade to snuff out the life of an organism that lived for possibly centuries.

I have tried my best to write about the woody plants of North America with respect, humor, and a little bit of awe, but I look at this book as a springboard to help you along on your own voyage of discovery—in thicket and backwoods, garden and yard.

ACKNOWLEDGMENTS

Special thanks to my editor at Houghton Mifflin, Frances Tenenbaum, for her encouragement, advice, and enthusiasm. Thanks as well to David DeKing, the director of the New England Wild Flower Society (NEWFS), for allowing me the time and support to complete this project, and to Barbara Pryor, our public information director and the photo editor of this book, for the countless hours she sat staring at images. Barbara, the results speak for themselves. I'm grateful to Katherine Scott, copy editor, for her editing skills, and to my horticultural colleagues Cheryl Lowe, Tom Smarr, and Pattie Scheuring, and especially my tireless assistants, Cayte McDonough and Andrea Hartcorn, for picking up the slack while I took time off to write. I also want to thank Cayte for all her help with the native plant societies and nursery sources sections. My appreciation to Chris Mattrick for his feedback about invasive plants and Bill Brumback for his propagation advice. Many thanks to Greg Lowenberg, Bonnie Drexler, and the NEWFS Library Committee — Dorothy DiSimone, Margaret Flannagan, Ruth Nastuk, Betty Porter, Mary Walker, and Nancy Webb — for assembling and maintaining such an outstanding reference collection, which made my research incalculably easier, more thorough, and more fun than it would otherwise have been.

Thanks, too, to the Visual Images Committee for assembling such a vast collection of wonderful slides; to Melinda Dillen, Dottie MacKeen, and Laura Schaufeld for the time they devoted to labeling and cataloguing the images for this book; and to the many talented photographers who have donated their work to us at the NEWFS over the years. I am indebted to Jean Baxter, Frank Bramley, Catherine Heffron, Hal Horwitz, William Larkin, Dorothy Long, John Lynch, Walt and Louiseann Pietrowitz, Adelaide Pratt, Willa Schmidt, and Mary Walker — some of the photographers responsible for the Society's outstanding slide collection. Thanks also to the Massachusetts Audubon Society for allowing us to use slides from their Albert Bussewitz Collection of woody plant images. I am fortunate to work with a tremendously talented and dedicated group of nursery volunteers. Thanks to Helga Andrews, Christine Bogonian, Christine Cofsky, Susan Dumaine, Jeremy Franceschi, Carol Fyler, Ann Hanscom, George Hibben, Lynn Luck, Sheila Magullion, and Sara Silverstein.

Finally, a personal thanks to my parents, Trudy and William Cullina; my sister, Susan; and my brothers, Kevin and John, for their love and support. Last, but certainly not least, thanks to Melissa, for everything!

THE NEW ENGLAND WILD FLOWER SOCIETY

Established in 1900, the New England Wild Flower Society is the nation's oldest organization dedicated to the conservation of wild plants. Its founders were part of the burgeoning turn-of-the-century wilderness appreciation and "return to nature" movements that sparked the campaign for a national park system and nurtured the fledgling conservation movement. In its early years, the Society focused on educating the public through a series of publications and lectures about our native plants and the disastrous effects that large-scale wild collection combined with habitat destruction were having on wild populations.

Although the Society's principal conservation interests are in New England, many people are surprised to learn that our mission is to promote the conservation of all temperate North American flora through education, research, horticulture, habitat preservation, and advocacy. To further these goals, the Society manages four nationally recognized programs.

EDUCATION PROGRAM IN NATIVE PLANT STUDIES. Through courses, field trips, garden tours, teacher training, family programs, and publications, the Society teaches thousands of people every year about native plants and their habitats. No other botanical organization or university in the country offers such an array of educational opportunities on the topic of native plants. The Society's award-winning Certificate Program attracts hundreds of continuing education students to study field botany, ecology, and native plant conservation.

GARDEN IN THE WOODS. The Society owns and operates Garden in the Woods, the largest landscaped collection of wildflowers in the Northeast, as its botanical garden and living museum. Garden in the Woods was founded in 1931 by Will C. Curtis and Howard O. Stiles to research the science and practice the art of growing native plants. Curtis and Stiles cultivated their Garden for nearly thirty-five years. In 1965, they entrusted it to the Society. Individual gardens include Woodland Groves, the Lily Pond, the Pine Barrens, and the Western Garden. The Garden is a center for conservation horticulture, propagation, and cultivation research. Today, our nursery offers the largest selection of propagated native plants in New England.

NEW ENGLAND PLANT CONSERVATION PROGRAM (NEPCOP). The Society founded and administers this program, a collaboration among botanists, federal and state agencies, and conservation organizations throughout the New England states. It is one of the leading plant conservation collaborations in the United States. NEP-CoP's activities include rare plant monitoring, rare plant reintroductions, invasive exotic plant control, habitat restoration, and habitat management.

PLANT CONSERVATION VOLUNTEER CORPS. The Society's Volunteer Corps surveys, monitors, and acts to preserve New England's native plant communities. These well-trained, knowledgeable volunteers assist conservation organizations such as state heritage programs and land trusts as they strive to manage plant populations on public and private lands. The Plant Conservation Volunteer Corps is part of the Society's ambitious strategy to revive interest in amateur field botany as a passion and pastime.

Nationally, the Society has a long history of collaboration and leadership in order to promote the conservation of native plants. We were one of the original institutional sponsors of the Center for Plant Conservation, a collaboration of more than thirty botanical institutions in the United States dedicated to preventing the extinction of native plants. Also, the Society is a member of the American Association of Botanical Gardens and Arboreta.

We believe that one of the first acts of conservation that people can do is to nurture native plants in their own gardens. The personal experience of growing native plants seems to stimulate the desire to conserve them in their native habitats. Gardeners make some of the best conservationists.

We invite you to enjoy the exciting experience of cultivating native plants in your garden and to support plant conservation efforts in your region or state. For more information on the Society, please visit our Web site or write us at our headquarters in Framingham, Massachusetts.

New England Wild Flower Society
180 Hemenway Road
Framingham, MA 01701-2699
Phone: (508) 877-7630
Fax: (508) 877-3658
E-mail: newfs@newfs.org
Web site: www.newfs.org

NATIVE TREES, SHRUBS, AND VINES

Introduction

Plants have an ability that no animal does: they can, theoretically, live forever. An orchid living in the duff on the forest floor simply grows a complete new self each year—new roots, new stem, new leaves, new flowers. Barring some catastrophe like a systemic disease or the chomping jaws of a burrowing rodent, a herbaceous plant like the orchid can go on this way for eons like the phoenix rising anew from the ashes each spring.

Woody plants differ from herbaceous plants in that they retain the same framework from year to year, pasting on a new layer of living tissue over the dead bones of tissues past. Unlike the orchid, a shrub or tree pastes on a veneer of new tissue atop those preceding it. An old, massive oak is simply a thin, living skin stretched over a long-dead framework of supporting wood. Woody plants were the first master builders, laying down lignin and cellulose to strengthen their stems and lift their leaves higher and higher above other plants that would otherwise shade them, or browsers bent on eating them. After the invention of photosynthesis—whereby leaves manufacture carbohydrates from carbon dioxide, water, and light—the invention of wood was the next great leap forward that allowed trees and shrubs to dominate all the places where liquid water is abundant enough to nurture their lofty canopies.

Inevitably, this very woody framework that is their strength is also their undoing, as fungi, ants, and termites discover it and begin to slowly but relentlessly undermine it from within. Trees do not die quietly. Their bleached skeletons remain like whale bones on the beach long after their living skin has withered. Colonizing plants like box huckleberry and quaking aspen combine the strategies of the oak and the orchid, outliving even the most ancient woody tree by sending up new stems or trunks from

a slowly spreading root system. DNA testing has shown that individual colonies of aspen or huckleberry, which may stretch over many acres, consist of a single individual that has gradually been expanding over the last 10,000 years. Barring climate change or human interference, it could easily go on for 10,000 more!

Woody plants have been called the "bones" of the garden, and you could say the same of their role in the wild as well. They are the structure that holds everything together, both physically and aesthetically. It takes a little getting used to, planting things that will long outlive us and that we may not see reach maturity. (Rapidly growing wildflowers are much more satisfying in this regard.) In fact, it is hard to really get to know individual trees or even large shrubs because they go about their business above our heads, out of view—mysteriously. Most of the time we can catch mere hints of a tree's ongoing life processes—a falling leaf, a discarded cone, or an intricate, spotted caterpillar that has dropped from somewhere above. So planting a tree is in some senses an act of faith: faith in my own longevity maybe, faith in the future probably, faith in the power, importance, and mystery of trees certainly.

I have met very few people interested in native plants who are not also interested in the rest of life on earth. One of the things you quickly learn about woody plants is the staggering number of birds, small mammals, insects, and fungi, not to mention people, that depend on them directly for their existence. Sara Stein, the author of the *Noah's Garden* series, told me recently of her unrestrained delight upon finding pipevine swallowtail butterfly caterpillars feeding on the Dutchman's pipe she planted in her yard. Truly, if you plant it, they will come. It is with the same sense of satisfaction that I watch

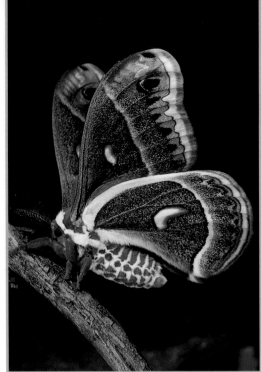

(LEFT) *A greater gray tree frog* (Hyla versicolor) *on white oak* (Quercus alba). *The mottled skin of this charming little frog has evolved to closely mimic the bark of certain trees. If the trees are cut down, the frog has nowhere to hide. You can hear the shrill, bird-like call of H. versicolor echoing through forests across eastern North America, especially after a warm summer rain.*

(RIGHT) *Many insects rely on native plants for food and shelter. The cecropia moth* (Hyalophora cecropia), *one of our largest and most spectacular moths, eats little as an adult, but its young feed voraciously on a variety of native trees. Look for the thumb-sized, mint green caterpillars on cherries and maples in late summer. Planting native trees and shrubs brings beauty to your yard in many ways.*

migrating birds feeding ravenously on the winterberry holly I planted out back near the terrace or bees buzzing around my sweet pepperbush. So, planting a tree, or vine or shrub is also an act of faith in the marvelous complexity of life — a complexity that is impossible to really comprehend but truly awesome to behold. Go plant a tree.

What Is a Native Plant?

For the purposes of this work, "native" means plants growing in North America prior to European settlement, and the term "woody plant" means any species with at least a woody (or lignified) trunk or base. The use of native plants in landscaping has become very politicized in recent years, and this is unfortunate. Like the noted writer-philosopher Wendell Berry, I am suspicious of movements, and do not want to see the enjoyment and appreciation of our wonderful flora needlessly polemicized under the auspices of a native plant *movement*. Therefore, I think both the term "native" and some of the reasons for choosing to grow these plants need further clarification.

It is natural for us humans to think of time in terms of our own life spans, and it is certainly understandable that we see organisms that live and die over longer intervals as having an air of permanence. A Douglas fir that has lived 1,000 years is incomprehensibly old to us, and to think, further, of the land itself as having a life span is nearly impossible. In geological time, 1,000 years is roughly equivalent to 10 min-

utes in the life span of a person. In this sort of relative time, it has been about two years since the age of the dinosaurs and about two hours since the last Wisconsin glaciers retreated north. If we could only view the earth with some sort of super-time-lapse photography for a few minutes, geological time would be understandable as the powerful dance of continents, mountains, ice, and water, where forests ebb and flow like waves on a beach and ancient trees are mere momentary bubbles in the changing surf. With this sort of perspective it becomes clear that what we see in the wilds at this particular moment in time is but a split-second-long freeze frame in a much larger process, and to draw too many conclusions about particular elements in this composition without putting them into a geological context is a dangerous proposition. This becomes particularly important when one is discussing rarity and extinction or even the concept of what is a native plant. In geological time, a plant is native somewhere only as an airplane's transient vapor trail is native to a particular place in the atmosphere. Species are always in a state of flux, advancing and receding, evolving and disappearing, their presence in any one place only transitory. Even the land itself is constantly moving, shifting, and recombining. How can we then say that anything is native anywhere? It is equivalent to taking a photograph of a busy street and from then on assuming that these people caught in mid step have always resided on this bit of pavement and will always continue to, unless some great catastrophe intervenes. To argue this point would be an exercise in futility.

The important point, then, is not simply what it means to be native, but what possible consequences

Coast redwood (Sequoia sempervirens) *with sword-fern* (Polystichum munitum) *understory. The magnificent redwoods are the dominant plant in the strip of land called the redwood belt along the northern California and southern Oregon coast. Once these trees grew over a much wider range, but because of climatic and geological change they are now restricted to this band of cool, foggy habitat.*

displacing a particular species from a particular place may have on the ecosystem as a whole. This is the key argument for what ecologists call the preservation of biodiversity. Individual species do not exist in a vacuum—the actions of one species radiate outward like ripples on a pond, affecting many others. For example, say the eggs of an insect that feeds on hemlock trees are transported halfway around the globe by some freak weather event (or with human assistance). The hemlocks in the new region have never experienced this pest, have no defenses against it, and begin to die out over much of their range. As the range of the hemlock recedes, so too do the ranges of the fungi that feed on its wood, the birds that feed on its seeds, the caterpillars that consume its needles, and so on. The gap left in the forests by the death of these trees allows the advance of other trees that could not grow in the shade of the hemlock, and as this may well have been the climax tree in the forest succession of the region, the whole life cycle of the forest itself is altered. Should the diversity of life be great enough, other organisms that depend on these advancing species will move forward as well, and a few may eventually adapt to feed on the hemlock pest itself, reversing the tide and restoring some kind of balance. In a healthy ecosystem, such disturbances can over time actually increase biodiversity, and the more species there are in a particular region, the more flexible and proactive the whole ecosystem will be. Just as it is easier to write poetry with a vocabulary of 10,000 words as opposed to 200, so too will a large number of species be more responsive to change and able to restore balance after disturbance or insult. The elimination of biodiversity dams this flow, so to speak — the water

still trickles by, but the salmon cannot swim and the bears cannot feast, the dragonfly nymphs have less to feed on and it is hard to say whether even the quality of the mud doesn't change for the worse. More than any other species on the planet, we humans have the ability to shape our environment. I firmly believe that if we all decide to make an effort to restore some of the local plants to our landscapes, we will in no small way help make our own piece of the world a richer, more diverse, and by consequence a heathier place. This is not politics; it is simple truth.

How to Use This Book

Three years ago, when I decided to write *The New England Wild Flower Society Guide to Growing and Propagating Wildflowers of the United States and Canada,* I did so with the conviction that there was a vital need for a comprehensive guide to the culture, personalities, ecology, and propagation of these plants. But wildflowers are only part of the story. What about trees, shrubs, and vines? There is certainly more information available on native woody plants than on their herbaceous companions, but it tends to be either regional in focus or written in outline or table format. So I present to you here the companion to my book on wildflowers: a comprehensive reference on woody plants, which I hope will be useful for the novice and expert, gardener and naturalist alike, with information presented in a style that is approachable and easy to read but still informative and accurate. The plants are arranged alphabetically by genus, each entry beginning with an overview that includes anecdotes and relevant information to serve as an introduction to the group. This is followed by notes regarding basic cultural advice, garden uses, and, if relevant, the plant's importance for particular wildlife. Each entry concludes with a list of representative species and their particularities. General cultural information and detailed notes on propagation are in a separate section at the end of the book.

I have sought to include woody plants from all of temperate North America so that you can select species that are well suited to your individual climate, light conditions, and soil. While I encourage you to grow and appreciate the plants of your area, I also know that we all as gardeners like to seek out the challenge of something new and different, so whenever possible I have included information to aid you in growing a particular plant successfully outside its native range.

Latin Names: Family, Genus, and Species

I realize that Latin is no one's first language, and it can be a bit ponderous to use if you are not used to it. I have liberally used Latin in the text, not to impress you with my erudition, but because it really is valuable to know the Latin names and to become comfortable using them, for two reasons. First, common names are often wonderful and poetic, but many common names, like maple, are generic, so it is diffi-

cult to know which plant someone is referring to. Even more confusing are names like ironwood or sage, which get applied to multiple genera. Second, the Latin binomial name can tell you a great deal about a plant because it is part of a system of classification based on a plant's familial or evolutionary relationships and individual characteristics. The plant kingdom has been split into categories and subcategories on the basis of characteristics of their vasculation, seeds, reproductive structures, and other features, starting with the most global categories and working down to the most specific. This classification system works as follows:

There are two divisions in the plant kingdom. The first, Pteridophyta, includes all the plants such as ferns and mosses, also known as bryophytes. These are plants that reproduce without flowers or seeds, relying instead on spores. The second division is the Spermatophyta, or seed plants, which encompasses most of the plants now on earth; they are more recently evolved than the Pteridophyta. The Spermatophyta are divided next into gymnosperms and angiosperms. Gymnosperm means "naked seed" — the ovules, or eggs, are not enclosed in an ovary. In this group are all of the conifers and a few related plants. Angiosperm means "covered seed," because these evolved coverings or fruits for their ovules or seeds. This is the biggest group of plants alive today. The angiosperms are next divided into two classes:

the monocots, plants with only one cotyledon (the first, or embryonic, leaf), and dicots, which have two cotyledons. Among the monocots are grasses, lilies, orchids, irises, palms, bromeliads, sedges, and a few others, so it is clear that they are pretty successful evolutionarily. The monocots are a personal interest of mine. However, most of the plants we work with are dicots, a large and highly successful group.

Both the monocots and dicots are subdivided into a series of families. A family is a fairly manageable grouping of plants that share certain recognizable characteristics. (All family names end in "aceae." This is a nomenclatural convention that makes it easy to tell a family name from a genus or species name.) The members of the orchid family (Orchidaceae) are monocots in which the sexual parts are united into a structure called a column; the composites (Asteraceae), are dicots with flowers aggregated into distinct daisy-type inflorescences. It is very helpful to know the family a certain plant belongs too, as it gives many clues, especially regarding its propagation and habits. Certain families, like the Ericaceae and Rosaceae, have a disproportionate number of wonderful garden plants, and knowing

this will help you narrow your search for new possibilities.

Families are further subdivided into genera (genus is the singular form). A genus is a smaller grouping of plants with very similar characteristics. Oaks are in the genus *Quercus*, honeysuckles in the genus *Lonicera*, and firs in the genus *Abies*. Though beeches and oaks are in the same family, they have been split into separate genera because they differ anatomically and cannot interbreed. Conveniently, plants within a genus share many of the same characteristics, so I have used this as the organizing principle of the book.

Genera are further divided into species. A species is a group of genetically very similar plants or animals that are distinct from other species in the genus. Humans are a species—*Homo sapiens*—that is distinct from other (now extinct) species in the genus *Homo*, such as *Homo erectus*. The Latin binomial (two-name) system consists of the genus name, capitalized, and the species name, written lower case. The genus name and species name are always italicized. The binomial system is sort of like our system of phone numbers, with area codes and exchanges,

Franklinia (Franklinia alatamaha), *like the camellias and stewartias, belongs to the horticulturally desirable tea family* (Teaceae). *The hard seed capsules form in late fall, overwinter on the tree, and finish developing the following summer, finally cracking open above and below to release the seeds.*

Common witch-hazel (Hamamelis virginiana) is one of only two native species in the genus. Striking flowers decorate its branches in fall just as the leaves are turning and dropping. Spring witch-hazel (H. vernalis), blooms in winter, but occasionally the bloom periods of the two species overlap. If they are growing near each other, hybrid offspring with intermediate form and blooming habit may result.

which allow for a great many possible combinations. Thus *Fraxinus velutina* and *Quercus velutina* are two very different plants with the same specific epithet. Knowing that *velutina* means "velvety" tells you something about the plants too. With plants, the separations between species are usually more blurred than with animals. This means that you cannot assume that two plants are of the same species if they produce fertile offspring. Though you can tell from just looking that *Ilex glabra* is different from *I. opaca*, a species is an artificial construct, and plants are always in a state of flux and evolution. (Note that a repeated genus name is often abbreviated, as in the preceding example—*I. opaca* rather than *Ilex opaca*.)

When a plant occurs over a wide range or in geographically isolated areas, often there are distinctive races, called subspecies (abbreviated ssp.), which are judged to be too similar to be separate species, but are distinct enough from each other to be recognizable. *Erigeron chrysopsidis* ssp. *brevifolius* (meaning "short-leaved") is slightly different from *E. chrysopsidis* ssp. *austiniae* (meaning from Austin, Texas). More commonly, there are minor variations within a species—like flower color, size, level of hairiness—that are not extreme enough to be given a subspecies designation. These are noted as varieties (abbreviated as v. or var.). Botanically speaking, a variety represents some consistent, natural, and minor variation that occurs within a given population of the species. In practice, the term "variety" is often confused and

applied to all sorts of things, both horticultural and botanical. *Juniperus virginiana* var. *glauca* is a blue-needled form of juniper found growing with populations of green-needled forms. *Chrysogonum virginianum* var. *australe* is a larger, clumping type of the species *C. virginianum,* or goldstar. The key here is that a variety is something that differs from the "typical" species in some relatively minor way. By analogy, people with red hair could be *Homo sapiens* var. *aurantiaca* (meaning "orange"). Except for this minor difference, they are just like everyone else in the species. The term "variety" was intended to refer to natural or wild variants, but horticulturists began to use it also to refer to cultivated strains that appeared or were bred in gardens. To keep wild and human-selected variants separate, the term cultivar was developed. A cultivar is a clone or seed strain selected for a particular trait or traits. The cultivar name is written in roman type, with single quotes: *Hydrangea quercifolia* 'Snowflake'. There are also cultivars of varieties or subspecies. A human cultivar might be *Homo sapiens* var. *aurantiaca* 'Woody Allen'. *Chrysogonum virginianum* var. *australe* 'Allen Bush' would be a cultivar of the variety *australe* selected for vigor and long bloom. The key is the single quotes: if you see *Chrysogonum* 'Allen Bush' in a catalog, this is shorthand for the particular cultivar I just mentioned and will be exactly like all the other 'Allen Bush's out there (unless a careless nursery person mixed up their labels).

When two species hybridize or interbreed naturally in the wild, the offspring's binomial is written with an ×, to signify that it is of hybrid origin. So when two hawthorn species, say *Crataegus crusgalli* and *C. succulenta*, hybridize, they produce a new species, *Crataegus × nuda*. Hybrids made by humans are not usually given a new species name but are written with an ×. An example is *Coreopsis ×* 'Moonbeam', a tickseed cultivar of hybrid origin.

Taxonomy

Taxonomic name changes are a common and often (to gardeners) frustrating result of ongoing research in the field of plant classification. The system of plant classification is in a constant state of flux as old information is clarified and new research tools uncover hidden relationships or differences. However, I am cognizant as well of the meaning names take on beyond the confines of taxonomic research. Names, like all language, are conventions that allow us to share ideas and concepts, and thus take on a life of their own whose importance should not be minimized. Therefore, though I sympathize with the goals of taxonomists, I am reluctant to embrace every new name change and revision that comes along, because I think these need time and debate within the professional botanic community before they are accepted, and even more time in the horticultural community before they are wholly adopted. I have tried to indicate where I have used a new name as well as where I have declined to—not out of obstinacy but out of a desire for clarity based on consensus and tradition.

The primary authorities I used for both Latin and common names are Morin et al., *Flora of North America;* Gleason and Cronquist, *Manual of Vascular Plants of the Northeastern United States and Adjacent Canada;* Kartesz, *A Synonymized Checklist of the Vascular Flora of the United States, Canada, and Greenland;* and Hitchcock and Cronquist, *Flora of the Pacific Northwest.* Complete references for all sources cited in the text can be found in the Bibliography, page 338.

Pronunciation of Latin Names

Words communicate information, and I believe there is no right or wrong way of pronouncing them as long as the information comes across. Latin, like any language, has certain rules of grammar, and botanical Latin has evolved from it. However, whether you pronounce *Chamaecyparis* as "kam-ay-sip-AIR-iss" or "kame-ee-SIP-ar-iss," people will understand, rules or no rules. With this in mind, I have given suggested pronunciations, based on horticultural convention, in parentheses for each genus, with the accented syllable in capital letters.

The Genus Entries

Each genus entry has introductory text, followed by four sections: Culture, Uses, Wildlife, and Propagation.

CULTURE: This section is intended to give a quick idea of how hard or easy it is to grow the plants in the genus and specific requirements (such as transplanting times and soil type), to help you decide if it is appropriate for your conditions. If individual species are quite different from the rest of the genus, I try to single them out here or in the species descriptions. I have avoided pointing out every possible pest or disease that might afflict the genus, mentioning only those serious enough to threaten the health of well-sited, otherwise vigorous individ-

Carolina silver-bell (Halesia tetraptera), foreground, and Canada redbud (Cercis canadensis), background, light up the spring woodland understory at Garden in the Woods.

(LEFT) *Redbuds are fairly easy to propagate from seed, and even young seedlings flower profusely.*

(BELOW) *Bumblebee on a crabapple (Malus sp.). Animals and insects depend on native trees and shrubs, but the plants depend on the animals, too. The pollination service this bumblebee provides while gathering nectar and pollen for its young will result in a good crop of crabapple fruits later in the year. Birds and mammals that feed on the fruits will in turn disperse the seeds.*

uals. See the chapter on propagation (page 261) for more comprehensive information.

USES: Here I briefly list some of the possible situations and uses the particular genus is suited for (for example, shade tree, hedge, groundcover, soil stabilization), again to give you some ideas, but not to limit your own imagination. See also "Native Trees, Shrubs, and Vines for Various Sites and Uses" on pages 303–311.

WILDLIFE: One of the strongest reasons for using locally native plants is their inestimable value to myriad nonhuman organisms that have evolved with, and come to depend on, these plants for food and shelter. There is not a great deal of information available about plants' relationships with specific beetles, moths, fungi, or bacteria, but there is more on their benefits to birds, mammals, and butterflies, and so I have concentrated on the latter groups. Butterflies in particular are fascinating not only because they are beautiful and well studied and documented, as compared to moths or fungi, but also because their larvae often depend on just a few species or genera of native plants for food. Planting a pipevine and watching the pipevine swallowtails show up in your yard where before there were none fosters one of the most direct and powerful connections between your own action—planting this native species and not a nonnative vine—and the benefit to biodiversity of allowing a species to reproduce in an area where it formerly could not. I like to think of butterflies as the poster children for hands-on efforts to increase the biodiversity in your own backyard, though they represent just the tip of the iceberg as far as the total number of native species that might benefit in some way when you plant a pipevine, American beech, or California sycamore.

PROPAGATION: I realize that not everyone is interested in propagation— but you should be, you really should be! Accordingly, I have organized the propagation information in a table that begins on page 277. Under the genus description in the main body of the text, I have briefly indicated the general ease or difficulty of propagating from seed or cuttings for the genus as a whole. The four categories are easy (can be propagated by a beginner with little specialized equipment), moderately easy (some experience required, but again, requiring little specialized equipment), moderately difficult (requires experience, specialized equipment, or is slow to propagate), and difficult (challenging even for an expert with specialized equipment).

The Species Entries

Each species entry provides information in the following categories: Zones, Soil, Native to, Size, and Color. This is followed by a general description of the species.

ZONES: I have based winter-hardiness on the revised USDA Plant Hardiness Zone Map (pages 336–337). The map breaks down North America into a series of zones, from 1 to 10, experiencing gradually colder average minimum winter low temperatures. The coldest zone is Zone 1; the warmest, Zone 10. A hardiness zone indicates the areas where the average minimum winter temperatures in a given year fall between a certain range. For example, Garden in the Woods, in Framingham, Massachusetts, lies in USDA Zone 6, where average winter minimums are –10 to 0° F, though in many years we have lows well above zero and once in a great while there are years where they fall below –10° F. For each of the featured species, I have included a hardiness range that I have arrived at on the basis of personal experience, references such as Dirr's *Manual of Woody Landscape Plants*, and the natural range of the plant. I include an upper and lower zone limit for each

plant, the lower limit (smaller number) being the coldest zone in which it will grow and the upper being the warmest limit it can tolerate. This warmer limit needs further explanation. When I state a plant's range as Zones 4–7, I mean to indicate not only its cold tolerance, but also its unsuitability for gardeners in most of Zones 8–10, where summers are too long and warm for the plant to thrive. (An exception is the Pacific coast, which benefits from a cool maritime climate where both winters and summers are mild.) In some cases, I have included a zone in parentheses—for example, Zones (4)5–7—to indicate that a particular species may be more cold (or heat) tolerant if sited carefully.

I have found hardiness ratings to be a useful general guide when selecting plants to try, but please keep this information in perspective. There is much more to determining a plant's hardiness in a particular situation than simply its tolerance of cold. Other climatic factors include the amount of annual solar radiation, the altitude, the average relative humidity, patterns and amounts of rainfall and snowfall, reliability of snow cover, average summer high and low temperatures, and length and severity of extreme hot and cold temperatures. Prolonged temperatures

The vase-shaped silhouette of American elm (Ulmus americana, right) is distinctive even from a great distance. It is winter-hardy in Zones 3 through 9—essentially all of the United States and southern Canada.

Devil's club (Oplo-panax horridus) *is a shade-adapted under-story plant. Its large, thin leaves are designed to capture the dim light that filters through the upper tree canopy in the dense coniferous forests of the Pacific Northwest. Don't plant devil's club in the sun, which will damage the leaves.*

below 20° F or above 90° F are much harder for many plants to endure than a brief chill or heat wave. Furthermore, factors like the windiness of the site, the freeze-and-thaw patterns and depth of soil frost, and seasonal day length at a particular latitude all play a part in determining a plant's hardiness. So even though Sable Island, Nova Scotia; Cape Cod, Massachusetts; Raleigh, North Carolina; Albu-querque, New Mexico; and Juneau, Alaska, are all within USDA Zone 7, they have vastly different cli-mates and it is rare to find a plant that will thrive in all of them. Plant hardiness is a subject on which I could easily write a book, but rather than developing more sophisticated hardiness ratings, I think it is simply far less complicated to grow the plants native to your area whenever possible and, further, to seek out genotypes that originate nearby if you can. An *Acer rubrum* from Florida will likely grow better in Georgia than one originating in Maine. If you want to grow plants from farther afield, look first for

species with ranges that are close to yours in latitude or longitude. A plant from southern New Mexico will have a better chance in Georgia than Wisconsin, and a gardener in Alberta will be more likely to over-winter plants from Saskatchewan than New Brunswick. Pay close attention to soil recommenda-tions and remember that a healthy, established plant has the best chance of survival.

After the hardiness zone in the species entry is the preferred sun exposure. "Sun" means full sun, or at least six hours of direct sun daily in midsummer; "part sun" means two to five hours of direct sun and the rest of the day in shade (this sun does not have to come all at once, as long as the total exposure is at least two hours); and "shade" means less than two hours of direct sun. Granted, sunlight is difficult to quantify like this. As you get closer to the equator, the sun becomes more intense, so gardeners in the Deep South can accommodate plants in shade that can grow happily only in full sun in the north. Where I have given a range, say "sun to part sun," assume that in southern Mississippi the plant may benefit from some afternoon shade, whereas in Quebec, it will likely require full sun. Shade is even more difficult to quantify, as it represents a whole range of light from nearly full sun to almost darkness. There are few plants that will grow in what I call deep shade — the shade found beneath dense evergreens or in the small spaces between tall buildings. By "shade" I mean to indicate high or open shade, the kind you find on the north side of a building open to the sky or under a broken forest canopy where the tree limbs begin 20 to 30 feet above the ground. In this type of shade, if you pass your hand over the plant it should cast a visible shadow. We regularly limb up the trees in our woodland — raise the roof, so to speak, by cutting off lower limbs, because this favors the growth of most shade plants. Sometimes I have used the term "light shade," and by this I mean a spot that receives maybe an hour or two of direct sun or dap-pled sun for most of the day.

SOIL: Finding plants to suit your soil or vice versa is one of the keys to successful gardening. Most horti-cultural works, including this one, greatly simplify the classification of soils for the sake of brevity — and, frankly, because we have much to learn about the interrelationship of plants and soil. In the wild, certain species are often associated with particular soil types, like sands or clays, or soils derived from certain minerals like serpentine or limestone rock. Other plants are generalists and grow on a wide vari-ety of substrates. Fortunately, most woody plants are fairly accommodating if you can provide a soil with-in a certain range of water-holding capacity, pH, and fertility. The Soil section for each featured species provides basic moisture ranges as follows:

"Wet" means a soil with a high water table, where standing water is visible within one foot of the surface when you dig down with a shovel. Typically, the water table fluctuates during the season, and periodic standing, or surface, water is tolerated by most wetland plants. Obviously wetlands are sensitive ecosystems important to wildlife as well as to many plants, so if you have this type of soil, be aware that your state and local authorities may have strict regulations and guidelines regarding wetland disturbance or alteration. If your wetland area has been damaged, restoring it with native flora is one of the most satisfying and beneficial things you can do for your local ecosystem.

"Moist" means a soil where the water table is at least 1 foot below the surface, but it is a soil that never dries out completely, or only for brief periods. The soil 2 to 6 inches below the surface should be cool and damp to the touch. Obviously, this is an ideal soil for most plants and one that in practice is difficult to find. We all have wet and dry years, but think of this as an average condition. Many gardeners rely on occasional supplemental irrigation to keep soils evenly moist, but please consider more drought-tolerant alternatives if you find that you constantly need to water. The addition of organic matter and a

(ABOVE) *Hobblebush* (Viburnum lantanoides) *is a true shade-loving shrub, with large, crinkly leaves to catch any light that penetrates the tree canopy above. It is also one of the most interesting shrubs for fall color; the leaves pass through shades of burgundy, pink, lime green, pale yellow, and brown before dropping off.*

(LEFT) *Western desert soils contain a large proportion of coarse sand and gravel, which allow water to drain through very quickly. Plants adapted to these soils have little tolerance for waterlogged conditions around their trunk and roots.*

Mighty Sitka spruce (Picea sitchensis) *growing in the temperate rainforests of the Pacific Northwest establish themselves more readily on fallen logs than on the forest floor. These "nurse logs" provide the young seedlings with moist, well-drained conditions and higher light levels than they might receive on the floor below. Even after centuries, trees growing in a row still reveal that all once germinated on a single fallen log.*

good layer of mulch will help hold water and cool the soil as well.

"Dry" soils feel dry to the touch a foot or more below the surface for at least part of the year. Often these soils are moist or wet in winter and spring and dry over the course of the summer. This is a common condition in many gardens, and fortunately there is a host of native plants adapted to dry soils that are excellent alternatives to a dependence on irrigation.

Plant roots need oxygen as we do, and certain plants, especially those from dry, sandy soils and alpine environments, will easily suffocate if a soil holds too much water. A "well-drained" soil contains a high percentage of sand or gravel, which promotes air exchange and sheds water quickly. "Moist, well-drained" soils strike a balance between air exchange and water retention. They have a good balance of organic material and grit but require regular rainfall or irrigation. "Dry, well-drained" soils are gritty enough to shed water even during times of rain. A heavy clay or gumbo soil would not be considered well-drained, even if it is dry.

By "acid" or "acidic" I mean soils with a pH below 5.5; "alkaline" means a pH above 6.5. Most trees and shrubs can be accommodated in soils with a pH between 5.5 and 6.5, so I have mentioned only the exceptions. For more detailed discussion of soils and pH, please see the Soil section under "Ecological Gardening," page 17.

NATIVE TO: Here I supply information on the plant's habitat and range. The typical habitat a particular species prefers, for instance, swamps and wet prairies, gives you clues as to where you can best accommodate it in your own garden. I find this information extremely valuable when trying to place a plant or choose species for a given location. The range, for instance, "Wisconsin to Alberta south to Texas and Missouri," is a very generalized range for the plant. If you drew lines on a map of North America connecting these areas, it would roughly contain the range of the species. Therefore, in this example, you might expect to find the plant in a suitable habitat in Minnesota and Oklahoma, but not New Mexico or Nova Scotia. Of course this does not necessarily mean that the plant could not thrive in a garden in Nova Scotia or New Mexico or, conversely, that it occurs within every state within the range.

I compiled habitat and range information from a number of the sources listed in the bibliography, especially Gleason and Cronquist, *Manual of the Vascular Plants of the Northeastern United States and Adjacent Canada;* Hitchcock and Cronquist, *Flora of the Pacific Northwest;* Radford, Ahles, and Bell, *Manual of the Vascular Flora of the Carolinas;* Morin et al., *Flora of North America,* vols. 1 and 2; Cronquist et al., *Intermountain Flora;* Steyermark, *Flora of Missouri;* Martin and Hutchins, *A Flora of New Mexico;* Munz, *A California Flora; Hortus Third;* and the Great Plains Flora Association, *Flora of the Great Plains.*

SIZE: The height given is the average height under cultivation. A wide height range—say 20–60 feet—usually indicates that the plant height varies depending on conditions. Some species (*Abies grandis,* for example) can attain a great height in the wild; in such cases I include that height in parentheses just as a matter of interest, not as a realistic reflection of what to expect in cultivation. The figure given for width is the plant's expected width within 5 to 25 years in the garden, depending on the plant's rate of growth and whether it is a long-lived tree or shrub. This figure should give an idea of necessary spacing. Again, I have occasionally included a third number in parentheses to indicate potential size of very large wild individuals. Most vines vary greatly in both height and width, depending on how they are supported.

COLOR: I have tried to be as detailed as possible about flower color. Many entries list a range, say from violet to purple or white, that you might find within the species as a whole. For conifers, whose flowers are enclosed in cones, not petals, I give the cone color at the time of flowering. Similarly, for plants that produce catkins (birches, for example), I give the color of the catkins. As for flowering season, I list the time of year rather than specific months, since the weather month by month varies greatly from region to region. If your spring lasts from early March until late May (aren't you lucky!) then a flowering time of late spring would be mid to late May.

(LEFT) *Tulip tree* (Liriodendron tulipifera) *is one of the tallest trees in the eastern United States, typically ranging from 70 to 120 feet when mature. Occasionally an individual in a protected valley may top out at 175 feet! In the text, such an unusual height range is given as "70 to 120 (175) feet," with the number in parentheses indicating the extreme.*

(RIGHT) *Though its yellow-green flowers are barely noticeable in spring, the blazing fall color of the sugar maple* (Acer saccharum) *is impossible to miss.*

❧ Statement on Wild Collecting ❧

THE NEW ENGLAND WILD FLOWER SOCIETY originated in response to unrestrained plant collecting that was devastating populations of certain vulnerable ferns, club mosses, and woodland wildflowers. Although collection of plants by individuals can damage local populations, the commercial collection of wild plants for the nursery trade poses much more of a threat. Short of direct monitoring, there is never any assurance that wild collection is not depleting local populations beyond their capacity to regenerate. The New England Wild Flower Society strongly recommends purchasing propagated plants and strongly recommends against purchasing any wild-collected plants.

Just as a rise in the demand for fish has nearly exterminated all the commercial fish species of the North Atlantic, so too the increasing popularity of native plant gardening threatens the health and stability of wild populations everywhere. The vast majority of plants sold today are nursery-propagated (grown from seed or cuttings/divisions of nursery stock), but the slow-growing woodland and bulbous species are especially vulnerable and are still harvested in unconscionably high numbers. These include many of the lilies and lily relatives such as trilliums, mariposa lilies, and trout lilies, bloodroot, bluebells, hepaticas, lady-

slippers, and gingers, to name a few. Some shrubs, like rosebay rhododendron, are routinely cut back, dug, and sold as "cut-offs" for a fraction of the price charged for nursery-raised plants.

Forestry practices that put maximum profit above the health and persistence of ecosystems are equally disturbing. The mindless cutting of our last stands of old-growth timber and the replacement of species-diverse wild forests with genetically engineered, industrial forest monocultures makes about as much sense to me as cutting off your foot when you can't get your boots untied. The only way to stop this depredation is to eliminate the demand. When buying woodland plants, balled and burlaped shrubs or trees, or even lumber, ask your supplier about their source. If the supplier is unsure or if the price seems too good to be true, look somewhere else. Be skeptical of supposedly "rescued" plants (plants dug from areas about to be developed or paved over). I know from personal experience of unscrupulous collectors who market supposedly rescued plants actually dug from safe, healthy populations. While I hate to see plants being destroyed under a bulldozer, the term "rescued plants" is too open to interpretation and abuse at this point to be anything more than a loophole for disreputable collectors.

Ecological Gardening

The term "ecological gardening" describes an environmentally friendly way to grow plants. Traditional gardening can involve tremendous labor and expense to modify an existing site to accommodate plants that may be unsuitable and require extensive resources in maintenance to keep the plants going. Certainly all gardens need some annual care—that is precisely what makes them gardens and not wild areas. However, there is no question that it is far easier in the long run on both you and the environment if you make it a policy whenever possible to find plants to fit the site rather than trying to make a site fit unsuitable plants.

The central purpose of this book is to show you the possibilities that abound in our native flora so that you can choose plants that are both appealing *and* adapted to the climate and soils of the region in which you live. I have been frustrated myself by the lack of good information available on native trees and shrubs. With few choices in plants, you inevitably have to spend time and expense modifying your site to fit the needs of the available plants. Of course, if you have a place where "absolutely nothing will grow," do not expect natives to fare much better than more exotic plants. Fortunately, such situations are rare if you take the time to consider your conditions and plan accordingly.

A basic understanding of the fundamental, interrelated environmental factors that determine which plants will grow where, combined with the ability to recognize them and choose plants accordingly, is all you really need to be an excellent horticulturist. The paragraphs on cultivation for each genus focus on narrowly targeted advice. This section on cultivation, in contrast, is a brief introduction to the fundamentals of plant biology and ecology. I intend it as a sort of prologue as well as an attempt to explain some of the reasons behind typical gardening advice.

Plants live under the restraints of their environment just as we all do. The important limiting factors for plant life are the availability and quality of light, soil (which includes its physical structure, fertility, and moisture-holding capacity), water, and temperature. Matching plants to a particular set of these conditions is the essence of good gardening, whether you choose to call it ecological or not.

Certain plants are especially good at growing in a specific combination of environmental constraints, such as full sun in sandy, dry soils with temperatures that are hot during the summer and mild during the cloudy winter, when most of the rainfall occurs. This combination is a fairly harsh one for plant life, and those species that can survive in it do so mainly by becoming specialists, with a physiology, anatomy, and life cycle finely tuned to get the most out of a limiting environment. For example, cacti have been able to thrive in extreme environments by losing their leaves and evolving water-holding stems, and deep roots. They are limited to certain rigid sets of environmental conditions by this, but within them, they compete exceedingly well.

Other plants, considered generalists, are adapted to a range of conditions—sun to shade in silt or clay soils of average fertility and moisture content, consistent rainfall, and temperatures that are not too

Hackberry (Celtis occidentalis) *is a rugged tree that thrives in harsh, dry conditions and a range of soil types. The leaves and fruits are important food sources for butterflies and birds. These characteristics combine to make hackberry a fine tree for ecologically minded gardeners.*

hot in the summer or too cold in winter. They have evolved to grow moderately well in a wider range of environmental conditions, but still, they cannot grow just anywhere. Most popular woody plants are generalists to some degree, thus the labels say, "Grow in sun to shade, moist to dry soils, Zone 3–10." However, if you limit yourself to these "easy" or adaptable plants, you are ignoring a host of wonderful native plants that are more exacting in their requirements, but not difficult to grow if they are chosen carefully and sited correctly. When considering the plants in this book, keep this in mind and look at the constraints present in your own garden as opportunities to grow some wonderful specialist plants exceedingly well.

Light

Obviously plants need light to grow. The ability to transform the energy in sunlight into stored chemical energy is the fundamental miracle of life that makes everything else possible. The intensity and duration of sunlight that strikes a particular spot is easy to quantify in a lab. One of my more interesting laboratory tasks when I was working in horticultural research was to collect the printouts from a machine, set up at an experimental farm, that plotted the intensity and duration of solar radiation from day to day on a graph. Sunny days showed up as even bell curves peaking around noon. Partly cloudy days looked like jagged mountain peaks because the intensity would vary abruptly as the sun came and went. Cloudy days resembled low, rounded hills. We measured the light from spring until fall, and you could see marked differences in the height and width of the curve between readings taken in late June and those taken in the waning days of September. After I had the graphs for the season, I carefully cut out the bells, craggy mountains, and low hills with a razor knife and put them in a machine that measures surface area. By using some mathematical calculations I have since forgotten—so many square inches of graph paper equaling so much solar radiation—I neatly quantified the total amount of sun that had shone on that particular spot during the growing season. I know there are computer programs that can collect and output this data more easily, but somehow cutting out those little blobs made the whole thing more real.

My point here is that it is helpful to think of sunlight as a quantity, just as it is easier to think of rainfall as a number of inches, or fertilizer as a number of pounds. Certain plants need a specific quantity of sunlight both daily and over the course of the season to grow their best, and you need to consider this when siting them in the garden. A whitebark pine at 12,000 feet in the Colorado Rockies receives huge amounts of sunlight, say, 40 buckets a day (an artificial unit of measurement I've made up for convenience) during the growing season because the days are long and the high altitude means that the sun has not had to pass through much light-refracting atmosphere. However, the growing season is short at this altitude, so the plants quickly accumulate their necessary 1,600-bucket yearly quota and go dormant. A rose growing on the cloudless plains of Kansas may receive an average of 30 buckets of sun daily, but over a longer growing season, this could amount to a whopping 3,000 buckets—a quantity it needs for stocky growth, prolific flowering, and long life. A mapleleaf viburnum from western Virginia may receive 20 daily sun buckets for a few weeks in spring before the trees leaf out, then only about 3 buckets

Mountain heather (Cassiope mertensiana), which grows at high elevations in the western mountains, requires strong sun and a short, cool growing season to thrive. Specialized plants like this need to be sited carefully in the garden.

for the rest of the long season, for a total of only 900 buckets, even though it may ideally prefer 1,200 for flowering and setting seed. It has adapted as best it can by emerging early and getting as much growing done as possible before the light dims.

All of these species will grow best if they receive both the daily intensity and seasonal totals they were designed for. Cassiope is an evergreen native to the northern parts of the Northern Hemisphere—Zone 2. If you grow a cassiope at sea level in Seattle—Zone 8—it may not get the strong sun it needs unless it is sited very carefully, and in the long growing season the plant will likely "burn its candle at both ends," so to speak, shortening its life in cultivation. Alternatively, the mapleleaf viburnum from the Appalachians will likely thrive in the longer growing season on Puget Sound, which allows it to come closer to its ideal of 1,200 sun buckets annually.

One final point to consider is day length. Plants are able to sense day length and use it to tell time. The timing of many plants' growth and bloom is based more on the length of the day than on the air temperature or availability of water. Between March 21 and September 21, in northern latitudes the days increase and then decrease in length more extremely than in southern latitudes. Many late-blooming plants time their flowering to a particular day length. A September-blooming species from northern Illinois begins to initiate flower buds in August, when the days are, say, 14½ hours long. The same species in southern Louisiana has its internal clock set for August days that are only 13½ hours long. If the Illinois plants are grown in Louisiana, they may bloom in July, and the southern plants, if transplanted near the Great Lakes, might not bloom at all because by the time the days get short enough to trigger flowering, cold has set in. Adaptation to day length is important to consider when you are choosing plants from a markedly different latitude.

Soil

One of the hardest aspects of plant cultivation to grasp and yet perhaps the most vital to understand is the concept of soil. We cannot see what happens underground, so it is more difficult to determine what might be going wrong down there when a plant is declining. I realize that "out of sight, out of mind" applies here, but before you doze off or skip to the next chapter, remember that understanding something about what goes on below ground is really the key to successful gardening. For ease of discussion, I have broken up this section into soil's physical structure, fertility, and pH. Really, though, these are three facets of a larger whole, all of which influence each other.

Sand dunes on Cape Cod. The relatively large particles in sandy soils shed water quickly and do a poor job of holding nutrients and organic matter. Certain plants, like the pitch pine (Pinus rigida) pictured here, are well adapted to nutrient-poor, shifting sands. These stunted landscapes have a picturesque, timeless quality that I find especially inspiring.

Soil's Physical Structure

THE MINERAL COMPONENT

Soil is a mixture of minerals and the recycled remains of plants and animals that serves to anchor a plant in place and hold reserves of water and nutrients vital for growth. The mineral component comes from eons of weathering, which has broken down parent rock—anything from limestone to granite or volcanic ash—into tiny pieces of sand, silt, and clay. Soils are classified on the basis of particle size, with sand particles the largest, then silts, and finally clays. The type of parent rock is important in determining the types and concentrations of different minerals in the soil and thus its fertility, but not its particle size classification. Thus, quartz sand and granite sand have different chemical properties, but they hold and shed water the same way. Take a minute to think about this process of weathering. Imagine taking a rock and splitting it into four chunks with a hammer, just as rain and frost slowly wear away mountains. You have revealed what was formerly interior rock and thus have created more exposed surfaces than there were before. As you continue to break it down into smaller and smaller pieces (wear eye protection and sing prison work songs when you are doing this), the volume of rock has changed very little, but

more and more interior surface is exposed. Water is an electrically charged molecule that clings to the surfaces of these particles just as it does to your skin after a shower, and the smallest particles—which have the greatest surface area for a given volume—will hold on to the most water. The gaps, or pores, between the particles also get smaller as the particles themselves decrease in size. These pores are important channels that allow air exchange in the soil. Sandy soils have larger particles and larger pores and thus abundant air flow. Their large pores are also harder for water to "fill up." A fine clay soil has a tremendous surface area that can hold much more water, and furthermore, its pores are smaller, so the water routinely fills up all the pores in the fine soil, preventing oxygen from entering and fostering a condition known as saturation. One of the ways that scientists classify wetlands is by the level of oxidized iron or rust present. Waterlogged soils are typically gray in appearance, not brown, because iron cannot oxidize to the familiar rusty brown without free oxygen. Roots need air to breathe just as we do, and waterlogged, heavy soils can suffocate them. Woody plants like buttonbush and tupelo are adapted to waterlogged soils, so they have roots that can "hold their breath," so to speak, and so are good choices for places with high water tables and wet, clay soils; however, they are intolerant of droughty soils. On the other hand, plants adapted to coarse soils, like pinyon and broom crowberry, will quickly suffocate in a heavy, wet soil. Conversely, sandy soils (which have less surface area and so hold less water) often have too little water for many plants; only those with deep roots, like bearberry, will thrive.

Accordingly, as a gardener you need to either stick with plants that are adapted to your soil's physical type and water table or modify the soil to suit the plants. Take a pinch of soil and hold it between your thumb and forefinger, then dip the lot in a glass of water. Now rub the moistened soil between your fingers. Does it feel gritty or very smooth and sticky? Is the color brown or gray? Gritty soils are more sandy; sticky-smooth are clay. Silts fall in between. Although you cannot easily change the water table, you can make a heavy clay soil more aerated by adding sand and make a sandy soil hold more water by adding silt or clay.

THE ORGANIC COMPONENT

Between 2 and 15 percent of a soil's volume is made up of organic matter—plant and animal remains in various states of decay. Organic matter has important effects on a soil's physical structure, water-holding capacity, and fertility. Organic compounds stain soils deep brown or black, and it is no wonder that this is the color we associate with fertility (and the makings of a good layer cake). Organic material in the form of leaf and bark mulches, tilled cover crops, or composts added to soil will act like a sponge in sandy soils, allowing them to hold more water. In clay soils, the organic material will actually open up and aerate the soil by gluing the small particles together into larger ones. In both cases, organic material is a key component for creating an ideal rooting environment. In all soils, organic as well as clay, colloids (decay-resistant particles with electrically charged surfaces and large surface area) are vital in what is called cation exchange. The nutrients a plant needs are available to it only in ionic, or soluble, form. For example, ammonium nitrate, a fertilizer salt, breaks down into the ammonium ion NH_{4+} and the nitrate ion NO_{3-} when dissolved in water. Only in these forms can the nitrogen ions be absorbed through a root's cell membranes. These ions would easily be washed out of the soil in rainwater except that they are held by the electrically charged colloids like books in a library until a plant needs them.

To add organic matter to a new planting, spread 3 to 4 inches of well-rotted compost (meaning there are no big chunks of identifiable leaves, wood, or dung in the material and it is not hot to the touch) and mix it in thoroughly before planting. In addition, put down a mulch of shredded leaves or aged pine bark or wood chips as a mulch every spring on estab-lished beds. Over time, worms, fungi, and other creatures mix this mulch with the lower layers, creating deep, dark, rich topsoil that is perfect for most plants.

Earthworms are like little pellet factories, breaking down organic material and extruding the remains in the form of dung, called castings, which are rich in fertilizer salts. They "till under" vast quantities of organic material annually. What most people do not realize is that all the worms in northeastern and central North America are introduced species brought here accidentally from Europe. They have rapidly taken over habitat left worm-free for millennia because the native species had been driven south by the glaciers and had not yet returned. These introduced worms are aggressive, voracious scavengers, and it is difficult to say what effect they might be having on plants and ecosystems not adapted to their presence. They are still in the process of displacing the less noticeable native worms in the southern United States. Worms have come to be seen as benign and friendly creatures that help the soil and feed wildlife. They are certainly welcome in the disturbed, heavily cropped soils of vegetable gardens, but I suspect that in undisturbed, stable forest communities, exotic worms can have negative effects. In the rich, organic soil we have built up at Garden in the Woods, worms transform the yearly mulch of leaves mixed with topsoil into a six-inch layer of spongy pellets that fine-rooted plants are simply unable to take root in. I am guessing that the fine sandy soil we have is especially good for making worm castings, and the upshot is that many plants have become difficult to grow well. I have been adding builder's sand to new plantings, which I think is too coarse to pass through the worms, so this soil is not pelletized, and the results have so far been encouraging. Nevertheless, our resident crows are quite happy with the writhing abundance of worms. They come in at 5 P.M. every day when the trails close to rake though the mulch, and they get quite upset with me when I work late and interrupt their dinner.

Soil Fertility

Plants need minerals in their diet just as we do. Whereas we take a mineral supplement when our diet does not provide enough of certain nutrients, we give plants fertilizers. Look on a vitamin label and compare it to a fertilizer label. You will likely see potassium, phosphorus, magnesium, boron, calcium, and iron, among others. Think of fertilizing as providing mineral supplements to plants growing in soils depleted by improper care or outright abuse. Giving plants fertilizers in moderation to supplement what is lacking in the soil will make them grow better and help them fight off the effects of stress and disease. All successful gardeners learn to recognize the importance adequate fertility plays in helping a

The massive trunk and root system of a giant sequoia (Sequoiadendron giganteum) *scavenges and holds most of the available nutrients found in the ground beneath, leaving little for understory plants. In the garden, careful and moderate use of supplemental fertilizers will help ensure that all plants, large or small, receive what they need to grow their best.*

garden really shine. However, you can easily have too much of a good thing with fertilizer, so aim toward eventually building a healthy, stable soil that recycles all the nutrients plants need and needs little supplementation. While fertilizers are useful tools when properly applied, too much fertilizer can be toxic, and just as there are USDA daily allowances for vitamins and minerals, there are manufacturer recommendations for fertilizer rates, which should not be exceeded. Plants that evolved in nutrient-poor environments like bogs are especially prone to fertilizer poisoning. Inorganic or chemical fertilizers especially are basically just salts that can literally suck the water out of roots, just as salt dries fish if applied too liberally. Overfertilizing can also affect a plant's internal processes and cause distorted or unseason-

ably late growth. Excess nutrients that are not taken up by plants leach into water systems and cause further problems for humans and wildlife. I always recommend that you have your soil tested by a lab when you start your garden, so that you will have a base line for recommendations about how much fertilizer to add, and every few years you should retest the soil. Call or write to your local agricultural extension office for the soil-testing lab nearest you.

All fertilizers are not created equal. Most agricultural fertilizers contain the big three — nitrogen, phosphorus, and potassium — which are given as a percentage of the gross content of the bag. A 20-10-10 fertilizer contains 20 percent nitrogen, 10 percent phosphorus, and 10 percent potassium by weight, with the rest consisting of other nutrients, fillers, and impurities. Certain inorganic, or chemical, fertilizers are "incomplete," meaning that they contain adequate levels of only the three major nutrients and little or none of a dozen nutrients needed in smaller amounts, like boron and molybdenum. Other products include large amounts of one nutrient — for example, lawn fertilizers contain a lot of nitrogen — can be toxic to plants other than those for which they were designed. The nutrients in inorganic fertilizers, like 10-10-10 or the common liquid 10-10-10 plant foods, are water-soluble, meaning that although most of the nutrients dissolve into their ionic form immediately when mixed with water, and thus can be taken up quickly by plants, they are also easily washed out of the soil by rain or irrigation and drain into water supplies. These inorganic fertilizers are manufactured in the form of salts like potassium nitrate and ammonium nitrate. They cause rapid greening and lush growth, but they need frequent replenishment — it is like living on a diet of candy.

Organic fertilizers, which range from manure composts to dried and bagged products containing such things as cottonseed meal, crab meal, bone meal, and dehydrated manure have a greater percentage of their nutrients in nonsoluble form. These compounds must be broken down by microorganisms over time before they can become soluble and thus available to plants, just as the complex sugars or starches in a potato are released more slowly into our systems than the simple sugars in a candy bar. Thus, organic fertilizers are in a sense "time-release" — they do not overwhelm and poison the plants or wash away as quickly as inorganic fertilizers do. We prefer organic fertilizers at Garden in the Woods for this reason and also because they are fairly complete, containing a good balance of the necessary minerals. Furthermore, they promote the growth of soil microflora (bacteria, fungi, earthworms, and insects), which feed on and break down the organic materials. A soil without a healthy microflora can be compared to a person who has just taken a course of antibiotics. The system is a "blank slate," more easily colonized by pathogenic organisms because the benign inhabitants have been killed off. We use primarily blended granular organic fertilizers with an analysis approximating 5-5-5 applied in spring before growth begins and occasionally reapplied in early summer. Fertilizing trees and shrubs after midsummer, especially with nitrogen, is not a good idea unless they are severely deficient, as this can lead to prolonged growth that leaves them vulnerable to early cold snaps. When planting in fall, it is a good idea to amend the area with well-rotted compost, as this will provide a bit of fertilizer to help them establish without forcing new growth. Composts, especially properly prepared manure composts, are excellent sources of both organic matter and nutrients, and they are the best way to build a healthy, fertile soil over the long term. These are best applied to existing plantings as spring mulch, which will be slowly incorporated into the soil over the season. A healthy soil is a fragile thing, but annual additions of compost and careful and judicious use of fertilizer combined with perennial plants to prevent erosion will restore just about any ravaged soil in three to five years.

Recently there has been much talk about mycorrhizal fungi and the supposed advantages of products that contain these beneficial organisms. Most plants form mutually beneficial associations with specific species of mycorrhizal fungi. The fungi are present in healthy soils and penetrate or envelop a seedling's feeder roots. Infected roots develop swollen or highly branched shapes and it is these composites that are the mycorrhizae. The fungi produce fine, threadlike structures called hyphae, which vastly increase the surface area of a plant's root system, and aid in the uptake of certain nutrients, primarily phosphorus as well as copper, manganese, and zinc. Plants in the rhododendron family have well-developed mycorrhizae that efficiently scavenge nitrogen in the nutrient-poor, acidic soils they frequent. One of the best-known mycorrhizal fungi is the truffle of gourmet fame, which colonizes the roots of oaks and hazels.

Mycorrhizae are of obvious value in nutrient-poor environments, but I am very skeptical of the efficacy of so-called mycorrhizal supplements that are sold as growth-boosting magic bullets. In rare cases, such as the revegetation of strip-mine tailings or other sterile, "dead" soils, inoculating transplants of mycorrhizal fungi has been shown to improve growth. However, a typical garden soil should already contain a host of mycorrhizal fungi, and further, their benefit is negligible if the soil is fertile. I have seen mycorrhizae develop on perfectly healthy bearberry plants grown in a soilless potting mix in our nursery; most likely the fungi blew into the pots as spores. Lastly, certain fungi are hosted by specific groups of plants, and a purchased inoculant mix is

not guaranteed to match the plants you are growing. Unless you are involved in land reclamation, I think you would be better off putting your money into a good yearly shot of compost and leaving the rest to Mother Nature.

Soil pH

A soil's pH is a measurement of its relative acidity/alkalinity, which in turn refers to the relative abundance of hydrogen (H+) ions and hydroxyl (OH–) ions in the soil solution. Soil pH is an important factor in fertility and in rates of biological activity. The parent rock from which a particular soil is derived has the greatest influence on its pH. Certain

Coast azalea (Rhododendron atlanticum). Rhododendrons and other members of the heath family (Ericaceae) form symbiotic relationships with specific mychorrizal fungi. The fungi live in the roots and help the plant scavenge nitrogen more efficiently than it could on its own.

types of rock contain high levels of calcium and/or magnesium, two important plant nutrients that also affect the soil's chemistry. Limestone, which originates from marine deposits of coral reefs, shells, and the like, is very high in these nutrients, and ground limestone is an important fertilizer for several reasons. Calcium is not added to many premixed fertilizers because it affects the solubility of other components. However, calcium and magnesium are two of the most soluble and thus easily rain-leached minerals. In wet climates they become scarce in soils not derived from limestone rock, so such soils may have to be supplemented with dolomitic limestone (a type of limestone that contains both calcium and magnesium). The nutrients in limestone are important in plant growth, but they also affect the soil's pH, making certain other nutrients more or less available, depending on their levels.

pH is measured on a scale of 1 to 14, with 1 being the most acid, 7 being neutral, and 14 being least acid (basic). Soils typically range in pH from 4.0 to 8.0. Remember that when a molecule (in this case, water) is dissolved, its components split into electrically charged ions—the form that can be absorbed by cells. At a low pH, there are more hydrogen ions floating around than hydroxyl ions, and at a high pH, the situation is reversed. Adding limestone raises the pH of the soil, making it less acid, by displacing hydrogen ions with calcium. Certain minerals become more soluble in the company of H+, whereas many others become more soluble around OH–. For example, iron, which is abundant in all soils, is only readily soluble at a low pH. Phosphorus is more soluble and thus available to plants at a higher pH. Acid-loving plants do not really love acids; rather, they have evolved on a diet rich in iron but low in most other nutrients, so they are "lazy" about scavenging iron but very efficient at gathering up nutrients like phosphorus. When you grow an acid-loving plant, such as rhododendron, in alkaline soil, it cannot gather the necessary iron it needs, and so develops a deficiency. Fertilizers sold to "rescue" iron-deficient, acid-loving plants contain the mineral in *chelated* form, meaning (at least as far as fertilizers are concerned) it has been combined with an agent that makes it soluble at a higher pH. Furthermore, since acid-loving plants are adapted to a life of scarcity when it comes to most other nutrients, they can be easily overwhelmed by excess. At a higher pH (less acid), most of the important nutrients become more soluble, and, like people living on a high-fat diet, they accumulate too much in their tissues, which can be toxic. Conversely, lime-loving plants evolved in less acid soils under conditions of relative abundance, and they quickly suffer deficiencies when the soil is too acid.

Another, more subtle indirect effect of pH is its influence on soil microflora and fauna such as bacteria, nematodes, and fungi, including those responsible for disease. At either a very low pH (say, below 5.0) or a very high pH (above 7.0), the growth of many fungi and bacteria is inhibited. For example, in a very acidic soil mix, I can raise fetterbush quite successfully. If, with limestone, I raise the pH to 6.0 (slightly acidic), the plants easily succumb to phytophthora root rot, a fungus that grows more vigorously under less acidic conditions. It is not only the detrimental fungi that are affected, but also mycorrhizae and decomposing organisms.

In the wild, the availability of calcium and magnesium—and thus the soil's pH—is one of the key factors determining which plants grow in a particular place. Subtle changes in a soil's chemistry tip the balance to certain plants that are best able to cope with the particular abundance or lack of nutrients and with "good" and "bad" microorganisms. If you are naturalizing plants in a meadow or woodland or restoring an area disturbed by human activities, it is important to select species that are best suited to the site. In a garden situation, though, small competitive advantages are not so important; suffice it to say that a nearly neutral to slightly acid pH (5.5 to 6.5), combined with good, balanced fertility, will be suitable for most of the plants in this book. I have indicated acidic or alkaline for particular genera or species when I am aware of their specific affinities. A soil test will measure your pH and give recommendations for adjusting it accordingly.

Temperature

Effects of Cold

In the scope of possible temperatures found in the universe, life as we know it can exist in only a very small range. Although some plants can survive periods of temperatures below zero or above 100° F, most require a range of about 45° to 85° F to grow and reproduce. Plants are not warm-blooded, as we are, so the danger of cold involves the disastrous effect of expanding, piercing ice crystals on cell membranes. Winter-hardy plants have ways of decreasing their relative water content and concentrating dissolved chemicals in their tissues to act as "antifreeze." This is a metabolically costly process, so plants produce only the minimum amount of antifreeze they need to endure the conditions they evolved in. A red maple from the moderate climate of Florida will likely perish if planted in Quebec, whereas local red maples will come through the winter fine. Cold-hardiness is primarily genetically predetermined; it varies moderately from plant to plant and tremendously from species to species. This is another reason why provenance is important when selecting garden plants. Fortunately, many plants—*Magnolia ashei*, for example—are much hardier than their native range would suggest because they have a genetic capacity for antifreeze production that is probably a holdover from colder times. Further, if you raise your own plants from seed, you can often select certain ones that are a little hardier and over time increase the survival odds a bit.

Root hardiness, like stem hardiness, has to do with preventing ice formation. The earth holds tremendous quantities of heat through the winter and is slow to warm in summer, so soils rarely suffer the extremes of temperature found aboveground. Roots therefore can afford to be less cold-hardy than tops, and this is why even winter-hardy plants in unprotected pots rarely survive a cold winter. Mulch (in addition to its other benefits, like weed suppression and addition of organic matter) acts like a blanket that helps to retain heat in winter and moderate fluctuations in soil temperature that cause dangerous frost heaving during successive freeze-thaw cycles. So mulching is an especially good practice in cold, snowless climates (snow is an excellent insulator, as most gardeners know). In moderate climates, even subtropical plants will prove winter-hardy through occasional cold snaps if the ground remains unfrozen. Since lower water content equals higher levels of plant antifreeze, well-drained soils help many marginal plants survive the winter.

Effects of Heat

All chemical reactions speed up and slow down at different temperatures. Plants, like animals, use enzymes to catalyze, or "manage," the chemical reactions needed to produce and use energy, and enzymes are designed to work most efficiently in a certain range of temperatures. Plants from cool climates have enzyme systems that operate well at lower temperatures, but bring them into warmer conditions, and enzyme activity accelerates so much that it may simply cease, leading to a slow loss of vigor and death; the plant literally burns itself out. Conversely, plants from hot climates have metabolisms that can become sluggish when they are grown too cool; the plants may fail to bloom or to store enough food reserves to survive a long winter. Though a healthy individual can usually tolerate occasional fluctuations from its ideal temperature range, in the long term this can translate into a failure to thrive. Night temperature is almost more important than day temperature in terms of enzyme function, since many metabolic processes involved with energy production happen only during the night.

(TOP) *Nootka cypress (Chamaecyparis nootkatensis) hails from the cool Pacific Northwest, so it is able to withstand winter temperatures well below zero, but it tolerates summer heat poorly.*

(BOTTOM) *Arizona cypress (Cupressus arizonica), on the other hand, is very heat-tolerant but will be killed if temperatures drop below 100° F. It languishes in the type of cool climate that Nootka cypress loves.*

Transplanting

Containerized Plants

Bog rosemary (Andromeda polifolia) looks great in a container—sometimes better than it does after a few years in the garden. When selecting container-grown plants at a nursery, examine the soil in the pot. Does it look old, crusty, or weedy? The quality of the potting soil (and thus the roots) is as important as the healthiness of the branches and leaves. Select plants with fresh-looking soil and avoid those that are pot-bound or top-heavy (the above-ground portion appearing too large for the size of the pot).

Moving woody plants from containers to the ground is fairly straightforward if you pay attention to a few things. When a plant is grown in a pot, its entire root system is obviously contained in this pot—unless it has worked its way out of the drainage holes and into the ground below, which happens more often than you might think. However, there are a few key differences between this container root system and one growing in the ground. First of all, a container-bound root system is usually smaller and more concentrated. A 6-foot-tall sapling can be contained in 3 gallons of soil (a 12-inch pot, or about 1 cubic foot of soil), but in the ground, it would likely spread out 6 feet in the top 1 to 2 feet of earth (roughly 25 to 40 cubic feet of soil). Therefore, a contained root system relies on far less surface area and far less soil volume to support its leaves with moisture and nutrients. In the nursery, the containerized plant is watered frequently (as much as twice a day) and receives a constant stream of fertilizer that is either injected directly into the irrigation water or applied through time-release pellets. Modern container nurseries practice what is really almost a form of hydroponics by using coarse, relatively sterile growing media as "soil" supplied with a regular stream of nutrient-laden water. The result is tremendous top growth,

since even a small root system can readily supply a lush, fast-growing crown. The plants are readily portable and cheaper to produce than their labor-intensive, field-grown and -dug counterparts. However, container-grown plants do present potential problems once the tree or shrub is taken off life support and planted in the ground.

Whether selecting a tree or shrub in the nursery or raising your own, aim for a plant that has a good proportion between the size of the container and that of the crown. The crown volume should ideally be no more than two times the volume of the pot—more than that and you will have to provide extra water to get it established. How does the container soil look? Does it seem to be fairly fresh, or is it old and choked with roots and weeds? The quality of the container soil affects the water needs of the plant, and also the condition of the roots themselves, which I'll address a bit later. If you are planting early or late in the season, before the crown has leafed out or sent out new growth or after growth has ceased for the year, you can choose a more top-heavy individual.

The next thing to be aware of is incompatibility problems between container mixes and field soils. Containers are watered frequently and hold water differently than the ground does. Containers have what is really a perched water table, meaning that water pools in the bottom of the pot, so container soil needs to be very well drained (or else the pot becomes a swamp) and must have a very coarse tex-

ture. The addition of composted tree bark or aggregates like sand, gravel, perlite, vermiculite, or pumice helps the pot shed excess water, but this mixture will require more frequent watering than all but the most gravelly field soil. When a root ball contained within this coarse mix is set into the finer soil of the garden, water does not readily move from the finer to the coarse (see "Soil's Physical Structure," page 18). In fact, water can actually be pulled from the root ball by the greater capillary attraction of the finer field soil. This poses a special challenge for very fine rooted plants like rhododendrons, whose roots are especially vulnerable to dehydration.

To counter both the limitations of a small root system and soil incompatibility issues, it is important to follow a few basic rules. First—especially if the plant has been growing in a highly organic container mix—amend your field soil with organic material such as compost before planting. To avoid creating what is in effect a larger container, mix the compost into the top 4 to 6 inches over a large area, say, 4 to 6 times the diameter of the pot, rather than in a deep, narrow area. The compost will help create a transitional zone between the field and container soil. If the plant is not terribly root-bound and its roots are relatively coarse and tough, I try to remove about one-third of this mix by sloughing it off from the bottom and sides of the roots, using my fingers or a cultivator tool. Leave the center intact and cover loose, exposed roots with field soil when you backfill the hole. If, when you pop or cut the plant out of the container, you find it has delicate, threadlike roots, or the roots are thick and hopelessly tangled, it is better to slice the ball rather than try to break it up. I usually set the ball on the ground and use a sharp digging spade to slice into the sides about 1 to 2 inches, creating four vertical slits that go clear through the bottom. This allows the ball to be spread out (butterflied) as it is set in the hole, giving greater field and container soil contact, and at the same time prunes circling or girdling roots and does not overly disturb fine roots. In either case, set the ball so its top will sit even with or slightly above grade when watered in. Tamp the field soil down thoroughly around the ball with your fist, your heel, or the butt of a shovel to establish good soil-to-soil contact and eliminate air pockets.

For the first three to six months (more if the tree or shrub was especially root-bound and top-heavy), it's critical to provide supplemental water. Remember that the container-grown root system was able to support an oversized top only because it was frequently watered, and this will still be the case until a larger root system can grow. In spring and summer, I like to water newly planted shrubs and trees every day or two for the first three weeks (unless it rains or the ground is naturally boggy). I curtail watering to once or twice a week after that, but continue water-

ing through the first growing season. Fall-planted specimens will need to be thoroughly watered once a week until the ground freezes, and then again for the first month or so after new growth begins again in the spring. Remember that most of the roots are still right there in the root ball around the crown, so concentrate watering there. Also, take care to keep the surrounding soil moist, to prevent it from wicking water away from the root ball. The faster you can get new roots out into the surrounding soil, the better. Light fertilization with either a balanced granular or liquid will aid this tremendously in spring and summer. If you are planting in fall, use a low-nitrogen, high-phosphorus and high-potassium fertilizer like bone meal mixed with muriate of potash. This will encourage roots without forcing late top growth, which would easily be damaged by frost. Apply a more balanced fertilizer in the spring.

It takes up to two to three years in the ground for a containerized root system to completely catch up with the canopy, and some supplemental watering during droughts, even a year or two after transplanting, may be necessary.

Digging and Transplanting Field-Grown Plants

Until recently, nearly all trees and shrubs were grown to size in the ground, then dug, wrapped with burlap, wire, or wood planking, and moved to their new location. Field-grown material has certain advantages over container-grown. Generally, it is possible to acquire larger specimens, since over time they are much more cost-effective to raise in the ground than in huge pots. Furthermore, soil incom-

Fine-rooted species like this Cumberland azalea (Rhododendron cumberlandense) are especially sensitive to physical incompatibilities between the coarse soils of containers and finer field soils. When planting container-grown fine- or fibrous-rooted trees and shrubs, remove the pot and tease the outer 1 to 2 inches of roots out of the container soil, then plant the ball and tamp the field soil firmly around the exposed roots.

Bald cypress (Taxodium distichum *var.* distichum) *grows in flooded bays and swamps with low levels of soil oxygen. The trees produce these peculiar "knees"—swellings from the roots—that may act as snorkels to allow the roots to breathe.*

patibility and root girdling/circling are much less of a concern with balled and burlaped material. On the down side, field-dug plants are heavy, must be handled carefully so that the ball is not crushed or loosened, are difficult to keep watered once they are out of the ground (especially during the growing season), and are harder to successfully transplant once active growth has begun.

A shrub or tree growing in the ground typically extends its root system well beyond its drip line (the limits of its leaf canopy) in search of surface water and nutrients as well as deep into the soil in search of groundwater lying below. Even a sapling with a 6-foot-diameter crown cannot be excavated with its entire root system intact—the weight would be tremendous, the ball difficult to keep intact, and the cavity left behind costly to refill. Consequently, trees and shrubs are dug with only a small portion of their roots, maybe the innermost 10 to 20 percent. So unlike a container plant, whose crown can be supported by its dense root ball if the plant is given enough water, a field-dug plant likely won't have enough roots to support an intact crown, no matter how much water is provided.

Nurseries circumvent this problem partially through root and top pruning. Root pruning is done a year or two before the plant is due to be dug, and is especially important with plants that, like magnolias, firs, and persimmons, have thick and fleshy but few-branched roots. Before growth begins in spring, using a sharp spade, cut through the roots in a circle 10 to 12 inches deep roughly 8 to 24 inches smaller in diameter than you plan to make the finished ball a

year hence. For large or valuable specimens, you can cut half the circle the first season and finish it the next. At the same time, remove about one-third of the canopy, either by pruning back all the branches or removing the lower or weaker ones. The severed roots will branch and regrow over the course of the next year or two, and a smaller crown will be easier for them to support. When you are ready to dig up the plant, make a ball 1 to 2 feet larger in diameter than the pruning circle, so you don't sever all the new roots that have formed in the interim. I like to further reduce the canopy by about 20 percent at this point, to alleviate some of the stress on the root system during the coming growing season.

Because soil interface problems are less of an issue with field-dug and transplanted material, there is debate about the efficacy of amending the planting hole with organic material or topsoil before planting. I think you have to look at the soil quality in each particular situation, and if it is poor—light-colored, low in fertility, excessively sandy—the addition of 3 to 4 inches of compost worked into the top 6 inches of soil over an area 4 to 6 times the diameter of the root ball seems warranted to help the roots reestablish quickly. If your soil is reasonably good, no additional amendment, other than possibly some fertilizer, may be necessary. If the ball is wrapped with real biodegradable burlap, simply peeling or cutting off the top half once the ball is in the hole may be all that is required. The less the ball is broken or loosened, the better. If the plant came in a wire basket, try to cut or remove as much of the wire as possible. If the wrapping is synthetic or plastic burlap, it must all be cut away and completely removed—preferably once the ball is sitting in the hole. Plant the same way you would a containerized specimen, tamping down the soil around the ball—don't stomp on the ball itself!—and make sure that the finished grade is equal to and not above the level of the soil ball itself. Water as described for container plantings. I like to make a little moat by walling up soil or mulch in a circle around the plant which can be filled with water without its running off, so there is time for it to soak into the soil where it is needed.

Again, for several reasons, field-dug trees and shrubs are for the most part best handled before they begin growing in the spring or after growth slows in the fall. This gives the root system time to reestablish before the stressful summer season. As an added benefit (and this applies to all plants), getting the tree situated before it leafs out will allow it to adjust the thickness and size of its leaves to the light levels of the chosen spot. Often these vary quite a bit from the place it was being grown, and plants already in leaf may drop their leaves or have them burned off as they try to adjust to a new place.

Trunk Flare

Increasingly these days I see trees, lawn trees especially, with a ring of color-enhanced mulch piled up in a distressing ring around the trunk. The base of any plant, be it tree, shrub, or herbaceous perennial, is the interface between the aboveground parts (trunk or stem) and the belowground (roots, rhizome, bulb, or corm). Roots and rhizomes, being underground structures, are necessarily rot-resistant when exposed to dark and dank, some roots more than others. Trunks and stems, on the other hand, rot very easily if they are buried underground, with obvious and unfortunate consequences to the party involved. Therefore, it is vitally important to keep the upper portions of the crown aboveground. You can determine where this point is by looking for what is called the trunk flare, the point where the roots begin to bulge out from the base of the stem and head off into the ground. If you examine wild trees, this flare, sometimes called the trunk crown, becomes immediately apparent. Equally apparent under cultivation are trees or shrubs that shoot straight out of the ground without any noticeable change in diameter, like big lollypops stuck in the ground. This is a sure sign that the crown has been buried, either during construction on the site or by overzealous mulching. At Garden in the Woods we have this problem around the fringes of the parking lot, where snow and gravel are continually dumped over the winter, and the crowns of the bordering trees are eventually buried. Arborists have told me that trunk flare burial is the leading cause of accidental death in trees between the ages of 10 and 60. What can you do? First, take care in planting that you do not bury the crown. Sometimes, balled and burlaped trees will have soil pushed up around them during digging, and this must be stripped back when they are replanted. A tree service can help you remove soil from around large trees (there is a new device that uses compressed air to blow away debris), or you can carefully excavate the trunk using a spade, trowel, and your fingers so as not to chip the bark. Lower the grade to the point where you see individual roots differentiating from the trunk like big toes; root bases can adapt to life aboveground more easily than trunks can to life belowground, so err on the side of removing more soil. After that, pile on mulch in moderation—1 to 2 inches a year is plenty—leaving the flare free.

Lawn trees such as this sourwood (Oxydendrum arboreum) are particularly vulnerable to crown burial. Notice how the homeowner has piled mulch right around the base of the tree, covering the trunk flare. This puts the tree at risk of injury from rot diseases.

Pruning and Wound Healing

The art of pruning is truly that—an art—and I cannot hope to do it justice here. However, knowing a few basic points will greatly improve the health and longevity of your patients. First, remember that only wood exposed to air and water is subject to rot. When a trunk is completely sealed, it is very decay-resistant. Wounds—to the bark, at the point where limbs attach, or to the truck flare and root base—allow bacteria, fungi, and insects like carpenter ants a foothold that can eventually weaken the tree or shrub to the point that it topples over. Just as with humans, the object of wound healing is to allow the injured area to close up cleanly and quickly, and the faster the bark seals up, the less potential structural damage will be inflicted. When I was a kid, the prevailing wisdom was to paint over wounds with tar or shellac to retard rot. However, subsequent research showed that painting doesn't help and may actually hurt by trapping moisture and retarding wound-tissue formation. Woody plants heal by producing fast-growing callus tissue that grows out over the injury and eventually meets and joins the callus coming from the other side. A wound to an area of the trunk will heal and look like an eye lying along the trunk, because callus grows more quickly from the sides of the wound than from the top or bottom. Wounds at the point of branch-trunk union usually heal so they look like a doughnut because where the limb meets the trunk, there is a ring of callus tissue, called a branch collar. Many woody plants naturally shed branches as they become shaded, and the need to heal after such shedding explains the presence of this branch collar, though only partially developed, on healthy branches.

For wounds to bark and trunk, there is little you can do other than to cut away any loose bark or debris that might interfere with wound closure. If a limb breaks or you prune it off, always cut the branch cleanly just above the branch collar, usually evident as a slightly swollen ring where the branch and trunk meet. Try to cut the branch perpendicular to its plane of growth, both to reduce surface area and to avoid removing part of the collar accidentally. It usually slants down and away from the trunk, so the cut would be made, say, a quarter-inch from the trunk in the branch crotch and slanted downward so that at the bottom it was an inch or so out from the trunk.

The best time to prune woody plants is when they are dormant. At this time they have drawn much of their carbohydrate reserves into the roots, so the loss of some limbs is not quite as serious. Deciduous plants' branch architecture is also much easier to see clearly in dormancy, and the branches are lighter without the leaf load. I do most pruning in late winter, as I can clean up after winter storms while I'm at it. The exceptions are genera that "bleed" excessively if cut in spring (maples, dogwoods, birch) because

(LEFT) *With proper pruning, a wound will heal quickly and cleanly. Large wounds may take years to fully close over. The only sign of a former wound on this hackberry* (Celtis occidentalis) *is a telltale bull's-eye pattern of callus tissue on the trunk.*

(RIGHT) *Some trees, like the American elm* (Ulmus americana), *require little if any pruning. The tree naturally drops its lower limbs as it grows.*

they experience quite a bit of root stress at this time of year. These trees are best worked on in the fall.

Rejuvenative Pruning

Healthy trees and shrubs recover from injury much faster than old or weakened individuals, and there comes a time in every plant's life when you have to ask, would it be better just to cut it down and start over? Many shrubs and some trees benefit from what I call one-step, or rejuvenative, pruning. This sophisticated procedure involves cutting some or all of the trunks to within a foot of the ground, using a chain saw or sharp pruning saw. Shrubs that are naturally suckering and multistemmed (and these are legion) respond to this treatment very well, provided that (1) it is done when they are dormant, (2) the cut stems are alive and still reasonably vigorous, and (3) you don't get carried away and cut out all the roots as well. The fast-growing sprouts that spring from the stumps may need to be thinned the following winter. The net effect of this intimidating and severe pruning, should the operation be a success (and it usually is), is a marked improvement not only in vigor but also in flowering, fruiting, and general appearance. Some plants (spireas come to mind) can be handled this way every season, but most others need it only every 5 to 15 years. A less severe technique is to remove one-third of the large stems each year for three years, or just cut out limbs or stems as they become weak and die (dead limbs are less likely to resprout).

Diseases

I do not discuss diseases and pests at any great length in this book for several reasons. This is not because native plants are problem-free—on the contrary, they are fed on by a host of organisms, most of whom have coevolved in the rich web of checks and balances of the local ecosystem. Most plants are attacked by something, and we should thank God for that, as it is all that prevents them from running amok. Focusing on disease is an easy way to get medical schoolitis, where you start to think you have every affliction you read about. If you can minimize environmental stress by choosing plants suitable for your light, soil, and temperature conditions, most of them should grow reasonably well, and if not, try them in another spot or get something else. I firmly believe there is no plant worth growing if it must be maintained by applications of poisons. Please do not needlessly expose yourself and your children to these chemicals. Find your tolerance for what might be called acceptable damage, and if the plant exceeds that, pull it out, period. I have run my nurseries and gardens with few

pesticides by practicing good housekeeping, selecting resistant plants, and letting natural predators do the work. After decades of overreliance on pesticides, many gardeners are almost shocked to discover that plants are not intensive-care patients in need of a constant chemical assault to survive. To most people 10 years ago an organic apple meant a small, arthritic lump riddled with worm holes, and in the same way it is easy to envision an organic garden as a place overrun with pests, where a few pitiful blooms attempt to open through a net of spider mites, and leaves disappear under a barrage of fungi and bacteria, like targets at a shooting gallery. Not true—believe me, really not true. An organic garden is a place buzzing with life.

This being said, I do think there is a real threat coming from abroad to many if not all of our native trees. With the ease of airplane travel and container shipping, organisms are moving around the planet at a frighteningly fast rate. Already pines, ashes, chestnuts, elms, hemlocks, spruces, and firs are suffering terribly under the onslaught of introduced insects and diseases to which they have little resistance and for which there are few if any natural predators. What can be done about this, other than stopping all importation of plants and plant products while greatly increasing the power of the USDA, is beyond me. In weak moments, I worry that our great-grandchildren will have few trees left.

White ash (Fraxinus americana), *one of our great forest trees, is now declining as a result of diseases and pests, often aided and abetted by the mistakes of well-meaning people.*

Encyclopedia of Plants

Abies grandis

Abies (AY-bees)
Pinaceae
Fir

When I think about firs, the word "noble" comes immediately to mind. These are grand plants of the cold North and high mountain peaks, growing comfortably at or just below the timberline, an imaginary boundary on mountains and tundra beyond which the rigors of weather make it impossible for trees to survive. They are often lumped in with spruces in forestry texts, as the two inhabit many of the same places, and both have the narrow, conical shape of the classic Christmas tree, which has evolved to shed huge weights of snow quickly and easily. Snow is something that goes hand in hand with firs, and I cannot attempt to understand them without continually reminding myself of this.

A little memory aid that I learned as a kid was "Firs are friendly, spruces are not." Fir needles whorl in a semicircle around the upper side of the twig, each needle curving gently upward and ending in a rounded or blunt tip that is bristly yet soft to the touch. Spruce needles end in a tiny point that will prick your fingers if you shake hands with a branch. Another difference is that fir needles attach to the branch with what looks like a little suction cup, whereas spruce needles stand on little stalks. In firs the stomata (the pores that allow gas exchange) are concentrated in bands along the lower surface of the needles, and these appear like two light-colored stripes along the midrib,

giving the undersides a whitish cast that contrasts subtly with the typically deep, glossy green upper surface.

The way fir needles curve up in a brushlike arrangement makes the twigs supremely adapted for catching snow, and this used to puzzle me. It makes sense, though, if you observe firs in winter. The needles trap a small amount of snow, which weighs down the small branches and forms an icy skin over the tree, which then sheds additional snow faster than a toboggan shoots down a ski slope. The snow cannot penetrate this outer barrier and settle on the larger branches, where its accumulated weight could topple the tree. This brushlike arrangement also means that from any angle, you see the tops of some needles and the striped bottoms of others. This two-toned effect is one of the fir's most ornamental characters.

To complete the picture, fir branches are supported by a thick, relentlessly vertical trunk that inches slowly skyward each year to evenly balance the load. The trunk is smooth and green or gray when young and covered with light brown, flaking bark when older. Like most conifers (cone bearers), this conical form results from strong dominance of the tree's apex, which allows only the uppermost bud on the tree to grow. This perpetuates the straight trunk. Other buds grow out horizontally to form the branches. At first these branches angle upward, but the accumulated weight of needles and snow eventually forces them down. Branches partway down become horizontal, and the oldest and lowest finally become pendulous and draw closer to the trunk. Thus the fir's characteristic form is tall and narrow, with the lower branches clothing the tree like an apron. The sausage-shaped female cones are interesting as well, growing staunchly upright like the tree itself and clustered in bunches at the very top of the tree, where the seeds have the best chance of being carried by the wind.

Of course, firs also *smell* good. Like many conifers, they produce a resinous sap designed to protect the tree from infections. In pines and spruces, this resin suffuses the wood, ready to ooze out at the slightest bruise. Firs have a different strategy, filling little pockets in their outer bark with resin. The pockets have the look and jiggly feel of the blisters you get on your hand from chopping wood all day, and any insult to the bark causes them to pop and ooze resin. The more volatile components of this stuff quickly evaporate, bringing to the nose that heady and unmistakable smell of balsam or camphor. What remains is a thick, tarlike resin that retards decay and discourages insects like bark beetles from penetrating the tree. This congealed resin will continue to dry for years; slowly releasing its scent—that is why balsam pillows remain fragrant for so long—until it has reached the almost rocklike consistency of amber.

Of the eleven species native to North America, all

Abies grandis. *The needles of giant fir have a lustrous quality that shines through in all seasons. They are arranged in two distinct ranks, like the barbules of a bird feather.*

but two firs grow in the mountains of the West, especially in the conifer-friendly Cascade and Sierra mountains, where Pacific storms dump huge loads of snow in good winters. *Abies balsamea* is the common fir species in New England and up through the boreal forests of eastern and central Canada. The only other species in the east is the Fraser fir of the southern Appalachians, thought by many to represent an isolated population of balsam fir that has recently evolved into a new species.

CULTURE: Most firs inhabit places where the growing season is remarkably short, but they make the best of it with evergreen needles that can photosynthesize as weather permits, and a cold-tolerant root system that functions well even near freezing. This need for cool, moist soils and a short growing season does restrict firs' use in the landscape. Except for white fir, most of the species suffer from a bewildering variety of fungal infections at lower latitudes and altitudes, diseases that are suppressed in the wild by the cold. White fir is the only species that has proved fairly adaptable in cultivation, and it is commonly used as a screening and windbreak tree in the Northeast and Midwest. No firs do well in urbanized areas or in the humid Southeast.

Site them in an acid soil, preferably one that remains shaded, moist, and cool. Some firs are shade-tolerant, but they are really just biding their time until faster-growing competitors eventually die and they can come into their own. Sun encourages dense growth and a well-balanced crown. Light fertilizing can help the trees grow more quickly when young, but firs are not heavy feeders. Soil temperatures in containers tend to be high, making containers generally unsuitable for firs. Most available trees are field-grown. Balled and burlaped trees transplant fairly well in spring before growth commences.

USES: Specimens, windbreaks, screening, Christmas trees.

WILDLIFE: Seeds are of some importance to birds, and the dense evergreen branches provide them with excellent protection in winter and nest sites in spring

PROPAGATION: Difficult from cuttings, moderately easy from seed.

Abies amabilis
Silver Fir

ZONES: 5–7; part sun, sun
SOIL: Moist, acidic
NATIVE TO: Coastal and subalpine forests; British Columbia to southern Alaska south to northern California
SIZE: Height 75 (200) feet, width 2–25 feet
COLOR: Male cones red, female cones purple; blooms in spring

Silver fir is one of the grand old trees of Pacific northwestern forests, favoring cool, middle elevations in the Cascades and Olympics. It gets its name because many of the 1-inch-long needles are held vertically and pointing forward, which reveals the stomatal bands and gives the tree a silvery appearance. It is one of the more shade-tolerant species, able to exist under the canopy of Douglas fir, hemlock, and noble fir until they begin to thin out and it can take its place in the sun. In outline it is tall and narrow, with deep green needles. It will grow in the East, though never coming close to the grandeur it achieves in its native haunts.

Abies balsamea
Balsam Fir

ZONES: 3–6; part sun, sun
SOIL: Moist, cool, acidic
NATIVE TO: Cold, boreal forests; Labrador to Alberta south to Iowa, New York, and Connecticut and in the mountains to Virginia
SIZE: Height 60 (80) feet, width 12–18 feet
COLOR: Male cones red-purple to orange, female cones gray-purple; blooms in spring

Balsam fir is familiar to most people in the East as a Christmas tree cut in Canada and brought down for a few weeks of decoration. In northern Maine, however, it is a major component of the forests. It is a stiff, relatively fast-growing, narrowly pyramidal tree when young, often getting topped and broken up in the crown with age. Needles are usually less than an inch long, medium green above and silvery-green below. When used in landscapes balsam fir is usually a rather small, stressed looking tree, even in Zone 6.

Abies concolor
White Fir

ZONES: 4–7; sun
SOIL: Moist to moderately dry
NATIVE TO: Moderate- to high-elevation mixed coniferous forests; Colorado to Idaho and southern Oregon south to Nevada and northern Mexico
SIZE: Height 80 (120) feet, width 15–25 feet
COLOR: Male cones red-purple, female cones olive green; blooms in spring

This is a wide-ranging fir in the mountains of the West, typically with glaucous blue-gray, widely spaced needles that can be over 2 inches long. The long needles and their uniform color above and below give the plants a characteristically soft, muted appearance in the landscape. It grows 10 to 12 inches a year, with a strongly conical shape and a grayish bark that gets corky with age. White fir is by all accounts the most drought-tolerant and adaptable of the native firs for landscaping, and in its bluest forms, it rivals Colorado blue spruce in color. It has a sharper smell than balsam fir—a mix of orange peels and camphor. Individual stands are geographically and thus genetically isolated, so many local varieties have been recognized. Some authors treat Sierran California races as a separate species, *Abies lowiana* (Sierra white fir). This differs mainly in its greater potential height and needles that lack a glaucous bloom, at least on the upper surface.

Abies fraseri

Fraser Fir

ZONES: 4–6; part sun, sun

SOIL: Moist to moderately dry

NATIVE TO: High elevations in the southern Appalachians, Virginia south to Tennessee

SIZE: Height 50 (80) feet, width 12–18 feet

COLOR: Male cones yellow to reddish, female cones dark purple; blooms in spring

There is some debate as to whether this is merely an isolated variety of the widespread balsam fir. Although they are in many ways identical to the casual observer, Fraser fir is a bit more heat- and drought-tolerant, and has become the tree of choice for Christmas tree growers south of Connecticut. It does offer the consumer the characteristic peppery-sweet balsam fragrance. The main difference is in its seed cones and needles, which are about 50 percent shorter than those of balsam firs.

Abies grandis

Giant Fir, Lowland Fir

ZONES: 4–7; sun

SOIL: Moist, well-drained

NATIVE TO: Seasonally moist, lowland to middle-elevation conifer forests; Montana to British Columbia south to California and southwest Idaho

SIZE: Height 80 (200) feet, width 18– 30 feet

COLOR: Male cones purple, red or yellow, female cones gray-purple to blue; blooms in spring

Giant fir has proved to be a vigorous grower in our gardens, notable for its strongly two-ranked needles, flattened in a single plane like a bird feather, which are deep, glossy green above and blue-green below. It has a distinctive and dignified presence when young, and a tall, narrow habit like silver fir when older. Selections from the colder parts of its range should prove fairly hardy and suitable for use around the Great Lakes and New England. The crushed needles have a strong citronella odor.

Abies lasiocarpa

Subalpine Fir

ZONES: 4–7; sun

SOIL: Moist, cool, acidic

NATIVE TO: Coastal and subalpine coniferous woodlands and glades; northern California north in

the Cascades through British Columbia and Alaska to Yukon

SIZE: Height 40–60 feet, width 12–18 feet

COLOR: Male and female cones purple; blooms in spring

This species is wide-ranging, and current thinking is to split off the Rocky Mountain form, which is found on the length of the Continental Divide from New Mexico to the Yukon, as *A. bifolia* (Rocky Mountain alpine fir). Horticulturally, I would treat them the same, though geographic races are important when selecting plants adapted to a specific region. This is a noble tree, whether it is gracing the edge of a subalpine meadow framed by glaciated peaks or standing as a narrow sentinel in the garden. The needles average over an inch in length—typically a striking glaucous blue above and silvery blue below. The needles whorl haphazardly around the twig, giving the plants a shaggy, lovable aspect. It has performed very well in Framingham, growing slowly but steadily for twenty-five years now without problem. Like all firs, it holds its foliage for years, so the plants soon become visually impenetrable.

Abies procera

Noble Fir

ZONES: 5–7; sun

SOIL: Moist

NATIVE TO: Mixed coniferous forests at middle elevations; extreme northern California to Washington

SIZE: Height 100 (240) feet, width 25–40 feet

COLOR: Male and female cones red to purple; blooms in spring

This is a grand tree, with short, blue-green needles in whorls on the upper half of each twig like a thick

Abies lasiocarpa. The shaggy, steel blue needles of subalpine fir trap the first snow, creating a slick surface that sheds additional snow, which falls abundantly during the long alpine winter.

bristly coat. Older specimens have a shaggy, peeling bark on trunks that shoot straight up out of sight in the canopy. *A. magnifica* (red fir) is a close relative that extends south through the California Sierras. It has longer, deep green needles and massive seed cones up to 8 inches in length that sit like purplish kielbasas at the top of the tree late in the season. Both tend to shed their lower limbs as they mature, which only serves to heighten the sense of their massive size. They are also among the longest lived of firs, some topping the four-century mark. Regrettably, they are not well adapted to life outside their native range.

Acer circinatum.
Many-fingered leaves and a delicate carriage combine with brilliant fall color to make vine maple a fine addition to the woodland garden.

Acer circinatum

Acer (AY-ser)
Aceraceae
Maple

I admit I have a love/hate relationship with maples. Growing up in New England, where red maple and sugar maple have been elevated to the level of patron saints, it is dangerous to admit this. As long as I can remember, though, I have been allergic to maple pollen. I clearly remember the moment I discovered the source of my itchy eyes and throat. One April when I was about twelve, I wandered out to the backyard, stuck my nose in some red maple flowers, and inhaled deeply (I can't remember now what prompted me to do such a thing). Burning waves of pain coursed through my sinuses, and from then on I have known the face of mine enemy. Luckily, the spring rains quickly wash maple pollen from the air

and the irritation from my memory. By June, all is forgiven and maples become just another shade tree overhead. Come fall, though, as their leaves begin to glow in unbelievable combinations of fiery orange, sultry red, and shimmering yellow, I'm seized with the urge to run up and down the street handing out seedlings for my neighbors to plant, so that one day the whole town will be a kaleidoscope of color for a few magical weeks each fall.

Not all members of the genus *Acer* are trees, nor do all color vibrantly in autumn, but the *Acer* tribe is surely one of the most versatile and recognizable genera of woody plants on the continent. Maples are opposite-leaved, which gives their branches a certain unmistakable rhythm and familial form. With the exception of *A. negundo,* their leaves are palmately lobed, with tissue stretched between strong leaf veins that radiate out from the base like on a duck's webbed foot. The flowers grow in bunches or dangling chains colorful enough to give the trees a soft yellow or red glow for a week or two in late spring. Individual trees may bear male or female flowers or a combination of both. Maples seem to be evolving either toward or away from insect pollination. The trees are often abuzz with bees, but the pollen is light enough to be transported on the winds and up the nasal cavity. Speaking of wind, most everyone is familiar with the aerodynamic refinement of maple samaras, or keys. The flattened seeds develop in pairs joined by a seam along the bottom and each is provided with a curved membranous wing. Its sole purpose is to postpone the seed's inevitable fall from grace for as long as possible so the wind can carry it farther from the shade of the parent tree. Though a seedling will have a better chance of establishing away from the smothering limbs of its parent, maples are as a rule agreeably shade-tolerant trees. Their large, flat leaves are adept at capturing the dim remains of the sun that survive the trip through the upper canopy. The smaller species are generally understory trees in mature forests, and the larger ones, like sugar maple, can establish under other trees, waiting for a gap in the canopy for a chance in the sun.

Sugar maple sap has a very high concentration of sugar (2 to 6 percent). As with some of the birches, if winter storms shear off branches, in late winter the trees will weep prolifically from the wound as sap begins to rise from the roots. As this sap runs over the bark and evaporates, a sticky sweet glob or sugary icicle develops, and Native Americans learned to collect the sap and freeze it or boil it down into a concentrated syrup. Yum.

CULTURE: Maples are on the whole shallowly rooted, which makes spring or fall transplanting easy, but the combination of a shallow root system and the dense shade they cast makes growing much of anything beneath them rather difficult. They are fast-growing when young, with indeterminant twigs that will keep on lengthening well into summer if conditions are good. The understory species are fairly sensitive to drought, heat, and pollution, but perform beautifully in a sheltered or woodland setting. The death of many old sugar maples along roadways has been linked not only to old age but to the effect that road salt has on them indirectly via their associated mycorrhizal fungi: the fungi are killed by the salt runoff, which hampers the tree's ability to compete for nutrients. I also wonder what effect indiscriminately applied lawn fungicides may have on these and other beneficial fungi. In wet years, many maples suffer from anthracnose, which attacks the expanding leaves and can leave the tree looking sparse and shriveled until new leaves are produced. Fortunately, this doesn't happen every year, and trees that are growing in open situations in the landscape typically suffer less because of the enhanced air movement around them. The bark disease called nectria canker (caused by *Nectria galligena*) is sometimes a problem, especially when an individual is weakened by other problems. Pruning is best done in the fall to minimize sap bleeding.

USES: Specimen tree, shade tree (large species), personal sugar factory (sugar maple).

PROPAGATION: Easy to propagate from seed.

Acer circinatum
Vine Maple

ZONES: (5)6–8; part sun, shade
SOIL: Moist, acidic
NATIVE TO: Cool, moist woodlands; northern California north on the western side of the Cascades to southern British Columbia
SIZE: Height 10–15 (30) feet, width 8–12 feet
COLOR: Red; blooms in spring

I think of this species as the North American equivalent to *A. palmatum,* the Japanese maple. It grows as an understory shrub or multistemmed small tree in the rainforests of the Pacific Northwest along with *Taxus brevifolia* (Pacific yew) and *Oplopanax* (devil's club). It weaves around other plants amid the giant buttressed trunks of Douglas fir, Sitka spruce, and hemlock, its sinuous trunks often draped in a thick coat of moss and trailing along the ground at times, ready to trip you as you gaze in awe at the canopy high above. The leaves are rounded in outline, notched less than halfway toward the center into 7 to 9 lobes, again suggesting the Japanese maples. It is one of the best natives for fall color in the maritime west, blushing red, orange, or yellow as the rains begin again in early autumn. We are growing it at Garden in the Woods and it survives, but it does suffer twig dieback in winter and demonstrates a susceptibility to nectria canker and a general hesitancy in this region that I would call simply failure to

thrive. It has perhaps the most striking flowers of any of our maple species. The females have 5 deep red sepals surrounding smaller white petals that form a ring around the immature samara waiting to expand in the center. Male flowers are long and wispy as if to catch the slightest breeze in the forest. The samaras are typically pinkish red, much like those of red maple, and are also attractive.

Acer glabrum
Rocky Mountain Maple

ZONES: 4–7; sun to light shade
SOIL: Moist to moderately dry
NATIVE TO: Cliffs, slopes, wooded hillsides; western Nebraska north through British Columbia to coastal Alaska, south to California and New Mexico
SIZE: Height 8–20 (40) feet, width 6–15 feet
COLOR: Yellow-green; blooms in spring

A. glabrum ranges throughout the mountainous West at higher elevations where moisture is adequate. It is a twiggy, multistemmed shrub or small tree with small, leathery leaves that are sharply toothed and 3-lobed, resembling gooseberry leaves, though leaves produced later in the season, especially in shady sites, are actually trifoliate. The foliage is glossy dark green in summer and golden yellow in fall. Not widely used as an ornamental, it is a tough and adaptable plant in cooler climates. The trees are generally dioecious.

Acer leucoderme
Chalk Maple

ZONES: 5–9; sun to shade
SOIL: Moist to moderately dry
NATIVE TO: Moist ravines and upland woods; piedmont of North Carolina south to Alabama and eastern Mississippi
SIZE: Height 20–30 (40) feet, width 15–25 feet
COLOR: Greenish yellow; blooms in spring

Chalk maple is a close relative of sugar maple, in fact when I first moved to North Carolina I assumed that they were sugar maples. It differs in several ways, the most important one being that it is a distinctly smaller, multitrunked understory tree, rarely reaching the upper canopy, with a chalky white-gray color to the younger bark. It is beginning to catch on in the Southeast as a more drought- and heat-tolerant, space-saving substitute for its cousin, and its fall color is equally stunning. *A. barbatum* (Florida maple) ranges over much of the same area, just dipping down into the panhandle of Florida. It is only marginally distinct from chalk maple and can be used in a similar fashion.

Acer macrophyllum
Big-leaf Maple

ZONES: (5)6–8; sun to shade
SOIL: Moist, acidic
NATIVE TO: Lowland forests, streamsides, ravines, mountains farther south; California north along the coast to southern Alaska
SIZE: Height 40–60 (100) feet, width 20–50 feet
COLOR: Yellow; blooms in spring

Few hardwoods can compete for light in the conifer-dominated Pacific Northwest. Though big-leaf maple never attains the great height of its cone-bearing neighbors, it is certainly the largest deciduous tree in these forests. In the rainforests of the Olympic peninsula, *A. macrophyllum* grows to 80 feet or more, which in this forest of giants makes it still an understory tree. Because it loses its leaves in winter and lets the sun into its branches, the larger limbs are festooned with comically thick coats of the *Selaginella oregana* and of licorice fern (*Polypodium glycyrrhiza*), which do most of their growing in winter. In drier environments, the tree is restricted mainly to floodplains, where it can get moisture in summer. The leaves are as much as 12 inches across in the shade, deeply lobed like those of a large silver maple, and the effect of an old tree is ponderous but beautiful in all its substantiality. At low elevations fall color is typically yellow, but higher, where the air is crisper in fall, it takes on more of an apricot shade. It is grown as a street or yard tree in the Pacific Northwest, and it is hardy in cool temperate areas of the East, though rarely grown in favor of local natives.

Acer negundo
Box Elder

ZONES: 3–10; part sun, sun
SOIL: Moist to dry
NATIVE TO: Floodplains, disturbed areas, roadsides; New Hampshire west to British Columbia south to Mexico and Florida
SIZE: Height 20–40 (60) feet, width 15–30 feet
COLOR: Green; blooms in spring

Box elder is a short-lived, small to medium-sized, dioecious tree adapted to a life of floods and their associated disruptions. So it is not surprising that it thrives on human disturbance as well, and has taken up residence along with tree of heaven (*Ailanthus altissima*) in sidewalk cracks, roadside waste places, and just about anywhere else it can get a roothold. In its natural habitat it has value, helping to stabilize banks and watercourses with its tenacious roots and resprouting trunks, but outside this context, it has become almost weedy. It is certainly a very adaptable species, and we have extended its range throughout much of the United States. It may have use in the landscape where alternatives are few, and if limbed up (lower limbs removed) to form a single trunk, it makes a passable tree. Leaves are pinnately compound like ash (an alternate common name of boxleaf elder is ashleaf maple); they are borne on stout twigs that break easily in storms. Fall color is yellow to yellow-green.

Acer pensylvanicum
Striped Maple, Moosewood

ZONES: 3–7; part sun to shade
SOIL: Moist, cool, acidic
NATIVE TO: Damp woods, ravines; Nova Scotia and southern Quebec to Minnesota south to Michigan, Pennsylvania, and in the mountains to Georgia
SIZE: Height 15–20 (30) feet, width 7–10 feet
COLOR: Greenish yellow; blooms in spring

Moosewood is an understory tree or multistemmed shrub of the northern hardwood forests. Moose do indeed love it. The clear-cuts around the family camp in northern Maine abound with sorry-looking stump sprouts kept pruned to 2 to 3 feet by the large, lumbering herbivores. The bark on younger trunks is an evocative, photosynthetic green laced with serpentine stripes of white and black. The effect is subtle and beautiful, especially in winter. The leaves are large, distinctly 3-lobed, and well adapted for life in the shade. They turn a luminous, moonlight yellow

Acer pensylvanicum. Sinuous, chalky white tracings highlight moosewood's brilliant green bark. Chlorophyll in the bark can continue to photosynthesize after the leaves have fallen in autumn and again in early spring, an important advantage for this small understory tree, which must eke out a living in the shade of forest giants.

in fall that I especially love. Moosewood is not a long-lived tree, nor is it happy in heat and drought, but if you have a spot where the soil is cool and moist and where its leaves will be sheltered from the full force of the noonday sun, this is a tree well worth establishing.

A cultivar worth mentioning is the selection 'Erythrocladum' (coralbark maple), which I first saw at the Arnold Arboretum, near Boston. The normal green background color of the young bark is replaced in this selection with coral red, which becomes especially vibrant when cold returns in autumn. By the time the leaves are gone, the twigs are a positively fluorescent coral red. It is not easy to find, but I was able to obtain some grafted plants and hope to produce more when they mature. *A. spicatum* (mountain maple) has a similar leaf, habit, range, and ecology, but lacks the lovely striped bark. It carries its yellow-green flowers in upright racemes, and because they are usually at eye-level, it is pretty in bloom.

Acer rubrum
Red Maple

ZONES: 3–9; sun to light shade
SOIL: Wet to dry; prefers moist, rich soils
NATIVE TO: Woods and swamps; Newfoundland to Manitoba south to eastern Texas and Florida
SIZE: Height 40–75 (110) feet, width 20–50 feet
COLOR: Red; blooms in early spring

Red maple has the widest range of any of our maples and will grow just about anywhere. In moist, fertile soils this tree is at its best, with a wide-spreading, rounded crown, somewhat plated gray-black bark, and brilliant orange to crimson and scarlet fall color. It rarely gets as large or old as sugar or bigleaf maple, but red maple is becoming a shade tree of choice because of its adaptability, fast growth when young, and fair degree of pollution tolerance. Many cultivars have been selected for reliable fall color or canopy shape, but be careful to select plants of local provenance whenever possible. A red maple originally from Georgia will not perform well in Quebec and vice versa.

Acer saccharinum
Silver Maple

ZONES: 3–9; part sun, sun
SOIL: Moist to moderately dry
NATIVE TO: Primarily floodplains and riverbanks; New Brunswick and southern Quebec to South Dakota south to Oklahoma and Georgia
SIZE: Height 60–75 (100) feet, width 30–50 feet
COLOR: Greenish yellow; blooms in spring

You can find silver maple along most of the major rivers in the East, growing where occasional high water inundates its roots for a few weeks in spring. It bears deeply cut, almost lacy leaves with a white bloom on the undersides that flickers in the wind, and its bark is distinctly shaggy in appearance. This is a very fast-growing tree when young, and for this reason it was a popular shade and street tree in the building boom after World War II. However, as these baby boomers have matured and begun to rain branches and large limbs down on houses and cars during storms and snows, they have fallen out of favor. Silver maple is a weak-wooded tree, and older specimens inevitably show the gaping scars of past indiscretions. In habit it is rangier than sugar maple, with many lower limbs angling up and away from the base of the trunk. Fall color is unremarkable—usually butterscotch yellow with some green mixed in.

Acer saccharum
Sugar Maple, Rock Maple

ZONES: 3–8; sun to light shade
SOIL: Moist, preferably only slightly acidic
NATIVE TO: Rich woods, especially on limestone; Nova Scotia to Minnesota and eastern South Dakota south to Missouri and Virginia and in the mountains to Georgia
SIZE: Height 60–80 (100) feet, width 25–50 feet
COLOR: Yellow-green; blooms in spring

Certainly this is one of our finest forest trees. When given enough space, the lower limbs set off horizontally, then curve upward in the amiable arm-waving, bent-elbowed way of the saguaro cactus. I must quote the effusive comments of Donald Culross Peattie in his classic *A Natural History of Trees* on the fall color of this species:

The most magnificent display of color in all the kingdom of plants is the autumnal foliage of the

Acer saccharum. *Sugar maple's legendary fall color develops as the leaves are dying in autumn, when excess sugars trapped in the leaves are converted to red-orange pigments called anthocyanins. Why this happens remains a mystery.*

trees of North America. Over them all, over the clear light of the Aspens and the Mountain Ash, over the leaping flames of Sumac and the hellfire flickerings of poison ivy, over the war-paint of the many Oaks, rise the colors of one tree—the Sugar Maple—in the shout of a great army. Clearest yellow, richest crimson, tumultuous scarlet, or brilliant orange—the foliage of Sugar Maple at once outdoes and unifies the rest. It is like the mighty, marching melody that rides upon the crest of some symphonic weltering sea and, with its crying song, gives meaning to all the calculated dissonance of the orchestra. (p. 454).

A bit over the top, perhaps, but this is the kind of fevered emotion that a sugar maple in full fall regalia can unleash in my heart as well. *A. grandidendatum* (bigtooth maple) is a closely related tree, smaller in stature and adapted to more alkaline soils, which ranges throughout the Southwest in scattered pockets. *A. nigrum* (black maple) is yet another questionably distinct species, identified mainly by the drooping margins of its darker green leaves.

Aesculus pavia

Aesculus (ay-ES-kew-lus)
Hippocastanaceae
Buckeye

Aesculus pavia. *Red buckeye is a perfect tree for the smaller garden. It blooms at an early age, and the flaming red flowers are spectacular for a few weeks in spring. Bold, droopy foliage carries through until fall.*

In the wild, buckeyes are minor members of the forest community. Many are understory trees favoring richer soils, though a few of the largest occasionally find a place in the upper tree canopy. Their wood is light-colored and extremely soft and weak, so they have been ignored by loggers in favor of walnuts or oaks. They might be relegated to horticultural obscurity if not for their beautiful flowers, which decorate the branch tips in colorful panicles or racemes for a few weeks in spring or summer. Buckeyes' distinctive foliage, too, has helped popularize

them. Their leaves are palmately divided like the five fingers of an outstretched hand, these arranged in pairs coupled by their long petioles. The petioles adjust in length as the leaves are expanding, so that those below are not shaded from those above. This petiolar compensation helps give the plants a certain tiered, well-spaced confidence that looks distinctive and dynamic. The leaves expand in a remarkable flourish each spring from a very large, resinous, terminal bud with a sharp pointed tip. Tubular flowers appear at the ends of many twigs as the leaves have more or less expanded. Most of the species have cupping petals and a tuft of stamens that protrude just beyond them, but in the bottlebrush buckeye and California buckeye, these stamens lengthen to look like flittering eyelashes winking at potential pollinators as they pass by.

Generally these are slow-growing plants, especially the horticulturally desirable *A. pavia* and *A. parviflora*. This is understandably discouraging to the nursery grower who wants to turn over inventory rapidly. As a general rule, large seeds like oaks, walnuts, and buckeyes have evolved to nourish a substantial seedling taproot. Thus, buckeyes put much of their resources the first few years into growing a deep taproot, which needs to be accommodated in a large container. The long and the short of this is that you will have to pay what seems like a considerable sum of money for a stubby little plant in an oversized pot and wait a good deal longer for it to amount to anything in the landscape. Buckeyes are wonderful things; just give them some time.

Most references I have come across warn of the poisonous effects of buckeyes, but the information in the literature is confused, in part because much is inferred about North American species from experience with the European horse chestnut *(A. hippocastanum)*. The seeds of red buckeye have been used as a fish poison and ground to yield a starch with insecticidal properties that was used in bookmaking. When washed to remove saponins and other bitter chemicals, however, the seeds of all buckeyes produce a highly nutritious flour. The few poisonings I could find reference to may have resulted from improper preparation of the seeds or misuse as a medicinal (see Millspaugh, *American Medicinal Plants*, pp. 167–170).

CULTURE: Buckeyes need a fairly rich and moist but well-drained soil to look their best. This will speed growth when young and produce consistent flowering when mature. Transplant in early spring and fertilize lightly for the first few years, but don't overdo it. I defoliated some red buckeyes one year with overzealous fertilization aimed at speeding growth. Even small seedlings have remarkable carrot-thick taproots that can be trimmed by a third without harm to the plant. The smaller species will begin to bloom when very young, and as painful as it sounds, removing the inflorescences on young plants in spring as soon as they are visible will encourage another flush of vegetative growth. Though most of the species can tolerate shade, they are best with at least 3 to 4 hours of sun. Ohio buckeye suffers from leaf blotch caused by the fungus *Guignardia aesculi*, the same disease that plagues horse chestnut and leaves the tree looking scorched by late summer. Thankfully, the other species are much more resistant to this disease, and resistant selections of Ohio buckeye are available.

USES: Specimen.

WILDLIFE: The nuts are a valuable mast for mammals. *A. pavia* attracts hummingbirds.

PROPAGATION: Easy from seed, though slow to grow.

Aesculus californica
California Buckeye

ZONES: 7–9; sun
SOIL: Moist in spring
NATIVE TO: Canyons and slopes, California
SIZE: Height 10–20 (35) feet, width 8–15 feet
COLOR: White to pale pink; blooms in late spring

California buckeye is a magnificent plant in flower, with dense pure white or light pink racemes suggesting in the way they rise up vertically from the mass of the plant, a stockier, bolder-looking bottlebrush buckeye. It is a chaparral species, tolerant of fire and summer drought, with a multistemmed, rounded habit whether it remains a single tree or spreads to form small thickets. I grew this in North Carolina after seeing it at the J. C. Raulston Arboretum, in Raleigh, and it proved perfectly hardy but never adjusted to East Coast time. When the heat and drought of summer return, it sheds all of its leaves, spending the rest of the season as a thick-branched, lifeless-looking thing in the landscape. This is a logical adaptation in a Mediterranean climate, where the rains come early and the drought lasts all summer. Certainly it's a valuable native for California gardens as well as for Southeasterners who want to stump their friends and annoy their neighbors.

Aesculus flava (octandra)
Yellow Buckeye, Sweet Buckeye

ZONES: 4–8; part sun, sun
SOIL: Moist, deep
NATIVE TO: Rich, moist woods and bottoms; the southern extreme of Pennsylvania west along the Ohio River to Illinois and south in the Appalachians to Tennessee and Georgia
SIZE: Height 40–80 (130) feet, width 20–35 feet
COLOR: Yellow or yellowish white suffused with red; blooms in spring

Yellow buckeye is our largest species of *Aesculus*, and

well-grown trees out in the open or in a favored spot in the forest have a broad, burly longshoreman presence. The warm gray bark peels off in irregular, curling strips and adds a certain shagginess to the tree's visage. You can distinguish it from Ohio buckeye (*A. glabra*) because it lacks a foul odor when you bruise the bark, and the seed husks are spineless. The flowers vary in color, but are typically a creamy yellow with a patch of red at the base of the upper petals. They are borne in short, branched panicles, and a plant in full bloom is pretty but not stunning. When open-grown the limbs fork low on the trunk, sending up a few stout branches so that the tree takes on a broadly oval outline. The heaviness of the bare branches in winter is not for everyone, but it makes a fine albeit somewhat messy shade tree with much better disease resistance than Ohio buckeye.

Aesculus glabra
Ohio Buckeye

ZONES: 4–7; sun
SOIL: Moist, well-drained
NATIVE TO: Alluvial woodland, often on calcareous soils; Pennsylvania north to southern Ontario and Wisconsin south to Kansas, Texas, and Alabama
SIZE: Height 30–40 (120) feet, width 20–40 feet
COLOR: Greenish yellow; blooms in spring

In habit this tree is much like *A. flava*, and in the Victorian era it was planted commonly as a street and lawn tree. I lived in a house for a few years in college that had an old one out front, and it tolerated life on a very busy street fairly well. However, it was one of the last trees to leaf out in spring and then got attacked by leaf blotch every fall so that by September it was bare again. I found myself secretly embarrassed and publicly apologetic for this lack of verdure. The flowers are not especially noticeable, but I do like the tree's hulking winter outline. There are some definable geographic races that are sometimes given specific status. *A. glabra* var. *arguta* (Texas buckeye) is found on limestone soils in central Texas and Oklahoma, and differs in having smaller size and more leafets per petiole (9 to 11 instead of the typical 5).

Aesculus parviflora
Bottlebrush Buckeye

ZONES: 4–8; part sun, sun (will grow but not bloom well in heavy shade)
SOIL: Moist, though it tolerates some drought
NATIVE TO: Alluvial soils, rich woods; confined mostly to central Alabama, but crossing into western Georgia along the Chattahoochee River
SIZE: Height 4–8 (18) feet, width 6–15 feet
COLOR: White; blooms in summer

Bottlebrush buckeye is a sublime shrub if you can

give it some breathing space and time to develop. In the forest it is a gap species, traveling around by root suckers in search of breaks in the tree canopy. Its scraggly look in the wild belies the lovely spreading mound it can become when grown in the open—a rounded, multistemmed semicircle studded with wispy racemes at a time when few plants are blooming. In winter it has a twiggy aspect, with larger stems toward the center and new sprouts coming up from the edge. It bears its flowers on the branch tips like its cousins, but they take their time to mature, growing longer all spring before finally bursting into bloom. Since the foliage is by this time fully expanded and a rich medium green, the flowers stand out beautifully above it. Fall color is a slow fade from green to soft yellow. This was a popular plant a century ago, and I've seen quite a few nice old specimens marking the remains of Victorian gardens. The one drawback is that the plants look a tad rangy for a few weeks after the flowers fade, as the stalks yellow and die. Var. *serotina* is a horticultural entity with flowers that appear a few weeks later, so it's nice to combine with the species if you can find one.

Aesculus pavia
Red Buckeye

ZONES: 5–9; part sun, sun
SOIL: Moist
NATIVE TO: Fertile woodlands and margins; along the coastal plain from North Carolina through northern Florida and Texas, then north to western Tennessee and southern Illinois
SIZE: Height 10–25 (40) feet, width 10–20 feet
COLOR: Bright to pinkish red; blooms in spring

We planted a red buckeye outside my office, and when it is in bloom, it rivals the rhododendrons in color and vibrancy. The relatively large petals are arranged like a hood to force the heads of foraging hummingbirds against the pistil and stamens. The stamens of each flower mature earlier than the pistils to encourage cross-pollination. The leaf petioles are often tinged red as well, and this contrasts with the deep, glossy green of the leaves. In habit it is an understory tree, with one or two trunks and a crown that is narrower than tall. Branches are rather stout for their size, regularly forked and ascending. It is fairly slow-growing (6–8 inches a year at Garden in the Woods), but with time, open-grown plants become gumdrop-shaped in outline. It does not appear to sucker like many of the smaller species, and the foliage remains in good condition all season. Overall, this is my favorite species, and its size makes it a great addition to smaller gardens if you have some patience while it matures.

Aesculus sylvatica
Painted Buckeye

ZONES: 6–9; light shade to sun
SOIL: Moist
NATIVE TO: Fertile woodlands; mostly in the piedmont from Virginia to Mississippi and Tennessee
SIZE: Height 5–20 feet, width 4–10 feet
COLOR: Creamy white to yellow or pink; blooms in spring

Like bottlebrush buckeye, this is a suckering, forest-gap species, and wild plants around my home in Durham, North Carolina, went completely unnoticed for the 50 weeks a year they were not in flower. It is closely related to red buckeye, and pink-flowered plants are likely to be natural hybrids. It naturalizes well in open woodland, but doesn't have the ornamental attributes of some of its relatives. I have read reports of brilliant red-orange fall color, but have seen only yellow myself.

Alnus rubra

Alnus (ALL-nus)
Betulaceae
Alder

Alders are not highly refined plants for the well-manicured landscape, but they are great healers of lands scarred by floods, logging, mining, or even glaciers. In a sonnet written in the early seventeenth century, the poet William Brown wrote, "The alder, whose fat shadow nourisheth / Each plant set neere

Alnus rubra. *Red alder typically forms almost pure stands along watercourses. This fast-growing grove is probably only twenty years old, although it appears much more mature.*

him long flourisheth" (quoted in Schwintzer, *Biology of Frankia*, p. 15). This may be the first documented observation of the benefits that nitrogen fixation by alder can have for the local ecosystem. Unlike legumes, which accumulate nitrogen through their symbiotic association with bacteria in the genus *Rhizobia*, *Alnus* and many other woody pioneer genera like *Comptonia*, *Ceanothus*, and *Dryas* use the services of bacteria in the genus *Frankia*. These plants have an unusual root morphology that enables them to colonize nutrient-poor areas, build up the soil, and make these areas fit for other plants to follow.

Alders are for the most part fine-branched, thicket-forming shrubs of watersides, bogs, and tundra. They are constantly sending up new suckers from the base and roots, and are unrivaled in their ability to colonize and stabilize the banks of turbulent mountain streams. Almost any unmanaged brook or river in the northern third of the globe will have its compliment of alder. The exception in this shrubby clan is red alder, which can grow to 100 feet or more in ideal spots and resprout remarkably quickly after cutting or fire. It is now being coppiced as a pulpwood tree in the Pacific Northwest — grown like a crop in agricultural fields and cut every decade or so like so much wheat.

Like their relatives the birches, most *Alnus* species produce both male and female catkins that form in the fall and overwinter half-developed and tinged purple on the ends of the twigs. The males elongate when the weather begins to warm in spring, dangling like yellow tassels from the branch tips. The females are stubbier; more like little pine cones, and remain on the trees a year or more, even after the seed is shed. In the winter, these are easy to spot and help identify the plants. The shrubby types are very similar in appearance, though there are minor differences in catkin size, leaf shape, and the toothiness of the leaf-margin.

CULTURE: Transplant readily into moist, wet, or even seasonally saturated soils. They will survive in drier soils but there are better plants for such sites. Alder being used for watercourse stabilization will need to be pinned or held in place with fiber mats until established. Container plants that are destined for areas where alder are already growing should become adequately inoculated with nitrogen-fixing *Frankia* once transplanted, but if there is a question, you can dig a few handfuls of soil from around established wild plants and mix this into water to form a thin slurry with which to water the containers. *Frankia* is sensitive to fertilizer salts, so after inoculation or transplanting into the field, do not fertilize the plants heavily. This will also help them maintain an advantage over competing weeds. Older plants can be renjuvenated by hard pruning when they are dormant; cut back the stems to within 6 inches of the ground.

USES: Reforestation, reclamation, bank stabilization.

WILDLIFE: Alder provide food and cover for goldfinches and grouse, and beavers seek out the twigs. They are host to the alder aphid, a large, sucking insect covered with white cottony hair, and these aphids are one of the primary foods for our only carnivorous butterfly, the harvester (*Feniseca tarquinius*), whose larvae prey on aphids much as ladybugs and lacewings do. Alder is one of the larval food plants for the tiger swallowtail and pallid tiger swallowtail butterflies (*Papilio glaucus* and *P. eurymedon*) as well as the colorful white admiral (*Limenitis arthemis*), green comma (*Polygonia faunus*) and mourning cloak (*Nymphalis antiopa*).

PROPAGATION: Easy from seed, moderately easy from division or hardwood cuttings.

Alnus incana
Speckled Alder, Thinleaf Alder

ZONES: 2–7; part sun, sun
SOIL: Moist to wet
NATIVE TO: Pond and streamsides, bogs, swales, *A. incana* ssp. *rugosa* from Labrador to Saskatchewan south to North Dakota, Iowa, and West Virginia; *A. incana* ssp. *tenuifolia* from Montana north through Alberta to northern Saskatchewan and Alaska south to California and New Mexico
SIZE: Height 8–15 (30) feet, width 6–20 feet
COLOR: Dull purple; blooms in early spring
Speckled alder is a circumboreal species represented in North America by two subspecies, one east and one west of the Continental Divide. *A. incana* ssp. *rugosa* (often listed as simply *A. rugosa*, speckled alder) is the most common *Alnus* species in southern New England. It is usually a thicket-forming shrub growing in colonies in wet, sunny locations. Its leaves have a jagged, doubly serrate margin like a page torn out of a book, and white lenticels dot and speckle the trunk. *A. incana* ssp. *tenuifolia* (thinleaf or mountain alder) is so called because the leaves are thinner in texture. In the Old West, spying some mountain alder meant that precious water was near at hand.

Alnus maritima
Seaside Alder

ZONES: 4–8; part sun, sun
SOIL: Moist to wet, somewhat salt-tolerant
NATIVE TO: Pond, stream, and riversides, Wicomico and Nantikoke rivers of Delaware and Maryland, also in south central Oklahoma
SIZE: Height 10–20 (30) feet, width 6–12 feet
COLOR: Purple-brown; blooms in late summer to fall
This is a very interesting plant for plant geographers, as it represents the only North American member of

the Asian group of fall-blooming alders, which develop catkins during the summer that flower before the leaves are shed. Seeds complete development over the following summer and are shed as the next crop of flowers mature—the same reproductive rhythm as common witch-hazel (*Hamamelis virginiana*). *A. maritima* is now restricted to two very small areas in the mid-Atlantic states and Oklahoma, which probably represent the last fading remnants of a far wider distribution in postglacial times. Horticulturally it is much like the other shrub species, albeit somewhat larger, but ecologically it is yet another fascinating reminder that plants are not passive and immobile, but rather are wanderers, advancing and retreating at a pace that is merely too slow for us to perceive.

Alnus rubra

Red Alder

ZONES: 4–7; light shade to sun

SOIL: Moist to wet

NATIVE TO: Floodplains, streamsides; central California north along the coast through southern Alaska, with a disjunct population in the Idaho panhandle

SIZE: Height 50–80 (100) feet, width 15– 25 feet

COLOR: Purple–brownish yellow; blooms in early spring before leaves emerge

Red alder is a common sight in the Pacific Northwest. It is capable of tremendously fast growth (up to 10 feet a year for stump sprouts), though it is not very long-lived. Young stands develop a striking matte white bark that rivals that of paper birch, but this becomes obscured by patches of moss as the trees age. *A. rubra* (*rubra* refers to a red dye extracted from the inner bark) yields a light but fairly strong wood used for interior surfaces of furniture and as a source of paper pulp. In the landscape, it can provide quick screening and shade, eventually yielding to slower-growing shade-tolerant conifers like western red cedar. In the drier parts of Oregon and California, it is replaced by *A. rhombifolia* (white alder), a smaller tree that is more tolerant of low humidity and drier soils.

Alnus serrulata

Smooth Alder, Common Alder

ZONES: 3–10; part sun, sun

SOIL: Moist to wet

NATIVE TO: Stream banks, swales, bogs, and lakeshores; Canadian Maritime Provinces south along the coast, then west to southern Missouri, then south again to eastern Texas and Florida

SIZE: Height 8–15 (25) feet, width 6–15 feet

COLOR: Purple–brownish yellow; blooms in early spring

This is the most heat- and humidity-tolerant species,

and thus it is the alder of choice for the Southeast. In habit and appearance it is much the same as speckled alder, and the two interbreed, making identification a frustrating and fruitless task for the aspiring young botanist or *Alnus* aficionado.

Alnus viridis

Green Alder, Sitka Alder

ZONES: 2–7; sun

SOIL: Moist to wet

NATIVE TO: Stream banks, swales, bogs, tundra, and lakeshores; most of Canada south of the high Arctic, south to northern California and Montana and east through northern Minnestota and southern Ontario to New England, with isolated populations in the Appalachian Mountains to North Carolina

SIZE: Height 4–10 feet, width 3–8 feet

COLOR: Green-purple; blooms in spring

This species is northern, traveling clear across Canada and the Aleutian Islands to Siberia. As you might expect, it has responded to its frigid and windswept environs with smaller size and a twiggy tenacity. Male catkins develop in the fall, but the females remain sheltered under a protective blanket of scales through the winter. Where green alder overlaps with other alders, this lack of visible immature female flowers in winter is an easy way to distinguish it. Like *A. incana*, *A. viridis* has been divided into eastern and western races that I'll make note of because they are often listed as separate species. *A. viridis* ssp. *crispa* (green alder) ranges from Greenland to Alberta, to be replaced by the larger-leaved *A. viridis* ssp. *fruticosa* (Siberian alder) as it ranges toward the Northwest Territories and the larger-growing Sitka alder (*A. viridis* ssp. *sinuata*) as it drops down the Pacific side of the Rockies.

Amelanchier

(ah-mel-LANK-eer)

Rosaceae

Serviceberry, Sarvisberry, Shadbush, Shadblow

Amelanchier alnifolia

The serviceberries are all lovely variations on a theme. There are 20 or so species in this mostly North American genus; all are shrubs or small trees with silvery gray bark and delicate white flowers that appear in little bunches from the bare twigs in early spring. The airy and precocious appearance of these blooms gives the plants a soft, frosted look, as though they've been dusted with late-season snow. They freely interbreed where ranges overlap, creating a vast and notorious hybrid swarm that has driven sober botanists to drink. You really never know for sure what you are going to get when you grow these promiscuous rascals, but generally there are three types that blur together along the edges. The first are the trees, *A. laevis* and *A. arborea*, capable of topping a four-story building but commonly in the 20-to-30-foot range with 6-inch-diameter trunks appearing singly or in small clumps. Then there are the tall shrubs, notably *A. canadensis*, with trunks possibly as big as your wrist or as small as your thumb growing in multistemmed clumps that can be forced with judicious pruning of the stems to form attractive small trees with an oval crown. Finally there are the suckering shrubs, like *A. sanguinea, A. bartramiana, A. utahensis,* and *A. stolonifera*, which prefer open or disturbed ground and spread to form rounded clumps or thickets. So there is a shadbush for every situation, and all bring to the garden a certain untamed refinement lost in the highly bred forms of crabapples and cherries. Their flowers have a charming informality; the five petals are arranged unevenly like a disheveled star with a yellow spot of stamens in the center. These appear with the unfolding leaves from spear-shaped buds and are all the more welcome and vivid because of the barrenness of the season.

Amelanchiers have many common names. "Serviceberry" is a corruption of the word "sarvisberry," in a reference to the berries' faint resemblance to the fruits of the sarvis tree or European mountain ash. The moniker "shadbush" results from the fact that they bloom concurrently with the yearly spawning migration up eastern coastal rivers of the shad (an anadromous fish of eastern rivers). A plethora of common names is a good indicator of a plant's past value to people, and in this case it boils down to fruits, small but delectable fruits that are among the tastiest and most uniquely flavored wild fruits this

continent has to offer. Together with the nectar they provide for awakening insects, this fruit puts them near the top of the list in terms of value to wildlife. The blueberry-sized berries ripen to a deep purple or red in summer. Saskatoon serviceberry has the sweetest fruits, and was long an important staple of the Cree tribes of the Canadian prairies, who crushed and dried the fruits with buffalo meat to form pemmican, which saw them through the long winters. These berries ripen over a few weeks in early to midsummer, but, like freestone peaches, the fruit bruises easily and deteriorates quickly, so they are never likely to be-come widely available. You will have to grow them yourself to really enjoy them—provided you can beat the birds to them, that is. Serviceberry leaves are oval, often finely toothed along the margin, gray-green above and lighter underneath. Fall color can be very good, ranging from golden yellow through blotchy oranges and reds in a good year.

CULTURE: Serviceberries are extremely adaptable and transplant readily into a range of soils, and many can tolerate very dry, poor conditions once established. Root systems are fibrous and shallow and thus easy to move. The wood is very dense and strong, so the tree species are very resilient in storms. All of them can be renewed by hard pruning, and older, weak stems should be removed when they start to show decline to prevent them from acting as reservoirs for disease. Like most members of the rose family, *Amelanchier* species suffer from leaf spot, rusts, and stem cankers, which may leave the plants somewhat defoliated before fall. Many of the more commonly available cultivars are resistant to diseases, though, and if you choose a species that is appropriate for your area, disease is usually not severe. Their understated beauty, fruits, and importance to birds and mammals put them near the top of my list of natives for the landscape.

Amelanchier alnifolia. The juicy, ripe berries of saskatoon are among the continent's most delectable wild fruits. I would describe their flavor as somewhere between cherry and pear, with a hint of almond mixed in. Many birds, including thrushes and grosbeaks, rely on high-energy Amelanchier *fruits to sustain them during the breeding season. The branches are festooned with informal flowers for a week or so in early spring.*

USES: Specimens, foundations, woodland edge, soil stabilization (stoloniferous species), fruit production.

WILDLIFE: Besides their value to birds and mammals, serviceberries are one of the primary larval foodplants of the tiger, pallid tiger, and two-tailed tiger butterflies (*Papilio glaucus, P. eurymedon,* and *P. multicaudata,* respectively), as well as the viceroy, white admiral, and western admiral (*Limenitis archippus, L. arthemis,* and *L. weidemeyerii*) and the western hairstreak (*Satyrium californica*).

PROPAGATION: Moderately difficult from cuttings, moderately easy from seed.

Amelanchier alnifolia

Saskatoon Serviceberry, Western Serviceberry

ZONES: 2–6; sun

SOIL: Moist to moderately dry

NATIVE TO: Stream banks, thickets, rocky slopes; Manitoba northwest to central Alaska south to northern California, New Mexico, Colorado, and western Minnesota.

SIZE: Height 4–10 (20) feet, width 4–10 feet

COLOR: White, lightly fragrant; blooms in early spring

As you might guess from the specific name, *alnifolia,* meaning "alder leaf," this colonial, shrubby species has oval leaves flattened along their base and jagged margins, suggest an alder in appearance. It is the most common species in the West, and produces clusters of inch-wide, dark reddish purple fruits in summer. "Saskatoon" is likely a corruption of the Cree word for the fruit; it is superior to most others in flavor, and there are a number of cultivars that have been selected for good fruiting. One word of caution: the sugary pulp moves through a bird's digestive system remarkably fast, so watch where you park your car during berrying season.

I can confirm Michael Dirr's observations (*Manual of Woody Landscape Plants,* p. 93) that the shrub performs poorly in the humid East, suffering from defoliating leaf diseases that bother local species far less. In my garden, it blooms a week earlier than the eastern species and ripens its fruit earlier as well. The closely related and equally tasty *A. humilis* (low serviceberry) grows in calcareous soils farther east and may prove a decent substitute. This particular species provided my introduction to serviceberry fruit when I was on a canoe trip in western Ontario after high school. It is very good indeed. To give you an idea of the range of shrubby, spreading *Amelanchier* species, I will mention *A. sanguinea* (New England serviceberry), a northeastern plant favoring dry soils and bearing red twigs and new growth, later flowers, and slightly smaller, edible fruit; *A. utahensis* (Utah serviceberry), from the Great Basin; and *A. nantucketensis* (Nantucket shadblow), a rare endemic restricted to sandy soils in a few spots along the northern Atlantic coastal plain.

Amelanchier arborea

Downy Serviceberry

ZONES: 4–9; light shade to sun

SOIL: Moist but well-drained to dry

NATIVE TO: Upland woods, rocky outcrops; New Brunswick to southwestern Ontario south to Oklahoma, Louisiana, and northern Florida

SIZE: Height 20–30 (50) feet, width 8–15 feet

COLOR: White; blooms in early spring

I have seen this species growing as a canopy tree on dry ridge tops where the competition was forcibly reduced in stature, but in general it is relegated to the understory and woodland edge. Downy serviceberry bears new leaves covered in soft gray fur on branches covered in muscled cool gray bark laced with darker vertical striations. When open-grown, it becomes a handsome single or multitrunked small tree with a narrow oval crown. The flowers come in long sprays from the opening buds, and the regrettably unpalatable red-purple fruits are borne on short (<1-inch) pedicels.

Amelanchier bartramiana

Mountain Serviceberry

ZONES: 3–6; part sun, sun

SOIL: Moist to moderately dry

NATIVE TO: Moist, often acidic soils of bogs, streamsides, swamps, and also rocky slopes; Labrador to Manitoba, south to Minnesota, Vermont, and Maine

SIZE: Height 3–6 feet, width 3–4 feet

COLOR: White; blooms in spring

I was very impressed with this species when I saw it in full bloom at the Arnold Arboretum, near Boston, and later in the wilds on the Gaspé Peninsula of Quebec. The new leaves may have a bronze cast like Allegheny serviceberry, maturing small, oval, and gray-green in color, and the flowers are also small but very numerous on plants in the sun. It tends to be a tight, many-branched, rounded little shrub—the plant at the Arnold Arboretum is roughly 4 feet high and 3 feet wide after 15 years and shows no sign of stoloniferous tendencies (spreading by shallow horizontal stems). Fruits are small, dark purple, and edible, though I haven't tried any for flavor. I think this species has great potential as a tough landscape and foundation plant for northern gardens.

Amelanchier canadensis

Canada Serviceberry, Shadbush

ZONES: 4–9; light shade to sun

SOIL: Wet to moderately dry

NATIVE TO: Swamps and low woods; mostly within 200 miles of the Atlantic coast from Newfoundland to Mississippi

SIZE: Height 10–20 feet, width 5–10 feet

COLOR: White; blooms in early spring

Although this serviceberry is restricted to moist soils in the wild, it is adaptable in cultivation and makes an attractive small tree taller than wide when some of the smaller stems are removed. Bark is uniformly smooth and cool gray and the fruits are small, dark purple, and edible. I like to use this shadbush near foundations or in mixed borders where some height is desired.

Amelanchier laevis
Allegheny Serviceberry

ZONES: 4–8; light shade to sun

SOIL: Moist to dry

NATIVE TO: Woods and ridges; Newfoundland southwest to Minnesota and Iowa, east to Maryland and in the mountains to Georgia

SIZE: Height 25–40 feet (60) feet, width 8–18 feet

COLOR: White; blooms in early spring

In habit and adaptability Allegheny serviceberry is much like its close relative *A. arborea*. It differs in a few important ways, however, which make it the tree *Amelanchier* of choice for gardens. The new growth emerges a bronzy purple, which contrasts remarkably well with the large flowers, and it produces delicious dark purple fruits. The two occasionally hybridize in the wild to produce *A. × grandiflora* (apple serviceberry), also listed incorrectly as *A. lamarkii* or *A. canadensis* 'Lamarkii', a superior plant with a winning combination of hybrid vigor and downy, bronzed new growth, as well as even larger, more numerous flowers and edible fruit.

Amelanchier stolonifera
Running Serviceberry

ZONES: 4–9; sun

SOIL: Dry, well-drained

NATIVE TO: Sandy and rocky soils, cliffs, dunes, and upland woods; Newfoundland to Ontario south to Minnesota, Michigan, and Virginia

SIZE: Height 1–6 feet, width 3–10 feet

COLOR: White; blooms in spring

I have chosen this species to represent the highly stoloniferous complex of low serviceberries that are the true taxonomic black hole within the genus. Others that are basically equivalent are *A. obovalis* (coastal serviceberry) from the southeastern coastal plain, as well as *A. pumila* (dwarf serviceberry), and *A. spicata* (spicate serviceberry), the latter two often reduced to synonymy with running serviceberry. Because of their low, scraggly habit, this group has the fewest applications in the landscape, but could be used where a drought-tolerant spreading ground-cover is needed to weave in with other plants. I am growing *A. stolonifera,* and it spreads at the same rate as lowbush blueberry, making it a good companion. I have interplanted the two along with sheep laurel on a dry, acid bank in front of my house. We'll see which one is victorious.

Andromeda polifolia

Andromeda polifolia (an-DROM-eh-da)
Ericaceae
Bog Rosemary

ZONES: 2–6; part sun, sun

SOIL: Constantly damp but not sodden, cool and acidic

NATIVE TO: Acid bogs, circumboreal; Labrador to Alaska south to British Columbia, Indiana, West Virginia, and New Jersey

SIZE: Height 12–20 inches, width 16–28 inches

COLOR: Light pink; blooms in spring

The finest bog rosemarys I have ever seen were growing in containers at a large wholesale nursery. The confines of a pot and a "just this side of lethal" dose of fertilizer produces tight little mounds of narrow, leathery blue-gray leaves smothered with bubble-gum pink buds and softer pink, bell-shaped flowers in clusters from the ends of the twigs — just in time for spring sales. There is no cuter plant than a well-grown *Andromeda* in a 2-gallon pot, but alas, this foliar and floral affluence begins to thin out after a few years in the garden. Bog rosemary has an undeniable charm; I just want to warn you that its true nature will not be revealed until it leaves the container for the open soil. In the wild, it is often a sparse, traveling shrub of sphagnum bogs and alpine tundra, where the soil is cold and damp, infertile, and extremely acidic. It creeps along slowly like the

Andromeda polifolia. A well-grown bog rosemary forms a neat little mound of ice blue, leathery leaves, topped in earliest spring with bright pink, jug-shaped flowers. Careful, light shearing during early summer will help keep the plant full-looking.

smaller *Vaccinium* species, sending up new stems clothed in 1-to-2-inch leaves that spiral their length, branching more and more finely over the next few seasons. Its buds are set along the branch tips in fall, so they are ready to expand quickly as the ground warms and the bog becomes a buzzing cacophony of feasting bees. I am very fond of bog rosemary, and if given a peaty spot, full sun, and no competition, it can live up to its potential. We have patches of it mingling informally with bog laurel (*Kalmia polifolia*), leatherleaf (*Chamaedaphne calyculata*), and Labrador tea (*Ledum groenlandicum*) in our bog gardens at Garden in the Woods—an ericaceous smorgasbord of sorts where none stands out above the rest but the overall effect is just right.

A. polifolia var. *glaucophylla* ranges much farther south and east than the typical form of the species. It is a bit taller, with narrower leaves coated in woolly white pelt underneath, which contrasts subtly with the leathery blue uppers like a fur collar on a winter coat.

CULTURE: Transplant from containers in spring to a sunny spot with damp, loose, acid soil (the 1:1 peat moss–sand mix I use for bog gardens is appropriate). Do not crowd bog rosemary, or it will thin out. The older stems can be removed to rejuvenate the clump, but not much else is required. Does not do well in hot climates, where root diseases prove fatal. Fertilize sparingly when established.

USES: Bog garden, tundra simulation experiments.

PROPAGATION: Moderately difficult from cuttings or seed.

Aralia spinosa. In winter the stout, few-branched trunks of Hercules club might be mistaken for sumac, which also thrives along roadsides and woodland edges. However, once summer comes, there can be no mistaking the humongous, intricately divided foliage of this Aralia, which has some of the largest leaves of any plant in temperate North America. Colonies are especially beautiful in fall, when ethereal clusters of flowers and fruits festoon the canes.

Aralia spinosa

Aralia spinosa (a-RAY-lia)
Araliaceae
Hercules Club, Devil's Walking Stick

ZONES: 4–9; light shade to sun
SOIL: Moist to wet; best in fertile soils
NATIVE TO: Low woods; Delaware to Indiana and Missouri south to Texas and Florida; naturalized in New England and parts of the Great Lakes
SIZE: Height 6–15 (40) feet, width 4–10 feet
COLOR: White and purple-pink; blooms in late summer

Hercules club is a first-rate ornamental except for two flaws: its ability to spread remarkably far underground and then pop up in embarrassing places, coupled with an armament of stout, nasty thorns that line the petioles, branches, and trunk to rebuff your loving embrace. The thorns are interesting in that, though most numerous on the twigs, they continue to grow slowly along with the bark, so that older stems are smooth to the eye but prickly to the touch. It is a forest-gap species with shallow, wandering roots that test for breaks in the canopy every 10 feet or so by erecting very stout, pithy stems supporting elaborate, tropical-looking thrice pinnately compound leaves up to 3 feet long and 2 feet wide gathered near the tops of the stems—in fact, I think these are the largest leaves of any plant in the North American flora. When *Aralia spinosa* finds a spot with some sunshine, up it goes a few feet a year, broadening out into the understory on a few muscular branches. On the edge of the woods, it can act like a sumac, forming tropical-looking groves fit for lounging in front of in your Hawaiian shirt, with your parrot and colorful umbrella drink. A word of caution, though: as I discovered the hard way, Hercules club is a sleeping giant. We had an old specimen growing in a garden I was maintaining, and as it is not a long-lived tree, the trunk was showing signs of decline. I cut the plant back to the ground to rejuvenate it, and rejuvenated it was, popping up here and there every 10 feet or so from dormant buds on its spreading roots. As with sumacs and sassafras, a healthy tree seems to keep its root sprouts in check, but removing the main trunk(s) unleashes buds long lying in wait.

A. spinosa has an airy, palm-tree effect all summer and a coarse, unique, stubby look in the winter, but fall is truly its finest hour. As summer begins to wane, the tip of each branch develops a flattened, compound panicle composed of dozens of small flowers arrayed in wagon-wheel umbels. The creamy white flowers give the plants a frothy, clouded appearance when they first appear. As individual flowers are pollinated (they are always buzzing with bees), their pedicels turn grape-juice purple in anticipation of the dark purple berries to follow. Since the inflorescences bloom sequentially, by early fall the whole is a glorious crazy-quilt jumble of cream, pink, and purple. The pedicels help advertise the berries to birds, who quickly eat them, and soon the leaves yellow and drop off.

CULTURE: Transplant from containers or move sections of root and stem in early spring. It prefers a moist, rich soil—even the edge of a swamp. Certainly Hercules club is not for the smaller garden, but it is an easy plant for the woodland edge or an island in the lawn. It will grow as a fairly well behaved small tree as long as the crown is not damaged, but expect some root sprouting eventually. In the right situation, it is a feast for the eyes as well as the birds.

USES: woodland edge, contained specimen, massing.

PROPAGATION: Easy from seed.

Arbutus menziesii

Arbutus (ar-BEW-tus)
Ericaceae
Madrone

Madrone is one of those rare trees possessing a jaw-dropping sinuous elegance that almost everyone can recognize as something special. *Arbutus* species are relatives of rhododendrons, with rich, glossy evergreen leaves and sweetly fragrant bell-shaped flowers hung from a gnarled, thickly branched trunk. The flowers are a translucent greenish white—not tremendously showy, but visible enough to lend a whitewashed effect to the canopy when they bloom. Pollinated flowers develop into leathery yellow then vivid orange fruits that hang from the branches for months in vivid Halloween contrast with the leaves. The true joy of these trees, though, is their multicolored bark, a luminous coppery orange on the younger branches eventually peeling away in patches like a bad sunburn to reveal rippling inner bark that is dull olive green. The trunks become so smooth at this stage that the bark looks more like sculpted clay than living tissue. Finally very old trunks develop a checkered, warm gray bark puckered at the base with a burl of dormant buds ready to sprout in case fire kills off the current canopy. Madrone's wood is reddish brown, and along the coast between northern California and Washington, local craftspeople sculpt furniture from it, some of the best pieces preserving in their form the gnarled and twisted quality of the tree.

CULTURE: Even though Pacific madrone grows as far north as rainy British Columbia, it is found there in dry microclimates in the rain shadow of mountains, where rainfall is limited to 20 inches or so a year. They are plants of rocky, dry soils that need some attention when young but are extremely tough and long-lived when established. I have never seen impressive specimens outside their native range, and in the Southeast, I would imagine only gardeners directly along the coast could grow them at all. They are intolerant of excessive soil moisture in the summer, but are adaptable to varying levels of acidity. Their reputation for being difficult to transplant may stem in part from people trying to dig wild-grown

Arbutus menziesii. The brick red color and smooth-as-clay texture of an adolescent Pacific madrone creates quite a statement in the landscape. As the tree grows, gray and brown tones will replace the red on the lower trunk.

plants. Nursery-grown containerized specimens will transplant, provided they are watered carefully so that a deep taproot can become established, which takes one to two years. After this they require little water or care. Like many members of the Ericaceae, they associate with nitrogen-scavenging mycorrhizal fungi, which limits their need for fertilizer.

USES: Specimen.

WILDLIFE: Excellent nectar plants, and the mealy fruits are valued by birds.

PROPAGATION: Moderately easy from seed.

Arbutus arizonica

Arizona Madrone

ZONES: (8) or 9–10; sun

SOIL: Well-drained

NATIVE TO: Mountain slopes, canyons (4000–8000 feet); southeastern Arizona and southwestern New Mexico south in a line through west central Mexico

SIZE: Height 20–40 feet, width 15–25 feet

COLOR: White; blooms spring to summer, as rains permit

This extremely handsome tree is a close relative of the Pacific madrone (*A. menziesii*), which may have evolved from it. The Arizona species is restricted to higher elevations at the edge of the Sonoran Desert, where higher rainfall allows it to survive. It differs from Pacific madrone in that its older bark is white to gray, rather than olive, its leaves are narrower, and its fruits ripen closer to scarlet.

Arbutus menziesii
Pacific Madrone

ZONES: 8–9; sun
SOIL: Well-drained
NATIVE TO: Dry slopes, canyons, beach heads; California north to southwest British Columbia along the coast
SIZE: Height 20–50 (100) feet, width 20–50 feet
COLOR: Greenish white; blooms in spring

Besides featuring ornamental bark, flowers, and fruit, this tree puts on a show as it sloughs off its two-year-old leaves when the newest ones are coming out in early summer. The old leaves turn brilliant red before they fall, adding yet another shade to this tree's psychedelic palette. The fruits are said to have a mildly narcotic effect, but I cannot find any confirmation of this.

Arbutus texana
Texas Madrone

ZONES: 8–10; sun
SOIL: Well-drained, slightly acid to alkaline
NATIVE TO: Hills and mountainsides in scattered populations through southwestern and south-central Texas and northern Mexico
SIZE: Height 20–40 feet, width 15–30 feet
COLOR: White; blooms in spring

This species of madrone, like *A. arizonica*, just crosses into Texas from the tribe's center of diversity in mountainous Mexico. It has dark green leaves that are gray below and scarlet berries that light up the tree like Christmas decorations in late summer. Typical specimens have a gray, smooth bark, but individuals with combinations of orange, deep rusty red, olive, and brown tones can be found. Texas madrone is well loved in its home state and is used in landscapes to some degree, though its reputation for being difficult to transplant limits its widespread use.

Arctostaphylos patula
Arctostaphylos
(ark-toe-STAF-ee-los)
Ericaceae
Manzanita, Bearberry, Kinickinick

Arctostaphylos **species** have found the Mediterranean climate most to their liking in California, where every mountain range and peninsula seems to have its own complement of unique species and varieties. Despite this diversity, all the manzanitas have certain things in common. They are broadleaf evergreens in the Heath family, with dull or glossy, leath-

ery leaves on short petioles arrayed along branches covered with peeling bark in lovely shades of maroon, bronze, green, and cinnamon. They are some of the finest groundcovers and shrubs in our flora, all sharing a fondness for craggy or sandy places, where water drains quickly away and nitrogen is in limited supply. Like *Arbutus* and most of the other Ericaceae, *Arctostaphylos* can scavenge nitrogen with tremendous efficiency by associating with mycorrhizal fungi. Fire is a friend to these shrubs, and after a conflagration many will resprout vigorously from a burl or crown covered in a knot of dormant buds. They are primarily groundcovers or rounded shrubs, though a few can attain the stature of a small tree with age. Manzanitas continue to grow through the season as conditions permit, and the fresh new leaves contrast with mature ones light against dark. As the growing season begins to wane, small clusters of flowers develop from the tips. When these are partially mature, they cease expanding and go through the winter ready to resume growth quickly in spring. The flowers are urn-shaped, with petals fused into a hanging bell cinched together at the bottom so that the opening is just big enough for a bee to access nectar with its tongue. They range from white to pink, often with a light, honey-sweet fragrance that permeates the air when they are warmed by the sun. Of course, bees and flowers give rise to fruits, usually large red berries that are dry and mealy but relished by many mammals, including, of course, bears—hence the common name bearberry.

The bewildering array of species, subspecies, and

Arctostaphylos patula. *On parched, windswept outcrops, greenleaf manzanita takes on wonderfully picturesque twisted forms that suggest the finest bonsai. A thick, burly trunk forces its way through crevices in the rock and stands ready to send out vigorous new sprouts from myriad dormant buds should fire damage the branches.*

varieties of manzanita along the West Coast are in the midst of rapid speciation, and myriad variation in leaf and fruit form and color, size, and bark characters can be found as the result of hybridization and genetic isolation. I will attempt to cover a decent cross-section of the species. Though most are hardy only along the Pacific coast, controlled crossing with hardier forms has the potential to produce a plethora of more adaptable shrubs with outstanding leaf and bark characteristics, if only someone would undertake it.

CULTURE: These are rugged drought-, wind-, and salt-tolerant plants once established. I have tried to grow the hardy forms of *A. patula* and *A. nevadensis* in the dry-land garden at Garden in the Woods, and they seem to wither away—not in winter, but in the muggy days and sultry nights of late summer. The leaves get blemished and spotted, and the plants are prone to what is probably a root rot but could also be drought stress brought on by poor root establishment. What puzzles me is that the plants grow well in the nursery, weathering winter and summer too, but fail to establish in the garden. This gives me hope that I have just not found the proper microclimate for these lovely shrubs. I suspect that part of the problem may be incompatibility between the container soil mix and a gritty garden soil, and careful attention to watering is necessary for the first year or two until the root system can establish both deep roots for water and a network of fine feeder roots to scavenge nutrients. *Arctostaphylos* needs well-drained soil, typically acidic, though a few of the Californian species are endemics in that state's serpentine soils. I saw an interesting planting at the Holden Arboretum in Kirtland, Ohio, where some bearberry was planted on a sandy mound. During some dry years it spread into the adjoining clay, but after a very wet year, the plant died off right along the margins of the sand.

Light fertilization will produce vigorous new growth and aid establishment, but this is playing with fire because too much will promptly kill the plants. It is best to withhold all fertilizer once transplants have settled in. Transplant container-grown plants in spring. The groundcover types can be layered, and the rooted sections carefully lifted the following spring with some success. Established plants should never be moved.

USES: Groundcover, massing, bank and dune stabilization, seaside planting, and xeriscaping (landscaping with drought-resistant plants); large species can be used as specimens.

WILDLIFE: The fruit is eaten mainly by mammals. Bearberry is a food plant for the larvae of the northern zigzag fritillary *(Boloria freija)* and hoary and brown elfins *(Callophrys polios* and *C. augustus).* The flowers are an important nectar source for early-season foragers.

PROPAGATION: Moderately difficult from cuttings, difficult from seed.

Arctostaphylos alpina
Alpine Bearberry

ZONES: 2–6, part sun
SOIL: Moist and cool, acidic, well-drained
NATIVE TO: Tundra and alpine ridges; Greenland to Alaska south in the mountains to Maine and New Hampshire
SIZE: Height 3–8 inches, width 8–16 inches
COLOR: Pink; blooms in spring

This cold-climate species is one of the characteristic low groundcovers of the alpine summits of New England and eastern Canada, where tundralike conditions allow it to survive far south of its main range in northern Canada and Alaska. It is a small shrub, with puckered, spatulate leaves that are shiny and thinner in texture than most of the group, and that blush burgundy in fall, then tend to brown off during winter. Jet black berries adorn the plants in autumn. We are growing this species in a partially shaded, mossy area of the garden where seepage from the slope above keeps the ground cool and boggy during the summer.

Arctostaphylos canescens
Hoary Manzanita, Silver Manzanita

ZONES: (6)7–9, part sun, sun
SOIL: Well-drained, moderately dry
NATIVE TO: Dry or gravelly slopes and coniferous forests at moderate elevations; southern Oregon south to central California
SIZE: Height 3–6 feet, width 3–4 feet
COLOR: White to light pink; blooms in early spring

Dusky silver leaves and contrasting cinnamon bark combined with a manageable size make this manzanita one of my favorites.

Arctostaphylos columbiana
Hairy Manzanita, Bristly Manzanita

ZONES: 8–9, part sun to sun
SOIL: Moderately moist to dry
NATIVE TO: Dry slopes, coastal scrub and coniferous forests; coastal Bristish Columbia south to northern California
SIZE: Height 3–7 (10) feet, width 3–6 feet
COLOR: White; blooms in spring

Hairy manzanita gets its name from the bristly hairs that coat the twigs. It can be found up the Pacific Coast in wetter habitats than most of the other species. It is a fast-growing shrub or even small tree with pointed, green leaves covered in a thin gray pubescence when young, bright red fruits, and sinuous, muscled trunks covered in brown bark peeling to expose brighter red underneath. It is a common sight in recent clear-cuts in the coastal ranges of Oregon and Washington.

Arctostaphylos edmundsii
Little Sur Manzanita

ZONES: 8–9, sun

SOIL: Well-drained

NATIVE TO: Ocean cliffs and bluffs, Monterey County, California

SIZE: Height 1–2 feet, width 3 feet

COLOR: Light pink; blooms in winter at the onset of the rainy season

Little Sur manzanita is one of a number of distinct species restricted to the rugged coast of Monterey County. It is an especially lovely species, with bronzy new growth that contrasts with the glossy green of mature leaves. In habit it is a spreading, mounded shrub with red-brown fruits ripening in spring. Several cultivars with colorful new growth have been introduced and are available from California nurseries.

Arctostaphylos glandulosa
Eastwood Manzanita

ZONES: 7–9, part sun, sun

SOIL: Well-drained, gritty

NATIVE TO: Gravelly or sandy chaparral and coniferous forests to 6,000 feet; Oregon to southern California

SIZE: Height 3–8 feet, width 3–8 feet

COLOR: White; blooms in late winter to early spring

Eastwood manzanita is a wide-ranging and variable species complex with six to eight named varieties. The typical form has tightly congested glossy, vibrant green leaves, white flowers, and red-brown fruits covered in sticky glands like the twigs. It favors

Arctostaphylos uva-ursi. I like to shear back bearberry's vigorous trailing stems in early spring to encourage a denser carpet. Alternatively, you can pin down these long growths with a galvanized wire staple. The pinned stems will layer, or root, where they contact the ground, and, when well rooted, can easily be lifted and transplanted.

fire-prone areas and develops a large knotted burl at the base of the smooth, dark red trunk.

Arctostaphylos glauca
Bigberry Manzanita

ZONES: 9, sun

SOIL: Well-drained, dry

NATIVE TO: Chaparral of lower mountain slopes; southern California

SIZE: Height 6–10 feet, width 6–8 feet

COLOR: White to light pink; blooms in late winter

I include this tender species because it is arguably the largest of the genus, becoming a rounded, multi-trunked small tree. The leaves typically are paddle-shaped, with a glaucous bloom so that the whole has a blue-gray cast in the best forms. Mahogany twigs give way to peeling bark and sport large, branching clusters of blooms on hairy pink pedicels. The berries are also very large (up to 1 inch wide) and ranging in color from dull red to orange. *A. manzanita* (common manzanita) is similar in size and habit, with deep green leaves that are the perfect foil for pure white flowers and fruits that are white ripening to red.

Arctostaphylos hookeri
Hooker's Manzanita

ZONES: 8–9, part sun, sun

SOIL: Sandy, well-drained

NATIVE TO: Dunes and dry, open woods; Monterey County, California

SIZE: Height 1–3 feet, width 3–4 feet

COLOR: Light pink; blooms in spring

Lovely glossy red fruits that are pointed at the apex distinguish this mounding species from the central California coast. The fruits remind me of cranberries the way they color strongest on the side facing the sun. Dull to shiny green, spoon-shaped leaves tightly clothe the stem. *A. tomentosa* (woolyleaf manzanita) grows in the same region but it is shrubbier in character, with lanceolate leaves with woolly petioles, shaggy red-brown bark, and more rounded but equally glossy red fruits. *A. densiflora* (Sonoma manzanita) is a spreading, low shrub or groundcover layering where it touches the ground. It hybridizes with some of the taller species to produce low, mounded shrubs.

Arctostaphylos nevadensis
Pinemat Manzanita

ZONES: 6–8, sun

SOIL: Well-drained, moderately moist to dry

NATIVE TO: Outcrops and open woodland; Washington south to northern California with isolated populations east in the Rockies to Colorado.

SIZE: Height 8–24 inches, width 20–36 inches

COLOR: White to pale pink; blooms in spring

A congested (dense), low shrub or groundcover with bronzy, peeling bark and spoon-shaped leaves ending in a small point. As with most of the manzanitas, leaf color is variable, though dusty green seems to be the norm in plants I have seen. This is one of the hardiest of the western species, though still marginal in Zone 6 without consistent snow cover. The twisted, colorful stems and thick evergreen leaves make it an excellent garden plant where it can be grown. Fruits are a ruddy brown when ripe.

Arctostaphylos patula
Greenleaf Manzanita

ZONES: 5–8, sun
SOIL: Rocky, well-drained
NATIVE TO: Open forests and glades to 9,000 feet; Colorado to Washington south to California, Nevada, and Utah
SIZE: Height 3–6 feet, width 3–6 feet
COLOR: Medium pink to white; blooms in spring

The gnarled, sculptural trunk of this shrub, veiled in a thin cinnamon and green exfoliating bark, is a sight not soon forgotten and is enough to spur my continued efforts to cultivate it in the East. The stiff, leathery leaves are spoon-shaped with more or less flattened bases and a fairly long petiole and range in color from dusty gray-green to medium green in color. Material from the hardiest Coloradoan forms is available from specialty nurseries.

Arctostaphylos uva-ursi
Bearberry, Kinickinick

ZONES: 3–8, part sun, sun
SOIL: Sandy, acidic, well-drained
NATIVE TO: Dunes, sand barrens, ridges; circumboreal, Labrador to Alaska south to California, New Mexico, Indiana, and Virginia
SIZE: Height 3–8 inches, width 2–4 feet
COLOR: Light pink; blooms in spring

Certainly this is one of our finest groundcovers, and also the most adaptable species. The specific epithet, *uva-ursi*, means literally "berry of bear." It forms fast-creeping mats of glossy, spatulate leaves that are deep green in summer and bronzy red in winter. Peeling, shiny mahogany bark covers older stems, which is often obscured by foliage. Bearberry will survive heat and humidity that will kill the other species, provided it has perfect drainage. The fruits are large, ⅜ inch, bright to dark red, and very attractive when not hidden in the leaves. My two reservations regarding widespread use of this plant are its intolerance for all but poor, acid sand and the difficulty I have raking leaves from the mats in autumn — the rake tends to snag and uproot long sections of stem.

Aristolochia tomentosa

Aristolochia
(a-ris-toh-LOH-kia)
Aristolochiaceae
Pipevine, Dutchman's Pipe, Snakeroot

Pipevines are grown more for their foliage than for their flowers—in this case, immense, heart-shaped rich green leaves growing on a twining vine. The foliar canopy continues to thicken through the summer, so that by fall it is completely impenetrable to the eye—imagine a small and well-behaved kudzu and you'll get the picture. A hundred years ago, when porches were more common and people actually used them, Dutchman's pipe was a popular way to create a living curtain, trained up wires or a trellis to screen the porch from heat and nosey neighbors in summer and still allow light to stream through in winter. The decline of the porch has left the pipevine without a horticultural niche, but its vigor, shade tolerance, and easy nature may yet find it a place in modern gardens. These vines need a framework to get started, but once up to a height of 5–8 feet, the woody, corky-barked older branches provide some support of their own. We use pipevine as a screen on an old wooden fence and as a "shawl" for our garden cottage's chimney; we also allow one plant to scamper through old rhododendrons as it would in the wild.

Aristolochia is a primarily tropical genus of vines and stoloniferous perennials. In our flora, we have

Aristolochia tomentosa. If you can find them among the large leaves, pipevine flowers are fascinating little things. The long, curved tube lures and traps small flies until they are well dusted with pollen, finally releasing them after twenty-four hours or so. When I cut open flowers, I often find only dead flies trapped too long in the pipe, which may explain why we have such poor seed set on our plants.

three true woody vines and six herbaceous species, including *A. serpentaria, A. pentandra, A. erecta,* and *A. reticulata,* which are interesting in their own way but are outside the scope of this volume. The flowers of some tropical species are among the largest and most ornate in the world, with sepals that fuse together at first to form a curved tube like the kind of old-fashioned curved tobacco pipe that Sherlock Holmes always puffed on. As the calyx comes out of the curve, it flares widely from a narrow opening to form a large bib patterned in burgundy, white, or tan, suggesting well-marbled meat. The look and texture of the flowers combined with a fetid odor attracts small flies that land on the bib and crawl into the small opening and down the crook of the tube. Flowers that have just opened and are releasing the most scent have down-curving hairs lining the tube, which function like tire spikes—the flies can crawl in but they can't get out. They are held in the chamber at the base of the flower while the stigmas are receptive and hopefully will pollinate the plants with pollen brought in from their last imprisonment. After a day or so, the anthers mature and the hairs in the tube wither, so the pollen-dusted flies can set off for their next adventure. Although our native species produce flowers that are tiny and drab in comparison to the tropical pipevines, the method of pollination is the same. Strangely, we never get any pods to form on our plants. I have dissected flowers and found each one occupied by a few dead fungus gnats usually stuck to the stigma. I am not sure whether the flies died of natural causes or not, but my guess is that we lack a pollinator long-lived and strong enough to survive confinement, for we are north of the plant's native range. I have tried hand-pollinating the flowers by stripping off the calyx, but either the plants are self-sterile or the period of receptivity is very short, as this has so far failed to produce results. Strangely enough, I saw a very healthy *A. macrophylla* loaded with pods at Leach Botanic Garden in Portland, Oregon, even farther outside the native range. The mystery deepens.

Aristolochia has a long history of medicinal use worldwide. It has been used to treat snakebites and a wide variety of ailments from arthritis to smallpox and pneumonia, and it has mild stimulating and diuretic effects when taken in small doses. The physiologically active chemical is aristolochic acid, which has been linked to the development of certain cancers in people taking *Aristolochia* as a component of Chinese herbal weight-loss preparations. In fact, there is even a syndrome called Chinese-herb nephropathy related to abuse of *Aristolochia*.

CULTURE: Best transplanted from containers in spring, though rooted divisions are also a possibility if available. Support the vines with wire cable or fencing if you want the plants to scale a solid fence or wall; they climb by twining, not by aerial rootlets.

Pipevines will grow in considerable shade, but growth will be thinner and lax. Shade seems to encourage root suckering as well, as the plants travel around looking for a gap in the canopy. Given at least a few hours of sun and a fertile soil, the vines will grow luxuriantly, sending out new shoots all summer from a few woody trunks to become a mounded, tousled heap of big bold leaves. When leaves drop in winter, the tangled mass of thin stems looks a bit scandalous, so I would recommend giving the plant a haircut down to the thicker stems. By late spring, the vigorous new growth will completely make up for any lost height.

USES: Screening, woodland edge.

WILDLIFE: Pipevines are well known among lepidopterists as larval food plants of the pipevine swallowtail butterfly (*Battus philenor*), one of our lovely black, orange, and blue swallowtails. Like the brightly colored monarchs, the dark purple caterpillars use prominent orange spots to alert would-be predators to their toxicity. They concentrate aristolochic acid from the leaves in their bodies, making them unpalatable to birds. Interestingly, though the butterflies feed willingly on non-native, ornamental pipevines, at least one, *A. elegans,* is toxic to them and kills the feeding larvae. (Scott, *The Butterflies of North America,* p. 185).

PROPAGATION: Moderately difficult from cuttings, easy from seed.

Aristolochia californica

California Snakeroot

ZONES: 8–9, light shade to sun
SOIL: Moist
NATIVE TO: Stream banks, wet thickets; northern California
SIZE: Height 4–15 feet, width 3–6 feet
COLOR: White and maroon; blooms in spring

The leaves and stems of this species are densely silvery and woolly when young. They are smaller than the eastern species, averaging only 2 to 3 inches in diameter. Its flowers have a large, inflated pouch where the tube bends, and the flare is like a three-pointed star that never quite opens. These pouches are white with red veins; the whole gives an impression of a yawning pelican with a full gullet.

Aristolochia macrophylla (durior)

Dutchman's Pipe

ZONES: 4–8, shade to sun
SOIL: Moist
NATIVE TO: Wooded slopes, ravines, and gaps; mostly confined to the Cumberland and Blue Ridge mountains from West Virginia to Kentucky, Ten-

nessee, and northern Georgia; naturalized elsewhere in the East

SIZE: Height 6–30 feet (depending on support), width 4–10 feet

COLOR: Ochre, brown, and burgundy; blooms in spring to early summer

This and the following species are very similar in habit and requirements. *A. macrophylla* has potentially larger leaves—up to a foot or so in diameter is possible in shade—lacks downy pubescence, and produces inch-long flowers that—at least from what I have seen—tend to be darker colored where they flare open. It is reported as more common on limestone soils, but we have had no trouble growing it in typically acidic woodland conditions.

Aristolochia tomentosa
Pipevine

ZONES: 4–9

SOIL: Moist

NATIVE TO: Stream banks and floodplains; Illinois to southeastern Kansas south to eastern Texas and the Florida Panhandle

SIZE: Height 6–40 feet (depending on support), width 4–15 feet

COLOR: Ochre, brown, and burgundy; blooms in spring to early summer

The most distinctive characteristic, as you might guess from the Latin name, is the woolly pubescence (*tomentosa* means "woolly") that coats the new growth and gives the floral tube a bristly look up close. With leaves in the 4-to-6-inch-diameter range, I find *A. tomentosa* to be less texturally obtrusive than *A. macrophylla*. On the basis of its natural range, I would imagine this to be a bit more heat-tolerant as well.

Aronia arbutifolia
Aronia (a-ROH-nia)
Rosaceae
Chokeberry

There are many types of wetlands in North America—bogs, pocosins, marshes, tidal flats, and swamps—each with its cohort of plants and animals, each with a characteristic look and feel. Among these varied wetlands, there is a certain type of open swamp that I call berryland, where trees are sparse and hummocked and shrubs proliferate in a great suckering sea. This is where you are most likely to find chokeberries. Berryland is heaven for robins, a place where blueberries, viburnums, hollies, spicebush, dogwoods, mountain holly, and chokeberries adorn themselves in a veritable fruited feast each summer and autumn. Chokeberries contribute clus-

ters of scarlet, black and purple fruits that hang like little cherries from the axils of the branches on long pedicels. These are sour and mealy when ripe, so they are passed over in the initial feeding frenzy and hang on the shrubs, slowly fermenting, often until the robins return hungry in spring. In their preferred habitat, *Aronia* species are suckering, colonizing shrubs sending up vigorous sprouts that grow to 6 feet or so, then start to branch near the top. Thus the plants have a narrow vase shape when young, broadening to a rounded, arching clump in old age. Musky-sweet-smelling flowers grow in little rounded clusters from short spur branches on the older wood, so for a few weeks in spring the plants are frosted white. The blooms have a typical rose family appearance, akin to pears, serviceberries, and wild cherries. Each of the five petals narrows to a stalk, making the flowers look like little fan blades with a cluster of deep red stamens in the center.

CULTURE: Chokeberries are amazingly adaptable given their restricted natural habitat. They will grow in wet or dry soil, clay or sand, but certainly look their best in a spot that is somewhere in between. In wet conditions, plant them on hummocks or mounds so the roots have an aerated zone around the crown. They are moderately shade tolerant, but lack of sun spurs them to run about, looking for light, and the growths are weak and few-fruited. With a few hours of sun, they bloom and fruit very well, and the plants tend to stay as a single, multi-

Aronia arbutifolia. *Lustrous, pleasantly plump chokeberries look their best in fall but taste best (to birds, anyway) after winter's frosts have softened them up.*

stemmed clump. You can remove some of the new sprouts each year to encourage a vase-shaped habit with branching beginning about 3 feet off the ground—plenty of legroom for smaller companions around its base. They transplant easily from containers or rooted suckers in spring. *Aronias* do suffer from some of the same leaf diseases as apples and the like, and in a wet year, some of the leaves may begin to turn color and drop off slowly in late summer, in effect prolonging the fall color season, so I don't mind it at all.

USES: Massing, shrub border.

WILDLIFE: Fruits are good late-winter forage for birds; flowers favored by bees.

PROPAGATION: Moderately easy from cuttings, easy from seed.

Aronia arbutifolia
Red Chokeberry

ZONES: 4–9, part sun, sun

SOIL: Wet to dry

NATIVE TO: Swamps and bogs, also drier thickets; Newfoundland to Florida, south directly along the coast to New England, then spreading farther west to Ohio, Kentucky, and Texas

SIZE: Height 5–10 feet, width 4–8 feet

COLOR: White; blooms in spring

Red chokeberry is the most ornamental *Aronia* species, boasting bright red fruits that slowly shrivel like maroon raisins in winter, and a striking brilliant scarlet to pinkish orange fall color. It has downy twigs and smooth gray bark with a hint of purple running through it on trunks up to 2 inches in diameter. The 1-inch, elliptical leaves are rough textured and a dark green in summer. With a little careful shaping, it can become a well-behaved small tree similar to Canada serviceberry in shape. Virtually all the red chokeberries available in nurseries are the cultivar 'Brilliantissima', with large, brightly colored fruits and consistent red fall color.

Aronia melanocarpa
Black Chokeberry

ZONES: 3–8, part sun, sun

SOIL: Wet to dry

NATIVE TO: Swamps, bogs, and thickets; Newfoundland west through southern Quebec and Ontario south to Iowa, Tennessee, Virginia, and in the Appalachians to northern Georgia

SIZE: Height 3–8 (10) feet, width 3–6 feet

COLOR: White; blooms in spring

Black chokeberry's fruits ripen first dark purple, then black, shriveling up and losing effectiveness earlier in the winter than those of *A. arbutifolia*. In the wild, this is typically a smaller shrub than its red-fruited relative though the plants in our gardens are

virtually indistinguishable in habit. Fall leaf color is somewhere between purple and burgundy, and it makes for a more subdued but still lovely contrast with the fruit. The two species occasionally interbreed where their ranges overlap, resulting in a hybrid species, *Aronia × prunifolia* or just *A. prunifolia* (purple chokeberry). This is a species in the process of evolving, with characteristics intermediate between the two parents: the fruits are purplish and the twigs are less downy than red chokeberry.

Artemesia tridentata

Artemisia (are-te-MEE-sia)
Asteraceae
Sagebrush

Sagebrush is synonymous with the West. Under the wide-stretching sky, tumbleweeds may tumble, bunchgrasses bunch, and antelope roam, but sagebrush is king. It is capable of surviving with little water on hardscrabble soils where temperatures can swing 150°F from the windy depths of winter to the searing heat of summer. Sagebrushes are a subtle study in shades of gray, suffused with a pungent, sweet turpentine sharpness that is certainly familiar to anyone who has spent time in the Great Basin after a summer rain. There are a number of shrubby *Artemisia* species in our flora, all bearing deciduous or semi-evergreen, silvery gray leaves on twisted, soft-wooded stems and each exploiting a slightly different ecological niche. They are evolving away from insect pollination. Consequently, flowers are small and inconspicuous individually—little five-petaled things enclosed in a set of hairy fish-scale bracts—but they are borne in dense balls or plumy heads held up away from the leaves to catch the ever-present winds and send pollen aloft. The volatile oils that give the plants their distinctive aroma make the leaves unpalatable to cattle, so sagebrush has become the enemy of ranchers set on improving their rangelands. Ironically, when cattle selectively graze the

---

Artemisia tridentata. *Big sagebrush is one of the cornerstone plants of the cold desert. Fundamentally important to that ecosystem, it brings a strong regional identity to the garden. Using native species in the garden helps us appreciate and celebrate the unique plants of our region.*

bunchgrasses that are sagebrush's competition, they encourage the latter to grow, so it is now more abundant than it was 150 years ago. Deer are able to digest the leaves because they expel the oily cud after they have extracted the more nutritious parts. One wonders whether buffalo can do the same.

Sagebrushes are so ubiquitous on the great western rangelands, deserts, and steppes that it is hard when you are surrounded by them to see them as plants special enough for the garden. Yet, like sugar maples in New England and palmettos on the Gulf Coast, they help to define their region and give it its unique character, all the while providing food and cover for a host of animals that have come to rely on them. Gardening with such hallmark plants helps bring genuine regional focus to a garden — a potent antidote for the "malling" (or mauling) and homogenization of the North American landscape.

CULTURE: Easily established in sunny, well-drained sites. These plants are happiest in the drier parts of the West. Transplant from containers in spring. Older stems and branches die off occasionally, and these can be removed at any time. They benefit from rejuvenation pruning every three to five years, which produces a flush of vigorous new growth from the base in spring. Sagebrushes will grow very quickly with a little extra water and fertilizer, but you have to be careful not to overdo it. Lush growth one year will leave the plants looking sagging and unkempt the next.

USES: Massing, background plants in borders, xeriscaping.

WILDLIFE: Forage and cover for mammals and birds.

PROPAGATION: Difficult from cuttings, easy from seed.

Artemisia arbuscula
Dwarf Sagebrush, Little Sagebrush

ZONES: 4–8; sun
SOIL: Dry, well-drained
NATIVE TO: Shallow soils of dry plains and slopes up to 10,000 feet; Colorado to Washington south to California, Nevada, and Utah
SIZE: Height 4–16 inches, width 2 feet
COLOR: Yellowish; blooms in summer

Dwarf sagebrush is a smaller version of big sagebrush (*Artemisia tridentata*); it is adapted to poorer soils and consequently has shrunk itself in size. It has the same three-fingered leaf tips, but their color is a bit darker gray. It grows best at slightly cooler temperatures than its larger relative, so it's found generally at higher elevations. Black sagebrush (*A. nova*) is a very similar later-flowering plant with darker leaves and a laxer habit. It grows through most of the Great Basin as well.

Artemisia cana
Silver Sagebrush

ZONES: 3–8; sun
SOIL: Dry to moderately moist
NATIVE TO: Creek sides and bottomlands in somewhat moisture-retentive soils; northwestern Nebraska north through Saskatchewan to British Columbia south to northern California, Utah, and New Mexico
SIZE: Height 2–4 feet, width 2–3 feet
COLOR: Silvery yellow in effect; blooms in late summer

Silver sagebrush favors moister sites than the other sagebrushes, so it is a good choice for heavier soils. It is a suckering, spreading shrub with many small branches and narrow, deciduous leaves that are about the size and color of lavender leaves (*Lavendula officinalis*).

Artemisia filifolia
Sandhill Sage

ZONES: 4–10; sun
SOIL: Sandy, well-drained
NATIVE TO: Dunes and sandy deserts; Nebraska to Wyoming and Utah south to Arizona and Texas
SIZE: Height 2–4 (6) feet, width 2–4 feet
COLOR: Yellow-gray; blooms in mid- to late summer

Sandhill sage is a lovely, wispy species with thin, almost threadlike gray-green leaves on vertical stems. It lends an unmistakable softness to the landscape but needs a sharply drained, sandy soil to thrive. Many of the spicy-sweet–scented leaves remain on the plant through the winter, taking on a darker green color as some of the gray pubescence wears off.

Artemisia spinescens
Bud Sage

ZONES: 4–10; sun
SOIL: Dry, well-drained
NATIVE TO: Dry, arid, often alkaline soils at middle elevations from western Montana to Oregon south to California, Arizona, and New Mexico
SIZE: Height 6–24 inches, width 1–2 feet
COLOR: Silvery yellow; blooms in spring

Bud sage is nearly herbaceous, but it does have a well-developed, woody base protected by old flowering stems that double as spines once the blooms wither. It is adapted for growth during the winter-spring rains, and leafs out and blooms very early, then drops its foliage and goes sort of lifeless in the summer heat. Certainly not as useful an ornamental as the semi-evergreen sagebrushes, but a curiosity.

Artemisia tridentata
Big Sagebrush

ZONES: 3–10; sun

SOIL: Dry, well-drained

NATIVE TO: Dry plains, hills, and mountain slopes to 10,000 feet; Nebraska to North Dakota, Alberta, and British Columbia south to California, northern Mexico, and New Mexico

SIZE: Height 3–6 feet , width 3–6 feet

COLOR: Silvery yellow; blooms in mid- to late summer

In spring growth, big sagebrush is a billowing cloud of silver shimmering like a mirage in the desert heat. Its specific epithet refers to the three teeth, or lobes, at each leaf tip, giving the leaves a bird's-foot appearance. In fall, the leaves lose their luster and become a darker gray-green through most of the winter. This is one of the most common plants in the West, growing over a wider range of soil and climatic conditions than the other sagebrushes. Old, shattered trunks often splay at the foot of the plants in the wild, adding to their aura of immutability.

Asimina triloba. Lurid maroon pawpaw flowers hang from the branches as the leaves expand in spring. Each pollinated flower develops into one to three kidney-shaped fruits about the size of a fist. The meaty color and fetid aroma of the blooms are designed to attract flies and beetles rather than butterflies or bees, and their heavy substance withstands the insects' roughhousing.

Asimina triloba

Asimina (ass-eh-MEE-nah)
Annonaceae
Pawpaw

Back in the old days—that is, the real old days, say 75 million years ago, before I was born—bees hadn't been invented yet, so it was up to beetles to pollinate the first flowering plants. Beetles are not attracted to the sultry, musky perfume favored by moths or the yellow and purple colors noticed by bees. They like their flowers white or maroon, preferably with the smell of overripe fruit or old socks. Pawpaws (and also magnolias and sweetshrub) are survivors from that distant time when insect pollination first developed. Beetles are attracted to the flowers by smell and color, then feast on a heavy crop of pollen as well as specialized tissue produced at the base of the petals and presented as a reward for services rendered. Pawpaws are largely restricted to the warm, humid sections of the southeastern United States, reveling in a climate that probably is little changed from the one they first evolved in millions of years ago. Most of the two thousand or so members of the Annonaceae, the custard apple family, are truly tropical, and only one, our common pawpaw, *A. triloba*, is hardy in the North. It is a distinctive small tree with long, drooping leaves that lend it a heavy, almost ponderous, appearance in the landscape. It spreads by root suckers, popping up here and there, commonly forming understory groves or thickets in fertile soil. The others are shrubs, the majority restricted to peninsular Florida and typically with smaller, stiffer leaves and a multistemmed habit.

Pawpaw flowers range from the beautiful to the mildly obscene, each a unique variation on a simple pattern. They are unusually large and of heavy substance (beetles are rough customers), with three big outer petals that splay out flat and three or four smaller inner petals that curl lovingly around a ball of stamens and pistils. *Asimina triloba* and its smaller sibling *A. parviflora* have fleshy, voluptuous, foul-smelling blooms that look as though they might decorate the parlor of a red-light district establishment. Others, like *A. reticulata* and *A. obovata*, have chaste, cream-colored or lemon flowers that rival magnolia blooms in size and in shape.

Of course, then there are the fruits, which are technically berries. Common pawpaw has the distinction of bearing the largest edible fruits of any of our native plants; they are lumpy, kidney-shaped, and about the size of a child's fist—cultivars have been developed with much larger fruits still. We harvested a bunch and passed them out at a staff meeting a few years back. About half of the staff liked them, describing the flavor as somewhere between banana and melon (I won't say what the other half reported). The other species have smaller fruits, all containing large seeds that cling to the pulp and so get passed through the guts of raccoons, opossums, and other mammals that relish the fruits and disperse their seeds. Each flower can potentially produce four or more fruits, but usually all but one to three are sloughed off as they begin to develop.

Deeringothamnus pulchellus (beautiful pawpaw) and its relative *D. rugelii* (Rugel's pawpaw) are rare, fire-adapted low shrubs of south central Florida with flowers that look a bit like *Calycanthus* and have a fruity-sweet fragrance as well. They are one of the many victims of human fire suppression, flowering heavily only on resprouting stems that arise after fire has killed the plants back to the ground and opened the canopy above.

CULTURE: Pawpaws are taprooted plants that resent transplantation. Small container-grown plants will transplant well in the spring, but young seedlings are sensitive to strong ultraviolet radiation and do best if lightly shaded for the first few years. *A. triloba* needs a fertile, loamy soil to thrive, and if open grown it will become a pyramidal small tree casting dense shade and only occasionally sending up root sprouts, which can be removed as needed. I have little experience with the smaller shrubby species, but they prefer sandy, acidic soils in the wild so I would imagine a similar situation would suit them in the garden. They have a twiggy, running habit like some of the blueberries, so are best used in informal situations. *A. longifolia* and *A. obovata* are both spectacular native shrubs that deserve much wider use in warmer parts of the Southeast. Extracts from the bark have been found to be insecticidal, which may help to explain *Asimina*'s pest-free nature. Research into potential cancer-fighting effects is also promising.

Much has been speculated about pawpaw pollination and consequent fruit set. Growth tends to be clonal, and fruit set can be sparse, even on older specimens. Therefore, it is recommended that you plant at least two unrelated individuals for good cross-pollination. However, I have seen several pawpaws, including one in the Garden in the Woods, that set copious fruit with nary another tree in sight. It may be that appropriate pollinators are not always available, or that trees need time to settle in before bearing.

USES: Specimen, screen, naturalizing.

WILDLIFE: Pawpaws are a valuable food for raccoons, opossums, and other mammals—but you might not want to attract them. Because of the size of the seeds and the fruit's habit of falling under the tree when ripe, it is conceivable that some long-extinct large herbivore was once the main vector for the seeds. Pawpaw leaves are the larval food for the glorious white-and-black-striped zebra swallowtail butterfly (*Eurytides marcellus*), whose range is confined to that of the plants it feeds on.

PROPAGATION: Easy from seed.

Asimina incana (incarna)
Polecat Bush

ZONES: 8–9; light shade to sun
SOIL: Moist to dry, sandy
NATIVE TO: Sandy soils, oak-pine woodlands and pas-

tures; southeastern Georgia to northern Florida
SIZE: Height 3–5 feet, width 3 feet
COLOR: Creamy white with a blotch of yellow in the center; blooms in spring

Polecat bush produces large, elegant, sweet-smelling flowers from the previous season's growth as the leaves are beginning to expand. The big outer petals droop a bit, so you have to peer around to see the yellow blotch hidden in the center. It has oblong leaves, and its 2-to-3-inch edible fruits ripen in late summer.

Asimina longifolia (angustifolia)
Narrow-Leaf Pawpaw

ZONES: 8–9; light shade to sun
SOIL: Sandy, well-drained
NATIVE TO: Flatwoods, pastures, and sand ridges; southern Georgia to southeastern Alabama south to northern Florida
SIZE: Height 4–6 feet, width 3–4 feet
COLOR: Creamy white with a deep crimson blotch at the base of the inner petals; blooms in late spring to early summer (continuing into fall after fire)

This is a very distinctive species, with narrow, willowy leaves up to 8 inches long but less than an inch wide (they remind me of oleanders in leaf). The lovely flowers, about 4 inches across and "cherries and cream" in color, hang from the new growth among the expanded leaves. The flowers' long outer petals look almost like sheets hung out to dry on the branches. *A. longifolia* can be trained to form several upright trunks, and makes a fine specimen shrub in the garden. Fruits are small and knobby and develop in irregular clusters of two to six.

Asimina obovata
Flag Pawpaw

ZONES: 8–10; light shade to sun
SOIL: Sandy, acid
NATIVE TO: Sandy soils, ridges, and dunes; central peninsular Florida
SIZE: Height 6–10 (15) feet, width 4–7 feet
COLOR: Creamy white outer petals, white to pink inner petals, with a dark red basal blotch; blooms in late winter to early spring

This is a plant I wish I could grow outdoors. It erects large, irregular blooms from the previous year's wood as the leaves are just expanding. Flag pawpaw's flowers hang down like *A. longifolia's,* and they are similar in size and color, though with a pronounced citrus scent and an overall rounder appearance, more the shape of an egg. The flowers seem completely out of scale with the thin twigs. Some forms have inner petals on which the basal blotch suffuses through the entire surface, lending the flower a two-toned effect that is quite beautiful. It can be trained

Betula papyrifera. Birch seeds need bare soil for good germination, so you'll find the highest concentrations of seedlings on land that has recently been burned or cleared and then abandoned. The bark of paper birch is highly flammable, and I have often wondered if it is designed to encourage forest fires, which might kill the parent tree but clear a space for the off-spring.

as a multistemmed shrub or even a small tree. As in *A. longifolia*, the new growth is covered with a cinnamon-colored pubescence that adds to the attractiveness of the leathery, oblong leaves. *A. reticulata* (also called flag pawpaw) is a smaller, twiggier plant with similar coloring, smaller leaves and flowers, and an overlapping range.

Asimina pygmaea
Dwarf Pawpaw

ZONES: 8–9; part sun, sun
SOIL: Sandy, acidic, moderately moist
NATIVE TO: Sandy peatlands and savannas; southeastern Georgia to central Florida
SIZE: Height 8–15 inches, width 2 feet
COLOR: Maroon; blooms in late spring to early summer.

This is a curious little spreading shrub adapted to fire-prone savannas. It sends up arching stems with two-ranked narrow leaves and fetid flowers that are huge for the size of the plant—about 2 inches in diameter—followed by 2-inch fruits. *A. tetramera* (four-petaled pawpaw) is a similar species from central Florida distinguished mainly by its larger size (to 4 feet).

Asimina triloba
Pawpaw, Dog Banana

ZONES: 4–9; light shade to sun
SOIL: Moist, fertile
NATIVE TO: Bottomlands, rich woods; New York and southern Ontario west to southeastern Iowa and Nebraska south to eastern Texas and the Florida Panhandle
SIZE: Height 8–25 (40) feet , width 6–10 feet
COLOR: Maroon; blooms in spring

When sited well, in a spot where the soil is moist and the sun shines down, this pawpaw becomes a pyramidal tree with 6-to-12-inch drooping oblong leaves alternating in two ranks from stout branches. In poorer spots, it remains a scraggly multistemmed shrub traveling around looking for a break. I have tried it in a drier spot, and it languished—it survived but it died back in a drought. If left to itself, *A. triloba* can expand to form incredibly dense, shady thickets in the understory. Cultivars have been selected for good fruit production and flavor, and plants certainly fruit better in the sun. Since raccoons will raid the trees, I shake down the nearly ripe but still firm and green fruits in fall (wear a hard hat—they come down like missiles) and let them ripen indoors like bananas until they are soft and more yellow-green. *A. parviflora* (small-flowered pawpaw) is half the height of *A. triloba*, bearing smaller flowers and 1-inch fruits. It is a good substitute if you want the foliage effect on a plant with smaller stature.

Betula papyrifera

Betula (BETCH-yew-la)
Betulaceae
Birch

The birches are consummate cold-climate plants, one of the few genera of deciduous trees that can compete with firs and spruces in the vast cold reaches of the boreal forest. Their seeds fall mostly in winter and blow across the snow-scoured landscape looking for a bit of mineral soil to germinate in when the weather warms. Birches find landscapes scrubbed clean by glaciers much to their liking, and unlike many species that fled south to escape the ice, they stayed close to its edge, ready to pop up whenever it retreated. Most of our birch species are opportunists — short-lived trees or shrubs that establish themselves after disturbance and are slowly replaced by other species. A few, like the yellow birch, can be found in more stable communities, growing into impressive old specimens in the company of maple and beech.

Colorful bark is synonymous with birches — the chalk-white paper birch, the golden yellow birch, and the salmon-colored river birch. Birch bark is very thin on all but the oldest limbs and trunks. As the tree grows and outer layers give way in response to internal expansion, the bark rolls off in thin parallel strips that twist madly when detached in little dangling curls. The fresh, new bark exposed underneath is unblemished by soot, lichens, or moss. This continual replacement of its skin keeps the trunk looking colorful for many years, until gradually the new layers of bark become rougher and dark, losing their luster. Of course not all birches have exceptional bark. Many are sort of a drab gray-brown, but because of the spectacular few, birches have been accorded a place of honor in the suburban landscape that they are in many respects ill prepared for. Hot, dry expanses of lawn are a far cry from the glacier-scarred, snow-covered lands that white birches especially relish, and they suffer as a result. River birch, which is our only truly warm-climate species, is becoming a popular replacement.

Some of the species are important lumber trees, providing fine furniture woods with close grain and a light blond color. Black birch sap contains high concentrations of wintergreen oil (methyl salicylate), and has long been tapped for use as a flavoring for foods and to produce the root beer–like birch beer. The trees bleed excessively when cut or tapped in the spring, and the syrup can be boiled down like sugar maple's. When we have late-winter ice storms that snap off black or yellow birch branches, the trees build up cloudy icicles where the sap oozes out, providing me with a little frozen treat when I'm out in the icy woods.

Birches all have more or less oval, finely serrated leaves borne alternately on fine branches. Fall color is usually a pretty bright or golden yellow. The fine branches hold themselves at a tight vertical angle, forming a narrow oval crown supported by limbs and trunks that are relatively thin for their length, even on older trees. This makes birches prone to bending and breakage during snow and ice storms. Often, trees on the edge of the forest have a telltale lean to the trunk—lasting memories of heavy ice and snow loads. Like their relatives the alders, birches bear flowers of different sexes separately on the same tree. The inflorescences form in fall and overwinter tightly closed but ready for spring. Male catkins are visible in winter as little tails hanging from the branch tips. These expand rapidly in early spring as the leaves begin to swell, tripling in size like a dry sponge dropped in water and releasing their pollen to the wind. Female flowers hide farther down the twigs on little spur branches, becoming little cones of tightly packed three-pronged scales interspersed with small winged seeds. The cones gradually disintegrate in winter, releasing seeds onto the snow like confetti.

CULTURE: Birches prefer moist, slightly acid, cool soils. They are fibrous-rooted (do not have a taproot) so transplant fairly easily in spring either as balled and burlaped or container-grown plants. Container-grown birches are not as prone to root girdling problems as taprooted trees, but I still root-prune the ball before setting it in the ground. As I intimated above, try to avoid pruning birch in late winter and spring to avoid excessive bleeding of sap. Fall, just after leaf drop, is the best time to prune.

Since the paper-barked species lose their color as the trunks age, cutting the trees to the ground every twenty years is a way to keep them colorful and, in the case of river birch, of a manageable size for the smaller landscape. They resprout quickly.

USES: Specimen, massing.

WILDLIFE: *Betula* spp. are very important to a host of insects including an array of moths and butterflies. They host many species of moth larvae, including the orange-striped oakworm moth (*Anisota senatoria*), our magnificent cecropia moth (*Hyalophora cecropia*), rusty and whitemarked tussock moths (*Orgyia antiqua* and *O. leucostigma*), and the spear-marked black moth (*Rheumaptera hastata*). Butterfly caterpillars that feed on birch include the viceroy and white admiral (*Limenitis archippus* and *L. arthemis*), green comma (*Polygonia faunis*), comma tortoise shell and mourning cloak (*Nymphalis vau-album* and *N. antiopa*), willow-bog fritillary (*Boloria frigga*), and aspen dusky wing (*Erynnis icelus*). A few birch-feeding insects can become troublesome in the landscape. Bronze birch borer (*Agrilus anxius*) is a native beetle that looks a bit like a small firefly. Larva feed on the cambium, making winding tunnels under the bark and weakening or girdling the tree. They cannot attack healthy trees, and only specimens stressed by other problems are vulnerable. Birch leaf miner (*Fenusa pusilla*) is a European sawfly whose larvae feed on the leaf mesophyll of paper birch and gray birch, and affected trees can lose most of their foliage for a time in early summer. Other species of leaf miner sawfly are also becoming established, but it is hoped that introduced predatory wasps will eventually bring these insects under control (Johnson and Lyon, *Insects*, p. 184). The seeds provide food for overwintering birds like kinglets, chickadees, and juncos, and the fine twigs provide good nesting sites in summer. The shrubby species are important forage for herbivores like rabbits, deer, and elk.

PROPAGATION: Difficult from cuttings, moderately easy from seed.

Betula alleghaniensis (lutea)
Yellow Birch

ZONES: 3–7; shade to sun

SOIL: Moist to moderately wet

NATIVE TO: Rich woods and bottomlands; southern Newfoundland, Quebec, and Ontario to Minnesota, south to Indiana, Maryland and, in the mountains, to Tennessee and northern Georgia.

SIZE: Height 60–80 (100) feet, width 15–30 feet

COLOR: Rusty yellow; blooms in late spring

Yellow birch is a common tree in the northern hardwood forest. It is fairly shade-tolerant, and can persist in the understory for many years until it finds an opening in the canopy. In favored sites it can become an enormous old-growth tree with a thick primary trunk and a wide network of finer branches. The bark of even older trees is bronzy golden in color, peeling off in thin curling sheets like little rolled-up carpets and lending the tree a shaggy appearance from a distance. The bark has a satin as opposed to glossy patina, which gives the trunks a subdued glow. It is the primary timber birch, valued for veneer and furniture wood, and the sap has a wintergreen smell like that of *Betula lenta,* its closest relative. Within its native range, it makes a fine tree for the larger landscape, but it is planted only a fraction as often as the white-barked species.

Betula lenta

Black Birch, Sweet Birch

ZONES: 4–7; shade to sun
SOIL: Moist to moderately dry, cool
NATIVE TO: Rich forests, rocky outcrops; Maine and southeastern Ontario south to Ohio and Virginia and in the Appalachians to northern Georgia and scattered spots in Mississippi
SIZE: Height 40–60 (80) feet, width 10–25 feet
COLOR: Yellow-brown; blooms in late spring

This species is the most common one in southern New England, often a successional tree in areas of disturbance and occasionally living long enough to reach 2 feet diameter. Older trees often suffer from nectria canker, caused by the widespread fungus *Nectria galligena,* which produces a characteristic target, or bull's-eye, wound on the trunk and shortens the trees' average lifespan. The fungus kills the lip of callus tissue around the circumference of the wound when the tree is dormant, and then a new ring of callus of slightly larger diameter forms the following growing season, only to be killed again in winter. Eventually these cankers become quite large on older trunks, with two or more overlapping and seriously affecting the tree's vasculature. The cankers don't kill the tree outright, they just weaken it so that drought or insects can finish it off. Black birch is not widely grown as a landscape tree. Its bark is a dull, purplish gray and peels off in thick, rectangular plates only on older trunks. It is an important component of the eastern hardwood forests, however, and should be left to grow wherever possible. Fall color is a glowing shade of bright yellow. *Betula uber* (Virginia roundleaf birch) is likely a mutated form of black birch with rounded leaves ending in a pointed tip. It was first described in 1918 from a tiny population in the Blue Ridge Mountains area of Virginia and then was lost again for over 50 years before being rediscovered in the same area.

Betula nigra

River Birch

ZONES: (3)4–9; light shade to sun
SOIL: Moist to moderately dry, acidic
NATIVE TO: River banks and floodplains, often subject to periodic flooding; Massachusetts to New York, Pennsylvania, Illinois and Minnesota south to eastern Texas and northern Florida
SIZE: Height 60–80 feet, width 15–25 feet
COLOR: Yellow-brown; blooms in late spring

River birch is a common floodplain species in the East, with a characteristic pinkish or orange-red exfoliating bark that curls off much like yellow birch's. As its native range indicates, it is the most heat-tolerant birch species, and thus has become the birch of choice for landscaping. Like black birch and yellow birch, it is not susceptible to the borers and miners that plague the white birches. 'Heritage', a cultivar introduced by Heritage Nursery, is virtually the only river birch offered in the trade. It was selected for vigor, dark green leaves, and bark that is lighter than typical, a sort of pink-flushed white aging to darker pink then warm bronze. I worry that excessive use of this one clone will lead to some disease epidemic, a fate that seems to befall all monocultures in time.

Betula occidentalis

Western Birch, Water Birch

ZONES: 2–7; part sun, sun
SOIL: Moist to wet
NATIVE TO: Stream banks and swampy ground, mountain slopes; Ontario west through the Northwest Territories to Alaska, south to California, Nevada, and New Mexico
SIZE: Height 10–20 (30) feet, width 6–12 feet
COLOR: Yellow-brown; blooms in late spring

Commonly this western birch is a large, multistemmed shrub found in moist pockets even in the drier areas of the Great Basin where streams drain snowmelt from the high mountains. However, it is also the only western birch that can reach the size of a small tree. It is in the white birch group with *B. papyrifera,* though its bark is bronze or coppery in color and does not peel.

Betula papyrifera

Paper Birch, Canoe Birch, White Birch

ZONES: 2–6; light shade to sun
SOIL: Moist, acid
NATIVE TO: Forests; Newfoundland west across northern Quebec to the Northwest Territories and southern Alaska south to Washington, North Dakota, Indiana, and New Jersey
SIZE: Height 60–80 (100)feet, width 20–30 feet

COLOR: Yellow-brown; blooms in late spring

I never get tired of this tree. Its bright white bark, often with a hint of salmon underneath and punctuated by black "eyebrows" where branches attach, is one of the joys of the northern landscape. Despite its problems, if sited in a spot where the soil remains shaded and cool and never dries severely, paper birch makes an outstanding specimen. It is not a long-lived tree, typically coming in after logging, fire, or windstorm. The bark contains flammable oil that erupts as if it had been soaked with kerosene when you put a match to it. I have always wondered whether this flammable bark evolved as a way both to spread fire to clear competitors and to let the flames burn themselves out quickly near the trunk so that internal damage is minimized. In any case, nothing beats it for getting a campfire going. Never strip bark off live trees, as this damages the tissue and prevents the white bark from growing back.

B. cordifolia (heartleaf birch) is an amazing tree that my wife, Melissa, first introduced me to in northern New England. It takes over from paper birch at higher elevations, and can be distinguished by its heart-shaped leaf bases and a peeling bark that is far pinker in color. A population I saw on the Gaspé Peninsula of Quebec had beautiful mahogany and cherry red bark with no hint of white except on the smaller branches—truly stunning. With some cultivar selection, this tree has great potential for northern gardeners. *B. populifolia* (gray birch) is a ruddy gray and white, early successional tree often found colonizing abandoned agricultural land in the Northeast. It is a small, short-lived white birch with leaves that are heart-shaped rather than broadly oval.

Betula pumila

Bog Birch

ZONES: 2–6; sun

SOIL: Moist, cool

NATIVE TO: Tundra, bogs, fens, lakeshores; Newfoundland to northern Alberta and the Northwest Territories south through British Columbia and the Cascades to northern California, in the Rockies to Colorado, and in the east to Indiana, Ohio, and New Jersey

SIZE: Height 3–10 feet, width 3–6 feet

COLOR: Yellow-brown; blooms in late spring

Bog birch is a species characteristic of northern tundra and boggy seeps high in the mountains farther south. It becomes a rounded, finely branched shrub, typically with a short main trunk that splits into a number of equal branches just above the ground. The leaves are broadly oval, almost rounded in outline and held close to the twigs on short petioles. We are growing this species quite successfully in a partially shaded, damp spot below the nursery, and I

have seen it used elsewhere on boggy hummocks, but there is honestly little to recommend it for use in the landscape. The bark is a dull gray brown, and the branches tend to get matted down by snow and regrow at an awkward tangle. This is one of a group of closely related shrub birches that freely interbreed where ranges overlap, so identification is difficult. *B. glandulifera* (dwarf bitch or swamp birch) is nearly identical, but a bit smaller in size and ranges across all of northern Canada and the high peaks of New England and the West. *B. nana* (Arctic birch) grows as far north as the Arctic Circle and is usually a spreading, low shrub 1 to 2 feet high with 1½-inch, oval leaves. I have seen it used in a few rock gardens in New England, where it grows but doesn't seem to bloom.

Bignonia capreolata

Bignonia (Anisostichus) capreolata

(big-NOH-nia)

Bignoniaceae

Cross-vine

ZONES: (5)6–9; light shade to sun

SOIL: Moist

NATIVE TO: Woods and thickets; Virginia to southern Indiana and Illinois south to eastern Texas and Florida

SIZE: Height 5–80 feet, depending on support, width 3–10 feet

COLOR: Typically bronze with yellow on the flare, but cherry red, scarlet, maroon, orange, and yellow forms are available, many bicolored with yellow in the throat; blooms in spring from previous year's wood

Cross-vine is one of our showiest native vines, but it is not nearly as well known as its equally flam-

Bignonia capreolata. Cross-vine's colorful, gaping flowers add a tropical flair to the landscape, and the vines can easily be controlled with occasional pruning. Fences, cedar posts, or the rough bark of larger trees all make good supports for this spectacular climber.

*Callicarpa americana.
Some colors seem decidedly unnatural, and topping my list is the outrageous silvery magenta of beautyberry fruits. These likable berries remain colorful well into fall and even winter, before a hard freeze deflates them or birds carry them off.*

boyant cousin, trumpet vine *(Campsis radicans)*. Cross-vine sports large, flaring blooms with the petals forming a tube for two-thirds of their length, then reflexing back away from the opening in five rounded lobes. The color ranges from bronze to maroon, orange, red, and yellow — bright, hot colors to attract pollinating hummingbirds. They are almost as large as trumpet vine blooms, and the buds have the same inflated anticipatory feeling, as if their cheeks are coloring up from holding their breath for too long. They have a sweet, chocolaty smell if you can get your nose close to them.

Cross-vine has very unusual compound leaves that are divided into a matched pair of lanceolate leaflets with a little tendril in between where a third leaflet should be. The leaves are borne in opposite pairs up the stem, so the effect is one of four leaves arrayed unevenly around each node. In the wild, cross-vine travels up the corky bark of pines and gum trees, and is capable of extending 10 to 15 feet in a season and sending its little tendrils into the fissures of the tree's bark to knit the vine in place. These tendrils remain until the following year, when aerial roots emerge from the mature stem to provide a permanent means of attachment. It is common to see the sets of leaves working up the clear lower sections of some large forest tree on their way up into the sun, where they bloom out of sight. They will also grow on fences or barns — really any place they can get started — and this is where you are more likely to see the flowers. They are usually not overpowering like the introduced wisteria, kudzu, or English ivy, which can strangle and bring down their host in time.

CULTURE: Prefers a moist soil and sun. On a fence in my yard in Durham, North Carolina, it remained pretty well behaved, clustering along the top and sending up more stems each year from the roots. The foliage remains on the plants through the winter, usually bronzing a bit and burning in cold weather. It has proved winter-hardy at Garden in the Woods, in Zone 6, where we have it working up an old white pine. It burns back a bit in winter and has yet to flower, but I am optimistic. Since flowering is on older growth, wait until after it blooms to trim the vines. If things are getting too unkempt for your liking, cut it back hard in winter and forgo a year of flowering. Cross-vine is a rapid grower, and requires little in the way of fertilizer once established.

USES: Screen, fences, naturalized on trees.

WILDLIFE: Pollinated by hummingbirds as well as bees.

PROPAGATION: Moderately difficult from cuttings, easy from seed.

Callicarpa americana

Callicarpa americana
(kal-lee-KAR-pah)
Verbenaceae
American Beautyberry

ZONES: (6)7–10; part sun, sun

SOIL: Moist

NATIVE TO: Moist woodlands, mostly along the coastal plain, southern Maryland to North Carolina and Arkansas, south to Texas, Mexico, and Florida

SIZE: Height 3–8 feet, width 3–6 feet

COLOR: Light pink; blooms in summer

American beautyberry is a one-season shrub, but what a spectacular season it has. Most of the year, it's a rather nondescript plant, but for few months in late summer and fall, the shrubs are covered in clusters of remarkable, silvery magenta berries that are closer to some shocking shade of teenager's nail polish than anything you'd expect to see in nature. The effect is stunning. Beautyberry has a mounding, open habit a bit like *Forsythia*'s, with arching, caney stems and pairs of large oval, pointed leaves tapering slowly to a petiole and held out perpendicularly from the twigs. Clusters of small pink, four-petaled flowers are borne sequentially in the leaf axils as the new growth continues to expand in summer. By late in the season, ripe fruits become evident low on the canes, while higher up the plants are still flowering. In this way, fruiting extends well into fall or even winter in the deepest parts of the Deep South. The quarter-inch fruits are bunched tightly together in the leaf axils — each stem suggesting a large necklace of brilliant purple beads strung on stout twine. A white-fruited form, 'Lactea', is not nearly as showy.

CULTURE: Beautyberry transplants easily into fairly moist, even seasonally wet soils, preferably in a spot that receives at least a few hours of direct sun to encourage heaviest fruiting. Treating the shrub almost like a herbaceous perennial keeps it much neater and prolific. I take my cues from the North Carolina Botanical Garden, which maintains a dazzling patch of these shrubs that are summarily cut back to within 6 to 10 inches of the ground late each winter. The vigorous growth that ensues in spring restores the plants to 4-foot mounds by early fall, when the thick clusters of berries reach their peak. We have tried to establish the plants at Garden in the Woods (Zone 6) a few times without luck, and I imagine we need to plant them near a foundation where the ground freezes less severely or take more care in mulching the roots in winter. In general these are trouble-free plants. Scale insects are about the only pest I have noticed.

USES: Massing, mixed borders.

WILDLIFE: Long bloom makes this a good species for the butterfly garden. Birds are not especially fond of the fruits, but they eventually eat them later in the fall and winter, spreading the seeds around abundantly.

PROPAGATION: Easy from cuttings and seed.

Calocedrus decurrens

Calocedrus (Libocedrus) decurrens

(kal-oh-SEED-rus)
Cupressaceae
California Incense-cedar

ZONES: 5–8; part sun, sun
SOIL: Moderately dry to moist; prefers moist
NATIVE TO: Montane, mixed conifer forests; northwestern Nevada and eastern Oregon south through the Siskiyou and Sierra mountains to Baja California
SIZE: Height 25–40 (150) feet, width 8–20 (30) feet
COLOR: Rusty yellow; blooms in late winter and spring

California incense-cedar has an unmistakable, feathery grace that ranks it near the top of my admittedly long list of favorite conifers. Almost everyone has had their fingers and teeth clamped around a piece of it at one time or another, for its wood is used in the manufacture of pencils, yet few are acquainted with this magnificent, rich green pyramid from the

Sierras. *Calocedrus* (literally, "beautiful cedar") has the same flattened, scale-like leaves as its relative arborvitae *(Thuja)*, though the branchlets have a knobbier "finger bone" appearance as they splay out in fan-coral fashion. The fans often tilt so their flat side is toward the viewer, and arrange themselves in overlapping layers like the pages of a book. This layered effect enhances the rich, soft texture provided by the deep green of the needles. One of the nice things about the leaves is that they remain deep green into early winter, developing a hint of the bronze seen in arborvitae when temperatures drop into the teens. In form the trees remind me of scale models of the giant sequoias they share their home with—the same broad trunk flaring widely at the base, the same dark pyramidal crown lending an air of stocky stability, all this in a much more manageable size. The bark of incense-cedar flakes cinnamon brown in youth and becomes fluted and fissured on

older trunks, in stark and lovely contrast with the rich green plumes of foliage. Its decay-resistant wood has made it, like many of its relatives, a valued lumber tree. The fragrant heartwood is used for cedar chests, and the essential oils are extracted for use in fragrance manufacture.

CULTURE: It is hard to believe that a tree so restricted in the wild could be so adaptable in cultivation, but like the dawn redwood (*Metasequoia glyptostroboides*), incense-cedar was far more widespread in the geological past and so retains an adaptability belied by its current limited range (the only

Calocedrus decurrens. *California incense-cedar juxtaposes graceful, vivid green foliage with a stout, shaggy trunk to create a composition that is at once delicate and substantial, formal and impressionistic.*

other living *Calocedrus* species are found in southern China and on Taiwan). It has proved hardy and agreeable in the Northeast, and many arboretums contain stalwart specimens with stocky, buttressed trunks. This stockiness combined with the overlapping branchlets, which act like roof shingles, make it less prone to winter storm damage than arborvitae, and I think it makes an excellent replacement for this reason. It transplants moderately well from containers in spring, but balled and burlaped plants are more difficult to move and establish. Some larger, balled specimens we have purchased had little more than a gnarled stub of a taproot when unpacked, so be wary when buying larger trees. In the wild, broken-topped, old-growth trees regularly approach 150 feet in height; in the landscape, a mere fraction of that is likely. Unfortunately, deer do seem to relish the needles as much as those of arborvitae. *Calocedrus* is not extremely fast growing, but new growth is indeterminate, so under good conditions, it can add 12 inches a year when young.

USES: Specimen in formal landscapes, screening.
PROPAGATION: Moderately easy from seed.

Calcanthus floridus 'Athens'. This chartreuse-flowered form of the normally maroon sweetshrub is one of the most wonderfully fragrant plants at Garden in the Woods. Though the flowers may go unnoticed amid the leaves, it is impossible to miss the rich, tropical-fruit aroma drifting around the plant in spring and summer.

Calycanthus floridus 'Athens'

Calycanthus floridus
(kal-ee-KAN-thus)
Calycanthaceae
Sweetshrub, Allspice, Strawberry Bush

ZONES: (4)5–9; light shade to sun
SOIL: Moist to dry
NATIVE TO: Deciduous woodlands, streamsides, bottomlands in Maryland southwest to Mississippi and east to the Florida Panhandle; also scattered populations in Ohio, West Virginia, and Pennsylvania
SIZE: Height 4–10 feet, width 4–12 feet
COLOR: Maroon or occasionally greenish yellow; blooms in late spring to summer and sporadically until fall

One of my favorite stops when I give summer tours at Garden in the Woods is at our *C. floridus* 'Athens', so that I can introduce people to its intoxicating fragrance. *Calycanthus* is another in the ancient line of beetle-pollinated magnolia relatives. Healthy plants produce wave after wave of oddly shaped flowers, which release a fruit salad perfume of strawberry, banana, mango, and peach guaranteed to get your stomach rumbling. These blooms are 1 inch in diameter, with curving, layered tepals set one inside the next like a miniature magnolia or water

lily. The plants themselves are adapted to life in the forest. Wild plants mosey around with root suckers searching for light gaps in a lax and unwieldy fashion. However, given a cultivated situation with a few hours of sun and a reasonably fertile soil, sweetshrub plumps up and fleshes out quite agreeably. A well-provided-for individual may sport forking branches an inch or more in diameter, but these become obscured by smaller shoots coming from the base and roots so the whole takes on a leafy verdure and wide-mounded shape. Sweetshrub's leaves are bold in texture, broadly oval in outline, and arranged in two alternating ranks up the stems so that the plants have a recognizable, slightly drooping and layered character. The foliage is marked with prominent veins and shaded a glossy or matte medium green,

which fades slowly to soft yellow in fall before dropping to expose the strange, misshapen pods. These pods inspire metaphor, looking most like small puckered sacks of potatoes hung here and there from the branches. They are chock full of huge, interesting seeds that resemble legless beetles or exotic, polished mahogany and gray beans.

C. occidentalis (California sweetshrub) is restricted to moist soils along streams in central and northern California with a disjunct population near Seattle, Washington. Generally it is similar, though potentially a larger shrub, with tepals that are rounded, not pointed at the tips. It has arisen after becoming genetically isolated from the main population center on the East Coast. When crushed, its leaves have the same, spicy odor as its eastern cousin, and the flowers have a faint fruity or even fetid aroma. It is cultivated far less than *C. floridus* and is hardy only in Zones 8–9.

CULTURE: Adaptable, but best with some sun and moist soil. We have plants scattered in many locations, including a damp, limestone slope that receives about an hour of sun in summer; a heavily shaded dry, acidic bed under oaks; and another in rich, moist, chocolate-cake loam. All grow and bloom, but not surprisingly the last has the fullest shape and longest blooming period. The flowers are borne at the tips of the new growth in spring and will continue as long as the plant is actively growing. Hard pruning in winter (which will compromise flowering the following spring) or light shaping in summer is very helpful to keep a balanced canopy. Older stems can also be selectively removed when they start to lose productivity.

USES: Massing, naturalizing, mixed border.

PROPAGATION: Moderately easy from root cuttings and seed.

Campsis radicans

Campsis radicans
(KAMP-sis)

Bignoniaceae

Trumpet Vine, Trumpetcreeper

ZONES: 4–9; light shade to sun

SOIL: Moist to dry

NATIVE TO: Moist woods, hedgerows, roadsides; New Jersey to Ohio and eastern Iowa south to Texas and Florida; naturalized farther north

SIZE: Height 6–40 feet or more, depending on support, width 4–10 feet

COLOR: Orange, red-orange, or yellow; blooms in summer

Trumpet vine has an unabashedly tropical appeal, with its immense, fluorescent coronet flowers and compound leaves bedecking stout, ambling vines. *Campsis* climbs with clinging rootlets that emerge along the stems and proliferate wherever they bump up against something, cementing the vine in place. Leaves are borne in pairs, each one pinnately compound like an ash, with 6 pairs of leaflets crowned by one terminal leaflet, all jaggedly toothed and reasonably dark green in color. It would look as much at home over the door of a palm-thatched island hideaway as it does climbing up a pine in Virginia or an arbor in New York. The big, bodacious flowers of trumpet vine appear successively in congested racemes for a month or so in summer. Blooms burst

out of a toothy, dark orange calyx that surrounds the base of the flower like a skirt, and in any one inflorescence you can usually find 1 to 2 open blooms as well as fat, lipstick-sized buds and a few developing pods. The flowers are indeed shaped like 3-inch trumpets flared open with a flourish, with anthers and stigma pressed up flat against the roof. The anthers mature first, ready to smear pollen on the forehead of any hummingbird that sticks its head in for a drink. Bumblebees also visit the flowers, but I am unsure, given their smaller size, whether they can effectively

Campsis radicans. *A cluster of spectacular trumpet vine blooms awaits the arrival of a local hummingbird. If some are pollinated, the corollas will fall away and long, cigar-shaped pods about the size of an overgrown string bean will spring out of the calyx. Each pod contains hundreds of flaky seeds shaped a bit like a fried egg.*

pollinate them. The peeling, warm gray bark of older stems, a bit like a grapevine in appearance, is attractive in winter when the leaves are gone.

When I first went to college, I passed by a trumpet vine every day that had scaled a neighbor's house. I was so enamored of the hot orange blossoms that when the plant was hung with its ponderous seedpods, I couldn't resist plucking a few and growing up some plants. Then I played Billy Trumpetseed, giving the seedlings away to everyone and anyone who had what I deemed to be suitable quarters for my vines. I planted one in a little bed out on my parents' flagstone terrace where it could climb up a plastic trellis. Little did I realize in those heady days, that my beloved trumpetcreeper would creep more than trumpet, coming up in the cracks between the stones and returning twice as abundantly after eventual attempts to root it out. It persisted there for 15 years, constantly being cut back and chided and thus never flowering, until finally renovations finished it off. Learn from my mistakes, dear friends, and put some thought into location before establishing this lovely but rambunctious vine.

CULTURE: *Campsis* is a very amenable vine, growing in light shade or sun equally well, though flowering will be better in sun. It is tolerant of a range of soils and moisture levels, too. Vines can grow 10 feet or more in a season, and the rootlets will pull off paint from the house or shed if you let it get too close. I think the best way to handle it so that it doesn't overtake your property is to train one or two main stems up a sturdy support, then cut all the long shoots back to within 6 inches of these main stems every winter. Since flowers come from the tips of new growth, blooming will be unaffected by even severe pruning, short of cutting it all the way back to the ground. The vines still get a little crazy-looking by late summer when pollarded this way, but all in all they remain quite civil, and the blooms will show to good effect on new shoots that grow out horizontally from the trunk. Root sprouts may emerge some distance from the trunks, and these can be summarily removed with a spade. Alternatively, you can just allow it to scramble over a fence or hedgerow or climb a dead tree.

USES: Trellis, screen, arbor.

WILDLIFE: Attractive to hummingbirds.

PROPAGATION: Moderately easy from cuttings, easy from seed.

Carpentaria californica. One of the rarest woody plants in North America, carpentaria is the last surviving member of an ancient lineage.

Carpentaria californica

Carpentaria californica

(kar-pen-TARE-ia)
Saxifragaceae (Philadelphaceae)
Tree Anemone, Carpentaria

ZONES: 8–10; sun

SOIL: Moist, well-drained

NATIVE TO: A few moist slopes in the Sierra Nevada foothills, Fresno County, California

SIZE: Height 3–7 feet, width 3–4 feet

COLOR: White; blooms in summer

One of North America's rarest plants, carpentaria is found at only a few sites in central California. It is what taxonomists would call a living relic — the last surviving member of an ancient lineage on the verge of natural extinction. It is an extraordinarily lovely shrub, suggesting an evergreen viburnum covered incongruously with bouquets of roselike blossoms. The rich green leaves are a good foil for the 2-inch, 5-petaled flowers centered with a puff of orange anthers. On first glance, carpentaria bears lit-

tle resemblance to its closest relatives, the mock-oranges, but its sweet citrus perfume betrays a distant familial relationship. In habit it is a stiffly upright, many-stemmed, suckering shrub with thin, brown peeling bark on four-angled stems, again much like mock-orange *(Philadelphus)* in character. The leaves are lance-shaped, glossy green, and leathery above, lighter and pubescent below, and hang in pairs on twigs flushed purple where they face the sun. Flowers come clustered at the tips of new growth, and the plant is virtually smothered in white for a few weeks in summer. When a flower is pollinated, the pointed ovary in the center of the flower begins to swell through its collar of stamens while the petals slowly dry and reflex back against the stem. By the time the seeds have ripened, the capsule is the shape of the dome atop a Turkish minaret, with the remains of the withered petals forming a skirt below.

CULTURE: Although it is native to a summer-dry, Mediterranean climate, carpentaria does well in an evenly moist yet well-drained soil with moderate fertilization. I have grown it as a container plant in a cool greenhouse and moved it outside in summer, and the floral show was well worth the space and effort. There are cultivars available in Europe that are

reliable in Zone 8, where the ground does not freeze severely.

USES: Specimen, foundations.

PROPAGATION: Moderately difficult from cuttings or seed.

Carpinus caroliniana v. virginiana

Carpinus caroliniana (kar-PYE-nus)

Betulaceae

American Hornbeam, Musclewood, Blue Beech

ZONES: 3–8; sun to shade

SOIL: Moist to seasonally wet

NATIVE TO: Streambanks, floodplains, bottomlands in rich woodland; southeastern Quebec to southern Ontario and Minnesota south to Arkansas and the piedmont of Georgia and South Carolina

SIZE: Height 15–20 (30) feet, width 12–18 feet

COLOR: Yellow tinged reddish purple; blooms in late spring

The sinuous, rippled trunks of American hornbeam, resembling muscled arms straining under some Herculean task, are a common sight in the understory of low woods throughout the East. It is rare to find them anywhere but under the shade of floodplain species like maple and ash, with trunks leaning and contorting this way and that in search of any available light. The fluted stems of even the oldest trees are shown to advantage by smooth, blue-gray bark laced with striations of a deeper hue. The bark is quite smooth to the eye but rough to the hand when rubbed against the grain, much like the bark of American beech, with which it is occasionally confused. Unlike the mighty beech, though, *C. caroliniana* is a small understory tree with a crown wider than tall supported by stout, outspread branches that begin near the ground as a short single trunk. Its twigs are thin and freely branch to form a flattened deck to display its oval, deep green leaves to best advantage. The leaves have a saw-toothed edge narrowing to a pronounced, pointed tip. Fall color can be outstanding, especially in the sun: yellow blended with orange, scarlet, even maroon. As in its close relative hop hornbeam *(Ostrya virginiana)*, the male flowers hang in long slender catkins from stem tips in spring, just as the leaves are unfolding. Female inflorescences are shorter and stockier, each ovary sheltered by a leafy, three-lobed involucral bract (bracts set below the flowers). The bracts are strung together like a cluster of hops, and they are quite ornamental for a few weeks late in the summer as they turn from light green to almost white, then tan. These persist into early winter, slowly disintegrating and dispersing the seed as the bracts catch the wind. When open-grown, American hornbean has a neat, rectangular canopy, and it's especially lovely if limbed up a few feet when young to expose the beautiful muscled trunk. It is not extremely long-lived and not as formal looking as the larger European hornbeam *(Carpinus betulus)*, and older stems succumb to fusarium cankers after 20 to 30 years, especially when stressed by drought. Still the trees are fast growing and it is one of our most ornamental small trees for winter effect that thrive in shady, damp situations.

Carpinus has a very hard, light wood, and the European settlers used it much as they did the Old World species, to make sturdy tool handles, mallet heads, and the like. The wood takes a smooth polish like the surface of horn, hence the common name hornbeam: "beam" comes from the German word *Baum,* tree. The species has been divided into two overlapping subspecies: *C. caroliniana* ssp. *caroliniana* from south of the boundary of Pleistocene glaciation, which has smaller leaves (1 to 2 inches long), and the more northern *C. caroliniana* ssp. *virginiana,* with leaves in the 2-to-3-inch range. The two are very similar in appearance, but nursery-grown material is often of the southern race, which is far less hardy in the North.

CULTURE: Easily transplanted from containers, though Donald Wyman mentions in *Trees for American Gardens* (pp. 168–169) that it is difficult to move older, field-dug plants. I have moved a few balled and burlaped trees in the 2-to-2½-caliper range in spring before leaves emerged, and they settled in after two years. This is hardly a scientific sampling, but I have planted more from containers (3-to-7-gallon) and they generally move well if root-pruned and planted in spring. Although this is a wetland species in the wild, American hornbeam does grow well in somewhat drier cultivated situations, though it prefers a moist, fairly fertile soil in either light shade or sun.

Carpinus caroliniana var. virginiana. *This beautiful photograph captures details of a tree that might go unnoticed if you walked past it in the forest. Clusters of ripe hornbeam seeds stand out vividly like Chinese lanterns against the autumn leaves.*

Carya glabra. Pignut hickory is so named because the nuts — relatively small, hard to crack open, and bitter tasting — are considered fit only for swine. But in fact many mammals relish them. Squirrels will chew through the intensely bitter, tannin-soaked husk and gnaw away at the shell to get at the nutmeat inside. Deer wait for the husks to split, then swallow the seeds whole.

Fertilize lightly in spring for the first few years and take the time to shape the plant a bit when young, so the tree will have a single trunk for the first 16 to 24 inches above ground. Multitrunk trees develop narrow crotches that accumulate water and debris, which shortens their life considerably. The stems bleed somewhat in spring, so try to limit pruning to fall and early winter.

USES: Specimen in informal landscapes, naturalized in understory plantings. It can be sheared and shaped into hedges as is done with the European *C. betulus.*

WILDLIFE: Nuts are eaten by birds and mammals; the leaves are one of the foods for the adaptable white admiral *(Limenitis arthemis)*, striped hairstreak *(Satyrium liparops)* and tiger swallowtail *(Papilio glaucus)* butterflies

PROPAGATION: Moderately difficult from seed.

Carya glabra

Carya (ka-RYE-ah)
Junglandaceae
Hickory

Few plants profiled in this volume stand less chance of becoming common landscape plants than the hickories. Not that hickories are "bad" trees in horticultural terms; on the contrary, these are some of the tallest, stateliest, and longest-lived hardwoods of the eastern forests. They just take their time about things. Hickories, like oaks, have large seeds, which nurture the development of a deep taproot that allows many to live in dry, upland forest in an association called, logically enough, oak-hickory forest. Seedlings can establish under adult trees, but grow poorly in the shade. Ground fires, drought stress, or browsing may nip the young trees back to the ground, and each time they will come back more vigorously from an ever-expanding root system. When I

worked as a forest ecologist counting tree reproduction, most of the hickory seedlings in a given area showed telltale signs of dieback and resprouting. No one knows how long these seedlings can persist like this—20, 50, even 100 years seems possible—waiting for an eventual catastrophe to raze the forest. Then the patient seedlings grow in earnest, putting on 2 to 3 feet a year to take their place in the canopy. These sprouts, together with those that come from larger stumps, can grow far faster than a seedling just springing from a nut.

Hickory wood burns hotter than just about any other, and in many colonial woodlots it was selectively harvested for firewood. The big nuts do not fall far from the parent unless moved by squirrels or jays, so some overharvested areas have but a few trees. The wood has remarkable tensile strength, making it the wood of choice for the very ax handles used to chop it down. Hickory heartwood is deep brown graded irregularly with blond, and it makes a bold-grained furniture wood as well. This same resiliency gives the trees a great deal of snow, wind, and ice resistance. A broken crown is much rarer among hickories than oaks, maples, or beeches. In habit, the trees have a straight, narrow trunk, usually much smaller in diameter than oaks of a similar age and clear of branches at least half way up. When grown in the open, the canopy is somewhat broader, especially with pecan and shellbark hickory. The crown is narrowly oval, composed of stout twigs that meander and turn in shallow S-curves. I stared at a large pignut all winter as I wrote my last book, and the effect of fresh snow caught in the bows of these curving twigs was quite beautiful — fragmented, really, as if I were looking through shattered safety glass. Pinnate leaves burst dramatically from large, oval, sapsticky buds in spring and zigzag along the lengthening twigs. Flowers and nuts often grow from the terminal bud on older twigs, with vegetative growth commencing from one of the smaller side buds, and this, combined with the zigzag growth, explains their vaguely serpentine branching character. Fall color is typically a pretty golden yellow or apricot orange mixed with rusty brown.

Many of the hickories have edible nuts, but of course it is the oily-sweet pecan that is truly outstanding and second only to walnut in commercial value among our native trees. Shellbark hickory is next in flavor; with huge nuts almost the size of walnuts and a sweet meat with a bit more of a tannin bite. Shagbark has slightly smaller nuts with a pungent sweetness, and all of the others except water, pignut, and bitternut hickory have small but edible meats. Large hickories can produce 500 pounds or more of nuts in a good year, and the nuts can be collected as they fall to the ground—or you can use a handy tree shaker like the ones the professionals use. The pungent husks will crack into quarters as they dry, and you can then peel them off to get at the nuts. Be warned, however, that wild hickories have not been bred to have the thin, easily cracked shell of commercial pecans.

CULTURE: Small, container-grown seedlings or, in the case of pecan cultivars, grafted scions are sometimes available from nurseries. I worry about raising hickories in containers because of problems arising from distortion and constraint of their extremely long taproot. Very deep, narrow band pots (3 inches wide, 10 to 12 inches deep) are preferable for the first year to get seedlings started, but they should not stay long in confinement. It is better to collect seeds in fall, store them in damp peat in the refrigerator for the winter to protect them from rodents, and sow the seeds in place in the garden in spring. The seedlings spend a few years getting rooted before beginning top growth in earnest. If you have some seedling hickories on your property, you can encourage them by removing adjacent plants and cutting the stem back to the ground in winter. A vigorous new sprout or two will spring up the next season. These sprouts usually have better form than the original seedling. Many insects, animals, and fungi feed on hickories, which makes them extremely important members of the forest community, but can lead to some unsightly leaf drop and the like. Pecans are notoriously messy trees, and some of the others are as well, but hickories generally are not planted in formal landscapes, so a bit of untidiness won't be noticed.

USES: Naturalizing, nut production, shade tree, hedgerow.

WILDLIFE: With the demise of the chestnut, hickories have become important nut trees for forest animals. They bear nuts more regularly than oaks, so can bridge the gap when oaks are between mast years. The leaves feed a variety of insects, including the bizarre walking sticks (*Diapheromera femorata*), moths such as the hickory tussock moth (*Lophocampa caryae*), whose larvae wear a luxuriant white coat spotted with black, and butterflies like the striped, hickory, and banded hairstreaks (*Satyrium liparops, S. caryaevorus*, and *S. calanus*), and gray hairstreak (*Strymon melinus*). Their most remarkable dinner guest is the great hickory horned devil (the larva of the royal walnut moth, *Citheronia regalis*), our largest caterpillar at 5½ inches; it rears up to greet you with large yellow eyespots — certainly a startling sight to come upon in the woods.

PROPAGATION: Moderately easy from seed.

Carya aquatica
Water Hickory

ZONES: 6–9; part sun, sun
SOIL: Moist to seasonally wet
NATIVE TO: Floodplains, bottomlands often temporarily inundated in spring; along the Atlantic coast from Virginia to Florida then west to eastern Texas and north up the Mississippi River to southern Illinois
SIZE: Height 60–90 (140) feet, width 25–40 feet
COLOR: Yellowish green; blooms in spring

Water hickory has the same slender leaflets as the pecan (*C. illinoinensis*), its closest relative. It grows in slightly wetter soils and has a narrower crown than pecan, and warm gray bark that peels off in wide strips much like shagbark hickory. All in all the fine leaves and exfoliating bark make this a very ornamental hickory that should be encouraged where it is growing wild. The nuts are very bitter, unfortunately.

Carya cordiformis
Bitternut Hickory

ZONES: 4–9; part sun, sun
SOIL: Moist to moderately wet
NATIVE TO: Bottomlands, floodplains, moist slopes often over limestone; southern Maine and Quebec to Minnesota south to eastern Texas and the Florida Panhandle
SIZE: Height 70–100 (160) feet, width 25–40 feet
COLOR: Yellow-green; blooms in spring

Bitternut ranks as one of the tallest eastern forest trees, commonly growing over 100 feet on fertile alluvial soils and easy to distinguish, if you can get close enough, by its sulfur yellow, naked winter buds. It has fairly narrow leaflets, with fewer (7 to 9) to a leaf than either water hickory or pecan. Its cool gray bark is relatively smooth and doesn't flake or sheet off like the bark of many of the other species. Like the other hickories, even very tall trees have a relatively narrow trunk, which tapers very gradually to the branches high above.

Carya glabra
Pignut

ZONES: 4–9; part sun, sun
SOIL: Seasonally wet to dry
NATIVE TO: Floodplains and riverbanks to rocky or gravelly soils and ridges; southern Maine to southern Minnesota south to eastern Texas and central Florida
SIZE: Height 60–80 (100) feet, width 25–35 feet
COLOR: Yellow-green; blooms in spring

Pignut is so named because its small, bitter, thick-walled nuts were deemed fit only for swine and other livestock. Its cool gray bark tears apart in an interwoven lattice without peeling back in broad sheets like that of shagbark hickory. It develops a narrow, oval crown, even when grown in the open. This species is the most widely adapted to varying habitats, favoring drier uplands as well as richer alluvial soils. It is the most common hickory in my neck of the woods, mixing with oaks on well-drained, acid soils.

(Northern forms have been called a separate species, *C. ovalis*, by some authors.) Shagbark and bitternut hickory mostly displace it on the better sites.

Carya illinoinensis
Pecan

ZONES: 5–10; part sun, sun
SOIL: Moist, deep and fertile
NATIVE TO: Floodplains and bottomlands; Indiana to Iowa south to Texas, Mexico, and the Mississippi Delta of Louisiana
SIZE: Height 6–90 (130) feet, width 30–45 feet
COLOR: Yellow-green; blooms in spring

The mighty pecan is most at home in the hot and humid South, where long summers allow it to ripen bumper crops of fruit. So many nuts are produced in good years that many a household and waistline become overwhelmed with pecan pies and the rest go to rot or to squirrels out in the yard. This tree tends to be lower-branched and wider-crowned than the other hickories, with narrow leaflets and a warm gray bark that peels off in little squares or scales rather than strips. Selection work has been done to breed hardier cultivars for northern growers, and I have seen mature trees in New England that produce some filled nuts (the Bartlett Arboretum of the University of Connecticut has some good fruiting trees), but not nearly in the abundance seen in the Deep South. It can be grown in irrigated valleys of the Southwest, where the dry climate prevents many of the diseases that befall it eastward.

Carya laciniosa
Shellbark Hickory

ZONES: (4)5–9; part sun, sun
SOIL: Moist, fertile
NATIVE TO: Floodplains and rich bottomlands; Delaware and New York west to southern Iowa and Kansas, south sporadically to eastern Texas, Mississippi, and Georgia
SIZE: Height 60–80 (120) feet, width 25–40 feet
COLOR: Yellow-green; blooms in spring

Back when I lived in western New York, I was introduced to this species by a friend who made a yearly pilgrimage to a big hedgerow tree to collect the large, delicious nuts. I cannot easily distinguish it from shagbark hickory in winter, though the leaves typically have 7 to 9 leaflets, as opposed to shagbark's 5 to 7. The bark tends to sheet off in larger sections, and the nuts are walnut-sized, ridged, and solid tan, not marbled like pecans. It is certainly not a common tree, as it favors fertile river-bottom soils that mostly have been converted to agriculture. In fact, all the trees I have seen have been remnants left behind in hedgerows between farm fields.

Carya ovata. The unmistakable silhouette of a full-grown shagbark hickory has a certain tattered stoicism about it, as if the tree were wearing the accumulated weight of history on its weary limbs.

Carya ovata
Shagbark Hickory

ZONES: 4–9; part sun, sun
SOIL: Moist to moderately dry
NATIVE TO: Bottomlands, slopes, and upland forest; southern Maine and Quebec to southern Minnesota, south to eastern Texas and Georgia
SIZE: Height 70–100 (140) feet, width 20–35 feet
COLOR: Yellow-green; blooms in spring

I have always admired the bark of this tree. It peels off in great sheets, at first torn and split as the trunk expands, then peeling away from both ends like corrugated aluminum roofing tearing off in a hurricane. The sheets seem reluctant to give way completely and hang there forlornly, so the whole tree takes on a shaggy, unshaven aspect with age. It ranks at the top of my list for ornamentality and also for personality — the bare trees seem quite alive and almost sinister on a wet, foggy day. Shagbark hickory is fairly adaptable concerning soil moisture and fertility, but it is not as tolerant of poor soils as *C. glabra*.

Carya texana
Black Hickory

ZONES: 5–9; sun, part sun
SOIL: Moist to dry, well-drained
NATIVE TO: Sandy or rocky hills, often steep, eroded hillsides; southern Indiana to eastern Kansas south to central Texas and the Mississippi Delta region of Louisiana

SIZE: Height 20–60 (140) feet, width 10–30 feet
COLOR: Greenish yellow; blooms in spring
Black hickory develops the same tight, knitted bark as pignut, dark gray to almost black in color. In eastern Texas and adjacent states, it can grow to enormous heights, but it is very drought- and heat-tolerant, growing on sterile soils in central Texas as a small, narrow tree barely 20 feet high. It grades into sand hickory (*C. pallida*) to the east of the Mississippi River, a narrow tree of moderate height native to sandy pinelands in the southeastern United States.

Carya tomentosa
Mockernut Hickory

ZONES: 4–9; part sun, sun
SOIL: Moist to dry, well-drained
NATIVE TO: Sandy or rocky soils, slopes, and ridges
SIZE: Height 60–80 (100) feet, width 20–30 feet
COLOR: Yellow-green; blooms in spring
Mockernut hickory is superficially like pignut, with which it shares its habitat. In this case, the cool gray bark is ridged and patterned in diamond shapes a bit like ash bark, and it does not peel. The leaves are broad and covered in a sticky coating of hair.

Cassiope mertensiana

Cassiope (kas-EYE-o-pee)
Ericaceae
Mountain Heather, Moss Heather

Cassiope—the word rolls off my tongue like soil rolling off my shovel as I bury another dead one in the depths of my compost pile. These little heaths of cold, alpine bogs and tundra are beguilingly beautiful, and sooner or later every rock gardener must test his or her mettle and plant a few in the garden. Like the true heaths of the Old World (*Erica* spp.), these are small spreading or mounding shrubs with deep green needles or scale-like leaves on short branches that get matted down by the snow and root where they touch the peaty, damp ground they prefer. Lovely bell-shaped white flowers (large for the size of the plant) hang from the stem tips after the snow has melted. They are one of the joys of a summer hike in the Cascades or the Rockies, growing intermixed with their cousins the *Phyllodoce* species in large hummocky swaths along moraines and sheltered slopes. In the east, *Cassiope* drops into the United States only at the summits of some of the higher mountains of Maine and New York, about as close to the subarctic as this country can provide.

Mountain heath, *Phyllodoce*, is often lumped with *Cassiope* horticulturally because the plants have sim-

ilar requirements. The most obvious difference is the color of their flowers, which in the common species like red mountain heath (*Phyllodoce empetriformis*) is a strong rose pink. In other ways, though, the two genera are very much alike. Mountain heaths are also small, mounded shrubs clothed in evergreen, needle-like leaves crowded along short stems. Red mountain heath is common at high elevations in the Cascades and Rockies. It is related to the circumboreal Arctic mountain heath (*P. coerulea*), which has similar leaves (like small hemlock needles, really) and nodding, rose pink to bluish pink bell flowers held above the mound on long peduncles. It is most common in the tundra of northern Canada and Alaska and in the high mountains of northern New England. Cream mountain heath (*P. gladuliflora*) is more similar in effect to *Cassiope* species, as it bears pale yellow to almost white flowers. It is sympatric (shares habitat) with red mountain heath.

Cassiope mertensiana. *Mountain heather's deep green, needlelike leaves set off its pure white flowers beautifully. It is one of the easier species to grow if you can afford it a cool, peaty soil.*

CULTURE: Those who succeed with mountain heathers and mountain heaths plant them in pure peat or peat mixed with sand in a spot that remains cool through the season, preferably with some seepage of spring water. Very low pH (4.5 or so) may help suppress root diseases that would otherwise imperil the threadlike root system. High in the mountains, they receive full sun, but at lower elevations, morning sun or high shade will help prevent overheating. During hot spells, you may want to rent an industrial ice machine so you can liberally sprinkle the cooling crystal at their delicate feet. Alternatively, try snaking a coolant coil from an old air conditioner through your bed and set it to a thermostat that kicks in when the soil temp climbs over 55°F. In suitable conditions the little plants are trouble-free.

USES: Rock garden, peat garden.
PROPAGATION: Difficult from cuttings or seed.

Cassiope lycopodioides
Clubmoss Cassiope

ZONES: 3–6; light shade
SOIL: Moist, cool, well-drained and acid
NATIVE TO: Bogs, tundra; Alaska across the Aleutians to Siberia
SIZE: Height 8–12 inches, width 12–16 inches
COLOR: White; blooms in spring

It is surprising, given its northern range, that this species is probably the most amenable to cultivation. Its leaves have been reduced to adpressed scales that cover the whiplike branches, creating an almost reptilian look. Bell-shaped flowers poke out from between the scales at the tips of ascending branches in a charming way.

Cassiope mertensiana
Mountain Heather

ZONES: 3–6; light shade
SOIL: Moist, cool, well-drained and acid
NATIVE TO: Alpine meadows and bogs at high elevations; Montana to British Columbia and Alaska south to California, Nevada, and Colorado
SIZE: Height 8–14 inches, width 12–18 inches
COLOR: White; blooms in spring

Large, starkly white flowers stand out beautifully above the deep green foliage of moss heather, each a perfect little dangling bell. The effect of a patch in bloom is understated elegance. Mountain heather is one of the easier of this difficult genus to grow. It is a common, even dominant constituent of the subalpine meadows and glades that grace the Cascades, growing intertwined with *Phyllodoce empetriformis* in damp, glacier-fed moraines and bogs. Four-angled mountain heather (*C. tetragona*) is a very similar species with an overlapping range and flowers only about one-half as large.

Cassiope (Harrimanella) stelleriana
Moss Bush

ZONES: 3–6; light shade
SOIL: Evenly moist, well-drained, acidic
NATIVE TO: Alpine meadows and bogs; Alaska south to Washington in the mountains
SIZE: Height 3–8 inches, width 10–14 inches
COLOR: White; blooms in spring

A low, creeping plant with small, needle-like leaves on short ascending stems that branch here and there. In appearance it is somewhere between a heather and a clubmoss. The flowers of this species are upfacing and not fused into a bell (this is one of the reasons it has been split into a separate genus by some). Rather, they are distinctly five-petaled, not opening fully. The floral display is not as copious as

Castanea pumila. Chestnut flowers burst from the saw-toothed leaves in late spring. Their rich, heavy perfume must be irresistible to bees, wasps, and beetles, for every spray quivers with the patter of tiny feet. Sadly, by the time an American chestnut flowers, it is likely to be killed by blight, since dying trees shunt their remaining energy into a last-ditch attempt at reproduction. Chinkapin, shown here, is no more resistant to the blight than the other species.

in some of the other *Cassiope* species, and it is difficult to grow. *C. (Harrimanella) hypnoides* is a circumboreal species, similar in habit but with pure white, rounded flowers streaked with bits of red. It is equally challenging to grow, but a lovely sight in the wild. It ranges as far south as Mt. Katahdin in Maine.

Castanea pumila

Castanea (kas-TAY-nia)
Fagaceae
Chestnut

The blight that has caused the near extinction of the American chestnut ranks, in my opinion, as the single greatest catastrophe that has befallen the eastern broadleaf forests since the arrival of Europeans nearly 400 years ago. It is an epic tragedy not only because the tree was so important to myriad animals and insects, as well as to indigenous people, but also because this magnificent tree — so supremely adapted to life in the humid temperate forest — was struck down by a disease we humans undeniably aided and abetted. Part of what made chestnut so successful was its ability to persist in the shade of other trees and rise steadily up through them into the canopy to eventually replace them. Chestnuts in clear-cuts that have survived after the blight as resprouting root systems grow two to three times as fast as any other tree. It is common to see clumps released by clear-cut logging that have grown to 15 to 20 feet, only to be killed back by the blight and forced to sprout all over again — but they are still taller than neighboring oaks and maples that haven't experienced such travails. Chestnuts are related to oaks and beeches, and the shiny brown nuts nestled in a sea-urchin husk are about the size of a hazel. The leaves are broadly lanceolate, up to 10 inches long and serrate, with regularly spaced, forward-pointing teeth like the business side of a particularly aggressive-looking handsaw. If you are fortunate enough to see them, chestnut flowers are among the most ornamental in the beech family. The long male catkins spring out in all directions from the new growth in large, drooping, kitten tail plumes while the females, already with a small spiny husk in evidence, nestle in axils a bit lower down. Old trees developed a knitted, roughened bark that covered one of the strongest, most decay-resistant woods on the continent. Amazingly, you can still find bleached and weathered hulks of chestnut trees still intact on ridge tops where they fell 75 years ago. Chestnut was once the building material of choice within its native range, and though timber-sized trees are no longer available, a small industry has grown up to recycle chestnut beams from old barns and use them in new house construction.

Not surprisingly, such remarkable trees, capable of fast growth on a variety of soils, were the dominant hardwood through much of the East prior to 1904, when the fungus *Cryphonectria (Endothia) parasitica* was accidentally imported on Asian chestnuts brought into New York City and began to spread like wildfire through native stands. The trees have virtually no immunity to the disease, which starts out as a telltale sunken area of bark that cracks and erupts with rusty orange fruiting bodies called stromata. The trees try to contain the rapidly growing infection by producing a ridge of corky callus tissue around the circular lesion, but the fungus rapidly advances and girdles the tree, often in one season. Ironically, the very tannins that normally suppress diseases help feed the growing fungus. Insidiously, the disease attacks many trees just as they become large enough to begin flowering, either because of added stress or hormonal changes induced by flowering or because blooms attract boring insects, like the two-lined chestnut borer *(Agrius bilineatus)*, that spread the disease. By killing the trees before they can reproduce, the fungus prevents natural selection for disease resistance from proceeding.

Crossbreeding the American species with blight-resistant Asian chestnuts does confer immunity, but almost all the hybrids are small, spreading trees like their Japanese or Chinese parents. They are acceptable for orchards but certainly are no replacement as a forest tree. Some scattered native chestnuts show some natural immunity. At the Connecticut Agricultural Experiment Station in Hamden, there is a collection of resistant cultivars. Typically these plants can slow and concentrate the fungus in their bark, which becomes swollen and rough with some target-like cankers developing much like nectria cankers on walnut or birch. Researchers are trying to defend against the fungus by developing strains of it that are weakened by what is thought to be viral infection. The aim is to have the weakened strain colonize a tree and supersede infection by more virulent strains that would kill the tree. This approach has worked very well on European chestnuts, which are a bit more naturally resistant. A hypovirulent strain was released many years ago at Garden in the Woods, and we do have some fairly large chestnuts coming up in the woods, but there is little evidence as yet that they will survive once they begin fruiting.

I am an optimistic person by nature, and I still hold out hope—buoyed by the fierce tenacity of millions of resprouting chestnut roots—that somehow, someday, this majestic tree can beat the disease and take its former place in our forests. I hope I live to see that—nothing could make me happier.

CULTURE: Transplant when fairly young to a well-drained location, though chestnuts are not too fussy regarding soil. There is really no way to prevent *Cryphonectria* from infecting the tree if you live within the historic range of chestnut, so it is doubtful that many people will be rushing out to grow them. However, though an individual tree will usually perpetuate itself through resprouting, the species is completely dependent on humans for establishment of new seedlings. Planting chestnut seedlings has that aura of tireless optimism that we Americans are famous for, so get out those shovels. The American Chestnut Foundation (p. 333) is a clearinghouse for information about the tree and about breeding resistant strains.

USES: As a reminder of the importance of persevering in the face of terrible odds.

WILDLIFE: Formerly the primary mast species in many areas, providing nuts for mammals and ground feeding birds like jays, grouse, and turkeys. Like hickory, these trees host three species of hairstreak butterfly larvae—the striped hairstreak, hickory hairstreak, and banded hairstreak *(Satyrium liparops, S. caryaevorus,* and *S. calanus)*—as well as the banded oak dusky wing *(Erynnis brizo)*.

PROPAGATION: Moderately difficult from seed, mostly because seed is hard to find.

Castanea dentata

American Chestnut

ZONES: 4–9; sun to shade

SOIL: Moist and fertile to dry and rocky

NATIVE TO: Slopes, ridges, and bottomlands in deciduous forest; Maine to Michigan south to Louisiana and northwest Florida

SIZE: Height formerly 70–100 feet, now typically 10–15 feet, width formerly 30–50 feet, now 5–8 feet

COLOR: Yellow; blooms in summer

Catalpa speciosa.
*Northern catalpa's
bodacious blooms are
laced with cues to guide
pollinators to their
reward. A tracery of
purple lines flags the
route a bee must take,
and yellow dots on the
fertile flowers simulate
pollen as further adver-
tisement.*

Castanea pumila (alnifolia)
Chinkapin

ZONES: 5–9; sun to light shade
SOIL: Moist to dry, well-drained
NATIVE TO: Woodlands and sandy pine barrens;
coastal Massachusetts south to Florida and
southwest through Pennsylvania, Kentucky, and
Arkansas to eastern Texas
SIZE: Height formerly to 30–40 feet, now typically
6–10 feet, width formerly 10–15 feet, now 4–10
feet
COLOR: Yellow; blooms in late spring

This smaller species grows as a shrubby tree in poor,
sandy barrens or as a taller understory tree on better
soils. It flowers three weeks earlier than *C. dentata*
and is easy to distinguish when in fruit, as the husk is
in two, rather than four sections, and there is never
more than one seed inside. Ozark chinkapin *(C.
ozarkensis)* is a larger species with distribution centered in the Ozark Mountains of Arkansas and
adjoining states. It may represent a past hybrid
between *C. dentata* and *C. pumila*, as in many ways it
is intermediate between them.

The western chinkapins *(Chrysolepis*, commonly
listed as *Castanopsis)* are Pacific coastal counterparts
to the chestnuts, with leathery evergreen leaves that
are nearly smooth along the margin and smaller but
equally spiny nuts that are edible if you can extract
them. Giant chinkapin *(C. chrysophylla)* can grow to
150 feet in height in the redwood belt and Coastal
Ranges of northern California, Oregon, and Washington, but it is often dwarfed by the immense
conifers of the region and must get by as primarily
an understory tree, even at great heights. It has the
ability to resprout after fire, giving it an advantage
over Douglas firs after a conflagration or, more commonly in these heavily managed forests, clear-cut-
ting. The new twigs and undersides of the leaves are
coated in waxy, golden scales, and the upper surface
of the foliage is sort of a yellow-green that makes the
trees easy to spot amid darker evergreens. Old trees
develop a knitted, reddish brown bark, and the trees
bloom with the same musky virility as the American
chestnut. Upright, creamy white, foxtail catkins
cover the trees in a lovely display in early summer.
Bush chinquepin *(C. sempervirens)* is a shrubby,
chaparral species restricted to the California Sierras
and the extreme southwest corner of Oregon.
Although as yet unaffected by chestnut blights, neither of these is widely grown, as they have a difficult
reputation that stems in part from their long taproots that make all but seedlings difficult to move.
They are partial to the mild Pacific climate and hardy
only in cool-summer parts of Zones 8–9 (perhaps
Zone 7 or even 6 for the smaller species).

Catalpa speciosa

Catalpa (ka-TAL-pa)
Bignoniaceae
Catalpa

Catalpas are coarse, ponderous trees that for a
week or two each spring decorate themselves with
large, frilled flowers possessing a hothouse beauty
strangely at odds with the visage of the tree itself.
The effect is akin to a heavyweight boxer in drag. In
habit catalpas are heavy-limbed, medium-sized trees
with heart-shaped leaves up to a foot long and 8
inches across. The leaves grow in sets of two or more
commonly three from each node—an unusual
arrangement that helps identify them in winter (few
other trees have three leaf scars per node). Fall leaf
color is a muddy yellow fading to black. As in its
cousins *Campsis* and *Bignonia*, the seeds are reared
in long, cylindrical pods pointed at both ends. The
liberally produced pods turn chocolate brown as the
leaves begin to fall, then hang on through most of the
winter. The pods collect near the branch tips, giving
the trees a weeping look, which adds to the general
impression of their gravity-bound bulk. Wild catalpas are confined to river systems, so it seems possible
that the pods are designed to drop off and float to a
new place before releasing seed. The origin of the
name catalpa is a Creek word, *kutuhlpa*, meaning
"head with wings," in reference, I imagine, to the
shape of the seed. The flat seeds ripen stacked in the
pods like those of *Campsis*, and each has a flattened
embryo with cotyledons outspread and centered in
the middle of two long, feathery paper wings that

help with wind or perhaps water dispersal. It does look like a little head with wings sprouting out of it.

Catalpa flowers are white overall, with what appear to be four flaring, ruffled petals narrowed into a short tube at the base; two of the five segments are fused. The opening of the tube is traced with purple lines and speckles framed by two rows of orange dots that disappear down the throat. The orange turns to yellow as the flowers mature, which simulates pollen; the patterning acts as an effective nectar guide to lead bees into the tube to accomplish pollination. The flowers are displayed in large, branched panicles from the terminal of every twig as the leaves are nearly expanded. The trees are a bit late to leaf out, so flowering doesn't commence until very late spring. In Britain, catalpas are valued as one of the choicest flowering trees North America has to offer, and they were once planted widely as a landscape tree on this side of the Atlantic as well. Like the European horse chestnut, which they resemble a bit in floral exuberance, catalpas were popular trees in the Victorian era, where florid excess was a virtue, not a vice. Today, we value convenience over the rococo, and the pods, large leaves, and brittle wood make for a messy tree that few homeowners want to bother with. It is rare to see anything but mature trees here and there in older neighborhoods.

CULTURE: There are two species of catalpa, both similar, and both are highly adaptable trees that are easily transplanted, either balled and burlaped or from containers, into a range of soil types and moisture conditions. Their flexibility is surprising given the preferred habitat and very limited natural distribution of both species. Catalpas do need full sun to flower well. I have seen them used just for bold foliage effect where the stems are cut back to the ground every two to three years. The vigorous sprouts have especially large leaves and are capable of 6 feet or more in annual growth. The cultivar *C. bignonioides* 'Aurea', with golden-green leaves, is employed to nice effect this way in a mixed border at the Tower Hill Botanic Garden in Worcester, Massachusetts.

USES: Lawn and park tree.

WILDLIFE: The leaves host the black, yellow-lined catalpa sphinx moth *(Ceratomia catalpae)*, which feeds on them, often in great numbers. In the past, fisher folk planted the trees solely to harvest the caterpillars for bait when needed. (The fierce-looking caterpillars are plucked off and gruesomely turned inside out by poking them from one end with a twig, then impaled on a hook.) I have seen some trees outside of Washington, D.C., that were largely defoliated by caterpillars, but most of the caterpillars had been parasitized by braconid wasps and hung there paralyzed with a load of eggs/pupae on their backs.

PROPAGATION: Easy from seed.

Catalpa bignonioides
Southern Catalpa

ZONES: 5–9; sun
SOIL: Moist to dry
NATIVE TO: Riverbanks, floodplains; in a limited area of the Florida Panhandle north to southwest Georgia, southern Alabama, and southeast Mississippi
SIZE: Height 30–40 feet, width 25–30 feet
COLOR: White marked with reddish purple and yellow; blooms in early summer

This species is the smaller and less winter-hardy of the two catalpas. Its slightly smaller flowers are displayed in larger panicles, and the leaves emit an unpleasant odor when crushed.

Catalpa speciosa
Northern Catalpa

ZONES: 4–8; sun
SOIL: Moist to dry
NATIVE TO: Riverbanks and floodplains, in a 50-to-100-mile belt along the Mississippi and lower Ohio rivers; southwest Illinois and southern Indiana south along these rivers to eastern Arkansas and western Tennessee
SIZE: Height 40–60 (80) feet, width 20–40 feet
COLOR: White marked with reddish purple and yellow; blooms in late spring

The fast-growing *C. speciosa* was once planted in coppice plantations in the Midwest; the trees were harvested for use as rot-resistant fence posts, telegraph poles, and the like.

Ceanothus americanus.
For the gardener seeking attractive plants that will thrive in inhospitable sites, Ceanothus offers many possibilities. New Jersey tea is one of the best species for the East, and its frothy white flowers are an exceptional source of nectar for bees and butterflies.

Ceanothus americanus

Ceanothus (see-a-NOH-thus)
Rhamnaceae
California Lilac, Wild Lilac, New Jersey Tea, Redroot, Ceanothus

Ceanothus species are a bit of an enigma in the world of native shrubs. Along the East Coast there is but one species, New Jersey tea *(C. americanus)*, a low, suckering shrub growing in difficult locations that goes mostly unnoticed for all but a few weeks in summer, when the branch tips are abuzz with all manner of insects attracted by its plumes of fine white honey-scented flowers. A few similar species are spread throughout the drier parts of the United States and southern Canada, but sunny California is virtually awash in species—40 of our 50 *Ceanothus* species grow only in the Golden State. Californian ceanothuses are not just abundant, they are extraordinarily beautiful. White flowers abound, but so do frothy cerulean blues, fragrant lavenders, and cool violets, on shrubs with glossy, typically evergreen leaves attractive even when the plants are out of bloom. Flowers are borne either in panicles at the tips of the new growth or along the older growth from axils or small spur branches in flat-topped or rounded cymes. Each five-petaled flower is small, but the blooms are produced in abundance. The leaves of many Californian *Ceanothus* species are leathery, reduced in size, and spread along stout twigs singly or in pairs with fairly long internodes. This is an adaptation to the dry-summer Mediterranean climate, a climate that ceanothuses obviously thrive on.

Like *Alnus* and *Myrica*, *Ceanothus* can fix atmospheric nitrogen with the aid of bacteria in the genus *Frankia*. Thus they can grow in eroded or generally poor soils with limited moisture for part of the year.

Why then, you might ask, aren't there more ceanothuses in the dry Great Basin just east of the Sierras? The likely explanation lies to the south, in Mexico. When California's climate began to dry out, about 4 million years ago, cool-climate plants retreated into the mountains, leaving the door open for plants from the subtropical areas of Mexico to migrate north. These include the Pacific madrone as well as several sclerophyllous (having tough, evergreen leaves) *Ceanothus* that began to speciate like mad in this brave new world that lacked much in the way of competition.

Pacific *Ceanothus* species, though too tender for most of North America, are justifiably popular in their home states, and many cultivars have been selected and planted in gardens and parks and even along highways. That would probably be the end of the story, except that although the showy-flowered sclerophyllous species are very different from New Jersey tea and its relatives like prairie red root *(C. herbacea)* and snowbush *(C. fendleri)*, remarkably, all ceanothus species can freely hybridize (which helps explain their rapid speciation). This trait has been used to advantage in Europe, where in the 1800s hybridizers began to combine the cold- and humidity-tolerance of the eastern species with the striking flowers of some of the Californian ones. The result is an array of great garden plants with pink, violet, lavender, and even mesmerizingly true-blue flowers. A few of these are hardy in the eastern United States, especially the *Ceanothus* × *pallidus* hybrids that have both *C. americanus* and *C. herbacea* as well as the very tender Central American *C. coeruleus* in their background. We have grown some of these, and they are lovely in flower, though the spent panicles stand up above the foliage for the rest of the summer looking a bit stark, and the stems die back to the ground when the temperature falls to below about −5° F. The flowers come on new growth, so this is not a problem, and the plants can almost be treated like perennials.

Little breeding work has been done in this country outside of California, though I think this genus holds tremendous possibilities for producing hardy, floriferous, blue-flowered garden shrubs that are both heat- and drought-tolerant. This may succeed especially by substituting some of the hardier blue species for *C. coeruleus*.

CULTURE: Ceanothuses require several things in order to do well. They are full-sun plants, though the deciduous species can handle partial shade. They are intolerant of wet soils, and the sclerophyllous species especially will succumb to root diseases if the soil is too wet during the heat of summer. These are not plants for the Southeast, for high humidity combined with summer rainfall will quickly kill them. Ceanothus can be cut back to the ground when dormant if they become rangy. Most are fire-adapted, disturbance-oriented plants that thrive with this sort of harsh pruning treatment. I have grown the eastern species as well as some of the hybrids, and find them generally easy to raise in containers and to transplant into the garden in spring. Healthy container plants, growing in a well-drained mix, developed actinorhizal nodules on the roots while in the nursery (the nodules have the same knobby look as those on legumes' roots). Problems usually arise from either poorly drained soils or lack of sun, though the absence of suitable actinorhizal bacteria in the chosen site may play a part. (Advice about *Frankia* inoculation is the same as given for *Alnus*.) Of 60 bare-root *C. americanus* plants I potted last spring, 7 developed curled, chlorotic foliage and eventually died. In the past, I have had interveinal chlorosis appear in container plants that I attributed to iron deficiency brought on by our hard water. But this was a different sort of pattern, which may still represent a nutrient deficiency or imbalance, and I need to investigate it further.

USES: Massing and border for the smaller, herbaceous species; foundations, screens, and bank stabilization as well for the larger.

WILDLIFE: *Ceanothus* species are premier nectar plants for many insects, including butterflies, bees, and beneficial parasitic wasps and hoverflies. The long list of butterflies whose larvae feed on the plants include the pallid tiger swallowtail (*Papilio eurymedon*), orange-tip admiral (*Limenitis lorquini*), western tortoise shell (*Nymphalis californica*), coppermark (*Apodemia nais*), western and buckthorn hairstreaks (*Satyrium sylvinus* and *S. saepium*), green hairstreak (*Callophrys affinis*), turquoise hairstreak (*Erora laeta*), spring azure (*Celastrina argiolus*), mottled dusky wing (*Erynnis martialis*) in the East, and buckthorn dusky wing (*Erynnis pacuvius*) in the West. I would rank the ceanothuses among the top 10 native shrubs for butterfly gardens.

PROPAGATION: Moderately difficult from cuttings and seed.

Ceanothus americanus
New Jersey Tea

ZONES: 4–9; part sun, sun
SOIL: Well-drained, acidic
NATIVE TO: Sandy or rocky soils, woodland edge, pine barrens; Quebec to Minnesota south to Texas and Florida
SIZE: Height 2–3 feet, width 2–3 feet
COLOR: Creamy white; blooms in summer
This is the most adaptable *Ceanothus* species for eastern gardens, tolerating rain and humidity provided the soil is well drained. It has narrowly oval, dark green 2-to-3-inch leaves with prominent sunken veins arranged oppositely up the stem. Foliage is deciduous, and fall color is an unspectacular yellow-green. The habit is a finely branched, many-stemmed shrub bearing elongated panicles of frothy flowers in mid summer, when few other plants are in bloom. Flowers come from the axils of the new growth on long peduncles clustered toward the top of the shrub. Occasional hard pruning in winter combined with sun and good drainage keep it looking best.

Ceanothus cuneatus
Buckbrush Ceanothus

ZONES: 7–9; sun
SOIL: Summer-dry, well-drained
NATIVE TO: Chapparal and mountain slopes and ridges; California and southern Oregon
SIZE: Height 3–8 feet, width 3–4 feet
COLOR: White, occasionally light blue; blooms late in spring
Buckbrush is one of the most common species in the California chapparal, forming large stands on drier slopes and covering itself with a glorious coat of white flowers for three weeks in spring. It is a fairly stiff, upright shrub with small, thick evergreen leaves borne on short spurs along the twigs. The foliage is spatulate, gray-green above and with a dense coat of white wool underneath to help prevent water loss. Relatives include Monterey ceanothus (*C. rigidus*), a densely branched, arching low shrub with wonderful bright blue flowers and very small, spiny evergreen leaves. It grows on sand flats in and around Monterey Bay. Coast ceanothus (*C. ramulosus*) is a more widespread Pacific coast species that grows as far north as Oregon and may represent a hybrid between *C. cuneatus* and *C. rigidus*.

Ceanothus diversiflorus
Pinemat, Trailing Ceanothus

ZONES: 7–9; part sun to light shade
SOIL: Moist, well-drained
NATIVE TO: Coniferous forest and margins in the Sierras, between 3,000 and 6,000 feet in elevation; northern California
SIZE: Height 6–12 inches, width 2–4 feet
COLOR: Blue, occasionally almost white; blooms in late spring
An unusual ground-covering species in that it is adapted to fairly heavy shade; it trails around in the forest understory on scandent stems lined with alternating, thin, fuzzy leaves that are evergreen, oval and 1 inch long. Flowers are borne in small rounded clusters on leafless axillary branches.

Ceanothus fendleri
Snowbush

ZONES: 4–9; sun
SOIL: Moderately dry, well-drained
NATIVE TO: Valleys and rocky hills in open ponderosa pine forest, occasionally exposed ridges; western South Dakota (Black Hills) to Colorado and Arizona, New Mexico, and Texas
SIZE: Height 10–18 inches, width 1–3 feet
COLOR: White; blooms in summer

Snowbush lives up to its name, smothering itself in balls of bright white flowers for a short time in summer. The foliage is small, up to an inch long and narrowly ovate, alternating up thin stems. Small side branches terminate in stout spines to protect the plant from deer, who relish the new growth before the spines stiffen. The overall effect of the plant is densely twiggy—a low mound beset with thorns.

Ceanothus gloriosus
Point Reyes Creeper

ZONES: 8–9; sun
SOIL: Well-drained, moderately moist
NATIVE TO: Ocean bluffs and slopes; Point Reyes area of central California
SIZE: Height 4–12 inches (taller out of the winds and salt spray), width 3 feet
COLOR: Deep blue to purplish blue; blooms in spring

An attractive groundcover with opposite, dark, evergreen leaves that are oval and strongly toothed and small but numerous clusters of rich blue flowers borne on short axillary branches from the previous season's growth. Var. *exaltatus* is a more upright, sprawling shrub from farther inland.

Ceanothus herbaceus (obovatus)
Prairie Red Root

ZONES: 4–8; sun
SOIL: Well-drained
NATIVE TO: Sandy or rocky soil of prairies, occasionally woodland edge farther east; Michigan west to Montana south to northwestern Indiana, Texas, and Arkansas with scattered populations in Vermont, New York, and Quebec
SIZE: Height 2–3 feet, width 2–3 feet
COLOR: White; blooms in early summer

This species differs from New Jersey tea in that its more broadly oblong leaves and flowers are mostly terminal, not axillary. I have grown them side by side, and prairie red root is a looser-looking shrub with larger, bolder foliage and a less spectacular flower effect because the blooms are more concentrated toward the tip of each stem.

Ceanothus impressus
Santa Barbara Ceanothus

ZONES: 8–9; sun
SOIL: Well-drained, summer-dry
NATIVE TO: Dry sandy mesas in Santa Barbara and San Luis Obispo counties, California
SIZE: Height 1–6 feet, width 6–10 feet
COLOR: Deep blue; blooms in spring

This is a very ornamental species that is being used very effectively as a bank cover at the Santa Barbara Botanical Garden. It appears to be a fast-spreading, low shrub forming colonies of stiff, twiggy stems covered in very small, narrow, but beautifully glossy leaves. The flowers form in large, domed panicles above the foliage over 3 to 4 weeks in spring. Its rapid spread and drought tolerance make it a prime candidate for roadside plantings where it can be grown.

Ceanothus prostratus
Mahala Mat

ZONES: 6–7; sun to light shade
SOIL: Dry, well-drained
NATIVE TO: Drier mountain slopes, either as an understory plant in mixed coniferous forest or on more exposed, rocky, slopes; Idaho to Washington south to California and Nevada.
SIZE: Height 2–6 inches, width 2–8 feet
COLOR: Deep blue to almost white, fading to pink; blooms in spring

A fantastic, ground-hugging evergreen with spiny, holly-like leaves much like those of *C. purpureus*. Ball-shaped heads of brightly colored flowers grow from the nodes on short, upright stems.

Ceanothus purpureus
Hollyleaf Ceanothus, Napa Ceanothus

ZONES: 8–9; sun
SOIL: Dry, well-drained; tolerates some summer moisture
NATIVE TO: Dry, west-facing slopes and ridges in Napa County, California
SIZE: Height 2–4 feet, width 2–3 feet
COLOR: Dark, blue-purple; blooms in spring

This is one of the most beautiful of all the California ceanothuses, and is one of our finest native shrubs. Small, spiny, holly-shaped leaves clothe the stiff stems in pairs in a curious sort of way. They are a deep, glossy green, curve down like a tongue, and are set close together with short internodes. Flowers coat the outer branches, opening first as a ball on the tips and working their way down the stems in little axillary clusters. Muskbrush (*C. jepsonii*), named for the musky smell of the flowers, is similar.

Ceanothus sanguineus

Red-stem Ceanothus, Oregon Tea-tree

ZONES: 4–8; sun

SOIL: Well-drained

NATIVE TO: Rocky hills, Montana to British Columbia and extreme northern California with a disjunct population in northern Keweenaw, Michigan

SIZE: Height 3–10 feet, width 3–4 feet

COLOR: White, occasionally light blue; blooms in early summer

This fascinating species is widespread in the Pacific Northwest but, like thimbleberry (*Rubus parviflorus*) it is also found far to the east along the Keweenaw Peninsula, which juts into Lake Superior in northern Michigan. It is the only large shrub ceanothus that grows this far east. It has flat-topped clusters of flowers borne in the axils of oval 2-to-3-inch-long deciduous leaves from the previous year's growth. The youngest twigs are stained red, and the habit is oval and upright. It is a very attractive shrub—certainly one of the undiscovered beauties of our flora—and it has great potential in hybridization work.

Ceanothus velutinus

Sticky Laurel, Mountain Balm

ZONES: 4–8; sun

SOIL: Dry, well-drained

NATIVE TO: Rocky slopes, open coniferous forest, especially sites of past fire; South Dakota to British Columbia south to California and Colorado

SIZE: Height 2–5 feet, width 3–5 feet

COLOR: White; blooms in early summer, possibly into midsummer

Sticky laurel is the hardiest of the evergreen *Ceanothus* species; its large, oval leaves are coated with a gummy, balsam-scented resin that makes them highly flammable and deviously designed to actually spread the flames and thus eliminate competitors. Once it establishes after a fire, it can persist for a long time, limiting the growth of other plants possibly with alleopathic chemicals (compounds released by one species to inhibit the growth of others) and so becoming a pest in the eyes of foresters. Horticulturally it is a pretty mounded plant, with a light, airy flowering effect that is nicely framed by the shiny, rich green foliage, its gloss enhanced by the resin.

Celastrus scandens

Celastrus scandens

(se-LAS-trus)

Celastraceae

American Bittersweet

Celastrus scandens. The fruits of American bittersweet have all the flamboyance of its Asian relative, and the vines are far more easily contained.

ZONES: 3–8; sun to shade

SOIL: Moist to dry

NATIVE TO: Moist clearings, thickets, roadsides in Quebec and Ontario to Manitoba south to Wyoming, extreme northern Texas and Alabama and in the Appalachians to northern Georgia

SIZE: Height 5–15 feet or more, depending on support, width 4–15 feet

COLOR: Greenish white; blooms in late spring

I **have always liked** the name bittersweet, because I think it perfectly captures the essence of this deciduous vine. Bitter because it will strangle and scramble over everything in sight, sweet because the red-orange and yellow berries that develop on female plants in fall look very sweet in a seasonally appropriate sort of way. Its inherent aggressiveness pales by comparison to the introduced *Celastrus orbiculatus* (Asian bittersweet), which is choking many areas of the Northeast—a pest that makes *C. scandens* look positively polite. Asian bittersweet is a very close relative, so close, in fact, that there is some evidence that the two are hybridizing, raising the possibility that the true native vine may disappear like a spoon sinking into a vigorous hybrid soup.

Celtis occidentalis.
Hackberries have a fair-
ly consistent shape when
young, which lends
them to use in allees and
as street trees. Select cul-
tivars that are resistant
to witches' broom to
avoid that unsightly
infection.

American bittersweet produces racemes of small, hardly noticeable flowers at the terminus of the new growths, whereas *C. orbiculatus* flowers in little clusters from the axils all along the stem tips. Thus, *C. scandens* has fruits in 2-to-3-inch-long clusters of 10 to 20, like small bunches of grapes hanging out away from the leaves, whereas the introduced bittersweet has little groups of 2 to 4 fruits alternating up the stems amid the yellowing foliage. The native species typically has narrower, ovate leaves ending in a pronounced tip, and Asian bittersweet has fuller, almost rounded leaves. However, these are minor distinctions, and honestly I often have trouble distinguishing the true species from what appears to me to be a cocktail of hybrid intergrades. Both produce twining, fast-growing shoots that will coil around each other if there is nothing else—when a bunch have grown together the effect is much like twisted cable. Both species have seeds enclosed in a bright red fruit that ripens protected in a three-valved jacket, similar to the fruits of the related genus *Euonymus*. When the seeds are ripe the yellow-orange jacket opens up like the bays on a space shuttle, exposing the red fruit nestled inside.

If you do want to grow the native species, first be sure about your identification. I have received hybrid plants obviously grown from a native female that was pollinated by a *C. orbiculatus* male. Since they are dioecious, you have to have both a male and female for fruit set, and this, combined with problems of hybridization, makes cuttings taken from confirmed, sexed adults the best method of propagation.

CULTURE: Bittersweet is very adaptable and will grow almost anywhere in the northeastern United States and southern Canada. I am sure it will grow well in the Pacific Northwest, but I would caution gardeners there against introducing it, as it might well become rampant. Fruiting is, of course, best in sun. Bittersweet will send up sprouts from its shallow, bright yellow roots at some distance from where you plant it. Without doubt, the native species does seem more content scrambling over stonewalls or fences than its Asian counterpart, which readily climbs up into 60-foot trees and chokes them. If you have a steep bank or other difficult spot, and you like the fruits in decorative arrangements, this may be just the vine for you.

USES: Screening for difficult areas, walls, fences, the old, rusting Chevy that you honestly mean to haul off to the junkyard someday, or your neighbor's unfortunate garden statuary.

WILDLIFE: The fruits are relished by songbirds.

PROPAGATION: Moderately easily from seed or cuttings.

Celtis occidentalis

Celtis (SEL-tis)
Ulmaceae
Hackberry, Sugarberry

Growing up at the fringes of hackberry country, in New England, I have never gotten to know these trees as I have tulip poplar, elm, beech, or sugar maple. However, I have come to appreciate them and their rugged, adaptable nature, which makes up in resiliency what it might lack in flamboyance. The eastern *Celtis* species enjoy the good life of a rich bottomland, sharing the deep soils along rivers and streams with their cousins the elms. The western species grow in drier situations, but all hackberries can stand seasonally parched soils in cultivation. They bear elliptical or lance-shaped leaves edged with fine teeth and netted with veins. The base of the leaf is slightly uneven, as if mischievous children had snipped off one side with scissors. In open situations, the larger ones will form a broadly oval, low-branched crown much like sugar maple in shape. Smaller branches are often disfigured by witches' broom, which causes a characteristic knotted, ball-of-twigs effect in the canopy that helps identify the trees from a distance. The witches' brooms are caused by a small mite, *Eriophyes celtis,* which crawls under the scales of a dormant bud and begins feeding and multiplying in spring. Infected twigs are also attacked by a powdery mildew (*Sphaerotheca phytoptophila*), which exacerbates the disease. Bud tissue proliferates, causing many small shoots to grow from a central knot in summer and die off in winter. Badly infected trees look terribly compromised, but they can continue to grow and fruit and otherwise live to a ripe old age. There are broom-resistant cultivars available, and these have proved to be very useful street trees in urban or windswept environments where few other species survive. Throughout parts of the South, upper Midwest, and Great Plains, hackberries are increasingly evident, casting welcome shade on parking lots, backyards, and side streets.

Hackberries get their name from the hard little fruits they produce in quantity. Trees produce male and female flowers, both of them small and inconspicuous, blended in with the emerging leaves. Female flowers are interesting on close inspection. They consist of a ring of green sepals and maybe a few petals spaced like a saucer with a bottlelike ovary set teacup fashion in the middle. Two feathery stigmas stick out of the bottleneck like miniature peacock plumes to catch drifting pollen. If all goes well, the ovary will swell into a round, ½-inch drupe containing one stony seed. The fruits are green until fall, when they ripen to a dull red, orange, blue-black, or, most commonly, a ruddy brown patina similar to that of a polished leather armchair in a gentlemen's club. Each fruit is attached, cherry style, to a long, thin pedicel by a little suction cup disk. The sugary-thick fruits are very important fall-winter forage for both migrating and overwintering birds as well as mammals. They remain hanging on the trees well into winter, but are not very noticeable to us on the ground.

The genus is a confusing one to sort out taxonomically, for individual plants as well as geographical races are quite variable in size, leaf shape, etc. Following *Flora of North America*, I have grouped several species, like *C. pumila* and *C. douglasii,* in with other, more widely ranging complexes.

CULTURE: Hackberries are not fussy about soils. They transplant well into heavy as well as sandy soil, in moist or seasonally wet locations as well as those that dry out in summer. Certain species (*C. occidentalis* and *C. reticulata*, for example) are more common on limestone in the wild, but low pH does not appear to be a problem in cultivation. They are reasonably shade-tolerant, but certainly do best in the full sun, though open-grown trees are more susceptible to witches' broom attacks. There is not much you can do about the broom, though there are selections of *C. occidentalis* and *C. laevigata* on the market that are reasonably resistant. Not surprisingly, healthy trees will fare better.

USES: Street or shade tree, especially for difficult sites.

WILDLIFE: These are excellent trees for wildlife, with fruits that are highly nutritious for birds and mammals, and leaves that feed larvae of many host-specific butterflies, including the tan, brown, and white hackberry butterfly (*Astrocampa celtis*) and its relatives desert hackberry and tawny emperor (*Astrocampa leilia* and *A. clyton*). Other butterflies that feed on hackberry include the purple and silver emperors (*Doxocopa pavon* and *D. laure*); subtropical butterflies that come over the border from Mexico to feed on hackberries in the Southwest like snout butterfly (*Libytheana carinenta*), small curvy wing (*Caria ino*), and Mexican sister (*Limenitis fessonia*); and finally, the less host-specific species question mark (*Polygonia interrogationis*), and mourning cloak (*Nymphalis antiopa*). Of course, where insects feed, trees loose leaves, and these butterflies can nearly defoliate trees on occasion.

PROPAGATION: Moderately easy from seed.

Celtis laevigata
Sugarberry

ZONES: 5–9; sun to light shade
SOIL: Moist to dry
NATIVE TO: Rich bottomlands and slopes; Maryland to southern Illinois and southeastern Kansas south to Texas and Florida
SIZE: Height 60–80 (100) feet, width 40–60 feet
COLOR: Greenish white; blooms in spring and summer
In appearance sugarberry begs to be compared with beech, in both its wide, densely leafy canopy and the smooth, muscled cool gray bark that clothes its limbs and trunk. The sweet fruits, described by some as date-like in flavor, ripen from red to almost black-brown in autumn. It is a fairly common street and shade tree in the South, with a wide-spreading canopy that arches out over the street from a single trunk often forked near the base into several thick limbs. Its leaves are smaller than the more northern *C. occidentalis*.

Celtis lindheimeri
Lindheimer Hackberry

ZONES: 7–10; sun
SOIL: Well-drained
NATIVE TO: Ravines; south-central Texas and northern Mexico
SIZE: Height 15–25 (40) feet, width 15–20 feet
COLOR: Greenish white; blooms in late winter to spring
This rare species is related to the widespread netleaf hackberry (*Celtis reticulata*). It has a wide-spreading, rounded crown, corky bark, and leaves with a noticeable gray tomentum on the lower surface, which gives the trees a grayer appearance than netleaf hackberry. The ripe fruits are usually light brown as opposed to red in the netleaf. It is also notable as the only known host of the beautifully patterned Mexican sister butterfly, which is limited in the United States to the few counties in central Texas where this hackberry grows.

Celtis occidentalis
Hackberry

ZONES: 3–9; sun to light shade
SOIL: Wet to dry
NATIVE TO: Rich bottomlands, slopes, occasionally drier ridges; southern Quebec and Ontario to southern Michigan, then north to southern Manitoba south to northern Texas, Alabama, and North Carolina
SIZE: Height 30–70 (100) feet, width 20–70 feet
COLOR: Greenish white; blooms in early spring

In rich, closed canopy forest, *C. occidentalis* takes on a tall, high-crowned shape like a rain-forest species, but in the open it, too, develops wide, rounded branches. The distinctive cool gray bark of this species is ridged, the ridges rounded into bumps or warts. The effect is like wax that has come too close to a flame and become melted and smoothed along the edges. The eastern genotypes are large trees, but as you move west and rainfall decreases, the trees adapt with progressively smaller stature. Small hackberry *(Celtis pumila)* is the name given to these diminutive populations, which represent merely geographical variations. Fruits of this species are red-orange to dark blue—blue-black when ripe.

Celtis pallida
Desert Hackberry

ZONES: 8–10; sun
SOIL: Well-drained, seasonally dry
NATIVE TO: Canyons and mesas, typically in sandy or gravelly soils along seasonal waterways; southern Texas to Arizona and south into Mexico, also in southern Florida
SIZE: Height 3–10 feet, width 3–8 feet
COLOR: Greenish white; blooms in late winter to spring

This is a thorny scrub species with smooth gray bark and fruits in the yellow-orange-red range. The leaves are thick, 1 inch long, and bear a few large teeth. The more eastern dwarf hackberry *(C. tenuifolia)* lacks thorns and is generally twice the size of desert hackberry.

Celtis reticulata (douglasii)
Netleaf Hackberry

ZONES: 4–9; sun
SOIL: Dry
NATIVE TO: Dry hills, ravines, cliffs, typically alkaline; Colorado to Utah, north to central Washington and south through the Great Basin to southern California and Texas
SIZE: Height 5–25 feet, width 5–20 feet
COLOR: Greenish white; blooms in late winter to spring

Netleaf hackberry develops a low, flat crown often wider than tall, with rough leaves conspicuously veined below. It will grow in the Northeast, retaining its small character but also developing witches' broom to quite an extent. Certainly this is should be a small tree of choice through large parts of the West, for both its toughness and its benefits to wildlife.

Celtis tenuifolia (georgiana)
Dwarf Hackberry

ZONES: 4–9; sun to light shade
SOIL: Wet to dry
NATIVE TO: Stream banks and rich slopes; New Jersey to Pennsylvania north to southern Ontario and west to Missouri, south to eastern Texas and northern Florida
SIZE: Height 12–25 feet, width 8–15 feet
COLOR: Greenish white; blooms in spring

Dwarf hackberry was named decades before the even smaller western species were known to science, and the name has stuck. It is smaller than the sympatric sugarberry *(Celtis laevigata)*. It has blunt-tipped leaves that are gray-green and a bit smaller than *C. laevigata*'s. Its bark is warty and furrowed like that of *C. reticulata*, but its crown is narrower and taller. From what I have seen, this hackberry seems especially prone to marginal chlorosis of the leaves, possibly due to improper pH or to nutrient deficiency. This results in a crown that is very blanched and unattractive.

Cephalanthus occidentalis

Cephalanthus occidentalis
(sef-fa-LAN-thus)
Rubiaceae
Buttonbush

ZONES: 4–10; sun to light shade
SOIL: Moist to wet (flooded)
NATIVE TO: Swamps and stream sides, often emergent in shallow water; Nova Scotia and New Brunswick to southern Quebec and eastern Min-

Cephalanthus occidentalis. The ring of pistils projecting from the core of each buttonbush flower creates a saintly halo that softens what would otherwise be a rather coarse bloom.

nesota, along the Mississippi river to Texas and Florida and Mexico. Scattered also in New Mexico, Arizona, and the central valley of California

SIZE: Height 3–8 feet, width 3–6 feet

COLOR: Creamy white; blooms in summer

Few of our native shrubs are as subtly distinctive as buttonbush, in both its floral appearance and its preferred habitat. Its common name refers to the 1-inch balls of flowers that grow from the branch tips in summer. These perfect spheres look distinctly tropical to me, like something one would see on a mimosa in Hawaii, and nothing at all like its closest native relatives, bluets (*Hedyotis* spp.) and partridge-berry (*Mitchella repens*). The musky-sweet flowers emanate from a green core of ovaries, each one a 4-petaled, tubular bloom projecting a long style from the core so that the appearance is of a perfectly round ball surrounded by a semitransparent ring (the way you might draw light emanating from the halo of a saint). These globes appear successively over a month or so in summer, set against a background of glossy, dark green leaves growing in whorls of three along thick twigs. The leaves have a bold texture and an oval to lance-shaped outline, and are usually creased and folded upward along the midvein to expose the thick, creamy veins that net the lower surface. They emerge fairly late in the spring, after all danger of frost has passed. In the wild, buttonbush could be viewed as the freshwater mangrove of the north, growing in standing water at the edge of ponds or swamps, usually in muddy flats where the water recedes in summer and leaves a telltale trace of pondweed and debris clinging to the trunks to indicate the high-water mark earlier in the season. In this stressful environment, the shrubs typically grow up and die back repeatedly, so that the stand has a rough, haphazard appearance, especially in winter when the leaves are gone. In moist soils in a garden situation, however, the plants can become quite large, developing into low-branched shrubs or even small trees with smooth bark that is greenish gray with sinuous gray-brown striations. The leaves cluster toward the outer canopy, giving them an open look ideal for underplanting. In colder parts of Zones 5 and 4, buttonbush will die back in severe winters, and it can be treated as a perennial in a mixed border: cut it back to 6 to 12 inches every winter or three and it will regrow to a 3-to-4-foot rounded mound by flowering time. Since flowers come from new growth, hard pruning will not eliminate them. I have seen buttonbush used very effectively this way in southern Ontario.

CULTURE: Site buttonbush in moist or wet soils, as it is intolerant of drought. If you want to naturalize it along a pond, plant it just at the edge, so that it will be inundated in spring but will be out of the water in summer. The plants spread underground in such situations, so it will adjust itself as needed. Away from the water in more managed situations, prune the young shrub to one trunk or two and remove dead twigs as needed in winter. Full sun and moderate fertilization in spring will produce the best flowers.

USES: Naturalize on banks and in shallow water, use as a specimen or for massing, or treat as a woody perennial.

WILDLIFE: *Cephalanthus* is a great nectar plant to incorporate into butterfly gardens or naturalized plantings. The tubular flowers attract the large, showy species like tiger swallowtails and fritillaries.

PROPAGATION: Moderately easy from cuttings or seed.

Cercis canadensis 'Forest Pansy'

Cercis (SER-sis)
Fabaceae
Redbud

Each spring, as the world begins to color up again, our woods fill with the soft, hazy purple flowers of redbuds lacing through the lower canopy. They are one of our loveliest small flowering trees, invaluable specimens in smaller gardens and just as lovely naturalized through the woodland understory or forest edge. Part of their unique charm comes from the way their flowers are displayed. The blooms are pealike in shape, with three upper petals splayed out like ears and two lower ones combined into a beak or lip, all a uniform purple-pink in color. The calyx is dark pink, and it completely encloses the unopened petals and wraps around the base of open ones for a subtle two-toned effect. Blossoms hang in little clusters all along the twigs, branches, and even older trunks, perfectly silhouetting the entire tree in hot pink as if it were lit from within. The trees flower early in the season, before their leaves have emerged, so they have a wonderful soft texture at this time. As the blooms fade, heart-shaped leaves begin to grow from ends of the twigs in a zigzag arrangement with new ones continuing to form well into summer if conditions are favor-

Cercis canadensis 'Forest Pansy'. Many plants produce burgundy pigments in response to cold. Though most eastern redbuds carry a hint of garnet in their young, expanding spring leaves, 'Forest Pansy' retains this color in the mature foliage as long as night temperatures remain below 65–70 degrees.

able. The leaves get fairly large (4 to 5 inches wide and a bit less in length is possible), and they droop slightly on long petioles so that you never see their undersides unless you crawl underneath the tree. A tree in leaf has a tiered, emboldened look much different from the fine effect it has in flower, and this textural metamorphosis is another great quality of redbuds.

When young, redbuds can grow very quickly—4–6 feet per year is not uncommon in youth. Vigorous shoots tend to arc out in a curve, and the most vigorous come from near the tips of the previous season's growth. Thus, young trees develop a fanned, vase-shaped habit with a crown that gradually spreads wider and wider once the trees have reached their mature height of 15 feet or so. In the southeastern United States, redbud comes into bloom a week or two earlier than flowering dogwood (*Cornus florida*), and in mild years where late frosts don't cut things short, the two overlap for a few weeks in a fugue of white and pink that is beautiful beyond description. Both are understory species that can grow and flower well in the shade of taller trees, but they certainly produce more abundantly where they receive some sun. Redbud seeds develop in a 2-to-3-inch-long flattened pod. Wild trees out in the sun are often hung with so many dark brown pods that the plants look as though they have grown a beard. This unshaven look persists from fall into winter, until the pods all shatter and fall. Typical redbuds develop a yellow or yellow-green fall color, but the outstanding burgundy-leaved cultivar 'Forest Pansy' turns orange in our garden before the foliage drops.

CULTURE: Redbuds are easily transplanted in early spring, either from containers, as balled and burlaped trees, or even as small bareroot whips. They prefer moderately moist, fertile soils, but will grow tolerably well in summer-dry locations once estab-

Cercis occidentalis. Western redbud adorns every branch with a rich veneer of brightly colored blooms. Few small trees can rival redbud for sheer visual impact, and its manageable size makes it appropriate for smaller gardens.

lished. *C. occidentalis* and the western varieties of *C. canadensis* are especially drought-tolerant and thrive in rather poor soils. Like flowering dogwood, redbud is a typically short-lived tree; 20 to 30 years is a normal life span. Stresses brought on by drought, severe cold, or excessive shade will weaken the trees and pave the way for attack by the opportunistic canker fungus *Botryosphaeria dothidea*, a widespread disease that also attacks apples, sycamores, and sweetgums, among others. Affected redbuds develop sunken areas on the trunk surrounded by a collar of callus tissue much like nectria cankers on birch or sassafras. A severely affected tree can have one canker after the next up the trunk, and they eventually girdle the branch completely. Eastern genotypes are most prone to attack; water during drought, light fertilization in spring, and a spot that receives at least an hour or two of direct sun will help them live to a ripe old age. Infected branches can be removed and disposed of, but this will not remove the underlying stress that allowed the disease to take hold.

USES: Specimen, naturalizing in forest understory, woodland edge, or scattered around in the open.

PROPAGATION: Easy from seed.

Cercis canadensis

Eastern Redbud

ZONES: 4–9; sun

SOIL: Moist

NATIVE TO: Moist woods and hedgerows, southeastern New York to Pennsylvania, Michigan, and eastern Nebraska south to northern Mexico and Florida

SIZE: Height 12–25 feet, width 10–20 feet

COLOR: Bright pink, occasionally white; the color of redbuds is remarkably consistent, and except for occasionally white-flowered individuals, the color of all is a bright, almost magenta pink; blooms in early to late spring

The typical variety is a small tree with dark, reddish brown bark exfoliating in thin strips and large leaves that are shiny and flushed with purple when young, maturing to a matte light green when mature. Seed from northern genotypes is far hardier in Zone 4–5, and care should be taken to ensure that local races are planted whenever possible. Most of the commercial production comes from the Southeast and Northwest, using southern genotypes, and lack of winter hardiness can be a problem. This is one of my favorite small trees, and no garden should be without at least a few. In the Southwest and the mountains of northeastern Mexico, there are two distinct races that have been given varietal or even species status. *C. canadensis* var. *mexicana* (Mexican redbud) hails from northwest Mexico and southwestern Texas, growing on dry limestone soils in its home territory. I have grown a few plants that I obtained from the J. C. Raulston Arboretum in Raleigh. It looks much like var. *texen-*

sis, though the new growth is covered with a downy pubescence. It suffered dieback in Durham, North Carolina (Zone 7), so I would rate it a Zone 8–9 plant for the drier parts of the South. In habit it has the same vase shape and magenta flowers as the species, albeit with smaller stature overall. *C. canadensis* var. *texensis* (Texas redbud) is another plant that I first obtained through J. C. Raulston, and we sold it for a time at Niche Gardens, in Chapel Hill. It is a bit hardier, Zone 6, possibly 5, and its range extends from Oklahoma and Texas into Mexico. Its beautiful leaves are only 2 inches or so wide—about half the size of those of *C. canadensis*—and are glossy bronze, aging dark green, with a wavy margin. Like the Mexican form, it tends to be a smaller tree, with lighter bark and multiple trunks. Selections like the cultivar 'Oklahoma' are wonderful, both in leaf and in flower, but they need hot summers to do well. I have tried several times to establish Texas redbud in Massachusetts, and the plants never seem to get growing in the summer. Perhaps I'll try it next in a very warm microclimate, such as against a south-facing wall.

Cercis occidentalis

Western Redbud

ZONES: 8–9; sun

SOIL: Summer-dry, well-drained

NATIVE TO: Dry slopes, canyons, and chapparal up to 4,500 feet in the Sierras; central California, with scattered populations in southern Nevada and Utah following the Colorado River into northern Arizona

SIZE: Height 8–20 feet, width 6–15 feet

COLOR: Bright pink; blooms in early to late spring

This geographically isolated race is not terribly different from the others in shape or flower color but is distinct enough to be called a separate species. Like those of Texas redbud, with which it was combined at one time, its glossy leaves are 2 to 3 inches wide, borne on shrubby, multistemmed plants that will grow into small trees if given a good location. It is well adapted to dry summers, full sun, and mild winters. I do not know whether plants from the disjunct stations in Utah and Arizona, sometimes called *C. occidentalis* var. *orbiculata*, have been well tested in western gardens. They may prove more adaptable in the interior West, as good specimens are growing in gardens in the Salt Lake City, Utah, area.

Cercocarpus ledifolius

Cercocarpus
(ser-ko-KAR-pus)
Rosaceae
Mountain Mahogany

Mountain mahoganies are hard-wooded shrubs or small trees in the rose family most recognizable by their fluffy, colorful styles that are barely visible at first but expand after the flower is pollinated to form a long, twisted tail covered in hairs. In this it is much like its relative Apache plume. The flowers themselves are small, with five reflexed petals and a dense cluster of anthers that contribute more than the petals to the overall color and texture of the blooms. They cluster in small bunches set among the leaves. The seeds and styles remain on the plants all summer and into fall, and when backlit by the sun, the myriad fine hairs give the plants a striking, soft-focus glow. The hairs can irritate the skin, though, which explains the colorful common name hellfeathers, bestowed by cowpokes who had to ride through stands when tending the herd. Mountain mahoganies are actinorhizal—they have nitrogen-fixing *Frankia* bacteria on their roots—so they have a distinct competitive advantage in poor, dry soils. This trait, combined with an interesting, thick-twiggy shape and elegant foliage, has made them increasingly popular landscape subjects throughout the drier areas of the West. The irritating styles make them hard to use around foundations and other areas where people are likely to contact them, but mountain mahoganies are valuable for reclamation, highway planting, and soil stabilization projects. The leaves are either evergreen or deciduous, depending on the species; they are borne on short axillary twigs that look like the spur branches on an apple and that are prominently marked with consecutive leaf scars spaced closely together. The four species are closely

Cercocarpus ledifolius. After pollination, the fuzzy style centered in each curl-leaf mountain mahogany flower grows out in a crazy, twisting curlicue. The fine hairs catch the sun and lend the tree a haunting, silvery glow.

related, but each is adapted to different levels of soil and atmospheric moisture, which is reflected by the relative size of their leaves. *C. montanus* and *C. betuloides* have oval leaves, whereas *C. ledifolius* has narrower blades that are rolled inward slightly around the margin to cut down on surface area and thus conserve water. *C. intricatus* takes this to the extreme, having narrow leaves rolled under and covered below with a thick felt much like the leaves of Labrador tea. All have a resinous, spicy aroma when warmed by the sun, and hard, dense wood that burns hot and long.

CULTURE: Transplant as young container plants in spring to well-drained soils. *Cercocarpus* species are well adapted to low-humidity, low-rainfall environments, but suffer in the heavier climate farther east. I have tried to get *C. montanus* established in our dry-land garden, but the plants grew extremely slowly and were set back in rainy summers, which eventually killed them. I imagine that *Frankia* inoculation can be accomplished, as for alder or ceanothus. Western nurseries are producing mountain mahogany in containers, so I think my problems are climate-related and are not due to any inherent resentment of confinement.

USES: Restoration, soil stabilization, massing where irritation from styles will not be a problem.

WILDLIFE: The evergreen species provide good cover for wildlife. Larvae of western hairstreak (*Satyrium californica*) feed on the leaves, as do those of chaparral hairstreak and orange hairstreak (*S. tetra* and *S. behrii*).

PROPAGATION: Moderately easy from seed.

Cercocarpus betuloides
Western Mountain Mahogany

ZONES: (6)7–9; sun
SOIL: Well-drained, moderately moist in season
NATIVE TO: Chaparral, dry slopes and washes; southwest Oregon through California
SIZE: Height 6–20 feet , width 5–15 feet
COLOR: Creamy yellow; blooms in spring

This species has oval leaves about an inch long that are strongly pleated along the lateral veins in a fishbone pattern, like those of *Hamamelis*. Several varieties have been named according to the shape and pubescence of the leaves. They are dark, glossy green above and whitish green below. The habit is broadly oval, about as wide as tall, with silvery gray twigs and smooth gray bark on the older stems that is very pretty, especially in winter when some of the leaves fall and you can really see into the center. *C. betuloides* is a common, widespread component of the Californian chaparral.

Cercocarpus intricatus
Littleleaf Mountain Mahogany

ZONES: 5–8; sun
SOIL: Dry, well-drained
NATIVE TO: Dry ridges, cliffs, and brushlands; southwestern Colorado to Utah and California, then east to Arizona and New Mexico.
SIZE: Height 3–8 feet, width 3–8 feet
COLOR: Creamy yellow; blooms in spring

Littleleaf mountain mahogany's narrow leaves roll under to such an extent that the white wool that covers the lower surface of the leaf is almost completely obscured. The leaves tend to cluster on short spurs that are widely spaced on the twigs, so that there is a ball of leaves here and there amid the intricate, spiny branches. The evergreen foliage is glossy and very dark green at first, but turns rusty brown as it ages. The styles are short, about an inch long, and barely protrude from the cluster of leaves, so the mix of green and rusty red laced with silver gray has a weird hoarfrost-on-leather beauty about it. In habit this species tends toward a low, multistemmed shrub with silvery gray bark and gnarled twigs. It is closely related to *C. ledifolius*, and in many ways is a morphological extreme of that species adapted to the driest habitats.

Cercocarpus ledifolius
Curl-leaf Mountain Mahogany

ZONES: 4–9; sun
SOIL: Dry, well-drained
NATIVE TO: Rocky slopes at middle elevations (3,000–9,000 feet); Colorado and Montana to southeastern Washington south to California and Arizona
SIZE: Height 6–24 feet, width 5–30 feet
COLOR: Creamy yellow; blooms in late spring to early summer

This wide-spreading, twisted tree has bark that is bright silvery white when young, but furrowed and darker, rusty gray with age on the stout, lower trunks. From a distance, it looks much like hawthorn. Its leaves are thick and leathery, wider than those of *C. intricatus*, but more or less outfitted with wool below and taking on a reddish patina during the winter. "Curl-leaf" refers to the way the end of the blade curves upward like the tip of a ski. These come from the tips of ever-lengthening, meandering spur branches that are heavily ridged with the scars of past petiolar attachment. Groves of older trees are usually browsed up as far as deer or cattle can reach, which exposes the lower trunks and gives the plants a bonsai appearance. Overall, I think it is the most ornamental of the genus.

Cercocarpus montanus

Alderleaf Mountain Mahogany, Birchleaf Mountain Mahogany

ZONES: 4–8; sun

SOIL: Moderately dry, well-drained

NATIVE TO: Dry hills and sagebrush slopes, open juniper-pinyon woodland; western Nebraska and South Dakota to Idaho and Oregon south through California to Arizona, Texas, and Mexico

SIZE: Height 5–15 feet, width 5–15 feet

COLOR: Creamy yellow; blooms in late spring

C. montanus is the widest-ranging and most adaptable species in the genus, typically bearing reluctantly deciduous leaves somewhat toothed and creased along the veins, glossy above and gray or downy pubescent below. Where the range of *C. montanus* overlaps with that of the larger *C. ledifolius*, hybrids can be found that intergrade between the two. Generally though, *C. montanus* prefers slightly higher rainfall. Where it is not heavily browsed, it can become a small, smooth-barked tree similar in shape to the other species.

Chamaecyparis nootkatensis

Chamaecyparis
(kam-may-SIP-a-ris)
Cupressaceae
False Cypress, White Cedar

These soft, elegant conifers cluster at the edges of our continent, as if the sound of the distant surf is a requirement for growth. More likely, I suppose, false cypresses are attracted to the fogs and rain that frequent the coasts and bathe their twigs and roots in replenishing moisture. You don't need to live in a fog bank or a locker room to grow these conifers, but their successful culture is limited to the milder, more humid parts of the United States and Canada. *Chamaecyparis* is closely related to *Thuja*, with needles reduced to flattened scales that alternate up the twigs in a tightly fitted, overlapping arrangement. This herringbone pattern makes the twigs look like miniature stylized trees that have been flattened to a single plane with a rolling pin. All three *Chamaecyparis* species are minor components of their respective floras, restricted to narrow habitats, but within these habitats they are fairly common. Their limited habitat range in the wild belies a greater adaptability in cultivation, and may be due to competitive disadvantage rather than inherent obstinacy. Atlantic white cedar *(C. thyoides)* is a denizen of coastal bogs, slowly colonizing the peatlands and forming dense stands. The trees are never extremely tall, but they develop wide, fluted trunks containing valuable rot-resistant heartwood, which was formerly harvested so extensively that few old trees remain. The other two species grow in the Pacific Northwest, where they can become sizable trees, though they are still dwarfed by the towering redwoods, firs, and spruce they share the canopy with.

In the landscape, false cypress has a narrow, pyramidal shape that is formal in character even with age. The native species are not as widely used as their Asian cousins, *C. obtusa* and *C. pisifera*, whose many forms and cultivars are ubiquitous in eastern landscapes. All have soft-textured, dark green foliage that holds its color reasonably well in winter, and sport spherical, segmented, blue-green cones that develop with the new growth, often in such abundance that they cast a bluish shadow over the trees until the expanding needles obscure them. Bark is tan or reddish brown, peeling and cracking in thin strips much like *Thuja*'s. Beyond this, all three native false cypresses are quite distinctive.

Nootka false cypress *(C. nootkatensis)* is probably best known as one of the parents of Leyland cypress (× *Cupressocyparis leyandii*), an intergeneric cross between it and Monterey cypress *(Cupressus macrocarpa)*. Extremely fast growing, tough, heat- and salt-tolerant, and generally far more adaptable than either of its parents, Leyland cypress has become the screening tree of choice throughout the Southeast. When I worked at a small full-service nursery in North Carolina we couldn't keep Leylands in stock. The deep green trees have a formal character and can grow 3 feet a year when young, taking on a soft, pyramidal shape quite quickly. The cross originated in England, where some of the original trees are over 100 feet tall now. I would be surprised, though, if they

Chamaecyparis nootkatensis. Spectral? I think so. The branches of Nootka cypress seem barely able to resist gravity's pull. It is one of my favorite trees, possessing an animistic, melancholy personality that adds genuine character to the landscape.

get that big in the Southeast, where the atmosphere is far less—how should I say—sodden. It is hard to believe, really, that two fairly restricted, cool-climate species from separate genera could produce a plant with such marvelous hybrid vigor. Offspring of Monterey cypress should be expected to be quite tender, so Leyland cypress is risky in colder parts of Zone 6.

CULTURE: Generally, moist, acidic but well-drained soils and fairly high atmospheric moisture are necessary for good growth. I have planted *C. nootkatensis* in fairly dry, sandy soil and it has grown very slowly—nothing like what it can do in a better soil. Port Orford cedar *(C. lawsoniana)* grows on a range of soils in the wild—sandy and fairly dry to wet, swampy soils and even serpentine slopes in the Siskiyous. Sadly, though, an introduced root disease *(Phytophthora lateralis)* is wiping out the tree throughout most of its limited range. Despite massive intervention on the part of government and private groups, the fate of this noble conifer is really in question, and Port Orford cedar has become difficult to grow within its wild range, though it thrives surprisingly well in the northeastern United States as well as in Western Europe. Atlantic white cedar is more adaptable, tolerating summer heat, wet soils (as long as the crown remains above water), even moderate drought. Transplant all three in spring, either balled and burlaped or from containers. The roots are generally fibrous and coarse, and relatively fast top growth (1-2 feet in year) can be expected in good, moist soil and sun.

USES: Specimen, screening.

PROPAGATION: Moderately easy from cuttings and seed.

Chamaecyparis lawsoniana

Port Orford Cedar

ZONES: 5–8; part sun, sun
SOIL: Moist but well-drained
NATIVE TO: Coniferous forests, mostly in the Coast Ranges of southwestern Oregon and northern California, with scattered populations in California's Siskiyous and on the slopes of Mount Shasta
SIZE: Height 35–40 (150) feet, width 10–30 feet
COLOR: Yellow to red; blooms in early spring

This is the most formal of the native false cypresses in shape, with a dense, narrow-pyramidal form and a straight trunk capable of great heights in the wild but typically under 50 feet in cultivation. The cones are relatively large (½ inch wide), and are a bluish purple mixed with green. Dark green as well as lovely blue-needled cultivars exist. Unless the situation changes, the species may soon be extinct in the wild and persist only in cultivated situations outside of the range of the root disease.

Chamaecyparis nootkatensis

Alaska Cedar, Nootka Cypress

ZONES: (4)5–8; part sun, sun
SOIL: Moist, well-drained
NATIVE TO: Coniferous forests of the Coast and Cascade ranges from Oregon north to the end of the temperate rainforests near Ancourage, Alaska
SIZE: Height 20–40 (120) feet, width 10–25 feet
COLOR: Yellow; blooms in spring

There are few conifers whose outline evokes the dripping, moss-hung rainforest as effectively as Alaska cedar. The trees develop a narrow, pyramidal crown composed of a network of downward-arching branches hung with pendulous twigs. Wild specimens have a droopy effect that seems appropriately melancholy on cloudy, drizzly days. The most widely available cultivar is 'Pendula', with even more exaggerated, downward-swooping branches and weeping blue-green branchlets. The species and especially the cultivar have become reasonably popular as specimen trees in the Northeast as well as in the Northwest, where they grow very well. It is one of my favorite conifers, standing out in the garden like a silent emerald ghost that draws the eye like no other.

Chamaecyparis thyoides

Atlantic White Cedar

ZONES: 4–9; light shade to sun
SOIL: Moist to wet, acid
NATIVE TO: Bogs and wooded swamps, primarily along the coastal plain from Maine to South Carolina and the Piedmont of Georgia, then along the Gulf of Mexico from Florida to Louisiana
SIZE: Height 20–40 (55) feet, width 6–15 feet
COLOR: Yellow-brown; blooms in spring

The familiar, shaggy brown trunks of Atlantic white cedar encircle coastal bogs ands swamps like a death knell, signaling the eventual end of the open vegetation. The trees can get fairly tall in the South, but farther north snow and ice damage leave the older crowns broken and younger trees bent over, limiting their use to the immediate coast where snows are usually not as heavy. The branches of *C. thyoides* are finer than those of the other species, forming a crown that is more irregular but still generally tall and narrow. It has a slightly unkempt, dark, dark silhouette that I really like, and we used to have quite a number planted in the garden, until a bad winter storm broke off most of them five years ago.

Chamaedaphne calyculata

Chamaedaphne calyculata (kam-ay-DAF-nee)
Ericaceae
Leatherleaf

ZONES: 2–7; part sun, sun

SOIL: Moist to wet, acidic

NATIVE TO: Bogs, circumboreal; in North America from Newfoundland to Alaska south to British Columbia, Iowa, and New Jersey and in the mountains to northern Georgia

SIZE: Height 2–3(4) feet, width 2–3 feet

COLOR: White; blooms in early spring

Leatherleaf is a consummate bog plant, as common and essential to these floating wetlands as the sphagnum moss that knits together the mats on which it floats. In the wild, *Chamaedaphne* is a scraggly, suckering shrub forming large, radiating colonies in open heathland, but given a modicum of room and a wet place to settle, it becomes an attractive, mounded evergreen, getting slowly wider as the years go by. It grows and blooms in a distinctive way, with vigorous shoots coming from the roots clothed in 1-to-2-inch narrow, oblong leaves that are glossy and dark green above and rusty-scaly below. When these vertical shoots get to be a few feet high, they send out nearly horizontal twigs with progressively smaller leaves that are angled upward in two zigzaggedy ranks, every leaf nurturing a little flower bud in its axil. Each successive leaf is about 20 percent smaller than the preceding, so that the smallest at the end of these shoots are only ½ inch long. Because of this, the shrubs have a very angular, horizontal crown over a stiffer, vertical core. Early in spring, dormant buds swell, bedecking the horizontal twigs with double rows of lovely white bellflowers hung on light brown pedicels that contrast nicely with the cockscomb crest of leaves arrayed above. Flowers are replaced by woody capsules that retain the long, threaded style that formerly protruded from the flower. These are rusty green at first, aging to a grayish-white. The capsules are ornamental in an understated way, primarily because they add a frosty tone to the dark, dominant green and burgundy of the leaves in winter. Older stems continue to send out new flowering branches each year, so the plants become quite dense and twiggy, with a low, mounded shape.

CULTURE: Leatherleaf requires damp but not flooded, very acidic soils and cool summers to thrive. We grow it beside our pond as well as in peaty areas in the company of bog rosemary (*Andromeda polifolia*) and Labrador tea (*Ledum groenlandicum*). Best growth and flowering take place in full sun, but the plants perform well with as little as four hours of direct sun. When the soil is wet, place the root ball on a mound or hummock to keep the crown above the water. Once established, no fertilizer is necessary, and pruning is limited to selectively removing the older, less vigorous stems.

USES: Low shrub for massing in bog garden or at pond side.

WILDLIFE: Flowers are a good early-season nectar source. It is one of the preferred food plants for the larvae of the brown elfin butterfly (*Callophrys augustus*).

PROPAGATION: Moderately difficult from cuttings; moderately easy from seed.

Chamaedaphne calyculata. *Leatherleaf's leaves become progressively smaller toward the ends of the branches, making this shrub easy to recognize among its bogland neighbors. Neatly ranked flower buds form in summer but remain tightly closed through the winter, unfolding in early spring just after frost has left the ground.*

Chilopsis linearis. The familial relationship between desert willow and catalpa (p. 74) is clear if you focus on the flowers.

Chilopsis linearis

Chilopsis linearis
(kye-LOP-sis)
Bignoniaceae
Desert Willow

ZONES: 7–9; sun

SOIL: Well-drained, dry, as long as water is available deeper in the soil

NATIVE TO: Washes and dry creek beds; Texas, New Mexico, and Arizona to California south into Mexico

SIZE: Height 10–25 feet, width 10–15 feet

COLOR: Typically, white lined with yellow or purple; also, purple-red, pink, or rose; blooms in early to late summer

As the West has dried over the millennia, rivers that formerly ran aboveground have retreated below, betraying their subterranean existence only by the scoured outlines of their old beds and the preponderance of vegetation that grows there. Certain desert trees and shrubs, called phreatophytes, are able to extend very deep roots through gravelly soil until they hit this underground water, and so flourish luxuriantly in an otherwise harsh, arid environment. Many oasis species have this ability, forming lush pockets of vegetation without visible sign of water. Desert willow is one of these phreatophytes, growing in dry creek beds where it can access deep water to nourish fast-growing stems tipped with large, beautiful flowers. Willow is a fitting name, for although they are related to catalpas, not true willows (*Salix* spp.), these shrubs or small trees have a lax, open crown and long, thin leaves much like willows in character. Flowers are shaped like those of catalpa, with two, nearly fused upper petals and three lower ones forming a lip striped with yellow or purple lines to act as a guide for pollinators. The sweetly fragrant blooms are ruffled and frilled, opening a few at time on terminal spikes that keep coming in flushes during the summer as long as moisture is available. The fine-textured leaves are up to a foot long and only ½ inch wide, and though the shrubs have a sort of floppy, untidiness about them, the charming flowers find them a place in southwestern gardens. Cultivars with darker flowers ranging from reddish purple through to light pink are available, and since the flowers come on new growth, plants can be pruned hard in winter to keep them a bit more orderly.

Chilopsis has been crossed with *Catalpa* to create × *Chitalpa tashkentensis,* basically a hardier, more cold- and humidity-tolerant desert willow with wider leaves and flowers in the white to pink range. It is grown by some of the large California nurseries, and you see it touted in mail order catalogues with seductive close-ups of its bodacious blooms. However, the plant has the same floppy tendencies as its desert parent, and suffers from mildew in the more humid climate of the East.

CULTURE: Desert willow needs some supplemental water to get established in the first two years, but after that it will require little other than an occasional pruning. Site in full sun, in gravelly or sandy loam, if possible where the water table is within 30 to 40 feet of the surface. The trees can be cut back to near the ground every few years in winter to keep them dense and shrubby without compromising blooming.

USES: Screening, background, naturalizing.

PROPAGATION: Easy from seed.

Chionanthus virginicus

Chionanthus virginicus

Chionanthus virginicus (kee-o-NAN-thus)

Oleaceae
Fringetree, Old Man's Beard

ZONES: (4)5–9; sun to light shade

SOIL: Fairly wet to moderately dry

NATIVE TO: Rich woods, streamsides, and swamp margins; New Jersey to West Virginia, Tennessee, Louisiana, eastern Texas and Florida, with scattered populations in Ohio, Kentucky, Missouri, and Oklahoma

SIZE: Height 10–20 (30) feet, width 10–20 feet

COLOR: Bright white; blooms in late spring

Every spring I am completely enchanted by this tree when it fluffs into flower. There are few more transcendent sights than its thick twigs hung with clouds of sweetly fragrant, delicate flowers like so much cotton or fleece. Fringetree's flowers grow in little clusters on leafless branchlets from the lower buds of the previous season's wood, and each blossom is pure white, with 4 very thin, drooping petals about ½ inch long. The topmost sets of buds on each twig sprout leaves instead of blooms, so the developing foliage appears skirted by a fringe of flowers. Plants are dioecious, with males supposedly showier in flower owing to their longer petals. I have looked at plants side by side and tried to guess by flower size which were males, and I was right about half the time. Thus, either I need glasses or there really isn't much difference. If you have males and females (though occasionally a lone female will pollinate itself), the latter will set a good crop of dark blue fruits roughly one-third the size of an olive and similarly shaped. The leaves are narrow ellipses with a strong central vein and a satin finish, and the foliage has a pleasingly heavy texture when the flowers fade.

When young, fringetrees are characterized by regular, alternate branching in much the same way as their relatives the ashes. If you look down on a fringetree from above and picture a clock face centered on the ground below it, the branches would come in pairs from the trunk, the first two at 12 and 6 o'clock, the next two at 3 and 9 o'clock, the next pair back to 12 and 6. The branches themselves and even the flower panicles sprout this way, so the tree has an ordered, broad-pyramidal shape. After about 15 years of age, though, the fringetree frees itself from the regularity imposed by the arrangement of its buds, and begins to take on a more open, irregular shape with large limbs that arch down and around, even touching the ground. Old trees still have a broadly rounded crown when cloaked in leaves, but as these

yellow and drop in fall, the crazy, meandering trunks and twisting branches suggest that a certain madness has descended on the venerable old man's beard.

CULTURE: For the most part, these are easy-to-please shrubs or small trees. I have worked mainly with container-grown plants, both large and small, and these transplant easily enough in the garden. It is well worth a little time pruning the small tree to have 1 to 3 trunks when young, unless you would like to encourage the wilder look of a many-stemmed plant. The seedlings are a bit slow-growing at first, and I have had trouble with small ones getting bent and matted down by snow. If this happens, pruning back a 2-to-3-year-old seedling in winter nearly to the ground will generate a few vigorous, straight shoots the following spring and establish a good framework for the future. Old, broken stems can be removed with similar results. Fringetree is at its best in a moist, fertile soil with at least 3 to 4 hours of sun, though it will take drier soil and less light with reasonable success. They grow fairly slowly—8 to 16 inches a year is average—but begin to bloom when only 4 to 5 years old. The fruits are kind of pretty, and the birds like them, but there is really no way of sexing the trees, which are all raised from seed. To hedge your bets, plant three or four within 50 feet of each other.

USES: Specimen.

PROPAGATION: Moderately difficult from seed.

Chionanthus virginicus. The airy white flowers of a fringetree in full bloom glow magically against a dark, wooded background. This tree grows at Niche Gardens in Chapel Hill, North Carolina.

Chrysothamnus nauseosus

Chrysothamnus nauseosus
(kry-so-THAM-nus)

Asteraceae
Rubber Rabbitbrush

Chrysothamnus nauseosus. *Like a cumulus cloud on a warm summer day, rabbitbrush billows up in a southwestern garden.*

ZONES: 4–9; sun

SOIL: Well-drained, dry

NATIVE TO: Dry plains, roadsides, ravines, rangelands; North Dakota and Montana to Utah, south to Arizona and Texas

SIZE: Height 3–6 feet, width 3–6 feet

COLOR: Bright yellow; blooms in late summer to early fall

One of my most vivid memories of New Mexico is the billowing gray and soft yellow rubber rabbitbrush that lines the roadsides. Rabbitbrush is sort of a half perennial, half shrub in the aster family that sends up dozens of narrow, white stems hung with long, thin, aromatic gray leaves from a short woody trunk or low, gnarled branches. Late in the summer, dense, broccoli-shaped heads of lovely yellow flowers crown the plant, which fade slowly to a warm, tannish gray as the pappus develops on the seeds. The plumes remain soft and attractive into the winter, even as the leaves fade and all that is left are the stark, chalky white shoots. What I like is the subtle metamorphosis from silver to gray, then yellow and tan, each so characteristic of—and essential to—the rhythms of its particular season. Rabbitbrush is adapted to disturbance, so it has flourished since the arrival of people to the desert. Overgrazing, mowing, and construction create just the sort of open ground that it needs to establish and persist.

The white latex sap that oozes from a broken branch has long been used as chewing gum by the native peoples of the Great Basin, and during World War II it was extracted and refined into a high-grade rubber called chrysil. It was never exploited because it is not produced in large quantities—it was estimated that all the millions of rabbitbrush plants in the desert would yield only about 30,000 tons of refined rubber, hardly worth the effort of extraction (see Mozingo, *Shrubs of the Great Basin,* p. 289). This latex makes the plants unpalatable to livestock, and ranchers view it as a pest that displaces better forage on overtaxed rangeland. In fact, however, rabbitbrush is part of the natural cycle of succession that leads eventually to sagebrush and bunchgrasses if the land is left undisturbed. So it's here to stay.

There are about a dozen species of *Chrysothamnus* in the West, all basically similar in overall character and centered in and around the Great Basin. They include *C. albidus* (alkali rabbitbrush), which has small, narrow leaves and white flowers rather than yellow, *C. teretifolius* (green rabbitbrush), which bears thick, green leaves covered in a resinous varnish, *C. parryi* (Parry's rabbitbrush) with flowers in narrower spikes, and *C. pulchellus* (beautiful rabbitbrush), a small dune-loving plant with large, flattened heads of yellow flowers that are big in proportion to the leaves and stems. Below the flowers are large, scaly bracts set like the scales of a fish.

CULTURE: In drier areas of the West, *Chrysothamnus* are carefree, very drought-tolerant, mounded shrubs. I have seen them used quite effectively in landscapes, either massed or incorporated into mixed borders. They bloom on new wood and naturally die back to the main trunk and branches each year, so a hard pruning in winter—after seeds have shed if you like their ornamental quality; before they shed if you are worried about seeding in—to remove all the thin flowering stems is appropriate and will help to keep the plants looking respectable. Rabbitbrush can send roots down 20 to 30 feet in search of water, but supplemental irrigation for the first year is necessary to get them going. Small self-sown seedlings or container plants can be set out in spring. I collected some seed the last time I was in New Mexico and brought it back to Garden in the Woods. We have established plants in our smaller rock and dryland garden, but they are hardly thriving. The morning dews and humidity of summer gets to the leaves, which spot and fall, and even some of the stem tips wither, so I have yet to get any flowers.

USES: Xeriscaping, massing, mixed border.

WILDLIFE: Cattle don't like them, but wild herbivores like deer and rabbits make *Chrysothamnus* an important part of their winter diet. The leaves are eaten by the larvae of two butterflies, the cream checkerspot and pearly checkerspot *(Chlosyne palla and C. gabbii).*

PROPAGATION: Easy from cuttings or seed.

Cladrastis kentukea (lutea) (klad-RAS-tis)

Cladrastis kentukea

Fabaceae
American Yellowwood

ZONES: 4–8; sun to light shade

SOIL: Moist

NATIVE TO: Rich bottomlands, cove forests, river bluffs; western North Carolina to Kentucky and Tennessee and northern Alabama, scattered populations along the White River in southern Missouri and adjacent Arkansas as well as eastern Oklahoma

SIZE: Height 30–50 feet, width 40–50 feet

COLOR: White or pale pink; blooms in late spring

One of the plant explorer André Michaux's most sensational finds as he journeyed about the Southeast in the late eighteenth century was a large tree with smooth gray bark that looked to him much like the Japanese sophora *(Sophora japonica)*, which had become popular in Europe. He named his new find *Sophora lutea* (later changed to *Cladrastis lutea* and finally *C. kentukea*), and it is among the rarest trees in our eastern flora. Michaux discovered it in the Cumberland region of north central Tennessee, near what is now the town of Gainesboro. Its scattered occurrence in the southern Appalachian and Cumberland mountains suggests that this tree was driven nearly to extinction by the advance of the glaciers but managed to survive in small, sheltered valleys that remained warmer than their surroundings. In Missouri and Arkansas, the trees leave the rich forests for limestone bluffs along rivers, and it is possible that the waters catch and distribute its hard seeds.

In habit they are wide-crowned, medium sized trees with smooth, beechlike gray bark and short trunks that fork quickly into two or three stout branches. The pinnately compound leaves are easy to recognize, as the leaflets tend to alternate up the rachis (the main stem of a compound leaf) instead of pairing up as in ash, hickory, or locust. Additionally, the terminal leaflet is larger than the successively reduced 5 to 8 lateral ones. The leaves attach to the thick mahogany twigs with a large cupped base that completely hides the bud protected inside. The leaves, which emerge one after the other along the zigzag twigs, have a beautiful, golden yellow fall color. The name "yellowwood" refers to the light yellow color of the freshly cut heartwood, which yields a yellow dye once employed to color homemade cloth.

The true glory of these trees is the magnificent, panicled chains of snow white flowers that hang from the branch tips when the leaves are nearly expanded (a pink form, 'Rosea', has been developed

Cladrastis kentukea. To avoid future problems, this American yellowwood sapling should be pruned to remove all but one or two of the branches that are forking out a foot above the ground. If left alone, the crotches are likely to crack or split as their branches become larger and heavier.

and distributed by the Arnold Arboretum). These have often been compared to wisteria blooms, and they have the same banner-and-lip pea shape of most in the pea family. Each slender flower curves down and out, with a large dorsal petal standing erect and four smaller ones folded together and down like a beak. These dangle on long central chains with smaller chains hanging off them, so the tree literally drips with white. The flowers are most fragrant after dark, possibly to attract moths, though bees frequent them during the day, and clusters of flattened pods similar to redbud's result from the service. This spectacular tree is as rare in gardens as it is in the wild, though some nurseries do sell the plants. I think there are several reasons for this rarity. First, yellowwood is fairly slow growing and very slow to flower, especially when shaded, and even older trees flower heavily only every 2 to 3 years. We have a 22-year-old tree planted in our woodland that has yet to produce a single bloom, though I have seen younger plants flowering in the open at the University of Connecticut. Second, they look a bit coarse and gangly when young, so they don't look appealing in a container. Third, they tend to grow quite wide in the open—40 to 50 feet is possible—which makes them hard to integrate into smaller properties. Despite these obstacles, I think this is one of the greatest and yet most underappreciated of our flowering shade trees.

CULTURE: American yellowwood seems to transplant easily enough. I have spring-transplanted containerized seedlings as well as balled and burlaped saplings, and we even dug out a few saplings bareroot from a growing bed in the fall and they established without problem. The tree has a strong desire to fork low on the trunk, sending out several simultaneous branches that are prone to split at the crotch as the crown ages. Try to prune saplings to a single lead, and space branches along the trunk. After a late-winter ice storm, I had to prune off some broken limbs from one specimen, and the poor tree nearly bled itself to death, so try to limit pruning to late fall. Yellowwoods grow on limestone soils as well as slightly acid ones, and seem adaptable regarding both pH and moisture, though rich, moist soil is preferable to dry and poor. A spot that receives 3 or more hours of sun will lead to faster flowering.

USES: Specimen, shade tree.

WILDLIFE: Good source of nectar.

PROPAGATION: Moderately easy from seed.

Clethra alnifolia. Summersweet grows remarkably fast in sun and fertile soil. This planting is only three years old, but already the plants have filled in to create an unbroken mass of white and green in midsummer, when the languid air is redolent with clethra's sweet clove and musk perfume.

Clethra alnifolia

Clethra (KLETH-ra)
Clethraceae
Summersweet, Clethra

In the past ten years, summersweet has gone from the relative obscurity of swamps and woods to one of the best-selling native shrubs in the East. It is a beautiful plant in flower, with intoxicating, musky sweet spires covering the plants in the languid days of midsummer. But just as important, it grows extreme-

ly fast in a container. At Niche Gardens in North Carolina, we could take cuttings in spring, pot them in two weeks, and have a full, 16-inch-high, flowering plant ready by August. Few woody plants can provide such fast growth. In the wild, clethras are suckering shrubs that form thickets in low areas of woodland or open swamps. This characteristic of summersweet almost cost me my life when I was employed as a forest ecologist. I was working during hunting season, decked out in my most flattering fluorescent orange outerwear, which I figured would make me visible from outer space, let alone from 20 feet. As I was counting the thin, chocolate stems of a thick stand of summersweet, I heard a man and his young son walk by, then crunch around in the opening 10 yards away. I stood up to say hello, only to see the barrel of a shotgun aimed in my direction. Fortunately the guy had his finger off the trigger, because when he jumped back with a startled "ehhgggahh!!" the gun would otherwise have discharged. He apologized profusely, informing me that he thought I was a pheasant (I didn't know whether to be flattered or insulted), and he was just trying to flush me out. After that I always brought a radio with me.

Clethra is unusual in that vigorous basal sprouts can grow up and actually branch, then bloom their first season. This gives plants a very dense, casually mounded appearance, neat enough for the landscape but with a touch of wildness that suits the more informal style of gardening popular today. The leaves are a fresh, bright green at first, aging to dark, glossy green when mature, and because the plants continue growing most of the summer, the two-toned effect is quite pretty. Each leaf is widest beyond the middle, finely toothed, and deeply furrowed along the veins. The flowers appear from the growing tips amid the fresh green leaves, first green themselves with little round knobs set thickly on slender racemes. Blooms open sequentially from the bottom up, lending them a narrow pointed aspect like a Gothic steeple. A stand of clethra in bloom is almost overwhelming in a giddy, nose-tingling sense, and all manner of insects come to dine on the nectaral feast, which goes on for a month or so. In fall, as the seed capsules are ripening, the leaves turn golden yellow etched with brown before curling and dropping to the ground.

CULTURE: Clethra is an easy plant for all but droughty areas of the garden. It grows almost like a perennial in the way it quickly establishes and begins to bloom. New stems come from the base and roots, and the plants become a mounded mass of indistinct stems. You can cut the shrub to the ground in winter if it is getting too rangy; new growth will come back in droves the next year and flower at 3 to 4 feet high. Probably best suited to most gardens are the more compact cultivars of *C. alnifolia* ('Compacta', 'Hummingbird'), and the rose-flowered selections like Broken Arrow Nursery's fabulous 'Ruby Spice'. Cinnamon clethra *(C. acuminata)* is a bit harder to intergrate because of its size, but it has proved pretty adaptable for us. We have dug out sections from our larger patch and moved them without difficulty. New growth on *C. acuminata* can be amazingly fast (5 to 6 feet for new sprouts), and the lovely bark begins to develop in the third season. Michael Dirr reports that cinnamon clethra performs poorly in the Deep South, suffering from heat and drought (*Manual of Woody Landscape Plants,* p. 243). In our New England garden, plants in rich soil and some sun have grown faster and become small trees, while others in poorer, rocky soil and shade are only 6 feet high after 20 years, with stems less than 1 inch in diameter.

USES: Massing; pond side planting; mixed borders; hedge; naturalizing in woodland understory.

WILDLIFE: Superb mid summer nectar plants visited by butterflies and friends. A patch of blooming clethra is a buzzing cacophony of tiny wings.

PROPAGATION: Easy from cuttings, moderately easy from seed.

Clethra acuminata
Cinnamon Clethra

ZONES: 5–7; sun to light shade (more shade further south)

SOIL: Moist

NATIVE TO: Rich mountain woods, on slopes or coves along streams, mostly in the southern Appalachians; southwestern Pennsylvania to eastern Kentucky, south to Tennessee and northern Georgia

SIZE: Height 8–15 (30) feet, width 4–8 feet

COLOR: Creamy white; blooms in summer

The striking, burnished cinnamon, tan, purple, and brown exfoliating bark of cinnamon clethra is one of the finest of any native shrub's, and it stands out even from a distance in the verdant mountain woods. In the wild and in the garden, this becomes almost a small tree with age, occasionally sending up another stem a few feet from the last to grow in the colony. In shade, the branches cluster near the top of the stems, which exposes the bark to the eye without much effort with the shears. It is less of a stand-alone shrub than summersweet, needing an underplanting of ferns or wildflowers to skirt its lower extremities. The flowers are similar to summersweet's but are borne in longer, wider racemes a week or two earlier. Unfortunately, they have but a trace of musky-sweet perfume, but they are still visited by all manner of flies, bees, wasps, and butterflies. Its leaves are 4–6 inches long, larger than summersweet's, with a covering of fine hair that gives them a gray tone. Bark color varies from plant to plant, developing most kaleidoscopically on older trunks, which can be as much as 3 inches in diameter.

Clethra alnifolia
Summersweet

ZONES: 4–9; sun to light shade

SOIL: Moist to wet

NATIVE TO: Swamps and moist woods within 100 miles of the Atlantic coast from southern Maine to northern Florida and along the Gulf of Mexico to eastern Texas

SIZE: Height 4–9 feet, width 4–12 feet

COLOR: Ivory white; blooms in summer

Summersweet is something that no gardener should be without. Its carefree disposition, fragrant blooms —which appear during the midsummer lull when not much else is in bloom—and glossy, deep green leaves are as at home in a formal garden as they are naturalized in a swamp. Interestingly, cultivars like 'Hummingbird', found at Calloway Gardens in Stone Mountain, Georgia, appear to be fairly hardy in the North. We have not had any dieback on this cultivar in Zone 5–6 and it does well at the Berkshire Botanic Garden in Sturbridge, Massachusetts, which is a true Zone 4 in most winters.

Corema conradii. *Though its maroon flowers are so small as to escape the notice of the casual observer, broom crowberry begins to bloom toward the end of winter, a welcome sign that spring draws nigh. This colony is growing in a heathland community on Cape Cod along with bearberry (Arc-tostaphylos uva-ursi).*

Corema conradii

Corema conradii (ko-REE-ma)
Empetraceae
Broom Crowberry

ZONES: 4–7; sun to part sun

SOIL: Well-drained, acidic, but not overly dry

NATIVE TO: Pine barrens along the north Atlantic coast, Newfoundland to New Jersey

SIZE: Height 10–20 inches, width 1–3 feet

COLOR: Dark red; blooms in early spring

I am drawn to some plants for reasons that are hard to explain, and broom crowberry is one. This small, mounded evergreen resembles a heath in both its overall shape and the needled appearance of the

Empetrum nigrum. *Though its needlelike leaves resemble Corema's, black crowberry produces juicy black berries instead of small, hard capsules.*

small, dark green leaves, whorled up thin forking stems. Its flowers are small and barely noticeable, grouped at the tips of its twigs in little clusters before new growth commences in spring. The flowers are butted up against the uppermost leaves and are hard to see from a distance, but they create a subtle maroon haze that settles over the plant for a week or two just as the garden is beginning to stir again. There is nothing spectacular here, nothing that will send the heart into thudding palpitations when you first see one, but the broom crowberry has something—perhaps an erudite sophistication—that sets it apart from its companions. It grows along the windswept Atlantic coast, favoring the peat-laced sandy soils that build up in time as dunes cut off from the waves flatten and settle, or rocky depressions fill with moss and duff. Crowberry is one small step removed from the Ericaceae, and you can see this in its pattern of growth: a set of 3 to 8 new twigs sets off each year from the tip of last year's progress, casually building a more and more complex architecture from a few stems at the base. The shrubs gain only 2 to 4 inches in height and spread each year, but in time they become neat flattened mounds shaded deep green. The female plants develop clusters of small round fruits nestled in a basket of bracts, again not showy but fitting in character.

In the garden, broom crowberry provides a stabilizing influence, settling in among companions like bearberry, trailing arbutus *(Epigaea repens)*, and low rhododendrons. It can also help lend structure to herbaceous plantings of acid-loving plants in much the same way as the heaths do.

Two other genera closely related to *Corema* are *Empetrum* and *Ceratiola*. Empetrum, also called crowberry, grows farther north along the coast in boggy soil as well as in alpine areas and tundra. The main difference is that *Empetrum* species have axillary flowers that yield to pulpy, black or red berries (about as big as a blueberry) ripening in summer. Their foliage is darker green and a bit thicker, but it is otherwise similar in appearance and arrangement to broom crowberry's. *E. eamesii (rubrum)*, red crowberry, with cranberry red to purple fruits, ranges through northern New England and eastern Canada. *E. nigrum* (black crowberry) is circumboreal, descending south along the northeast coast and high mountains as well as the upper Great Lakes. Both species make cute little evergreen mounds in a peaty, damp spot, and I have seen great green cushions along the northern New England coast that are positively luxuriant. The two species are virtually indistinguishable when not in fruit.

Ceratiola ericoides (sand hill rosemary) takes over from *Corema* in the Southeast, growing in similar habitats, sandy acidic soils of settled dunes along the coast from South Carolina to Florida and Mississippi. It differs in a few distinct ways: leaves are on the average twice as long, the plants are on the whole a bit stiffer and larger in appearance, and it bears its flowers more like *Empetrum*, in the leaf axils along the stems of the previous season's growth. It is obviously the plant of choice for the Southeast, and can be utilized in a similar fashion. However, *Ceratiola* needs extremely good drainage to survive, so gardeners in the piedmont clay belt will only succeed with it if they plant it in a rock garden or raised sand bed. Propagation is as for *Corema*.

CULTURE: *Corema*, *Empetrum*, and *Ceratiola* species are not terribly difficult if you have sandy, acidic soils to begin with. They need a place where they can grow unmolested by aggressive neighbors, and thrive best where the soil has a good amount of peaty organic matter but low fertility. They develop a network of hairlike roots from a central woody one, and are best set out in spring from containers in a location that receives at least a few hours of sun. In the wild, they are able to grow in the understory of the pygmy pine–scrub oak forests that develop along the immediate coast, but tend to become threadbare from lack of sun. We have had good success with *Corema*, provided its soil requirements are met, but I imagine it is suited only to climates where broadleaf rhododendrons thrive. Eventually, *Corema* can spread to the point where a winter haircut is warranted, and healthy specimens respond well to removal of one-third of their canopy when they are dormant as well as a less drastic, light shave off the new growth in early summer.

USES: Massing, low border, or scattered in acid-soil heath or rock gardens.

PROPAGATION: Moderately easy from cuttings, moderately difficult from seed.

Cornus (KOR-nus)
Cornaceae
Dogwood

Cornus alternifolia

Be it a flowering dogwood *(C. florida)* with its matchless beauty when in bloom or the gray dogwood *(C. racemosa)* and its ilk with their utilitarian flexibility, the dogwoods have settled into our gardens as easily as autumn leaves settle in a mossy pool. The patriarch of the family, the tree that elevates the clan to the horticultural aristocracy, *C. florida*, comes as close to perfection as nature is willing to tread, with the balance and austerity of a Japanese line drawing. Greatness is rare in all aristocracies, so it is no surprise that most of the other members of the clan are more proletarian than noble. Still, some essence of what you might call *Cornus*-ness survives in the shape of their leaves, the pattern of branching, or deep burgundy fall color.

Dogwoods have small, usually four-petaled flowers packed together in balls or flat-topped heads to form a platform for insects to walk around on as they sip nectar. Though the individual flowers are small, en masse the groupings have a pretty, soft white appearance that makes them reasonably ornamental in flower. In this they are similar to many viburnums. Flowering dogwood *(Cornus florida)* and Pacific dogwood *(C. nuttallii)*, as well as the little herbaceous groundcover bunchberry *(C. canadensis)* go further, surrounding the flowers with enormous white bracts to further advertise the blooms and lend the plant a rich white nobility. Pacific dogwood differs from its eastern sibling mainly in that the flower heads are surrounded by five or six bracts, instead of the symmetrical four that encircle each inflorescence on flowering dogwood. This simple difference changes the whole rhythm of the tree, lending it a much more camellia-like appearance, even though in leaf and habit the two dogwoods are nearly the same.

Birds, attracted by red, white or blue-black fruits with a sweet or starchy pulp, are the primary seed dispersers of dogwoods. The fruits of many species are quite ornamental, as is the bark of both young twigs and older trunks. The shrubby species construct twiggy thickets that provide cover and stabilize slopes and wetlands. All have leaves with lateral veins that branch out from the midvein, then travel up and along the margin of the leaf in a distinctive way. The foliage is usually lighter gray-green underneath, a fact that becomes clearer when upper surfaces of the leaves turn ruddy burgundy in the fall and contrast nicely with the lighter shade below. The final thing that makes most dogwoods recognizable even in winter is their pattern of branching. New growth begins from a pointed bud set between two leaf scars. Except for vigorously growing branches, all the new twigs have a swooping, out-and-up shape like antlers, with one shoot jutting out farther than the others in its rack. Year after year of arcing twigs set one after another lends the branches a scalloped appearance, especially when draped with snow.

CULTURE: Most dogwoods are natives of damp or swampy ground, though many have proved reasonably drought-tolerant in cultivation. The shrubby species are easy to establish in wet to moderately dry soils, with full sun needed for dense growth and strong twig color. They respond very well to rejuvenative pruning. The tree species bleed excessively from wounds received in early spring, so limit pruning to fall after the leaves have fallen. Most of the shrubs are moderately stoloniferous, forming spreading, many-stemmed colonies that may eventually need to be thinned and can be divided and replanted when dormant. Cut the plants back to 6 inches, and use a sharp spade to slice off sections from the perimeter of the clump. All dogwoods can get powdery mildew later in the year, especially in wet climates, which can severely disfigure and defoliate the plants. Good air circulation and sun coupled with decent culture are the best remedies, though some years there is not much you can do to prevent it, short of using fungicides. Usually, the plants can recover without problem the next season.

Then of course there is dogwood blight, which has eliminated many of the flowering dogwoods from the northern sections of the species' range since the 1970s. The disease is caused by the aptly named anthracnose fungus *Discula destructiva*, which infects leaves and twigs and can grow down into branches, partially killing off whole sections of the tree. The branches die quickly in early summer, leav-

Cornus alternifolia. *Sugary berries ripen on the pagoda dogwood in midsummer. For the seeds to germinate expediently, the fruits should be picked when they first turn blue. Mash them in a strainer under running water, pick out the small, light brown seeds, and sow them immediately. The seeds of summer-ripening* Cornus *species require warm, moist conditions prior to winter if they are to germinate the following spring.*

ing dried leaves on the twigs; this and excessive sprouting below the dead sections are characteristic diagnostic features of the disease. When I was growing up, our woods in Connecticut were full of flowering dogwoods growing in the understory, but few remain. Unlike chestnut blight, though, this disease is opportunistic and will not kill healthy trees. Drought, cool rainy weather in spring when the leaves are emerging, and a shaded location all make the trees more susceptible. I have found that the single best thing you can do to stem this disease is to water dogwoods deeply during summer droughts. An open, sunny location also helps to keep them vigorous, and the leaves dry more quickly, discouraging the fungus. Additionally, a few handfuls of fertilizer broadcast around the tree in spring will help not only flowering but also disease resistance. No one should be afraid to use this beautiful tree in landscapes, provided they can be given moist soil and some light and air around the crown. Further, since wild trees continue to survive and multiply, I wager that resistance will develop more strongly in wild populations within the next century.

USES: Specimen; massing; bank stabilization (depending on species).

WILDLIFE: Berries and twigs are valuable as food and shelter for birds and small mammals. Since fruits ripen from summer to fall, depending on the species, planting more than one kind will provide the widest offering to birds.

PROPAGATION: Easy to moderately difficult from cuttings, easy from seed.

Cornus alternifolia

Pagoda Dogwood, Alternate-leaved Dogwood

ZONES: 3–8; sun to light shade
SOIL: Moist to wet
NATIVE TO: Low or rich woods, swampy thickets and hedgerows; Newfoundland to Minnesota south to Arkansas, Alabama, and northern Florida
SIZE: Height 10–25 feet, width 6–15 feet
COLOR: Creamy white; blooms in late spring

This is the only dogwood with alternate, not opposite, branching. Pagoda dogwood cannot match the other tree species in flower, but it has a graceful, tiered branching pattern suggestive of the architecture of a pagoda that is unmistakable and quite beautiful. It puts up a straight central leader that grows up a foot or two, then sends out a set of nearly horizontal side branches. These continue to get wider each year, but remain visually separated from the layers above and below. The flowers—dense cymes of small blooms from the tips of the previous season's growth—appear with the new leaves and possess a musky-sweet aroma you can smell from quite a distance. The fruits mature fairly early in summer, turning from green to pink, then bright,

dark blue, often with all three colors present for a time on each juicy red cyme. These are very pretty as they are turning, but birds relish the sugary pulp and the fruits are quickly stripped. The cyme remains colorful for an additional two weeks. Though dogwood blight does not seen to bother it, pagoda dogwood does suffer badly from powdery mildew in some years, and older, stressed trees are easily killed by what I believe is the same stem canker that affects redbud and many other trees. Again, vigor and freedom from drought stress are your biggest allies. I have seen some remarkable, aged specimens growing along pond or streamsides in the open, and the flat plane of water is a perfect foil for the tiered branches.

Cornus amomum

Silky Dogwood

ZONES: 4–8; sun to light shade
SOIL: Moist to wet
NATIVE TO: Wet woods, thickets, and streamsides; Maine and Quebec to Minnesota south to Oklahoma, Arkansas and Georgia
SIZE: Height 3–10 feet, width 3–6 feet
COLOR: Creamy white; blooms in late spring

C. amomum lacks many of the features that make other dogwoods so ornamental. It is a twiggy, many-stemmed shrub with older stems becoming lax and arching outward somewhat. It does have larger leaves, oval in outline and usually 3 to 4 inches long. The fruits mature cobalt blue, and are fairly ornamental for a short time in late summer. Overall, this plant is probably best reserved for naturalized situations or left to grow for the benefit of wildlife.

Cornus florida

Flowering Dogwood

ZONES: (4)5–9; sun to light shade
SOIL: Moist, slightly acidic
NATIVE TO: Woods; southeastern Maine to southern Ontario and Michigan south to Illinois, Oklahoma, northeastern Mexico and Florida
SIZE: Height 12–20 (30) feet, width 8–15 feet
COLOR: Ivory white streaked with maroon or occasionally pink; blooms in spring

Flowering dogwood produces very showy, crimson berries in small knobby clusters at the branch tips that ripen in fall. Healthy trees in the sun can be so loaded with the fruits that robins sit in the branches, drowsy from gluttony. The leaves turn deep burgundy sometimes flushed with red, and color develops early in the fall, coinciding with fruit ripening to help attract the attention of birds. Chipmunks also eat the fruits, though I think they are mainly interested in the seed, which they digest and thus, unlike the birds, do not spread. The warm gray bark on older trees has a square-patterned alligator-hide quality that is also

Cornus florida. *The beauty of flowering dogwood comes as much from the graceful tiered arrangement of its branches as from the balanced symmetry of its four-bracted flowers.*

ornamental. Trunk diameters over 6 inches are uncommon, but the hard, split-resistant wood of larger trees has been used to fashion bowls, pipes, and mallets, among other things.

Cornus nuttallii

Pacific Dogwood, Mountain Dogwood

ZONES: 7–9; sun to light shade

SOIL: Moist

NATIVE TO: Forests and woodland edge at middle elevations in the mountains; central California to British Columbia with a disjunct population in the Idaho Panhandle

SIZE: Height 10–30 (50) feet, width 8–15 feet

COLOR: Ivory white, occasionally pink; blooms in spring

Pacific dogwood is much like flowering dogwood in both shape and preferred habitat, but bears five or six to even eight bracts around the tight ball of flowers. Fruits are orange-red and cluster in a knobby ball. This is a beautiful tree, distinctive and different from the eastern species in flower, but, alas, not well adapted to warm summer regions. The population from Idaho has yielded more winter-hardy genotypes, but these are still susceptible to diseases exacerbated by summer stress when grown in the East.

Cornus racemosa

Gray Dogwood, Swamp Dogwood, Red-panicled Dogwood

ZONES: 3–8; sun to light shade

SOIL: Wet to moderately dry

NATIVE TO: Stream banks, old fields and thickets; Maine to southern Quebec and Manitoba, south to Illinois, Missouri, and Virginia

SIZE: Height 3–8 feet, width 3–8 feet

COLOR: Creamy white; blooms in spring

Gray dogwood has a wild, unrefined character similar to that of red osier (*C. sericea*), and I like to use it in naturalized situations. Cool gray, smooth bark covers the older stems, which sprout in great quantity to form ever-widening clumps. Each stem grows up for a time, then branches profusely, so the shrubs have a fairly fine texture, both when clothed in small gray-green leaves and when bare in winter. Flowers are borne on pedicels that develop a lovely deep red color as the fruits turn white in late summer. The contrast between stem and fruit is quite nice, and though the fruits are quickly eaten by a host of bird species, the pedicels remain bright and attractive for several more weeks, adorning the branch tips like little colored trees. This is fairly drought-tolerant as dogwoods go, and I would put it on my short list of shrubs important to wildlife. Similar species from swampy habitats include *C. drummondii* (rough-leaved dogwood), with wider leaves, greater height (it can become a small, 15-foot tree), and a more midwestern range, as well as southern swamp dogwood (*C. stricta*), found mostly along the southeastern coastal plain. This is basically the southern extension of gray dogwood, with pale blue fruits and leaves whose undersides are more light green than white.

Corylus americana. *American hazelnut trees guard their precious nuts in a porcupine pelt of tiny, bristly hairs — a challenging mouthful for a hungry rodent to chew through.*

Cornus sericea (stolonifera)

Red Osier Dogwood

ZONES: 2–7; sun to light shade

SOIL: Wet to moderately dry

NATIVE TO: Swamps, stream banks, and thickets; Newfoundland to Alaska south in the western mountains to northern Mexico and in the East to Illinois and Pennsylvania

SIZE: Height 3–10 feet, width 4–8 feet

COLOR: Creamy white; blooms in spring

In the wild, red osier is a suckering, layering tangle of caney branches that forms dense thickets in wet soils. It has white fruits and twigs that are greenish in summer but develop a dark red, maroon, or blood red color as temperatures and leaves drop in autumn. It is grown mainly for this winter twig color, which can be stunning poking up through the snow. In the landscape trade, this is much confused with its close relative from Eurasia, tartarian dogwood *(C. alba)*, and the two are difficult for me to tell apart, especially in the nursery. Our native species is a bit more rank and stoloniferous in growth, and in general, I think it is best to handle this as a perennial and cut it back to near the ground before growth begins in spring to encourage vigorous, well-colored canes to sprout in season. I have never found this plant to be very satisfactory in formal situations, as the pruning necessary to develop good branch color doesn't allow the shrub to be anything but a twiggy, resprouting mound that lacks the character that comes with age.

Western forms of red osier are designated ssp. *occidentalis,* though in practice they are hardly distinguishable from eastern genotypes, distinguished as ssp. *sericea.* In the drier parts of the West, it is found only fairly high in the mountains, growing beside water with the likes of speckled alder *(Alnus incana* ssp. *tenuifolia).* The names *C. baileyi* and *C. interior* have been applied to regional variations of ssp. *sericea* and have little real merit. Round-leaved dogwood *(C. rugosa)* has much larger leaves, up to 6 inches long and 4 inches wide, and almost suggests hobblebush viburnum in aspect; the twigs are merely mottled with red and have an overall larger, coarser branching habit. It ranges from Quebec to Manitoba south to Iowa and New Jersey, but I have seen it mainly in the mountains, growing in gravelly slopes under birch and maple. I am not sure *C. rugosa* has wide application in horticulture, but I like the bold foliage and large mounded shape.

Corylus americana

Corylus (KORE-i-lus)
Betulaceae

Hazelnut, American Filbert

It **is surprising** to many people that wild versions of the heart-shaped filberts we eagerly crack open during the winter holidays grow throughout much of the United States and southern Canada. The problem is, people are not the only ones who relish the sweet meat of hazelnuts, and squirrels especially will guard and check the hazelnut shrubs like worried farmers for any sign that they are ready to harvest. For me, these *Corylus* are the true harbingers of spring, among the first woody plants to bloom in our woods each season and a welcome sign to the winter-weary that all will soon be right again. Pairs or triplets of half-expanded male catkins on the twigs in autumn elongate into dripping, yellowy locks as the frost leaves the ground in spring. The female flowers are more sublime, just fine ruby red stigmas that poke out from knobby buds like little snake tongues to lick up pollen. The two native hazelnuts are very similar in appearance. I can tell them apart in winter only because *C. americana* has stalked hairs on the newest twigs, and its male catkins hang on short stumps as well. Both American hazelnut and beaked hazelnut *(C. cornuta)* are spreading, understory shrubs able to grow higher and drier on the slope than many of their competitors. Seedlings establish a few main stems with slightly zigzagging, alternate leaves that are broadly oval, silhouetted by a row of irregular, jagged teeth and covered with a rough down that feels unshaven as it passes through your fingers. The foliage is diaphanous, a thin green film stretched between the ribs of prominent veins and trimmed off on one side of the base. The first seedling shoots get to a foot or so then send out more vigorous shoots from their roots, which grow higher than the first, then branch out somewhat horizontally. This pattern is repeated and the clump gets gradually taller and wider, becoming with time a loose, twiggy amalgamation with an irregular, vaguely flattened appearance and warm gray-brown bark on stems rarely more than an inch in diameter.

If you shuffle around in the foliage during summer, you are likely to find a few developing nuts, and it is here where the differences between species become brilliantly clear. American hazelnut wraps its nut in a soft, elaborately filigreed pair of bracts colored just like the leaves and ending with a stiff ruffle. The clusters of 2 to 3 nuts taken together resemble a Victorian drawing of a ruffled tulip or peony. Beaked hazelnut is demure in comparison, its bracts drawn tightly around the nut and stretched into a long, narrow beak with just a hint of ruffle poking out like a shirtsleeve from a coat. The 1-inch beaks arc away from the oval fruits wrapped at their base, and this, combined with the slight flaring of the tube tips, gives the appearance of duck heads bunched together. Beaked hazelnut protects its seed in a coat of bristly hairs that will poke your skin if you try to pinch one without gloves on (I can't imagine what they do to a squirrel's tender little lips). Hazels are shrubs to naturalize in the understory or at the edge of the woods. They have an inescapable wildness about them that is hard to incorporate into managed landscapes unless you plan to grow them in an orchard for the nuts.

CULTURE: Hazelnuts establish themselves easily in a wide range of soils, tolerating considerable dryness in summer but never wet feet. They will grow happily as an understory shrub, though fruiting will diminish in shade. I have never tried to screen the trees from rodents, but if you want to harvest nuts, select a spot that gets a few hours of sun, and plant at least half a dozen in an attempt to overwhelm the squirrels with abundance. I think the black bird netting recommended for blueberries, cinched up tight at the base of the shrub or pegged to the ground, might help. Certainly a squirrel could chew through it, but they do seem to hate the feel of the mesh on their paws, so it can act as a deterrent. Nothing short of a wire cage can completely protect hazels.

USES: Naturalizing, nut production.

WILDLIFE: Certainly valuable for the nuts, which feed small mammals and large birds like turkeys and grouse. Larvae of the fairly uncommon (at least in the East) turquoise hairstreak (*Erora laeta*) feed on the leaves.

PROPAGATION: Moderately difficult from seed.

Corylus americana

American Hazelnut

ZONES: 4–8; part sun to shade

SOIL: Moist to dry

NATIVE TO: Woods and clearings; Maine to southern Ontario and southeastern Alberta south to North Dakota, Iowa, eastern Kansas and Oklahoma, Louisiana and southern Georgia

SIZE: Height 5–12 feet, width 4–8 feet

COLOR: Yellow-green (male) and red-purple (female); late winter to early spring

Corylus cornuta

Beaked Hazelnut

ZONES: 3–8; part sun to shade

SOIL: Moist to dry

NATIVE TO: Woods and clearings; Newfoundland west through southern Quebec and Ontario to central British Columbia, south through California (ssp. *californica*) and scattered at higher elevations in the Rockies, in the East south to Iowa, Michigan, Pennsylvania and in the mountains and Piedmont to Georgia and Alabama

SIZE: Height 5–14 feet, width 4–8 feet

COLOR: Yellow-green (male) and red-purple (female); late winter to early spring

Populations along the Pacific coast (*C. cornuta* ssp. *californica*) are differentiated from the widespread *C. cornuta* ssp. *cornuta* by their fatter leaves, shorter beaks, and the presence of glandular hairs on the twigs.

Cotinus obovatus

Cotinus obovatus
(ko-TYE-nus)
Anacardiaceae
American Smoketree, Chittamwood

ZONES: 4–8; sun to light shade

SOIL: Moist, moderately acidic to neutral

NATIVE TO: Rare and restricted mostly to limestone outcroppings in scattered localities in Tennessee and northern Alabama as well as Oklahoma and central Texas

Cotinus obovatus. *American smoketree is more fire than smoke, and what a glorious conflagration it can produce. Intense red and glowing orange fall color develops best on plants that receive at least four hours of direct sun. The color also varies from one individual to the next; this particular tree, outside my office, is consistently the best in our collections.*

Crataegus phaenopyrum. Holly-red fruits ripen on Washington hawthorn before the leaves have dropped in fall and hang on most of the winter in scarlet profusion. The hard, sour fruits are usually ignored by birds in the fall but are readily devoured in the spring as flocks migrate north

SIZE: Height 15–30 feet, width 8–15 feet

COLOR: Yellow-green with hints of maroon; blooms in spring

This small tree has so much to offer us, it is a mystery to me why it is virtually unknown in gardens. It is a relative of the familiar European smoketree *(C. coggygria)*, which is grown not for flowers or fruit but for the fuzzy pedicels that support the developing seeds. These bearded stalks change from purple to smoky silver over the course of the season, persisting on the branches a bit too long, like the guest who wouldn't leave. What is at first a rich and beautiful cloud eventually becomes a tiresome collection of dust-bunnies hung from the branches. Our native species is a different sort of plant altogether. Its pedicels have the same bearded character, but the beards are shorter and are borne in much smaller terminal panicles, so the smoky effect is not so pronounced. In addition, they don't set as much seed, so the pedicels fall with the small yellow-green flowers and never develop. The trees are mostly dioecious, which further complicates pollination. For a few weeks when the European species is smoking like a signal fire, I wish ours could do the same, but after that I am glad it knows when to quit.

C. obovatus offers large and benevolent leaves shaped like tennis rackets with an oval blade and a long petiole. The foliage emerges with a burgundy wash, especially along the margins, and evolves into a beautiful blue-green above and silvery below that shimmers like a tropical lagoon with the slightest breeze. New growth comes from the tips of the twigs, which grow at narrow angles away from the center so that the younger trees have an open but stiffly upright form that becomes more rounded as the crown matures. The bark is cool gray and smooth, aging dark and scaly. I feel fortunate that the garden crew planted a couple of smoketrees outside my office window; in autumn the green leaves begin to glow, as if lit from within. The leaves regain some of the burgundy they had in spring, now mixed with purple, red, and orange like the clouds at sunset. It is truly one of the most spectacular things in the garden at this time of year. The plants outside my window receive about 4 to 5 hours of direct sun, and these certainly color more profoundly than older specimens we have growing in more shade. I suspect that sunlight is the important factor here, though clonal differences may be responsible as well. Certainly, the trees in light shade rarely flower, unlike the ones in the sun.

American smoketree has a strong but not overpoweringly bold texture, either when trained to a single leader as a narrowly upright tree or when allowed to become spreading and multitrunked —a big rounded shrub suitable for massing. It does not have the spreading tendencies of its relatives the sumacs, though it will resprout if cut back hard for

some reason. The wood is much harder than sumac, but has similar orangey heartwood, which was used to produce a yellow dye during the nineteenth century and was harvested to such a point that the scarce trees were nearly eliminated. Since the branches are fairly broad but not closely set, we have not had problems with snow damage in the garden.

CULTURE: Smoketree has grown well for me in both fairly acidic soil (pH 5.2) and nearly neutral soil that we amend with limestone gravel (pH 6.8). With decent moisture and fertility, the young ones can grow 2 to 3 feet in a season, leveling out at about 15 to 20 feet. I like to train the tree to a single leader when young, so that it becomes a fairly narrow, small specimen that can be underplanted with shrubs of perennials, which contrast and highlight the texture and color of the foliage. Transplant in spring from containers (field-dug trees are difficult to move), and if the seedling has grown awkwardly, let it grow for a year or two then cut it back hard so it will sprout another leader. Trees are not sexed in nurseries, though a few cultivars selected for fall color are occasionally found, so if you want smoke, you will need to plant three or four and hope for more females than males. The plants do not root easily from cuttings, nor do they graft well, which makes selection of superior cultivars difficult.

USES: Specimen, massing.

PROPAGATION: Difficult from cuttings, moderately easy from seed.

Crataegus phaenopyrum

Crataegus (kra-TAY-gus)
Rosaceae
Hawthorn

Hawthorns can be thought of as the prodigal sons of apples, who have left the comfort of rolling orchards for a rough-and-tumble life in the wild. The hard life has toughened them, clothed them in wizened and cocksure thorns, and given them the support of roots able to eke out a life in hardscrabble places not fit for their pampered brethren apples and crabs. They prefer open situations like old fields, fencerows, and savannas, where they can develop a flat rounded crown that is wider than tall, composed of interlaced branches lined with 1-to-3-inch back-curved thorns that are really modified axillary twigs honed to a needle-sharp point. Leaves are typically triangular in outline, with a rough-toothed margin divided more or less into three or five shallow lobes. Hawthorns have a wistful way of flowering, the branches hung with myriad clusters of five-petaled blooms typical of the rose family, bunched together like bouquets on small spurs. These are followed in late summer by clusters of brilliant red or orange fruits tipped with a persistent gray calyx crown, much like a rose hip. If the leaves have weathered their various trials and last until autumn, then they may blaze with color similar to the fruits'.

Because of their many ornamental characteristics, hawthorns have been widely grown in landscapes, especially windblown open areas around office parks, universities, and parking lots, where their inherent toughness serves them well. If you wish to grow unimproved wild hawthorns, you must prepare yourself for a series of afflictions that force the foliage into early retirement most seasons, leaving the tree's fruits, thorns and interesting form to carry you through the eight succeeding months until it leafs out again. But selections have been made from a number of our native species with far superior disease resistance coupled with consistent fall color, large fruits, and attractive form. Over 1,100 species have been named worldwide, but as few as 100 to 200 are considered valid species. Though I usually favor the genetic diversity inherent in seed-grown plants, in this case, for all but the wildest situations, the cultivars should be sought out.

CULTURE: Transplant in early spring, either balled and burlaped or from a container, into well-drained soil in a sunny location. Full sun and air circulation, in addition to a moderate dose of balanced fertilizer (don't overdo it), will help curtail the rusts, scabs, and fire blight that defoliate the wild trees. The thorns are pretty nasty if you catch one in the eye or hand, and they seem to reach out and grab you when you get near the tree. Thornless or less thorny cultivars are available for use where contact with children or stumbling adults could be a problem. As far as I know, the hawthorns seem to be able to self-pollinate well enough, as mass plantings of single clones set good quantities of fruit.

USES: Specimen, massing.

WILDLIFE: The fruits are passed over initially in fall, but through the winter and early spring they slowly shrivel and gradually disappear down the gullets of resident birds. Leaves feed a number of butterflies and moths, including the larvae of the pallid

swallowtail butterfly (*Papilio eurymedon*) and striped hairstreak (*Satyrium liparops*) and moths such as the cecropia (*Hyalophora cecropia*), red-humped caterpillar moth (*Schizura concinna*), western tussock moth (*Orgyria vetusta*), and the whiteline leafroller (*Amorbia humerosana*). The last of these feeds voraciously—along with a host of mites, aphids, sawflies, treehoppers, crickets, and borers—often to the detriment of the tree.

PROPAGATION: Moderately difficult from seed.

Crataegus aestivalis
May Haw

ZONES: 5–9; sun
SOIL: Moist to wet
NATIVE TO: Pond shores, low woods; mostly coastal North Carolina to Florida and Mississippi
SIZE: Height 8–15 feet, width 6–12 feet
COLOR: White; blooms in spring

A shrubby species with long straight thorns up to 1½ inches long, small spoon-shaped leaves that lack much in the way of toothiness, and large fruits in clusters of 1 to 3 that are widely harvested to make may haw jelly. Other southeastern relatives include blueberry hawthorn (*C. brachycantha*), with glossy leaves of similar shape and pretty but unpalatable fruits turning from dark red to blue then blue-black, much like blueberries. It likes similar habitats, and can become quite large and oval in outline. Hollyleaf may haw (*C. opaca*) is a swamp tree that can grow to 40 feet. Its large red fruits are ridged like little pumpkins and are harvested much like cranberries, by skimming them from the water after they are shaken down.

Crataegus crus-galli
Cockspur Hawthorn

ZONES: 4–7; sun
SOIL: Well-drained, moist to dry
NATIVE TO: Fencerows, abandoned fields, roadsides, and clearings; southeastern Quebec and Ontario to Michigan south to Illinois, Tennessee, and Maryland
SIZE: Height 20–30 feet, width 20–35 feet
COLOR: White; blooms in spring

This hawthorn, common in the Midwest, is widely used in landscaping because of its toughness; attractive glossy leaves, which are more or less spoon-shaped and are protected by recurved thorns up to 2 inches long; a thick, layered, flat-topped shape that gives it an "acacia on the African savanna" look; good scarlet-orange fall color; and dark red fruits that hold on long into the winter. *C. crus-galli* var. *inermis* is a better subject for landscaping than the species, as it lacks the fierce thorns. The northeastern fleshy hawthorn (*C. succulenta*) is similar, with large, lustrous fruits in big clusters, as is pear hawthorn (*C. calpodendron*), which has distinctive, pear-shaped fruits that turn dull red in autumn.

Crataegus douglasii

Black Hawthorn

ZONES: 4–8; sun

SOIL: Well-drained

NATIVE TO: Thickets, floodplains, edges of wet meadows; Saskatchewan to Alaska, south to California and South Dakota with isolated populations in northern Michigan, Minnesota, and southern Ontario.

SIZE: Height 15–25 feet, width 15–20 feet

COLOR: White; blooms in spring

Even the resilient hawthorn has met its match in the Great Basin deserts, and the genus dwindles to but one species, black hawthorn, found in moist soils at medium elevations in the mountains throughout the West. It has typical shallowly lobed leaves and sparse, 1-inch thorns. The flowers are relatively small, and the fruits mature blue-black.

Crataegus marshallii

Parsley Hawthorn

ZONES: 5–9; sun, part sun

SOIL: Moist

NATIVE TO: Moist soils, floodplains, swamp forests; Virginia to Florida and Texas and north in the Mississippi Valley to southern Illinois

SIZE: Height 15–25 feet, width 15–20 feet

COLOR: White; blooms in spring

Parsley hawthorn gets its name from its deeply lobed, lacy leaves, which make it fairly easy to distinguish. The fruits are red and the flowers, large and showy. Thorns are slender and not too abundant. It also boasts striking, burnt orange and gray peeling bark.

Crataegus mollis

Downy Hawthorn

ZONES: 4–7; sun

SOIL: Well-drained, moist to dry

NATIVE TO: Fencerows, abandoned fields, roadsides and clearings; northwestern New York and southern Quebec to Ontario and Minnesota south to Oklahoma and Tennessee

SIZE: Height 20–40 feet, width 20–35 feet

COLOR: White; blooms in early spring

A large, wide-spreading, domed tree with a thick pelt of down on the new leaves that combines with the silvery twigs to give the trees a pronounced grayish cast. Large, red fruits are produced in fall from flowers that have a musky, off-putting scent.

Crataegus phaenopyrum

Washington Hawthorn

ZONES: 4–8; sun

SOIL: Well-drained, moist to dry

NATIVE TO: Moist woods, fencerows, abandoned fields, roadsides and clearings; Pennsylvania to Illinois south to Missouri and Florida

SIZE: Height 25–30 feet, width 20–25 feet

COLOR: White; blooms in late spring

Washington hawthorn is one of my personal favorites, for its nice oval silhouette, its excellent disease resistance and its heavy crops of large, red fruits. It is widely planted in the East and was the only hawthorn planted around the University of Connecticut that held its leaves well into fall. 'Princeton Sentry' is a narrow, upright form, and 'Clark' is notable for especially heavy fruit set. Like the species, these cultivars are well armed with large thorns.

Crataegus pruinosa

Frosted Hawthorn

ZONES: 3–6; sun

SOIL: Well-drained, moist to dry

NATIVE TO: Moist or dry woods, fencerows, abandoned fields, roadsides, and clearings; southern Vermont and southern Ontario to southern Michigan, and Iowa, south to Missouri and the mountains of North Carolina

SIZE: Height 20–35 feet, width 10–20 feet

COLOR: White; blooms in spring

This distinctive hawthorn has a narrow, oval crown taller than wide, large red to yellow-orange fruits, silvery gray bark, and typical lobed, triangular leaves. The fine branches are well armed with thorns. Scarlet hawthorn (*C. coccinea*) is very similar and is a fairly common old-field hawthorn in New England and southeastern Canada.

Crataegus punctata

Dotted Hawthorn

ZONES: 4–7; sun

SOIL: Well-drained, moist to dry

NATIVE TO: Fencerows, abandoned fields, roadsides, and clearings; southern Maine and Quebec through southern Ontario to Minnesota and eastern South Dakota, south to Missouri and Tennessee and in the Appalachians to northern Georgia

SIZE: Height 15–25 feet, width 20–30 feet

COLOR: White; blooms in late spring

This hawthorn is typically a small, flat-topped tree wider than tall with oval leaves and long, thin thorns. The fruits are oval and deep red. The thornless cultivar 'Ohio Pioneer' is an attractive and fairly disease-resistant selection with a flat-oval silhouette like that of many crabapples. The fruit drops off the tree punctually in late fall. *C. punctata* and *C. phaenopyrum* are the last hawthorns to bloom.

Crataegus viridis

Green Hawthorn

ZONES: 4–7; sun
SOIL: Well-drained, moist to dry
NATIVE TO: Old fields, pastures, and forest margins; Delaware to Florida and Texas and north along the Mississippi River to southern Indiana and Missouri
SIZE: Height 20–35 feet, width 20–35 feet
COLOR: White; blooms in spring

Typically green hawthorn has a very dense, upright oval shape, silvery branches, and dark green, triangular to almost diamond-shaped leaves. It produces clusters of enormous fruits that are a velvety red in color and is one of the best among this large genus for fruiting effect. The cultivar 'Winter King' is being widely planted in the Midwest and the East, and it has a more vase-shaped, angular look and still larger fruits. Green hawthorn is certainly one of the best of the native hawthorns for gardens, with fruits that rival many crabapples in winter effect, scarlet-orange fall color, exfoliating bark, and good disease resistance second only to Washington hawthorn in my experience. Glossy hawthorn *(C. nitida)* is similar and possibly a hybrid of *C. viridis* and *C. crus-galli*. It is an attractive tree with dark, shiny leaves that are fairly long and narrow with good fall color. Its shape is a wide, flattened dome hung in fall with dark red fruits and set with thin but very sharp thorns. It is native to a 200-square-mile area around the confluence of the Ohio and Mississippi rivers.

Crataegus viridis. *Green hawthorn develops a regular, oval crown. This tree is about ten to twelve years old.*

Croton alabamensis

Croton alabamensis
(KROH-ton)
Euphorbiaceae
Alabama Croton

ZONES: 6–8; part sun to light shade
SOIL: Moist to moderately dry
NATIVE TO: Limestone bluffs and rocky cliffs along the Cahaba and Black Warrior rivers in central Alabama and reported also from Tennessee
SIZE: Height 3–8 feet, width 4–8 feet
COLOR: Yellow-green; blooms in spring

If you're used to thinking of crotons as multicolored tropicals in the genus *Codiaeum* (the houseplant croton), or weedy annuals like *Croton glandulosus*, the enigmatic Alabama croton comes as a bit of a shock and a puzzle. It is a very rare shrub, barely surviving the last ice age in a few sheltered river valleys near Birmingham, Alabama. I would describe it as an upright or spreading understory plant with dark green, elliptical, blunt-pointed leaves that are sparsely sprinkled with silver scales on the upper surface and densely silvered beneath. The petioles and young stems are white-scaly, as are the three-chambered capsules that develop in loose terminal racemes during the summer. Alabama croton forms loose, spreading clumps that can form large, mounded colonies in time, but it can also be trained as a lovely single-trunked shrub with a thick, rounded crown. The main ornamental features are its 2-to-4-inch-long leaves and white twigs, the leaves being fairly stiff and

Croton alabamensis. I feel privileged to have seen the rare Alabama croton in its native haunts in north-central Alabama. The scraggly, twisted stems clinging to gray-black limestone outcrops bear little resemblance to the full, rounded specimens that develop under cultivation. The habitat is under pressure from development, and the survival of this fascinating relic is sadly in question.

bold in texture, with bright green upper surfaces that contrast well with the scales of the stem and fruit. The leaves are semi-evergreen, with older ones gradually turning hunter orange blended with yellow and green before falling, and the youngest persisting at the branch tips. By spring, most or all of last year's leaves are gone, showing the emerging leaves with their felted coats as well as the willowesque little racemes of bright yellow flowers to best effect on bare branches. This is yet another botanical curiosity from our complex and wonderful flora that I don't foresee becoming a top ten foundation plant. However, it is certainly interesting in naturalized situations and can be quite beautiful massed in light shade or trained as a specimen where you can enjoy the leaves. The Birmingham (Alabama) Botanic Garden has some excellent plantings on display.

CULTURE: Transplant from containers, or if an established plant has spread, divide off pieces of the main clump in spring with a sharp shovel and plant in moist soil out of the noonday sun—leaves tend to bleach out in full sun. Seedlings will often appear underneath established specimens, and these are easily transplanted in spring or fall. A bit of careful pruning when the plant is young can shape it into an attractive, thick-twigged shrub.

USES: Specimen; naturalizing in woodland or woodland-edge situations.

PROPAGATION: Moderately difficult from cuttings and seed.

Cupressus arizonica

Cupressus (koo-PRESS-us)
Cupressaceae
Cypress

The genus *Cupressus* is restricted mainly to California, where a closely related group of six species has evolved from one or two originals isolated from each other by volcanic eruptions, climate change, and other obstacles. Cypresses are stiff, scale-leaved evergreens much like the taller junipers in habit and habitat requirements. Steely blue forms of Arizona cypress have been promoted in recent years by the J. C. Raulston Arboretum, and cultivars like *C. arizonica* 'Blue Ice' are certainly some of the most striking silvery blue screening conifers you're likely to find. I was quite taken with them, and I am not alone—witness the haircuts the Raulston Arboretum's stock plants received from nursery people taking cuttings. The branchlets of this and others like Sargent cypress (*C. sargentii*) have a distinct, blunt stockiness and waxiness to their branching that is different from junipers. Alas, the last time I was at the J. C. Raulston Arboretum, they had taken some of the plants out because in the long run they are not well adapted to clay, heat, and humidity all at once. Among the Cali-

fornian species, *C. bakeri* may prove growable in the Northeast, as it lives at high elevations in the Sierras. There are, however, better conifers for most of the country, and though they are beautiful, *Cupressus* species are probably best used only within their native range.

Cypress cones are of the soccer ball type, like those of their relatives *Chamaecyparis* and *Thuja*, often persisting on the branches for many years before being steamed open in a fire. They have very pretty, peeling or curling bark and knobby, fluted older trunks and branches. In exposed locations, the central leader keeps getting burned off by the wind,

allowing lower side branches to sweep up and become part of the crown

CULTURE: Cypresses are best in full sun and well-drained sandy or gravelly soils. They are very drought-, wind-, and salt-tolerant, and are easily transplanted from containers or balled and burlaped in fall or early spring. They are lovely narrow screening or specimen plants in the landscape. Older trees develop deep roots, and should not be moved. Stem canker, caused by several fungi, can become a serious problem, especially for previously stressed trees.

USES: Screening, specimen, windbreak.

WILDLIFE: Primarily valuable as shelter for birds and small mammals.

PROPAGATION: Difficult from cuttings, moderately difficult from seed.

Cupressus arizonica 'Blue Ice'. Striking foliage, formal habit, and a tough, drought-tolerant constitution have made Arizona cypress cultivars like 'Blue Ice' favorite landscape plants in the Southwest.

Cupressus arizonica

Arizona cypress

ZONES: 7–9; sun
SOIL: Well-drained, moderately moist to dry
NATIVE TO: Canyons, open montane woodland, chaparral; scattered localities in Texas, New Mexico, Arizona, southern California, and Mexico
SIZE: Height 20–40 (75) feet, width 4–15 feet
COLOR: Green; blooms in spring

This handsome species reaches its greatest expression in the mountains of southern Arizona, where large old specimens with silver-blue needles mix with pines and junipers on higher slopes. It is a popular screening tree in the Southwest, offering gardeners transfixing needle color, beautiful peeling silver and brown bark, and a narrow, stiffly columnar form when young, becoming pyramidal with age. In the Southeast, it will perform best if planted on a well-drained, droughty soil with good air circulation around the canopy. Sargent cypress (*C. sargentii*) is a broad-crowned coastal Californian relative with glaucous foliage and dark gray bark. It is restricted to serpentine soils in the wild, but will grow on other substrates in cultivation. MacNab cypress (*C. macnabiana*) is an even wider-spreading dark green tree, with nearly horizontal branches and a short trunk. It is also a serpentine endemic from northern California.

Cupressus bakeri

Baker's Cypress, Modoc Cypress

ZONES: 5–7; sun
SOIL: Moist, well-drained
NATIVE TO: Mixed coniferous forest 3,000 to 7,000 feet in the mountains of northern California and southern Oregon
SIZE: Height 40–60 (70) feet, width 15–20 feet
COLOR: Green; blooms in spring

This cypress grows high in the Sierras and Cascades in the company of incense cedar and lodgepole pine. A rare species usually found in small stands stranded from each other by past volcanic eruptions that may have nearly extirpated it at one time, it has a tall narrow silhouette tapering to a rounded point, dark green needles, and shiny, reddish brown to gray bark covering a ramrod straight trunk. Baker's cypress is probably the only *Cupressus* species that is reliably hardy in the Northeast.

Cupressus macrocarpa

Monterey Cypress

ZONES: 7–9; sun, part sun
SOIL: Moist, well-drained
NATIVE TO: Coastal headlands on the Monterey Peninsula in California

SIZE: Height 30–40 (80) feet, width 15–30 feet
COLOR: Green; blooms in spring

Monterey cypress is the signature tree of the picturesque Monterey peninsula: its stunted, contorted form perfectly captures the mood of life at the edge of the Pacific. It is one of the rarest trees in the world, found only in two little groves on rocky cliffs in the fog belt, where dews and condensation help it through the summer drought. However, it has been widely planted along the Pacific coast as far north as Washington and is also used as a timber and specimen tree in the British Isles, Asia, and New Zealand, where the cool maritime climate is much to its liking. Away from the coastal wind and salt spray, it develops a narrow, pyramidal crown similar to that of its famous offspring, the Leyland cypress (× *Cupressocyparis leylandii*). Its needles are dark green, almost black, and its bark, shaggy gray.

Cyrilla racemiflora

Cyrilla racemiflora
(sye-RIL-a)
Cyrillaceae
Titi, Cyrilla, He-huckleberry

ZONES: 6–9; part sun, sun
SOIL: Moist to wet
NATIVE TO: Low sandy woods, pocosins, stream sides, and open shrub bogs; southeastern Virginia along the coast to Florida and Texas, south to Central America
SIZE: Height 4–15 (30) feet; width 4–8 feet
COLOR: Creamy white; blooms in summer

Titi (pronounced "tie-tie") is a familiar sight in the dense longleaf pinelands of the southern coastal

Cyrilla racemiflora. *Pyrotechnic floral displays are titi's claim to fame. The flowers give way to hard capsules that crack open when ripe to release dozens of small seeds. These germinate readily if scattered on the surface of damp soil and placed in a warm, bright location. Cyrilla is also easily rooted from cuttings taken when the plants are in flower.*

plain. Its preferred habitat is damp, sandy pocosins, where it sends up new shoots from the roots in ever-expanding colonies. Individual stems can be an inch or more in diameter, with leaves and branches clustered near their tops. The very fragrant off-white flowers are displayed in 3-to-10-inch long tasseled racemes that open from base to tip, and the masses of tiny flowers look beautiful framed against the shiny green leaves. The blooms burst exuberantly in all directions from just below the current year's growth like starburst fireworks, either splayed out horizontally amid the leaves or, more commonly, drooping down in long, lazy racemes. The plants have a weeping, soft-explosive appearance in bloom that is visually dynamic and beautiful, and they are always covered with pollinating bees out to make some titi honey back at the hive. The somewhat leathery leaves are 2 to 4 inches long and less than an inch wide with a rounded tip. Older leaves color red and drop in fall, but a few of the last leaves to form on the stem tips hang on through the winter.

Like most plants, titi exhibits some variation over its range, both in overall size and length of leaves. In Florida, several common ecotypes have been given their own names, including littleleaf titi *(C. parvifolia)*, with leaves about half the typical size, and *C. arida* (no common name is available, so how about pygmy titi), from sandy scrublands, which is smaller overall and a good candidate for dry, sandy soil.

Cliftonia monophylla (buckwheat bush, black titi) is a little-known relative from the boggy flatwoods and pocosins of Georgia and Florida to Louisiana. Out of flower it is difficult to tell it from *Cyrilla,* as it has similar leaves on short petioles arrayed along the twigs at fairly short intervals. Its leaves are darker in color, truly evergreen, and with a pale waxy bloom below. In flower, though, it is quite distinctive, with upright or arching spires of five-petaled flowers, each about ½ inch wide and tinted translucent white or sometimes light pink. The lightly but sweetly fragrant flowers grow from the tips of the previous year's growth in early spring before new leaves emerge on long, stiff racemes 4 to 8 inches in length. They explode out from among the leaves as do *Cyrilla*'s but the effect is more refined and demure. In habit this is a stiff shrub or small tree spreading (like many wetland species) into large, many-stemmed colonies with an open, informal character. As with *Cyrilla,* judicious pruning and shaping in winter will accentuate the form and make it suitable for more formal situations. Flowers are followed by four-winged capsules that are green at first, ripening light brown. These do bear an uncanny but purely coincidental resemblance to the fruits of wild buckwheat *(Eriogonum* spp.), and probably act as flotation devices to distribute the seed. Woodlanders Nursery in Aiken, South Carolina, has done much to promote this lovely evergreen, but it remains virtually un-

known, even in the Deep South where it thrives. It is hardy in Zones 7 to 9 and possibly mild Zone 6 (I am about to test some in our garden). It prefers damp, acid soil and full sun for best flowering.

CULTURE: I have grown *Cyrilla* both in North Carolina, where it can be trained into a narrow, semi-evergreen treelet if you remove most of the smaller suckers each winter, and in New England, where it remains a 3-to-4-foot rounded shrub tenaciously clinging to a few tattered and burned leaves by winter's end. In a sheltered garden in Zone 5, I got it to bloom well, but we have had trouble with it at Garden in the Woods (Zone 6), I think because it is planted down by the pond, where early and late frosts do not do it justice. The twigs die back in winter, which eliminates all the flower buds. Titi grows well at the New York Botanical Garden without any evidence of dieback. For best effect give it some sun and a moist to wet, acidic soil.

USES: Shrub border, pond side, naturalizing.

WILDLIFE: Excellent nectar plant for predatory wasps, day-flying moths, beetles, bees, and butterflies — it is always covered in insects when in bloom.

PROPAGATION: Easy from cuttings and seed.

Decumaria barbara

Decumaria barbara
(day-kew-MARE-ee-ah)
Hydrangeaceae
Wood Vamp, Climbing Hydrangea

ZONES: (5) 6–9; part sun to shade

SOIL: Moist, acidic, humus-rich

NATIVE TO: Damp woodlands, riverbanks, and swamps, on the trunks of canopy trees or scrambling over rocks and logs; Virginia to Florida and Louisiana

SIZE: Height 10–30 feet, depending on support, width 3–8 feet

COLOR: White; blooms in late spring to early summer

Decumaria barbara. *Wood vamp is a good, albeit deciduous, substitute for English ivy, a plant that is becoming invasive in parts of the southern United States and the Pacific Northwest.*

The word "vamp" can mean either a seductive woman or a patch used to cover something up, and though the origins of the name wood vamp are unclear, both meanings fit this scrambling, deciduous vine. *D. barbara* is closely related to hydrangea, and boasts alluring, deep green oval leaves narrowed to a pronounced, pointed tip. In the wild it is content trailing over rocks or logs, rooting as it goes in duffy soil, or climbing up the lower trunks of tall trees, its fat cinnamon brown stems sprouting a pelt of short, hairy roots that work into the tree's bark and anchor it firmly in place. In many ways it is our native equivalent for English ivy *(Hedera helix)* (albeit a deciduous one) in the glossy dark luster of the leaves, its clinging rootlets, and a proclivity toward flowering only when it has climbed up into the tree canopy. The flowers of *D. barbara* are soft and puffy looking, but not terribly showy, as they lack the ring of large, sterile bracts around the circumference that make many hydrangeas so colorful and bright. They grow in flat corymbs from the tips of the new growth as the leaves are finished expanding. Climbing hydrangea is a vigorous plant, and we had quite a patch of it growing almost to the point of weediness over a loblolly stump outside our office at Niche Gardens in North Carolina, from which we would readily pilfer rooted pieces to pot up and sell. This particular ground-bound plant never flowered, but we grew it mainly for the foliage, and—after the leaves yellowed and fell in autumn—for the twisted, woven mass of thick stems that was exposed all winter. We are growing this species at Garden in the Woods, and it has overwintered well in containers and also in the ground, though we have yet to find it a spot where it luxuriates as it does down South.

CULTURE: Wood vamp can handle considerable shade, though it grows best in light shade or morning sun with roots sunk in a rich, acidic, humus-rich soil with adequate moisture. It tolerates drought, but the vine shows its moderate displeasure by dropping some of its leaves prematurely. It does well as a solid groundcover under shrubs or trees, but is too vigorous to mix with herbaceous plants or other groundcovers. Shear back the stems in late winter if you need to temper its spread. Transplant from containers in spring or fall, or transplant rooted layers in early spring before new leaves emerge.

USES: As a deciduous groundcover for shade, or to skirt the lower trunks of trees.

PROPAGATION: Easy from cuttings, layers, and seed.

Diervilla lonicera

Diervilla (dye-er-VIL-la)
Caprifoliaceae
Bush-honeysuckle

Diervilla lonicera. *Bush-honeysuckle flowers form in the axils of the new growth, so blooming can last for several months as long as conditions favor continued growth. With this indeterminate habit, growth theoretically could continue indefinitely, but in reality it is cut short by the end of the growing season.*

I **have come to appreciate** the bush-honeysuckles for their ruggedness, long bloom, and freedom from pests and diseases. Certainly, they lack the star power of an azalea or ceanothus, but as we search for low-maintenance alternatives for difficult situations, the bush-honeysuckles are gaining the attention of nurseries and gardeners alike. Their leaves are either matte or glossy in finish, lance-shaped, tapered to a point, and paired on arching, deep red stems in a ranked arrangement a bit like that of forsythia. The foliage emerges with a copper wash which fades to green with a hint of red remaining on both the midvein and blade as the leaves mature. They do have that sort of caney, unfettered growth habit of forsythia, especially in richer soils, and a proclivity toward spreading from the roots quite joyously at times. This can pose problems in a small, crowded garden but it is a real advantage when you are trying to stabilize a bank or establish a mass planting. The flowers are tubular, split halfway up into 5 equal petals that curl outward and reflex back a bit. These grow in bunches from the axils of the topmost sets of leaves on each stem, much like the true honeysuckles. All the species have bright yellow blooms, which have the habit of reddening slightly as they are pollinated, adding to the generally multicolored effect of the shrub. The stem tips arch over toward the ground with the little trumpets held above them, where they can be noticed. If conditions are at all favorable, bush-honeysuckles will continue growing through the season, which means you can continue to enjoy highlights of bronze new growth and scattered flowers after the main flush has passed. The red color of new leaves, twigs, and veins is most noticeable in the sun. A few cultivars with bronzy leaves that turn reliably reddish purple or scarlet in the fall are available, as are compact forms with deeply colored flowers.

CULTURE: Easy to transplant into a range of soils. They will grow in fairly dry, well-drained soils and luxuriate in moist rich locations. A spot somewhere between the two will facilitate the restrained exuberance of the shrub at its best. We planted a few dwarf bush-honeysuckle (*D. lonicera*) in a chocolate, fertile soil recently, and the root sprouts are beginning to colonize a large area at an alarming rate. Nearby, in a summer-dry, partial-sun location, a southern bush-honeysuckle (*D. sessilifolia*) has stayed put and performed well for 20 years now, but certainly lacks the luster of the former in its favored root run. They will grow in fairly heavy shade but lose all ornamentality.

USES: Bank stabilization, massing.

WILDLIFE: Butterflies frequent the flowers, and because they can bloom for such an extended period, we have incorporated some into our butterfly garden.

PROPAGATION: Easy from cuttings, root cuttings, and seed.

Diervilla lonicera
Dwarf Bush-honeysuckle

ZONES: 3–7; sun to light shade
SOIL: Moist to dry
NATIVE TO: Rocky soils, cliffs, and forest gaps; Newfoundland to Saskatchewan south to Minnesota, Illinois, and Virginia, and in the Appalachians to North Carolina and Tennessee
SIZE: Height 2–4 feet, width 2–5 feet
COLOR: Sulfur yellow often fading red; blooms in summer to early fall

The genus divides neatly along the Mason-Dixon Line, with this smaller species to the north. The leaves, somewhat more oval than those of *D. sessilifolia,* sit on a short petiole. I have read in several books that this is the less vigorous of the two species, but I have found it just as strong in flower and leaf. It makes a nice subject for naturalizing and massing in the North.

Diervilla sessilifolia
Southern Bush-honeysuckle

ZONES: 4–8, sun to light shade
SOIL: Moist to dry
NATIVE TO: Woodlands, cliffs, rocky banks; mostly in the mountains from North Carolina to West Virginia south to Tennessee, Alabama, and Georgia

SIZE: Height 3–5 feet, width 3–6 feet
COLOR: Sulfur yellow often fading red; blooms in summer to early fall

D. sessilifolia seems to be more common in the nursery trade than *D. lonicera,* perhaps because of its larger size and lusty growth in a container. It will provide you a low-maintenance cover for difficult spots, and some of the tinted-leaved cultivars are quite beautiful. Nursery growers like them because they root easily and fill a pot quickly. Georgia bush-honeysuckle (*D. rivularis,* also listed as *D. sessilifolia* var. *rivularis*) is similar, though the leaves and twigs have a slight downy pubescence when young. It has a comparable range and habitat preference.

Diospyros virginiana

Diospyros (dye-oh-SPY-ros)
Ebenaceae
Persimmon

Diospyros is a Greek word meaning "fruit of Zeus," or "fruit of the gods," a moniker you will no doubt dispute if you happen to bite into an unripe persimmon. The small, squishy fruits of our native species are quite delicious when fully ripe, with the same smoky-sweet taste of the cultivated varieties, but immature fruits are loaded with tannin that will pucker your mouth better than ten lemons. Persimmons are lovely trees with clean, glossy leaves, dark green in summer and rich reddish purple in fall, beautiful bark, and a well-mannered habit, so it is a mystery to me why they are so uncommon in gar-

Diospyros virginiana.
Delectable persimmons can be yellowish, red, orange, or nearly black when ripe. To avoid a tongue-puckering surprise you'll not soon forget, eat only soft, fully ripe fruits (the flesh should give way to light pressure, much like an overripe avocado).

dens. The trunk has the same dark heartwood as the timber ebony, but trees rarely get to timber size (the ebony used in woodworking is obtained from a tropical species, *D. ebenum*). Our common species is a plant of fencerows and forest margins, much like sassafras, spreading by root sprouts to form little groves or thickets if conditions are right. The new twigs and even the petioles can be tinted bright red, and in late spring the young twigs are decorated with small but very fragrant flowers that look like the little urns of blueberries and huckleberries. These are white at the base with four flaring tips painted soft yellow and splashed like a jam pot with a bit of purply-red inside. Male trees bear clusters of 2 to 3 flowers in each axil, while female trees produce only one flower per leaf, which are also larger and already subtended by the four-part calyx that forms the little hat on ripe fruit. These fruits (technically they are berries) are 1–1½ inches in diameter, usually apricot flushed with red or purple when ripe and masked with a gray, waxy bloom. Occasionally even almost black-fruited trees (*D. virginiana* forma *atra*) can be found. Female plants selected for their good-flavored fruits are occasionally offered as grafted stock. If you raise your own trees, plan on growing up three to four plants and then, to ensure pollination, thinning out all but one male once they have begun flowering (this takes 5 to 7 years when grown from seed). Ripe fruit should be soft, and it will drop from the tree late in the year once it is ready. Don't shake the partially ripe fruits down unless you are prepared to leave them ripening indoors for a few weeks. The fruits are full of seeds, so they are best used in pies, jams, or jellies or made into wine, which can be distilled into potent 'simmon beer—just the thing to sip during those cold winter nights with your feet up by the fire.

CULTURE: Persimmons have interesting black fleshy roots, and I have had no trouble transplanting bareroot seedlings or container plants. They have a reputation, like sassafras, for being difficult to transplant that may come from people trying to dig and move root sprouts, which lack the fortitude to make it on their own. The seedlings grow easily enough, so I would recommend collecting some fruits and starting some this way. They grow in a range of soils, and I have often seen them coming up into worn-out agricultural land stripped of everything good and gracious by years of overfarming. They will also thrive in richer soils, but cannot compete with faster-growing species on such sites without your help. Like many colonizing trees, if conditions are good and you allow the trunk to go unmolested, persimmons will rarely sucker badly. They seem generally free from disease, though fall webworms (*Hyphantria cunea*) can be a problem some years, forming ghostly veils over the branches and partially defoliating the tree. (Interestingly, fall webworm is one of the few insects native to North America that have escaped in Eurasia and it is now becoming an uncontrolled pest there.)

USES: Naturalizing along forest margins and fencerows, home orchard.

WILDLIFE: When persimmons flower, they positively roar with the accumulated fluttering of myriad pollinators. The fruits are important fall and winter food for many mammals, including deer, opossum, raccoon, and even bears fattening up to sleep away the winter (isn't that a nice thought).

PROPAGATION: Easy from seed.

Diospyros texana
Chapote, Texas Persimmon

ZONES: (6)7–9; sun, part sun
SOIL: Well-drained, moist to dry
NATIVE TO: Rich bottomlands, fencerows, even dry outcrops; Texas south into Mexico
SIZE: Height 10–40 feet, width 7–20 feet
COLOR: White and yellow; blooms in late spring

Chapote rivals sycamore and even madrone in its beautiful exfoliating bark, which is reddish brown to gray, sloughing off to reveal chalky white patches underneath. Chapote grows as a multistemmed small tree or suckering shrub in the drier half of Texas, holding on to some or all of its leaves during winter in the southern part of its range. The 1-inch, hairy black fruits are interesting ornamentally, but full of seeds and not too tasty. They will stain everything—including your tongue, if you wish to scare your loved ones—a nice shade of grayish black. It is certainly one of the finest small trees for ornamental winter bark, though it needs a warm, fairly dry climate to grow well. The fruits, and perhaps the leaves as well, release allelopathic (growth-inhibiting) chemicals that retard other plants, and this may explain why the trees can become a problem on rangelands.

Diospyros virginiana
Common Persimmon, Possumwood

ZONES: 4–9; sun to part sun
SOIL: Moist to dry
NATIVE TO: Thickets, forest margins, and hedgerows; southern Connecticut to Iowa and Kansas south to Texas and Florida
SIZE: Height 30–50 feet, width 15–25 feet
COLOR: White and yellow; blooms in late spring

The bark of older trunks takes on a thick, alligator-hide checking that is very attractive. The species reaches its northeastern limit near New Haven, Connecticut, and I have grown plants descended from this population, not so much for winter hardiness as earlier fruit ripening. Trees of southern provenance don't finish ripening if we have an early winter.

Dirca palustris

Dirca (DER-ka)
Thymelaeaceae
Leatherwood, Wicopy

Dirca palustris.
*Leatherwood turns a
unique pale yellow in
fall, a color that lights
up the shade like a sun-
beam on a cloudy day.
Dirca actually prefers
light shade to sun, mak-
ing it a valuable speci-
men shrub for woodland
gardens.*

Leatherwood is yet another unique native shrub unaccountably absent from cultivated landscapes. It has grayish brown bark covering twigs possessing a strange, rubbery flexibility that suggests the common name (the elastic bark was used by Native American peoples for bow strings). These twigs get quite knobby, both where they join branches and where they attach to the leaf petioles, and this knuckled appearance carries on into the larger branches as well. These put on girth out of all proportion with their size, so a well-grown plant has a pleasantly bloated silhouette, with a swollen trunk and forking branches tapering quickly to knobby twigs, like a miniaturized oak tree. It is the same "big tree in miniature" aesthetic that makes bonsai so appealing, and I can't think of any other shrub that carries it off so well without pruning or shaping. Early in spring, just as the leaf buds are beginning to expand, little tubular flowers with protruding stamens poke out from between the bud scales and hang down like little chartreuse earrings. It is a subdued floral effect, but charming in its own way on the stocky, naked branches. You can even cut the branches in late winter and force the flowers indoors, to nice effect. As the leaves continue to expand they become egg-shaped and matte gray-green above and grayish white below. In fall, these turn a unique shade of soft yellow to almost white mixed with green.

Leatherwood is a refined plant for the woodland garden but lacks the "container appeal" so important in our modern-day cash-and-carry nursery business, and I imagine this partially explains its scarcity in the trade. The seeds ripen very early, one day hanging

like little olives among the leaves and the next dropping off and disappearing with nary a hint of color change. They are hydrophilic and, interestingly, germinate best if sown immediately outdoors with the pulp still attached. Dry seed or seed that has been kept in the refrigerator and the greenhouse will stubbornly refuse to germinate. Peter Del Tredici wrote a very humorous article about his trials and tribulations that is well worth the read (in *Arnoldia* 44 (1): 20–24). Since nursery people have their hands full with many other things in late spring, it is easy to miss the fruits, and the problem of production becomes clearer. We had two beautiful specimens below the nursery that I collected seed from, but an early, wet snow bent one down so far that it split apart where the two main branches met. I bolted these together to cinch up the break, but the wound never healed and we eventually removed it (the stump didn't resprout as so many shrubs do). After that, fruit production on the other one dropped way off until I planted another for cross-pollination. When I worked at the Connecticut Agricultural Experiment Station, we had two monstrously thick leatherwoods in our native shrub display garden, and under these was a solid carpet of seedlings.

CULTURE: Best in moist, slightly acid to neutral soils with protection from the noon sun. Plants in the full sun bleach out where the leaves face the sun, and the shrubs are definitely happier in a partial shade or even heavily shaded situation. In the wild I have seen them mostly in alluvial woodlands, where they tend to be sparse and twiggy from competition. The biggest problem is breakage at narrow crotches, for although the branches are extremely flexible, they attach at narrow angles that makes snow and ice loads a danger. It will help greatly if you try to shape the young plant to one central trunk for the first 12 inches.

USES: Specimen for the shade or woodland garden, planted where its form can be appreciated all year long.

PROPAGATION: Moderately difficult from seed.

Dirca occidentalis
Western Leatherwood

ZONES: 6–8; partial sun to shade
SOIL: Moist
NATIVE TO: Moist, wooded hills around San Francisco Bay
SIZE: Height 2–6 feet, width 3–4 feet
COLOR: Yellow-green; blooms in late winter to early spring

This very rare species is probably the remnant of a population stranded and cut off from the larger eastern range of *D. palustris* because of climate change. It differs mainly in the color of the ripe drupe — dull red as opposed to the yellow-green of *D. palustris*.

Dirca palustris
Leatherwood, Wicopy

ZONES: 3–8; part sun to shade
SOIL: Moist, tolerates pH from 5.5 to 8.5
NATIVE TO: Rich alluvial woods, bottomlands, and swamp margins, often over limestone; Nova Scotia and southern Quebec, Ontario, and Minnesota, south to Iowa and Missouri and western North Carolina and Virginia, with scattered populations throughout the Gulf Coast states
SIZE: Height 3–6 feet, width 4–6 feet
COLOR: Light yellow-green; blooms in early spring

Dryas (DRY-as)
Rosaceae
Mountain Avens, Dryas

Dryas octopetala

It is tremendously illuminating to study a plant in the wild that you had previously known only in cultivation. Recently I had the chance to follow a friend of mine, the dedicated botanist George Newman, around the Gaspé Peninsula of Quebec, an amazing geological amalgamation of limestone, serpentine, and granite that hosts a fantastic blend of northern, eastern, and western species all within a day's drive of Montreal. One of the interesting things we saw were great mats of yellow avens (*D. drummondii*) growing on a cobbled limestone bar in one of the major rivers. I had tried unsuccessfully to establish this plant in a well-drained, south-facing rock garden, not realizing that what it really wants is a moraine, with excellent drainage but a free flow of cooling water running beneath.

Mountain avens are charming, low evergreen shrubs for the rock garden that are well worth establishing if you can find the right spot. They creep out slowly from a central crown on radiating woody stems bristling with persistent petioles and set with whorls of small, narrow, leathery leaves finely scalloped along their edges. These are puckered and rich, deep green on the upper side and more or less white, wild, and woolly-waxy beneath. *Dryas* are actinorhizal plants supremely well adapted to growing along the fringes of melting glaciers where the soil is tousled, rocky, and low in fertility. Typically, they grow in limestone areas, though they seem to adapt to acidic soils pretty well in cultivation. Before the new leaves emerge, the mats erect very large, upfacing flowers that are yellow or white, typically with eight petals and a dense puff of stamens in the center. As the flowers set seed, the pedicels elongate to lift the heads up into the wind and each seed grows a long fuzzy tail to aid its eventual flight. The developing seed heads have a frenetic energy pleasingly in contrast to the calm green mats of leaves. As new foliage grows, the leaves that are on the lower side of the wood splay flat on the ground while those on the upper side angle upward, so both the white undersides and dark tops of some leaves are visible from any perspective.

CULTURE: Though growing these little shrubs is not terribly difficult, they are challenging enough to give them an aura of respectability among the loftiest rock gardening circles. Choose a spot that is shaded in the afternoon and has soil amply amended with gravel but that does not dry out terribly (try adding some peaty duff as well). We had white mountain avens (*D. octopetala*) growing for many, many years in our rock garden (they were, sadly, finished off by a herd of deer three years ago) whose mat would wax and wane a bit through the years, but it always put up at least a few lovely flowers in spring. These are not plants for hot, humid summers, but otherwise they are pretty trouble-free once established. Transplant them from containers in spring and water them carefully the first year. The trailing stems root a bit as they go, and you can snip off a section and establish it as you would a cutting and then set it out.

USES: Specimen or groundcover in the rock garden.

PROPAGATION: Moderately difficult from cuttings and seed.

Dryas octopetala.
White mountain avens holds its pure white blooms proudly above mats of foliage on long, slender stems. As the flowers turn to seed, this patch will be awash in bearded gray, tousled heads.

Dryas drummondii
Yellow Avens

ZONES: 2–6; part sun
SOIL: Well-drained, slightly acidic to basic, moist
NATIVE TO: Gravel bars, limestone scree, tundra, and sandy deposits; Alberta to Alaska south to the Cascades into Washington, to the Rocky Mountains into Montana, and in the East to northern Ontario and Quebec
SIZE: Height 1–6 inches, width 1–2 feet
COLOR: Light yellow; blooms in early spring

Although the flowers of yellow avens never open completely, it is still an attractive plant, with stubby, elliptical leaves heavily ridged and dark green above and white woolly below.

Dryas octopetala
White Mountain Avens

ZONES: 2–6; part sun
SOIL: Well-drained, slightly acidic to basic, moist
NATIVE TO: Gravel bars, scree, tundra, and sandy deposits; circumboreal, in North America from Greenland to Alaska south in the Rocky Mountains to Montana and British Columbia
SIZE: Height 1–6 inches, width 1–2 feet
COLOR: White; blooms in early spring

This is a bit larger in overall habit than *D. drummondii,* with cheery, up-facing flowers that open flat. It has a scalloped margin to the leaves, which distinguishes it from *D. integrifolia,* which has smooth, revolute margins but is otherwise similar.

Elaeagnus commutatus. *Silverberry's striking pewter cast comes in part from the myriad waxy scales that cover its leaves, twigs, and fruits. The scales refract light like tiny lenses, so the plants shimmer with a metallic sparkle unmatched by most other silver-leaved shrubs.*

Elaeagnus commutatus

Elaeagnus commutatus
(ee-lee-AG-nus)
Elaeagnaceae
Silverberry

ZONES: 2–6; sun
SOIL: Well-drained, slightly acidic to alkaline
NATIVE TO: Sandy or gravelly soils and plains, slopes, riverbanks, and shores; northern Ontario to Alaska, south to British Columbia, in the Rockies to Colorado, and east to western Minnesota and Iowa with isolated populations in eastern Quebec
SIZE: Height 1–7 feet, width 3–8 feet
COLOR: Silvery yellow; blooms in late spring to early summer

Two non-native *Eleagnus* species, Russian olive (*E. angustifolia*) and autumn olive (*E. umbella-*

ta), have become scourges in the East. They were originally distributed by federal, state, and local government agencies to stabilize soil and provide food and habitat for wildlife, but they have run amok, taking over abandoned fields with a vengeance and shading out native shrubs that would normally grow in these successional habitats. As a point of contrast I present to you our native species, *E. commutatus*. Silverberry is a low, suckering shrub of poor, stony soils and windswept plains. An actinorhizal species, it thrives in that big section of central Canada and the northern tier of the United States that is always shaded the coldest color on TV weather maps. Silverberry's leaves are strikingly beautiful, dressed in silky pewter that seems to literally shine softly in the sun. Its weedy cousins from the Old World are more of a dirty gray in color. Silverberry's leaves are elliptical if laid flat, but the leaf margins turn up and crinkle a bit, so the foliage looks somewhat lance-shaped and fluted in outline. Small, four-petaled tubular flowers are borne in clusters in the axils of the leaves as new growth matures, and they emit a delicious spicy fragrance that perfumes the air. The leaf petioles and young twigs are cinnamon brown and are overlain with the silvery brown scales that scatter over the berries and give the shrub its name. These berries are green turning orange then red with a metallic sheen, and birds readily devour them. Older branches develop a shiny mahogany bark and a gnarled twisted shape.

Though silverberry is one of our most beautiful shrubs in foliage effect, its running habit makes it difficult to use in all but very naturalized situations or contained areas like parking lot strips. In my experience, it spreads easily but lacks the inherent aggressiveness of autumn olive. It is a shimmering shrub valuable for birds, and perfect for massing in difficult, windswept locations in the North.

CULTURE: Prefers well-drained, nutrient-poor soils and full sun. I have seen it growing on limestone soils, so I imagine a near neutral to alkaline pH is preferred. The stolons run fairly deep in the soil, making rooted sections difficult to separate with enough roots to survive. Transplants easily from containers in spring.

USES: Massing in difficult areas, bank stabilization.

PROPAGATION: Easy from seed.

Elliottia racemosa.
Georgia plume's flowers form at the tips of new twigs, coming in a flush in summer and continuing sporadically into fall.

Elliottia racemosa

Elliottia racemosa
(ell-ee-OT-tia)
Ericaceae
Georgia Plume

ZONES: 6–9; sun to light shade

SOIL: Moist, well-drained, acidic

NATIVE TO: Pine-oak savanna and sand ridges, mostly along the coastal plain of Georgia and possibly South Carolina

SIZE: Height 5–25 feet, width 5-15 feet

COLOR: White; blooms in mid- to late summer, often then sporadically into fall

The southeastern United States has a staggering diversity of woody plants, including many relict or isolated genera, like *Nevusia, Torreya,* and *Elliottia,* that have managed to hang on, but barely, through the millennia and others, like *Franklinia,* that have not. The Appalachians are one of the oldest mountain ranges in the world, and at one time, according to evidence derived from the study of plate tectonics, the Southeast was at the center of the supercontinent Pangea, which was thus literally the core of the world. *E. racemosa* is a plant that *looks* old in an evolutionary sense. There is something of a work in progress about it that is at once charming and curious, a stilted, uncomplicated beauty that makes it both a stunning garden shrub and a fascinating study in persistence and the will to survive. Georgia plume's foliage reminds me a bit of sourwood (*Oxydendrum arboreum*) in both shape and arrangement—3 to 6 inches long and lance-shaped, with margins rolled up a bit along the edges and narrowed to a long point. The leaves alternate along the twigs but are separated by such short internodes as to appear almost whorled. The plants I've grown have shed some of their leaves that were still green, and others turned a mix of brilliant scarlet, yellow, and purple before falling. The fragrant flowers are carried on long spikes out away from the foliage at the tips of the new growth as it matures, much like bottlebrush buckeye without the frills. The plant keeps growing late into the season, and flower spikes appear in a flush in summer, then sporadically into early fall. They have five petals that separate and splay outward from a shallow tube, as do some of the azaleas. It is a denizen of sandhills and oak-pine forest along the coastal plain, where fire is common in dry summers. Accordingly, it forms suckering, scrubby thickets of rather stiff, fast-growing stems reddish brown in color that resprout liberally from the roots after disturbance.

Elliottia was discovered by Steven Elliot in Waynesboro, Georgia, around 1800 and later across the Savannah River in South Carolina. For many years after that, it was feared that it had been driven extinct by land clearing for agriculture around the original locality, until populations were eventually relocated there and also in central Georgia. The Arnold Arboretum has been working with this very rare species for many years, and Al Fordham, the former propagator who, sadly, passed away in 2000, worked out methods to propagate it so that plants could be

Ephedra viridis. Once you get past the strange, leafless appearance of green jointfir, you'll find that it offers interesting textural possibilities in the dry-land garden.

distributed to various public gardens and arboreta. Like *Franklinia* and *Stewartia,* among others, Georgia plume is surprisingly hardy north of its almost subtropical home. The important thing to realize is that it goes dormant very slowly in the fall, especially when young and growing vigorously. This is not a problem in south Georgia, where winter creeps in gently, but farther north the plants are subject to winterkill when cold comes fast and hard. The Arnold Arboretum tried three or four times to get the plants established, but without success, and finally resorted to digging them up and putting them into cold storage every year. A larger plant was left in the ground one fall and it has thrived ever since (this is similar to my experience with *Franklinia).* Young seedlings need to be protected for the first three winters, until the plants adjust, growth moderates, and they begin to go dormant earlier in the fall. We wrap young trees in a tent of closed-cell foam insulation (Microfoam) and then a sheet of white plastic supported by a teepee of tomato stakes. The tent is constructed in mid-November and removed in March. This may sound extreme, but it makes a big difference when trying to establish marginal species should you be so inclined.

Tar-flower *(Befaria racemosa),* also called flycatcher, is a relative from similar habitats along the coast of southeastern Georgia south into central Florida. It is a 3-to-6-foot shrub with stiff branches and alternate, dusty gray, narrowly oval leaves sessile on the stems. Its flowers stand above the plant proudly on loosely branched inflorescences, opening during the summer as new growth matures. These remind me of rhodora *(Rhododendron canadense)* or even the herbaceous guara *(Guara lindheimeri)* in shape—the loose, spoon-shaped white or pink petals are stained deep pink at the base and spread wide like a wagon wheel with a tuft of stamens in the center. Unlike rhododendrons, though, each flower has 6 to 7 petals, and the blooms emit a light, sweet fragrance. The calyx and resulting seed capsule are tacky and resinous, hence the common names. It is a spectacular sight in full flower, a perfect blend of gangliness and grace that rivals many perennials in the exuberance of its bloom, but without the refinement necessary to be accepted easily by the horticulture industry. It is hardy in Zones (7)8–9.

CULTURE: *Elliottia* transplants readily from containers or as sections grubbed out from the periphery of an established clump in early spring. Plant them in a moist but well-drained acidic soil. In the Southeast, it may suffer from *Phytophthora* in heavy soils and needs to be sited accordingly.

USES: Specimen, massing.

WILDLIFE: Excellent nectar plants for many insects.

PROPAGATION: Moderately difficult from root cuttings, difficult from seed.

Ephedra viridis

Ephedra (ef-FED-ra)
Ephedraceae
Jointfir, Mormon Tea, Ephedra

Ephedra species certainly rank as one of the weirdest bunch of shrubs covered in this book. They are gymnosperms distantly related to *Taxus,* but they look more like a twiggy horsetail *(Equisetum* spp.) than a conifer. Mormon tea has gotten quite a bit of press lately because of its widespread use as an herbal stimulant for weight loss and bodybuilding. The shrub's tissues contain high concentrations of ephedrine alkaloids, including ephedrine, pseudoephrine, norpseudoephedrine, norephedrine, and methyl ephedrine. These are precursors of many synthetic amphetamines, and increase heart rate, blood pressure, and alertness and lessen appetite and fatigue. Ma huang *(E. sinica)* is an Asian species that is most commonly used in herbal preparations, but all *Ephedra* species contain some cocktail of these alkaloids. A recent study ("Adverse Cardiovascular and Central Nervous System Events Associated with Dietary Supplements Containing Ephedra Alkaloids," *New England Journal of Medicine* 343: 1833–38) linked consumption of the drug to stroke, seizures, and death in otherwise healthy young subjects—findings that illustrate the dangers one risks when taking unrefined herbal medications. The genus favors dry, desert habitats where food is sparse and nutrients precious, and so the plants produce these chemicals as a defense against herbivores. Obviously the chemicals are effective, because the plants thrive and grow without the benefit of thorns or spines in areas where grazing is widespread. Cattle do eat them, which makes one wonder whether they enjoy a little jolt once in a while.

Jointfirs have the same whisk-broomy habit as Scotch broom *(Cytissus),* with needles reduced almost to nonexistence on stiff, grooved, photosynthetic stems. New branches grow in pairs or whorls and bear either male or female cones along their length in winter or early spring. The male plants develop cones in fall and these overwinter as little green nubs, then send out bright yellow anthers from under each scale in spring, turning the plants the color of hardened butter for a few weeks. Female plants produce one or two hard, teardrop-shaped seeds, and the bracts of their cones are translucent yellow, orange, red, or a less vibrant brown. Once you get used to the "knocking on heaven's door" quality of these leafless, twiggy gymnosperms in an otherwise verdant summer landscape, they can be quite effective textural accents in the dry-land garden. Older branches develop gray or brown bark and tend to lean or sprawl under the weight of dense tufts of younger, stiffly ascending stems. The overall habit is a finely textured mound usually wider than tall.

CULTURE: The adaptability of these curious plants has left me pleasantly surprised. While certainly not fast-growing, both *E. nevadensis* and *E. viridis* have done well in a sunny, gravelly spot in our dry-land garden. I have yet to try some of the others, but I suspect these two may be the most amenable. Overall, many of the jointfirs are very similar in garden effect, so I have not gone out of my way to establish a comprehensive collection. It is normal for the plants to dry out and die back some in winter, with new growth returning in a flush in spring. From my experience, they are pretty fibrous-rooted and transplant fairly easily provided you site them correctly. We do not provide any supplemental water or fertilizer.

USES: Accent and textural effect in the dry-land or xeriscaped garden.

PROPAGATION: Moderately easy from seed.

Ephedra culteri
Navajo Ephedra

ZONES: 5–8; sun

SOIL: Well-drained, dry

NATIVE TO: Sandy flats and rocky slopes; centered in the Four Corners area of Colorado, Utah, Arizona, and New Mexico

SIZE: Height 1–3 feet, width 3–6 feet

COLOR: Male cones yellow, female cones yellow-brown; blooms in late winter to spring

A fine-textured rhizomatous species forming spreading colonies of bright green stems turning yellow-green in winter. From a distance it looks almost like grass sprouting from stocky, chestnut-colored trunks.

Ephedra nevadensis
Nevada Jointfir

ZONES: 5–8; sun

SOIL: Well-drained, dry

NATIVE TO: Dry slopes and rocky hills; southwestern Utah through Nevada to southern Oregon, south to southern California and northwestern Arizona

SIZE: Height 8–28 inches, width 1–2 feet

COLOR: Male cones yellow, female cones yellow and green tinged with pink; blooms in late winter to spring

Nevada jointfir is sparser in branch than the other species, so it has a coarser texture in the garden, with a low-mounded habit and stems at first gray-green, aging to gray.

Ephedra torreyana
Mormon Tea

ZONES: 5–9; sun

SOIL: Well-drained, dry

NATIVE TO: Rock or sandy flats and slopes; western Texas through New Mexico and western Colorado to Utah, Arizona and southern Nevada

SIZE: Height 1–3 feet, width 1–3 feet

COLOR: Male cones yellow, females cones green to yellow-orange; blooms in spring

Typically a stiffly upright shrub with leaves and branches in sets of threes. The twigs are blue-green fading to gray with age. Other related species include Death Valley jointfir *(E. funerea)*, which has funereal, bone-gray stems and is found only in the Great Basin desert along the California-Nevada border, and Mexican tea *(E. trifurca)*, the tallest species, which becomes a large shrub 15 feet high and wide in favored spots and has pale green twigs and fissured gray bark. It ranges along the U.S. border with Mexico and south.

Ephedra viridis
Green Jointfir

ZONES: (4)5–8; sun

SOIL: Well-drained, dry

NATIVE TO: Rocky slopes and canyon walls; western Colorado and southwestern Wyoming through Utah and Nevada to California south to northern Arizona and the Four Corners area of New Mexico.

SIZE: Height 1–4 feet, width 2–3 feet

COLOR: Male and female cones yellow-green; blooms in spring

This is one of the most ornamental jointfirs, boasting bright green twigs fading to a deep gray-green in winter and a dense, upright growth of wispy branches supported by silvery gray trunks.

Fagus grandifolia. A grove of American beeches is a delight for the senses. In spring the large, pointed buds unfold into soft green leaves; in summer the high, dense canopy offers cool respite from the heat; in fall the leaves turn magnificent shades of primrose yellow and auburn; and in winter the magnificent elephant-hide trunks rise amid persistent brown leaves rustling in the breeze.

Fagus grandifolia

Fagus grandifolia
(FAY-gus)
Fagaceae
American Beech

ZONES: 4–9; sun to shade

SOIL: Moist

NATIVE TO: Rich woodlands, deciduous and mixed forest; Nova Scotia to southern Quebec and southern Ontario to eastern Minnesota south to Illinois, Missouri, and eastern Texas and northern Florida

SIZE: Height 50–70 (90) feet, width 25–50 (100) feet

COLOR: Yellow-brown; blooms in spring

One of the strangest things that has ever happened to me in the woods centers around a large (16-inch-diameter) beech. I was out with a botany class in a rich woodland one spring day—one of those days when the air is sweet and still and the birds are chirping away—when we heard a slight popping and cracking, looked back, and saw the mighty beech we had just walked under slowly tear up its roots and come crashing down. I can only imagine that some combination of root trauma, latent winter injury, and newly softened, muddy soil coupled with the increasing weight of a new crop of leaves finally brought about the tree's inevitable surrender to gravity. Most likely it had been slowly tilting farther and farther over for some time, and we just happened to be there to see the result. We see trees down in the woods all the time, but witnessing one's sudden and unexplainable top-

pling is something else, like seeing a great whale beach itself for no apparent reason. Was it a sign, a portent, a gift, or just the random coincidence of paths crossing at the right second in time? The image has remained vividly etched in my memory ever since.

Of course, beech trees don't fall over easily. Beech is one of the grandest, most majestic of our eastern trees; slower in growth than maple, oak, or elm, but capable of inching up under their canopy and eventually replacing them in the sun. Like aspen and sassafras, beech is a master at vegetative reproduction. Its roots are shallow and wide-spreading, liberally initiating new sprouts that ring older trees like a dense family of seedlings and saplings in various stages of maturity. Whether it is some combination of allelopathy, dense shade, or aggressive roots, nothing much can survive under a mature beech except its own root sprouts. These draw sustenance from the main trunk and are thus able to grow quickly and relentlessly upward in shade that would stifle a seedling that had to fend for itself. It is more likely that you will see groves of beech than single specimens, all linked to one original root system as one supertree. Interestingly, beech trees in the southern United States are less likely to send up root sprouts than they are in the North. Whether this is a climatic or genetic effect is unclear.

American beech is one of the most easily identifiable trees in the eastern forests. Its pewter gray bark is smooth to the eye and rough to the touch like the skin of an elephant. Even young trees develop a rippled, fluted trunk that bulges below each branch to suggest tendons flexed in an effort to keep the leaves aloft. Just as familiar as the pachyderm bark are the hopes and admonitions of young lovers carved crudely into it whenever a beech grows near a sylvan path. They carry these brands—"DL loves MR," "Josh Was Here '77," "School Sucks"—for decades, the letters slowly stretching and fading in the cracked and roughened, healed-over surface.

Beech trees produce a thick, verdant leaf canopy supported by a dense network of fine gray branches tipped in winter by large, chestnut-brown, spear-point-shaped buds. Each leaf emerges a striking chartreuse, and a silvery grove hung with developing leaves is a beautiful sight. The foliage matures to glossy, dark green, each leaf with a regularly toothed margin and a visible network of herringbone veins that give the blade a pleated texture, especially as it emerges and again as it fades. Finally, the leaves develop a burnt sugar and gold fall color that glows resplendent once again against the silvery gray bark. Many of the lower leaves dry and curl to a warm tan but hang on the branches until spring. As the leaves are turning, spiny capsules along the twigs open up and drop three-sided, teardrop-shaped beechnuts on the ground for squirrels, chipmunks, and jays to gather. The tree relies on abundance to ensure dispersal. If it drops enough of the ½-inch nuts, the animals will carry them off and sequester them in larders, where a few may lie forgotten until they can germinate and unfurl their large cotyledons in spring.

CULTURE: The American beech is a magnificent tree, but its sheer size and habit of forming a tangle of root suckers (unlike the European species, *F. sylvatica*) make it difficult to incorporate into smaller properties. Further, the dense crown makes cultivating anything but moss underneath it impossible unless the tree is limbed far up the trunk and supplemental water and fertilizer are provided each year. Although root sprouts are impossible to move, small, container-grown seedlings as well as balled and burlaped saplings can be transplanted successfully in spring or fall. The trees prefer fertile soil and moisture, which helps them fend off beech bark disease, an often fatal combined attack of two imported pathogens that has destroyed hundreds of thousands of trees since it was accidentally introduced into Nova Scotia around 1920 on trees imported from Europe. A cottony scale insect begins the attack, colonizing patches of the smooth bark and causing lesions that are disposed to infection by nectria bark canker (*Nectria coccinea* var. *faginata*). The cankers develop large sunken lesions on the trunk, which can kill the tree. Spotted, roughened bark erupts with crimson fruiting bodies (tiny spherical mushrooms) in fall. Fortunately, healthy trees can resist attack by the scale and subsequent infection by the fungus. A mature wild tree in my parents' yard has had some scale for as long as I can remember, but it shows no sign of stress other than some roughened patches of bark. It is growing in a rich, moist soil, as are many of the native beech in the area. During the gypsy moth outbreaks of the 1960s and '70s, repeatedly defoliated trees often died from beech bark disease, but now that the moth has come under natural control, this added stress is no longer nearly the problem that it was.

USES: Specimen and shade tree for large properties, naturalizing in woodland.

WILDLIFE: An important mast species for small birds and mammals as well as deer, turkey, and grouse. The larvae of the turquoise hairstreak (*Erora laeta*) and eastern oak dusky wing (*Erynnis juvenalis*) are known to feed on the leaves.

PROPAGATION: Moderately difficult from seed.

Fallugia paradoxa

Fallugia paradoxa
(fa-LEW-gia)
Rosaceae
Apache Plume

ZONES: 5–9; sun

SOIL: Well-drained, dry

NATIVE TO: Foothills, canyons, and washes; Colorado to southeastern California south to Arizona, western Texas, and northern Mexico

SIZE: Height 3–6 feet, width 3–6 feet

COLOR: White; blooms in spring to summer, as weather permits

Among the many plants I've killed, Apache plume remains a solid favorite. In the Southwest, it is an easy and vigorous shrub that forms dense, spreading mounds of woolly brown twigs and shaggy gray trunks dotted through the growing season with demure, five-petaled flowers. These are shaped like wild roses with margins and tips rolled back informally, cupping a yellow puff of stamens. The plants are either male or female, though female plants sport a beard of sterile anthers in the center so the effect is the same. Flowers grow on long, thin, nearly leafless branchlets that spurt out from the mass of foliage to display the blooms to good advantage. The female flowers produce wispy cat-tail styles that lengthen as the seeds mature and take on a striking rosy purple hue before drying to warm gray. Since the plants bloom over the course of the summer, there are always flowers and, on the females, fruits in various stages of colorful development. The leaves are small and stiff with that healthy, dark green glow that comes from a diet rich in nitrogen. They grow in little fascicles of 2 or 3 that alternate up the thin twigs; they sometimes persist through the winter. They have a three-toed shape with the center one forked again into three smaller toes. Thus the plant has a pleasing, fine dark texture that is a fitting backdrop for the blooms and seed.

CULTURE: As I have discovered after several years of failure, Apache plume has little patience for high humidity. It is an easy species to germinate and grow, provided you can give it well-drained soil, strong sun, and the sort of air that parches the lips and dries the throat. It is a common species in the Southwest, and has found its way into the nursery trade there as

Fallugia paradoxa. *Apache plume is a fabulous plant for a dry climate. It is fast-growing and requires little in the way of fertilizer or supplemental water. Prune out older stems during the winter to keep the clump vigorous and shapely.*

well. Transplant small, container-grown seedlings, or sow the seed directly in place at the beginning of the summer rainy season. *Fallugia* is an actinorhizal (nitrogen-fixing) genus related to *Cercocarpus*. *Frankia* inoculation can be accomplished as for *Alnus*. Since both sexes are necessary for fruit production, allow at least 3 to 4 seedlings to grow, or propagate sexed plants by stem cuttings or division. A bit of supplemental water during the summer will help prolong blooming. The plants can be cut back hard in late winter to rejuvenate them.

USES: Massing, hedging, xeriscaping.

PROPAGATION: Moderately difficult from cuttings and seed.

Fothergilla major

Fothergilla (foth-er-GIL-ah)
Hamamelidaceae
Fothergilla, Witch-alder

Fothergilla major.
Among the many large fothergillas in our garden collections, one plant consistently develops intense, red-orange fall color. It is a self-sown seedling growing on a hummock in an open swamp. The shrub barely clings to life in this saturated environment, and I wonder if the stress of its continued existence contributes to its exuberant autumnal display.

Some shrubs are blessed with such virtue and merit that they hardly need me to tout their charms or apologize for horticultural shortcomings. Fothergillas fall comfortably into this group. They resemble civilized witch-hazels in the flattened, fan-shaped and ascending way the branches grow, their scalloped and ribbed oval leaves zigzagging up buff colored twigs atop thin trunks that grow from a central root system to form a dense, spreading colony. There are only two species of fothergilla, both native to the southeastern United States. They bloom in spring, before the leaves emerge, so the delicate flowers are well displayed at the tips of the bare twigs. In shape these remind me of brushes on the motorized shoe-shiners you see in gentleman's clubs — a cylinder of bristly stamens that are lime green maturing milky white. The flowers are a handsome sight in early spring, and they release a heady, honeyed perfume

that hangs in the garden as food for the nose. During the summer, the matte blue-green leaves of fothergillas recede into the background, but they "flower" once again as frost settles on the garden in fall. This time it is the leaves that bloom — a spectacular blazing cacophony of apricot, orange, maroon, and crimson. They have the habit of coloring from the outside in, so the center is patterned with a zone that is a shade or two darker than the margin itself.

Fothergilla capsules ripen in summer, first cracking open, then constricting a membrane that surrounds the shiny brown seeds to such an extent that they are forcibly expelled at great velocity and can travel 15 feet or more, well away from the shade of the parent to a spot amenable for growth. The two species divide neatly along both dimensional and geographic boundaries. *F. gardenii* is a short plant of the coastal plain, and *F. major* is a taller, understory shrub of mountain cliffs and glades. The two can hybridize, and the popular cultivar 'Mount Airy', intermediate in size between the parents, is likely the result of just such an encounter.

CULTURE: Best in moist but well-drained, acidic soil, especially in the South, where root disease can be a problem in heavier soils. We have one patch of large fothergilla planted on the fringe of the skunk cabbage swamp, and it has seeded in or been planted actually in the middle of the swamp as well, so the roots are underwater in spring and the soil dries to muck in summer. It has survived there for many years, but remains somewhat stunted. It does color up about two weeks earlier than plants in drier locations, though, and the visage of a glowing red orb in the midst of mud and mire is very pretty. Fothergillas will bloom and color best with at least 2 to 3 hours of direct sun, especially in the North. *F. major* does need some room after a time. We have a patch that now covers about 500 square feet and is spreading. To control spread, you have to remove the root sprouts that come up at the fringes of the clump and keep it pruned to several larger central stems.

WILDLIFE: Rich source of nectar for insects.

PROPAGATION: Moderately difficult from cuttings and seed.

Fothergilla gardenii
Dwarf Fothergilla, Dwarf Witch-alder

ZONES: 5–9; sun to light shade
SOIL: Moist to moderately wet
NATIVE TO: Damp pocosins and savannas along the coastal plain; North Carolina to Florida and Mississippi
SIZE: Height 3–6 feet, width 2–6 feet
COLOR: White, tinged with green; blooms in spring Glaucous blue-leaved forms of both species occur in the wild, but only 'Blue Mist', a cultivar of *F. gardenii*, is widely available. *F. gardenii* is also variable as to

height and leaf size. The typical form has leaves in the 1-to-2-inch range and becomes a rounded, spreading mound. There are forms that approach *F. major* in height and size of leaf, and here the boundaries between the two become indistinct. In general, dwarf fothergilla flowers a bit earlier and has smaller blooms than *F. major*. I have used it to good effect in foundation plantings, and clients have appreciated the fact that it presents a neat, mounded appearance, even when the leaves are off in winter, that never needs pruning or hedging.

Fothergilla major
Large Fothergilla, Large Witch-alder

ZONES: 4–8; sun to light shade

SOIL: Moist (wet) to dry, well-drained

NATIVE TO: Ridge tops, riverbanks, and dry slopes in the southern Appalachians from North Carolina and Tennessee to Georgia and Alabama with one disjunct population in north-central Arkansas

SIZE: Height 4–15 feet, width 6–12 feet

COLOR: White, tinged with green; blooms in spring

I am continually amazed, given this species' preferred ridge-top habitat, that it performs so well for us in two fairly boggy locations. You will occasionally see reference to *F. monticola,* which some believe to be glabrous, less upright, and more prone to spread than *F. major*. This is likely not a valid distinction, yet I do feel that the degree of spreading is variable among different clones, and most of the plants we have at Garden in the Woods represent the wandering extreme. This is a rare species in the wild, but it makes a great garden plant, especially along a fencerow, woodland edge, or in a larger mixed planting. The flower clusters are more elongated than the preceding species', to brilliant effect.

Franklinia alatamaha

Franklinia alatamaha (frank-LIN-nia)
Theaceae
Franklinia, Franklin-tree

ZONES: (5) 6–9

SOIL: Moist, acidic, well-drained

NATIVE TO: Formerly found along the Altamaha River in eastern Georgia

SIZE: Height 12–15 feet, width 8–16 feet

COLOR: White with brilliant orange-gold stamens; blooms in fall

If there is a plant that has achieved lasting martyrdom, it is unquestionably franklinia. This charming relative of the camellia was discovered in 1770 by the plant explorer extraordinaire John Bartram

along the banks of the mighty Altamaha River near its mouth, where one third of Georgia's runoff flows summarily into the Atlantic Ocean. It's likely that franklinia was already on the verge of natural extinction, and after an unconfirmed sighting in 1803, near what was then Fort Barrington in swampy McIntosh County, Georgia, it has never been seen in the wild again. Legend has it that all franklinia plants in cultivation today are descended from the few that Bartram removed to his own Pennsylvania garden in the late 1700s. Franklinia's disappearance is one of the great unsolved mysteries of botany, and it serves as a poster child and lasting symbol of the plight of native species suffering under human onslaught. That it is extinct in the wild seems pretty well settled, but *why* is another question. Like many relict genera, including *Elliottia*, it had likely been nearly eliminated by climate change and the cascade of problems that affect small, isolated populations (inbreeding depression, vulnerability to disturbances like fires or hurricanes, etc.). It is possible that Europeans merely stumbled upon it coincidentally just as it was about to die out. Another theory has it that an introduced root disease, brought in with cotton during the days when the coastal plain was under wholesale conversion to the valuable fiber, may have finished off the last stands of the tree. Franklinia is very susceptible to *Phytophthora cinnamoni,* the root pathogen that thrives in poorly drained soils and is a major problem for rhododendron nurseries. The upshot is that although the small tree thrives in southern New Eng-

Franklinia alatamaha. *Like common witch-hazel, franklinia chooses a strange time of year to flower. Only in midautumn, when its leaves are turning and beginning to fall, do its pearly buds finally unfurl. The sumptuous flowers are all the more precious at this time of year, when one's thoughts have turned to the approach of winter.*

land and parts of the Mid-Atlantic region and the Midwest, it cannot be grown anywhere in its native haunts for long. Attempts at reintroduction have ended in failure, though there is speculation (mentioned to me by Robert McIntosh) that the trees' locality may have been misrecorded by Bartram as swampy ground when it really grew higher and drier on sand ridges.

Where it can be grown, franklinia is a splendid, small, multistemmed tree. It produces long, tapered leaves that are dark glossy green above and dusty green below. The flowers develop at the tips of the branches slowly during the summer as if consciously trying to hold back to let the anticipation build to a frenzy. The buds look like big pearls until the scale-like calyx begins to peel back one section at a time to expose the balled petals. Each lightly fragrant flower is about 3 inches across, with five odd-sized white petals and a deep golden orange ring of stamens gracing the center. These gorgeous blooms finally open a few at a time over about a month in late summer. They are followed by curious woody capsules that ripen over the course of the next year, so that by the time the flowers open, last year's seeds have begun to shed farther down. Each capsule cracks open into five chambers, like a half-opened orange, with each segment cracking also part way up the middle from below. Because the flowers develop at the branch tips, new growth initiates the following spring from farther down, usually only one or two buds setting out at an angle and hooking around in an arc as they grow. Thus franklinia develops a picturesque, curving shape much like that of some dogwoods, its bark reddish gray patterned with lighter gray striations as the underbark is exposed in cracks. In the fall, many trees develop spectacular scarlet and burgundy fall color just as the last flowers have faded.

Loblolly bay (*Gordonia lasianthus*) is a beautiful evergreen tree that I became quite smitten with when I moved to North Carolina. A close relative of franklinia, it has glossy, dark green leaves and a narrow, upright growth habit that reminds one instantly of sweetbay magnolia, a tree it shares its swampy home with. White flowers similar in size and shape to franklinia's appear sporadically through the summer. It grows remarkably fast in containers—6 feet or more in a season—and I managed to procure half a dozen 5-gallon specimens from a friend. Four went to the garden at the nursery, and two down to the creek below my house. Within the year, all had died. Even taking my lack of gardening ability into account, this was a distressing failure, and I was glad to read that others have had similar problems establishing loblolly bay. Mike Dirr in *Manual of Woody Landscape Plants* (p. 390) theorizes that a root pathogen may be the culprit in cultivation. Anyway, it is a pretty plant coming up through the longleaf pines and cypress in the wild. Its range is from Virginia to Florida and Louisiana in

coastal swamps and it is winter-hardy in Zones (7)8–9. Propagation is the same as for franklinia.

CULTURE: North of the cotton belt, franklinia does very well in gardens *once it is established.* In warmer parts of Zone 5, it needs a sheltered location and protection for the first few years (see *Elliottia* entry, p. 116, for our method), as it starts off slowly in spring and has trouble cycling down for the winter. Well-drained, moist soil seems preferable, though good specimens at the Holden Arboretum were growing in an area that is seasonally wet during most springs. Established trees will suffer winterkill when temperatures drop below about −10°F, but sprouts will grow back quickly below the killed part. This is not an easy tree to get established. The seedlings take a few years to settle in, and we have lost several that never adjusted. In containers it can grow extremely fast (4 feet in a season) but 8 to 18 inches a year is normal in the ground. What can I say . . . there are easier specimen trees to grow, but few with the aura of mystery and intrigue that surrounds franklinia.

USES: Small specimen tree.

PROPAGATION: Easy from cuttings, moderately easy from seed.

Fraxinus americana

Fraxinus (FRAX-in-us)
Oleaceae
Ash

Basic choices made early in life can have lasting ramifications. From the time its first leaves emerge, an ash tree chooses the symmetry of pairs: pairs of leaves arranged at each node, pairs of leaflets along each compound blade, pairs of branches that set out confidently from the main stem. It is a pattern that carries through the tree and gives it a recognizable presence in the forest or garden. Ashes are famil-

Fraxinus americana. A paired arrangement of leaves and branches translates into a distinctive forking pattern that makes white ash easily identifiable from a distance.

iar trees in the eastern woods, choosing places where the soil is fertile and water plentiful to spread rounded crowns of finger-thick twigs that curve out and up, much like the tines of an old-fashioned pitchfork. Many of the species look superficially similar in leaf, but they vary in size from small trees to forest giants. Most are dioecious, with female trees producing copious quantities of paddle-bladed samaras that spin down from the canopy in the fashion of maples. Though most ashes are unremarkable in flower, *F. cuspidata* is truly outstanding, with a flower display that rivals that of its distant cousin the fringetree (Chionanthus) both in floral frothiness and the intensity of its sweet perfume. A few of our species are planted as shade or street trees valued for bright yellow, burgundy, or deep red fall color and symmetrical form in youth. White ash and green ash are also important lumber species prized for their light-colored, durable wood.

In the last 50 years, seemingly healthy white ash, black ash, and green ash have been dying mysteriously throughout the Northeast and Midwest. I have watched many trees suddenly begin to drop leaves earlier than normal in fall, then over the next year or two suffer rapid dieback of the crown, and death. This puzzling affliction, known as ash decline, is thought to be a lethal combination of environmental stresses and disease that overwhelms the trees' defenses. Drought, pesticide, and salt residues that kill roots and mycorrhizal fungi, ozone pollution, and a recently discovered disease called ash yellows have all been implicated in this disturbing phenomenon. Ash yellows is caused by an amorphous creature called a mycoplasma-like organism (MLO) that is similar to a virus but lacks any definable cell walls; it enters the phloem tissue of the tree, presumably in the saliva of feeding insects like leaf-hoppers or spittle bugs, and begins to damage and plug it up. Sick trees typically show dieback and sometimes attempt to resprout from witches' brooms lower on the trunk. The disease also prevents the tree from cycling down and preparing for winter normally; this in turn makes the tissues susceptible to winter injury and explains why many just never leaf out again after beginning to show symptoms the previous summer. There are many unanswered questions regarding this disease and the other possible causal agents of ash decline. However, there does appear to be variability in resistance to ash yellows, and good culture, including preventing drought stress, helps prevent symptoms from developing—once a tree begins to show signs of the disease, there is not much that can be done. Keep in mind that although there are a number of superior cultivars on the market that have been selected for brilliant autumn color, drought tolerance, and good form, little if any selection has been done for disease resistance that I am aware of. The ashes are fast-growing and beautiful

trees, but until ash decline is better understood, use them with caution in the Northeast and Midwest.

CULTURE: Ashes can be transplanted readily in spring or fall from containers or as balled and burlaped saplings. The larger species are best in moist, fairly fertile soil and sun. They will tolerate drier soils, but this can predispose them to disease. Selections are widely available that tolerate the windy, dry conditions of the upper Midwest and Plains, and green ash has become a popular street tree in Denver, Colorado, and Billings, Montana. Some bleeding will occur if pruning is done in spring, so prune in fall.

USES: Street or shade tree.

WILDLIFE: Ashes are popular host trees for butterfly caterpillars, such as the two-tailed tiger swallowtail *(Papilio multicaudata)*, mourning cloak *(Nymphalis antipa)*, Baltimore *(Euphydryas phaeton)*, and the striped hairstreak and banded hairstreak *(Satyrium liparops* and *S. calanus)*.

PROPAGATION: Moderately easy from seed.

Fraxinus americana
White Ash

ZONES: 4–9; sun to light shade
SOIL: Moist
NATIVE TO: Rich woods; Nova Scotia to Minnesota south to eastern Texas and northern Florida
SIZE: Height 60–90 (120) feet, width 25–60 feet
COLOR: Yellow; blooms in spring

White ash is the largest and one of the most common and widespread of the genus. Its leaves are composed typically of 7 oblong leaflets, 3 pairs plus 1 at the tip of the rachis, that are medium green in color. Its bark is dark gray, and diamond-shaped fissures develop on older stems that help identify it in winter. In New England, its leaves turn a distinctive purple or maroon color in fall that adds depth and contrast amid the maples and birch it shares ground with. This is probably the most susceptible of the *Fraxinus* species to ash yellows, and I have seen whole forests of white ash almost completely killed in recent years, as well as numerous dead trees along streets and in side yards. It is tremendously disheartening for me to see yet another of our beautiful canopy trees succumbing to disease, and at times I wonder whether in 50 years any tree will remain in our forests.

Fraxinus anomala
Single-leaf Ash

ZONES: 5–8; sun
SOIL: Moist to dry, well-drained
NATIVE TO: Pinyon-juniper and oak-manzanita woodland, western Colorado to southern Utah and Southern California east to northwestern New Mexico

SIZE: Height 3–15 feet, width 3–12 feet

COLOR: Yellow; blooms in spring

Single-leaf ash is anomalous for the genus, with its single or rarely trifoliate leaves suggesting lilac more than ash. It is a shrub or small tree of drier soils in the Southwest. In moister habitats within the same region you can find the pretty little 30-to-40-foot velvet ash (*F. velutina*), which looks like the eastern ashes, with 5-parted, pinnate leaves shiny green above and covered with a coat of down on the undersurfaces, especially when young. *F. velutina* has been planted extensively as a street and yard tree in Texas and the Southwest, but it is fairly susceptible to attack by borers and the wood is weak.

Fraxinus cuspidata

Flowering Ash, Fragrant Ash

ZONES: (6)7–9; sun

SOIL: Well-drained, summer-dry

NATIVE TO: Rocky slopes and ledges; scattered locations in Texas, New Mexico, Arizona, and Mexico

SIZE: Height 6–15 feet, width 5–12 feet

COLOR: Creamy white; blooms in spring

Unlike the other ash species, flowering ash produces billowing masses of 4-petaled, sweetly fragrant flowers each about 1 inch long and hung in dense panicles amid the new growth, very much like fringetree (*Chionanthus*). Its leaves average 7 to 9 leaflets, each leaflet rather narrow and stiff. It is a beautiful sight in flower, but as far as I know, it is not frequently cultivated.

Fraxinus latifolia

Oregon Ash

ZONES: 7–9; sun to light shade

SOIL: Moist

NATIVE TO: Rich soils along streams, floodplains and coastal forest; western British Columbia south in the mountains and along the coast to central California

SIZE: Height 30–60 (120) feet, width 25–40 feet

COLOR: Yellow; blooms in spring

Once classified as a variety of *F. americana,* this Pacific Northwest species is in many ways similar to white ash. It is a common tree of waterside habitats at lower elevations and valleys in Oregon and Washington, and it will make an attractive shade tree, with a rounded crown that turns yellow or rusty yellow in fall. Its chief drawback is a propensity to drop its foliage in September—good if you like an early shot of fall color, bad if you want to postpone the bleakness of winter for as long as possible.

Fraxinus nigra

Black Ash

ZONES: 4–8; sun to light shade

SOIL: Moist to wet

NATIVE TO: Wooded swamps; Newfoundland and Quebec to Manitoba south to Iowa, Indiana, and Delaware

SIZE: Height 30–50 (75) feet, width 15–25 feet

COLOR: Yellow; blooms in spring

Other than a darker, more tightly knitted, slightly peeling bark and a preference for mucky soils, this species closely resembles white ash, and can be used as a passable substitute in waterlogged situations, although it has narrower habit and slower rate of growth. *F. caroliniana* (pop ash, water ash) is the smaller-leaved, southeastern extension of *F. nigra,* populating swampy forests along the Atlantic and Gulf coasts from Virginia to Texas. These and blue ash can be differentiated from the others in the genus by their samaras, which lack the little ridge that runs like a crest on top of the seed, perpendicular to the larger wing.

Fraxinus pennsylvanica

Green Ash, Red Ash

ZONES: 3–9; sun to light shade

SOIL: Moist to dry

NATIVE TO: Moist to wet woods and wooded swamps; Nova Scotia to Alberta south to Wyoming, Kansas, Texas, and Florida

SIZE: Height 40–60 (75) feet, width 20–30 feet

COLOR: Yellow; blooms in spring

What a run this tree is having. An array of cultivars offering natural adaptability, ease of transplanting, and tolerance for tough urban or windswept situations has made green ash one of the most widely planted street trees in the northern United States and Canada. Most of the cultivars share the species' tightly oval habit, furrowed, red-gray bark, and a glimmering yellow fall color. Like Oregon ash, this tree colors up early in the year, maybe 7 to 10 days earlier than white ash, and it is in the fall that I notice it everywhere, casting its shade in parks and lining the macadam with a regularity of outline that landscape architects love. In maturity, this species takes on a more irregular outline, much like that of *F. americana,* in which several broad branches interrupt the smooth flow of leaves. The pairs of leaflets are nearly sessile, and tend to get larger as they move up the rachis. The lower surfaces of the leaves can be more or less covered in rusty pubescence, with hairier plants called red ash and the glabrous called green ash. It is a pretty minor distinction when you get out of the herbarium and into the forest. In general, this species seems to be able to live with the disease ash yellows better than white ash. This trait, coupled with its better tolerance of urban environments and heat, make green ash preferable in landscapes, despite its less spectacular fall color.

Fraxinus profunda (tomentosa)
Pumpkin Ash

ZONES: 5–9; sun to light shade

SOIL: Moist to wet

NATIVE TO: Wooded swamps and river bottoms; scattered from New Jersey to Ohio and Illinois, south to Missouri, Louisiana, and western Florida

SIZE: Height 50–80 (120) feet, width 25–60 feet

COLOR: Yellow; blooms in spring

If you stare at a collection of ashes long enough, you begin to see subtle differences in what had until then looked like a uniform amalgamation of pinnate leaves, opposite branches, and reticulated bark. Whether this is due to eyestrain, suggestion, or enhanced perception born of patient meditation I am not sure, but the fact remains. Enter pumpkin ash, a polyploid plant thought to have originated from past hybridization between white ash and green ash, with leaves that are a bit larger and bolder in effect than those of *F. americana* but with similar fall color. The easiest way to tell it from the others is its larger samaras (2 inches long and approaching ½-inch wide).

Fraxinus quadrangulata
Blue Ash

ZONES: 4–7; sun to light shade

SOIL: Moist to moderately dry, slightly acidic to alkaline (pH)

NATIVE TO: Moist woods and limestone outcrops; Ontario and southern Michigan to eastern Kansas south to Oklahoma, West Virginia and in the Appalachians to Georgia

SIZE: Height 50–70 (100) feet, width 20–30 feet

COLOR: Yellow; blooms in spring

Superficially not much distinguishes blue ash. The twigs are noticeably four-sided in cross section; the leaflets sweep to a long, narrow tip; and it is capable of growing in high-pH soils, like *F. pennsylvanica*. I don't recommend this, of course, but if you take a whack at the bark with a hatchet, the exposed wood will turn bluish as it dries, hence the common name. Fall color is light yellow.

Fremontodendron californicum

Fremontodendron (Fremontia) californicum
(free-mont-o-DEN-dron)

Sterculiaceae

Flannelbush

ZONES: 8–10; sun

SOIL: Well-drained, summer-dry

NATIVE TO: Dry, rocky foothills and seeps at altitudes of 3,000–6,000 feet in the mountains; California and Arizona

SIZE: Height 4–15 (20) feet, width 5–15 feet

COLOR: Bright, soft yellow; blooms in late spring

Called the queen of California's spring-flowering shrubs (despite some pretty spectacular competition), flannelbush is another of the Golden State's strange and beautiful endemics. In the fossil record, it becomes evident that this genus was not always so restricted in range. Sixty million years ago, when the area was more languid and tropical, flannelbush flourished among cycads and tree ferns. As the mountains rose and the climate dried and cooled, flannelbush adapted to some extent, but its range is limited now to the lower slopes of the mountains, where rainfall is higher and the winters are mild. This species has leathery, evergreen leaves that are slightly lobed and about 1 inch in diameter on vigorous shoots. Its habit is a combination of sprouting and sprawling, with leaves alternating along long stems that arch out from the clump. Come late spring, flannelbush blooms in a glorious flush that lights up the hillsides in bright lemon yellow. The flowers emerge singly from the leaf axils up and down the stems. Each has 5 petals (or, rarely, 4), the petals having a thick waxy coating and rounded tips that narrow to a distinctive little point. The base of each petal has a swollen pit or gland that is suffused

Fremontodendron californicum. *Flannelbush is a spectacular shrub that came into existence more than 80 million years ago in the Cretaceous period, the end of the dinosaur age. It has weathered climate changes both large and small, and survives now in a few small mountain enclaves in California and Arizona.*

with Kelly green and that I imagine is a nectar gland. *Fremontodendron* is a distant relative of the mallows (Malvaceae), as shown by its sexual parts, which like the mallow's are partially fused into a stout column —five anthers ringing one tail-like style— that rises from the center of the wide-spreading petals. When the flowers first open, the anthers are swollen and burnt orange in color, quickly fading to yellow as the pollen is shed. This same red-orange pigment returns in the petals as the flowers begin to fade, so a bush in full bloom has a noticeably two-toned appearance. Flowers are followed by woody, five-valved capsules much like those of hibiscus and other mallows.

Southern flannelbush (*F. mexicanum*) is distinguished by its more deeply lobed leaves, more stiffly upright carriage, and a habit of blooming off and on down among the leaves, where the flowers do not make quite the same splash. It grows in southern California and into the Baja Peninsula, so it is only hardy in Zones 9–10.

CULTURE: *Fremontodendron* will grow well only where the soils remain fairly dry in summer. It is a highly ornamental species, and I have seen it used effectively as far north as coastal Washington as well as throughout California in gardens without too much summer irrigation.

USES: Specimen, screen.

PROPAGATION: Easy from cuttings, moderately easy from seed.

shade of conifers as well as in openings and clear-cuts, either rooted in the duff or springing directly from seed left in rotten stumps and fallen logs where a bird or small mammal once paused for a morning constitutional after dining on the fruits. Salal's blue-black berries ripen about the size and texture of blueberries and are hung enticingly on slender, arching racemes that rise from the uppermost leaf axils along the stem. The bell-shaped blooms that precede these fruits are translucent white, heavily suffused with the same shade of deep red that blends with green on the stems and petioles. In the sun, even the glossy oval leaves take on a reddish cast, especially underneath, but sun or shade, the foliage has a distinctive un-ironed, undulating quality that makes salal easily recognizable. "Salal" is a Native American word for this plant, whose berries were processed into a dried pemmican cake or sugary syrup.

Gaultheria shallon is one of the most common shrubs in the wetter areas of the Pacific Northwest. It is a very beautiful evergreen for massing and covering larger areas, and is as much a part of the regional character as the Douglas fir and vine maple.

CULTURE: Salal is best reserved for those areas of the West under the influence of the mild Pacific air currents. We have grown it for many years in a shady, acidic spot in our garden, and it has survived and sometimes even prospered, but every few years a cold and snowless winter knocks it back enough that it has never luxuriated. Though it will grow in sun, it is

Gaultheria shallon.
When I see drifts of salal carpeting mossy banks, I know I am in the misty forests of the Pacific Northwest. Using local plants in the garden gives it a regional identity that is fast disappearing in this increasingly homogenized world.

Gaultheria shallon

Gaultheria shallon

Gaultheria shallon
(gall-THAIR-ria)
Ericaceae
Salal

ZONES: 6–9; sun to shade
SOIL: Moist to somewhat dry in summer
NATIVE TO: Wooded slopes and clearings; British Columbia south through Washington and Oregon and the redwood belt of northern California and sporadically farther south
SIZE: Height 1–5 feet, width 3–8 feet
COLOR: White more or less suffused with pink; blooms in spring

I **covered the smaller** wintergreens in my book on wildflowers, but this leaves one species undescribed, the ubiquitous and ever-lustrous salal. This spreading, understory shrub fills the same ecological niche in the Northwest as dog hobble (*Leucothoe fontanesiana*) in the Appalachians, forming a impenetrable, tangled mass of arching stems clothed in evergreen leaves that spring each season from an ever-widening root system. It can grow in the dense

perhaps best reserved for dry shade, as this is a more difficult situation to fill with other plants. Sections of sod or rooted stems as well as containerized specimens are easy enough to transplant in fall or winter. If your planting has begun to grow too exuberantly and threatens to overtake the space, cut it to the ground before new growth commences. It will come back a bit stunted for a year or two but will eventually regain its former size.

USES: Massing, large groundcover for moist or dry shade.

WILDLIFE: Berries for birds, mammals, people.

PROPAGATION: Moderately difficult from cuttings, moderately easy from seed.

Gaylussacia brachycera

Gaylussacia
(gay-loo-SAY-shah)
Ericaceae
Huckleberry

To the casual eye, there is very little difference between huckleberries and blueberries—same twiggy habit, oval leaves, cute little upside-down urnshaped flowers—the same gestalt. I commonly find black huckleberries growing intermixed with lowbush blueberry in dry, upland woods, fire-prone sand scrub, or thin-soiled rocky balds. Huckleberry's leaves are less blue, and the berries are almost black, containing seeds large enough to crunch between my teeth as I gorge on them in summer. Blueberry seeds are more numerous but smaller, so if you notice seeds, chances are you are munching on huckleberries. Dangleberry *(G. frondosa)* is larger than the others, much like one of the taller blueberries, with black fruits and leaves that blaze red or orange before they fall. Box huckleberry is the standout among *Gaylussacia* species, a plant that rises above the fray, in a horticultural sense. It boasts glistening, evergreen leaves about the size of a squirrel's ear that are deep ivy green in the summer but washed with burgundy like the twigs as they emerge in spring and again as cold nips them in fall and winter. Box huckleberry is a fairly rare species throughout most of its range, with a scattered distribution centered in the Appalachians of West Virginia. This sort of spotty occurrence suggests that the species was nearly eliminated by past glacial advances, surviving precariously in a few protected refuges that remained ice-free. It does not appear to reproduce readily from seed, relying instead on a slow vegetative advance on sympodial stems. We have large swaths in the garden, and they spread only 6 to 12 inches a year, slowly forming a solid, redolent colony. Genetic studies done on one 100-acre stand in central Pennsylvania suggest that it is indeed all one massive plant that has been patiently advancing a foot or so a season for the last 12,000 years!

CULTURE: All *Gaylussacia* species relish sharply acid soils like those suitable for rhododendrons and their kin. Black huckleberry is very drought tolerant, and can be intermixed with lowbush blueberry to provide subtle textural and genetic diversity. Dangleberry and dwarf huckleberry prefer the moist soils and swampy hummocks where you are likely to find highbush blueberry growing well. Finally, box huckleberry does best in a damp but well-drained situa-

Gaylussacia brachycera. *Box huckleberry has tremendous garden potential, but its slow growth has made it hard to produce cost-effectively in nurseries. Thus it is an ideal plant for the backyard propagator, who is not so constrained by the demands of the bottom line.*

tion. I have tried it in a fairly dry, sandy soil, and it never established. We have it established on lightly shaded banks, where some water seeps down from above, and it performs magnificently. Huckleberries are reasonably shade tolerant, producing some flowers and fruit with only an hour or two of sun, but the more light, the merrier.

USES: Groundcover, massing.

WILDLIFE: Important nectar source for bumblebees; berries loved by birds and bears.

PROPAGATION: Moderately easy from seed.

Gaylussacia baccata
Black Huckleberry

ZONES: 4–9; sun to shade

SOIL: Moist to dry, acidic and well-drained

NATIVE TO: Upland woods, rocky slopes, sandy barrens; Newfoundland and Quebec to Manitoba south to Missouri, Alabama, and Georgia

SIZE: Height 1–2 (3) feet, width 2–4 feet

COLOR: Light pink; blooms in late spring

Black huckleberry spreads on shallow, buried stems, sending up new shoots each season from the outskirts of the colony. These grow up and arch over, then sprout a network of fine branches hung with 1-inch oblong leaves shading dangling racemes of little flowers and, later, blue-black fruits that lack the dusty bloom of many blueberries. Fall color is usually a burgundy or deep red, which contrasts well with the scarlet flames of turning lowbush blueberry leaves. Dwarf huckleberry (*G. dumosa*) is similar in habit and general appearance, though on average a bit shorter, and it ranges along the Atlantic coast from Newfoundland to Florida. It is distinguished by its larger flowers produced singly or in pairs from the leaf axils, coupled with a love of damp places like the margins of bogs or coastal swamps.

Gaylussacia brachycera
Box Huckleberry

ZONES: 5–7; sun to light shade
SOIL: Moist, well-drained, acidic
NATIVE TO: Slopes and banks, mostly in the Alleghenies and Appalachians; Maryland and Delaware to Pennsylvania and West Virginia south to Kentucky and eastern Tennessee
SIZE: Height 8–12, width 2–3 feet
COLOR: Light pink; blooms in late spring

The glossy, slightly cupped leaves of box huckleberry do suggest boxwood in a way, though it would have to be a boxwood dipped in glossy, deep green paint. In habit it is much like the other small species, creeping along on stems just below the ground that send up out-curving branches along the margins of the clump, which get twiggier and denser over the next few seasons. When I first came to Garden in the Woods, I wondered aloud why this species was not readily available to gardeners, as it is one of the best groundcovers in our collection. After working with it, though, I have come to understand that it is not the easiest plant to please; it is slow to propagate and get established in the garden and thus must be elevated to the status of specialty plant for the wizened gardener. If you have a good spot for some, though, you can't beat it for draping over swaths of ground around taller acid-loving plants.

Gaylussacia frondosa
Dangleberry

ZONES: 5–9; sun to light shade
SOIL: Moist to wet, acidic
NATIVE TO: Swamps, thickets, and rich woods, mostly along the coast; southeastern New Hampshire to Florida, inland occasionally to Ohio, Tennessee, and Alabama
SIZE: Height 3–6 feet, width 3–4 feet
COLOR: Light pink; blooms in late spring

This is the largest species, typically a rounded shrub taller than wide, with medium green, 1-to-2-inch leaves that are long and blunt-tipped, interspersed with branched panicles of little bell-shaped flowers. The fruits are very dark blue, almost black, which helps distinguish it from sympatric highbush blueberry. Two other dangleberries, *G. tomentosa* and *G. nana,* are recognized as distinct species by some authors, because of both smaller stature and fruits

that are lighter blue. Both grow along the southeastern coast, and have shorter stems (less than 3 feet) topped with a nest of flattened, spreading twigs. *G. tomentosa* has woolly hair on the twigs and undersides of the leaves.

Gelsemium sempervirens

Gelsemium sempervirens
(jel-SEH-mium)
Loganiaceae
Carolina Jessamine, Yellow Jasmine

ZONES: 6–10; sun
SOIL: Moist to moderately dry
NATIVE TO: Thickets, fencerows, mixed forests: eastern Virginia to Tennessee and Arkansas south to Texas, Mexico, and Florida
SIZE: Height 3–20 feet, depending on support, width 3–10 feet
COLOR: Bright yellow; blooms in early spring

Fences make good neighbors, but also good places on which vines can scramble, and all throughout the Southeast, fencerows and thickets are decked out in spring with the daffodil yellow trumpets of Carolina jessamine. These flowers pop out of dormant little buds in the upper axils of every stem tip just as the air begins to warm in spring. They have a light, sweet fragrance not unlike jasmine and a tubular shape reminiscent of trumpet creeper or cross-

Gelsemium sempervirens. Carolina jessamine is a consummate vine for the garden. It provides lovely flowers, glossy evergreen leaves, and a restrained habit of growth, and it will grow just about anywhere.

vine. In the wild, *G. sempervirens* is a sparse, twining vine found poking out of the crowns of red-cedar or dogwood or twining around deadfalls in the company of honeysuckle and greenbriar. Give it a spot of its own, though, and it really shines, forming a thick mound of foliage as stems weave into stems and the glossy, evergreen leaves take on a reddish tint where the sun and cold have touched them. When trying to gain altitude, the vines grow quickly with paired leaves barely formed and widely spaced along reaching stems. As the vines luxuriate at their chosen height, however, the internodes (stem length between leaf nodes) decrease and the leaves grow larger, being typically 1½ to 2 inches long and lance-shaped in outline. New growth comes from the base to replenish the canopy, though the plants are pretty well behaved at ground level, unlike many that rely on others for support. It is a great ornamental, and it is widely planted on mailboxes, fences, trellises, and arbors in the South. We have grown it at the Garden, but the stems often suffer winterkill, leaving us flowerless in spring, even though the vines return from the roots. I am testing some hardier selections, including 'Margarita', which may prove more suitable here.

Swamp jessamine *(G. rankinii)* is a rarer species from swamps along the southeast coast, which I sold quite a bit in North Carolina chiefly because it blooms in late fall and continues once weather warms in spring, so you could mix it and *G. sempervirens* together and handily extend the bloom period. In leaf and habit the two are virtually indistinguishable, but swamp jessamine's flowers are about one-third smaller, lack fragrance, and have pointed as opposed to rounded petal tips.

CULTURE: These are best transplanted from containers in spring or fall into moist soils receiving at least 3 to 4 hours sun—the more sun, the better the flowering. Carolina jessamine is pretty tough and adaptable, though, and it can take a fair amount of drought as well as sandy or heavy clay soils combined with a good bit of shade. Judging by its habitat, I would guess that swamp jessamine prefers a wetter soil, though it grew well for me under average garden conditions. Fertilize both in spring after blooms have faded. Since they climb by twining rather than holdfasts or rootlets, provide some sort of support like a trellis, post, or fence for the vines to get started on. These do not develop large, heavy trunks, so you don't need an industrial-strength support as you might for wisteria. Alternatively, you can just let the vine trail over the ground or a wall as an informal groundcover. It does get a bit addled when you deny it support and attempts to climb by twining around itself in a futile attempt to gain altitude.

USES: Screening when trained to walls, arbors, trellises, fences and the like; or use as a scampering, twisting groundcover.

PROPAGATION: Easy from cuttings or seed.

Gleditsia triacanthos

Gleditsia triacanthos
(gle-DIT-sia)
Fabaceae
Honeylocust

ZONES: 4–8; sun, part sun

SOIL: Moist to dry

NATIVE TO: Rich woods, floodplains, often on limestone; Pennsylvania to southern Minnesota and South Dakota south to Texas, Tennessee, and Florida

SIZE: Height 25–40 (70) feet, width 25–40 (80) feet

COLOR: Green; blooms in spring

Gleditsia triacanthos. *It's easy to find both small trees and tall trees, but if you are searching for a medium-sized specimen, say in the 25-to-30-foot range, the field of possibilities shrinks considerably. Honeylocust's intermediate size and soft shade may be just the thing for the smaller yard.*

Landscapes have a way of imitating art. As the influences of modern art, with its emphasis on abstract forms and simple geometry, trickled down from painting and sculpture to architecture and finally landscape architecture in the fifties and sixties, designers gravitated toward trees that approximated the purified ideal of tree or shrub embraced by this minimalist aesthetic. Honeylocust, with its predictably vase-shaped trunk and blocky, flattened crown, fit the bill quite nicely, and untold millions of the trees were plopped down in parking lots, corporate parks, and sidewalk tree pits. Honeylocust is a tough tree, with an unmistakable outline and fine-textured pinnate and bipinnate leaves that cast a light enough shade for grass to grow combined with the remarkable ability to just disappear after they turn burnt yellow and fall, meaning no raking!

(Really the small leaflets just bed down in the turf or wash away in runoff.) Fashions change, though, and the poor honeylocust has become as dated as the blue aluminum-and-glass buildings they tend to skirt. Overuse of the tree has made it monotonous; more insidiously, it has allowed the development and spread of a litany of diseases that are of less concern in scattered, wild populations. All in all, though, it remains a fine shade tree, and since all fashions come back around eventually, it will surely become popular again.

In wild honeylocust, all exposed surfaces are covered with remarkable, branching thorns up to 4 inches long and as thick as darning needles. These grow in bunches scattered like fortifications about the trunk and larger branches and ring the smaller ones like a prickly stubble. Why the trees arm themselves like this is a mystery to me, as no browsing animal currently alive could even reach up into the canopy. Perhaps spines are the honeylocust's equivalent of an appendix, evolved to ward off the advances of some giant herbivore that no longer exists. One thing is for sure—these impressive thorns would have prevented the tree from ever becoming popular as an ornamental if not for the discovery of one wild population, var. *inermis,* that lacked spines. This variety is the only honeylocust commercially available, though you may find an armed tree here and there in older public gardens. My woody ornamentals professor in college said he would give extra credit to anyone who could locate the one thorny specimen on the University of Connecticut campus, and of course I searched and searched all semester but never found it.

Flowers emerge with the new leaves and they are pretty much the same color, so you'd be apt not to notice them if not for the humming of bees and the heavy, honeyed fragrance that hangs in the air. In summer, very large, flattened and twisted pods develop along the branches. At first they are green, but come autumn they turn shoe-leather brown and begin slowly to fall from the tree. The foot-long pods are lined with a sweet pulp, which is relished by cattle (and some people, too), who browse fallen pods and thus spread the seeds. I can imagine that the long-lost herbivore may have been the natural seed vector for the trees. There is another species, water locust (*G. aquatica*), which grows in swamps and river floodplains along the southeast coast and up the Mississippi River drainage to southern Illinois. It is similar in size and shape to honeylocust, though the pods are much smaller (1 to 3 inches) and lack sweet pulp.

CULTURE: Easily transplanted as a balled and burlaped or containerized tree into a range of soils and moisture conditions. It will grow in light shade, but full sun is preferable. A number of diseases have been documented, including a debilitating canker,

Thyronectria austroamericana, powdery mildew, and rust, and the trees are regularly attacked by webworms, among other insects. However, when used in moderation, honeylocust is not particularly problem-prone, and I think often it is removed simply because it can eventually get quite large and tends to outgrow the space provided for it on the assumption that it will remain a small tree. The wood is extremely hard and strong and should be cut only while still green to save your saw.

USES: Street or shade tree where light shade is needed.

WILDLIFE: Valuable nectar source.

PROPAGATION: Easy from seed.

Gymnocladus dioicus

Gymnocladus dioicus (jim-no-CLAD-us)
Fabaceae
Kentucky Coffeetree

ZONES: 4-8; sun to part sun

SOIL: Moist to moderately dry

NATIVE TO: Rich, alluvial soils; New York to southern Minnesota and South Dakota south to Oklahoma, Tennesee, and Virginia

SIZE: Height 60-75 (100) feet, width 30-50 feet

Where honeylocust has been enthusiastically embraced by the nursery and landscape industry, the muscular Kentucky coffeetree, of the same family, remains virtually ignored. In the wild this large species is fairly uncommon, preferring river bottoms

---

Gymnocladus dioicus. *The visually delicate divided leaves of Kentucky coffeetree beautifully temper the heaviness of its trunk and limbs.*

rich with alluvial silt deposited over eons by spring floodwaters. I was taught that the seeds are adapted for water dispersal, a theory borne out by both their distribution along the major midwestern river systems and by the design of the seed itself. Female trees produce 4-to-10-inch-long leathery pods about the shape of a giant pea pod. These can hang on the trees all winter, and even after a year or two on the ground, many are still perfectly intact. The sweet mucilaginous pulp that surrounds the seeds contains the alkaloid cystisine (or cystisin), a nerve toxin that produces a distressing narcotic effect. Settlers even mixed the pulp with water and left it out to poison unsuspecting flies (see Pammel, *A Manual of Poisonous Plants*, p. 538). Accidental human poisonings are attributed to people mistaking the pods for the sweet, edible pods of honeylocust. Cattle are also made ill by the pods, which seems to support the idea that water, not some large herbivore, is the agent of dispersal. Each pod contains a handful of very hard, ¾-inch seeds almost the color of coffee, which at one time were ground and roasted to get rid of the bitter toxins and were used as a coffee substitute. The seed coat must be worn away with concerted effort before the seed germinates—just the sort of rough treatment it would have to endure as it tumbled down a swollen river in the remains of its boatlike pod.

Kentucky coffeetree is a unique and beautiful tree. There was a big one planted outside of my office window when I worked at the University of Connecticut. In winter, the thumb-thick twigs and beautiful fissured and curled brown and orange bark gave it a visual heaviness unmatched by any other native tree save black walnut. It is relatively fast growing when young, quickly developing a stout main trunk that begins to fork about ten feet up into several ascending branches. At this point, growth slows to 8 to 12 inches a year. The crown remains open and the branches are well spaced enough for the first few decades so that grass can grow right up to the trunk. Late in spring the twigs finally leaf out, adorning themselves with huge, bipinnate leaves up to 3 feet long and held perpendicular to the twigs to create a distinctively layered, parasol effect throughout the canopy. The flower racemes—5-petaled stars tinted pistachio green and white and enveloped around the base by a purple-gray calyx—grow from small side branches at the same time. The flowers are too small to make a visual impact, but, like those of honeylocust, they are sweetly scented and pollinating insects find them hard to resist.

CULTURE: Kentucky coffeetree seems fairly adaptable in landscape situations, tolerating a range of soils and moderate drought, though deep, rich soils are preferable. A few male cultivars are available, mostly in the Midwest, which eliminates the potential messiness and toxicity of the pods. Kentucky coffeetree really needs at least 6 hours of midday sun to perform well. This, combined with its large eventual size, makes it a good choice for parks or larger yards.

USES: Shade, street, or park tree.

WILDLIFE: Good nectar source for bees and wasps.

PROPAGATION: Easy from seed.

Halesia tetraptera

Halesia (hal-LEE-sia)
Styracaceae
Silverbell

Halesia tetraptera. *Flowers dangle from the bare branches of Carolina silverbell just as the leaves start to emerge. Halesia blooms at a young age. This particular plant, growing in our nursery, is only three years old.*

Silverbells play a crucial part in the boisterous, colorful spring symphony at Garden in the Woods. They are one of the essential understory trees of the Appalachian forests, adorning themselves early each season with row upon row of opalescent bells that dangle from every branch. These flowers appear just before the leaves, as do redbud's and flowering dogwood's, and the three combine to frame the garden in a haze of creamy pink. Each bloom has four petals that are fused at least half their length to form a parasol protecting the pistil and stamens from rain. The blooms grow from buds set along the previous season's growth, in effect tracing this network of twigs in the fashion of redbuds, which makes the two especially good companions visually.

There are four species, which differ somewhat in overall size and the size and shape of the blooms. In habit they are single or multistemmed, with slender trunks and branches patterned in a latticed gray-brown bark underlain with silver. Leaves are thin in substance, light green, oval in outline, and so finely toothed along the margins that they appear entire. *Halesia* leaves are large but not coarse, with a fall color I'd rate a passable medium yellow streaked with green. When the leaves are shed, curious fruits come clearly into view. These bear a striking resemblance to the feathers on darts: two or four thin wings projecting at right angles from a swollen central core containing the seed. In outline, these winged fruits are oval or almost teardrop-shaped, and hang like the blooms in little dangling clusters along the horizontal twigs and branches. As the leaves drop in fall, the fruits turn from light green to rosy green to brown and hang on the tree well into winter. In fact, the remains of old pedicels shag the branches for a year or more, implying by their resiliency that the fruits must be literally torn free by the wind. I suppose that the wings are indeed meant to catch the breeze and carry the seed, but its weight would require hurricane-force winds to keep it aloft for more than a few seconds. When the seeds are cut open, the embryo occupies only about a third of the seed, the rest taken up by corky extensions of the seed coat. Like the hollow bones of birds, this may have evolved to lighten the load in flight—or in float? At any rate, the fruits add a certain fecund ornamentality to the trees in autumn.

Carolina silverbell and mountain silverbell can become quite large in time. I have seen some that were obviously envisioned as dogwood-sized trees by the designer but that had grown into full-sized specimens about the size of a linden (*Tilia cordata*), with trunks 10 inches in diameter. In shade, though, they remain demure in relation to large canopy trees, and this combined with an ability to bloom heavily in only filtered light make them invaluable in the woodland garden.

CULTURE: Transplant silverbells in spring as balled and burlaped or containerized saplings. Michael Dirr reports mediocre results from balled and burlaped material in the South and attributes this to the plant's having a relatively small root system, not amenable to digging and transporting (*Manual of Woody Landscape Plants*, p. 413). We have installed a few 1-to-1½-inch-caliper field-dug specimens, including one poor soul that was forced in a spring flower show, and then was left outside to weather the ides of March, which perfunctorily defoliated it. We planted the leafless tree later that spring, and it suffered through the driest summer we've had in ten years, albeit with some root zone irrigation. Happily, the branches leafed out again, and after two years it recovered sufficiently to commence flowering once again. The same root-system qualities that make field-digging risky serve silverbells well in containers, and container-grown specimens can be set

into the garden without much worry about root girdling. As a point of taste and also structural integrity, I prefer trees that have been staked and pruned so that they develop a strong central trunk. The main drawback of silverbells is their propensity to suffer ice and snow breakage, and narrow crotches at the base of multistemmed trees are especially prone to splitting under a heavy load of ice — we lost a prime specimen in a bad storm a few years ago. Fortunately, if the tree is cut off at the ground, the roots will respond with a tremendous surge of new sprouts that are capable of 10 feet of growth the first season. Thin these down to the best stem or two the following winter. Silverbells bloom very young, and resprouted trees will resume flowering in 3 to 4 years. They all prefer a fairly fertile, moist, slightly acidic woodland soil.

USES: Specimen or understory tree.

PROPAGATION: Moderately easy from cuttings, moderately difficult (slow) from seed.

Halesia diptera
Two-winged Silverbell

ZONES: (4)5–8; sun to shade
SOIL: Moist, acidic
NATIVE TO: Bottomlands, swamps, and rich woodlands; mostly along the Gulf Coastal plain from southern South Carolina and Georgia to northern Florida and eastern Texas
SIZE: Height 15–25 (35) feet, width 12–20 feet
COLOR: White; blooms in late spring

This small, multistemmed understory tree lacks silvery white underbark, and its fruits have only two well-developed wings instead of four. Its flowers are distinctive as well, with petals that are not fused into a seamless bell and thus flair a bit, somewhat like those of the related *Styrax grandifolius*. Var. *magniflora* has larger blooms and is the one most often sold; it makes an especially lovely show in spring, blooming concurrently with flowering dogwood (*Cornus florida*). *H. diptera* blooms 10 to 14 days after *H. tetraplera*.

Halesia parviflora
Little Silverbell

ZONES: 6–9; part sun to shade
SOIL: Moist to moderately dry
NATIVE TO: Oak-pine woodlands and sand scrub; scattered locations in Georgia, northern Florida, and Mississippi
SIZE: Height 10–20 feet, width 6–15 feet
COLOR: White; blooms in spring

This is the smallest species, thought by some taxonomists to be merely a small-statured ecotype of the widespread Carolina silverbell (*H. tetraptera*). Its flowers are about half the size of the others', which makes it of less ornamental value, though its habitat suggests greater drought and heat tolerance, which could be valuable traits in the Southeast.

Halesia tetraptera (carolina)
Carolina Silverbell

ZONES: 4–8; sun to shade
SOIL: Moist, acidic
NATIVE TO: Rich wooded slopes and stream banks, mainly in the piedmont and mountains from West Virginia and North Carolina to Mississippi and northern Florida, with scattered outlying populations in Ohio, Kentucky, Arkansas, and Oklahoma
SIZE: Height 20–40 (80) feet, width 15–30 feet
COLOR: White or occasionally rose pink; blooms in spring

The Carolina silverbell is the most widely cultivated species, though its larger potential size should be considered when placing it. The striped and patterned bark and 4-winged fruits are ornamental in the winter, and the tree blooms about the same time as redbud. There is a pink form, 'Arnold Pink', or var. *rosea*, with flowers lightly flushed. These are exquisite in bloom, making a stronger statement than the typical form, which is admittedly muted in effect unless sited against a dark background.

Halesia tetraptera var. *monticola (H. monticola)*
Mountain Silverbell

ZONES: 4–8; sun to shade
SOIL: Moist, acidic
NATIVE TO: Rich mountain coves at higher elevations in the Appalachians; North Carolina to Tennessee and Georgia
SIZE: Height 30–50 (80) feet, width 20–35 feet
COLOR: White; blooms in spring

Mountain silverbell is just a larger version of Carolina silverbell. I have seen it growing as a 12-inch-diameter canopy tree in the Smoky Mountains, the flowers high overhead buzzing with bees. Its blooms are larger than those of the Carolina silverbell, and so the floral effect is more pronounced if you can see it.

Hamamelis
Hamamelis virginiana
(ham-a-MAY-lis)
Hamamelidaceae
Witch-hazel

You have to respect a plant that laughs in the face of winter, especially one, like witch-hazel, that unleashes a belly-shaking guffaw. Common witch-hazel (*H. virginiana*) has the audacity to bloom in autumn, just as leaves are falling all around and a tree's efforts should turn not to reproduction but to surviving the coming cold. Spring witch-hazel (*H. vernalis*) is even more impudent, hoisting its wispy 4-petaled flowers in the depths of winter, when few if any pollinators are available to service them. Why they bloom at such an odd time is indeed a mystery. Certainly they appear to be insect pollinated, and the blooms, especially of spring witch-hazel, emit a fruity perfume no doubt designed to attract six-legged creatures. Even in the depth of winter there are insects about—snow midges, flies, maybe an occasional beetle—and a plant blooming then would receive their undivided attention. Another advantage of cold weather is the way it prolongs blooming. The petals seem remarkably chill-proof, and they decorate the naked branches for a month or more, emitting fragrance only when the sun has warmed the air at least a few degrees above freezing (the petals coil and uncoil like little carpets as conditions dictate). Common witch-hazel flowers when many insects are still lingering around from the summer, so its flowers would seem to be more easily pollinated. Because the fall-blooming species tends to flower as its leaves are blazing yellow and falling, the blooms are not as easily seen, and breeding work is under way to select superior garden plants that drop leaves cleanly and quickly to display the flowers to good effect. On the Ozark Plateau, where the two species are sympatric, color variation in the flowers of *H. virginiana* suggests occasional hybridization

Hamamelis virginiana. *In this photograph of common witch-hazel, a cluster of new flowers is rolling open above one of last year's seed capsules, which has finally ripened after a year on the tree. Hamamelis seeds are launched from the capsules with remarkable velocity, sending them far away from the shade of their parent.*

with its more florally variable relative. There is great potential here for selecting good forms of both species as well as hybrids with different bloom times to extend the season of bloom.

Witch-hazels are consummate understory shrubs or small trees. They are invariably multistemmed, with a vase-shaped habit resulting from a style of branching seen also in elms and redbuds: the topmost few buds along the previous year's wood grow most vigorously, while those lower down grow progressively less so. In effect this creates a flattened, fan-shaped branch spread to efficiently catch what is left of the light that passes through the tree canopy above. The stems are covered with ruddy gray bark that remains smooth and unfissured, even on older trunks. Each slightly gray-green, alternate leaf is broadly oval and set with a textured, fishbone pattern of veins that roughly scallop the margin where each protrudes. The foliage of both species is bronzy red when it emerges, slowly transforming to green as the tissue fully expands. Flower buds form in the leaf axils during the year and bloom in season. If they are pollinated, fuzzy 2-parted capsules develop inside a calyx cap. These ripen a bit in winter, then continue through the next growing season, the seeds finally maturing as the weather cools again in autumn. Ripe capsules split open like the maws of two baby robins stretched wide in anticipation of a worm. Inside are four shiny seeds surrounded by a membrane that dries quickly on exposure to air and squeezes the seeds out at a velocity great enough to propel them up to 25 feet.

Witch-hazels have a distinctive shape that looks very appropriate in a woodland setting. They can grow happily in shade, where their older branches begin to arch out irregularly, and they will also do well in partial sun, which encourages tighter growth. They have a unique, apricot yellow fall color that can be truly outstanding at the edge of the woods. Shriveled leaves often remain to skirt the lower branches through the winter. I like this quality of the plants, mostly for the rustling sound the leaves make in this aurally depauperate time of year. For centuries witch-hazel bark has been steeped in water to produce a mild, spicy astringent, and Native Americans employed the trees to treat a range of ailments, including colds, eye infections, kidney problems, and hemorrhoids. The common name refers to the use of forked branches as divining rods to locate underground water; another term for dowsing is "water witching."

CULTURE: Best sited in partial sun to light shade and in a moist, slightly acidic soil. Plants grown in full sun and wind may exhibit signs of scorching and burning, though flower production is usually enhanced. Transplant in spring or fall as balled and burlaped or container-grown specimens. Both species can be rejuvenated with heavy pruning every 10 years or so to retain good form. Alternatively, you can selectively remove older trunks and encourage the more vigorous sprouts that come continually from the base. *H. vernalis* is more stoloniferous than *H. virginiana*, and if left to its own devices it will become a dense thicket after 20 years or so. In this case, judicious thinning and sucker removal after flowering will keep the clump within bounds.

USES: Specimen, massing, naturalizing in the forest understory.

PROPAGATION: Difficult from cuttings, moderately difficult from seed.

Hamamelis vernalis
Spring Witch-hazel

ZONES: 4–8; part sun to shade

SOIL: Moist to seasonally wet, moderately acidic to neutral

NATIVE TO: Stream banks, sand bars, and low woods; the Ozark plateau of Missouri, Arkansas, and eastern Oklahoma

SIZE: Height 6–12 feet, width 6–15 (25) feet

COLOR: Variable, from translucent yellow to bronze, or commonly orange or deep red; blooms in mid- to late winter

Spring witch-hazel is the smaller of the two species, with finer twigs and a shrubby, thicket-forming habit. The largest stems are often no more than 1 inch in diameter, with a stiff, upright carriage. The blooms start to appear during the first thaw of the year, with full bloom in the Garden (Zone 5) by early to late February, depending on the weather. Spring witch-hazel has the remarkable ability to bloom even when the ground is frozen and under a foot of snow. The blooms are 30 percent smaller than common witch-hazel's, but have the same ribbon-thin petals crosslike in a cupped, darker-colored calyx. At its best, the fragrance has a rich, dried-apricot fragrance that is a potent tonic for the winter-weary nose. Cultivars have been selected for both flower color and bloom time, though I think we have only just touched on the possibilities.

Hamamelis virginiana
Common Witch-hazel

ZONES: (3)4–8; sun to shade

SOIL: Moist to seasonally wet or moderately dry

NATIVE TO: Wooded slopes, floodplains, damp woods and thickets; Nova Scotia, southern Quebec and southern Ontario to eastern Minnesota south to eastern Texas and central Florida

SIZE: Height 8–20 (30) feet, width 8–20 feet

COLOR: Golden yellow; blooms in fall

Common witch-hazel is fast growing when young, with a slight zigzag pattern to the twigs as the leaves come out in their turn. It stays relatively concentrated as a clump, with branches spreading out widely from a narrow base. The flowers are like those of spring witch-hazel, though larger. The fragrance is similar to the other species, but usually very faint. It is an easy and adaptable plant for eastern gardens.

Hudsonia tomentosa

Hudsonia (hud-SOW-nia)
Cistaceae
False Heather, Beach Heather

There are few more difficult places for a plant to grow than in shifting sands. By nature, plants want to take root and stay awhile, confident that the soil around their crown will neither wear away dangerously nor pile up to such an extent that the branches become buried, as can easily happen out on the dunes. Aside from physical unpredictability, sand is an awfully poor substrate as water and nutrients go, so plants that make a home in it must be resigned to a spartan diet. Furthermore, anyone sandblasted during a windy day at the beach knows that blowing sand is dangerous stuff, capable of stripping and battering soft tissues relentlessly. The reward for persisting in such a limiting environment is that dune plants have precious little competition.

On the rugged, shifting dunes skirting the Atlantic coast and the Great Lakes you are likely to find *Hudsonia*. These small shrubs become attractive nested buns of thin vertical branches thickly clothed in small needles or scale-like leaves. They grow in pure sand, sending their roots down until they reach a steady supply of moisture deep in the dune. As blowing sand inevitably settles around and buries the crown, branches keep growing upward and outward to stay just above it. Eventually, old clumps can be 4 feet or more across, just a circle of separate, layered branches radiating from a central core in such a way to suggest they are all indeed connected at some center point deep in the sand. *Hudsonia* grows very slowly — 2 inches a year is about average — so an old mound is surely decades old. For most of the year they blend unobtrusively with the lichens, heaths, and sand, but for a week or two in spring, their cheeky little buns are covered in starry, 5-petaled flowers washing like a golden tide over the windswept dunes.

CULTURE: I have been fascinated by the picturesque quality of *Hudsonia* for many years, and have experimented quite a bit with both species. Unfortunately, they are generally less than satisfactory once taken out of the sand-scoured environment they thrive in. We are growing them in full sun in a gritty rock garden, and both species grow and flower, though for continued health they need very acidic soil, a supply of moisture below the surface, perfect drainage, and freedom from competition. In such a position, they do start to bush up and take on the lovable shape that makes them so pretty in the wild. Avoid fertilizing them once established, as growth gets a bit rank — at least by *Hudsonia* standards.

USES: Dune restoration, seaside plantings, acidic rock gardens; very tolerant of salt spray and saline soil.

PROPAGATION: Moderately difficult from cuttings or seed.

Hudsonia ericoides
False Heather

ZONES: 4–8; sun to part sun
SOIL: Moist but sandy, well-drained, acidic
NATIVE TO: Sand barrens and rocky headlands; mostly along the coast from Newfoundland south to Delaware and scattered to South Carolina
SIZE: Height 4–12 inches, width 8–20 (36) inches
COLOR: Golden yellow; blooms in late spring to early summer

False heather is more shade tolerant than beach heather, preferring slightly more stable dunes and pine scrub. The awl-shaped leaves are dull gray-green during the growing season and a warm brown where they persist in the winter. In habit it is generally similar to its sibling but a bit softer and more open.

Hudsonia tomentosa
Beach Heather

ZONES: 2–8; sun
SOIL: Sandy, well-drained and acidic
NATIVE TO: Open dunes and sand scrub; along the coast from Labrador to Rhode Island and inland in suitable habitats to Manitoba and the Northwest Territories, Wisconsin, and Minnesota south to West Virginia
SIZE: Height 3–12 inches, width 4–18 inches
COLOR: Golden yellow; blooms in late spring to early summer

Beach heather is smaller than false heather and is readily distinguished during the growing season by its knobby, adpressed scale-like leaves covered in a pelt

Hudsonia tomentosa. *For fifty weeks of the year, beach heather is a driftwood gray mound. A colony of it looks like a pile of cobblestones half buried in the sand. For a couple of weeks, though, the plants are awash with bright, starry flowers that illuminate the dunes.*

of gray hair. During the winter the dried leaves turn a light tan color, but persist on the stems until spring. I prefer this *Hudsonia* for its ornamental effect, mostly because of its tight habit and gray foliage. It can grow in more exposed habitats than false heather, often just behind the tide line of the outer dunes.

Hydrangea quercifolia

Hydrangea (high-DRAIN-ja)
Hydrangeaceae
Hydrangea

Hydrangea quercifolia. *The ornamental parts of a hydrangea bloom are the sets of four white bracts surrounding the little clusters of flowers. Oakleaf hydrangea produces long, cone-shaped panicles thickly set with bracts that open white, then fade to deep pink and green before finally turning construction-paper brown as the seeds mature.*

Neither of our two native hydrangeas can offer gardeners the designer pink or blue flowers of the Asian bigleaf hydrangea (*H. macrophylla*) and its relatives, but when all is said and planted, they are still fine, fine ornamentals. Hydrangeas have small, fairly insignificant fertile flowers clustered at the tips of the mature new growth. These are more or less ringed by large, 4-petaled sterile flowers whose sole purpose is to advertise the presence of the tiny flowers clustered about them. Some individuals have few if any sterile blooms, and these are decidedly unspectacular in flower. Others have no fertile flowers at all, just broccoli or even cabbage-sized heads of large sterile bracts. Because these gelded flowers can never set seed, they stay colorful for weeks, slowly changing from leprechaun green to chalky white, and then slowly flushing pink and green again before finally fading to papery brown. Oakleaf hydrangea produces a cone of sterile flowers with fertile ones hidden beneath; on sterile forms of this species the sterile flowers are either more thickly set or have multiple petals arranged in complex tiers. Wild hydrangea has blossoms with domed heads, and the sterile forms are rounded like snowballs.

CULTURE: Both species are woody, suckering shrubs with large, bold-textured leaves adapted to catch the dim light of the forest floor. The double forms of wild hydrangea as well as all forms of oak-leaf hydrangea are beautiful in flower, and they are popular garden subjects. Wild hydrangea has a running, thicket-forming habit, especially in good soils, so it is a bit difficult to use in formal areas unless massed. I think it is most satisfactory when treated as an herbaceous perennial that is cut to the ground every fall. Oakleaf hydrangea tends to be more of a multistemmed clump, and it too can be pruned hard every once in a while to maintain a mounded shape, although hard pruning will curtail flowering the following summer. The hydrangeas transplant easily enough from containers and grow quickly in good soil amended with a bit of fertilizer. Both have the habit of drooping in the hot sun, which indicates they are dry only if the leaves don't recover once shade returns.

USES: Massing, mixed border, scattered specimen in the shade garden.

WILDLIFE: Fertile forms are good nectar plants, but fully double ones are void of nectar.

PROPAGATION: Easy from cuttings or seed.

Hydrangea arborescens
Wild Hydrangea, Smooth Hydrangea

ZONES: 4–9; part sun, shade
SOIL: Moist
NATIVE TO: Hillsides, rich woods, and damp thickets; southern New York to Ohio south to Oklahoma, Louisiana, and Georgia
SIZE: Height 2–4 feet, width 3–10 feet
COLOR: White; blooms in early to midsummer

The wild form of this species is fairly weedy and the flower effect is minimal. Forms with a ring of sterile flowers around the edge (much like the *H. macrophylla* lacecaps) are better, but only the fully sterile cultivars like 'Annabelle' and the older, smaller-headed 'Grandiflora' make an impact in the garden. 'Annabelle' borders playfully on the absurd, with heads that enlarge to the size of basketballs on vigorous stems. Of course this enormous weight on top of rather thin stems means the plants have a tendency to bend over after a heavy rain. The flowers come from the new growth, and I prefer to cut the plant to the ground after the leaves drop in fall. This seems to curtail suckering, increase flowering, and generally improve the shape of the plant: with annual pruning, expect a broad mound; without it, a twiggy patch. Fertile forms hold their seed in dried capsules until late fall or spring, a fact that infuriated me for years because a colony downwind from the nursery would drift tiny seed into my flats, and I would have to constantly pull out little hydrangea seedlings with roots like cables, taking half the other seedlings with them. The 6-to-10-inch narrowly heart-shaped leaves are pretty and bold-textured in summer, and well-fed plants bear leaves of dark forest green that complements the whiteness of the blooms. Mildew can partially defoliate the plants by fall, when the remaining leaves turn yellow-green before dropping. Cut the flower heads when they are fully expanded and dry them upside down for use in dried-flower arrangements.

Hydrangea quercifolia
Oakleaf Hydrangea

ZONES: (4) 5–9; sun to light shade
SOIL: Moist to moderately dry
NATIVE TO: Bluffs and talus slopes, woodlands; Georgia and Tennessee south to Louisiana and Florida
SIZE: Height 3–10 feet, width 4–12 feet
COLOR: White fading to pink; blooms in summer

Oakleaf hydrangea is nearly a four-season shrub. In the winter, a few reluctant leaves cling to clumps of sparsely branched, vertical stems clothed in shaggy, rusty brown exfoliating bark. In spring, leathery, deeply lobed leaves emerge dramatically from the branch tips. The leaves do suggest one of the red oaks in shape, with deep sinuses carving a series of lobes. It is an undeniably course-textured plant in winter, spring, and even in summer, when the foot-long cones of white flowers appear from the stem tips. These remain white for a few weeks, and as the fertile flowers are pollinated, the sterile ones flush slowly with pink in a remarkable fashion. In the fall, the leaves begin to turn deep maroon, then fade to scarlet before shriveling. This species is moderately hardy north of Zone 6, usually suffering some winter dieback that keeps it from attaining the size it reaches in the south. The compact cultivars like 'Pee Wee' and 'Compacta' and the stunning double-flowered 'Snowflake' and 'Roanoke', among others, are all widely available. The small forms are certainly less rank in appearance, and I have used them successfully in foundation plantings where the wild species would look out of place.

Hypericum frondosum
Hypericum (high-PAIR-i-kum)
Hypericaceae (Clusiaceae)
St. John's Wort

There is something almost consciously optimistic about the pouffy flowers scattered over a blooming St. John's wort. *Hypericum* is a hop skip and a jump evolutionarily from *Stewartia*, and you can sense this kindred relationship in the big puff of stamens that juts out from the center of the flowers. In many species, the four or five golden petals reflex

back against the stem as if trying to keep their distance from this glistening fecundity. The abundant stamens produce an excess of pollen, and bees are adept at harvesting this golden bounty. I like to watch bees working on these flowers with the precision of a farmer. They land on the ball of stamens and then quickly zigzag back and forth around its circumference, buzzing as they go to jog the pollen free. It only takes a second or two, but they manage to cover the whole area very efficiently and add the harvest to their swollen leg sacks. Of course they inevitably brush against the stigma that struts out from the center and thus pollinate the bloom.

There are woody *Hypericum* species and some herbaceous ones, both annuals and perennials. The introduced herbaceous weed *H. perfoliatum* is the species whose flowers are harvested for use as a natural antidepressant. Most of the native woody species are concentrated in the southeastern United States, and many are fine ornamentals with interesting form, foliage, and pretty flowers. All have opposite leaves that are either narrow or oval in shape set on twiggy, shrubby plants with what is often very handsome, exfoliating bark. A few are evergreen, but assume the following are deciduous unless I mention otherwise. Flowers develop on short, leafless branches at the tips and upper leaf axils of the new growth in summer so the blooms stand out proudly just above the mass of leaves. There is a notable buttercup yellow consistency to the flowers of this tribe, though a few have petals that are stained with orange like the

Hypericum frondosum. *The bee-tickling ball of stamens that puffs out from each golden St. John's wort flower is loaded with pollen. I suspect the anthers release it only when bees vibrate or buzz them at the right frequency. You can simulate this by holding a tuning fork against the anthers. If you find the right frequency, pollen should come spurting out of the anthers upon contact with the fork.*

stamens, and at least one is more butter cream than buttercup yellow. Flowers yield to large, pointed oval capsules that are very conspicuous on the branch tips in late summer and fall, sometimes persisting into winter in their dried, dark-brown state.

CULTURE: With the exception of a few wetland species, St. John's worts are plants of well-drained, moist to even droughty soils and open sunny places. If afforded the same in cultivation, they will thrive with a modicum of effort on your part. Though many of the following species hail from the hot, humid Southeast, they tend to concentrate in the sandy soils of the coastal plain or the loams of the mountains, not the heavy clay of the piedmont, where they can be susceptible to root diseases in wet years. Transplant from containers in spring, and fertilize lightly early in the season to maintain good foliage luster and heavy flowering. Many will take considerable drought once established, but supplement water for the first year until deeper roots establish. The larger species can get a bit rangy after 5 to 7 years, so an annual light winter pruning in which you remove only the outermost 25 percent of the crown will keep them neater and denser without jeopardizing flowering or the formation of a thick, barky trunk.

USES: Massing, hedge, mixed border.

WILDLIFE: Valuable as a pollen source for bees.

PROPAGATION: Moderately easy from cuttings, easy from seed.

Hypericum buckleyi
Blue Ridge St. John's Wort

ZONES: 5–8; sun
SOIL: Moist, well-drained
NATIVE TO: Balds (exposed rock outcrops) and cliffs at high elevations in the southern Appalachians; North Carolina to northern Georgia
SIZE: Height 3–16 inches, width 1–2 feet
COLOR: Bright yellow; blooms in summer

A low, mounded species restricted mostly to rhododendron balds high in the Smoky and Blue Ridge mountains. It bears small, elliptical leaves less than 1 inch long and 1-inch flowers intermittently through the summer. Blue Ridge St. John's wort makes a good rock garden subject.

Hypericum frondosum
Golden St. John's Wort

ZONES: 5–8; sun, part sun
SOIL: Moist to dry
NATIVE TO: Glades, bluffs, and rocky banks; Tennessee and Kentucky to southern Indiana south to Texas and Georgia
SIZE: Height 3–6 ft, width 3–4 feet

COLOR: Bright yellow; blooms in summer

If I had to pick one *Hypericum* for my garden, it would be golden St. John's wort. It becomes a dense, rounded shrub with warm gray exfoliating bark covered in pretty blue-green 1½-inch linear leaves that are the perfect foil for very large, puffy flowers about as wide as the leaves are long. The cultivar 'Sunburst' is much more readily available than the wild type, and its more compact, 3-to-4-foot habit and larger flowers make it well suited to gardens.

Hypericum kalmianum
Kalm's St. John's Wort

ZONES: 4–7; sun, part sun
SOIL: Moist, well-drained
NATIVE TO: Dunes and rocky lake shores; common around the Great Lakes from the Ottawa River in Quebec to southern Ontario, Wisconsin, and the Upper Peninsula of Michigan south to Illinois and Ohio
SIZE: Height 2–3 feet, width 2–3 feet
COLOR: Golden yellow; blooms in summer

Kalm's St. John's wort is a good choice where a neat, mounded plant tolerant of poor, droughty soil is required. *H. kalmianum* holds its flowers in flattened panicles rather than in clusters on the upper leaf axils. Each bloom is about 1 inch wide, with a large pompon of stamens nearly obscuring the 5 petals. The dark green leaves are 1 to 1½ inches long, slightly rolled under along the margin, and almost linear in shape.

Hypericum prolificum
Shrubby St. John's Wort

ZONES: 4–8; sun, part sun
SOIL: Moist to dry, well-drained
NATIVE TO: Swamp margins, rocky ledges, open woods; New York to Minnesota south to Louisiana and Georgia
SIZE: Height 3–6 feet, width 3–6 feet
COLOR: Golden yellow; blooms in mid- to late summer

This wide-ranging, mounded shrub is one of the hardiest and most adaptable. It carries its 1½-inch, medium green leaves on twiggy, warm gray stems and covers itself with small, puffy flowers for 3 to 4 weeks in summer. There is obviously some confusion in the nursery trade regarding this species and *H. kalmianum*, as I have received plants labeled as the latter that turned out to be *H. prolificum*, which has a 3-, not a 5-chambered capsule and smaller (less than 1-inch) flowers. Shrubby St. John's wort is an easy-to-please species for difficult situations and will readily seed itself around, almost to the point of weediness at times. Dense hypericum (*H. densiflo-*

rum) is similar overall, but the leaves are narrower, so the plant has a finer, bushier look I personally prefer. It grows along the margins of bogs and on sandy or rocky soils from New Jersey to Missouri south to Florida and Texas. It performed reasonably well for me in clay soils in North Carolina. Bedstraw St. John's wort *(H. galioides)* is yet another attractive shrub from low woods and swamps of the southeastern coastal plain. In habit it is similar to *H. densiflorum,* but the leaves are longer and narrower than those of the other St. John's worts.

Hypericum suffruticosum
Trailing St. John's Wort

ZONES: 7–9; sun
SOIL: Sandy, well-drained and acidic
NATIVE TO: Sandy pinelands along the coastal plain from North Carolina to Florida and southeastern Louisiana
SIZE: Height 2–6 inches, width 1–2 feet
COLOR: Pale, creamy yellow; blooms in spring to early summer

Trailing St. John's wort is a low, ground-covering species with narrow, oval leaves scarcely ½ inch long on trailing stems covered in rough, reddish brown bark. Its flowers are 4-petaled and distinctly pale yellow, with a small cluster of stamens in the middle, and are set in the folds of two very large sepals. It reminds me of cranberry in growth habit—a tiny little plant, but worth growing for the color of the flowers. St. Andrew's cross *(H. hypericoides)* has similar few-stamened pale yellow flowers, but it is a stiffer, more upright plant of larger proportions, 1 to 3 feet high, with a rather narrow habit. The plant sends up a few tall, stiff stems that branch heavily near the top in summer and fall. Its range is from Virginia to Oklahoma south to Texas and Florida in a variety of moist to dry habitats

Hypericum tetrapetalum
Four-petaled St. John's Wort

ZONES: 7–10; sun
SOIL: Moist to moderately wet
NATIVE TO: Pine flatwoods (low forests along the coastal plain) and pond shores; southeastern Georgia to central Florida and Cuba
SIZE: Height 6–36 inches, width 1–3 feet
COLOR: Bright yellow; blooms in spring to fall

An attractive evergreen shrub from the southern pinelands, *H. tetrapetalum* has small, rounded leaves with a heart-shaped base that are so nearly sessile as to appear perfoliate. The foliage has a glaucous green quality like that of some of the other St. John's worts, and it sets off the relatively large, 1-inch-wide flowers quite nicely.

Ilex opaca

Ilex (EYE-lex)
Aquifoliaceae
Holly

Hollies have a special meaning for me that goes beyond the plants themselves. As I understand it, my last name, Cullina (kul-EYE-nah), is an anglicized form of the Gaelic for "place of the holly." In Ireland, as in the British Isles generally, the evergreen English holly *(Ilex aquifolium)* has long stood as a potent symbol of renewal and life during the dark days around the winter solstice. Its spiny, scalloped leaves and red fruits are as much a part of Christmas as mistletoe and Santa Claus. On this side of the pond, our American holly *(I. opaca)* is the only species that comes respectably close to the spiny, archetypal English holly, but we are fortunate to have quite a number of less prickly species, both evergreen and deciduous, that brighten up the fall and winter landscape with their brilliant red fruits. Hollies are preeminent berry plants and are fall and winter staples of robins and mockingbirds, among others. If the berries are not eaten in the fall, they remain reasonably plump through the winter because of fairly low moisture content. Flocks of robins returning north used to descend on the American holly out in my yard every spring and strip the remaining berries in an amazing 15-minute feeding frenzy. The deciduous species are especially spectacular in fruit, as the leaves quickly drop away to reveal the berries lining the twigs in crimson splendor. Of course it is only the females that fruit, for hollies are dioecious.

I am frequently asked how close a male holly has to be for good fruit set (it seems that everyone, including me, wants to sequester the male in some forgotten corner of the yard). The plants are insect pollinated, and in fact you would hardly notice that the little translucent flowers are there at all if not for the attention the plants garner from every bee and

Ilex opaca. A female American holly hung with a good crop of fruit is certainly a potent symbol of life during the midwinter darkness. The red and green colors of Christmas were very likely originally inspired by holly boughs.

hoverfly in the neighborhood when in bloom; there is a slight, honey fragrance to alert you as well. The real question, then, is how far the insects will fly and still accomplish pollination. I have certainly had good fruit set when a male was up to 50 feet away, and others have told me that even 200 feet will do the trick, but this seems a bit ambitious to me and I would try to stay within the lower figure. Cultivars of certain wide-ranging species, winterberry *(I. verticillata)* in particular, have been selected from both northern and southern genotypes; for best pollination, try to match up males and females that bloom at the same time. In the case of winterberry, the northern forms bloom a week earlier than the southern. If you are uncomfortable playing matchmaker, ask your local nursery or consult a reference like Michael Dirr's *Manual of Woody Landscape Plants.* Horticulturists, mostly men, I reckon, have had fun naming male clones with suggestive monikers like 'Apollo', 'Southern Gentleman', 'Stallion', and 'Jim Dandy'.

Of the evergreens, several, like the distressingly named *I. vomitoria* (yaupon) as well as inkberry *(I. glabra),* dahoon *(I. cassine),* and American holly *(I. opaca)* are widely used in landscaping more for their foliage than for their fruit. *I. cassine* and *I. opaca* form a natural hybrid, *Ilex × attenuata,* and a few of these *I. × attenuata* cultivars, including the lovely 'Fosteri' series, are among my favorites. They develop a much narrower, more pyramidal form than typical American holly, and the deep, evergreen leaves are spiny but much smaller than that parent's. Females tend to fruit very heavily, a trait acquired from *I. cassine.* (Hollies are promiscuous, and one species can stand in as a pollinator for another.)

CULTURE: Hollies are easily transplanted, either as field-dug burlaped specimens or smaller container plants. I have even moved them in the middle of summer, though judicious pruning to lighten the crown is a good idea if you would be so bold. Though I tend to shy away from overdependence on cultivars, in the case of hollies, most of the selections are far superior in form, leaf color, vigor, and fruit set than the wild types, with the added advantage of being previously sexed. Just by accident, I have made plantings of mixed wild and selected cultivars of *I. glabra,* and the cultivars stand out to the point where I have been tempted to pull out all the wild ones and start over. Many hollies can tolerate flooded soils and some shade, though not surprisingly, best fruit production is in the sun. As a rule, all want an acidic soil, and gardeners in limestone regions may see chlorosis develop. All in all you could not ask for a better group of native shrubs for fall and winter effect.

USES: Screening, specimen, massing, hedging, foundation plantings.

WILDLIFE: Fruits are important winter and spring forage for birds.

PROPAGATION: Moderately difficult from cuttings, difficult from seed.

Ilex amelanchier
Serviceberry, Sarvis Holly

ZONES: 6–9; sun to light shade

SOIL: Moist to wet

NATIVE TO: Swamps and floodplain forests; along the coastal plain from southeastern Virginia to Florida and Louisiana

SIZE: Height 6–12 (16) feet, width 3–8 feet

COLOR: Greenish white; blooms in spring

I have not had the opportunity to see many representatives of this rare species, but what I have seen has impressed me. Superficially it resembles winterberry, but the deciduous leaves have a nearly smooth margin and a fine pelt of grayish down that gives them a bloomy look a bit like mountain holly *(Nemopanthus),* and like it, the fruits have a lustrous, satiny patina that is quite distinctive and beautiful. It has proved hardy for us at Garden in the Woods, though fruit set has been minimal. We only have one female plant, so it must occasionally be getting pollinated by the male *I. opaca* or the *I. verticillata* that are abundant in that part of the garden.

Ilex cassine
Dahoon

ZONES: 7–9; sun to light shade

SOIL: Moist to wet

NATIVE TO: Cypress swamps and depressions, riversides; along the coastal plain from southeastern North Carolina to southern Florida and southeastern Texas

SIZE: Height 15–30 feet, width 6–10 feet

COLOR: Greenish white; blooms in spring

This species is not planted nearly as much the *I. × attenuata* hybrids, but it is nevertheless a fine, evergreen holly. Female flowers are borne in clusters of 2 to 6 at the base of the current crop of leaves, to spectacular effect. The fruit color ranges from almost red to more commonly orange or orange-yellow, and this is one of the best hollies for fruiting effect. I have seen it used quite a bit in Florida to provide some holiday cheer for snowbirds from the North (both human and otherwise). The spineless foliage is medium green and narrowly lanceolate. Habit is open and rounded to narrowly pyramidal, with ascending branches. The var. *myrtifolia* (also listed as a separate species, *I. myrtifolia)* has smaller (less than 1-inch) leaves and fruits and a more compact habit. Both are more tolerant of higher pH than most hollies.

Ilex decidua
Possum-haw

ZONES: 6–9; sun to light shade

SOIL: Moist to wet

NATIVE TO: Wet woods, swamps, and damp thickets, occasionally better-drained locations; chiefly along the coastal plain from Maryland to Florida and Texas and along the Mississippi River system to eastern Oklahoma, southern Indiana, and southern Illinois

SIZE: Height 15–30 feet, width 8–15 feet

COLOR: Greenish white; blooms in spring

Possum-haw differs from winterberry and the other deciduous species mainly in its smaller, lance-shaped to obovate leaves that are dark green above, lighter below; its pretty silvery gray bark; and a stiffer, vertical carriage to the branches. It freely sprouts from the base and roots, forming large, unkempt thickets in the wild. Most of the plants I have seen in cultivation have been 'Warren's Red', which has large, deep red fruits carried on little spur branches and a good upright form, as well as the even narrower 'Sentry'. 'Warren's Red' does very well for us, but fails to set much fruit despite the proximity of male *I. opaca* and *I. verticillata*. The southeastern Georgia holly (*Ilex longipes*) is similar, but the fruits hang on long peduncles like little cherries.

Ilex glabra
Inkberry, Gallberry

ZONES: (4)5–9; sun to part sun

SOIL: Wet to moderately dry and sandy

NATIVE TO: Wooded swamps, low woods, and thickets; mostly along the coast from Nova Scotia to Florida and eastern Texas

SIZE: Height 3–6 feet, width 3–6 feet

COLOR: Bronzy green; blooms in late spring

Inkberry has long been one of my design staples, because of its adaptability and its lustrous, deep evergreen foliage that shines even in winter—and, more important, because it has a certain billowy, mounded character that is wild yet formal at the same time. There are few shrubs that you can plant and just let go that will keep such thick, even shape as inkberry, and yet it never looks forced or overly styled as boxwood or Japanese holly can. The leaves are narrowly oval to obovate, with a nearly smooth margin, and the plants are fairly slow growing, even by holly standards; 6 to 8 inches a year is about average. The fruits of this species are black, so they are not too noticeable, but they do spend several weeks in fall as a lovely plum purple as they begin to ripen. I have never tested this out thoroughly, but I believe, from what I have seen, that predominately female plants must produce some male flowers, as I have seen good fruit set on very isolated pistillate plants. Cultivars like 'Shamrock', 'Compacta', and 'Nordic', among others, have a tighter, more formal shape than the wild species. The plants are moderately stoloniferous, with sprouts coming occasionally from the base and roots, which can be removed if necessary. Sweet gallberry (*I. coriacea*) is a larger rel-

ative, growing to 15 feet, from the southeast coastal plain. Its earlier bloom time prevents interbreeding where their ranges overlap.

Ilex montana
Big-leaf Holly

ZONES: 4–8; sun to light shade

SOIL: Moist

NATIVE TO: Woods; in the Appalachians from western Massachusetts to North Carolina, Georgia, and Alabama

SIZE: Height 8–20 (30) feet, width 6–15 feet

COLOR: Greenish white; blooms in spring

This winterberry relative is distinguished by its relatively large broadly oval leaves 2 to 4 inches long and an inch or so wide, and rather small, grooved fruits. To me it looks a bit like an apple tree in the shape and arrangement of the leaves.

Ilex opaca
American Holly

ZONES: (4)5–9; sun to light shade

SOIL: Moist, acidic

NATIVE TO: Woods and hedgerows; along the Atlantic coast from southeastern Maine to Maryland, then inland to Kentucky and southern Missouri south to Texas and Florida

SIZE: Height 15–40 feet, width 8–15 feet

COLOR: Greenish white; blooms in spring

This is the only native holly with spiny-toothed, evergreen leaves. The foliage has a fairly dull, matte finish, so it is easy to tell from the English holly and Chinese holly as well as from hybrids formed by it and the glossier dahoon. Its color is army green in summer, flushed yellow in winter. For this reason,

Ilex verticillata. *Winterberry fruits start to ripen when the leaves are still on the plant and are slowly revealed as the foliage yellows and falls. Be sure to have a male holly (preferably of the same species) within fifty feet or so to ensure good pollination.*

along with a sensitivity to several leaf spots and insect pests, the species is not used as much as others, but regardless, it is still a beautiful small tree with a juniper-like, pyramidal habit, smooth, warm gray bark, and a dense, leafy canopy, and there are many improved cultivars available if you search a bit. It reaches the northern limit of its range along the coast of New England, and here it is typically a round-topped shrub or small tree rarely more than 20 feet tall. In the South, it can become far more substantial, and narrow—30-to-40-foot trees are a common sight in the forest understory. This is really the only native evergreen holly that can reach a decent size in Zone 5, though a spot out of the winter wind is necessary to prevent leaf burn.

Ilex verticillata
Winterberry

ZONES: 3–9; sun to light shade
SOIL: Moist to wet, acidic
NATIVE TO: Wet woods, swamps, and thickets; Newfoundland and Quebec through Ontario to Michigan and Minnesota south to Indiana, Missouri, and Florida
SIZE: Height 6–10 (15) feet, width 6–10 feet
COLOR: Greenish white; blooms in spring
Winterberry is the hardiest of the native species, and the sight of females laden with fluorescent red fruits in the fall and winter landscape is spectacular indeed. It is typically found in wetlands, often where water stands in spring, but it has proved fairly adaptable in landscape situations provided the soil is not droughty. The leaves are oval, medium green, and slightly puckered on the upper surface where the veins intersect. The habit is stiff and somewhat upright when young, and broader and more open with age, but throughout its overall form is rounded and roughly as wide as tall, with new growth coming from the crown and larger roots to form thickets. The smooth bark is silvery, but not quite as lustrous as *I. decidua*'s. The popularity of this plant has skyrocketed in recent years, so there are a bewildering number of cultivars available, some with yellow fruits, or extra large red ones, others with dwarfed or compact habit. In addition, hybrids with the Japanese winterberry *(I. serrata)*, including the very popular cultivar 'Sparkleberry', are widely proffered and further complicate one's choices. Winterberry can have pretty nice fall color – sort of a smoky burgundy like the dogwoods, and the leaves fall early to expose the fruits. There is quite a bit of natural variation in this wide-ranging species. Southern forms (var. *padifolia*) tend to be larger, with wider leaves than the more northern, earlier flowering var. *verticillata*. Smooth winterberry *(I. laevigata)* is a very similar species, which, in our garden at least, tends

toward a wide, rounded shrub 6 feet high and 8 to 10 feet wide with large, orange-red to scarlet fruits that ripen a week earlier than those of *I. verticillata*.

Ilex vomitoria
Yaupon

ZONES: 7–10; sun to light shade
SOIL: Moist to wet (tolerates some drought)
NATIVE TO: Wet woods and swamps of the coastal plain; southeastern Virginia to Florida, Arkansas, and Texas
SIZE: Height 12–20 feet, width 6–12 feet
COLOR: Greenish white tinged purple; blooms in spring
Yaupon is an excellent evergreen shrub for gardens in the Southeast. The fairly small, flat leaves are toothed a bit on the margins and emerge with a purplish tinge, fading to deep, moderately glossy green. It is a good substitute for the ubiquitous and in my mind supremely boring Japanese holly *(I. crenata)*. The fruits are usually deep red and juicy-looking due to translucence in the skin. There are numerous cultivars, including compact, narrowly upright, and weeping or at least pendulous forms. The colorfully expulsive Latin epithet refers to the use of its leaves as an emetic and purgative by Native Americans.

Illicium parviflorum

Illicium (il-LIS-sium)
Illiciaceae
Anise, Anise-tree, Star Anise

Like pawpaws and magnolias, the anise-trees are an ancient line of beetle-pollinated flowering plants that have survived the vicissitudes of geological change in the great botanical refugium of the southeastern United States. They are shade-adapted, evergreen shrubs—not distinct in leaf but valuable for filling dark corners of the garden with a mass of green. The whole plant, including leaves and flowers,

Illicium parviflorum.
Yellow anise tilts its leaves and branches upward, giving the shrub a narrower, more tucked-in, formal appearance than its relative I. floridanum. The crushed leaves release the sharp, pungent odor of licorice.

is laced with volatile oils that hang over the area in a faint, pungent cloud. I could best describe the odor of a flowering anise as a blend of licorice and musk, which some find wonderful and which causes others to crinkle their noses and flee. The flowers attract beetles with the tangy aroma of unclean feet, while the leaves, especially when crushed, have a much more pleasant aniselike fragrance. These leaves are 3 to 6 inches long and narrowly oval, leathery-thick, and matte light to medium green. They alternate along stems of similar color when the crown is growing rapidly but tend to cluster mostly at the top on the less vigorous branchlets, much like broadleaf rhododendrons. In fact anise-tree serves a similar function in southern landscapes to that of catawba or rosebay rhododendron farther north: a reasonably bold, evergreen screen little troubled by diseases or insects. The individual stems have a noticeably upright, oval habit, with side branches coming off at low angles along main trunks and new sprouts coming from the base to widen the clump into a broad pyramid or rounded mound that can be judiciously pruned to keep it more formal in outline.

CULTURE: The volatile oils in the leaves and stems afford anise-tree excellent protection from insects and browsing mammals. *I. floridanum* grows on hummocks in swamps, and needs a fairly damp, organic soil and shade to thrive. I had a plant growing in half-day sun and the exposed leaves sunburned or yellowed in a most unfortunate way, especially in winter. *I. parviflorum* is more drought tolerant and thus has greater potential as a general-use evergreen for shade. Transplant from containers in fall.

USES: Screening, massing, background shrub for shade.

PROPAGATION: Moderately easy from cuttings or seed.

Illicium floridanum
Florida Anise, Stink-bush, Polecat Tree

ZONES: (6)7–9; part sun, shade
SOIL: Moist to wet, acidic
NATIVE TO: Moist ravines and stream sides, wooded swamps; northwestern Florida and southwestern Georgia through Alabama and Mississippi to eastern Louisiana and also in northeastern Mexico
SIZE: Height 6–10 feet, width 4–8 feet
COLOR: Crimson or, rarely, pink or white; blooms in mid spring to early summer

Florida anise is not as adaptable as the yellow anise, but it certainly provides more floral effect. The leaves have a long pointed tip and are a bit droopier than those of yellow anise. When crushed, they have a rich, musky, clove-like scent.

Florida anise produces deep red flowers from overwintering buds at the tips of the previous year's growth. These are 1 to 2 inches wide with spokelike linear petals much like those of *Calycanthus* in appearance. These are unusual in the ordered and consistent world of flowers in that they are quasi-composites of up to 33 petals, 21 pistils, and 50 stamens, with a knob of pistils surrounded by a ring of stamens and an outer ring of petals. The number varies considerably from flower to flower, but the proportion remains roughly 2:1:2. The name star anise comes from the curious seed capsules that form once the flowers fade, bloated dark brown wheels of boat-shaped pods, each splitting along the upper side to release a flattened, oval seed. The dried capsules remain on the plant, buried under the new crop of leaves, for up to a year, which helps identify them when they're out of flower.

Illicium parviflorum
Yellow Anise, Small Anise

ZONES: 7–9; part sun, shade
SOIL: Wet to moderately dry
NATIVE TO: Moist woods and swamps; restricted to a few small areas in southwestern Georgia and central Florida.
SIZE: Height 8–15 (20) feet, width 4–10 feet
COLOR: Yellow-green; blooms in late spring

This rare species is not closely related to the more widespread Florida anise, a fact borne out by the shape of its odorless flowers. The tepals are cupped, rounded, and pulled tight together to form a small bell that practically goes unnoticed even when the plants are in full bloom. Its leaves are thick, leathery, distinctly rounded at the tip, and a few shades lighter green than Florida anise's. The crushed leaves exude a sharp licorice aroma. They hold up much better in sun and drought, which serves to make this an excellent background and screening shrub. Individual stems are markedly narrow and upright, but the plants freely sucker to form broader colonies in time.

Itea virginiana. *Sweet-spire is an exceptional nectar plant that blooms in early summer, in the lull between frenzied spring and high summer. Later in the season, the reluctantly deciduous leaves turn red, orange, and maroon before finally dropping.*

Itea virginiana

Itea virginiana
(eye-TEE-ah)
Grossulariaceae
(or Iteaceae or Saxifragaceae)
Virginia Sweetspire

ZONES: 5–9; sun to light shade
SOIL: Wet to moderately dry
NATIVE TO: Swamps and wet woods; coastal plain from southern New Jersey and eastern Pennsylvania to Florida and Louisiana, then north along the Mississippi River to southern Illinois
SIZE: Height 3–6 feet, width 3–10 feet
COLOR: Ivory white; blooms in early summer

I got to know Virginia sweetspire in cultivation long before I studied it in the wild, and this is fortunate, for wild specimens are unseemly characters, lanky and weak-stemmed understory shrubs of wooded swamps—decidedly not the sort of fellows you'd think to invite into the proper garden or garden proper. Given a modicum of culture, though, sweetspire can really blossom into a wonderful shrub best described as an arching, informal mound covered with neat, leathery satin-finished leaves that alternate along the curving stems in an upturned fashion much like those of *Leucothoe* or *Diervilla*. The leaves are reluctantly deciduous, turning luminescent red, orange, yellow, and burgundy in fall, then slowly dropping by the time Thanksgiving draws near. In warmer climates, a few leaves will remain on the stem tips all winter. The species is a bit of an enigma to taxonomists, and has been forced to shuttle between different families like a foster child without a home. Gleason and Cronquist (*Manual of Vascular Plants*, pp. 226–227) place it in the gooseberry family (Grossulariaceae), which surprises a "gestalt" botanist like me, because there is little resemblance between this and other family members such as the prickly currants and gooseberries *(Ribes)*. I will leave this question to the taxonomists to decide, and get on with the description. In a superficial way it reminds me more of *Cyrilla racemiflora,* especially the way the kitten-tail flower spikes arch away from the mound of foliage like trailing fireworks. The starry blooms are tightly packed into 4-to-6-inch-long racemes that open sequentially from base to tip over the course of 2 weeks in early summer. Like *Cyrilla*'s, the flowers wait patiently until the new growth is well under way before festooning the shrub in a glorious helter-skelter, every-which-way-but-up bloomfest. The flowers are lightly fragrant and highly attractive to butterflies, which has helped popularize *Itea* in recent years. When pollinated, the flowers develop into 2-parted capsules which, like those of many saxifrages, can be used in dried arrangements.

The second reason I feel fortunate to have met this shrub first in the garden is that otherwise, I probably would have underestimated its adaptability. You would never guess that a lax understory plant in cypress swamps could perform so well in full sun and dry soils. I have even seen it thriving on a clay highway embankment in Raleigh, North Carolina. In the Southeast, swamps are safe havens for many species that cannot survive the frequent fires that ravage all but the dampest ground. Therefore, I think that many of the shrubs restricted to swamps in the wild can thrive in drier soils if fire is kept at bay—it's a theory, anyway, and helps to explain the horticultural flexibility of some wetland species.

Most of what is available from nurseries these days are cultivars, including the abundant 'Henry's Garnet', a selection found near Sharpsburg, Georgia, in 1954 by Mary Henry, who gave some to Swarthmore College. It boasts flower racemes larger than the typical form of the species and a beautiful plum purple fall color. There is a more compact version, too, called appropriately 'Little Henry'. There are other *I. virginiana* selections, including 'Merlot', with wine red fall color, and 'Saturnalia', which has mixed orange and red autumn tones. Nurseries like producing this plant because it roots easily, grows quickly to size in containers, and suffers few problems. Unfortunately, it leafs out late in spring, so its impact during the spring shopping season is less than spectacular. I have had a hard time convincing customers that the twiggy mass of reddened stems hung with a few burned old leaves is going to amount to much of anything in their garden. Have faith, people, have faith.

CULTURE: Virginia sweetspire can be readily transplanted from containers in spring or fall. It does best in a moist, moderately fertile soil with at least 4 to 6 hours of sun, but it will grow in dry or wet soils and in light shade, albeit more laxly. Prune after flowering or selectively remove some of the older stems during winter. With time, Virginia sweetspire can become a tad unruly, and severe rejuvenation pruning may become necessary.

USES: Massing, bank stabilization, informal hedge, and mixed border.

WILDLIFE: Esteemed as a nectar plant for butterflies and other insects.

PROPAGATION: Easy from cuttings or seed.

Juglans nigra

Juglans (JUG-lans)
Juglandaceae
Walnut, Butternut

It is sometimes difficult to see beyond the utilitarian aspects of trees. When I see a big black walnut, my mind's eye flashes to a scene where the limbs have all been sawed off and the log sits on rollers ready to be sawn into beautiful, chocolate brown lumber. Walnut heartwood is perhaps our most beautiful and valuable furniture wood, and enterprising colonists quickly cut vast forests of magnificent old-growth black walnut (*J. nigra*) in river valley forests of the Midwest and South to make the fine eighteenth- and nineteenth-century furniture that we pay such high prices for at antique stores today. The trees were harvested so ruthlessly that they were nearly eliminated from much of their former range, leading to a shortage of veneer-quality, large-diameter trees that has led ingenious "walnut rustlers" to steal big trees with the aid of a helicopter at night and sell an ill-gotten trunk for as much as $40,000. This also led to the widespread home-orcharding of walnuts, as enterprising backyard sylviculturists have been urged through magazine ads to plant seedlings as an investment for the future. The reality, however, is that good-quality walnut develops only on limestone-rich alluvial soil and takes 75 to 100 years to mature, so I imagine many of these plantings will never amount to much money-wise, but at least they are helping to increase the number of walnut trees. Walnut heartwood doesn't begin to develop until a tree is 20 years old or so; that is when the inner xylem gets too old to be functional conductive tissue and becomes plugged up with plant wastes and rot-inhibiting compounds including tannins, phenolic compounds, and gums. The accumulated compounds add strength and decay resistance, and, most important, the soft chocolate patina that gives walnut its unique appeal. In addition, these xylem tissues become occluded with a matrix of structures called tyloses, which act as physical barriers to rot and also help to physically strengthen the wood and reduce shrinkage when it's dried for use.

The extractives that infuse the heartwood of walnuts are not the only ones that deserve mention. The tannin juglone is an allelopathic chemical that is released from the leaves and has the notorious ability to retard the growth of many other plants that happen to be growing nearby—including Grandpa's prize beefsteak tomatoes! Other trees that are known to secrete these chemicals include balsam poplar, sugar maple, hackberry, and sassafras, but walnut's are some of the most widely studied.

Juglone also inhibits the growth of seedling walnuts, and this, combined with an intolerance of shade cast by the parent tree, means that these trees are usually found scattered through the forest rather than growing in stands. The largest are single-trunked trees branching above into several wide-spreading, stout limbs that support a big, rounded crown. The very stout twigs grow in an up-sweeping way and are marked with large, alternating scars where the heavy rachis of the big pinnate leaves was attached. Each compound leaf is 1 to 2 feet long and is composed of as few as 7 or as many as 25 (on *J. microcarpa*) oval or lance-shaped, finely toothed leaflets that droop a bit like a palm frond. The leaves as well as the husks surrounding the nuts are covered in glandular hairs that when bruised release a distinctive pungent tannin aroma. Of course nuts are the other things that walnuts are prized for. Next to pecans, walnuts are our most viable commercial nut species. As with acorns, the "meat" of the nut is really a pair of convoluted cotyledons that have swollen to act as a food source for the developing seedling, which then germinates hypogeally. After you collect the nuts, you have to rid them of their tacky husks, which contain a pigment that will stain the skin yellow-brown for days (wear gloves). *J. nigra* produces

Juglans nigra. A tree that has spent its life in the open will have a much different shape from that of a sibling that has grown up in a forest. This open-grown black walnut has a stocky trunk that divides low into wide-spreading limbs. The shape takes full advantage of the abundant sun and is less likely to suffer from buffeting winds than is a tall, single-trunked specimen.

baseball-sized husks that can be collected as they drop and run over a few times with the car or whacked with a mallet to free the nut inside. Butternut has smaller fruits, and these have a smooth, oily flavor. The others have even smaller nuts, which means you will have to invest more energy to extract quantities of the delicious meat.

CULTURE: All walnuts, including the southwestern species, prefer deep alluvial soils where their striker roots (secondary taproots) have access to underground moisture at all times. At least 3 to 4 hours of sun is necessary for fast growth and balanced crown development — but the more sun the better. Like most large-seeded species, walnuts develop a deep taproot as seedlings, making handling and transplanting difficult. You can buy bareroot whips or small, deeply potted seedlings, or just plant stratified seeds in place and wait for the large seedlings to emerge. Sadly, butternut is being exterminated by a canker with the staggering Latin name of *Sirococcus clavigignenti-juglandacearum* that was only described in the 1970s. It is unclear whether this is an endemic or introduced disease, but either way, it is causing phenomenal dieback throughout butternut's natural range. This was a fairly common tree in the woods when I was growing up, but now discovering one is worth celebrating. The canker affects twigs and branches as well as trunks and crowns, causing rapid tissue loss and death of the affected parts. It will infect weakened individuals of the other *Juglans* species, but not to this extent.

USES: Nut, timber, and shade tree.

WILDLIFE: Nuts are obviously valuable to mammals, and the foliage is consumed by the larvae of the hickory hairstreak and banded hairstreak butterflies (*Satyrium caryaevorus* and *S. calanus*).

PROPAGATION: Moderately easy from seed.

Juglans californica
Southern California Walnut

ZONES: 8–9; sun
SOIL: Well-drained but not excessively dry
NATIVE TO: Hillsides and canyons at lower elevations west of the Sierras in southern California
SIZE: Height 15–25 feet, width 7–15 feet
COLOR: Yellow-green; blooms in spring

Southern California walnut is a small tree or large shrub of the forested foothills near the California coast with blunted leaflets and 1-to-1½-inch fruits. The other Californian species, northern California walnut (*J. hindsii*) is larger and restricted to a few areas farther north, but it is becoming more widespread through its use as an understock in commercial production of English walnut (*J. regia*), whose own roots are too susceptible to drought stress and disease. After a time the understocks in abandoned orchards will resprout and the native species can then forcibly replace the grafted interloper.

Juglans cinerea
Butternut

ZONES: 4–8; sun, part sun
SOIL: Moist
NATIVE TO: Rich woods and floodplains, also drier, rocky slopes; formerly New Brunswick to Minnesota south to Arkansas, Alabama, and northern Georgia, but fast disappearing
SIZE: Height 50–70 (90) feet, width 20–40 feet
COLOR: Yellow-green; blooms in spring

The spread of butternut canker (see "Culture" section) means there is little point in planting this tree unless resistant strains can be found. When healthy, it develops into a smaller version of black walnut in both the size of the leaves and the overall crown. It ranges farther north than black walnut and seems to be able to thrive on more acidic soils. The heartwood is more of a blond-brown and was once a valuable furniture wood.

Juglans microcarpa
Little Walnut, Nogal

ZONES: 7–10; sun
SOIL: Well-drained but with access to underground moisture
NATIVE TO: Creeks, rivers, and washes; southern central Kansas to Oklahoma and Texas and New Mexico, south into Mexico
SIZE: Height 15–30 feet, width 6–15 feet
COLOR: Yellow-green; blooms in spring

Nogal is a pretty little tree with long leaves made up of many thin leaflets — quite a different texture than the other *Juglans* species and worth using where it can be grown. The bark of younger branches is silvery gray. It is a deep-rooted plant that can grow in washes where there is no visible sign of water. Arizona walnut (*Juglans major*) is another southwestern species distinguished by its larger size, fewer leaflets per rachis, and fruits that are twice as large as black walnut's (1 to 1½ inches in diameter).

Juglans nigra
Black Walnut

ZONES: 4–9; sun to part sun
SOIL: Moist, fertile, with a pH above 6.5
NATIVE TO: River bottoms, rich woods; Massachusetts and Vermont to southern Ontario, southern Minnesota, and eastern South Dakota south to Texas and the Florida Panhandle
SIZE: Height 70–90 (150) feet, width 30–60 feet
COLOR: Yellow-green; blooms in spring

Black walnut is a handsome, broad-crowned tree

whose size precludes its use in many situations. Typically, the straight trunk is clear of branches for the first 20 to 60 feet, and it is distinguished by a recognizable coal gray bark with a diamond-latticed pattern. Long compound leaves and drooping leaflets give the canopy a nice sawtoothed texture during the growing season. Quite a bit of selection is going on in an attempt to produce reliably superior nut and timber strains.

Juniperus horizontalis

Juniperus (joo-NIP-er-us)
Cupressaceae
Juniper

Junipers are durable conifers, but they take their time getting to an appreciable size, and this limits them in the wild to places where conditions are too rugged for faster-growing trees. They reach their greatest abundance in the interior western mountains at elevations between 3,000 and 10,000 feet. Here they mix with pines to form a dominant forest community, the juniper-pinyon woodland. At these elevations, rainfall is a bit higher than it is lower down in the sagebrush belt, but not high enough for the larger ponderosa and Jeffrey pines to get established and shade out the smaller junipers. In the East, junipers are relegated to an early serial or successional role, colonizing abandoned agricultural land and roadsides and flourishing until taller trees get established and shade them out. Only on shallow-soiled, hardscrabble balds (rocky outcrops), wind-blasted cliffs, and sandy scrublands do they have a chance to live to a ripe old age like their western counterparts.

Fortunately for junipers, stripped, degraded soils and hot, windy exposures are the hallmark of modern residential developments, and here they have found an important niche. Junipers are certainly one of the most often planted shrubs in suburban and commercial landscapes. They offer evergreen foliage combined with an extremely rugged constitution that makes them as close to fool-proof as a living plant can be (just remember "green side up," and they should be okay). The landscape market is dominated by the Asian species, especially Chinese juniper (*J. chinensis*), but we have many fine native species as well. Most of the North American junipers are small, single-trunked trees that develop stout, wizened trunks studded with short branches to form a rounded, narrow oval, or pyramidal crown. Their reasonable size and fairly predictable shape has helped them to become popular as screens and windbreaks for difficult locations. Two species, common juniper and creeping juniper, are low, sprawling groundcovers that have likewise become ubiquitous groundcovers in modern landscapes.

All junipers have small, pleasantly aromatic needles more or less covered in a waxy bloom. The leaves are classified as either awl-shaped, pointy "whip" leaves or flattened, twig-hugging "scale" leaves. Whip leaves are considered the juvenile form, so you find them on seedlings and nonfruiting branchlets. Even mature twigs will often produce a few of these pointy leaves early in the season, and each is tipped with a small but sharp point that can pierce the skin (and discourage herbivores). When I used to unload nursery trucks full of junipers, my forearms would develop a rash from the accumulated prickles. The rash quickly disappears unless you are very sensitive to the juniper oils, in which case be careful to wear heavy clothing when handling branches. The scale leaves are much easier on the skin because they flatten against the twig. The needles remain green for 3 to 5 years, helping to give the plant density and fullness in the landscape. In winter, the foliage will often develop a burgundy cast as a response to cold, which some people find unattractive—if you fall into this group, look for cultivars selected for green winter color. Juniper twigs are round, not flattened as in other familiar members of the family, and the genus is also unique in that the trees are predominantly dioecious. This fact becomes important to the ecologically minded gardener because juniper "berries" (actually female cones) are an important food for many birds, including the magnificent cedar waxwing (*Bombycilla cedrorum*) and its cousin, the Bohemian waxwing (*B. garrulus*). Some of the cultivars are sexed, but if you are growing the wild types from seed, be sure to plant at least 3 to 4 to increase the odds of getting a few females. If you have only female trees, I wouldn't be worried unless there are no male trees within 1,000 yards or so. The pollen travels well on the wind. The knobby, waxed seed cones ripen in one or two years, depending on the species, and on some forms of common juniper it can take up to three. The berries of all junipers have a pungent smell and a glaucous,

*Juniperus horizontalis.
Creeping juniper is a
tough customer. This
photograph was taken in
eastern Quebec on high
cliffs overlooking the
Gulf of St. Lawrence.
Only the most rugged
plants can survive the
bitter winter storms and
incessant winds blowing
in from the North
Atlantic.*

waxy color that is really quite pretty in the fall and winter landscape. Some female trees are so loaded with fruits that they appear to have turned from green to blue-gray. The oil found abundantly in the fleshy female cone is used to give gin its unique, resinous flavor.

Juniper oils suffuse all parts of the tree, and older specimens develop beautiful redolent heartwood stained deep red that has long been used to line cedar closets and hope chests as a natural moth repellent. These oils and resins make the wood highly decay resistant, and preserve the old, broken branches, which regularly protrude from the trunk of a venerable tree like silvered ribs. Long-dead but resilient snags are a common sight in regenerating forests in the East, testament to the former open condition of the land when the junipers colonized abandoned fields.

Junipers are the alternate host of the cedar-apple rust, a native fungus disease with a fascinating life cycle. In late summer and fall, the rust fungus releases a type of spore called an aeciospore that lands on wet juniper needles, germinates, and enters the vascular tissue, where it takes hold. Over the next summer and fall it develops into a small, hard, ruddy brown gall. The following spring, the galls wait for a warm, rainy night in late spring to swell up into a remarkable jellied creature composed of long, tendril-like horns that emanate from a spherical core and taper to a point. The whole looks and feels much like a saltwater anemone, and it is colored a uniform rusty orange that makes the 3-inch ball even more noticeable. The purpose of these gelatinized eruptions (called telia) is to release another type of spore, which floats out into the rainy night looking for an apple, hawthorn, or crabapple leaf to germinate on. When it lands on a leaf, a circular, discolored lesion begins to develop, and if the infection is severe, these lesions cause premature defoliation of the tree. Because of its effect on such an economically valuable crop as apples, attempts have been made to eradicate junipers from around orchard areas. Fortunately, a more sound approach—developing rust-resistant apples—is now the method of choice for combating this problem.

CULTURE: Junipers are easy to establish in well-drained soils, provided you take care to keep them watered the first season until roots are established. Like all conifers, they don't wilt to alert you they are under drought stress, they just quickly dry up and die. Established plants are very drought tolerant. Junipers need full sun and good air circulation to help fend off various fungus diseases; these can be a nuisance but they are only rarely life threatening. Junipers take light pruning or hedging pretty well, provided you don't cut them back too severely at any one time. Branches cut back to below the needle-covered twigs may resprout, but this severely weakens the tree.

USES: Screening, windbreak, foundation, hedge, groundcover, massing—you name it.

WILDLIFE: Great for birds, both as a food source and a dense, sheltered place to hide from the cold and build a nest. In fact, I would rate the tree forms of juniper as among the 10 essential plants to include in a bird-friendly landscape. The needles are eaten by the larvae of the widespread rusty orange, brown, and gray cedar hairstreak butterfly *(Callophrys gryneus)*, whose coloring echoes that of juniper bark quite nicely.

PROPAGATION: Moderately difficult from cuttings, moderately easy from seed.

Juniperus ashei
Ashe Juniper

ZONES: 6–9; sun
SOIL: Well-drained, alkaline
NATIVE TO: Limestone bluffs, hillsides, and glades; scattered in suitable habitat from southern Missouri and southwestern Arkansas to central Oklahoma and Texas then south into Mexico
SIZE: Height 20–35 (45) feet, width 15–30 feet
COLOR: Yellow; blooms in early spring

Ashe juniper has found a niche on limestone escarpments that mark the boundaries of an ancient reef system. It develops a round, wide-spreading crown of large scaffold limbs emanating from a single trunk, all covered in a shaggy, warm brown bark that exfoliates in long strips. The small, mostly scaly leaves are light to medium green, and the female cones are so large and dusky blue that they give the whole plant a gray aspect when mature. Other junipers with this broad, rounded shape include one-seeded juniper *(J. monosperma)*, a smaller species of rocky soils throughout the southwestern mountains, and alligator juniper *(J. deppeana)*, which has a similar distribution but prefers rocky soils higher in the mountains. It produces an attractive globelike crown supported by low-forked trunks covered in thin, plated bark.

Juniperus communis
Common Juniper

ZONES: 2–6 (7); sun
SOIL: Well-drained, acidic to alkaline
NATIVE TO: Old fields, rocky outcrops, tundra, mountaintops; circumboreal, in this hemisphere from Labrador to the Northwest Territories and Alaska south to British Columbia and in the higher mountains through the West, and in the East from Minnesota to Kentucky, western North Carolina, and Virginia

SIZE: Height 1–30 feet, depending on form, width 3–15 feet

COLOR: Yellow; blooms in spring

This plant has to rank as one of the toughest and most evolutionarily successful gymnosperms. It grows in a tremendous range of habitats through North America and Eurasia that have little in common save poor, stony soil that limits competition and gives this slow-growing species a chance to thrive. Typically it's a flat-topped shrub with many branches radiating out from a central trunk that develops just above the roots. *J. communis* is easy to identify because it is the only species that has only whip-type needles, which are about ½ inch long, green to silvery glaucous blue, and sharply tipped. Some forms are low, spreading groundcovers with upward-arching twigs growing from splayed branches that lie on top of the soil. Other forms are narrow, conical trees to 20 feet and rarely higher. The typical forms turn a sickly shade of red-brown in the winter, but both shrubby and groundcover-type cultivars with better winter color are available. Common juniper is a cold-climate species that does poorly in the Southeast.

Juniperus horizontalis
Creeping Juniper

ZONES: 2–8(9); sun

SOIL: Well-drained, acidic to alkaline

NATIVE TO: Dunes, sandy or gravelly soils, outcrops, and tundra; Labrador to the Northwest Territories south to British Columbia, Minnesota, and New Brunswick and scattered at higher elevations and along coasts farther south to about the 42nd parallel.

SIZE: Height 2–12 inches, width 3–6 feet

COLOR: Yellow; blooms in spring

If you want the living visual equivalent of Astroturf, then this is your plant. Creeping juniper, especially some of the popular prostrate cultivars, forms a ground-hugging carpet of mostly scale-needled twigs. Its only drawback is that it can't stand much foot traffic. I find the sweeping branches and gnarled trunk look especially picturesque careening over rocks and cliffs. Like common juniper, this is a plant of the glacier-scarred north, but it is certainly more heat tolerant than its prickly cousin. I have even seen it growing reasonably well in traffic islands in southern Florida, though that seems to be pushing it.

Juniperus occidentalis
Western Juniper

ZONES: 4–9; sun

SOIL: Well-drained

NATIVE TO: Dry, rocky soils and slopes; western Idaho to southern Washington, south through Oregon and California

SIZE: Height 25–40 (90) feet, width 15–25 feet

COLOR: Yellow; blooms in spring

Everything grows bigger in the Pacific Northwest, and junipers are no exception. In favored spots on the drier eastern flanks of the Cascades and Sierras, western juniper can become an impressive specimen with a stout, flaring trunk covered in glowing cinnamon brown bark that supports a gnarled, domed crown. The whole is knitted tightly to the rocks with thick, serpentine roots. Younger trees have a softer, more broadly pyramidal crown. They are reasonably fast growing when young.

Juniperus scopulorum
Rocky Mountain Juniper, Western Red-cedar

ZONES: (3)4–8; sun

SOIL: Well-drained

NATIVE TO: Rocky, exposed hillsides throughout the mountainous West above 3,500 feet and along the Pacific coast in British Columbia; western North Dakota to British Columbia south to eastern Oregon, Nevada, Arizona, New Mexico, and northern Mexico

SIZE: Height 10–25 (40) feet, width 6–20 feet

COLOR: Yellow; blooms in spring

As in its counterpart, eastern red-cedar (*J. virginiana*), form and needle color in this species are variable. The wild type tends toward a narrow oval crown becoming more rounded in age, but broad and narrow pyramidal forms are common as well.

Juniperus virginiana. *Female eastern red-cedars produce incredible crops of oily berries nearly every year — so many that the branches look distinctly blue when seen from a distance in fall. Birds such as waxwings, thrushes (including robins), and mockingbirds depend on the trees for winter and spring forage.*

The bark is warm gray and peels in thin strips. Forms with pendant to downright weeping branchlets can also be found, and some of these drooping selections, like 'Tolleson's Weeping', with its weeping-willow shape and blue-gray color, have become popular far east of its native range. This species is a valuable screen and windbreak used extensively in drier parts of the Midwest and throughout the Rockies.

Juniperus virginiana
Eastern Red-cedar

ZONES: 4–9; sun, part sun
SOIL: Moist to dry
NATIVE TO: Old fields, pastures, roadsides, balds, margins of swamps; southern Quebec to southern Ontario, Minnesota and southern Iowa south to Texas and Florida
SIZE: Height 15–35 (60) feet, width 3–12 feet
COLOR: Yellow; blooms in spring

Eastern red-cedar is a popular roadside distraction for me as I drive hither and yon. It becomes a small tree ranging in shape from a broad pyramid to a narrow exclamation point with no two in any one stand exactly alike in shape or needle color. I have puzzled over the evolutionary advantage of such polymorphism without coming to any conclusions—well, they are fun to look at, anyway. Red-cedar develops a gnarled trunk with a fluted, enveloping character. The trunk and stout branches are covered with a thin, gray-brown exfoliating bark that on some older trees becomes worn smooth. It is on these that the fluted bark becomes most picturesque, folding and swelling around each limb like hardened cellulite. Both male and female cultivars of both shapes have been selected, some with silver blue foliage as well. There are even dwarf bushy forms that are popular around foundations. Var. *siliciola* is a form found along the southeastern coastal plain with a consistently broad, pyramidal crown and smaller berries.

Kalmia angustifolia.
You are as likely to see sheep laurel growing above the tree line in the mountains as in dry scrublands along the Atlantic coast; it will thrive equally well in a cold bog and a dry, upland wood. Give it an acidic soil and some sun, and it is sure to please. Notice how the flower buds have sprung from the axils of the previous season's twigs just as the new leaves are emerging above.

Kalmia angustifolia
Kalmia (KAL-mia)
Ericaceae
Laurel

Only one hundred years ago, before airplanes made long-distance shipment of perishable commodities feasible, the florist industry relied on local growers to provide cut flowers and greens. Expensive hothouse flowers were heavily supplemented with cheaper wild-collected material that could be gathered by children paid pennies a bundle. By the early decades of the twentieth century, many people, including the founders of the New England Wild Flower Society, were growing alarmed at the wholesale eradication of trailing arbutus (*Epigaea repens*), clubmoss (*Lycopodium* spp.), ferns, and mountain laurel (*K. latifolia*) by industrious collectors who could ride the trolley out into the country and bring back their bounty to sell in the streets of New York, Boston, and Philadelphia. Part of the problem was that the hasty collectors would break off whole branches or rip out entire plants rather than just cut off a bloom or branchlet. Partly through the campaigning of the New England Wild Flower Society and partly because of the development of a commercial floriculture industry, this practice has mostly subsided, but one of the upshots of all the publicity was the adoption of mountain laurel as the Connecticut state flower in the 1920s. Fortunately, the harvest of untold millions of flowers did not eliminate the plant from eastern woodlands, though the growing populations of ravenous deer (or, as I like to call them, wood goats) are turning to its poisonous leaves when all else fails in winter and eliminating stands much more methodically than people did.

A typical *K. latifolia* has white flowers flushed pink in bud that erupt in a frothy display that makes mountain laurel unsurpassed among the broadleaf evergreens. This is the plant that I came to know growing up in New England, so imagine my surprise when I moved into my office at the Connecticut

Agricultural Experiment Station and found the drawers stuffed with photo after photo of pink, red-banded, plum- and raspberry-striped, speckled, and pure white selections, not to mention compact forms with smaller leaves. It turns out that my office was the former workplace of Dr. Richard Jaynes, the man who has single-handedly elevated the common mountain laurel to horticultural superstardom through his painstaking selective breeding program. Dr. Jaynes had retired just a year before I started, to put his full energy into a great specialty nursery that features a number of his cultivars along with a range of other ornamental woody plants.

Mountain laurel is only one of six native *Kalmia* species, all of them evergreen shrubs with leathery leaves. They bloom in summer from knobby buds set the previous fall, which mix with the newly expanding leaves. As with rhododendrons, the new foliage emerges in a flush, with leaves concentrated near the top of each growth so as to appear whorled. This lends the plants a tiered, picturesque form that adds to their charm. The blooms are all similar in shape: little satellite dishes composed of five fused petals with pointed tips and arranged in rounded clusters. Each petal is allotted two stamens, whose filaments are held under tension in a little cavity, like baited mousetraps waiting for an unsuspecting bee. As the bee lands on the flower and brushes the filament, it springs upward, dabbing the insect's abdomen with pollen as it forages for nectar at the base of the corolla.

CULTURE: All laurels require a strongly acidic soil and a moist, humid climate to thrive. If allowed this, both mountain laurel and sheep laurel are surprisingly drought tolerant once established, though the others need a boggy spot to do well. Full sun will produce the best flower effect. Only the southeastern *K. cuneata* and *K. hirsuta* are truly heat-adapted. Mountain laurel grows wild in the piedmont of North Carolina south into Florida, but it prefers north slopes, shaded streamsides, and other specific microclimates where the soil remains cool and moist.

USES: Specimen, screening, naturalizing, or bog garden, depending on species.

PROPAGATION: Difficult from cuttings, moderately easy from seed.

Kalmia angustifolia
Sheep Laurel

ZONES: 1–7; sun to light shade
SOIL: Acidic — boggy-wet to sandy-dry
NATIVE TO: Bogs, thickets, open woodland, sand barrens, tundra; Labrador to Michigan south along the coast to Virginia and inland to the mountains of North Carolina and Georgia
SIZE: Height 16–38 inches, width 2–4 feet

COLOR: Typically hot pink or red-pink, also white or light pink; blooms in late spring to summer

The vibrant flowers of this species develop in small, axillary clusters from the top section of the previous season's twigs. Because the new growth is well under way as the plants bloom, the flowers skirt below it in an almost tubular fashion. This is a very adaptable species that grows as happily in bogs as it does in rich woods or the pure sand of old dunes. It is a scurfy, suckering shrub in most situations, with thin vertical stems sprouting from a spreading, underground rhizome. After logging or especially after fire, it can resprout luxuriantly, and I have a vivid memory of working in a burned-over area awash in rich pink sheep laurel. The sub-opposite (almost opposite) or whorled leaves are narrow, leathery, and either slightly oblong or lanceolate with a whitish bloom underneath and a gray-green patina above. The twigs shed some of the lower leaves in winter and the rest turn deep burgundy for the duration. Like all laurels, the leaves contain andromedotoxin, a nerve poison that has been implicated in cases of livestock poisoning. Unfortunately, deer are partially immune to its effects, though it does seem to deter them if other sources of food are available. For difficult locations like dry banks, upland woods and the like, this is a good choice, but it will never compete ornamentally with its larger cousin, *K. latifolia*.

Kalmia cuneata
White Wicky

ZONES: 6–9; sun to light shade
SOIL: Moist to wet, acidic
NATIVE TO: Pocosins and swamps; coastal North and South Carolina
SIZE: Height 1–4 feet, width 1–2 feet
COLOR: White spotted with burgundy; blooms in early to midsummer

This rare evergreen is more of a curiosity than a great beauty. It has the same knobby flower buds as *K. latifolia*, but these never open fully, they just purse open enough to let a bee get its head in. The flowers remind me very much of barnacles in shape and color, and they form a ring around the current season's growth after it has finished developing. The leaves of this species are only 1 to 2 inches long and are narrowly spatulate, but they have a rough, lustrous, dark green color that is set off by rusty red twigs. It has lived for many years in our bog garden, but remains a thin, suckering shrub akin to sheep laurel in habit. It is the last *Kalmia* to bloom for us.

Kalmia hirsuta
Hairy Wicky

ZONES: 7–9; sun to light shade
SOIL: Moist to wet, acidic

NATIVE TO: Sandy bogs, flatwoods, and pocosins along the coastal plain; southeastern South Carolina to Florida and southeastern Louisiana

SIZE: Height 6–26 inches, width 12–18 inches

COLOR: Pale to deep pink, occasionally white, spotted with purple inside; blooms in summer to early fall

This is an unusual little species if one is accustomed to the more robust laurels. It grows from a horizontal, creeping rhizome that lofts thin vertical stems clothed sparingly in tiny, lance-shaped evergreen leaves that have a thin beard of long hairs along the margin. It is the sort of plant that goes unnoticed except when in flower, but it blooms far longer than any other laurel. The small but colorful saucers come in ones and twos from the axils of the uppermost leaves as the growths mature, not in a flush from overwintered buds as do the other species, thus there are a few open at almost any time during the summer. The flowers are pink overall, highlighted by a darker band of purple where the petals pucker to hold the stamen filaments. *K. hirsuta* has been crossed with *K. latifolia* in an attempt to produce heat-adapted, compact but showy ornamentals (see Dirr, *Manual of Woody Landscape Plants*, p. 530).

Kalmia latifolia. *My property is literally covered with an understory of mountain laurel. The land was lightly logged about ten years ago, and the laurel has responded to the higher levels of sunlight with incredible gusto. When they bloom in late spring, the woods are indescribably beautiful.*

Kalmia latifolia
Mountain Laurel

ZONES: (4)5–9; sun to light shade

SOIL: Moist to dry, acidic

NATIVE TO: Rocky woods, cliffs; southeastern Maine to southern Ohio south to southeastern Louisiana and western Florida

SIZE: Height 4–15 feet, width 4–8 feet

COLOR: Pink in bud, white or light pink in flower; rarely, deeper pink or maroon; blooms in late spring to early summer

This is certainly one of our finest flowering shrubs, and it has proved an adaptable plant in eastern landscapes, especially in Zones 5–6. It forms a large, rounded shrub supported by several trunks, often beautifully gnarled and twisted, that are covered in rich brown exfoliating bark. The plants come in so thickly in some forests, especially after logging has thinned the canopy, that they form impenetrable "laurel hells." The leaves of the typical form are 2 to 3 inches long and lance shaped, a bit wavy along the margins, and a rich, glossy green, even in winter. The leaves emerge in a bronzy flush before the flowers. Branches that flower heavily may not send out any new vegetative growth that season, which partially explains the alternate blooming of many individual plants (especially shade-grown ones). They do not run underground like other laurels, but the burl formed at the base of the trunks will sprout back copiously after fire or after the plant has been cut.

Kalmia polifolia
Bog Laurel

ZONES: 2–7; sun

SOIL: Moist to wet, acidic

NATIVE TO: Bogs; Labrador to Alaska south to California, Michigan, and New Jersey

SIZE: Height 1–2 feet, width 12–18 inches

COLOR: Dark pink; blooms in late spring

This is a rather sparse, spreading plant that is nearly invisible among other evergreens when not in flower. Its flowers are small, but they cluster proudly atop the stems in little flat bouquets. The very narrow, opposite leaves average about 1½ inches long, and they are usually deep, blackish green above and lighter blue-green and white-hairy below. The paired leaves are spaced evenly along very thin, almost scandent twigs that grow from a creeping rhizome. It is a cute little plant for naturalizing in bogs. Western forms of the species have been segregated into alpine laurel *(K. microphylla)*, which has leaves averaging less than 1 inch long, but is otherwise similar.

Larix laricina

Larix (LAIR-ix)

Pinaceae
Larch, Tamarack, Hackmatack

Nature thinks of everything, so the fact that there are deciduous conifers shouldn't be surprising. However, this does challenge one's unacknowledged preconceptions about the normally evergreen pine family, whose persistent needles freshen the sullen winter landscape and give the trees a jump on the season as soon as it's warm enough to begin photosynthesizing again. There is at least one other advantage to keeping one's needles. Before a tree drops its leaves, it must scavenge precious nutrients like nitrogen from them and store them in the stems. It is far less complicated and more efficient for the plant to simply shunt nutrients from older leaves to newer ones as needed. On the flip side, though, evergreen leaves are also a liability in winter because they must be sustained and protected from bitter cold. So larches have opted to drop their soft, wispy needles each autumn in a glorious flush of gold and apricot and wait out the cold as a leafless spire of blackened branches. This has allowed the larch to journey farther north than even the balsam fir — clear up into the frozen heart of the Northwest Territories, where it is so cold that regular thermometers are just about useless. Indeed, the larches are trees of cold, wet soils. At the southern extreme of its range, tamarack *(L. laricina)* is relegated to floating bogs where constant evaporation keeps the substrate cool, and extreme acidity limits competition. It is a strange thing to walk out gingerly on a floating mat of sphagnum moss and see larch trees swaying back and forth on the rippling waves created by your footsteps in the water hidden just below.

In the coniferous Shangri-la of the Pacific Northwest, larches can get to be enormous trees with 4-foot-thick, buttressed trunks covered in thin bark that support nothing but a shattered crown of twisted branches. All larches produce their needles in tight whorls on stubby spurs along the branchlets. It is as if these spurs are meant to imitate the fascicles or bundles of needles found in true pines (*Pinus* spp.). The spurs help give the larch its distinctive look of soft, knobby resiliency. In spring, spurs begin to swell at the tips and flush peppermint green as the new whorls of needles expand into small spokes studding every twig in an alternating, almost zigzag pattern. Even when mature, larch needles have a soft, light gray-green color that contrasts with the darker hues of sympatric trees. In habit, all but the oldest have a strongly pyramidal, Christmas-tree shape like spruce or fir, with a straight, vertical stem supporting tiers of nearly horizontal branches that radiate out from it in all directions. The burnt golden spectacle of turning needles rivals that of the birches and aspens in brilliance.

CULTURE: In cool and cold climates, *Larix* species will grow easily enough in all but droughty conditions. They seem to grow happily in averagely moist soils where the gardener has kept down competitors that would otherwise shade them out. This is not to say that larches are slow growing. I have seen young plants put on 2 feet or more in one season — not bad for a cold-climate conifer. Young trees have the ability to grow somewhat indeterminately, which allows them to respond to favorable conditions more readily than spruce or fir. Though they will never replace other more adaptable, evergreen conifers in the general landscape, they do have a prepossessing softness and lovely fall color that is well worth encouraging if you have the proper spot. In the colder regions of Canada and the mountains of the Pacific Northwest, larches will thrive in a variety of open habitats.

USES: Naturalizing, massing, restoration.

PROPAGATION: Moderately easy from seed.

Larix laricina

Tamarack, Hackmatack

ZONES: 1–6; sun, part sun

SOIL: Moist to wet, acidic and cool

NATIVE TO: Bogs, boreal forest and tundra margins, occasionally on well-drained soils; Labrador to the Northwest Territories and central Alaska south through eastern British Columbia to southern Alberta, Minnesota, northern Illinois, western Virginia, and New Jersey

SIZE: Height 30–60 feet, width 10–18 feet

COLOR: Dark red-violet (young female cones); blooms in spring

Larix laricina. *Tamarack is not evergreen, a fact it announces every fall with a brilliant apricot display as its soft needles prepare to drizzle down onto the mossy carpet below.*

Tamarack is a delicate-looking conifer found commonly in the boreal forests of the North and, less commonly, farther south, where it grows mostly as postglacial remnants isolated in cold sphagnum bogs. Although it can grow in well-drained soils, it is less fire tolerant than some of the other northern conifers, so tends to persist longest in wetter habitats.

Larix occidentalis
Western Larch

ZONES: 4–8; sun to part sun
SOIL: Moist, well-drained
NATIVE TO: Mountain valleys and lower slopes; western Montana to British Columbia south to Oregon and central Idaho
SIZE: Height 80–120 (200+) feet, width 20–40 feet
COLOR: Red-purple to yellow; blooms in spring

Western larch is a massive, fire-adapted conifer that develops a shaggy, blackened and gray bark and a narrow crown, but in leaf shape and color it is much like the tamarack. Though not as abundant in forests as Douglas fir, it is a valuable lumber tree yielding fairly strong, rot-resistant heartwood. Alpine larch (*L. lyallii*) is a much smaller (40-to-80-foot) tree restricted to the northern Rockies and the Cascades above 6,000 feet. It likely diverged from a common ancestor to exploit the more rigorous conditions near the timberline.

Ledum × columbianum. Chance hybridization between two species may give rise to a new species eventually, especially if the hybrid offspring is better adapted to a specific habitat than its parents or if it is genetically distinct enough that it cannot easily interbreed with them. Mountain Labrador tea, a naturally occurring hybrid between Ledum groenlandicum *and* L. palustre, *is found where the two parents grow sympatrically.*

Ledum × columbianum

Ledum (Rhododendron) groenlandicum
(LEE-dum)

Ericaceae
Labrador Tea

ZONES: 2–6; sun to light shade
SOIL: Damp, acidic, and cool
NATIVE TO: Bogs, pond shores, alpine and arctic tundra; Greenland to Alaska south to Oregon, Minnesota, and northern New Jersey
SIZE: Height 16–30 inches, width 2–3 feet
COLOR: White; blooms in spring

I have always thought that Labrador tea looks a lot like a small rhododendron, so its recent reclassification has not shaken me too badly. It is a common plant in sphagnum bogs and alpine summits in the northern parts of the United States, and like larch (*Larix*), ranges clear up and across northern Canada. A true evergreen, it hunkers down for the winter with its little lance-shaped leaves heavily felted underneath with a layer of rusty hair so thick and resplendent that you can even see a bit of it sticking out around the edge when you peer at the plants from above. Rhododendrons don't have the ability to shut down the stomatal pores in their leaves, so this heavy tomentum slows evaporation through the stomata, especially in winter. First-year twigs are also covered in a layer of fur, and when this glints in the sun you can pick up beautiful blond highlights in the auburn shag (oh, if my hair could be so lucky). Late in the season, fat little flower buds nestle and swell in the uppermost leaves so they can pop into bloom when warmth returns again.

These flowers differ from those of rhododendrons and azaleas in a few obvious ways, which is why Labrador tea has been classified separately in most systems. The first thing you notice about these starry little blooms is that the five petals are all separate and spread wide, clean down to the point where they fuse with the base of the ovary. Furthermore, the ovary is clearly visible as a little green swelling in the center of each flower. Most rhododendrons hide this precious seed chamber in a tube formed by the bases of the fused petals, giving them that familiar trumpet shape and forcing the anther filaments to cinch up against the long style. Since *Ledum* lacks this fused base, the stamens spread wide, like five small arms awaiting the embrace of a bee. Labrador tea flowers open sequentially in a rounded truss from a central core of green buds, and the plants are very pretty for two weeks in spring. The frothy, bright white flowers look especially radiant against the olive green leaves, which wait until flowers have passed to send up reinforcements. New growth comes out with leaves gathered toward the top as if whorled, each set building on the last to produce an elegant, layered scaffold that increases evenly in diameter each year. Branches that get buried under moss will layer, but most of the growth comes from a central crown, so the shrubs remain a discrete entity, not a suckering, spreading mat. Labrador tea, made from a suffusion of leaves, is an astringent drink used as a substitute for real tea, but it should be consumed in moderation, as the leaves contain some of the poisonous alkaloids common to the Ericaceae.

A very similar species, *L. palustre* (trapper's tea), which grows high in the Cascades of Washington and Oregon, is distinguished by its white (as opposed to rusty) tomentum. Where the two overlap, a hybrid, *L. × columbianum* (also listed as *L. glandulosum*—mountain Labrador tea), can occasionally be found. Neither has the low-elevation adaptability of the more widespread *L. groenlandicum*.

CULTURE: We can always learn a lot about a plant's needs and wants by studying its range and preferred habitat—in this case, a cool, strongly acidic soil (pH 4.0 to 5.5), well laced with humus. Moisture in both the ground and the air seems important, too, but Labrador tea is not really tricky to grow if you live where rhododendrons flourish. These plants generally take care of themselves: we do nothing but give them a fresh dressing of chopped leaves or pine straw in spring, then prune out dead wood in winter. Our largest planting did suffer some dieback during the severe droughts of 1995 and 1999, curtailing flowering the next spring and necessitating removal of some dead branches.

USES: Massed planting or specimen for heath or bog garden.

PROPAGATION: Moderately difficult from cuttings, moderately easy from seed.

Leiophyllum buxifolium (lee-o-FIL-um)
Ericaceae
Sand Myrtle

Leiophyllum buxifolium

ZONES: 5–8; sun, part sun
SOIL: Moist, acidic, well-drained
NATIVE TO: Barrens and balds; scattered through the mountains from North and South Carolina, Kentucky, Tennessee, and Georgia and also along the coast in southern New Jersey as well as in North and South Carolina
SIZE: Height 6–24 inches, width 1–2 feet
COLOR: White, tinged with pink; blooms in mid- to late spring

As one moves south along the Atlantic coast or down through the Appalachians, Labrador tea is replaced by its relative, sand myrtle (*Leiophyllum buxifolium*—such a long name for a such a diminutive plant). The two share certain characters, like evergreen leaves, low-mounding growth habit, and flowers with 5 free petals arranged in a star and carried in bouqueted half-rounds atop the plants in spring. There the resemblance ends, as sand myrtle leaves one with a much more delicate impression. It sends up stiff, vertical stems clothed in tiny (less than ½-inch), glossy green leaves suffused with burgundy

in winter. The newer twigs are bathed in a brighter shade of red, and this pigment drips into the flower buds as well, lending them a pinky cast that darkens the core of each domed inflorescence and fades to white as the flowers open. The anthers, too, have a dash of red, so the whole takes on a frothy whiteness punctuated by glimmers of red and pink. Blossoms are produced in such lavish profusion as to smother the foliage completely for 2 to 3 weeks in spring. It is a charming spectacle that has won this uncommon heath family member a place of honor in my garden.

I saw sand myrtle for the first time atop magnificent Grandfather Mountain in the Blue Ridge Mountains of North Carolina. It spilled around rocks in the company of turkeybeard (*Xerophyllum asphodeloides*) and many other ericaceous plants in that unique southern Appalachian plant community called the rhododendron bald. These mountains are too far south to develop true alpine vegetation on their summits, but the treeless balds, where a thin sheet of soil covers bare, acidic rock, are washed con-

stantly in a leaching bath of rain and fog. The form of *Leiophyllum* that grows on these peaks, *L. buxifolium* var. *prostratum*, develops as a low, spreading mat in response to the extreme wind, and this variety will remain true to form in cultivation. To find sand myrtle again, you have to travel all the way to the sandy pine barrens along the coast. Interestingly, this species has the same disjunct distribution as turkeybeard (*Xerophyllum asphodeloides*) and this gives some important clues about their culture. Like the balds, pine barrens have nutrient-poor soils. The coarse sand particles cannot hold mineral ions easily, and these are leached away quickly in rains. Thus rainwater filters down through the soil and pools in a water table not far below the surface, so although the soil appears dry, plant roots can travel down to find moisture cached below. Pine-barren genotypes are stiffer and taller, though older stems will lean over

Leiophyllum buxifolium. *If you can provide it with moist but well-drained, acidic soil, sand myrtle is a splendid garden subject, offering compact size, fine-textured evergreen leaves, and lovely flowers. The seedlings are almost microscopic when they germinate, but they steadily add tiny leaves if watered once a week with dilute fertilizer. Two months later, they are large enough to be visible at a glance, and by spring they'll be an inch tall.*

under their accumulated weight to produce a softer, billowing mound. New stems come from the base of the plant, so in time a spreading colony develops, with the neat yet informal character that I admire so much in inkberry holly (*Ilex glabra*).

CULTURE: After seeing *L. buxifolium* in the mountains, I made the mistake of assuming it needed sharp, rock-garden drainage, and I lost my first few plants. We have wonderful patches of it growing in our pine barrens at the Garden. This is an area of sand overlying a wetland, so both the well-drained surface and the access to water are achieved. Pine barren plants are well endowed with mycorrhizal roots, and we do nothing except apply a light layer of pine needles each spring as mulch. I raise sand myrtle from cuttings and seed, and we have planted out container-grown plants in spring, experimenting with them in drier soils but keeping them carefully watered for the first two years. They will establish, but I think for long-term survival this species needs a spot more akin to *Ledum*'s liking: damp, very acidic, but with some drainage around the crown. It is well worth the effort to get it established if you have a heath garden, though—truly a beautiful native shrub.

USES: Massing, edging.

PROPAGATION: Moderately difficult from cuttings and seed.

Leucothoe fontanesiana. Dog hobble is one of the most reliable, easy-to-please tall groundcovers used at Garden in the Woods. We employ it throughout the shady areas where a low-maintenance evergreen sward is desired. Crowded chains of delicate, jug-shaped flowers are a bonus in spring, as is the coppery color of the emerging foliage a few weeks later.

Leucothoe fontanesiana

Leucothoe (lew-ko-THO-ee)
Ericaceae
Dog Hobble, Leucothoe, Dog Laurel

I'll never forget the first summer I came to Garden in the Woods. It was in the middle of the worst drought in ten years, and Cheryl Lowe (horticulture director for the New England Wild Flower Society) and I decided to thin out a big patch of dog hobble that surrounded a fallen tree. We hacked out a couple of 3-foot-wide clumps and dragged them up the dry, west-facing slope that drops down from the entrance road into the woodland garden, and we just plopped them down on the surface of the leaf duff and kicked a few rotten logs up in front to level then off. After a perfunctory drink of water, which barely wetted the parched soil, we left them with the intention of coming back to plant them properly the following day. Life intervened in our plans, though, and we never did get back to plant them. You can imagine my surprise when, two years later, I wandered up the slope to check the fence only to find the *Leucothoe* rooted in and thriving—now that's a plant! Dog hobble (*L. fontanesiana*) is one of our garden staples. In the wild, it grows in tangled, verdant swaths in the rich forests of the southern Appalachians, and it makes an attractive, no-maintenance mound in difficult, shady spots or anywhere we need to skirt taller shrubs and trees in a fountain of its arching stems. Along the coastal plain, this species is replaced by the slightly smaller coast leucothoe (*L. axillaris*), which looks similar enough as a dried herbarium specimen that all hell has broken loose regarding the taxonomy of this genus. It seems that the type specimen for *L. catesbaei* was really a branch of *L. axillaris,* which, under the rules of nomenclature, makes the name invalid and thus the synonym *L. fontanesiana* becomes the proper moniker for the mountain species. To further complicate things, some references call dog hobble *L. walteri*, which is listed in Kartesz, *A Synonymized Checklist of the Vascular Flora of the United States, Canada, and Greenland* (p. 433), as a synonym for *Leucothoe* (now *Agarista*) *populifolia!* This is one of the few instances I can think of where the common names are less confusing and ambiguous than the Latin.

There is one deciduous species, *L. racemosa*, but the others are lustrous evergreens. All leucothoes arrange their lance-shaped leaves in two ranks along horizontal to arching stems, lending them a similar cascading textural effect as you might find with some larger ferns or Solomon's seals (*Polygonatum* spp.). Each year, new shoots arch up from the roots or from low on the existing stems and grow rapidly, adding to the colony and thickening the cover of leaves. The name dog hobble refers to the tangled layering colonies that are nearly impossible to walk through, especially if you are trying to scale a steep slope. As fall approaches, clusters of flower buds hang like little green bunches of grapes from the axils of other outermost leaves. These open early the following spring to create masses of dangling bells along the last foot or so of stem. The leaves hide the flowers somewhat, so the effect is not spectacular unless you can see it as an ant would (we have some flowing over a retaining wall that is very pretty to look up into). The flowers have a strong, honeyed fragrance and are very attractive to queen bumblebees out looking for energy to build the hive.

CULTURE: Leucothoes will grow well where rhododendrons thrive: in moist, acidic, duffy soils in shaded, deciduous woodlands. We grow *L. axillaris* and *L. fontanesiana* with ease in our woodland gardens, mostly as filler plants on slopes and under trees and tall shrubs. To look their best, they need a damp, humusy spot that receives morning sun. Though, as I mentioned, they will survive in dry, shady situations, they do not grow as lushly and are prone to leaf spotting. Sweetbells (*L. racemosa*) thrives as well, but it grows more like some of the taller blueberries (*Vaccinium* spp.), with arching twigs coming from upright stems and forming a loose, picturesque architecture that looks pretty laced with new fallen snow. In the piedmont of North Carolina, Florida leucothoe (now *Agarista populifolia*) performs much better than the leucothoes, and it survives at Garden in the Woods, though barely. Most winters it gets defoliated—burned back to the older stems or to the ground—so it has never gotten more than 2 feet high. I have little experience with Sierra laurel (*L. davisiae*), though I have some coming along in the nursery. It seems very picky about nutrition, and has developed marginal chlorosis that is tough to cure. The others take pruning and shaping pretty well. They tend to get scurfy and matted with fallen leaves unless you clean them up every five years or so. Hard pruning in winter will do little harm if it is done infrequently.

USES: Tall groundcover, massing, screening.

PROPAGATION: Moderately easy from cuttings and seed.

Leucothoe axillaris
Coast Leucothoe

ZONES: (4)5–8; part sun to shade
SOIL: Moist to moderately dry, acidic
NATIVE TO: Coastal swamps, streamsides; eastern Virginia to Florida and Louisiana
SIZE: Height 3–4 (6) feet, width 4–6 feet
COLOR: Creamy white; blooms in early spring

If eminent botanists like Asa Gray could not tell coast leucothoe and dog hobble apart, then I don't feel quite so stupid in my own taxonomic shortcomings. Both species form spreading colonies of arching branches, this plant with typically wider leaves and shorter racemes (less than 2 inches long with an average of 10 to 20 flowers on each). Compact cultivars are available, as well as some selected for especially intense new growth or winter color. The typical *L. axillaris*, like its cousin, produces leaves that are a

rich copper or bronze when young and which fade first to light green (which contrasts well with the burgundy-flushed leaves from the previous year) and finally to a deep, glossy green in summer and maroon in winter. The effect of the young foliage springing out of a tangled mass of stems is sumptuous indeed.

Leucothoe davisiae
Sierra Laurel, Black Laurel

ZONES: (5)6–8; full sun at high elevations, more shade is necessary at lower elevations
SOIL: Moist to wet, peaty and acidic
NATIVE TO: Seeps, wet meadows, and subalpine bogs at 6,000 to 8,500 feet in the mountains of northern California and southern Oregon
SIZE: Height 2–4 feet, width 2–3 feet
COLOR: White; blooms in late winter to early spring

Sierra laurel is very different from the eastern leucothoes, looking remarkably like mountain andromeda (*Pieris floribunda*) in effect. It has 1-to-2-inch very glossy, dark and leathery evergreen leaves that clothe ascending stems. The leaves are narrowly elliptical and rounded at the tip. The flower racemes rise up from the tips of the stems in tight, stiff bunches, just like mountain andromeda's. The plants form low colonies among rocks in the mountains but get taller in more protected sites. This is a lovely tall groundcover or mounded shrub that as far as I know is little used in horticulture. I have my doubts about its suitability in the East, where mountain andromeda and its hybrids are probably better choices.

Leucothoe fontanesiana (catesbaei)
Dog Hobble, Dog Laurel

ZONES: 4–7; part sun to shade
SOIL: Moist to moderately dry, acidic
NATIVE TO: Stream banks, shaded woods, and ravines in the Appalachian Mountains from Virginia and eastern Tennessee to northern Georgia
SIZE: Height 2–4 (6) feet, width 4–8 feet
COLOR: Creamy white; blooms in early spring

All comments under *L. axillaris* apply here as well. Dog hobble tends to have larger (over 2 inches long) racemes and subsequently more flowers per raceme than *L. axillaris*. The leaves tend to be a bit longer and more pointed as well. This is a plant that can survive repeated insult because it regenerates with a brand-new set of foliage and stems every spring. We had a big patch of this below a wall under hemlocks when I was growing up, and we used to jump and fall into it all the time, but it always persevered. The multicolored cultivar 'Girard's Rainbow' (often listed incorrectly as 'Rainbow') is a striking tricolored

Lindera benzoin. Spicebush leaves are the preferred food of the spicebush swallowtail butterfly caterpillar, which is colored white, gray, and black at first, to resemble bird droppings. After several molts, the larva turns either the blue-green of spicebush leaves or the soft orange of dried apricots, with two rows of turquoise dots down its sides and two remarkably realistic cartoon eyes on the last enlarged segment below its head. If you want a diverse group of butterflies to live in your yard, it is not enough to provide nectar sources for the adults; you also need to cultivate a wide variety of larval food plants.

clone that even someone like me who doesn't like most variegation can appreciate. The new growth comes out flushed dark pink laced with green, then the pink fades to white that is slowly replaced mostly by green by the time the leaf matures. In summer, the foliage looks just lightly streaked with golden white. Maybe I like it because it is truly garish for only a few weeks when in the flush and blush of spring.

Leucothoe (Eubotrys) racemosa
Sweetbells, Swamp Dog-laurel, Fetterbush

ZONES: 5–8; part sun to shade
SOIL: Moist, acidic
NATIVE TO: Swamp margins, hummocks, and low, sandy woods along the Atlantic coast; southeastern Massachusetts to Florida and Louisiana
SIZE: Height 3–5 feet, width 2–3 feet
COLOR: Creamy white; blooms in spring

Though it lacks the evergreen leaves and cascading habit of the other *Leucothoe* species, this pretty shrub carries its arching sprays of urn-shaped flowers up where you can see them, without leaves to obscure things. The flowers open just as the thin-textured, oval leaves are expanding. We have some planted next to mountain andromeda (*Pieris floribunda*), and the two are similar in floral effect. It is probably best used as a companion plant for blueberries and azaleas. Mountain fetterbush (*L. recurva*) is a closely related deciduous species from higher elevations in the southern Appalachians with larger leaves notable for their brilliant red fall color.

Agarista (Leucothoe) populifolia
Florida Leucothoe

ZONES: 7–9; part sun to shade
SOIL: Moist, acidic
NATIVE TO: Cypress swamps and hammocks (raised mounds in swampy areas) along the coast; South Carolina to Florida
SIZE: Height 5–10 feet, width 3–5 feet
COLOR: Creamy white; blooms in early spring

Florida leucothoe is a good species for the Piedmont and coastal plain in the Southeast. It is roughly similar in foliar effect to *L. fontanesiana*, though in my experience it wants to grow taller and spread more slowly, as more of an upright, cascading shrub than a flowing groundcover. It has vividly shining, medium green leaves with an oval base narrowed to a long, pointed tip that arrange themselves in two ranks on arching or pendant stems. The foliage is stiffer and smoother looking than that of *Leucothoe* species, but in flower it is similar, with hanging chains of little white bells coming from the old canes early in spring.

Lindera benzoin

Lindera benzoin
(lin-DAIR-ah)
Lauraceae
Spicebush

ZONES: 4–9; part sun to shade
SOIL: Moist to wet; grows on both acidic and slightly alkaline soils (pH 5.0–7.5)
NATIVE TO: Low woods, wooded swamps, and pond shores, more occasionally on uplands; Maine to Michigan south to Texas and Florida
SIZE: Height 8–15 feet, width 6–15 feet
COLOR: Soft, bright yellow; blooms in early spring

Spicebush exudes a manly after-shave scent when you scratch off the bark or crush the leaves — a mixture of cloves, anise, and musk that is one of my favorite woodland smells. This is a multistemmed, understory shrub usually as wide as it is tall, clothed in matte blue-green, droopy leaves that are a lighter toothpaste blue below. It's the sort of plant that fades into the lush background of rich woods and swamps during the summer, but reminds you of its presence in both spring and fall. Spicebush comes into flower here in early April, when the red maples have bloomed but all the other trees are still naked, and only skunk cabbage (*Symplocarpus foetidus*) and marsh marigolds (*Caltha palustris*) compete with it for insects' attentions.

The sweetly fragrant, light yellow flowers spring out from little round buds that have lain in wait along the previous season's twigs. The blooms cluster tightly in 4-to-20-flowered posies dotting the leafless stems, effectively tracing the outline of the plant the way redbud flowers do. The individual flowers are small and 5-petaled, with males and females on different trees. There is no difference in flower quality be-tween male and female plants, though a cluster of stamens give male flowers a faintly frillier appearance up close. A stand of spicebush in bloom is more of a warm, yellow suffusion than a forsythia-esque riot of color. They frequent low woods and hollows, so the soft yellow color looks like a luminescent fog settled among the trees. After the flowers have done their thing, dusky leaves begin to grow, each larger than the next, so that each twig displays the leaves' even progression in size from first to last. The largest leaves are up to 3 inches long and obovate in outline. The foliage of common spicebush appears to be heavier than the petioles were designed for, so the leaves droop in an attractive way. The rare Jove's fruit (*Lindera melissifolia*) has even heavier, drooping leaves, drawn to a narrow, pointed tip.

As summer passes into early fall, changes are afoot in the spicebush grove. Females have been slowly ripening shiny oval fruits (drupes) where the flowers clustered along the twigs, and as they begin to turn from green to yellow, then orange and red, the foliage takes its cue and flags brilliant yellow-gold to advertise to birds that the feast is at hand. The oily drupes must be tasty to birds despite their spicy smell, because they disappear remarkably fast if I don't collect them (for propagation) just as the skins begin to turn. Combine shade tolerance and early, fragrant flowers with radiant fall color and fruits, all on a pretty, flattened oval silhouette, and you have a first-rate ornamental. Certainly, spicebush is not as flashy as a redbud or dogwood, but it has a wild elegance about it that is perfect at the edge of the woods or scattered through trees. Though individual trunks can get to be 3 inches in diameter, all but the youngest twigs are covered in a dark gray-brown bark that is smooth to the eye but rough to the touch. Older stems spread out horizontally to catch the light, and new ones continually spring up vertically from the narrow base.

Depending on whom you talk to, there are two or three *Lindera* species in our flora. *L. benzoin* ranges throughout the eastern hardwood forests as well as the southeastern coastal plain, where it crosses paths with the two rarer members of the genus. Bog spicebush *(L. subcoriacea)* grows in scattered wetlands near the coast from Virginia to Florida and Louisiana. Superficially it looks similar, but the leaves are thick and almost leathery, about half the size of those of common spicebush, and mature foliage lacks the distinctive spicy odor when crushed. *L. melissifolia* grows in scattered places over much the same range, with historic records of its presence along the Mississippi River to southeast Missouri. Its lance-shaped leaves set it apart, as does its height: it's rarely more than 4 feet tall. To all but a botanist, the three species look pretty similar, so the rarer ones may be more common and confused than is now recognized.

Pond spice *(Litsea aestivalis)* is an extremely rare and visually distinctive relative of spicebush that grows mostly in limestone depressions and on the edges of vernal pools along the immediate coast (his-torically) from Virginia to Florida and southern Louisiana but now is likely extinct in parts of its former range. It has roughly the same branching habit and size, but the leaves are very small (about 1 inch long at best) and leathery in texture. The twigs and smaller branches display a noticeably zigzag pattern and female plants' fruits are very similar to those of *Lindera* in size and shape (about ⅜ inch long and half as wide). Although it may have limited use in general horticulture, it is a plant that is under extreme pressure from habitat loss due to coastal development, and thus all effort should be made to encourage it where it is found.

CULTURE: *Lindera* species are reasonably adaptable regarding soil, but they do best in moist, fertile loam where they can get a few hours of sun. I have planted them in drier soils as well as heavy shade, and though the rate of growth and flowering is reduced, they grow fairly well.

USES: Hedgerows, naturalizing in the understory, pond shores and swampy ground.

WILDLIFE: Good early-season nectar source, excellent forage for birds. Spicebush, along with sassafras, is the preferred larval host of the striking black, teal, orange, and white spicebush swallowtail butterfly *(Papilio troilus)*. The mint green caterpillars are large and menacing, with their prominent black-and-yellow-lined eyes at the top of the head to scare potential predators when they rear up.

PROPAGATION: Moderately easy from seed.

Liquidambar styraciflua. Sweetgum is a fast-growing, pyramidal tree that develops consistent red, burgundy, and orange fall color in the Southeast. In New England, early freezes often curtail the fall display before it develops fully, so green or yellow tones are all that can reliably be expected.

Liquidambar styraciflua

Liquidambar styraciflua (lik-kwid-AM-bar)
Hamamelidaceae
Sweetgum

ZONES: (5)6–9; sun to part sun

SOIL: Moist to dry; prefers moist

NATIVE TO: Mixed woodlands, fencerows, swamps, riverbanks; southern Connecticut south along the coast to New Jersey then inland to southern Illinois and southeastern Texas and central Florida.

SIZE: Height 60–100 (130) feet, width 30–70 feet

COLOR: Greenish yellow; blooms in spring

For anyone living in the southeastern United States, sweetgum is both a blessing and a curse. It is a fast-growing, pyramidal tree when young and is one of the few broadleaf trees that can keep pace with loblolly pine (*Pinus taeda*) on logged, burned, or abandoned agricultural lands. Seedlings are intolerant of shade, but they can form dense stands on old fields and race up and up with a dominant leader, eventually developing more of a rounded crown as the winners spread out in the canopy. Sweetgum puts on one of the most consistent and beautiful fall color displays of any southern tree, a fiery mix of reddish orange, yellow, and burgundy that really makes these individuals stand out amid the pines. The downside to these trees, known to anyone who has ever walked barefoot underneath one, are the vicious spiny gumballs (woody capsules) that drop to the ground in great quantities all winter after they have shed their winged seeds. These fiendish, medieval-looking things consist of many individual seed capsules balled together in a perfect sphere. Each capsule narrows to a sharp, spiny point, and no matter which way the fruits are lying, there are always a few points facing up to pierce the soft flesh of the arch or the callus of the toe. The balls are very durable, and unraked ground is usually littered with several generations of the resilient fruits. The flowers that produce these things are not showy, but they are interesting. The male flowers poke out from the twig tips in a pyramidal panicle, with a few of the ball-shaped female inflorescences dangling below it like oversized dime store earrings.

Sweetgum produces unmistakable 5-lobed palmate leaves resembling a maple leaf in shape. The middle lobe is largest and the two lowest (flanking the petiole) are proportionally reduced. However, the blade has a leathery, glossy-gummy texture that is heavier than any native maple's. The leaves alternate up shiny mahogany twigs that quickly develop a corky, winged bark. The winginess of the twigs and branches varies from individual to individual, and some can be so elaborately adorned as to be almost repulsive (I imagine these wings may serve some fire-retardant purpose). The wings wear away to rounded ridges on the largest limbs and trunk, which evolve finally into warm gray bark broken into narrow plates. The name *Liquidambar* means "liquid amber," a reference to the clear, yellow resin that has long been collected from trees and used as a natural chewing gum and a flavoring for soaps, tobacco, and incense (it has a balsamlike odor). This resin, called styrax or storax, is collected by slashing or stripping sections of the bark in late spring and coming back a few days or weeks later to scrape off the resin as it oozes out and collects. You can also see this tacky resin clinging to the large, dormant buds.

CULTURE: Transplant balled and burlaped or small container-grown seedlings in spring. The trees take a few years to settle in and grow in earnest, but when planted in full sun and a moist soil, they can grow prodigiously, and 2 to 3 feet a season when young is not uncommon. They grow indeterminately as long as soil conditions and day length permit. To avoid bleeding of the gum (pun intended), prune the trees after leaf drop in autumn. The cultivar 'Rotundiloba' bears leaves with rounded rather than pointed lobes, and rarely produces any fruit. This alone is reason enough to grow the plant if you want to use one as a street or lawn tree. It has a different rhythm to its canopy—more undulating, you could say.

USES: Shade tree.

PROPAGATION: Moderately easy from seed.

Liriodendron tulipifera

Liriodendron tulipifera
(leer-e-o-DEN-dron)

Magnoliaceae

Tulip Poplar, Tulip Tree

ZONES: 4–9; sun to part sun

SOIL: Moist

NATIVE TO: Rich woodlands, bottomlands; Vermont to southern Ontario and Michigan south to Missouri, Louisiana, and Florida

SIZE: Height 70–120 (175) feet, width 30–60 feet

COLOR: Orange and lime green; blooms in spring

I love everything about this tree – its tremendous height, the way it lovingly cups its youngest leaves in a protective jacket, the remarkable floral chalices it hides far up in the canopy. Tulip tree is the largest native magnolia relative and is arguably the tallest tree in eastern North America. Only sycamore (*Platanus occidentalis*) and eastern white pine (*Pinus strobus*) rival it in potential height. Forest specimens develop a straight, tall trunk with a broad pyramidal crown of branches beginning high above. The skin of young twigs is a shiny, tacky chestnut brown that develops into hard, warm gray, fissured bark on the trunks. The bark has a netted, V-shaped pattern much like that of white ash (*Fraxinus americana*). Tulip trees produce large leaves with two triangular lobes pointing out sideways and two more whose bases meet at the tip, so the two halves look like mir-

ror images of each other connected along a strong midvein. These emerge one at a time from a thumbless mitten made of two enlarged stipules that jacket the developing leaf and hide it from predators. If you backlight a growing branch tip, you can see the little leaf curled up in there like a salamander embryo in an egg sack. As the leaf expands, it hatches out of the flattened pod like a seedling from the soil, straightens out, and begins to enlarge in earnest. A vigorous branch can grow its distinctive leaves to almost a foot in diameter, though 5 to 7 inches is more likely. The tulip poplar is decidedly indeterminate, and new leaves will keep coming and coming late into the season till frosts strike them down. Because of this, the tree can grow remarkably fast on good soils. I watched a stand seed into a cleared area behind my house when I was in grammar school, and by the time I came back from college, the largest were 30 feet high, dwarfing the birch, oak, and ash that were attempting to keep up with them.

Like magnolias, some of the unsheathing buds unleash huge flowers instead of leaves. These are the size and shape of a garden tulip and consist of 7 key lime pie–colored petals that are stained orange at their base (the pattern of orange looks just like lapping flames in a fireplace) formed into a chalice enclosing a crown of stiff stamens and a central spike of stigmas. The whole has a rigid, industrial character, as if it had evolved in a time of championship wrestler–sized bees (or, more likely, beetles). If there is another tree nearby to cross with, the central spear point of ovaries will develop a crop of winged seeds that press up against it like stiff, green bird feathers. Since the flowers develop far up in the canopy of all but low-branched, open-grown trees, you rarely see a flower. I would find strangely colored petals in our backyard in spring and then ragged, spear-pointed structures with a few paddle-winged seeds attached in fall and have no idea where they came from. I think I was 10 or 12 before I discovered the source far overhead.

Tulip poplar is an important timber tree. Its wood is soft by hardwood standards, but develops straight and smooth, with few knots or scars. The heartwood is yellow when cut, fading to a greenish brown when dried, and is surrounded by white sapwood. It has long been used as a backing wood in furniture production, but now that lumber has become increasingly expensive in relation to composite materials, "poplarwood" tables and cabinets are becoming increasingly, well, pop'lar.

CULTURE: Garden in the Woods lies at the northeasternmost end of *Liriodendron*'s native range. We have two decent-sized trees growing down along the floodplain of Hop Brook, which winds through the property, and the winged seeds from these trees (the only ones I know of anywhere nearby) sometimes manage to loft uphill to the nursery and land in pots. With my fondness for this tree, I don't have the heart

Liriodendron tulipifera. The peerless flowers of tulip poplar give way to propeller-blade seeds that twirl down from the high crowns in fall and winter. The 1-to-2-inch, buff-colored seeds are easy to spot on lawns and pavement, and I collect handfuls quite easily this way. If seeds are sown immediately and left outdoors for the winter, a good crop of little seedlings will appear in spring and grow very quickly. I have a three-year-old seedling that is already 6 feet tall, and most of that height was added just this year!

Why Are Trees So Tall in the Pacific Northwest?

I have often wondered why trees grow so much taller in the Pacific Northwest than they do in the East. It is not for lack of rainfall. The East receives more precipitation than many areas of the Northwest, and it is spread evenly throughout the year, not dumped mostly during the fall and winter as it is out West. One of the first things that comes to mind is lightning. Thunderstorms are rare in the Northwest but common in the East. Since lightning seeks out the objects closest to the sky, there would be selective pressure against height. Yet some of the tallest trees in the world grow in the tropical rainforest belt, where thunderstorms and lightning are a daily occurrence. Also, if all the trees are tall, then there is no selective advantage to height. The answer to this riddle may lie in the physics of water. Water has weight. To pull a thin column of water high into a tree is to defy physical laws that say the molecular bonds that hold water molecules together will break when the accumulated weight of a water column gets beyond a certain point. Trees overcome this by creating very narrow water columns that limit the strain on any one point in the column. As water evaporates from the tree's leaves, negative pressure on the column that snakes unbroken down to the roots pulls more water up to the leaves.

In gymnosperms, like pines, firs, and redwoods, the xylem (the water-conducting tissues of the stem) is made of a long chain of narrow cells called tracheids butted up end to end to form chambered tubes. Individual tracheids can be opened or closed, effectively allowing or cutting off water flow at any point along the column. Angiosperms, especially ring-porous species like oaks, have xylem made of hollow tubes called vessels that bond together to form a thin but continuous pipe that water can flow through unimpeded. This has the advantage of creating less work for the tree, and also increased physical strength—one reason that conifers, or softwoods, are weaker-wooded is that the chains of tracheids are more easily ripped asunder than a long, cablelike tube of vessels—but it also means that the tube cannot be shut down if an air bubble develops. When trees are translocating water during times of stress—drought, cold, low atmospheric moisture, or excessive heat—the continuous column of water within the xylem can break, effectively eliminating its ability to pull water until the air bubble is eliminated. Gymnosperms can seal off this break and force out air, especially if they can draw on high atmospheric moisture (dew, fog) to force water down toward the roots from above. By contrast, if an oak suffers a break in its xylem vessels, especially the larger-diameter ones formed in the spring, the tube may be essentially useless for transport and retains usefulness only as a structural component. This explains why many temperate-zone trees produce wider xylem vessels in spring, when air is cool and water plentiful, and narrower ones in summer and fall, when the air is hotter and soil moisture tends to decrease. It is these alternating large- and small-diameter vessel-cells or tracheids that give wood its annual rings.

Thus it is no accident that gymnosperms like redwood, Sitka spruce, western red-cedar and eastern white pine are our tallest native trees. It is also not surprising that it is in the mountains of California and the Pacific Northwest, where the winters are mild, the summers cool and humid, and violent, stem-snapping hurricanes and tornados are rare, that these trees can attain their greatest height.

---

to toss them out, so I plant them around the property. Given sun and a fertile, moist soil, tulip poplar will grow quickly into a broad pyramid with a straight central trunk. If planted in the open, the lower branches will continue to grow up and arch away and down again in a distinctive pattern. The root system is fleshy and not particularly deep, so digging and moving are straightforward, but it takes a few years for the tree to get reestablished. Because of its fast growth, it is one of the few trees that you can actually sow in place and see grow into a decent sapling in five years. Despite the protection given new growth, aphids do relish the trees, and their honeydew drips to the ground below as well as onto other leaves, which may encourage unsightly sooty mold. Because of its size, this is not a species for small spaces, but if limbed up, it is a wonderful tree to garden under in a woodland setting.

USES: Shade tree.

PROPAGATION: Moderately easy from seed.

Lonicera (lon-ISS-air-a)
Caprifoliaceae
Honeysuckle

Lonicera sempervirens

The sultry fragrance of honeysuckle drifting through the warm night air is the bittersweet essence of Faulkner's gothic South. So it is perhaps poetic irony that this sticky-sweet perfume comes not from an indigenous vine but from the parchment-yellow blossoms of the rampant Japanese honeysuckle *(L. japonica)*, which strangles fences, hedgerows, and even a fellow too long sleeping under its twisting, ever-lengthening stems. Japanese honeysuckle releases this odor of jasmine and gardenia as the sun begins to set, continuing to loft it from fertile flowers well into the night to attract pollinating moths. We have some beautiful native honeysuckles, too, but these are bee- or hummingbird-pollinated. Their flowers are vividly colored, but lack as strong a scent. So here is the rub. To plant the invasive Asian honeysuckles is to invite trouble, but to stick with the natives, you must forgo penetrating fragrance. It is a difficult but important choice, and I hope you will choose the latter (maybe you could buy some bottled perfume and spray the native vines at sunset?!?).

We have over a dozen native *Lonicera* species in our flora, split equally between showy-flowered vines and not-so-showy shrubs or suffrutescent (dying back in winter to a woody base) perennials. All produce paired leaves at intervals along the stem, which is usually covered in finely shredded, peeling bark. The vines climb by twining and twisting, and most will keep on growing all season if conditions are good. Flowers are borne at the tips of new growth, and as the shoot turns its energies toward reproduction, the petioles of the new leaves dwindle, so that below the flowers they are at first sessile, with bases butted up against each other, and ultimately perfoliate—fused together into a cupped disk creased down the middle. Honeysuckle flowers consist of 5 narrow petals joined together for at least half their length into a long tube stuck in a little crown of a calyx. Wiry stamens and a long stigma with a gum-sticky tip protrude clawlike from the tube. The petals are rounded at the ends, and roll back at least a little in trumpet fashion. Some of the vining species orient the four lower petals into a lip, while others arrange all five in an even flair. There is sweet nectar hidden in the base of the tube, so insects or birds must jab their tongue down inside and in the process get dusted on the forehead with pollen. Since some of the vining types keep growing and producing new flowers all season, they are about the most reliable hummingbird feeders you could imagine. We have a large, vigorous *L. sempervirens* 'Alabama Crimson' planted on an arbor just outside my office window, and a female ruby-throated hummingbird *(Archilochus colubris)* stakes it out in spring and visits it about every 15 minutes all summer until she migrates south again in fall. It's as good as a man-made feeder, and I never have to clean or refill it. If the pollinator does its job, a soft, fleshy berry develops, first hard and green, then softening and going from yellow to orange and finally juicy scarlet. These make themselves available for other birds to eat, though a chipmunk climbs up into the one outside my window and takes most of the fruit as it ripens. Bird dispersal is one of the best ways for shrubs to move around, and our fine-feathered friends have moved some of the introduced species far and wide. Strangely, though, the native vines are much less prolific this way. I have rarely seen a volunteer seedling pop up from garden plants.

CULTURE: Though all honeysuckles are somewhat shade tolerant, insufficient sun means only one flush of blooms in spring. For best performance, site them in at least half-day sun in fertile soil that can be irrigated in times of drought. Honeysuckles transplant easily, either from containers or rooted divisions taken from the periphery of the main clump in early spring. You can liberally prune back the vines in winter, which will delay flowering but usually will not prevent it, as blooms come from short spurs on the older stems first, then the tips of more vigorous new stems later in the season. Provide some sort of support for the vines such as a trellis, fencing, or wire to help them achieve the desired height. After that they become thicker and woodier each year and provide their own support for reinforcements coming from the base. I like to leave the larger vines and just thin them out in late fall, pruning off some of the suckers from the base as well. Powdery mildew is a fact of life with honeysuckles, but full sun and good culture will keep it in check. (I find that the wild *L. sempervirens* gets mildew far less than the widely sold hybrid *L. × heckrottii*, Goldflame honeysuckle.)

Lonicera sempervirens 'Magnifica'. Although this cultivar does not bloom as freely as some of the other trumpet honeysuckle cultivars, I am quite fond of its rich red flowers. This vine is growing on an old oak stump. I give it a haircut in late winter to remove excessively long stems. By now the vine has developed a thick, stocky trunk that will support it once the trunk has turned to humus.

The year 2000 was especially cool and wet, and honeysuckle blight (*Isolibasidium deformans*) was especially prevalent, deforming and blackening soft new growth and causing it to drop prematurely. This can be especially troublesome under overhead irrigation, where leaves are continually rewetted. The best thing short of fungicide is to try to keep the leaves as dry as possible, plant them in a spot with good air movement, and remove weedy honeysuckles nearby that may be a source of reinfection. There is variation in susceptibility from plant to plant and species to species. I have seen much less problem on *L. hirsuta* and *L. dioica* than on neighboring *L. sempervirens*, and this resistance may be passed on to the hybrids.

USES: Train vining honeysuckles up trellises, along fences, up posts, even train tree fashion, like wisteria. The shrub honeysuckles can be naturalized in the forest understory or as fencerows.

WILDLIFE: The vining species are great for attracting hummingbirds, and the shrubs for bees. Berries are forage for birds and mammals.

PROPAGATION: Moderately easy from cuttings, moderately easy from seed.

Lonicera ciliosa
Orange Honeysuckle

ZONES: (4)5–8; sun, part sun
SOIL: Moist
NATIVE TO: Moist cliffs, riverbanks, mountain thickets; Montana to British Columbia south to northern California and the mountains of Arizona
SIZE: Height 2–18 feet (depending on support), width 2–6 feet
COLOR: Typically smoky orange; blooms in late spring to summer

This is basically the western form or extension of trumpet honeysuckle (*L. sempervirens*). It has pretty blue-green, glaucous, oblong leaves that are paler below; twining stems; and soft, gray-orange flowers that are similar in color to those of trumpet honeysuckle, but a bit shorter on average. They are followed by yellow-orange berries. Along the coast in drier soils, it is joined by California honeysuckle (*L. hispidula*), a lovely vine with similar leaves that are mostly evergreen and larger clusters of flowers from both the tips and upper axils of the stems. Flower color is more of a purple or pink, followed by large grapelike bunches of red fruits. I imagine this would be hardy only in Zones 8–9; in colder areas, limber honeysuckle (*L. dioica*) is a passable substitute.

Lonicera dioica
Limber Honeysuckle, Wild Honeysuckle, Smooth Honeysuckle

ZONES: 3–9; sun, part shade
SOIL: Moist

NATIVE TO: Moist woods and thickets; Quebec to Alaska south to British Columbia, Iowa, Oklahoma and New Jersey and in the Appalachians to North Carolina
SIZE: Height 4–10 feet, width 3–4 feet
COLOR: Yellow more or less suffused with pink; blooms in late spring to early summer, longer under good conditions

This is another great native vine to viny shrub in the perfoliate group, with leaves much like trumpet honeysuckle's that end in squat bunches of pretty, two-toned flowers each about 1 inch long followed by red fruits. Grape honeysuckle (*L. prolifera*) is more vine-like, and its small, yellowish flowers are not nearly as ornamental.

Lonicera hirsuta
Hairy Honeysuckle

ZONES: 4–7(8); sun to light shade
SOIL: Moist; often over limestone, but grows in acidic soils as well
NATIVE TO: Moist woods and thickets; Maine and Ontario to southern Manitoba south to Minnesota, New York, and Pennsylvania
SIZE: Height 4–10 feet, width 3–5 feet
COLOR: Bright butter yellow; blooms in late spring to early summer

I like hairy honeysuckle more and more each year. It has rough hairy leaves that can get quite large in the shade, 4 inches long and 2 inches wide, and it tends to bloom in one glorious flush, even under ideal conditions. In thicket situations, root suckers are sometimes produced as it meanders through the underbrush. The var. *hirsuta* from New England has larger flowers, to 1 inch long, than the more widespread var. *interior*. South of Pennsylvania, this species is replaced by yellow honeysuckle (*L. flava*), also a pretty, vine-to-shrub species with smooth leaves with a whitish bloom below and larger flowers, 1½ inches long on average, that have a hint more orange in the ones I've seen. It is hardy in Zones 5–9. Whether this represents a stabilized natural hybrid with trumpet honeysuckle (*L. sempervirens*), we can only guess, but the latter does cross with others (the genus is naturally promiscuous). Brown's honeysuckle, *L. × brownii* (*sempervirens* × *hirsuta*), is represented in cultivation by the widely planted cultivar 'Dropmore Scarlet', which seems to take mostly after the first parent in appearance but which has been more tolerant of honeysuckle blight than trumpet honeysuckle.

Lonicera involucrata
Twinberry, Bearberry Honeysuckle

ZONES: 3–7; sun, part sun
SOIL: Cool, moist, seems to prefer limestone
NATIVE TO: Cold woods and mountain meadows;

Quebec to northern Michigan and Alaska south to northern California and down the spine of the Rockies into northern Mexico

SIZE: Height 2–8 feet, width 2–6 feet

COLOR: Light yellow; blooms in summer

Twinberry is as much a curiosity as an ornamental. It grows as a low, twiggy shrub or large bush producing large, pointed oval leaves from vertical stems arising from the base as well as from the older, less vigorous woody branches. Pairs of tubular ½-inch flowers are produced on long peduncles that hang from the leaf axils. These are subtended by an elaborate boat-like ruffled pair of fused, red and green bracts with the small calyxes nestled inside the hull like two ship-wrecked sailors. Each calyx wraps around a green berry that ripens blue-black, at which point the bracts turn inside out to expose it and flash their own pink-waxy interiors to passing birds. The turned-out bracts have a cold-cut-on-a-plate quality—weird. We have tried to grow eastern genotypes (the smaller var. *involucrata*) without success, as they need a cool-summer climate. The larger, western forms are sometimes cultivated and are easy to grow from cuttings (see McMinn, *An Illustrated Manual of California Shrubs,* pp. 547–548).

Lonicera oblongifolia
Swamp Fly-honeysuckle

ZONES: 3–7; sun, part sun

SOIL: Moist to wet

NATIVE TO: Swamps and bogs; New Brunswick to Manitoba south to Minnesota, Ohio, and Pennsylvania

SIZE: Height 3–6 feet, width 2–4 feet

COLOR: Pale yellow; blooms in late spring

I am including this and the following shrubby species for reference, even though they have little to recommend them ornamentally. Swamp fly-honeysuckle has relatively large, almost egg-shaped leaves and small flowers paired on a long peduncle that give way to red fruits. Waterberry (*L. caerulea*) is a circumboreal, shrubby species with small, yellowish flowers borne in pairs hidden in the leaves, followed by pretty blue teardrop-shaped fruits. Other western U.S. shrubby species with small yellow flowers and red fruits include Utah honeysuckle (*L. utahensis*) and double honeysuckle (*L. conjugialis*). Fly-honeysuckle (*L. canadensis*) is a scraggly, running understory shrub found commonly in eastern woodlands.

Lonicera sempervirens
Trumpet Honeysuckle

ZONES: 4–9; sun to part sun

SOIL: Moist

NATIVE TO: Connecticut to Ohio and Oklahoma, south to Alabama and Florida

SIZE: Height 4–15 feet (depending on support), width 4–8 feet

COLOR: Orange, pinkish red, occasionally yellow; blooms in late spring and on to early winter with good conditions

Without question, this is the longest-flowering plant in our gardens. It starts in a flush in late spring and keeps on going in pulses until Christmas if the weather is mild. Granted, in shade it will limit itself to a month or so, but give it some sun, and wow. The leaves have a pretty glaucous bloom like that of *L. ciliosa,* as do the young stems. The typical forms have a wash of purple in the leaf veins, petioles, and twigs, but this is absent in yellow-flowered cultivars like 'Sulfurea' and 'John Clayton', making these easy to identify even out of bloom. The corollas average 1-to-2 inches long, and come one after the other in big, successively flowered bunches from the stem tips. Like most of the vining species, it is reluctant to drop its leaves, which hang on until late fall—there is no appreciable fall color. Fruit ripens yellow-orange-red.

Maclura pomifera. The beginnings of a large, puckered fruit are already evident in the remarkable flowers on this female Osage orange tree, photographed in full bloom at the venerable Arnold Arboretum in Jamaica Plain, Massachusetts. Each of the filamentous stigmas is attached to an ovary lying within one segment of the amalgamated syncarp (a cluster of united ovaries).

Maclura pomifera

Maclura pomifera
(ma-KLUR-a)

Moraceae
Osage Orange, Hedge-apple

ZONES: 4–8; sun

SOIL: Moist to dry

NATIVE TO: Thickets; originally native to a strip running through east-central Texas north into southeastern Oklahoma and southwestern Arkansas, now naturalized from Connecticut to Minnesota south to New Mexico and Florida

SIZE: Height 20–35 (50) feet, width 25–40 feet

COLOR: Greenish white; blooms in spring

Osage orange is certainly a curiosity. When I was growing up, a neighbor down the road must have

Magnolia virginiana.
Fragrance can add so much to our appreciation of a particular flower. Sweetbay magnolia blooms proffer a rich, melodious perfume that delights the nose, just as their color and shape delight the eye. The flowers never open fully; though they appear to be on the verge of flaring open resplendently, they don't follow through.

had a special fondness for it — perhaps he had moved east from the Plains, where it is planted commonly as a windbreak. He had planted 200 feet of road frontage with the trees, whose branches formed a sylvan arch over the macadam. Every fall, the sidewalk and gutter were littered with grapefruit-sized "oranges" that had dropped from the branches of female trees. Inevitably, one year a falling fruit smashed a passing windshield, and the town forced the guy to cut down all the trees. I always wished I had been there to scavenge the wood, for *Maclura* heartwood possesses a striking, orange-brown patina coupled with hardness, strength, and resistance to rot. It looks very beautiful fashioned into outdoor furniture (some of the benches at Garden in the Woods are made from it). The trees have a low-slung, spreading crown much like crabapple's or hawthorn's, supported by a short trunk forking near the ground into several limbs. The trunk is covered with a thin gray-brown bark splitting tantalizingly along fissures to reveal a bright orange inner bark. The twigs and smaller branches are armed with stout, stipular thorns that easily snag on skin and clothing. The bright green leaves, suspended on long petioles, are oval but narrow to a long, slender tip. Osage oranges are dioecious, the female trees clustering their flowers in a tight, pendent ball sprouting a furious Afro of stigmas to lick up the pollen necessary to develop their remarkable fruits (technically syncarps) — possibly the biggest fruits in our flora. These are really as big as grapefruits, though as a common name Osage grapefruit doesn't have quite the same ring, with a yellow-green rind that is patterned like hundreds of tiny lips or unroasted coffee beans stuck around a spongy core. If you smash open the milk-sticky rind, you find a hard whitish pulp with seeds scattered and embedded within. The fruits probably evolved for dispersal by large (now extinct) herbivores, but cows like to eat them once the frost has softened them up. The introduction of cattle, coupled with widespread planting as a natural barbed-wire fence, has greatly expanded the natural range of this once fairly rare tree. It seems possible that the North American extinction of large herbivores like the horse, and the rhinoceros in recent geological time, could explain its limited pre-Columbian distribution.

CULTURE: Osage orange is fibrous-rooted and is easily transplanted into a range of soils. It tolerates dry, windblown conditions remarkably well, but full sun is necessary for good crown development. Thornless male clones are available, mostly from nurseries in the Midwest and Plains states, and these are preferable to seed-grown material unless you want ponderous projectiles for your potato cannon or fodder for your pet rhinoceros.

USES: Hedgerows and windbreaks in difficult situations.

PROPAGATION: Easy from seed.

Magnolia virginiana

Magnolia (mag-NOH-lia)
Magnoliaceae
Magnolia

Magnolias are not wallflowers, not content to melt quietly into the background. Their large leaves and thick trunks loudly proclaim their presence wherever they are. Magnolias are special plants, and though they are not truly the first angiosperms, they are *among* the first, taking their place right after conifers on the phenological family tree. There is even the suggestion of pine or fir in the tacky, balsam-scented sap that oozes from their seed cones, but here the similarities end. Magnolias display two major steps forward in plant evolution: insect-pollinated flowers and jacketed seeds. They announce their achievement with remarkable blooms up to 10 inches across — more like architecture than flowers, really. Remember that petals are modified leaves transformed into banners to attract the attention of insects or animals, and this relationship is clear when you examine a magnolia's flower. The overlapping petals unfurl and curl back one at a time like developing leaves from a huge bud wrapped in a few protective, leaf-like bracts (the petals even suggest leaves somewhat in shape), and form a flattened saucer cupping a proud central cone elevated on a thick pedestal. A beard of stamens skirts the thumblike cone of ovaries, which makes up the bulk of the projection. The flowers emit either a fresh lemon-fruit or dirty-old-sock fragrance — the sort you'll recognize as an invitation to beetles. These large, rugged blooms are engineered to withstand the bacchanalian excesses of feeding and copulating scarabs, for like pawpaw *(Asimina)* and sweetshrub *(Calycanthus)*, magnolias evolved around 25 million years B.B. (before bees).

If all goes well with the beetles, the stamens drop off, followed by the petals themselves, and the ovary-cone begins to swell with developing seeds. Late in the season, the cone (really a collection of two-sided pods called a follicetum) flushes pink. Then the pods split along their seams, wither, and peel back, each releasing a corn kernel–sized seed wrapped in a pink or red skin. The seeds are attached by a weblike, fibrous strand that holds them to the outside of the cone like a safety rope, allowing them to dangle and twist in the breeze. This is an ingenious method of attracting birds, who are drawn by the bright color and the movement of the seeds. After a few days, if no birds happen by, the seeds drop to the ground under the tree to be squirreled away by rodents.

All of our native magnolias save cucumbertree (*M. acuminata*) are understory species. Nevertheless, most can develop an appreciable size and spread with time, even reaching the upper forest canopy in favored places. They are single- or multitrunked trees, at first somewhat pyramidal, then broadening with age. The main branches are decked with stout twigs that arch and meander in an irregular way. Most retain their sharkskin-gray, smooth bark even on the older trunks. Magnolias shield developing leaves in a pair of stipular bracts that wrap tightly around the bud, then crack and give way, remaining attached to the petiole base of the leaf below even after they have withered and browned. When young, the larger species can grow indeterminately, with central leaders gaining 2 feet in a growing season under ideal conditions. The majority of our species, including *M. ashei, M. frasieri, M. macrophylla, M. pyramidata,* and *M. tripetela,* are in the Umbrella group, characterized by large deciduous leaves—in some cases longer than your arm. *M. grandiflora* is truly evergreen, with smaller leaves, and *M. virginiana,* with even smaller foliage, is usually semi-evergreen in Zone 7 and warmer areas.

CULTURE: Magnolias produce fat, fleshy roots, and care must be taken when digging and transplanting, as it is hard to get a decent root ball that will hold together when moved from the hole. For this reason, I prefer to use container-grown material and plant it out in spring or early summer (fall in the South). By nature, these are trees of the moist, fertile soils found in rich coves, swamps, and floodplains, and a similar situation is best in cultivation. The ubiquitous presence of *Magnolia grandiflora* in all manner of situations in the southeastern landscape attests to its adaptability, and other large-leaved species will also grow in less-than-ideal conditions, albeit more slowly. All will tolerate light shade, where they develop an open, staggered canopy that usually lets enough light through for underplanted ferns or wildflowers. In the sun, the leaves come thick and fast, and trees will bloom more heavily and at an earlier age. Magnolias are not especially strong-wooded, and ice and snow breakage are occasional problems. We lost almost all our *M. virginiana* and the top of an *M. acuminata* during a heavy, wet, early-spring snowstorm.

USES: Specimen, understory tree, woodland edge.

PROPAGATION: Moderately easy from seed.

Magnolia acuminata
Cucumbertree, Cucumber Magnolia

ZONES: 4–9; sun to light shade

SOIL: Moist

NATIVE TO: Rich woodlands, ravines; New York and southern Ontario to southern Indiana and Missouri to eastern Oklahoma, south to Texas and western Florida (not found along the coastal plain)

SIZE: Height 50–80 (100) feet, width 30–40 feet

COLOR: Yellow or yellow-green, occasionally light orange; blooms in spring

One of the dilemmas for woodland gardeners is how to fill in the tree canopy as individuals die. Our garden has an overstory composed mostly of oak and white pine, many already over 100 years old, and we have to accept that they will not be around forever. From my experience with cucumber magnolia, this may be a suitable replacement species, as it grows well in the dappled shade under oaks and, should one of the larger trees die, can take its place in the upper canopy. This species is distinct from the other magnolias in that its deciduous leaves are evenly spread along the new twigs, not concentrated near the tip in a pseudowhorl. The leaf blade is 6 to 12 inches long and ovate to elliptical, narrowed to a blunt tip and rippled along the margin. The leaves come from fat buds capped in silver-furred bracts, the largest at the twig tip, as in all magnolias.

When mature, this is a stocky tree with rough-grooved bark and large limbs that arch away from the trunk. The common name cucumber tree refers to the strange, misshapen cones that vaguely resemble small cucumbers in shape and color when unripe, but which flush bright pinkish red as they begin to mature in late summer. Most cones seem to be poorly pollinated, as only scattered seeds develop, leaving the tissues in between sunken and twisted. Cucumber magnolia grows at a medium rate, and with time develops a strong, heavy presence. The flowers are small and relatively unremarkable for the genus, but their yellow color is imparted to hybrids, including the striking pale yellow cultivars 'Butterflies' and 'Elizabeth', both crosses with the smaller, larger-flowered Chinese *M. denudata* (Yulan magnolia).

Magnolia ashei
Ashe's Magnolia

ZONES: (4)5–9; sun to light shade

SOIL: Moist

NATIVE TO: Woodlands and ravines; endemic to the western Florida Panhandle

SIZE: Height 20–30 feet, width 12–20 feet

COLOR: Ivory white; blooms in spring

Ashe's magnolia differs from the more widespread bigleaf magnolia (*M. macrophylla*) in several ways. Its leaves are about half as long, 16 to 24 inches, and it is usually a smaller, multistemmed tree. It is a very rare plant in the wild, growing rarer every year as its six-county range in northwestern Florida gets paved over for cars and condos. It is surprisingly hardy, though, suggesting that this small tree was once far more widespread, but has been pushed to the bottom of the continent by glacial advances. It is a wonderful plant, with violin-shaped leaves and endearingly precocious flowering, beginning when the tree is only 4 to 5 years old. The giant leaves are chalky white below and gray-green above, turning a pretty apricot and brown before dropping in the fall, reminding me of curing tobacco leaves in form and color. Like all the large-leaved deciduous species, it lends a tropical, you might even say cretaceous, note to the garden that is hard to miss. Blooms average 6 to 8 inches across, and have a strong, honey-lemon fragrance.

Magnolia grandiflora
Southern Magnolia, Bull Bay

ZONES: (6)7–9; sun to light shade

SOIL: Moderately wet to moderately dry

NATIVE TO: Rich woods, bottoms, and hammocks; along the coastal plain from North Carolina to Florida and eastern Texas

SIZE: Height 25–50 (110) feet, width 20–60 feet

COLOR: Ivory white; blooms in late spring, sporadically into early summer

No plant is more characteristic of the Deep South than the nacreous, lemon-scented bull bay. It is the only completely evergreen magnolia in our flora, with broad oval leaves that are a rich bronzy green and incredibly glossy above and exquisitely contrasted with cinnamon below in the best forms. The leaf margins curl and undulate, and the trees form a thick, rounded canopy impenetrable to light. My sister-in-law Suzanne grew up with this tree and, like many southerners, she finds it coarse and messy. The foliage is so thick and resilient that when it dries and falls, it lingers like pieces of cardboard around the base of the tree. Since leaves fall sporadically through the spring and early summer, it requires frequent tidying up after when it's out in the front yard. The flowers can be up to 12 inches or more in diameter, second in size only to those of bigleaf magnolia, though most of the trees sold today are the smaller cultivars like 'Little Gem', which remains a manageable size and has leaves and flowers that are consequently reduced. Many people—myself included— feel that this is one our finest flowering trees and as such have attempted to force it to grow to the limits

of its winter-hardiness. Selected cultivars perform surprisingly well in Zone 6, though all tend to suffer leaf burn or become defoliated in late winter when the sun is strong, the wind is howling, and the ground is still frozen. I have had 'Edith Bogue' growing well on Cape Cod for ten years now, and we planted the lovely, russeted 'Braken's Brown Beauty' at Garden in the Woods in a sheltered nook behind our education building. Unfortunately, one winter's heavy snows bent it over, exposing the delicate leaf undersides to the winter sun and badly killing back the tree.

Magnolia macrophylla
Bigleaf Magnolia

ZONES: 5–9; sun to light shade

SOIL: Moist

NATIVE TO: Bottomlands and coves; through the southern piedmont from Virginia to southern Ohio, south through Tennessee to Louisiana and Georgia

SIZE: Height 25–40 (90) feet , width 20–35 feet

COLOR: Creamy white; blooms in spring

This is a remarkable deciduous tree. It has the largest undivided leaves of any woody plant in our flora – up to 3 feet long and 1 foot wide where they flare most broadly near the tip. Like those of *M. ashei*, the leaf margins undulate like the shell of a giant clam, revealing the chalky white undersurface in turns along their length. The sweetly fragrant flowers are extremely large as well—big, white saucers up to 16 inches across! It is the sort of plant that you have to site carefully in the garden, as it can be texturally overpowering among fine-leaved plant—even oaks and tulip tree are fine-textured compared to bigleaf magnolia.

Magnolia tripetala
Umbrella Magnolia, Umbrella-tree

ZONES: 4–9; sun to light shade

SOIL: Moist

NATIVE TO: Rich woods and coves, mostly in the Appalachians from Pennsylvania to southern Indiana south to Arkansas, Mississippi, and Georgia

SIZE: Height 25–40 (55) feet, width 15–35 feet

COLOR: Creamy white; blooms in spring

Umbrella magnolia is the hardiest of the bigleaf deciduous group, and it grows easily and even seeds about in our woodland gardens. Its 12-to-30-inch leaves—the "umbrellas"—are widest near the tip, tapering gradually to a narrow, un-lobed base. The flowers are not too spectacular, as the segments are rather thin, and they emit a rotten-socks odor when you get close to them. However, the tree is simply beautiful in the understory, with its large green umbrellas slung out flat from thick twigs to capture the light. It is the kind of tree you want to plant where you can walk under it and look up, as the leaves are especially striking when backlit from above. There is a large tree growing very well in the gardens designed by Fletcher Steele at Naumkeag (now open to the public) in Stockbridge, Massachusetts, where the wind and cold rush up unhindered from the Hudson Valley.

Magnolia virginiana

Sweetbay Magnolia, Swamp-bay

ZONES: 5–9; sun to part sun

SOIL: Moist to wet

NATIVE TO: Swamps, low woods and savannas, mostly along the coast from eastern Massachusetts and New York to Florida and eastern Texas

SIZE: Height 20–60 (80) feet, width 8–20 feet

COLOR: Creamy white; blooms in late spring and sporadically into summer, especially in the South

Sweetbay is a variable species: northern forms are reluctantly deciduous, multistemmed shrubs or small trees; southern forms are semi-evergreen and become narrow, single-trunked trees that climb through the understory and occasionally break out through neighboring cypress and tupelo into the sun. There is a famous remnant population out on Cape Ann, in Gloucester, Massachusetts, that has hung on for centuries after migrating north during the warm post glacial period 7,000 years ago. From this population, hardier, smaller forms have been introduced. I like the multistemmed northern race because it has an open, filtered canopy that allows underplanting, and the trunks develop a twisted, picturesque character like some of the Asian species. The leaves are small for the genus—3 to 4 inches long and 1 to 1½ inches wide—with a medium, gray-green upper surface and a whitish lower surface that looks pretty fluttering in the breeze. Selections have been made that retain their leaves more reliably in winter; still, I would not consider this a true evergreen. Even plants I observed in a south Florida swamp had dropped half their canopy by January. Flowers are small and cupped, 1½ to 2½ inches wide, and they open a few at a time over a month or possibly more. Though not as visually impressive as the large-flowered species, they are about the most heavenly sweet-smelling flowers you'll find in the genus.

Mahonia aquifolium

Mahonia (Berberis)

(ma-HOH-nia)

Berberidaceae

Mahonia, Oregon Grape, Grape Holly

Mahonia aquifolium. *Oregon grape is not static in the landscape. In spring it offers flowers and fresh new leaves mixed with older ones turning brilliant scarlet. In summer the dusty blue fruits are set against a shiny, deep green backdrop of mature foliage, and in winter the evergreen leaves chill to ruddy red against a blanket of snow.*

At their best, mahonias are dynamic textural plants with prickly, evergreen leaflets like American holly's strung into long, compound leaves like a sumac's. Oregon grape *(M. aquifolium)* is the most familiar in gardens, where it forms spreading clumps of unbranched stems covered in a warm gray, flaky bark and topped with a crown of shining, crinkly leaves. The foliage is beautiful when it comes out in spring all fresh and glistening, flushed bronze then chartreuse and finally deep, forest green. In fall the leaves turn burgundy when they are planning to last the winter and crimson if they are about to drop—a real study in red (leaves that survive the winter often color red and drop off as the next crop is maturing in spring). Mahonia flowers are also pretty. These open before the new foliage emerges in stiff panicles held up where you can see them atop the stems. The green immature buds become light, bright yellow as they develop, and open from the base of each cluster and work toward the tip. In summer, Concord grape–like clusters of bloomy blue fruit ripen among the new crop of leaves, and are quite effective well into fall unless the birds pick them off. Because the flowers are borne terminally, the new leaves flush out from one secondary bud just below. This results in a side-stepping, irregular crown, with old, unbranched shoots eventually topping out and new ones coming from the roots to replace them, helping to give the plants a more informal carriage than many broad-leaved evergreens.

There are other species of *Mahonia* throughout the West, including some with large, pinnate leaves and a group of dry-land shrubs with much smaller leaves, often beautifully tinted with reds and blue-grays. These last are intermediate between *Mahonia* and the true barberries, like Canada barberry (*Berberis canadensis*), which have simple leaves and two kinds of stems. Barberry's primary stems have thorns instead of leaves, and foliage is borne on short, spurlike axillary branchlets. In *Flora of North America*, Whittemore has consolidated all the mahonia species into *Berberis*, but in a horticultural sense the three groups (*Mahonia, Berberis,* and intermediates) are very different, so I will keep them separate. They also differ in their susceptibility to infection by wheat black stem rust (*Puccinia graminis*), one of several related rusts that affect *Berberis* and *Mahonia*. True barberries are the primary alternate host of this disease, which is an extremely serious pathogen of wheat and some other cereals. Therefore, susceptible species, like *Berberis canadensis* and *B. fendleri* (Fendler's barberry) as well as the introduced *Berberis vulgaris* (common barberry) are illegal to cultivate or transport in the United States and Canada. Some of the intermediate species, like algerita (*Mahonia trifoliata*), Fremont's mahonia (*M. fremontii*), and the striking Nevin's mahonia (*M. nevinii*) are also somewhat susceptible, and cultivation and transport are likewise prohibited. Fortunately, the large-leaved *Mahonia* species are all resistant to the disease, and therefore are legal to cultivate and transport, and consequently, these are the only species I will cover in detail.

CULTURE: The mahonias listed below generally prefer damp, acidic soils. They grow naturally in woodlands or forest gaps as well as on open, rocky slopes in the mountains, but heavily shaded plants become loose and spindly. They luxuriate in cool, maritime climates, and while the hardiest perform reasonably well in the Northeast and Midwest, they winter-burn in exposed situations. Gardeners in the South can also grow them well in a shaded, moist location. In colder climates, unless you live in an area with reliable, deep snow cover, plant them where they will be out of sight in late winter and early spring, until the new foliage emerges to restore their dignity. In other words, don't plant them next to your front walk!

USES: Foundations, shrub border, massing, groundcover.

WILDLIFE: Fruits scavenged by birds.

PROPAGATION: Moderately easy from seed.

Mahonia aquifolium
Oregon Grape, Grape Holly

ZONES: (4)5–7(8); sun to light shade
SOIL: Moist to moderately dry, acidic
NATIVE TO: Open woods and shrub lands from sea level to 6,500 feet; Montana to British Columbia south to California, Oregon, and the Idaho Panhandle
SIZE: Height 1–4 (12) feet, width 2–4 feet
COLOR: Bright yellow, mixed with green; blooms in early spring

Given the right location, this plant truly shines. In a spot protected from winter sun and wind, expect a slowly spreading shrub in the 2-to-3-foot range. It is the most adaptable of the rust-resistant species, with glossy dark-green compound leaves with typically 3 to 4 sets of lateral leaflets and one terminal leaflet—all the same size and very much like a holly leaf in shape. The leaves are lighter blue green on their undersurface. Several other species are reasonably similar, including Piper's mahonia (*M. piperiana*) from northern California and southern Oregon, which has wider leaflets that are tremendously glossy, even on the undersides, and shiny-leaf mahonia (*M. pinnata*), basically the California extension of *M. aquifolium*, from which it is hard to distinguish it.

Mahonia nervosa
Longleaf Mahonia

ZONES: (5)6–8; part sun to light shade
SOIL: Moist to moderately dry, acidic
NATIVE TO: Open woods, rocky slopes; southwestern British Columbia south along the west side of the Cascades and Sierras to central California, with an isolated population in the Idaho Panhandle
SIZE: Height 4–12 (48) inches, width 2–3 feet
COLOR: Bright yellow; blooms in early to late spring

Typically this is a low, spreading groundcover like *M. repens*, differing in the very large, long leaflets more like some of the Asian species both in size and horizontal, starched-shirt stiffness. The gray-green leaves can be up to 18 inches long, with as many as 9 pairs of lateral leaflets below one terminal. It is very shade adapted, often growing in dense Douglas fir forests in the Cascades. The leaves have less luster than those of *M. aquifolium*, but their size presents interesting textural possibilities when combined with other groundcovers. Like western dogwood and coast Douglas fir, an isolated population of this species grows far inland, in the area around the Snake River in northern Idaho. Seed from this station may be markedly hardier than coastal material.

Mahonia repens
Creeping Mahonia

ZONES: 4–8; sun to light shade
SOIL: Moist to moderately dry, acidic
NATIVE TO: Open forest, subalpine grassland, shrubby slopes and cliffs up to 9,000 feet; North Dakota to Idaho and British Columbia south to northwestern California, Nevada, and in the mountains to Arizona and New Mexico
SIZE: Height 2–12 (18) inches, width 1–3 feet
COLOR: Bright yellow; blooms in spring

This mahonia is a true groundcover, though it grows too sparsely to make a solid mat. The leaves are like the others', but are only 3 to 4 inches long and are composed of, typically, 5 leaflets. The blades are much thinner in substance and are matte army truck green like *M. nervosa*, and it flowers and fruits rather sparsely. This is the hardiest and most fire-tolerant species, though it seems adapted to areas with reliable snow or evergreen cover, as I have seen it winterburn badly when left exposed to the March sun. I would suggest pruning out older stems to keep it a more uniform height.

Malus coronaria

Malus (Pyrus) (MAL-us)
Rosaceae
Crabapple, Wild Crab

There are **four native** crabapple species in our flora, but they are cultivated far less than the Asian species and hybrids, mostly because of the native species' extreme susceptibility to cedar apple rust, which leaves them partially defoliated by late summer (see *Juniperus,* p. 148). Be aware that all *Malus* species freely interbreed, both with other wild species and more commonly with cultivated apples (*M. sylvestris* or *M. pumila*) and crabapple hybrids. Thus, to be assured of a wild crab's identity, you need to seek one growing in an area isolated from cultivated plants—a *Malus*-free zone (an "absence of *Malus*"?). Chances are it is a wild crab of some sort if the twigs are thorny, the flowers have red (not yellow) anthers, and the fruits are about 1 to 1½ inches in diameter and green to yellow-green when ripe (most hybrid crabs have smaller red or yellow fruits). Wild crab fruits are very sour; I will always vividly remember my fifth grade teacher's expression when she bit into one while we were on our weekly class nature walk in the old fields behind the school. Imagine someone trying to suck a pebble through a soda straw—lips puckered up like the base of a balloon. The fruits are certainly not the first choice of birds, but deer and a variety of other mammals eat

them, and with enough sugar and pectin, you could turn them into a passable jelly.

Despite their limitations, in flower the native crabapples are as lovely as any small tree, with pink-flushed, very fragrant, 5-petaled blooms decorating every branch as the leaves emerge in spring. There are some semidouble and double-flowered cultivars out there, and they put on a show to rival any Asian *Malus* in opulence. Wild crabs are all multistemmed shrubs or small trees of hedgerows and old fields, suckering at the base to form twiggy, thorny thickets—the perfect place for a bird to hide while it dines on the fruit.

CULTURE: A moist, open situation is best. Rooted suckers can be dug out and transplanted before flow-

Malus coronaria 'Nieuwlandiana'. This old, double-flowered cultivar of sweet crabapple is simply lovely in bloom. The flowers are not sterile, so yellow-green fruits will ripen later in the season.

ering. Though some selection for rust as well as scab resistance has been done for prairie crab, other than spraying and cutting down every poor juniper in the area, there is not much you can do about cedar apple rust other than marvel at the jelly-horned fruiting bodies as they poke out from a red-cedar.

USES: Naturalizing and planting for wildlife.

WILDLIFE: Crabapples provide fruit for mammals and birds, and the leaves are fed on at least occasionally by a variety of butterfly larvae, including the viceroy admiral, white admiral, and orange-tip admiral (*Limenitis archippus, L. arthemis,* and *L. lorquini*), striped hairstreak (*Satyrium liparops*), and spring azure (*Celastrina argiolus*).

PROPAGATION: Easy from seed.

Malus angustifolia

Southern Crab

ZONES: (5)6–9; sun, part sun

SOIL: Moist to moderately dry

NATIVE TO: Open woodland and thickets; North Carolina to Arkansas, south to Louisiana and northern Florida, occasionally farther north to New Jersey and Ohio

SIZE: Height 10–20 (30) feet, width 8–15 (25) feet

COLOR: Deep pink in bud, fading to light pink or white; blooms in spring

Southern crab is the common species in the Southeast, and it's very similar to the more northern *M. coronaria*, though it has narrower, oval leaves (as opposed to wide, pointed leaves with a rounded base). The two hybridize where their ranges overlap to form the intermediate *M.* × *platycarpa*.

Malus coronaria

Sweet Crabapple

ZONES: 4–8; sun, part shade

SOIL: Moist to moderately dry

NATIVE TO: New York to southern Ontario and Minnesota south to Kansas, Missouri, and scattered south in the mountains to northern Georgia

SIZE: Height 10–25 (30) feet, width 8–20 feet

COLOR: Deep pink in bud, fading to light pink or white; blooms in spring

Sweet crabapple develops a flat, horizontal crown wider than tall, with layered branches that are quite attractive in flower.

Malus fusca

Pacific Crab, Oregon Crab

ZONES: 5–8; sun, part sun

SOIL: Moist

NATIVE TO: Bog margins and mountain slopes; coastal Alaska to California

SIZE: Height 15–25 (40) feet, width 12–20 feet

COLOR: Typically white or flushed light pink; blooms in spring

Unlike the eastern species, Pacific crab has small fruits (½ inch in diameter) that turn yellow-green flushed with red when ripe. The fruits are relished by birds and continue to be an important winter food for Native Americans in the Pacific Northwest because their acidity keeps them from spoiling easily, and they become gradually sweeter over the winter. In habit it is a rounded, thorny shrub or small tree taller than wide.

Malus ioensis

Prairie Crab

ZONES: 4–8; sun, part sun

SOIL: Moist to moderately dry

NATIVE TO: Woods and thickets; Indiana northwest to eastern North Dakota, south to Oklahoma and Alabama, with isolated populations in Texas and Louisiana

SIZE: Height 15–30 (35) feet, width 15–25 feet

COLOR: Deep pink in bud, fading to light pink or white; blooms in spring

Prairie crab is the only one of the four crabs discussed here that is well represented in the nursery trade. Its scab (a leaf disease) resistance has been bred into many hybrids. Typically it is a small tree rather than a suckering shrub, with a single or branched trunk.

Menziesia pilosa

Menziesia (men-ZEE-zee-ah)

Ericaceae

Minnie-bush, False Azalea

Menziesia **species resemble** the deciduous azaleas in the way their leaves are held out flat and whorled around the tips of the twigs to catch the maximum amount of light filtering through the tree canopy. Also like the azaleas they become rounded, multistem shrubs with new shoots appearing from the crown or roots to fill in where older limbs have faltered. The flowers? Well, they're a different story. They are cute little bells arching out on curving, sticky-hairy pedicels from a central point like a miniature chandelier. The blooms are creamy white at the base and ringed with rosy pink around the petal edge, which is effectively the bottom edge, since they hang downward. In carriage, shape, and color, the blooms are nearly identical to those of the Japanese *Enkianthus campanulatus* (redvein enkianthus), though the eastern form, minnie-bush *(M. pilosa)*, will never attain the treelike proportions of an old enkianthus. Our one specimen of *M. pilosa* is in a difficult spot, and it is only 3 feet high and wide after 25 years. Its new leaves, stems, and pedicels are covered in white glandular hairs that give it a bristly

Menziesia pilosa. If you drive along the magnificent Blue Ridge Parkway winding up through the Smoky Mountains of North Carolina and Tennessee, you will find ample stands of minnie-bush growing from the foggy cliffs beside the road above 4,000 feet. Its cute little flowers dangle from the twigs as the new leaves are beginning to emerge.

halo when the sun hits it. These glands release a mild skunky aroma when crushed, much like the western species, *M. ferruginea*, which is nearly identical in many ways. It is possible to find wild plants of both species with beautiful cool blue-green foliage, and many individuals develop a fiery orange-red fall color like that of *Enkianthus*. Neither *Menziesia* is widely grown. Certainly they don't have the flair of the spectacular native azaleas nor the edible fruits of the blueberries (the fruit is a woody capsule), but they have a true, quiet charm in their dainty flowers and tiered leaves that I feel makes them well worth growing in the woodland garden.

CULTURE: Moist acidic soils and light shade as for azaleas seems appropriate. I have only limited experience with the genus, so I do not know how much sun and heat they can take, but our plant blooms well in moderate shade and soil that becomes fairly dry during the summer. My suspicion is that morning sun and better soil would really bring the shrub into its own, but it is quite pretty even in this location. The leaves may develop mildew during the course of the summer, a problem that could be remedied with a bit more sun.

USES: Specimen or naturalizing in the woodland garden.

PROPAGATION: Moderately easy from seed.

Menziesia ferruginea
Rustyleaf, False Azalea, Fool's Huckleberry

ZONES: 4–7; part sun, shade
SOIL: Moist, acidic
NATIVE TO: Damp woods, stream sides, subalpine and alpine meadows; coastal Alaska and British Columbia south in the Cascades and Rockies to California and New Mexico
SIZE: Height 3–6 feet, width 3–4 feet
COLOR: Creamy white suffused with pink, especially near the tips; blooms in spring

Rustyleaf is the western *Menziesia* species. On average, it has more blue-green to the leaves, which are oval and pointed, than the eastern species, as well as slightly smaller flowers with a less pronounced pink band. It can rival the best vine maple (*Acer circinatum*) in the intensity of its orange-crimson fall color. In the wild, rustyleaf can form extensive, suckering colonies under conifers like subalpine fir, and it will retain some of this colonizing habit in cultivation.

Menziesia pilosa
Minnie-bush

ZONES: (4)5–7; part sun to shade
SOIL: Moist, acidic
NATIVE TO: Damp woods, mostly in the Appalachians from Pennsylvania to Georgia
SIZE: Height 3–4 (6) feet, width 3–4 feet

COLOR: Creamy or greenish white banded in rose pink; blooms in spring

Both the western and the eastern false azaleas bloom with the emerging leaves, so the flowers mix and hang down among the foliage, which in this case is rather spoon-shaped and medium to mint green in color. Minnie-bush will sucker and spread, though more modestly than rustyleaf, and in the wild it remains mostly in discrete clumps. In the Smoky Mountains, minnie-bush mixes with *Rhododendron vaseyi*, *R. maximum*, *Pieris floribunda*, and several *Vaccinium* species in an ericaceous smorgasbord on misty cliffs above 4,000 feet.

Myrica pensylvanica

Myrica (MY-rik-ah)
Myricaceae
Bayberry, Waxmyrtle

Bayberries are shrubs you can depend on in difficult situations. For them, dry, sandy soils, low fertility, road salt, and wind are par for the course. All of the species are similar enough in leaf that you can say with a glance, "Oh, bayberry," even if you are not sure which one it is. Northern bayberry is the plant I have come to know best as it rings our yard on Cape Cod in a spicy-sweet necklace of slowly deciduous leaves. The foliage of all *Myrica* species contains aromatic oils that are released when the leaves are crushed, emitting a wonderful odor of camphor and oregano. This is the northeastern member of a species complex that stretches down the East Coast, growing anywhere dry soil and sun can be found. In the New Jersey pine barrens—that great melting pot of southeastern and northeastern flora—*M. pensylvanica* blends and hybridizes with its larger, more evergreen relatives *M. cerifera* and *M. heterophylla*, which displace it farther south. Across the cold North grows the completely deciduous, bog-loving sweet gale (*M. gale*), and along the Pacific coast you find

Myrica pensylvanica.
Making bayberry candles is an enjoyable way to connect with our colonial past as surely as a trip to the local historical society museum. These berries are ripe for the picking, which you can accomplish by rolling them off gently between thumb and forefinger and catching them in a bag or bucket held just below.

another large evergreen, *M. californica,* which differs from all the others in that male and female flowers occur on the same, not different, plants. Bayberry is yet another of the actinorhizal shrubs and trees that depend on an association with bacteria in the genus *Frankia* to fix atmospheric nitrogen so it is available for use by the plant. I have marveled at the way a bayberry can produce a rich green coat of leaves from a pile of pure, sterile sand. The southern waxmyrtles are able to grow in even hard, red clay, and they are employed ad infinitum as screening and roadside shrubs in the Southeast. Think of bayberries more as workhorses than thoroughbreds, and they will provide you with a dense, informal hedge without any maintenance.

The leaves are alternate, but they are arranged so thickly along the stem that they look nearly whorled. In color they can be dull or shiny, dark gray green above and lighter green to yellow-green below. New growth begins only from the tips of the previous season's twigs, so the crown has a tiered appearance like that of many azaleas. New sprouts come from roots at the margins of the branches, so the plant eventually becomes a rounded, spreading colony with an ordered but informal character.

Females of all but sweet gale produce tight little clusters of buckshot-sized hard gray berries along the length of the previous season's twigs, where nondescript flowers bloomed earlier that season. These consist of a seed covered in a thick, warty coat of wax, which must be nutritious, as birds slowly pick them off in fall and winter. The wax, called myricin, is the source of richly scented bayberry candles, which were one of the few room deodorizers available to early settlers along the coast. The candles are straightforward to make, and four pounds of fruits boil down to about a pound of wax. When they were harvested in earnest, people would set up camps in a stand of bayberry and cut off and strip branches—traumatic for the plant. You can roll off the fruits with your fingers and let them drop into a basket without harming the shrub. It does take some patience, but the smell of crushed berries will help make the time pass. When you collect a basketful, set a pot of water to boiling and dump in the berries. Keep the pot simmering and stir and smash the fruits occasionally to loosen the wax. The wax will rise to the surface, where it can be skimmed and dropped into cool water to congeal. The finished wax has a gray-green color like the leaves. Pick out the hardened chunks and let them dry. When you have done all your berries, melt the wax again by setting it in a clean coffee can floating in a pot of boiling water. Either pour it into candle molds or hand-dip your candles. Bayberry bark was also liberally employed by colonists as an emetic and purgative, and as a poultice helpful for curing sores and wounds.

CULTURE: All bayberries are best in full sun, but they are tolerant of a range of soils and moisture levels—in fact, I increasingly believe that they will grow nearly anywhere, provided they have enough sun. They need little care, though a bit of high-phosphorus fertilizer will speed growth. The taller species can be pruned to make a more formal hedge. The pungent oils help discourage insects as well as herbivores like deer and rabbits, and the only real problem I have noticed has been a progressive stunting of normal-sized *M. pensylvanica* (reduced and wrinkled leaves, shorter stems) that I am guessing is an insect-borne virus or mycoplasma, as it strikes only occasional plants in a colony, and once stricken these plants never recover in succeeding years. When I first noticed this in my garden, I thought I had found an interesting dwarf clone, but since then I have watched other full-sized plants develop the symptoms while their neighbors remained normal.

USES: Screening, foundations, hedges, massing, soil and bank stabilization, and habitat restoration.

WILDLIFE: Fruit and shelter for birds; foliage is eaten by the larvae of the red-banded hairstreak butterfly (*Calycopus isobeon*).

PROPAGATION: Moderately easy from root cuttings, moderately difficult from seed.

Myrica californica
California Bayberry, Waxmyrtle

ZONES: 7–9; sun
SOIL: Moist to dry, acidic
NATIVE TO: Bogs, dunes, headlands, moist meadows and hills; Vancouver Island south along the coast to southern California
SIZE: Height 6–20 (30) feet, width 5–15 feet
COLOR: Green; blooms in spring to early summer

California bayberry is sexually confused: a mix of male and female flowers can be found on the same plants. Possibly as a result of this, the amount of wax produced on the berries is variable. Waxy berries are whitish gray and unwaxed are dark blue-black. It can be trained as an adaptable screen or tall hedge, or if left to its own devices will become a wide dome of moderately glossy, rich green leaves. Amid the limitless number of evergreen shrubs that gardeners have to choose from along the Pacific coast, however, I doubt it will ever see much action.

Myrica cerifera
Southern Bayberry, Waxmyrtle

ZONES: 7–9; sun, part sun
SOIL: Moist to dry, acidic
NATIVE TO: Bog and swamp margins, sand barrens, dunes, open forests, and old fields; New Jersey south along the coast and lower piedmont to Florida, Arkansas, and Texas
SIZE: Height 8–20 (35) feet, width 10–25 feet
COLOR: Dark red and green; blooms in late winter to early spring

M. cerifera grows as a dense, informal shrub spreading by suckers into a rounded colony as wide or wider than tall. It has finer leaves than the other East Coast species, 1 to 3 inches long and narrowed to a slender tip. The waxy, gray-green foliage is quite handsome and the young twigs are a contrasting rusty brown, so it is a perfect evergreen screening plant for tough locations or less formal gardens. A related plant, *M. inodora* (odorless waxmyrtle) is restricted to the Florida Panhandle in the wild. It is a lovely evergreen shrub a bit like a beefed-up inkberry holly in shape.

Myrica gale
Sweet gale

ZONES: 2–6; sun to part shade

SOIL: Moist to wet, acidic

NATIVE TO: Swamps, bogs and pond and lake shores; circumboreal, in this hemisphere from Labrador to the Northwest Territories and Alaska south along the Pacific coast to Oregon and in the east to central Saskatchewan, Minnesota, and New Jersey, with isolated populations in western North Carolina

SIZE: Height 2–5 feet, width 3–6 feet

COLOR: Ruddy green and yellow; blooms in spring

Sweet gale is a densely branched, completely deciduous species with dark, gray-green leaves and seeds that form in little black clusters, almost like the pistillate "cones" of birch or alder. These are actually very interesting up close, as the scales are really little U-shaped bladders (bracteoles) that surround the seed like a life jacket, helping it to float off to shores unknown. It must be an effective means of dispersal, because *M. gale* grows clear across the boreal regions of the world. It is a dense, slowly suckering shrub that we have used effectively beside our pond. *M. hartwegii* (Sierra sweet-bay) is a similar species endemic to the California Sierras that was recently cut off from the main populations of sweet gale farther north in Oregon and has thus evolved into a new species.

Myrica pensylvanica
Northern Bayberry

ZONES: 4–7; sun to light shade

SOIL: Moist to dry, acidic

NATIVE TO: Dunes, pine barrens, dry forests and slopes, bog and swamp margins; Newfoundland south along the coast to North Carolina and inland to western New York, northeastern Ohio, and Pennsylvania

SIZE: Height 2–6 (10) feet, width 3–10 (25) feet

COLOR: Ruddy green; blooms in spring to early summer

I am always asked about substitutes for some of the grow-anywhere invasives like Japanese barberry and winged euonymus, and this is a good possibility. It doesn't have their brilliant fall color, but it will sur-

vive in a wide range of conditions (roadsides, dry slopes, even lightly shaded woodlands) and the billowing mounds are lovely in both formal and informal applications. Northern bayberry is reluctant to lose its leaves, and a few of the most vigorous sprouts retain them all winter (I just trudged through the snow to check the one out behind the garage to make sure). Most either drop off in fall or wither and brown on the plants in winter, exposing the interesting tiered architecture of the branches and the spreading, suckering progress of the colony. *M. heterophylla* (waxmyrtle, swamp candleberry) has nearly the same sort of narrowly spatulate leaf toothed a bit toward the apex, but it tends to hang on to most of its leaves in winter. Overall it is a bit larger, but basically it can be thought of as the southern race of *M. pensylvanica*. Its range is roughly that of *M. cerifera*, and it has proved reasonably hardy at Garden in the Woods (Zones 5–6), though its leaves burn off in winter.

Nemopanthus mucronatus

Nemopanthus mucronatus
(nee-mo-PAN-thus)
Aquifoliaceae
Mountain Holly

Nemopanthus mucronatus. *Mountain holly fruits have a unique, satiny luster and a vivid crimson shine that stands out amid the summer verdure. The knobby, spurred habit of the shrubs is a bit like that of crabapple or hawthorn.*

ZONES: 3–6; sun to light shade

SOIL: Moist to wet, acidic

NATIVE TO: Bogs and wooded or open swamps and shrubby mountain slopes; Newfoundland and Quebec to Minnesota south to Indiana, West Virginia, and New York and in the mountains (*N. collinus*) from West Virginia to North Carolina

Nyssa sylvatica. The blazing fall leaf display of a mature black gum announces to birds and squirrels that a feast of oily fruits is finally ready. Nyssa holds its turning leaves longer than most trees, and up to a month of brilliant color is possible before the foliage finally settles to the ground and the characteristic spokelike branches are exposed for the winter.

SIZE: Height 4–8 (12) feet, width 3–6 feet
COLOR: Greenish white; blooms in spring

On first glance, *N. mucronatus* looks quite a lot like one of the deciduous hollies. On closer inspection, though, it's clearly different. In winter this multistem shrub is an oval silhouette of stubby, silvery gray twigs—neater and more compact in form than most true hollies. Matte gray-green elliptical leaves appear in spring, attached to the twigs with petioles the color of a fine merlot. This purple pigment suffuses up the midvein a bit and plays tricks with the eyes, so the foliage too has a faint violet glow. During the long and languid days of midsummer, females are decorated with remarkable satin red fruits hung among the leaves on long red pedicels like splendiferous serviceberries. The fruits are borne on short leafy spur branches, and they look remarkably like the crimson velvet balls used to decorate the holiday tree. Though the fruits are around for only a week or two before the birds greedily devour them, they are such a visual treat in the heavy green days of summer that I anticipate them eagerly each July. The berries of true hollies are wonderful, too, but their color seems a notch less extraordinary amid the scarlet splendor of a New England fall.

Mountain holly is found in shrub bogs with the likes of *Aronia*, *Ilex*, and *Vaccinium* species—the fabled berryland I described under chokeberry (*Aronia*, p. 53). In the mountains, they grow on open slopes in the company of serviceberries and viburnums. So it would seem they are not too particular as to soil, as long as it remains relatively cool and moist, and fairly acidic. We sell cutting-propagated male and female clones to be assured of fruit set. Like male and female hollies, these should be spaced within 50 feet of each other. Southern Appalachian forms have a wider leaf with a more pronounced, narrow tip that lacks a mucronate (short, sharp, slender) point like the typical form. On the basis of this and other minor details, these forms are separated as *N. collinus* (Appalachian mountain holly), though the differences are negligible. The latter is a rare plant (or range extension) that runs south to North Carolina in the Appalachians, inhabiting cold mountain bogs and swamps.

CULTURE: Moist acidic soils and at least 4 to 5 hours of sun will produce more compact plants and more fruit than lightly shaded specimens, though even these will set some fruit.

USES: Massing, naturalizing, mixed border (the foliage is an attractive color that makes a good background for other shrubs and perennials).

PROPAGATION: Difficult from cuttings, moderately difficult from seed.

Nyssa sylvatica

Nyssa (NISS-ah)
Nyssaceae
Tupelo

I didn't realize it at the time, but the one acre of woods that surrounds my parents' home in Connecticut supports an amazing diversity of trees and shrubs for such a small area. I can count 24 species of native trees from memory, and there are probably more. Since leaving for college, I have never lived in a place that even approached this level of sylvan diversity, and it provided me with a living dendrology library from which to learn. My mother called one of the trees growing down in the hollow out back the umbrella tree, because it spread a crown of horizontal branches in all directions from a straight central trunk clothed in gray alligator-hide bark. As I later learned, this was none other than the tupelo (*N. sylvatica*), denizen of swamps and watersides throughout the eastern United States. The name is thought to be a corrupted version of the Creek words *eto opelwv*, literally, "tree swamp" (see Peattie, *A National History of Trees of Eastern and Central North America*, p. 498). The branches do come out like the spokes on a bicycle or the ribs of an umbrella, which you can clearly see if you rest your cheek against the trunk and look straight up. Bigger trees send up dozens of root suckers just like a beech, which grow up and die back to form a broomy skirt under especially effusive individuals. When you cut down a tree, it unleashes a madness of root sprouts, as I discovered by accident as I was clearing a space for a garden. (By the way, don't try to cut and split this crazy-grained tree for firewood—impossible! Because of this, there are some nice old-growth stands of tupelo that survived nineteenth-century land clearing.) The twigs of these sprouts, like the tree that produced them, have a slight zigzag pattern of growth, strong apical dominance, and oval, leathery leaves puckered down the middle and along a few major veins. Tupelos are among the few canopy-sized trees that produce bird-dispersed fruits (sassafras and cucumbertree are two others that come to mind). There certainly are quite a few berried shrubs and vines, but most trees have come to rely on their height to loft seeds into the wind or take advantage of the hording and forgetful habits of squirrels, chipmunks, and jays to transport and plant heavier nuts. Tupelo's blue-black fruits ripen during the last days of summer, but they hang among the leaves where they are easily missed. To let the birds know that dinner is served, the tree begins to burn magnificent shades of scarlet, orange, apricot, maroon, and crimson. It is one of the first trees to turn, and one of the finest of all—a warning to gardeners that autumn draws nigh. Interestingly, tupelos are dioecious, but the male trees color as well as the females bearing ripe fruit. I guess among *Nyssa* species, public relations are a family affair. Tupelo has forsaken the wind in flower as well. The blooms are small and inconspicuous to us, but bees relish them, harvesting nectar they turn into the sweet tupelo honey immortalized in the song by Van Morrison.

N. sylvatica has two relatives living in swamp forests near the coast and major rivers in the Southeast. Water tupelo (N. aquatica) grows with cypress in flooded bays and swamps. It develops a very similar buttress of roots to stabilize it in the mucky soil and a tall straight trunk capped by a flat canopy of large, leathery leaves. Ogeechee lime (N. ogeche) is a smaller tree that produces the largest fruits of the group: big olive-shaped things an inch or more long and almost as wide. This tree relies on the color of its red fruit, not spectacular leaves, to draw in the birds.

CULTURE: In the ignorance of youth, I tried to dig and move tupelo root suckers, and it never worked. The trees have a difficult reputation, especially *N. sylvatica*, which sends down a taproot that is sensitive to damage. I have grown and transplanted 1-to-2-gallon, 2-to-3-foot-high seedlings without any problem, and tupelo at least will grow well in a drier soil than its preferred habitat would suggest. Michael Dirr reports that *N. ogeche* is tolerant of dry soils and generally a bit easier to handle, root-wise (*A Manual of Woody Landscape Plants*, p. 683). Sun or partial sun is preferable, though lightly shaded understory situations can be endured, and this will force a tall, narrow trunk. I have not seen the degree of root sprouting on landscape trees as that which occurs in wooded swamps, so maybe this is a function of soil conditions or competition. The tupelos are not huge or fast-growing trees, but they can grow at a decent rate of 6 to 14 inches per year, in my experience, and more under nursery conditions.

USES: Lawn, street tree.
PROPAGATION: Moderately easy from seed.

Nyssa aquatica
Water Tupelo, Cotton Gum

ZONES: 6–9; sun to light shade
SOIL: Moist to wet, even inundated
NATIVE TO: Freshwater swamps, shallow standing water; along the coastal plain from Virginia to Florida and eastern Texas and up the Mississippi River system to southern Illinois
SIZE: Height 60–80 (100) feet, width 15–25 feet
COLOR: Green; blooms in spring

Although water tupelo is at its best in standing water, its buttresses flared and its branches hung with Spanish moss, this tall, narrow tree will grow at the edge of a pond or in a permanently damp spot in the yard. Its habit is similar to that of umbrella-like *N. sylvatica*, but the leaves are about 30 percent larger and the fruits twice so.

Nyssa ogeche
Ogeechee Lime

ZONES: 7–9; sun to part sun
SOIL: Moist to wet; tolerates some dryness
NATIVE TO: Swamps along the coast; South Carolina to Florida
SIZE: Height 30–50 (90) feet, width 15–30 (40) feet
COLOR: Green; blooms in spring

Ogeechee lime is the smallest of the three *Nyssa* species on average, but it bears the largest fruits. The thick, dark green leaves are more obovate than oval, and they don't often develop the intensity of fall color that is the hallmark of the genus. The leaf shape and carriage are very similar to those of sweetbay magnolia, and I have confused the two from a distance. Certainly this is a valuable tree for birds, and whole flocks of mixed species will descend on a ripe-fruited female and gorge until all the red drupes are gone.

Nyssa sylvatica
Black Gum, Sour Gum, Tupelo

ZONES: (4)5–9; sun to light shade
SOIL: Moist to wet; tolerates some dryness
NATIVE TO: Low woods, swamps, higher ground where the water table is close to the surface; Maine, southern Ontario, and Minnesota south to Texas and Florida
SIZE: Height 30–60 (80+) feet, width 20–35 feet
COLOR: Green; blooms in spring

Black gum has the regularity of outline (pointed oval, much like pin oak), glossy, dark foliage, interesting winter form, and striking fall color to make it a real four-season tree. It will become established away from water, although it cannot compete as effectively in more highly oxygenated soils because it grows more slowly than many other trees. I have a few coming up in sandy places in the yard that birds have seeded in from the kettle hole around the corner, and they have trouble keeping pace even with red-cedar. A bit of fertilizer and room when young will really help the tree to get settled and put on height.

Oplopanax horridus

Oplopanax horridus
(oh-plo-PAN-ax)
Araliaceae
Devil's Club

Oplopanax horridus. *Though devil's club is not a cuddly plant, it is easily accommodated in the garden. Its huge, rounded leaves are unsurpassed at bringing bold, tropical textures to the garden. The glistening red fruits are effective for several weeks in summer, and even in winter the thumb-thick, bristling canes (right) sculpturally trap the new-fallen snow.*

ZONES: (4)5–7(8); part sun, shade

SOIL: Moist, acidic

NATIVE TO: Deep, moist woods; Montana through British Columbia to Alaska south to northern California and Idaho with a disjunct population on some islands in Lake Superior, straddling the border between Michigan and Ontario

SIZE: Height 3–6 (10) feet, width: 4–8 feet

COLOR: Greenish-white; blooms in early summer

There is no more richly tropical-looking shrub than devil's club. It produces enormous, crinkly, palmate leaves from the top of thick, unbranched stems that literally bristle with a spiny coat of ½-inch thorns. It takes thorniness to an extreme unmatched by even roses or brambles: stems, petioles, peduncles, even leaf veins—all but the scarlet red berries are armed with them. Try to eat this one, Bambi! In the wet coniferous forests of the Pacific Northwest and the mountains of western Montana and northern Idaho, you will always find devil's club shuffling about the understory and unfolding its big leaves to catch the dim light that makes it to the floor. These leaves are palmately lobed, like maple leaves, but the lowest lobes overlap each other, so the leaf looks peltate at a glance. Artery-sized veins create deep channels in the blade, like a landscape scoured by

rivers. The tissue in between the veins is itself puckered and textured, and the leaves, arrayed as they are on very long petioles, create the impression of a rich green quilt that is just singing with design possibilities. As the leaves finish expanding, thick pyramids of flowers jut out from among them, and though these are not too much different from the leaves in color, they are followed by glossy red fruits flattened like those little cinnamon candies you see around Valentine's Day. In winter, the thumb-thick gray stems covered in thorns are sculptural as well, especially when snow settles on them and exaggerates their texture. The stems come from the roots and grow up straight and unbranched, with more beginning each year from the periphery of the clump, which takes on a broad, domed shape with age.

Obviously this is a plant that must be handled with kid gloves, as the thorns on the leaves will snag clothing and skin. When the railroads were being cut through the virgin forests of British Columbia, back in the days before bulldozers, engineers would divert the tracks around valleys especially thick with this shrub because the workmen found it so impossible to manage. We have a planting in the garden, though, that has remained a verdant, well-behaved clump for many years, and aside from a little gingerly care in fall clean-up (fall color is a passable yellow), it causes few problems. In one of the great examples of population disjuncture, there are stands of this species growing on some of the islands in Lake Superior, including the famous Isle Royale, studied by all bud-

ding ecologists because of classic predator-prey research done on its moose–wolf populations. How it jumped over 1,000 miles from the nearest populations in Idaho is still a mystery. It is possible that these are the last remnants of a once greater natural range, but it is also possible that birds carried seeds here from the Pacific Northwest and the plants were able to find purchase in a somewhat similar climate.

CULTURE: Moist, acidic soils and a spot sheltered from harsh wind and midday sun will let this shrub grow its best. It is pretty much deer-proof, but slugs can be a real problem, especially for seedlings still close to the ground. The stems grow slowly, maybe 4 to 6 inches a year, with the tallest centered in the middle of the clump. I imagine that this is not a shrub for lower elevations in the Southeast and lower latitudes in the Midwest.

USES: Bold textural accent in the woodland garden.

WILDLIFE: Birds slowly eat off the seeds as they ripen in summer.

PROPAGATION: Moderately easy from seed.

Osmanthus in flower. Wild olive is a pretty but decidedly informal sort of plant, its stiff stems forming an open, rounded crown decked in glossy, evergreen, lanceolate leaves hung in pairs on thin twigs. When planted in a sunny spot, wild olive becomes a large shrub or single-trunked small tree; in shade it is more of a spreading shrub. In shade the leaves are spaced enough on the stems that the canopy is light and broken – like gauze instead of a blackcloth screen. Late in the summer, nubby little buds shaped like miniature trees develop in the axils of the current season's leaves. In early spring, as soon as the frosts are reliably past, the buds begin to swell one at a time, opening tiny 4-petaled blooms that curl back on themselves and begin to loft great quantities of the heady aroma—so much in fact that a plant can perfume a whole yard with an odor of citrus and clove and even filter out into the neighborhood during the height of flowering later in spring. The plants are dioecious and if the females are pollinated, olive-shaped, blue-black fruits about ½ inch long develop over the course of the summer.

Osmanthus americanus. Where a filtering screen rather than an impenetrable hedge is desired, wild olive is just the thing. Its willowy crown lets in light and allows breezes to pass through, wafting the penetratingly sweet perfume of its tiny flowers hither and yon.

Osmanthus americanus
Osmanthus americanus (oz-MAN-thus)
Oleaceae
Wild Olive, Devilwood

ZONES: (5)6–9; sun to shade
SOIL: Moist to moderately dry
NATIVE TO: Woods, stream sides and swamp margins; coastal plain from southern Virginia to Florida and Louisiana
SIZE: Height 10–20 (40) feet, width 6–15 feet
COLOR: Greenish white with a yellow center; blooms in spring

One of the worst aspects of winter is the paucity of smells. Smell is the most evocative of our senses, able to transport us back to some other place and time far more completely than a picture or word. The coldness of winter stifles most fragrances, which need to evaporate to be captured by our noses. (To alleviate this olfactory boredom, I find myself wandering into the bathroom sometimes and taking a big whiff of suntan lotion—an odor that takes me right back to the beach.) Spring floods the senses in many ways, but no stimuli are more welcome than the torrent of forgotten smells—fragrances of mud, rain, and flowers rush in like water flowing into a parched landscape, and I'm born again. Deliciously fragrant, spring-blooming plants are especially precious for this reason alone, and few tingle the olfactory pathways like the lemon-spice scent of an

CULTURE: Wild olive is little troubled by pests, and wants only a reasonably moist, fertile soil and some protection from the midday sun (the leaves scald or yellow in the sun or if exposed in the winter). It has survived very well at the Arnold Arboretum (Zone 6), and in a place out of the wind it is remarkably cold hardy. Though not planted as widely as the more formal Asian species of *Osmanthus*, it is a great shrub to incorporate into woodland gardens and shrub borders. Transplant from containers in spring in the North, or fall in the South. It will take considerable pruning, which is best done just after flowering. The fruits are not especially ornamental, but they do provide food for wildlife. Most plants I have seen for sale were unsexed, so you'll have to take your chances.

Ostrya virginiana. The bark of hop hornbeam curls like old paint on a clapboard farmhouse. While not as flamboyant as paper birch or madrone, the tree is pretty in its own haggard way.

USES: Informal hedge or screen, massing.

WILDLIFE: Good early-season nectar source, fruits for birds.

PROPAGATION: Difficult from cuttings and seed.

Ostrya virginiana

Ostrya virginiana
(os-STRY-a)
Betulaceae
Hop Hornbeam, Ironwood

ZONES: (3)4–9; sun to light shade

SOIL: Moist to dry, well-drained

NATIVE TO: Slopes and the understory of upland forests; Nova Scotia, southern Quebec and Ontario to southeastern Manitoba south to eastern Texas and Florida

SIZE: Height 20–30 (55) feet, width 10–18 feet

COLOR: Yellow-green; blooms in early spring

In rich, fertile bottomlands there is a plethora of understory trees and shrubs, but climb to the uplands, and the number thins to only a handful capable of surviving the taxing combination of dry soil and shade. Ironwood is one of the understory trees you'll find growing in the shade of oaks and pines up on these hills or holding fast to steep ridges with a deep-anchoring root. It is a lovely small tree, with a shaggy, warm gray bark covering a single trunk studded its length with thin flattened branches of birch-impersonating leaves. Like the leaves of birches, which often grow with it, the blade of each leaf is a wide, rounded oval shagged down the edge with thin, irregular teeth. The first leaves to poke out in spring are small, about the size of a squirrel's ear, but each successive leaf on the zigzagging twig gets progressively larger. The male catkins overwinter as hard little dangles and elongate in spring until they become spongy and spread enough to release pollen to the wind. The yellow stuff is destined for little balls of stigmas that protrude from a scaly cone set among developing leaves. If all goes according to plan, seeds ripen one to a flattened, papery pod, which are strung together like fish scales or hops to form a little cone—hence *hop hornbeam*. These begin to dry in fall and turn from light green to warm gray, then slowly disintegrate after the last of the gilded leaves drop (a few papery dry leaves never drop off, rustling on through the bleak, leafless winter and helping you spot the trees from a distance). If you find a well-laden tree, give it a good shake, and the pods will come floating down. Each contains a teardrop-shaped seed about the size and color of a small sunflower seed but with a glossier sheen. I imagine the bladders help keep them aloft a bit longer so they can glide away from the parent. Per-haps the last to fall can more easily billow across snow with these inflated pads.

For general toughness, manageable size, and a well-ordered, oval canopy of dark green leaves, it is hard to beat ironwood. It is an important understory tree in eastern forests and thus deserves a place in managed landscapes as well. In the Sierra Madre of northwestern Mexico, where the climate and flora have much in common with the eastern United States, there are closely related species that have long been isolated from *O. virginiana* by the intervening deserts. Seeds from these Mexican plants have migrated up into the mountains of the Southwest, giving rise to a distinct species, *O. knowltonii* (western hop hornbeam), which is smaller throughout than its eastern cousin.

CULTURE: Ironwood is best moved as a container-grown plant or a carefully dug and balled sapling in fall or early spring. It will grow in a range of conditions, provided the soil is acidic and not waterlogged. It will develop a decent, airy canopy in dappled shade and a dense, visually impermeable cloak in sun. Growth rate is moderate; 8 to 16 inches per year is an average rate when young. The wood, which is very strong and resistant to ice damage, was employed for such things as airplane propellers and sleigh runners—hence the name ironwood. Wounds will weep in spring, so try to limit pruning to fall and early winter. The seedlings are quite drought tolerant once a deep root system is established, but will need supplemental watering for the first 1 to 2 years.

USES: Small yard or understory tree, especially

useful in dry-soil situations and urban applications where moderate size, fairly narrow crown, and pollution tolerance are important considerations.

WILDLIFE: The seeds are great forage for overwintering birds like chickadees and titmice.

PROPAGATION: Moderately difficult from seed.

Oxydendrum arboreum

Oxydendrum arboreum (ox-ee-DEN-drum)
Ericaceae
Sourwood, Sorrel Tree

ZONES: 5–9; sun to light shade

SOIL: Moist to moderately dry

NATIVE TO: Woods and fencerows; Pennsylvania to southern Indiana south to Louisiana and Florida

SIZE: Height 15–30 (60) feet, width 6–12 feet

COLOR: Creamy white; blooms in summer

The heath family has given rise to more ornamental shrubs and trees than any other in our flora. When I see Ericaceae in the description of a plant, I know it will be good in the garden, possibly great, because of their habit of growth and the sheer lavishness of their flowers. If I had to limit myself to only one group of woody plants, it would undoubtedly be this one. Sourwood is one of the most magnificent of this favored tribe, for, although it cannot compete with rhododendrons in floral extravagance, it is a tree that shines in the garden throughout the year. In the wild it favors the acidic soils of pine and hardwood forests, where it squeezes itself between the trunks of its taller companions with a narrow crown that climbs to the middle stories where the light is a bit brighter. It heads skyward on fast-growing leaders clothed like the side branches in drooping 4-to-6-inch lance-shaped leaves creased somewhat down the midvein. The upper surface is dark and shiny green and the lower, more green-gray—a fact you don't really notice until fall, when the foliage burns strongly scarlet and burgundy above and more whitewashed below. *Oxydendrum arboreum* blooms from the ends of the twigs after they've finished growing for the year. The blueberryesque little urns splay out on turkey-foot panicles to give the plants an impressionistic, weeping softness unmatched by any other tree, and it's all the more beautiful because it blooms in the sulking green heat of summer. These blooms are favorites of bees during this flower-poor time of year, and roadside stands throughout the south sell the rich brown sourwood honey that is the delectable result. The flowers yield to peppercorn capsules that are creamy-green as the leaves color—

Oxydendrum arboreum. *Pendulous chains of biscuit-colored seed capsules add a distinct textural note to the flaming crown of a sourwood in autumn. The thousands of tiny seeds that drift down in fall will germinate in the spring if they find a damp, mossy bit of ground to settle on.*

shaggy tassels silhouetted beautifully against the blazing canopy. As the leaves fall, the capsules turn from cream to brown, but hang on well into winter, adding just a touch of melancholy to the snow-laden branches. The main trunk develops a rough brown bark broken into irregular ridges the shape of shattered auto glass.

CULTURE: Sourwood prefers moist, acidic soils, though I have seen fine specimens growing on dry red clay. Sun will bring out the best fall color, and the trees look especially lovely drooping at the forest edge. They can develop into tall trees in time, though this is mostly in forest situations where they must climb up for light. In the open, they seem to get to a comfortable height of 15 to 25 feet and just stay there, slowly growing wider but still retaining their narrow, single-trunked figure. Like all the heath family members, it is heavily mycorrhizal, and you can feed the fungi with a yearly helping of rotted bark or leaves.

USES: Small specimen tree for the lawn, woodland edge, or even shade.

WILDLIFE: Sourwood is a vital source of midseason nectar favored by all manner of bees, wasps, beetles, and flies.

PROPAGATION: Easy from seed.

Parthenocissus quinquefolia. Fall color is Virginia creeper's claim to fame. This self-sown vine grows up a yellow birch at Garden in the Woods. Once you become familiar with the native plants in your area, you can encourage volunteers like this and give your garden designs more spontaneity.

Parthenocissus quinquefolia

Parthenocissus quinquefolia
(par-the-no-SIS-us)
Vitaceae
Virginia Creeper, Woodbine

ZONES: 4–9; sun to shade

SOIL: Wet to dry

NATIVE TO: Woods and clearings; Maine to Ohio and Nebraska south to Texas and Florida. (*P. vitacea* ranges from Maine and Quebec to Manitoba south to Indiana and New Jersey in the East and Wyoming, Utah, Arizona and Texas in the West.)

SIZE: Height 4–40 (80) feet (depending on support), width 3–15 feet

COLOR: Greenish white; blooms in early summer

If you've got an old rusty Chevy out in the yard that is becoming an eyesore, a stretch of gray concrete that you are tired of looking at, or a section of fence that is crying for greenery, then Virginia creeper is the plant for you. This familiar climbing vine of forests and fencerows grows without care in a variety of places. *P. quinquefolia* is well equipped for difficult ascents, as its tendrils can twine around wire or twigs or glue themselves to bark or walls with little suction-cup disks that grow from the tips. As the vine becomes established to its support, aerial rootlets grow out of the stem wherever it butts against something solid to more permanently attach it in place. A closely related species, *P. vitacea* (grape woodbine, also listed as *P. incisa*), more common westward, is nearly identical except that it lacks suction disks on its tendrils and the flowers and fruits are more cymose than panicled.

Virginia creeper produces 5-parted, palmate leaves that alternate up fast-lengthening, zigzag stems (4 to 8 feet of growth in a season is common). The middle leaflet is the largest, and the outermost (lowest) pair are the smallest, but all are creased down the midvein and jaggedly toothed along the margin like some forms of poison ivy. Of course, poison ivy has three, not five leaflets, but this hasn't stopped people from killing off thousands of innocent woodbines in unfortunate cases of mistaken identity. From the time the leaves emerge in spring until late in the summer, Virginia creeper provides a verdant blanket of leaves to cover whatever it grows on. The leaves screen walls and tree trunks, and they also hide fruits that have developed from insignificant flowers clustered on short panicles opposite some of the leaves. As fall approaches, the fruits turn purple-blue while the pedicels they're attached to become fluorescent scarlet in contrast. The leaves and petioles, too, begin to flag brilliant crimson or cherry red, for like leaves of flowering dogwood and tupelo, they help attract the attention of birds overhead. Virginia creeper is one of the first plants to turn in the fall, and it is a spectacular sight tracing red through the canopy of some still-green tree or hanging like a garland from a dead snag or fence. It is a vigorous plant that sends up new shoots from the roots as well as the shaggy-barked older stems. Thus it is probably too aggressive for a mixed planting or a mailbox, but if you have a wilder spot that needs covering, there are few finer natives, and none that will grow with such absence of care.

CULTURE: Virginia creeper will grow just about anywhere—swamps, dunes, shady woods, hot parking lot medians, etc. You can usually dig up rooted sections in spring (it's okay to cut the shoots back to remove the plants from their support and transplant them). Even without support, it will grow as a groundcover, but the plants definitely color their best climbing in the sun.

USES: Screening for walls (do not use on wood), arbors, fences, junk cars, and old appliances.

WILDLIFE: Fruit for birds, leaves feed the fantastic brown, yellow eye–spotted caterpillars of the Pandora sphinx moth (*Eumorpha pandorus*).

PROPAGATION: Easy from cuttings or seed.

Paxistima canbyi

Paxistima (pax-ISS-tim-a)
(Pachystima)
Celastraceae
Cliff Green, Oregon Boxwood, Paxistima

Paxistimas are studies in green. The new leaves emerge a fresh shade of Granny Smith apple green and arrange themselves in two orderly ranks up stiff twigs colored to match. As the foliage matures, it becomes progressively darker until it is a rich, glossy green contrasting nicely with the rusty red of the mature twigs. This contrast of light and dark green remains effective all season, for plants will keep growing until late in the year. As cold weather approaches, some of the leaves take on a bronze or maroon color, while others remain dark green. The plants spread slowly by root sprouts at the edge of the clump, so what starts out as a single clump of stems will become a small patch 2 feet across after 3 to 4 years. There are two species, one in the East and one in the West. The eastern form is a beautiful fine-leaved groundcover, whereas the western species grows more stiffly and gets about twice as tall. Both are carefree plants for sunny, fairly dry spots that look lovely when mixed with other groundcovers and perennials. I have planted a few clumps of *P. canbyi* in some bearberry to good effect. The bearberry has the same light and dark green leaves, but a lower habit and a bit coarser texture. Paxistimas can also be fashioned into a low clipped or unclipped hedge for parterres and knot gardens. The flowers, though tiny, do create a light green or ruddy red haze over the plants for a few weeks. The 4-petaled axillary flowers seem to attract small flies, which pollinate them and produce equally tiny podlike capsules containing 1 to 2 seeds. The seeds are surrounded by a fleshy aril that must attract Lilliputian ants to carry them off.

CULTURE: Paxistima requires full or part sun and well-drained soil. It's best to transplant it in spring, either from containers or older clumps that have been carefully teased apart. The plants look particularly appropriate growing amid rocks. Water carefully the first season until established, as a drought-stressed transplant will quickly die. They will grow with some shade, but in a looser and patchier way that is not nearly as effective. I have tried to grow Oregon boxwood (*P. myrsinites*), and it seems ill equipped to handle our summers or our winters. It may be a case of finding plants from the interior West as thrives in much colder areas in the Rockies. It is a beautiful and well-behaved low shrub.

USES: Edging, groundcover, rock garden, massing.

PROPAGATION: Moderately easy from cuttings, difficult from seed.

Paxistima canbyi
Cliff Green, Rat-stripper, Mountain Lover

ZONES: (3)4–7; sun to light shade
SOIL: Moist to moderately dry, well-drained, moderately acidic to alkaline
NATIVE TO: Rocky woods, limestone cliffs; mostly in the southern Appalachians from West Virginia to Virginia and eastern Kentucky
SIZE: Height 8–16 inches, width 16–24 inches
COLOR: Greenish white, tinged with red; blooms in late spring

P. canbyi is a rare plant in the wild, but it should not be in gardens. Cliff green is a lustrous evergreen groundcover whose leaves create an unusual, almost bristly texture (the leaves form a cross when viewed straight down from above). The older stems branch profusely, arching over under the accumulated weight as new shoots come up from below. The leaves are almost linear, with a slightly scalloped or revolute margin and a blunt, flattened tip.

Paxistima myrsinites
Oregon Boxwood, Myrtle Boxleaf

ZONES: (4)5–7; sun, part sun
SOIL: Moist to moderately dry
NATIVE TO: Openings in coniferous forests, rocky slopes and cliffs, mostly at middle and higher elevations; southern Alberta to British Columbia south to California, Utah, and New Mexico
SIZE: Height 1–3 feet, width 2–3 feet
COLOR: Yellow-green and reddish; blooms in late spring to early summer

This is a larger plant, with oval leaves that splay out more flatly than those of cliff green. The stems are a bit thicker than in the eastern species, so they remain upright instead of arching over. Rocky Mountain genotypes should be hardy into Zone 4 with consistent snow cover. It is reasonably shade tolerant, but it gets lanky (as do some of the smaller blueberries like *Vaccinium scoparium*, with which it grows).

Paxistima canbyi. Stem cuttings taken from cliff green in midsummer will root readily. Vegetative propagation is the most expedient method with this genus, as the seeds are very difficult to see, let alone collect efficiently. The two plants pictured here were produced from stem cuttings I started five years earlier.

Philadelphus inodorus var. grandiflorus. *The large, immaculate blooms of Appalachian mock-orange release a light but evocative citrus perfume.*

Philadelphus inodorus var. *grandiflorus*

Philadelphus
(fil-a-DEL-fus)
Saxifragaceae (Philadelphaceae)
Mock-orange

Throughout this book, I have tried to stress the special attributes of plants, be these beautiful bark, lustrous foliage, value for wildlife, or importance to the regional character of the landscape. Unfortunately, the mock-oranges have little to recommend them beyond the splendor of their blooms, and this has banished them to the edge of the modern landscape with the likes of deutzias and pearlbush. No one can question the purity and charm of a mock-orange flower: 4 glistening white petals cupping a tuft of orange anthers and lofting the intoxicating fragrance of orange blossoms to the breeze. The flowers are produced in crowded clusters from the stem tips as the new growth has just finished expanding. In a favorable spot, the whole plant is wreathed in white, and it is really quite lovely in a loose and delicate way. But they are somewhat awkward shrubs, with a caney, arching habit born of fast-suckering stems that bend under the accumulating weight of branches and leaves. The foliage is deciduous, arranged in pairs, and broadly oval in shape with a fairly thin texture tailored to a life in the understory (thinner leaves allow the light to penetrate more deeply into the tissues). Most have a few large teeth along the distal (toward the leaf tip) margins that are weakly defined, as if they are pushing

through gums, a feature that helps identify the plant as mock-orange. If you have a spot on the edge of the woods where a mock-orange can arch itself out from the shadows, it is well worth considering for the fragrance alone.

There is a group of closely related *Philadelphus* species in the various eastern mountain ranges, and a similar group in the West. None is grown in gardens as much as the more potently fragrant hybrids of the European species like *P. coronarius.*

CULTURE: *Philadelphus* species are tolerant of a range of conditions, including summer drought (which will cause wilting and even dieback, but not death) and shade. Best growth and bloom will occur in moist soils and at least part sun, and all the mock-oranges respond very well to spring fertilization. Older stems should be edited out of the clump in winter, or you can cut the whole thing down to the ground and forgo flowering for a year or two. The mock-oranges are best in moderate climates, and you can easily dig and move rooted sections from the main clump in early spring.

USES: Naturalizing along the woodland edge, shrub border.

PROPAGATION: Moderately difficult from cuttings, easy from seed.

Philadelphus hirsutus
Cumberland Mock-orange

ZONES: 5–8; sun to light shade
SOIL: Moist to moderately dry
NATIVE TO: Rocky cliffs and bluffs; North Carolina to Kentucky, Alabama, and Georgia
SIZE: Height 3–6 feet, width 3–5 feet
COLOR: Bright white; blooms in late spring
Cumberland mock-orange is the third of the eastern suite, distinguished by its smaller leaves tapering to a pronounced tip, and smaller flowers as well. The leaves and petioles are covered in a fine down, which gives the plants a visible softness, but in flower effect it is the least impressive.

Philadelphus inodorus
Appalachian Mock-orange

ZONES: 5–8; sun to light shade
SOIL: Moist to moderately dry
NATIVE TO: Stream banks, cliffs; mostly in the Appalachians of eastern Pennsylvania and western Virginia south to Alabama and northern Georgia
SIZE: Height 3–10 feet, width 4–6 feet
COLOR: Bright white; blooms in late spring
Of the three closely related eastern species, Appalachian mock-orange has the largest flowers, with blooms 1½ to 2 inches across (large-flowered individuals are called var. *grandiflorus*). It also has large oblong leaves about 3 inches long on the most vigor-

ous stems, arranged into paired ranks along the arching, shag-barked stems. At the Garden we have it growing in an inhospitable spot atop a shady esker, and it has become an open arching 9-foot shrub that still flowers despite its rough treatment. Most people take the specific epithet *inodorus* to mean it has no smell, but it does produce a light, citrus blossom fragrance, as does *P. pubescens*, from the Ozark Plateau (called, appropriately, Ozark mock-orange). Its flowers are smaller than those of *P. inodoratus* and are in denser racemes; its leaves are a bit larger still and are covered on their lower surfaces with a fine down. Additionally, its young twigs are gray instead of the chestnut brown common in the genus.

Philadelphus lewisii
Western Mock-orange

ZONES: 5–8; sun to part sun
SOIL: Moist to moderately dry
NATIVE TO: Stream sides, cliffs, openings in coniferous forests, fencerows; Montana and British Columbia south to northern California
SIZE: Height 3–10 feet, width 4–6 feet
COLOR: Bright white; blooms in late spring to early summer

P. lewisii is a lovely species with masses of large white, wonderfully fragrant flowers in late spring to early summer. Think of it as a western *P. inodorus* as far as leaf and flower size go. The coastal var. *gordonianus* is more heavily fragrant than the typical variety. I have seen *P. lewisii* thriving in fairly inhospitable, dry crevices and flowering so thickly as to obscure the stems beneath. All in all it is our most ornamental *Philadelphus* species and worth trying in the East as well.

Philadelphus microphyllus
Littleleaf Mock-orange

ZONES: (5)6–8; sun to part sun
SOIL: Moist to dry
NATIVE TO: Rocky soils, often rather dry, mixed pinyon-juniper woodland at moderate elevations; Colorado to California, Arizona and New Mexico
SIZE: Height 3–4 feet, width 3 feet
COLOR: Bright white; blooms in late spring to early summer

Littleleaf mock-orange has adapted to the trying conditions of the high desert by reducing its leaf area and overall size. The oval or lance-shaped blade averages under an inch in length and has a finer yet stiffer texture than the other mock-oranges. The small flowers are about the size of the leaves and release a strong, enveloping, fruity perfume. It seems reasonably adaptable to cultivation in more humid climates, but I have not grown it long enough to make any meaningful evaluation.

Physocarpus opulifolius

Physocarpus (fye-so-KAR-pus)
Rosaceae
Ninebark

Ninebark, like the mock-oranges, has become somewhat obsolete as a landscape shrub, for, although pretty in flower, it has a caney, almost rank habit one step from a bramble. There is basically a single species ranging across the continent that has adapted to local conditions with a variety of ecotypes (strains of a species adapted to particular regions), some of which have been given the status of separate species. All are multistemmed shrubs producing fast-growing shoots from a narrow base that arch out and away from the center as the weight of leaves and need for light dictate. Older stems can arch over all the way to the ground, with small side stems developing along their upper side from about midway on. Second-year and older stems are covered in an attractive, shaggy bark that sloughs off in long fibrous strips, but you have to do some judicious pruning to keep their bases in view (the common name ninebark probably refers to the many layers of peeling bark on older stems). A large plant has the same frenzied, out-of-control exuberance that has made mock-oranges fade from fashion, its canes swooping out willy-nilly in a crazy octopus way. So if a viburnum or shadbush is too staid for your liking, you might consider the ninebark instead. The smaller forms are better for less expansive gardens, as they are more compact and thus more ordered in their appearance.

You will recognize the rose family in the flowers of ninebark. They are 5-petaled, round-pointed stars set with a crown of stiff purple stamens and balled together in snowball heads about 2 inches in diameter. The flowers, like the small side branches that carry them, orient on the upper side of the canes

Physocarpus opulifolius. Ninebark's flowers bunch together in domed platforms that are easy for pollinating insects to land on. What a thoughtful design.

where they are most noticeable to us as well as the many insects that buzz and gather around their nectar. As the flowers fade, 5-pointed capsules (follicles) take their place, often tinged red and green and reasonably interesting through the summer. *Physocarpus* species have alternate, deciduous leaves with a flattened or rounded base suggesting a maple, especially where the blade is divided into three distinct, toothy lobes.

CULTURE: One of ninebark's best attributes is an ability to thrive almost anywhere, from dry shade to bitter wind and blazing sun. For this reason, it is used most extensively in the Plains states for screens and fencerows. Transplant from containers or dig and divide in spring. Like most suckering shrubs, ninebark can be cut to the ground in winter about once every decade (what I like to call a chainsaw crew cut) to clean it up and force a new flush of stems. Alternatively, you can annually shape and prune the shrub, removing most of the new suckers that will hide the pretty bark.

USES: Woodland edges, fencerows, mixed borders. Unpruned ninebarks get pretty dense and twiggy, making good shelter and nesting sites for songbirds.

WILDLIFE: Nectar, shelter for birds. Ninebark is one of the species preferred by the caterpillars of the spring azure butterfly *(Celastrina argiolus).*

PROPAGATION: Easy from cuttings or seed.

Physocarpus capitatus
Western Ninebark

ZONES: 4–7(8); sun to light shade
SOIL: Very moist to moderately dry
NATIVE TO: Stream sides, thickets, slopes, and open woods; Montana and Idaho to British Columbia south to northern California and Oregon
SIZE: Height 3–8 feet, width 4–6 feet
COLOR: White; blooms in late spring to early summer
Western ninebark is an ornamental, more compact version of *P. opulifolius* with 2-to-3-inch-wide corymbs that cover the plants in bloom. Its stamens protrude like white eyelashes, giving the whole a soft, frothy texture when in bloom. It is an arching, multistem shrub usually about 25 percent smaller than *P. opulifolius,* but in leaf size and shape as well as bark characteristics they are very similar. Western ninebark is less drought tolerant than the other *Physocarpus* species and is best in a moist to wet location.

Physocarpus monogynus
Small Ninebark

ZONES: (3)4–8; Sun to part sun
SOIL: Moist to dry, well-drained
NATIVE TO: Rocky hillsides and ledges, open woods;

South Dakota to Colorado, southwest to Arizona, and south to Texas
SIZE: Height 2–3 feet, width 3 feet
COLOR: White; blooms in early summer
This is a diminutive ninebark with deep green, 3-lobed leaves about an inch long, flowers borne in 1½-inch-diameter corymbs, and follicles with 3, not 5 sections. It forms a rounded, twiggy mound and grows under very difficult conditions. An even smaller species, *P. alternans* (dwarf ninebark) grows at higher elevations in the Great Basin. It is about half again as large in all its parts, with many individuals only 10 to 12 inches in height in exposed situations.

Physocarpus opulifolius
Ninebark

ZONES: (3)4–8; sun to light shade
SOIL: Moist to dry
NATIVE TO: Rocky soils, stream banks, lakeshores; Quebec to North Dakota, south to Colorado, Arkansas, and North Carolina
SIZE: Height 6–12 feet, width 6–10 feet
COLOR: White; blooms in late spring to early summer
Though it has been largely superseded in gardens, common ninebark can be effectively naturalized or used in restoration and soil stabilization. There is a gold-leaved cultivar ('Luteus', 'Dart's Gold') that emerges yellow highlighted with burgundy and fades to chartreuse. We have used this form in plantings, and the foliage color is light enough to provide a nice contrast without being sickly-looking, like some yellow-leaved plants.

Picea mariana

Picea (pie-SEE-ah)
Pinaceae
Spruce

In landscape situations I have a hard time telling the spruces apart at a distance, though in the wild I can narrow it down and take an educated guess. Spruces have a certain look: tall, conical, somewhat gnarled low down because they retain small dead branchlets for a while. It's the snow-shrugging shape of an A-frame ski lodge, and a landscape dominated by them has an unmistakable, deep green pointiness. Their 4-sided needles shag the twigs like foxtails, each set with a tiny barbed tip that pokes at your skin if you play too roughly. This sharpness, along with the tiny, persistent stalks at the base of the needles (sterigma), helps distinguish them from firs, as do the cones, which on spruce hang down from the upper branch tips instead of jutting up, fir fashion. Spruce is one of the most popular garden conifers in the northern half of the United States and southern Canada for one reason: they are rugged and adaptable, and thus are a better choice than firs if you want that classic, pyramidal Christmas tree shape. In the wild, spruces are tall and narrow, probably a response to competition and cold, but in the lower-elevation landscape they are broader at the hip and shorter too — as if the easy life has let them grow soft around the middle. They are also moderately important timber trees whose soft, white wood furnishes construction lumber and pulp, and finds a use as well in the construction of stringed instruments.

Like firs, these are plants of cool summers and snowy or wet winters. There are three species in the Northeast, two of which, black spruce and white spruce, set off across boreal Canada to become major players in the unbroken belt of coniferous forests stretching from the north Atlantic to the Pacific. The third, red spruce, hops from mountain peak to mountain peak south to North Carolina. Two others —Engelmann spruce and Colorado blue spruce— are common throughout the western mountains; the magnificent Sitka spruce is found only in the coastal rainforest belt of the Pacific Northwest. Unlike the firs, most spruces are thus quite wide-ranging, but one, *P. breweriana*, is restricted to a single mountain range.

CULTURE: Spruces prefer cool, acidic soils that remain reasonably moist through the year, though as a group they are more drought tolerant than the firs in landscape situations. The root system is shallow and fibrous, so balled and burlaped trees transplant well in early spring. They perform better in the ground than in containers, so most available material is field dug. Spruces are not as shade tolerant as firs, and they should be considered only for a sunny location, although they will survive in shade as slow-growing, ragged-looking saplings. Budworms, bagworms, and spruce gall aphids are a concern to foresters attempting to maintain vast spruce monocultures ("managed forests"), but healthy landscape specimens sited away from hot, dry situations are not troubled exceedingly by them.

USES: Screening, windbreaks.

WILDLIFE: The dense, needled spruce canopy provides excellent winter shelter, nesting sites, and fall-to-early-winter food (seeds) for many birds.

PROPAGATION: Moderately easy from seed, but slow.

Picea engelmannii
Engelmann Spruce

ZONES: 3–5(6); sun

SOIL: Moist, well-drained

NATIVE TO: Montane and subalpine forests above 3,000 feet in the Rockies and Cascades; Montana to Alberta and British Columbia south to northern California, Nevada, Arizona, and New Mexico

SIZE: Height 40–70 (150+), width 12–18 (30) feet

COLOR: Yellow and purple; blooms in spring

In the middle of its range, Engelmann spruce is a stately tree with a tall narrow spire of horizontal branches clothed in medium- to long-needled, more or less drooping branchlets. Like those of Colorado blue spruce *(P. pungens)*, the needles have a line of stomata on all four surfaces; though not as eye-popping a silver blue as in some forms of *P. pungens,* this nevertheless imparts a blue-gray cast to the tree all

Picea mariana. *Black spruce's immature female cones have a beautiful waxy purple color. By fall the cones will dry to dark brown and crack open to release little helicopter seeds to the wind.*

the more striking because of the pendulous, melancholy effect of the branchlets. On rich soils along watercourses in the mountains, this tree can live for hundreds of years and become rather thick about the trunk. Where Engelmann spruce crosses paths with white spruce in the northern Rockies, the two freely interbreed and effectively meld together in a confusing hybrid complex that is intermediate between the two. Seed from this complex lacks many of the ornamental features that distinguish *P. engelmannii.*

Picea glauca
White Spruce

ZONES: (1)2–6; sun to part sun
SOIL: Moist, acidic
NATIVE TO: Bog margins, mountain slopes and boreal forest; Labrador to the Northwest Territories and interior Alaska south to British Columbia, Montana, Michigan, and southern Maine
SIZE: Height 30–60 (90) feet, width 8–16 feet
COLOR: Cones yellow (male)/purple (female); blooms in spring

White spruce, so named for the ash gray color of its small needles and twigs, forms a narrow spire of stiff, horizontal branches. Closed-canopy trees retain a skin-scratching, eye-poking skirt of dead broken branches hung with moss and lichens that give the forests a certain weathered dreariness. It is a popular screen and windbreak tree in the North. The dwarf cultivar 'Conica', or Alberta spruce, stands like a sentinel beside doorways and headstones almost every-

where you look. (This most popular of all dwarf conifer cultivars is usually planted singly, but I have often thought that a whole grove of them planted like a miniature forest would be fun. You could set a little toy cabin in there complete with Little Red Riding Hood and the Big Bad Wolf . . .) White spruce grows sympatrically with the very similar black spruce (*P. mariana*), which has a vaguely darker green cast but is otherwise hard to distinguish. Black spruce is a bit fussier in the cultivated landscape, and so is less common there. Farther south in New England, it grows as a stunted little tree in cold sphagnum bogs.

Picea pungens
Colorado Blue Spruce

ZONES: 3–7; sun, part sun
SOIL: Moist to moderately dry
NATIVE TO: Midmontane forests (6,000–10,000 feet) in the Rocky Mountains; Wyoming to southeastern Idaho south to Arizona and New Mexico
SIZE: Height 30–50 (160) feet, width 10–18 (35) feet
COLOR: Cones yellow (male)/red-purple (female); blooms in spring

Colorado blue spruce has long, curved, and very sharp and stiff needles that are lined with a band of silvery stomata on all four sides. The tree has a cylindrical to pyramidal, tiered look, because the lower branches droop to form a dense, snow-shedding skirt instead of an ever-widening base. The banded stomata on certain trees are so conspicuous that they turn the crown silver-blue, a trait that has landed the tree in the landscaper's hall of fame. It seems every suburban yard has to have at least one of the blue-needled cultivars studding a bed of burgundy- and chartreuse-leaved shrubs (preferably ones that bloom hot pink). There is contrast and there is discordance, the first visually interesting, the latter optically painful. Unfortunately, this tree usually falls in with the latter. I like the blue-needled selections as much as the next guy, but please, use them in moderation before we turn our residential landscapes into ersatz amusement parks. When I first visited the Rockies, I half expected whole forests of silver, but in reality, this color extreme is rare. Most of the trees are more of a gray-green like *P. engelmannii,* and though the needles are bigger and shaggier, and tend to curve upward not outward, the rusty red branchlets droop in similar fashion.

Picea rubens
Red Spruce

ZONES: 4–6(7); sun, part sun
SOIL: Moist, acidic
NATIVE TO: Montane to subalpine and lower boreal forests; Nova Scotia to southern Ontario south mostly through New England and at higher elevations in the Appalachians to North Carolina

Picea pungens. *Cool Colorado blue spruces are used effectively in the wildlife gardens at the Holden Arboretum in Kirtland, Ohio. Local arboretums are superlative resources that can help you find trees and shrubs that perform well in your area, then show you how to artfully incorporate them into your landscape. The appendix on page 330 lists some great public gardens featuring native plants.*

SIZE: Height 30–60 (110) feet, width 10–18 (30) feet

COLOR: Cones yellow (male)/red-purple (female); blooms in spring

Red spruce is a small-needled species that is difficult to distinguish from white spruce and black spruce where their ranges overlap in the Northeast, but it is the only spruce that descends down the spine of the Appalachians. The twigs are covered with rusty pubescence, which gives the tree its common name and, together with a darker green needle color, helps distinguish it in side-by-side comparisons with its pale-faced cousins. It is suffering inordinately from acid rain in the southern Applachians, which both deteriorates the waxy cuticle of the leaf and, more insidiously, speeds leaching of mineral ions from the already poor soils. It can be used in much the same manner as white spruce in the landscape.

Picea sitchensis

Sitka Spruce

ZONES: (5)6–7; sun, part sun

SOIL: Moist, acidic

NATIVE TO: Coastal rainforests; southeastern Alaska south along the Pacific coast to northern California

SIZE: Height 100–140 (260) feet, width 25–40 (60) feet

COLOR: Cones yellow (male)/red-purple (female); blooms in spring

Nothing can prepare you for your first encounter with these enormous trees where old-growth stands have been preserved. Sitka spruce is the characteristic tree of the temperate rainforests in the Pacific Northwest, living for centuries and forming buttressed, smooth-barked trunks as big as a living room covered with all manner of ferns, mosses, lichens, and other bryophytes. The upper crown is composed of spoked, horizontal branches hung like clothes lines with pendulous branchlets. This distinctive habit makes the trees easy to distinguish from Douglas fir even at a distance. It thrives only in its native haunts, where the air is always cool and damp and the moss is ever soggy.

Pieris floribunda

Pieris floribunda
(pie-AIR-is)

Ericaceae

Fetterbush, Mountain Andromeda

ZONES: 4–6; sun to light shade

SOIL: Moist but well-drained, acidic (pH 4.5–5.5)

NATIVE TO: High-elevation mountain woods and balds; West Virginia to northern Georgia

SIZE: Height 2–4 feet, width 2–3 feet

COLOR: Creamy white; blooms in early spring

The magnificent heathland balds of the Great Smoky Mountains are a treasure trove of plants, and one of the gems that you'll find on these foggy summits is *Pieris floribunda*, a charming evergreen closely related to the Japanese andromeda *(P. japonica)*, that ever-popular foundation plant in the Northeast and West. Our native species has lance-shaped, leathery, dark gray-green leaves marked and creased along a strong creamy midvein much like mountain laurel. The blade is somewhat glossy and heavy enough that the leaves tend to droop a bit, showing themselves to good advantage. Like its Asian cousin, mountain andromeda's flower buds mature in autumn at the tips of the twigs. The forking racemes actually start to expand in the fall and early winter—enough so you can see the buds arrayed individually on the stems—so as soon as it warms in spring, these impatient flowers swell and come into bloom very quickly. *P. floribunda* is lovely in flower. The individual blooms are urn-shaped, like those of so many of the Ericaceae, pinched to a narrow opening and hung in two upside-down ranks along the stems. The racemes splay upward in a branching panicle like arms flung up for a hug, and their ivory white color contrasts elegantly with the rich, dark gray-green of the foliage below. In habit these are stiff-branched, bushy shrubs narrowed to a single trunk near the ground with a V-shaped canopy usually flattened a bit on top. Their early bloom, clean, upright habit, and glossy foliage make them valuable shrubs for foundation plantings and massing. The hybrid of *P. flori-*

Pieris floribunda. *The verb "fetter" means to shackle or restrain. It would take many, many years for a fetterbush to spread to the point where this moniker would seem appropriate, except for a creature the size of a ground squirrel. This slow-growing, mounded evergreen blooms in early spring, its flowers having been formed the previous season.*

Pinckneya bracteata.
Fever tree's flowers would be small and fairly nondescript if not for the occasional sepal that enlarges into a big pink shovel — no doubt to attract the attention of passing pollinators.

bunda × *japonica*, 'Brouwer's Beauty', is also an excellent plant if you are not a native-plant purist. It has a similar flat-topped, upright growth, but the racemes arch over a bit, a trait they received from the Asian parent.

In the cypress swamps of the southeastern coastal plain there is another species, *P. phillyreifolia* (vine-wicky) that takes the "Weirdest Growth Habit" award among the native Ericaceae. It sends up stoloniferous stems into the punky bark at the base of pond cypress (*Taxodium ascendens*), whose fibrous bark (like that of *Chamaecyparis thyoides* and *Sabal major*, its other hosts) fissures in long cracks that the vine-wicky can force its way into; it grows upward, wedged in the crevice and anchored by small rootlets encouraged by the abundant rain and dew in the swamp. These flattened, forking stems can travel as much as 30 feet up the trunk of the tree, poking out a few flowering branchlets here and there along the way. Its leaves are smaller than but otherwise similar to those of mountain andromeda, and the leafy side shoots produce small racemes of flowers in late winter from overwintering buds. In a landscape situation, where it has more light and freedom, it will grow as a rounded, shrubby evergreen, and does have possibilities in the Deep South, where *P. floribunda* cannot grow. Better still would be to establish it on a cypress or palm just to stump your know-it-all horticultural acquaintances.

CULTURE: The Achilles heel of mountain andromeda is *Phytophthora cinnamoni*, the fungus that causes root disease and subsequent wilt symptoms and dieback of the crown in many of the Ericaceae. Established garden plants are reasonably immune, but this has proved a difficult species to raise in containers and to get established in the garden. A very well drained, barky mix low in pH should be used in containers, and the plants need to be kept out of the heat and carefully watered. Even field-grown plants can suddenly die after transplanting, but if they survive a season, they are usually okay. Despite admonishment from nursery growers, I raise these plants in containers without problem (bark-based mix, pH 5.0, light liquid fertilizer only), but I admit they are touchy to move or to raise in a typical container nursery. I feel that this is a very underutilized species in the Northeast, and I am working to perfect a cultural regime that I hope will lead to greater availability. Its main advantage over Japanese andromeda is resistance to lacebugs, a pest that leaves the Asian plants stippled and pale by late summer. Certain native individuals, maybe 10 percent, in a seed crop do develop lacebug infestations, so some selection for lacebug resistance may be warranted.

USES: Foundation plantings, massing, mixed border, heath garden.

PROPAGATION: Moderately easy from seed.

Pinckneya bracteata

Pinckneya bracteata (pubens)
(pink-NEE-a)
Rubiaceae
Fever Tree, Pinckneya

ZONES: (7)8–9; part sun

SOIL: Moist to wet

NATIVE TO: Bogs, swamps, and bayshores; southwestern South Carolina to Georgia and northern Florida

SIZE: Height 6–15 (30) feet, width 6–10 feet

COLOR: Petals yellowish marked with purple-brown, showy sepals yellowish or light to dark pink spotted with darker pigment; blooms in early summer

Pinckneya, also called fever tree because its bark was used to treat malaria, is a remarkable plant that remains fairly obscure in horticultural circles because of its limited winter hardiness and intolerance of droughty soils. It is a relative of buttonbush (*Cephalanthus occidentalis*), sharing a love of mucky swamps and shallow ponds. In habit, too, pinckneya is somewhat like buttonbush — an open shrub or even small tree often spreading by root suckers to form a broad mound or colony at least half as wide as tall. Like *Cephalanthus*, it produces big, glossy, deciduous leaves arranged in pairs along the stem. These leaves are lovely in themselves — up to 8 inches long on vigorous shoots and broadly oval with a dewy shine that makes them always look as though they have just been rained on. The short petioles are tinted red, and this pigment often travels part way up the midvein before it peters out. The leaf veins mark the blade noticeably, giving it a bit of texture. As the leaves are finished expanding, a cluster of blooms develops from the stem tip and upper axils. The flowers themselves are about 1 inch long, with 5 petals narrowed into a slender tube except at the tips, which curl back on themselves like the lid of a sardine can after it's been rolled off. It is the sepals, not the petals, that are truly remarkable, though. At least one of the five sepals on scattered flowers expands into a leaflike, bubblegum-pink bract much like the bract of a pink poinsettia, except here they are oval and veined like the leaves. It is quite a sight to see these big bracts dangling from the twigs like pieces of tissue caught there by accident. The bracts are effective for a few weeks until the flowers have all faded, and small, knobby seed capsules begin to develop.

CULTURE: For best flowering and foliage, site *Pinckneya* in damp to wet soil where it gets morning sun. It can be trained as a single-trunk tree by removing the root suckers and lower branches in winter. It will survive in the warmer parts of Zone 7, but will be killed to the ground when temperatures drop below 0° F. Though it will resprout, flowering will be lost for the year.

USES: Specimen or massing near ponds, shrub borders.

PROPAGATION: Moderately easy from seed.

Pinus banksiana

Pinus (PIE-nus)
Pinaceae
Pine

There are few places in the continental United States and southern Canada where some species of pine does not grace the landscape. Pines are arguably the most wide-ranging and successful genus of trees on the continent, rivaled only by the oaks in their ability to grow in a diversity of climates. Like oaks, many pines send down deep roots to tap the water necessary to weather summer droughts. They can grow in hotter, drier landscapes than spruce, fir, or false cypress, and this ability helps make pines the dominant conifer in the East and at middle elevations in the West. Furthermore, they are just plain *beautiful* — I don't think anyone can argue with me there. Their long evergreen needles have an undeni-

able softness in the way they fracture light and whistle the wind. Like many conifers, they send out one flush of growth a year, and all the buds originate from the tip of the previous year's branches. During the winter, these new growths — or candles, as they are called — sit like the nubs of new deer antlers in the top whorl of leaves. In spring, all these candles have to do is streeeeeeeetch out, and as they do, bundles of needles spring up along their length. Pine needles are set into fascicles, each of which is a cluster of 2 to 5 needles cinched together at the base by crepe-paper scale leaves modified for this purpose. A particular species will have a consistent number of needles per fascicle, so white pines are often referred to as a five-needled pines and ponderosa as a three-needled pine. The bundles of needles are actually mini–side branches, and the advantage of this is that the pine can produce a thicker crop of needles along a given length of twig than, say a spruce, which produces its needles singly. This also explains why pines only branch from the tips: all the side branches have become bundles of needles. The result of this tips-only growth habit is a branching pattern that looks regular and segmented as one year's needles clearly build on the framework set down by the last. Pine cones, too, are modified branches. Some of the candles form overlapping woody scales instead of needles, and the resulting cones shield the developing seeds from harm.

I fear I cannot truly do justice to this very diverse genus in a limited space. Included within it is the tallest tree in eastern North America, eastern white pine *(P. strobus)*, and the oldest living tree in the world, intermountain bristlecone pine *(P. longaeva)*. It is hard to generalize very much about pines, and I think it is best to save further comment for the individual species entries.

CULTURE: For the most part pines are an adaptable lot. Many species are highly drought, fire, and heat tolerant, and some can withstand the salt spray of the ocean or the blistering cold of mountaintops with ease. Generally, though, pines are trees of the sun, preferring acidic, well-drained soils. As a rule, pines transplant well in the fall or early spring either as field-dug or containerized material. Most will shed their lower branches as they grow, both because they have become shaded and because the branches would otherwise act as a fire ladder to let flames leap into the canopy. Branch scars and wounds become plugged with a resinous sap, which limits decay and discourages insects. The wood of pines is not especially strong, but it is flexible, and a tree will often shed bits of its canopy in ice and snowstorms to avoid snapping the trunk. However, if the tree does lose its top, it cannot replace it easily like an oak or even other conifers like bald cypress or hemlock — technically this is because pines lack dormant axillary buds. Thus, helping the tree to establish a strong central

Pinus banksiana. My first introduction to the fire-adapted jack pine occurred on a long canoe trip in the Boundary Waters area of northern Minnesota and adjacent Ontario. We had to portage the canoes between lakes on a half-mile-long wooded trail that had burned five years earlier. Fast-growing jack pine seedlings had grown up so thickly that they nearly obscured the path, hiding the treacherous charred logs that lay across it. A portage that should have taken half an hour took most of the morning.

trunk by removing weaker forks and persistent dead limbs will greatly increase its chances in the long run. A number of insects, including sawflies and weevils, feed on pines, and in parts of the West and to a lesser extent in the East, white pine blister rust (whose alternate hosts are the *Ribes* species) is a significant concern, but there are no pest or disease problems great enough to warrant not planting pines.

USES: Shade, screening, windbreak, specimen, reforestation.

WILDLIFE: Common and widespread trees such as pines have many dependents, including birds and mammals that feed on the seeds and nest in the trunks. The larvae of the western pine white butterfly (*Neophasia menapia*) feeds on the needles, as do the eastern pine elfins and western pine elfins (*Callophrys niphon* and *C. eryphon*).

PROPAGATION: Easy to moderately easy from seed.

Pinus aristata
Rocky Mountain Bristlecone Pine

ZONES: 4–7; sun

SOIL: Well-drained

NATIVE TO: Subalpine and alpine ridges and slopes; Rocky Mountains of Colorado and New Mexico with one station in northern central Arizona

SIZE: Height 12–25 (40) feet, width 8–20 feet

COLOR: Cones red (male)/yellow (female); blooms in spring

The impossibly ancient bristlecone pines have recently been divided into two species. *P. aristata* represents the eastern species and *P. longaeva* (intermountain bristlecone pine)—from high elevation ridges in Utah, Nevada and southwestern California —the more western. *P. longaeva* is the longest-lived tree in the world, with some core samples from living trees estimated at 5,000 years old. It grows on dry ridges just at timberline, with sandblasted trunks clinging to life along narrow strips of live bark to support wizened old limbs. Both species have a rounded, densely needled crown because the deep green needles can remain living on the tree for 20 to 40 years. Young trees in the landscape remind me of the twisted-balloon creatures you see at children's birthday parties because of the way the bristly, persistent needles and segmented branches arrange themselves. The Rocky Mountain bristlecone is more amenable to cultivation, and since few of us care whether the tree lives for 1,000 or 5,000 years, this is the species most often grown. Provide it with a well-drained soil and full sun, and don't be alarmed if you see the needles flecked with little dots, as these are just bits of resin that ooze from ducts on the needle. In the garden, it will form a cuddly specimen with an oval outline, growing about 6 to 12 inches a year and quickly losing its single leader in favor of broad, ascending branches sweeping up from the trunk. Foxtail pine (*P. balfouriana*) is a related, taller-growing species native to a few locations in the California Sierras.

Pinus banksiana
Jack Pine

ZONES: 3–7; sun

SOIL: Moist to dry, well-drained, and acidic

NATIVE TO: Boreal forests, tundra margins, poor, sandy soils, especially following fire; Nova Scotia to northern Manitoba and then into the Northwest Territories south through Alberta to Minnesota, northern Illinois, and Maine

SIZE: Height 30–50 (85) feet, width 15–25 feet

COLOR: Cones yellow (male)/brown (female); blooms in spring

Jack pine is one of the serotinous species, meaning its cones remain unopened on the tree for many years until passing fire heats them up and melts off the sticky resin that binds them shut, releasing the seeds onto the newly scorched earth. Therefore, it is a common successional species in boreal forests, giving way eventually to longer-lived spruce and fir. It has 2-inch-long, twisted, gray-green needles in fascicles of two needles, and a scraggly open crown often lacking a central leader. Though it is one of the less ornamental pines, it is an important species in natural habitats as well as reforestation efforts, and it is the tree that gives character to the famous sand counties of Wisconsin as described in Aldo Leopold's book *A Sand County Almanac*. In the Southeast, the very similar Virginia pine (*P. virginiana*) fills the same ecological niche. It too is an irregular-crowned, 2-needled pine adapted to fire and the poor, open conditions along highways and old abandoned fields. Lodgepole pine (*P. contorta*), the provincial tree of Alberta, is another 2-needled serotinous species that ranges over most of the western mountains wherever meager rainfall allows it. As you can gather from its common name, the trunk grows strait and tall, up to 100 feet high, with a high narrow crown of 2-to-3-inch, deep green needles and cones containing seeds that may remain viable for 40 years or more, until fire releases them. Lodgepole pine is a common sight in ponderosa pine and subalpine fir forests, often forming pure stands in sections where intense fires recently raged.

Pinus edulus
Pinyon Pine, Piñón

ZONES: 5–7(8); sun

SOIL: Dry, well-drained

NATIVE TO: Dry mountain slopes and open woodland at 4,500–7,500-foot elevations; southwestern Oklahoma and Colorado to Utah south to Arizona, southern Nevada, New Mexico, and northern Texas

SIZE: Height 10–20 (50) feet, width 8–15 feet

COLOR: Cones yellow (male)/brown (female); blooms in spring

P. edulus is one of four related pinyon species growing in the Southwest. They are shrubs or small trees that mix with juniper to form vast, open woodlands at middle elevations in the southern Rockies. Pinyons, or pine nuts, the fruit of the pinyon pine, are an important nut crop in the United States. The pinyon seed or nut is very large by pine standards (about ½ inch long and ¼ inch wide), and lacks the papery wing that most pines use to help winds disperse their progeny. Instead the seeds are spread by industrious but forgetful jays and rodents, who collect the oily nutritious seeds and cache them in underground larders. Singleleaf pinyon (*P. monophylla*) has 1, not 2, needles per bundle, and it grows at somewhat lower elevations over the same range. It is our only native pine with 1-needled fascicles, though each one is stout and broad, and twisted so the crown looks full. Two other pinyons grow along the border with Mexico — Parry pinyon (*P. quadrifolia*) in southern California, and Mexican pinyon (*P. cembroides*) farther east and south. All are drought-tolerant, slow-growing (4 to 6 inches a year) species with stiff, gray-green needles. Both *P. monophylla* and *P. edulus* can be grown successfully in the Northeast, though I have never seen them set a bountiful crop of seeds.

Pinus flexilis

Limber Pine

ZONES: 4–6; sun, part sun

SOIL: Moist to dry, well-drained

NATIVE TO: Subalpine forests up to timberline, mostly in the Rocky Mountains, North Dakota to southern Alberta south to Idaho, Nevada, southern California, and New Mexico

SIZE: Height 30–50 (80) feet, width 20–30 feet

COLOR: Pale red/yellow; blooms in spring

When young, limber pine is hard to distinguish from eastern white pine and others in the 5-needle group, though it has a more prominent stomatal band along the needle so the foliage looks a bit more silvery blue. In the Rockies, it grows to enormous girth, with a short, muscular trunk and irregular crown (the silhouette looks very much like some of the white oaks from a distance). We have it growing in the Garden, and it seems to lose its leader early in life, instead developing several stout limbs. The young twigs are very flexible, which helps it resist wind and snow breakage. White-bark pine (*P. albicaulus*) is closely related. Its branches are very similar to those of Japanese white pine (*P. parviflora*) in appearance, with lovely, blue-green needles set in stiff foxtails at the branch tips. This rugged species grows at high elevations in the Northern Rockies and the Cascades, and older trees develop a very distinctive, scaly gray-

ish-white bark and a picturesque, gnarled crown in response to the tough conditions near timberline. In recent years, it has declined greatly as a result of repeated attacks by white pine blister rust. Sugar pine (*P. lambertiana*) is the largest pine in the world, occasionally attaining heights in excess of 240 feet through its range in the mountains of Oregon and California. The tips of its outswooping branches are decorated with mammoth cones nearly 2 feet long, which are often sold as Christmas decorations.

Pinus palustris

Longleaf Pine

ZONES: 7–9; sun to light shade

SOIL: Moist to dry, well-drained, acidic

NATIVE TO: Sandy uplands and flatwoods along the coastal plain; Virginia to Florida and eastern Texas

SIZE: Height 40–70 (150) feet, width 25–40 ft

COLOR: Cones purplish red; blooms in spring

Longleaf pine is a remarkable tree. Before plantation forestry, it was the dominant tree along vast stretches of the southern coastal plain. It is supremely fire dependent (fire eliminates faster-growing competitors), and seedlings spend their first 3 to 5 years as a grass-like tuft of soft, foot-long needles. These protect the growing bud from ground fires and nourish the development of a deep taproot, which inches down through the sandy soil until it hits groundwater. Once the seedling has stored enough food reserves, it bolts up 3 feet or more in one season, raising its stem tips above occasional fires. From then on it begins to develop a wide-spreading, open-branched crown hung with luxuriously long, soft-looking, medium green needles that cluster toward the shoot tips in a spray. The older trees also develop a thick, plated bark that is always charred by the fires that keep less resis-

Pinus edulus. *Most pines are tall trees that loft their winged seeds on long airborne journeys from their upper branches. Diminutive pinyons, lacking the advantage of height, have evolved large, nutritious seeds that are scavenged by rodents and birds, most notably the lovely blue pinyon jay (Gymnorhinus cyanocephalus), which caches the nuts in networks of small holes it drills into dead tree trunks. Forgotten seeds eventually drop out and germinate far from the shade of their parent tree.*

Pinus palustris. *Long-leaf pine is aptly named; its needles look more like long tufts of grass sprouting from the stout twigs than proper pine needles. The incongruous combination of long, languorous needles and stocky, brown-black, fire-scarred trunks gives this tree a unique and truly beautiful silhouette.*

more in the Sierras and Cascades; width 25–40 feet

COLOR: Cones yellow; blooms in spring

Ponderosa pine, like sagebrush, is synonymous with the West. It grows to be a tall, single-trunk, rounded or flat-topped tree with unmistakable platy bark that is gray flaking to reveal warm tan and red like the colors of the soil on which it grows; the inner bark is also beautifully patterned like a jigsaw puzzle if you view it up close. Like the longleaf pine, it sports a crown of long, shaggy needles, and it, too, is fire resistant especially when mature, growing often in open groves or glades where few other trees could survive. Each tree is spaced from the next so that all can scavenge enough water from the remains of the winter snows and the occasional summer storm. Jeffrey pine (*P. jeffreyi*), from the California Sierras, is very similar except that its needles are a lovely silvery blue to blue-gray. Both species grow reasonably well in the East if given some room, unpolluted air, and sun.

Pinus resinosa

Red Pine

ZONES: 3–6; sun

SOIL: Moist to dry, well-drained

NATIVE TO: Eastern boreal forests; Labrador to southeastern Manitoba south to northern Iowa and New Jersey

SIZE: Height 50–80 (105) feet, width 15–25 feet

COLOR: Purple; blooms in spring

From genetic studies it is clear that red pine, named for the reddish brown bark, was driven nearly to extinction during the last ice age, but managed to survive and recolonize cold forests in the Northeast after the last glaciers receded. As a consequence, there is very little genetic diversity among individuals, and an unthinned stand will grow thickly but slowly because individual trees have trouble gaining advantage over their nearly identical neighbors. Red pine has 4-inch-long medium green needles in bundles of 2 arranged stiffly on thick twigs, forming a narrow but fairly open canopy. Like jack pine, it will seed in after disturbance and be replaced by spruce and fir in time. In the 1930s the Civilian Conservation Corps planted red pine as a timber tree south of its natural range because it is fast growing and develops a straight, narrow trunk. These grids of even-aged red pines were a familiar sight in southern New England until an introduced scale killed them off in the 1970s and 1980s. For this reason, the trees are rarely planted anymore. The scale does not thrive within the tree's native range.

Pinus rigida

Pitch Pine

ZONES: 4–8; sun, part sun

SOIL: Well-drained, acidic, moist to dry

tant competitors at bay. When wounded by fire or boring insects, the wood secretes massive amounts of sticky pitch, which is used to advantage by the endangered red-cockaded woodpecker (*Picoides borealis*). Family groups laboriously tunnel out a cavity in healthy, old-growth trees over the course of 2 to 3 years, then peck smaller wounds around the trunk so that the whole tree is covered in pitch. This allows the dominant pair to fledge offspring safe from tree snakes, who find the sap irritating and so cannot climb to the nest. The resin-saturated stumps of longleaf pines are harvested for their valuable wood, which is split to make the highly flammable fatwood so good for starting a fire in the woodstove. Where natural fire has been suppressed, longleaf pine is replaced by faster-growing slash pine (*P. elliotii*), which matures more quickly and thus is more valued by timber companies. It can send out two or even three flushes of growth in a season, putting on up to 4 feet in height per year when young.

Pinus ponderosa

Ponderosa Pine

ZONES: 4–8; sun, part sun

SOIL: Well-drained, moist to dry

NATIVE TO: Foothills, canyons, drier mountain slopes; Nebraska and North Dakota to southern British Columbia south through California to western Texas and Mexico

SIZE: Height 40–70 feet in the Rockies, 100–200 feet or

NATIVE TO: Sandy soils of uplands, barrens, and, less often, bottomlands; Maine to southern Ontario south to southern Illinois, Tennessee, and in the Appalachians to Georgia

SIZE: Height 30–50 (85) feet, width 15–25 feet

COLOR: Cones yellow; blooms in spring

This is a scruffy species of poor, sandy, and salty soils in the Northeast. It is fire-resistant, one of the few conifers that can resprout from adventitious shoot buds on the base of the stump if cut or killed by flames. The stiff, 2-to-3-inch-long needles in bundles of 3 terminate in a sharp tip that can prick the skin. Needles and branches can develop from dormant buds on the larger limbs and trunk as well, lending the tree an unshaven shagginess that I like but others find coarse. Pitch pine was once widely planted on farms on Cape Cod and is now a dominant tree over much of the peninsula. Along the southeastern coastal plain, it is replaced by the very similar pond pine *(P. serotina)*, a medium-size tree that favors damp soils on the margins of bogs and swamps. It has a similar, flat-topped, craggy outline but longer needles more like loblolly's. The adventitious shoots that shag the branches and trunk, and bark cracked like the bottom of a dry mudpuddle, show its relationship to pitch pine. In the Piedmont and up to higher elevations in the Appalachians a third species, table mountain pine *(P. pungens)*, seldom becomes more than a large shrub on thin, rocky soils.

Pinus strobus
Eastern White Pine

ZONES: 3–8; sun to light shade

SOIL: Moist to dry, acidic

NATIVE TO: Forests; Labrador to southeastern Manitoba south to Iowa, Tennessee, and the mountains of northern Georgia

SIZE: Height 60–90 (220) feet, width 25–40 feet

COLOR: Cones purple (male)/red (female); blooms in spring

Eastern white pine is one of the most majestic trees in North America, and is the only eastern species that once rivaled western trees in height and girth. The big specimens have long ago been cut, many in the eighteenth century to become the large masts of vessels of the British Royal Navy, hence the moniker "king's pines." This is the only eastern member of the 5-needle group, with soft, gray-green needles that give it a fine wispy texture. *P. strobus* tends to seed into old fields or areas cleared by fire or storms, though seedlings can work their way slowly through to the canopy in a mixed forest. The woods around Garden in the Woods are full of suppressed white pines slowly inching their way up through oaks that probably seeded in when the chestnuts died out 75 years ago. It can grow 1 to 2 feet a year when young,

Pinus ponderosa. *Charcoal-black fire scars and cracked, furrowed auburn bark pattern the unmistakable trunk of an old-growth ponderosa pine. Young ponderosas are not especially fire resistant — their bark is not yet thick enough to withstand hot flames — so it is common to see scattered veterans like this rising above thick stands of pole-sized trees that have grown up since the last forest fire.*

and the knotty, white wood is prized for furniture and timbers. Open-grown or isolated trees are prone to attack by the eastern pine shoot borer *(Eucosma gloriola)*, a native moth that lays its eggs on the terminal shoot of vigorous trees. The caterpillars bore into the center of the shoot and eat down through the pith before pupating, killing the leader in the process. Loss of apical dominance causes one to four of the side shoots to take its place, creating forks in the single trunk that lower its value as timber and increase the chances of ice breakage. Since the egg-laying female moths are attracted to shoots growing in the open, dense stands or understory trees are less often affected.

Pinus taeda
Loblolly Pine

ZONES: 7–9; sun

SOIL: Moist to dry, acidic sand or clay

NATIVE TO: Flatwoods and swamp margins, naturalized on uplands; throughout the Piedmont, Maryland to Tennessee and eastern Texas east to Florida

SIZE: Height 70–90 (140) feet, width 20–35 feet

COLOR: Cones yellow; blooms in spring

Like slash pine and longleaf pine, loblolly pine possesses a light but strong, yellow wood with a prominent darker grain that is prized for building, cabinetry, flooring, and, increasingly, pulp. So fast growing are these pines that the Southeast threatens to replace the West as the pulpwood center of the United States. Loblolly comes from the name that English colonists gave the thick boiled porridge that they ate in times of scarcity. The heavy clay mud that this pine grew in reminded them of the sticky loblolly they ate, and so *P. taeda* became the loblolly pine. As settlers cleared the Piedmont of hardwoods, this pine seeded in, so now its range stretches much farther westward, away from the loblolly mud of the coastal swamps. It grows fast enough that plantations can be cut every 30 years, after which they are burned and replanted with seedlings. Every old field and roadside in the Piedmont is covered with loblollies. This is a taller tree than longleaf pine, with 5-to-6-inch needles held stiffly on a flattened oval high-branched crown. It grows with the sympatric shortleaf pine *(P. echinata)*, which can also grow into a tall, narrow tree hung with needles half the length of its neighbor's. The bark of shortleaf pine is rustier in color, with a lighter inner bark that gives the trunk a plated, cracked mud appearance like pitch pine's. Spruce pine *(P. glabra)*, a shorter species, is similar in needle size and arrangement to *P. echinata*'s, but its needles are a luminous, deep green even in winter, and the tree develops a softer, more informal crown than loblolly or shortleaf pine. (It reminds me more of a deep green eastern white pine in outline.) Its native range is primarily along the Gulf coastal plain, from South Carolina to Louisiana.

Platanus occidentalis.
Sycamore's military-style camouflage is anything but. The great mottled limbs of this noble tree beckon the eye like sinuous, living sculpture. Unlike most eastern trees, sycamore's rate of annual diameter growth does not slow once the tree reaches its full height. Consequently, the mottled base quickly attains a corpulence that seems out of scale with the tree's chronological age.

Platanus occidentalis

Platanus (PLAT-in-us)
Platanaceae
Sycamore, Plane-tree, Buttonwood

Sycamores can become massive, massive trees. There is an American plane-tree *(P. occidentalis)* growing by the Farmington River in Simsbury, Connecticut, that is easily 15 feet in diameter at the base — which soon divides into five huge limbs that loft a canopy of leaves covering a third of an acre. No other tree in the eastern United States can even approach this species in girth. California sycamore is a much smaller tree, which is surprising, given that the Golden State is the fabled land of forest giants. All sycamores slough off their bark like unwanted skin, revealing beautiful underbark that is at first white or light green, then olive, then dark green and finally brown before it falls off in irregular jigsaw puzzle patches. It is one of the most strikingly beautiful barks of any tree's; the color and patterning remind me of the earth tone desert camouflage that everything and everyone was painted during the Gulf War.

In winter, sycamores stand out like ghostly beacons, and old trees are especially pretty with their scruffy brown trunks and olive-white limbs supporting a network of fine twigs. In summer the trees are hung with very large leaves that partially obscure the bark, but these, too, are lovely in their fashion. They are palmately veined and divided into five lobes a bit like a maple, and the blade can be as much as a foot across from base to tip. The twigs grow indeterminately, with new leaves and stems being produced into late summer, so saplings can add 6 feet or more a season and rapidly colonize the fertile soils along the streams and rivers that the species prefers. When trees are young, the crown has a distinctly pyramidal shape that evolves into a wide or narrow dome as it matures. Old limbs will often break, then resprout along their upper side. As a result, venerable trees often have a bent-arm silhouette that is very recognizable. Sycamores produce balled fruits that hang from the branches like sweetgum balls, hence the

common name buttonwood. Fortunately, though, these fruits break into a pile of soft fluff, nothing like the spiky weapons of *Liquidambar*. The eastern species, *P. occidentalis*, produces one ball per peduncle, whereas the western one produces three or four in a chain. Additionally, *P. occidentalis* occasionally hybridizes with the Eurasian *P. orientalis* in cultivation. This tree, called the London plane tree *(Platanus × acerifolia)* for the city in which it was first discovered, is widely planted as a park and sidewalk tree in the eastern United States owing to its extreme tolerance of soil compaction and atmospheric pollution. In fact it seems second only to the introduced weed, tree of heaven (*Ailanthus altissima*) in its ability to thrive in that no-plant's-land between buildings and pavement—an ability incongruous with the rich floodplain soils preferred by the species in nature. You can distinguish the London plane tree from straight *P. occidentalis* by the fruits, which often hang two per stem, and the deeper olive color of the bark.

There is a widespread fungus disease, sycamore anthracnose (*Apiognomonia veneta*), that infects twigs and buds during the dormant season, when the trees are less able to combat it. As the trees leaf out in spring, the dead twigs become obvious; often these dead twigs amass in broom-like clusters from repeated dieback and resprouting. The large leaves are also vulnerable to attack in the cool, wet weather of early spring, and trees can become partially or even completely defoliated just as they are leafing out. However, within a few weeks a new crop of leaves begins to grow, and quickly rebuilds the canopy. Sycamore anthracnose can certainly be unsightly, and it must stress the trees, but they are able to shrug off the insult year after year and grow healthily all summer.

CULTURE: Sycamores transplant easily, preferably into deep, fertile soils, but they will tolerate some drought. They are best sited in full sun.

USES: Park or shade tree.

PROPAGATION: Easy from seed.

Platanus occidentalis
Sycamore, American Plane-tree

ZONES: 4–9; sun, part sun
SOIL: Moist
NATIVE TO: Floodplain forests, bottomlands, and occasionally uplands; Maine to southern Ontario, southern Minnesota, and eastern Nebraska south to Texas and northern Florida
SIZE: Height 70–100 (160) feet, width 40–60 (80) feet
COLOR: Green; blooms in late spring

Although its huge potential size and susceptibility to anthracnose make *P. occidentalis* a tough tree to integrate into smaller landscapes, it is one of our best plants for winter—and summer—bark effect. It is also one of the few trees that you could plant from seed when you are 50 and see it become a decent-sized specimen by the time you are 75.

Platanus racemosa
California Sycamore

ZONES: 7–9; sun, part sun
SOIL: Moist
NATIVE TO: Stream sides and canyons; California

SIZE: Height 30–50 (75) feet, width 20–40 feet
COLOR: Green; blooms in spring

California sycamore is a common tree along stream swales throughout most of California. It hangs on to some of its leaves long into the winter, often dropping the last ones as the new flush is beginning in early spring. For this reason it is pretty messy as a yard tree, but the whitish-gray bark is very appealing, and in the wild, the trees provide invaluable bank stabilization along flood-prone waterways. Unlike the eastern sycamore, whose leaves are shallowly lobed but scalloped noticeably along the margins, *P. racemosa* has deeply 5-lobed leaves, making it resemble those of a large sweetgum, and the margins are only faintly toothed. Arizona sycamore (*P. wrightii*) is a close relative restricted to ravines and waterways in Arizona and New Mexico, where its small crown can be seen leaning out over the water to get more light.

Populus tremuloides

Populus (POP-yew-lus)
Salicaceae
Poplar, Aspen, Cottonwood

Populus tremuloides. *Fast-growing and beautiful, aspens are well suited to the modern landscape. Nothing is more soothing than lying under the whispering, rustling leaves of a quaking aspen on a warm summer day. Should these trees become too large or begin to decline, they can be cut close to the ground; they will quickly be replaced by sprouts arising from the crown and roots.*

With a certain hastiness and coarseness to their branching, poplars have the look of something cheaply made. Even the name *Populus* suggests something abundant, common, and proletarian to the core. From an ecological point of view, poplars are the plant equivalent of a rapid response team, well adapted to colonizing disturbed or degraded habitats, stabilizing them, and eventually yielding to slower-growing, longer-lived trees. Like alders, poplars are the great healers of land that lies bleeding and torn, scoured or burned.

Cottonwood is a tree whose seeds most everyone has unwittingly collected. In early spring both male and female trees are hung with long catkins that sway unimpeded by leaves, which haven't yet emerged. Female trees quickly ripen their seed, and by late spring, the air is full of cottony fluff (the tiny seeds are outfitted with white, downy hairs) that gets caught on clothing and especially in the vent screens below automobile windshields. The abundant seed is so light that it can float great distances on the wind, and when it lands on moist, bare soil, the silk on the seed flattens against it, in effect gluing the embryo in place. There are some aspens growing about 500 yards from our nursery down near the railroad tracks that form the Garden's southern boundary, and by early summer newly potted plants become surrounded by little aspen seedlings that have blown in and sprouted. It is one of those weeds that—despite good sanitation and vigilance—no nursery can escape from without cutting down every aspen within a quarter-mile radius. Of course, cutting down a poplar would be really doing it a favor. The genus is famous for its ability to form vast, clonal colonies through prolific root sprouting, and this is only encouraged when you cut down the main trunk. One documented clonal stand in the mountains of Utah covers 107 acres and consists of 47,000 individual trunks originating from the same root system! It may well be that these groves of aspen are the largest living organisms on earth. Interestingly, the dry springs and summers of the western mountains are not conducive to seedling germination—they need a bare, consistently moist soil like that of our nursery—so seedlings are rare. Thus, many of these large clonal groves may date from just after the last ice age, when the climate in the Rockies was more humid and *Populus* seeds could blow in and become established. Now, although trees covering millions of acres produce tons and tons of seed, they are in effect at a reproductive bottleneck unless the climate changes for the better.

Populus species share certain characteristics, like oval or heart-shaped leaves narrowed to a tip and more or less flattened at the base, where they attach to a long, thin petiole. The leaves are borne alternately on thick twigs after they have spent the winter in large gum-sticky buds (a favorite winter food of the ruffed grouse). Most of the species are fairly small, narrow-crowned trees, though the cottonwoods can grow quickly to a very large size. Like their cousins the willows, poplars have soft, white wood that is prone to breakage in storms. Their bark is often green and smooth except on the lower trunk and on large limbs, and it is able to photosynthesize in late fall and early spring before the leaves take over. In fall the leaves of quaking aspen in particular take on a vibrant shade of bright yellow. They are to the Rockies what sugar maples are to Vermont.

CULTURE: Poplars are very easy to establish as 1-year-old container-raised seedlings planted out in early spring. All poplars can grow very rapidly, 2 to 6 feet a year, if given a moist soil and sun. Foresters will often plant alder with poplar to stabilize banks because the alder will fix nitrogen, some of which will be available to help the poplars grow quickly. Diseased or broken trees can be cut to the ground in winter, and copious root sprouts will emerge over the entire area come spring.

USES: Reclamation, naturalizing.

WILDLIFE: Poplar buds within reach are eaten by ground-feeding birds and mammals. The leaves are a primary or secondary food source of the white admiral, Western admiral, and orange-tip admiral butterflies (*Limenitis arthemis*, *L. weidemeyerii*, and *L. lorquini*), the green comma (*Polygonia faunus*), the comma tortoise shell and mourning cloak (*Nymphalis vau-album* and *N. antiopa*), and the aspen dusky wing (*Erynnis icelus*).

PROPAGATION: Easy from seed.

Populus angustifolia

Balsam Cottonwood, Narrowleaf Cottonwood

ZONES: 3–6(7); sun, part sun

SOIL: Moist

NATIVE TO: Stream and river sides in the Rocky Mountains; Montana and Alberta south to Nevada, Arizona, New Mexico, and northern Mexico

SIZE: Height 40–70 feet, width 15–35 feet

COLOR: Yellow-green; blooms in early spring

With a lance-shaped leaf more like a willow or cherry, balsam cottonwood is hard to mistake for any other poplar. It is a fairly common riparian species, with steeply ascending branches forming a round-topped, vase-shaped crown a bit like an elm's. Fall color is golden yellow. *P. × acuminata* (smooth-barked cottonwood), a natural hybrid of *P. angustifolia* and *P. deltoides*, has the smooth, photosynthetic bark of the narrow-leaved parent.

Populus balsamifera

Balsam Poplar

ZONES: 1–6; sun, part sun

SOIL: Moist

NATIVE TO: Wet woods, riverbanks, boreal forests, tundra margins; Labrador through the Northwest Territories to Alaska south to British Columbia, Colorado, Indiana, and Connecticut

SIZE: Height 60–80 feet, width 20–35 feet

COLOR: Yellow-green; blooms in early spring

Balsam poplar can grow quickly into a decent-sized tree with furrowed, gray bark and a rounded oval crown. It is instantly recognizable even from a distance because the oval, pointed leaves are covered especially on the undersides with an amber resin that gives the tree a rusty golden aura unlike others in the genus. The resin or balsam is highly volatile, and on any warm summer day the air of the north woods is filled with its heavy, redolent scent. This resin acts as a deterrent to herbivores, and it may have allelopathic effects as well. Leachates from the leaves have been found to inhibit germination, growth, and nitrogen fixation in alder (*Alnus* spp.), a plant of similar habitats (Schwintzer and Tjepkema, *The Biology of Frankia and Actinorhizal Plants*, p. 311). Bees are known to harvest the resin from poplars and use it as we use disinfectants, to keep the hive clean.

Populus deltoides
Eastern Cottonwood

ZONES: 4–9; sun, part sun
SOIL: Moist
NATIVE TO: Bottomlands, floodplain forests, shores, and damp prairie; Maine and southern Quebec to Minnesota south to Nebraska and Texas then east along the Gulf Coast to Florida
SIZE: Height 60–100 feet, width 25–50 feet
COLOR: Yellow-green; blooms in early spring

Eastern cottonwood and the related swamp cottonwood (*P. heterophylla*) are the only two eastern *Populus* species capable of growing to mammoth size. Often, when you find one in a forest, its trunk is twice as thick as the maples and ash that surround it, though they are likely all the same age. It is sometimes used as a street or lawn tree for this reason, but the wood is very weak and the trees drop many branches and twigs, not to mention seeds, so it is best left for naturalized situations.

Populus tremuloides
Quaking Aspen

ZONES: 1–7; sun, part sun
SOIL: Moist to moderately dry
NATIVE TO: Moist woods, bottomlands, disturbed areas, montane riparian communities, boreal forests, tundra margins; Labrador through the Northwest Territories to Alaska south in the western mountains to California, New Mexico, and northern Mexico, and in the East to Nebraska, Missouri, and Virginia
SIZE: Height 40–60 ft, width 15–25 feet
COLOR: Yellow-green; blooms in early spring

Quaking aspen, or "quakies," gets its name from the way the leaves quake and tremble in a light breeze. The leaves are about 1½ inches across, oval like those of most of the poplars, and hang on thin, flattened petioles up to 2 inches long. When wind hits the leaf, the blade rocks and twists from one side to the other, like a spoon-shaped fishing lure traveling through the water. This rocking exposes the light gray–colored undersides of the leaves as well, creating a visual as well as auditory flutter. The sound of a breeze rustling through the aspen leaves is very distinctive, a bit like the watery rattle of the bead-filled "rain sticks" you can buy from African import shops. I love to lie down near a quaking aspen on a warm, gusty day and listen to it sing. *P. tremuloides* is one of the most common and widespread trees in North America, and over its huge range it does vary as to the greenness or whiteness of its bark, but many of the trees that line every rivulet in the Rockies have a chalky olive-white bark that rivals paper birch's. Bigtooth aspen (*P. grandidentata*) grows in the Northeast. It is very similar except for a bit more green in the bark and a leaf blade that is coarsely, not finely, toothed. Both are small to medium-sized trees with single trunks and narrow, oval crowns of slightly ascending branches.

Potentilla fruticosa. *A long blooming period, neat, mounded habit, and tolerance of drought and dampness have long made shrubby cinquefoil a popular landscape plant. Most of the cultivars available in the nursery trade are European forms of this cosmopolitan species, but you can't easily tell which side of the Atlantic a particular plant hails from.*

Potentilla fruticosa

Potentilla fruticosa (Pentaphylloides floribunda)
(po-ten-TIL-a)
Rosaceae
Shrubby Cinquefoil

ZONES: 1–6; sun, part sun
SOIL: Wet to dry, but ideally moist, well-drained
NATIVE TO: Bogs, fens, calcareous outcrops, summits and tundra; circumboreal, in this hemisphere from Newfoundland to the Northwest Territories and Alaska south in the western mountains to California and New Mexico and in the East to Illinois and New Jersey

SIZE: Height 1–3 feet, width 1–3 feet
COLOR: Typically strong yellow, occasionally lighter yellow, gold, or white; blooms in summer

It seems hard to believe that there could be much in common between a cold bog and a dry, rocky outcrop. Strange as it may seem, though, the two do share some basic features that allow certain plants to grow in either. The most obvious thing these two environments share is low fertility, because overly wet and overly dry soils both limit decomposition and nutrient cycling. Bogs are also open places with abundant sun and few competitors — a rare situation in a generally forested landscape but one found as well in very dry soils. It seems likely that certain plants like shrubby cinquefoil, wax myrtles, and sheep laurel evolved first in dry, sterile soils and used this survival ability to colonize the equally open, nutrient-poor environments of bogs and fens. In the case of potentilla, which favors mineral-rich bogs and calcareous outcrops, the key to success seems to be an abundance of sun and the presence of limestone rather than a certain range of soil moisture. I have seen it in rich fens fed by underground waters passing through limestone as well as on windswept, dry outcrops, often composed of the same parent stone. What this means for the gardener is a plant that is highly adaptable to wetness or drought. Couple this with a neat habit, cold hardiness, and very long bloom time, and you have an invaluable landscape plant.

P. fruticosa is the only truly woody member of this large genus, erecting thin, twiggy stems from a twisted trunk and nest of fibrous roots that continually replenish the canopy and form mounding, matted clumps with time. It sports leaves that are pinnately compound, with leaflets so crowded together on their little rachis that they appear bird-footed, with 5 to 7 narrow little toes each about half an inch long and bristled with silky hairs underneath. Most of the gray-green leaflets curl upward slightly at the tip, lending a subtle dishevelment to what is overall a neatly ordered little mound. The word "cinquefoil" is an architectural term for a circular design composed of five arches with intersected bases that one sees in some Gothic windows — a pattern clearly borrowed from the cheery little *fleurs* of our subject here. Wild plants decorate themselves with rich yellow flowers about an inch across that lie flat against the outer reaches of the crown. The blooms open sequentially a few at a time from the new growth over a long season in summer. I was puzzled as to why wild selections do not bloom for as many months as the cultivars until I did a bit of investigation. Most of the garden cultivars have been selected from European races, which are dioecious tetraploids — male and female flowers are on different individuals. If you have a large planting of one of these cultivars, be it male or female, it cannot set seed and will therefore bloom and bloom in childless desperation. Our form (sometimes listed as a separate species, *P. floribunda*) is diploid and hermaphroditic — having male, female, and perfect flowers on the same plant — so if you have one of this type, it can still set seed, which will curtail bloom quite abruptly. Nevertheless, a month of flowers in the heart of summer is nothing to sneeze at. The shrubs also stay a very manageable size, since the older stems die off eventually and never get beyond a few feet in height.

CULTURE: Although this is a very adaptable plant in many ways, it is best in areas with circumneutral soils. Since it is truly a boreal and alpine plant, there is little hope for it in southern gardens. In most of the Northeast and Northwest, where acid soils predominate, a yearly dusting of lime will be required for growth to luxuriate as it does in the upper Midwest and Plains. Shrubby cinquefoil transplants easily from containers in spring and requires little care. Since the plants are deciduous, snow-matting is not as pronounced as on evergreens, but there may be a few disheveled weeks in spring before the new flush of stems has recovered its form. A bit of light pruning and deadwood removal can be accomplished at this time, but, as with roses, the older stems flower most profusely, so leave older stems if they are alive.

USES: Massing, possibly foundations, rock gardens. It is particularly effective integrated into perennial gardens to lend some permanent structure.

WILDLIFE: Summer nectar source. The leaves are the only food source of the cinquefoil copper (*Lycaena dorcas*), a small brown, black-spotted butterfly that ranges across Canada and the northern United States, wherever *Potentilla* grows.

PROPAGATION: Easy from cuttings, moderately easy from seed.

Prunus maritima

Prunus (PROO-nus)
Rosaceae
Plum, Cherry

When you think of cherries and plums, the delicious fruits and delicate ruffled pink flowers come to mind. The plums of orchards and horticulture are predominantly Eurasian, though. The North American members of this genus have bitter or small, stony fruits (called drupes) and fairly small, white flowers. However, if you come to our native *Prunus* species with a mind unclouded by visions of sugarplums and dancing rose petals, they are quite beautiful in their own right. Our natives are predominantly plants of hedgerows and old fields with fruits too sour for most of us but relished by birds, who spread the seeds very proficiently. The plums form spreading colonies often woven with thorns, and hung with fruits as big as large gumballs that are not bad to eat if you like a certain mouth-puckering astringency. Made into jellies or pies, they are quite tasty. The native cherries are more diverse, ranging from groundcovers to shrubs and successional trees to the occasionally massive black cherry with its incomparable satin-grained heartwood. All but *P. caroliniana* are deciduous, and in good years the fall color of plants like black cherry and pin cherry may rival the maples. All but the lovely pink-flowered desert peach cover themselves in white, 5-petaled blooms softened by a tuft of stamens that frill the flowers somewhat in profile. The plums and most cherries bear their flowers all along the branches on thin peduncles, tracing the form of the crown in a soft haze of white just as the leaves are beginning to unfold. Black cherry and chokecherry are the exception, producing long stiff racemes that spring haphazardly from the shoot tips after the foliage is nearly expanded. The leaves partially obscure the flowers, diminishing the floral effect.

With a few exceptions (*P. mexicana, P. hortulana, P. maritima,* and *P. caroliniana* are four that come to mind) our native *Prunus* species are a bit wild for civilized landscapes, but in a naturalized setting, they come into their own. Bees love the sweetly and strongly fragrant flowers, and mammals in addition to birds relish the fruits. The scrambled branches of the shrubby species provide an impenetrable fortress for a little animal to hide from hawks and cats.

CULTURE: For best effect, site in full sun. The shrubby species will do well in dry, sandy soil and can be used for bank and soil stabilization. For best fruit set, plant two or more individuals in close proximity. A number of insects and diseases afflict the genus, the most noteworthy being black knot (*Apiosporina morbosa*), an indigenous fungus disease that causes a section of twig or branch to swell markedly; most wild plums and cherries exhibit

Prunus maritima. *The little beach plum flowers with surprising extravagance considering the spartan conditions of its seaside haunts. Masses of flowers clustered along the twigs will yield an abundance of cherry-sized, bloomy blue fruits later in the season. I think the tart, ripe fruits taste great, but many people prefer them sugared up and slathered on toast as beach plum jelly.*

these numerous roughened areas scattered through the canopy. The surface of smaller lesions is smooth and black, like a piece of congealed tar washed up on the beach after an oil spill. Eventually, the limb may be girdled and forced to resprout below the infection. There is not much you can do to prevent the windborne disease, but pruning off and burning the knots below the point of infection will reduce the volume of potential spores. There is no question that good culture helps most plants tolerate the disease, which is often more of an eyesore than a lethal threat. Additionally, there are several native insects and parasitic fungi that prey on black knot, reducing its virulence significantly—not a possibility with many introduced diseases like chestnut blight, which have no natural enemies.

USES: Naturalizing, soil conservation, massing, edible fruit.

WILDLIFE: *Prunus* species provide fruit and cover for birds and other animals and nectar and foliage for insects. These trees are the preferred larval host plants for the tiger swallowtail, pallid tiger swallowtail, and two-tailed tiger swallowtail butterflies (*Papilio glaucus, P. eurymedon,* and *P. multicaudata*), coral hairstreak (*Harkenclenus titus*), western hairstreak and striped hairstreak (*Satyrium californica* and *S. liparops*), and alternate hosts for the viceroy admiral, white admiral, western admiral, and orange-tip admiral (*Limenitis archippus, L. arthemis, L. weidemeyerii,* and *L. lorquini*), as well as the gregarious spring azure (*Celastrina argiolus*).

PROPAGATION: Moderately easy from seed.

Prunus americana
Wild Plum

ZONES: 4–9; sun, part sun

SOIL: Moist to moderately dry

NATIVE TO: Fencerows, thickets, roadsides; New Hampshire to Montana and Manitoba south to Oklahoma and northern Florida

SIZE: Height 4–10 (18) feet, width 4–12 feet

COLOR: White; blooms in late spring

Usually when I have seen wild plum, it has been in large spreading colonies or thickets armed with thorn-like spur branches like those you find on the wild crabapples. Thus it is hard to utilize except in restoration or wildlife habitat situations, but a mass of the plants in bloom is light and airy. Fruits ripen red or yellow flushed with red on the side facing the sun and are covered with a waxy bloom like most plums. The leaves are 3 to 4 inches long, oval, and turn yellow in fall. Chickasaw plum (*P. angustifolia*) is similar but smaller, and the flowers come out well before the leaves in early spring, to good effect. It is a common sight along roadsides in the southeast coastal plain. Fruits are red but lack a glaucous bloom, and the leaves are noticeably narrower and only half as long as wild plum's. Canada plum (*P. nigra*) is another related species centered in eastern Canada.

Prunus andersonii
Desert Peach

ZONES: 5–7; sun

SOIL: Dry, well-drained

NATIVE TO: Sagebrush desert and washes; altitude of 4,000–8,000 feet in the Sierras of eastern California and western Nevada

SIZE: Height 3–6 feet, width 6–10 (50) feet

COLOR: Soft rose pink; blooms in spring

Desert peach is a silver-gray twiggy, thorny shrub that adorns itself with beautiful pink flowers (dark pink in bud) with wide-gapped petals like those of many *Amelanchier* species. The plants tend to occur as large, clonal colonies that are solid at first, but after hundreds of years become broken up into discrete patches as individual stems die out and sections become separated. It is an underappreciated native shrub that can be used to advantage at moderate elevations throughout the West. The fruits are stony and not edible.

Prunus caroliniana
Cherry Laurel

ZONES: 7–9; sun, part sun

SOIL: Moist to moderately dry

NATIVE TO: Hedgerows, open woods, stream sides, waste areas; formerly along the immediate coastal plain from southeastern Virginia to Florida and Louisiana, but now naturalized well inland throughout the Southeast.

SIZE: Height 20–30 (50), width 12–25 feet

COLOR: White; blooms in early spring

Cherry laurel, our only evergreen *Prunus* species, has been employed as an easy screen and hedge for many years in the Southeast, and it has thus been able to spread far beyond its once limited range. It is a wide, shrubby tree with fairly thick and glossy, elliptical or lance-shaped leaves 3 to 5 inches long that undulate and wave somewhat along the margin. The small flowers appear to be mostly just frothy stamens, as the petals reflex back to get out of the way, and these are borne in tight clusters amid the leaf axils where they are not readily seen. It is a good screening plant though maybe a little coarse and rank in a formal situation unless regularly clipped. The twigs are stiff and upright when young, and vigorous plants can grow 2 to 3 feet in a season.

Prunus maritima
Beach Plum

ZONES: 4–8; sun

SOIL: Sandy, well-drained

NATIVE TO: Sand dunes and barrens along the Atlantic coast; New Brunswick to Maryland, also on dunes along Lake Superior in Michigan

SIZE: Height 3–6 (10) feet, width 3–6 feet

COLOR: White; blooms in spring

Beach plum decorates its branches with frilly white blooms before the foliage emerges. The leaves are round-oval and hang stiffly on short petioles along spineless vertical shoots. Tart, red-purple plums develop in the fall. I have made some tasty jam out of them, but they are a bit tangy when you eat them raw. Like the other suckering plums, if you give beach plum some space and a modicum of culture, it will form a picturesque, round-spreading single-trunked specimen with beautifully sculpted, twisting branches.

Prunus mexicana
Bigtree Plum

ZONES: 4–9; sun

SOIL: Moist to moderately dry

NATIVE TO: Rocky, open woods and fields; southern Illinois and Missouri south to northern Mexico, Texas, and Alabama

SIZE: Height 15–30 feet, width 12–20 feet

COLOR: White; blooms in spring

Unlike the plums covered above, this and the following species are usually small trees rather than suckering colonies. Therefore, if you want to grow wild plums for fruit and don't have the space to devote to a free-running wild plum, I would suggest bigtree plum or hortulan plum, both of which have several heirloom varieties that are sometimes offered by specialty fruit nurseries. Bigtree plum has wide oval leaves and thorny twigs and produces rose red to purple fruits that make good eating despite their rather large pits. *P. hortulana* is another nonsuckering, edible plum that becomes a small, typically single-trunked tree branching low to the ground. It is found mostly in middle areas of the Mississippi Valley and makes a fairly attractive small specimen. The round, sweet fruits are red or reddish yellow and good for jellies. *P. monsoniana* (wildgoose plum) is more like *P. americana* in habit. Legend has it that the common name was coined after one Captain Means of Nashville, Tennessee, shot a wild goose and found a pit in its gizzard; he planted it and it grew into a superior, sweet-fruited cultivar (Steyermark, *Flora of Missouri*, p. 860). Both hortulan plum and wildgoose plum flower when the leaves are partially expanded, which screens the blooms somewhat.

Prunus pensylvanica
Pin Cherry, Fire Cherry

ZONES: 3–7; sun, part sun

SOIL: Moist to moderately dry

NATIVE TO: Forests, clearings (especially after fires), roadsides, and old fields; Labrador to southern Northwest Territories south to British Columbia, Minnesota, and Pennsylvania and at higher elevations to northern Georgia

SIZE: Height 20–40 feet, width 10–15 feet

COLOR: White; blooms in spring

Pin cherry is a short-lived species that is very commonly seen springing up after fire and invading abandoned fields and roadsides. It has a lovely, metallic coppery red bark marked with the distinctive horizontal stomatal bands found on the young bark of all cherries. Usually pin cherry forms a single, slender trunk set with whorls of thin branches that angle out to form a narrow oval crown hung with 3-to-4-inch lance-shaped leaves. These have perhaps the best fall color of any cherry, often a striking orange like the glowing flames that created its habitat.

Prunus pumila
Sand Cherry

ZONES: 3–6; sun

SOIL: Moist to dry, well-drained

NATIVE TO: Dunes and sandy soils, rocky woods and cliffs, beaches and sand bars; New Brunswick to Manitoba south to Wyoming, Wisconsin, New Jersey, and in the mountains to North Carolina

SIZE: Height 1–2 (3) feet, width 3–6 feet

COLOR: White; blooms in spring

Sand cherry has been separated into several distinct varieties, but all produce clouds of small flowers before the leaves. It favors well-drained soils, where it can spread and grow unimpeded. *P. pumila* var.

pumila from the Great Lakes and the widespread eastern *P. pumila* var. *cuneata* are upright, rounded shrubs lacking spines and, like the other native cherries, producing small black fruits. Two further varieties are lower and are more useful in landscapes for this reason. *P. pumila* var. *besseyi*, from the Rockies and Great Plains, is a flattened, sprawling shrub that can be shaped into a picturesque, almost bonsaied form as the branches arch toward and away from the ground in serpentine fashion. Var. *depressa* (creeping sand cherry) is a 3-to-8-inch-high groundcover favoring sand and gravel bars along rivers as well as limestone outcrops; it ranges throughout eastern Canada and the Northeast. It too has gray-green leaves arrayed on the upper sides of scandent stems that spread along the ground. Some of the plants in our collection develop a pretty orange and yellow fall color, and overall it is a fine groundcover if given sun and space to spread.

Prunus serotina
Black Cherry

ZONES: 3–9; sun to part sun

SOIL: Moist to moderately dry

NATIVE TO: Rich woods; Nova Scotia and southern Ontario to North Dakota south to Texas, northern Mexico, and Florida

SIZE: Height 50–70 (90) feet, width 20–30 (40) feet

COLOR: White; blooms in late spring

Black cherry is often struck down at a young age by black knot, but occasionally it can become a massive old tree with a tall, thick trunk that barely flares where it comes out of the ground. It has slender twigs and alternating buds, like birch, but when the

Prunus pumila *var.* depressa. *Test beds are valuable places to learn about unfamiliar species. I planted this creeping sand cherry in one of my nursery beds five years ago, when it was but a whip of a seedling. I've been very impressed with its sculptural, prostrate habit and its pretty flowers, so the shrub, now four feet in diameter, will be integrated into the garden.*

(LEFT) Prunus virginiana. *Choke cherry's pendent clusters of sugary fruits are irresistible to birds, which are sure to spread the seeds around.*

(RIGHT) Pseudotsuga menziesii *var.* glauca. *The Rocky Mountain form of Douglas fir, seen here in the wilds of northwestern Montana, is stockier and slower growing than its counterpart from the coastal rainforests of the Pacific Northwest. It has adapted over time to the more rigorous snowy winters it experiences high in the Rockies.*

bark is bruised, it has an acrid, cyanic odor very unlike the sweet root-beer smell of *Betula lenta.* The narrow oval leaves develop a burgundy red mixing with yellow in good falls, and the chocolate-colored bark peels like burned potato chips. The fruits are green, then red, then black. Because of its disease problems, it is rarely planted, but it is worth leaving if you have some as long as you don't have to garden underneath it: the fruits are loved by birds, but those that are not eaten drop to the ground and sprout like crazy in spring. Choke cherry (*P. virginiana*) is similar, though it remains a shrubby, weedy-looking understory or old-field tree, which ranges across most of North America in suitable climates. Bitter cherry (*P. emarginata*) is basically a western form widespread in the coastal areas of the West, with red changing to black fruits and reddish brown bark.

Pseudotsuga menziesii

Pseudotsuga menziesii (soo-doe-SUE-ga)
Pinaceae
Douglas Fir

ZONES: (3)4–7; sun, part sun
SOIL: Moist to moderately dry, acidic
NATIVE TO: Coastal and montane forest; Montana, southwestern Alberta to British Columbia south to California and western Texas

SIZE: Height 70–120 (300) feet, width 20–30 feet
COLOR: Yellow-red; blooms in spring

It is a bit intimidating to describe in a few short sentences a tree that is the warp and weft of an entire region. The mighty Douglas fir grows in large areas of the West, but it is in the wetter regions of the Pacific Northwest that it is especially abundant and massive. On the western side of the Cascades and Sierras, then north along the coast into British Columbia, their tall, furrowed trunks are everywhere apparent, huge flaring bases dwarfing the passing human. This is the largest form of the tree, *P. menziesii* var. *menziesii* (coast Douglas fir), capable of living over 750 years and growing to heights approaching 300 feet—the height of a 30-story building. Its needles are medium green with just a hint of yellow. East of the Cascades and Sierras, where the moisture has been rung out of the humid Pacific air, a smaller form called *P. menziesii* var. *glauca* (Rocky Mountain Douglas fir) has adapted to the less humid environment. This is the variety grown throughout the East as a Christmas tree and to a lesser extent as a garden subject because of its winter hardiness and the lovely blue-green color of its needles. A third, var. *macrocarpa* (bigcone Douglas fir) from Southern California, has cones and blue-green needles about twice as large as the coastal form. It is also listed as a separate species, *P. macrocarpa.*

Douglas fir is not a true fir, rather it falls between hemlock and larch in an evolutionary sense. Its inch-

long needles are soft and round-tipped like hemlock's, but they whorl evenly around the twig and tilt somewhat toward the tip. The twigs and leader come out in a whorled fashion like firs' and spruces' from the tips of the previous season's growth. A single dominant leader and 3 to 6 side branches set out in spring. At first these side branches are up-angling, but the middle ones gradually sag like an old mule to give the crown a certain sweeping pendulousness. Douglas fir is intolerant of shade, but after fires, logging, or storms have cleared a path, the trees seed in earnest and the saplings can grow remarkably fast. In the coastal Northwest, it is common to see stretches of 18 to 28 inches between each whorl of branches on trees between 5 and 30 years of age, as they climb rapidly toward the sun. Older trees develop an amazing furrowed and channeled corky brown bark up to 6 inches thick that acts like a blanket of insulation screening the cambium from fire. Most older trees are charred at the base from long-past conflagrations that have helped keep competitors at bay and opened up seedbeds for the Douglas fir's progeny. Without fire, these firs would gradually die out and be replaced by more shade-tolerant species like redcedar, true firs, and hemlock. Douglas fir cones are quite interesting, and along with the corky graybrown bark are the easiest way to identify the trees. Ranging in length from about 2 inches for var. *glauca* up to 8 inches for var. *macrocarpa*, the cones are shaped like giant hemlock cones with rather thin, rounded scales that overlap each other like shingles. A long bract pokes out from each scale like a threeforked snake's tongue. These bracts, which protect the seeds, are visible as the cones are developing and even after the seeds have been shed and the cone is lying on the ground.

The wood of this species is esteemed for its lightness and strength, and most of the old-growth forests that graced the West 100 years ago have been transformed into buildings throughout the country. Now the forests are managed as giant farms, where the trees are cut after about 75 years and made into pulp or lumber, and the whole process starts again. Because of its adaptability, disease resistance, and strength, Douglas fir is widely planted in plantation forests throughout the world, and many of these characteristics make it a superlative tree in the cultivated landscape too. In youth the tree has a narrow, conical habit and quickly develops a wide, corky trunk. Outside the Pacific Northwest, only the Rocky Mountain form should be used, and this will grow more slowly to about 60 to 80 feet. In the 1930s, the Civilian Conservation Corps planted it occasionally in the Northeast during reforestation efforts, and I come across 50-to-60-foot trees beginning to come of age in these plantings—nothing like the growth achieved in the Northwest by var. *menziesii!*

CULTURE: Douglas fir is about as drought toler-ant as many pines, though it can survive in fairly damp locations as well. Plant it in an acidic soil and full sun away from hot pavement and dry winds. It will transplant easily when field-dug, and bareroot seedlings can be easily purchased for use in Christmas tree and forestry operations.

USES: Screen, shade.

WILDLIFE: Almost 200 species of fungi have been found to form symbiotic relationships with this tree or feed on its decaying trunks. This is indicative of the vital importance it has in its native ecosystems. Many birds and small mammals feed on the cones and nest in the branches.

PROPAGATION: Moderately difficult from cuttings, moderately easy from seed.

Quercus alba

Quercus (KWAIR-kus)
Fagaceae
Oak

I **have to admit** being a tad overwhelmed by this amazing genus. With 90 species in North America alone, oaks are our most successful and widespread group of woody plants. Oaks are generally slow growing, but planting an oak is in a sense like sowing the seeds of your own immortality by helping something to take root that will likely live for 200 years or more. In fact, there are few broad-leaved trees that will reliably grow to a venerable age like an oak. A maple may wither, a pine may break, and a poplar may be just a distant memory when the huge limbs of a mighty oak still stand triumphantly to link earth and sky. As a whole they are very determined and determinate in habit, sending out one flush of more or less lobed, leathery leaves from a cluster of buds at the tip of last year's twigs. They grow in a segmented way somewhat like pines, developing an architecture than is jointed and craggy but undeniably noble in

Quercus alba. *I'd have to say that a big, opengrown white oak, with its massive limbs stretched to embrace the sky, is one of my favorite sights. All through New England, former fencerow trees like this now stand in the middle of second-growth forest that has sprung up since agricultural lands have gone back to forest.*

age. All this begins from a large nut filled mostly by a pair of swollen cotyledons that store food to nourish a developing taproot and the first flush of leaves. The starch-rich acorns help oaks become established in difficult conditions, but they also are of incalculable value to birds and mammals, as well as to native peoples, who learned how to mash and rinse the meal to flush out tannins, which would otherwise make the food bitter and inedible.

Beyond this it is difficult to generalize, so I will elaborate further in the individual species descriptions. Though species can often be rather particular in their habitat requirements, the genus has taken advantage of just about every niche available on the continent, and related species can interbreed to form new races quite easily, further diversifying and complicating things. Basically, though, there are two groups within the genus *Quercus*: section *Lobatae* (red and black oaks) and section *Quercus* (white oaks), with a small intermediate group called the golden oaks (section *Protobalanus*), restricted mostly to California and Arizona as well as northwest Mexico. The red oak group is so named for the beautiful red heartwood that develops in many species; the trees are characterized by rough, furrowed bark, leaves with lobes or margins tipped with small pointed teeth or bristles, and acorns that mature over the course of one or two years, depending on the species. Species in the white oak group have white or brown heartwood and leaves with rounded lobes or margins that lack bristly teeth, and acorns that mature in one year. The evergreen golden oaks differ from the white oaks in that the acorns take two years to mature. I will break the species up into these groups and cover a representative cross-section. For anyone who has the interest and space to collect oak specimens there is the International Oak Society (p. 333), devoted to their study and culture.

CULTURE: With the exception of a few floodplain species, oaks are taprooted plants that resent transplanting after only a few years of age and can suffer from roots becoming circled and girdled when started in containers. For this reason, ideally they should be planted directly as vernalized acorns or 1-to-2-year-old seedlings grown in deep containers, though I have had reasonable success with balled and burlaped trees, especially those that were root-pruned a year before final digging. These need some attention for a few years (water and fertilizer) and it takes 3 to 5 years before they really settle in and begin to grow again. (They form deep sinker roots to replace the taproot.) Select a spot with well-drained soil and at least 3 to 4 hours of sun. Oaks are medium- to slow-growing trees. I planted two-year-old seedlings of northern red oak and white oak in my yard when I was 15, and now after 20 years the red oak is becoming a real tree 30 feet high while the slower-growing white oak is about half that. You can encourage more rapid height growth by removing a few of the lowest branches

each winter as well as all but the strongest leader on top. Oaks are so knitted into the fabric of life on this continent that they are fed on by myriad moths, beetles, gall insects, fungi, carpenter ants, aphids, etc., but none are really life-threatening now that gypsy moths have come under natural control (though I have recently heard of a *Phytophthora* disease that is causing serious problems for some of the California oaks).

USES: Street or shade tree, reclamation, a lasting legacy.

WILDLIFE: Mast species for ground-feeding birds like turkeys and grouse, many jays, and mammals like deer, raccoons, squirrels, bears, chipmunks, and mice or voles. The list of butterflies that feed on the leaves is remarkably long, including: white admiral, western admiral, and orange-tip admiral (*Limenitis arthemis, L. weidemeyerii,* and *L. lorquini*), sister (*Limenitis bredowii*), Chiricahua metalmark (*Emesis ares*); many hairstreaks like live-oak hairstreak (*Habrodais grunus*), Colorado hairstreak (*Hypaurotis crysalus*), Hickory hairstreak, banded hairstreak, scrub-oak hairstreak, and gold-hunter's hairstreak (*Satyrium caryaevorus, S. calanus, S. edwardsii,* and *S. auretorum*), southern oak and rounded oak hairstreaks (*Fixsenia favonius* and *F. polingi*), white-m hairstreak (*Parrhasius m-album*), and finally turquoise hairstreak (*Erora laeta*); short-tailed Arizona skipper (*Zestusa dorus*), the dusky wings—banded oak, eastern oak, gamble oak, western oak, brown, and white-edged (*Erynnis brizo, E. juvenalis, E. telemachus, E. propertius, E. horatius,* and *E. tristis*)—and, last but not least, the golf-club skipper (*Pyrrhopyge araxes*).

PROPAGATION: Moderately easy from seed.

Red Oak Group
Section *Lobatae*
(Red and Black Oaks)

Quercus agrifolia
Coast Live Oak

ZONES: 8–9; sun

SOIL: Moist

NATIVE TO: Woods and hills within the coastal fog belt of California

SIZE: Height 3–60 (90) feet, width 30–60 (150) feet

COLOR: Yellow-green; blooms in late spring

The gnarled, twisted, black-barked trunks of coast live oak are a familiar sight along the California coast, but they are finding it increasingly hard to co-exist with a burgeoning human population. Open-grown specimens develop massive, meandering limbs decked in small holly-toothed evergreen leaves and supporting a heavy coat of epiphytic mosses and

ferns. It is home to one of the only arborescent sala-
manders, which hunts for food in its canopy and
rarely ventures down to the ground. Away from the
moderate climate along the coast grows interior live
oak (*Q. wislizenii*), a smaller evergreen tree or large
shrub adapted to drier conditions.

Quercus falcata
Southern Red Oak, Spanish Oak

ZONES: 6–9; sun, part sun
SOIL: Moist to dry, well-drained
NATIVE TO: Dry or sandy uplands; southeastern New
    York to southern Illinois and Oklahoma south to
    Texas and northern Florida
SIZE: Height 60–80 (100) feet, width 30–50 feet
COLOR: Yellow-green; blooms in spring

Southern red oak is a fairly common upland species
away from the coastal plain, becoming a large, stately
canopy tree with dark brown, slightly fissured bark.
It is reasonably fast growing (12 to 18 inches a year
when young). It is a taprooted tree, but if the initial
root is wounded, it can develop sinker roots after a
few years. The leathery leaves are divided into 3 to 5
sharp, narrow lobes like those of its cousin turkey
oak (*Q. laevis*), a smaller tree found closer to the
southeastern coast.

Quercus ilicifolia
Scrub Oak, Bear Oak

ZONES: 4–7; sun to light shade
SOIL: Dry, well-drained
NATIVE TO: Sand dunes and barrens, ridges, and rocky
    outcrops; Maine to southern Ontario south to
    West Virginia and Maryland and in the
    Appalachians to North Carolina
SIZE: Height 4–10 (15) feet, width 4–12 feet
COLOR: Yellow-green; blooms in spring

Scrub oak is a familiar shrub in sandy areas of the
Northeast, especially where occasional fire keeps
down taller competitors. Like all fire-adapted oaks, it
forms a large underground burl arrayed with dozens
of dormant vegetative buds where it can store reserves
in the event of damage to the crown, at which point
fast-growing sprouts spring up and grow 2 to 3 feet in
a season, quickly retaking lost ground. Typically these
are multistem, crazy-branched shrubs with smooth,
gray bark and sharply 3-to-5-lobed leaves only about
2 inches long. The foliage has a gray-green cast—
especially below—that I find quite attractive, and the
branches can be pruned and shaped into attractive
gnarled forms. Fall color is deep red and burgundy.

Quercus imbricaria
Shingle Oak

ZONES: 4–8; sun, part sun
SOIL: Moist to moderately dry

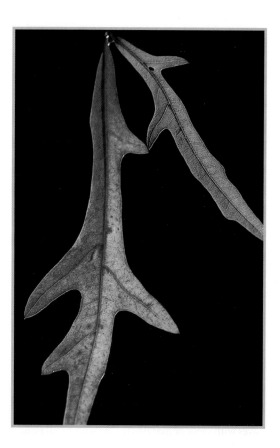

(TOP) Quercus falcata.
*The C-shaped indenta-
tions, called sinuses,
along the margin of this
southern red oak leaf
growing in the sun effec-
tively reduce its surface
area. This lessens water
loss while allowing some
sunlight to pass through
to the less deeply sinused
leaves growing toward
the center of the tree's
canopy. Notice the tiny
bristle at the tip of each
lobe, one of the distin-
guishing features of the
red oak group.*

(BOTTOM) Quercus ilici-
folia. *Developing bear
oak acorns are still
tightly cradled in their
corky caps. As the nut
matures, the cap loosens
and can be separated
with a bit of pressure
from the thumb.*

NATIVE TO: Slopes and upland forests; Pennsylvania to southern Minnesota and Iowa south to eastern Kansas, Arkansas, and western North Carolina

SIZE: Height 50–60 feet, width 25–35 feet

COLOR: Yellow-green; blooms in spring

Getting its common name from its use in making the rough shingles called shakes, *Q. imbricaria* is a distinctive oak with unlobed, glossy leaves 3 to 5 inches long and oval in outline. This small tree has a reputation for slow growth, but because it is fairly easy to transplant, I have seen it used quite successfully in parks and even some urban environments. In my experience it grows rather fast when young, putting out one or two flushes of leaves a year and forming a symmetrical pyramid of leaves on a smooth-barked, straight trunk. The foliage is deciduous, but reluctantly so, falling without appreciable fall color.

Quercus marilandica
Blackjack Oak

ZONES: 5–9; sun

SOIL: Dry

NATIVE TO: Ledges, ridge tops, old fields; southern New York and Pennsylvania to southern Illinois and Iowa, south to Texas and northern Florida

SIZE: Height 12–25 (40) feet, width 8–18 feet

COLOR: Yellow-green; blooms in spring

Blackjack oak is an unmistakable tree when in leaf, as the leaf blades swell from a narrow base to three large rounded lobes at the tip so as to appear almost triangular. The coarse foliage is shiny, dark green above and rusty brown and tomentose beneath. I have usually seen it up on dry ridges, where the twisted trunks become weathered from wind and drought and a thick, chunky bark develops to resist frequent fires. Although blackjack oak is not easy to transplant, it is a striking small tree that is worth the trouble to establish. It can find a foothold even on shallow soils overlying bedrock.

Quercus palustris
Pin Oak

ZONES: 4–8; sun, part sun

SOIL: Moist to moderately dry

NATIVE TO: Bottomlands and floodplains; Massachusetts to southern Minnesota and southern Iowa south to eastern Oklahoma, Arkansas, and North Carolina

SIZE: Height 50–80 feet, width 25–35 feet

COLOR: Yellow-green; blooms in spring

Like willow oak (*Q. phellos*), this bottomland species does not need a taproot, so it is relatively easy to transplant and is a popular street and park tree. It forms a symmetrical crown with a characteristic pattern: the lowest branches hanging down, the middle ones pointing straight out, and the highest tilted upward. In the forest, pin oak retains its straight thin-barked trunk and holds on to its dead lower branches longer than even scarlet oak, making it easy to identify among the elms, maples, and tulip poplar it shares the lowlands with. Pin oak leaves have the deep, C-shaped sinuses found in many within this section, which separate into 5 lobes splitting at their tips into smaller, bristled lobelets. Fall color ranges from red to burgundy, and can be quite pretty.

Quercus phellos
Willow Oak

ZONES: (5)6–9; sun, part sun

SOIL: Moist to moderately dry

NATIVE TO: Bottomlands, stream banks, and occasionally drier uplands; southeastern New York south along the coast to Florida, and inland to southern Illinois, Oklahoma, and Texas

SIZE: Height 60–80 (100) feet, width 30–60 feet

COLOR: Yellow-green; blooms in spring

Willow oak has very fine—2-to-4-inch-long by ½-inch-wide—deciduous leaves; an even, pyramidal form when young developing into a wide, thick-limbed crown with age; and a fibrous root system that makes transplanting even larger saplings fairly straightforward. Accordingly it is a popular street and shade tree in the Southeast and many suburban yards have been completely overtaken by a large willow oak that has outgrown its quarters. Fall color is usually yellow-orange fading to yellow-brown. Water oak (*Quercus nigra*) is a common southeastern species that looks very similar to willow oak, but its leaves are often wider toward the tip and will hang on well into winter. It is a shallow-rooted, twiggy-looking tree that looks a bit ratty by spring because of the persistent leaves, and I have noticed that mistletoe seems to prefer it over many other oaks for some reason. Laurel oak (*Q. laurifolia*) is a beautiful, wide-rounded tree of the southeastern coastal plain with willowy, semi-evergreen leaves that are wider than those of *Q. phellos*.

Quercus rubra
Northern Red Oak

ZONES: (3)4–8; sun, part sun

SOIL: Moist

NATIVE TO: Moist woodlands and slopes; Nova Scotia to southern Ontario and Minnesota south to Oklahoma, Mississippi, and Georgia

SIZE: Height 60–80 (100) feet, width 30–45 (60) feet

COLOR: Yellow-green; blooms in spring

The fastest growing of the northeastern oaks, *Quercus rubra* is one of the most important lumber trees in the region. Its heartwood is a rich, pinkish red (in fact, I am writing on a table I made from some beautiful red oak cut nearby in the Blackstone Valley). It develops channeled, silver-gray bark with lines of pink underbark visible in the cracks, especially when wet. As with most oaks the twigs are dark gray, and as I look out the window at snow melting off the branches, it occurs to me that dark branches make sense in a cold climate as they absorb more heat and melt off snow loads more quickly. The leaves are sectioned into 7 to 9 lobes separated by a U-shaped sinus, and each of these lobes is bristled by a few pointed (not sharp) teeth. Fall color is a rich mahogany most years. Red oak prefers better soils than its relatives black oak (Q. velutina), which has darker, scalier bark and leaves that are wider toward the tip, and scarlet oak (Q. coccinea), a smoother-barked tree with brilliant red fall color—one of the best for color in the genus. Both black oak and scarlet oak are common trees of ridges and upland forests throughout the East. They retain their dead lower branches much longer than red oak. I devised a way of telling red oak saplings from black oak and scarlet oak in my forestry days: if you whack the dead lower branches with a stick, they break off cleanly at the trunk if its Q. rubra, and come away rough and stubby if one of the others.

White Oak Group
Section *Quercus*

Quercus alba
White Oak

ZONES: (3)4–9; sun, part sun
SOIL: Moist to dry
NATIVE TO: Bottomlands, slopes, upland forests, ridges, sandy scrublands; Maine to southern Quebec, Ontario, and Minnesota south to eastern Texas and northern Florida
SIZE: Height 60–80 (100) feet, width 30–40 (70) feet
COLOR: Yellow-green; blooms in spring

I think white oak has always been my favorite tree, or at the very least in the top five. There is nothing more

picturesque than an open-grown white oak with its huge, twisted limbs and massive trunk clothed in warm gray shaggy bark. It is one of the most adaptable oaks, growing everywhere from the margins of swamps to dry ridges and stabilized dunes. In the Southeast, especially, it can grow a towering straight trunk that rivals the height of loblolly pine or even tulip poplar, ending with a flattened oval crown hung with leaves deeply scalloped into 6 to 8 rounded lobes. The blade is blue-green above and lighter below, and in fall it takes on a wine red or sometimes scarlet glow before eventually falling. Like all good things, though, white oak doesn't hurry, typically losing ground to faster-growing trees and biding its time in the middle canopy for decades before a gap opens up and it heads for the light. It is not easy to transplant, though I have moved 3-to-5-year-old containerized plants with good success and I'll continue to plant them, even though I will likely never see them reach full, glorious maturity unless some great advances in health care can extend my life for another 100 years. Overcup oak (Q. lyrata) is a southeastern U.S. species with leaves and bark much like white oak's except that the lobes of the leaves are slightly pointed. The cup on the acorn grows completely over the nut, leading me to think of it scandalously as the uncircumcised oak. Usually this is a small tree of swamps and wet, stick-in-the-mud woods.

Quercus bicolor
Swamp White Oak

ZONES: 4–8; sun, part sun
SOIL: Moist to wet
NATIVE TO: Swamp forests and floodplains; Maine and southern Quebec to Minnesota south to Missouri, Tennessee, and North Carolina
SIZE: Height 60–80 (100) feet, width 30–40 feet
COLOR: Yellow-green; blooms in spring

Swamp white oak looks like a cross between white oak (warm gray, shaggy, plated bark) and chestnut oak (oval, scalloped leaves). Like wetland species in the red oak group, it has a fibrous root system that makes it easier to transplant. It is not at all drought tolerant, but it can grow in heavy, poorly oxygenated soils. It grows slowly into a large oval, then rounded shape.

Quercus garryana
Oregon White Oak

ZONES: 7–9; sun
SOIL: Moist, well-drained
NATIVE TO: Open woodlands and mixed forests; British Columbia south to southern California
SIZE: Height 15–60 feet, width 15–40 feet
COLOR: Yellow-green; blooms in spring

Quercus alba. *Unlike the southern red oak pictured on page 207, this white oak leaf has no bristles at the tips of its rounded lobes.*

In rain-shadow areas of the Pacific Northwest, conifers give way to the Oregon white oak, which grows as an oval or rounded small tree with a lot of character. In the Willamette Valley of central Oregon, these trees are hung with great drapes of old man's beard *(Usnea)* and fishnet *(Ramalina menziesii)* lichens much the way live oaks are hung with Spanish moss in the Southeast. They have a shaggy, warm gray bark and round-lobed leaves like *Q. alba*'s. Shrub forms of this species with all parts reduced are called var. *semota* and var. *breweri*.

Quercus macrocarpa

Bur Oak, Mossy-cup Oak

ZONES: 3–9; sun, part sun

SOIL: Moist to dry

NATIVE TO: Prairies, bottomlands, typically over limestone; New Brunswick to Manitoba south to southeastern Montana, Texas, Louisiana, Tennessee, and Virginia

SIZE: Height 40–80 (120) feet, width 40–60 feet

COLOR: Yellow-green; blooms in spring

Quercus virginiana. *This image really speaks for itself. A massive old Gulf Coast live oak bearded with silver shocks of Spanish moss* (Tillandsia usneoides) *is one of the most evocative sights one could hope to find.*

Bur oak looks very similar to white oak in the color and slough of its bark, but its leaves have a couple of deep lobes toward the middle and a fan of shallow lobes toward the tip. The name mossy-cup oak comes from the tasseled fringe that decorates the big cap nearly concealing the acorn just like a too-large winter hat. This is the preeminent tree of the tall-grass prairies. Seedlings grow up and get burned back over and over again, slowly forming a huge burl; these burls astonished settlers trying to clear the land when they attempted to eradicate what looked like a little seedling and discovered a huge underground root not easily dislodged. During a wet cycle, when the prairie doesn't burn for 10 years, these patient oaks grow steadily upward, eventually growing up over the quick-moving flames and maturing into huge, wide-spreading trees. Now that fire suppression is the norm, bur oak glades are much more abundant in the prairie states.

Quercus montana (prinus)

Chestnut Oak

ZONES: 4–8; sun, part sun

SOIL: Moist to dry, well-drained

NATIVE TO: Rocky woods, cliffs; Maine and eastern Ohio south mainly in the Appalachians to Arkansas and Georgia

SIZE: Height 60–80 (100) feet, width 25–45 feet

COLOR: Yellow-green; blooms in spring

Chestnut oak is a common tree on the trap-rock ridges of central Connecticut where I grew up. It has a deeply channeled, purplish brown bark that is very easy to distinguish, and this thick bark travels up even to the medium-size branches—I imagine it helps protect the tree against fire. The 3-to-6-inch-long broadly oval leaves are neatly scalloped and flattened in such a way that they catch the light quite beautifully so that the crown looks emerald when you look up from underneath. It is closely related to and sometimes combined as one species with *Q. michauxii* (basket oak), which grows in damp to wet soils throughout the Southeast. Basket oak has larger acorns, over an inch thick, that are nearly covered by a large, shaggy cap; longer leaves that widen more toward the middle and are covered with loose felt below; and a bark that lacks deep V-shaped channels. Because herbarium specimens of both species have been labeled *Quercus prinus*, this name is no longer valid for chestnut oak. Chinkapin oak *(Q. muehlenbergii)* is yet another widespread eastern species in this group, with longer, thinner leaves very much like chestnut oak's in shape and color. It grades into the scrubby little dwarf chinkapin oak *(Q. prinoides)*, the only small, shrubby white oak in the East. This prefers acidic rather than the alkaline soils favored by its larger sibling, and it grows side by side with scrub oak in sand barrens from New England to Georgia and Texas. As a side note, an interesting natural hybrid between *Q. montana* and the English oak (*Q. robur),* called Sargent oak (*Q.* × *sargentii),* occurs sometimes where *Q. robur* has been planted or has escaped. It has the deep, furrowed bark of *Q. montana,* the picturesque, wide-spreading crown of *Q. robur,* and branch scars that pucker over in a strange, animistic way like giant eyelids. I have seen other white oak group hybrids occasionally in the wild, but they always lack vigor. This one is vigorous and it comes true from seed. The Arnold Arboretum has a beautiful specimen.

Quercus stellata
Post Oak

ZONES: 5–9; sun
SOIL: Dry, well-drained
NATIVE TO: Dry ridges and poor upland forests; Massachusetts to Illinois and southern Iowa south to Texas and Florida
SIZE: Height 25–50 (80) feet, width 20–30 feet
COLOR: Yellow-green; blooms in spring

Post oak is the white oak group equivalent of blackjack oak. The two grow together on dry ridges, and this species also has glossy leaves flaring into 3 wide lobes toward the tip that are rusty brown underneath. It is a scrubby tree that can occasionally get to be pretty large on a better site. Sand post oak (*Q. margaretta)* is basically a reduced, almost shrubby form that grows along the southeastern coastal plain from Virginia to Oklahoma and Texas.

Quercus virginiana
Southern Live Oak

ZONES: 7–9; sun, part sun
SOIL: Moist to moderately dry, well-drained
NATIVE TO: Hummocks and scrublands mostly along the coast; Virginia to Florida and Texas
SIZE: Height 40–80 (110) feet, width 30–60 feet
COLOR: Yellow-green; blooms in spring

The low-slung branches of an old live oak draped with long gray beards of Spanish moss and other bromeliads is the essence of the Deep South. This is a wide-spreading, mostly evergreen tree with small, oval leaves more or less lobed and toothed along the margins, though this varies from leaf to leaf and plant to plant. The upper surface is somewhat glossy and dark green and the lower, a rusty gray. It is easily transplanted and is much used as a street tree. The crown starts off sort of haywire, growing very quickly and sending out long twigs here and there on several flushes of growth per season, but after 15 years the tree settles down and begins to develop its alligator bark and fashions itself into an incomparable specimen. In sandy soils along the immediate coast, the trees are smaller—really just big, rounded shrubs most of the time. These are the closely related sand

live oak (*Q. geminata).* Interestingly, this and the other southern live oaks form a fleshy underground tuber from the cotyledons that fill the acorn. I have grown up seedlings of *Q. geminata* for bonsai, and these tubers make for interesting bases if you set them half in the ground. (Unfortunately, the twiggy growth habit of this species doesn't adapt well to the well-clipped ideal of the bonsai. You might call it bad-hair-day bonsai.) A third species, dwarf live oak (*Q. minima),* is more like an evergreen scrub oak, and it can spread around rhizomatously on stabilized dunes.

Golden Oaks Group
Section *Protobalanus*

Quercus chrysolepis
Canyon Live Oak

ZONES: 7–9; sun, part sun
SOIL: Moist to summer-dry
NATIVE TO: Ridges, canyons, and slopes; southwestern Oregon through California and Arizona to northern Mexico
SIZE: Height 10–35 (70) feet, width 10–40 feet
COLOR: Yellow-green; blooms in spring

This lustrous evergreen species looks like many of the eastern live oaks with its stiff leaves and ability to put out several flushes of growth in a good season to quickly form a rounded crown. Over its wide range, it is variable in size and leaf shape, becoming more shrublike in drier regions and a large tree in the foothills of the Sierras, where rainfall is higher. Leaves can range from lance-shaped to hollylike, sometimes on the same tree, but all the leaves are covered on the underside by a rich, rusty-felty indumentum that slows water loss and makes an attractive contrast with the glossy dark green above. Huckleberry oak (*Q. vaccinifolia)* grows at higher elevations in the Sierras, and becomes shrubby and almost a prostrate groundcover where harsh winds prevail. Palmer oak (*Q. palmeri)* lies between these two extremes, usually a shrub 4 to 8 feet high and wide with small, holly-pointed evergreen leaves.

Rhododendron atlanticum. *A good choice for smaller spaces, coast azalea becomes a 2- to 3-foot mound of blue-green leaves liberally studded with soft, fragrant, pink and white flowers.*

Rhododendron

(ro-doe-DEN-dron)

Ericaceae

Rhododendron, Azalea

For sheer eye-fluttering, spine-tingling beauty, it is hard to beat rhododendrons. Their large, trussed-up trumpets come in every shade of the rainbow save true green or blue, and these are displayed triumphantly on plants with a segmented architecture that is lovely in itself, flowers or no flowers. To make sense of this large and diverse group of plants, it helps to break them down into three sections. Lepidote (small-leaf) rhododendrons have small scales on their young stems and the leaf undersides. They are typically alpine species with relatively small evergreen leaves and in our flora are represented by only the *R. minus* complex and the little circumboreal *R. lapponicum.* Elepidote (large-leaf) rhododendrons are mostly forest plants with larger, evergreen leaves lacking scales. These are the archetypal rhododendrons. In our flora, *R. maximum, R. catawbiense,* and *R. macrophyllum* fall into this category. Finally there are the azaleas, which have (at least among our native species) deciduous leaves often more or less covered in sparse, bristly hairs, and flowers with 5 instead of 10 stamens. This is by far our largest native group, and most azaleas are fairly closely related and thus freely interbreed. The only exceptions are *R. canadense* and *R. vaseyi,* which are in their own section, and the unique *R. albiflorum,* which is not closely related to any of the others.

All rhododendrons form scaly, swollen terminal flower buds during the growing season that expand the following year into a "truss" or dome of large, colorful flowers. The petals fuse more or less into a funnel or bell narrowing to a base that surrounds the immature ovary. When a flower is pollinated, the whole bell falls away, first sliding over the long stamens and pistil before dropping to the ground. Vegetative buds are smaller but clustered at the tip as well, and these flush a single set of leaves in spring. Most species tend to concentrate their leaves toward the tips of the twig so they appear whorled, though vigorous shoots and suckers, especially on azaleas, have leaves alternating along most of their length. These vigorous sprouts can grow indeterminately as long as summer permits, so that new stems come along quickly to bolster or replace the existing crown. The evergreen species can produce fast-growing suckers as well, but usually do this only after the crown has been badly damaged or removed.

These are plants of acidic, nutrient-poor soils that develop in cool humid climates. The ancient Appa-lachian Mountains provide the perfect moist, humid atmosphere for these plants to thrive, and just as important, a damp, mossy seedbed for the seedlings to establish in. Rhododendrons are classic "moss-germinators": small-seeded, fine-rooted plants that have come to depend on mosses to provide a constantly damp, nutrient-poor environment for the seedlings to germinate on, root into, and begin to grow. Since mosses are small themselves and need light to photosynthesize, they grow only in places where fallen leaves don't settle, such as on old logs and stumps or rocks; fallen leaves would also smother a small seedling. In less water-saturated climates, rhododendrons tend to be restricted to swamps and swamp margins only because this is the best place to find damp, mossy carpets. As members of the heath family (Ericaceae) they employ mycorrhizal fungi that are very adept at scavenging nitrogen. In addition, they can actually inhibit the growth of mycorrhizal fungi needed by trees of various genera. This is one of the main reasons that treeless heathlands can develop and be maintained to the obvious benefit of the rhododendrons and their relatives.

CULTURE: As a rule, damp, organic soil with a pH of 4.0 to 6.0 is best. The rhododendrons grow best in a cool, humid, rainy climate as found in the Northeast, Northwest, and the higher elevations of the Southeast. The azaleas are the most adaptable, and the lower-elevation species do very well in the Piedmont and coastal plain of the Southeast. In the upper Midwest, high pH becomes a problem, but if you have acidic soils, you should be able to grow most of the species. Flowering will be better with at least a few hours of sun, but virtually all rhododendrons are very shade tolerant, so they make perfect understory shrubs. Interestingly, a fertile, nutrient-rich soil will inhibit the growth of ericaceous mycorrhizal fungi, and chemicals released by the roots of the plants that would normally be neutralized by the fungus can become poisonous. This, as well as a natural sensitivity to high levels of fertilizer salts, explains the "fertilizer burn" one often sees on rhododendrons suffering under the too-generous hand of a gardener or nursery person. Once rhododendrons are established, a yearly addition of organic mulch is the best fertilizer, as this will nourish rather than inhibit fungal activity. All species can be occasionally rejuvenated through selective removal of old or weakened stems during the dormant season, which will result in a surge of new growth from the roots.

Both the root-chewing larva of the black vine weevil (*Otiorhynchus sulcatus*) and the leaf-nibbling adults can be a problem with some evergreen rhododendrons, but in my experience the native species seem generally resistant. Some of the azaleas, especially *R. prinophyllum*, are defoliated by green fruitworms (*Lithophane antennata*), a rusty orange native moth whose caterpillars can attack buds and newly expanded leaves. Other problems, like azalea galls and stem borers, can be controlled by judicious removal of infected tissue if they become a problem.

USES: Specimen, shrub borders, foundations, naturalizing in the woodland understory.

PROPAGATION: Moderately easy to difficult from cuttings, moderately easy from seed.

Azaleas

Aside from *R. canadense*, *R. vaseyi*, and *R. albiflorum*, the azaleas are a group of distinct but closely related species that are approximately similar in growth habit: they form multistem suckering clumps with older stems growing up to height quickly, then branching out to form a rounded crown over a narrow base. Many azaleas are pollinated by hummingbirds and all have long, exserted stamens and a longer pistil that curls out and up from the corolla, which tends to be flatter and less bell-like than those of the evergreen species. With the three exceptions noted above, azaleas are highly interfertile, and in the wild, sympatric species are prevented from hybridizing mainly by their different bloom times. Thus, if you develop a collection of different species, you can have plants in bloom from early spring almost continuously until late summer or early fall.

Rhododendron albiflorum
White-flowered Azalea

ZONES: 4–6; sun to light shade
SOIL: Moist, cold, acidic
NATIVE TO: Stream sides and damp slopes, mainly subalpine; Montana to British Columbia and Oregon
SIZE: Height 2–6 feet, width 2–4 feet
COLOR: White; blooms in spring

When I first saw this plant in the wilds of the Oregon Cascades, I didn't recognize it as a rhododendron. It is a striking plant with lance-shaped, medium green deciduous leaves and 1¼-inch bell-shaped, rounded flowers that come not from the stem tips as in other species, but singly or in pairs from the axils lower down on the stem so that the blooms skirt the naked stems. It is very difficult, if not impossible, to grow, except in the cold, wet climate it prefers. It blooms when there is still snow in patches around its roots and is in leaf for only a couple of months before winter returns.

Rhododendron arborescens
Smooth Azalea, Sweet Azalea

ZONES: 5–8; sun to light shade
SOIL: Moist, acidic
NATIVE TO: Stream banks, moist wooded slopes; New York to Kentucky, south to Alabama and Georgia
SIZE: Height 5–10 (20) feet, width 4–8 feet
COLOR: White; blooms in early summer (occasionally later)

Smooth azalea is one of the most deliciously scented plants in my garden. It grows fairly fast into a rather large, rounded shrub with glossy, oval deciduous leaves and flowers that are pure white and redolent with the odor of vanilla and jasmine. The flowers are 1½ inches long with a long tube and blood red style and filaments, which creates a subtle but lovely contrast with the intensely white blooms framed against dark green foliage. Most plants bloom about the same time as *R. cumberlandense*, and seed grown from mixed plantings of these two species yields lovely peach and apricot, mostly fragrant, hybrids.

Rhododendron atlanticum
Coast Azalea

ZONES: (5)6–9; sun, part sun
SOIL: Moist, acidic
NATIVE TO: Hammocks, barrens, and moist woods along the coastal plain; Delaware to Georgia
SIZE: Height 18–36 inches, width 2–3 feet
COLOR: White tinged with pink; blooms in spring and occasionally again in fall

Coast azalea is an utterly charming smaller azalea that forms a dense, slowly expanding mound of narrow, glabrous, blue-green leaves. The buds and especially the tubular base of the flower are usually pink, opening to reveal a pure white interior, so the contrast of pink and white on a partially open truss is soft and pretty. The flowers have a light, sweet fragrance. Unfortunately, this species is only marginally hardy at Garden in the Woods, and it tends to wane and wax after hard and gentle winters, respectively. Coast azalea prefers a damp spot with more sun than some of the other rhododendrons. Alabama azalea (*R. alabamense*) is a relative with similar leaves and low, spreading habit from rocky woods in northern central Alabama and western central Georgia. The flowers — a fragrant blend of white, yellow and pink with a dark yellow splotch on the uppermost petal — open in early summer. It is hardy in Zones 7 to 9.

Rhododendron calendulaceum
Flame Azalea

ZONES: 4–8; sun to light shade

SOIL: Moist to moderately dry, acidic

NATIVE TO: Moist woods, slopes, stream banks; mostly in the Appalachian Mountains from Pennsylvania to Ohio, south to Alabama and northern Georgia

SIZE: Height 8–15 feet, width 5–8 feet

COLOR: Yellow through orange and red; blooms in spring

Flame azalea has the largest flowers of any of the native azaleas — each bloom 2 inches across and 2½ inches long, forming a big, ruffled trumpet. It is remarkably variable in flower color, though apricot

orange-yellow is typical and red the least common. Unfortunately, the flowers are only slightly fragrant. It is a tall, arching, many-stemmed shrub with a narrow, nonrunning base and a wide oval top. This is one of the backbone shrubs in our gardens — truly magnificent in flower. The leaves are about 4 to 5 inches long, oval, and light green in color. As with all the azaleas, in some years they can turn brilliant reds and maroons before falling. Florida azalea (*R. austrinum*) is a close relative from the southeastern coastal plain (Georgia to Florida and Mississippi) with smaller, earlier flowers of light apricot with a darker blotch. The flowers emerge before the leaves. It has a similar habit, fragrant flowers, and is a better choice in the Deep South; it is hardy in Zones 6 to 7. Oconee azalea (*R. flammeum*) is a smaller shrub from the Piedmont and coast of South Carolina, Florida, and Alabama with fragrant orange-red to crimson flowers that open between the bloom times of the other two in spring. It is hardy in Zones 7 to 9.

Rhododendron canadense
Rhodora

ZONES: 3–6; sun, part sun

SOIL: Moist to wet, cool, acidic

NATIVE TO: Low woods, bogs, and shores; Labrador to Quebec south to New York, Pennsylvania, and New Jersey

SIZE: Height 2–4 feet, width 2–4 feet

COLOR: Bright purple, occasionally white or light purple; blooms in early spring

This most northern of the azaleas blooms well before the leaves have emerged on naked, dark gray stems. These stems never get too big, as new ones are continually coming from the base and branching in a stiff, upright way so that the whole is a twiggy, mounded plant. The flowers have 5 separate petals. The uppermost one is the widest; it is flanked by two others that reflex back on either side; and two others splay out below. It needs a cool, humid climate to thrive, but it grows extremely well in the Garden in damp soil and partial sun, blooming profusely every year.

(LEFT) Rhododendron calendulaceum. *Flame azalea is one of the backbone shrubs in our Woodland Garden. Its large stature and luxuriant orange, yellow, or nearly red flowers contrast spectacularly with the predominant violets, blues, and whites of the wildflowers blooming beneath.*

(RIGHT) Rhododendron canadense. *For reasons I do not understand, rhodora and its closest relative, Rhododendron vaseyi, set copious viable seed every year without fail, whereas I have to hand-pollinate the flame and swamp azaleas to guarantee a decent crop of seeds.*

Rhododendron canescens
Piedmont Azalea

ZONES: 6–9; sun to light shade
SOIL: Moist, acidic
NATIVE TO: Moist woodlands, stream sides, pocosins; North Carolina to Arkansas and eastern Oklahoma south to eastern Texas and Florida
SIZE: Height 6–8 (15) feet, width 3–6 feet
COLOR: White and pink; blooms in spring

Piedmont azalea was the common woodland azalea around my home in Durham, North Carolina, and indeed through much of the central South. It is allied to pinxterbloom azalea (*R. periclymenoides*), and has the same wandering, stoloniferous tendencies, though its small, rounded leaves are more blue-green in color. The lightly fragrant flowers have a long, narrow tube and petals that curl back along the midvein. The tube is usually dark pink fading to white at the flair with pink again in the filaments, and the flowers form a ring, not a dome. This creates an interesting electric-wagon-wheel effect.

Rhododendron cumberlandense (bakeri)
Cumberland Azalea, Baker's Flame Azalea

ZONES: (4)5–7; sun to light shade
SOIL: Moist, acidic
NATIVE TO: Moist woods at higher elevations, mostly in the Cumberland Mountains from Kentucky to Tennessee and northern Georgia and western North Carolina
SIZE: Height 3–5 feet, width 3–4 feet
COLOR: Crimson to orange-red; late spring to early summer

A striking azalea, and one of my true favorites. It blooms just as spring turns to summer, when its glossy, dark green leaves are already fully expanded to set off the big, crimson claret cups. Its petals roll back a bit but they form the same, full, rounded trusses as flame azalea. It is reliably smaller in stature, decidedly clumping and narrowly upright-oval, and does well in New England, so I like to use it in foundation plantings and other situations where the larger azaleas would overwhelm. Flowers are not fragrant.

Rhododendron occidentale
Western Azalea

ZONES: (6)7–9; sun to light shade
SOIL: Moist, acidic
NATIVE TO: Coastal redwood belt from southwestern Oregon to central California
SIZE: Height 3–8 (15) feet, width 3–6 feet
COLOR: Combinations of white, yellow, pink, and red; blooms in spring

Growing in the cool, damp fog belt under redwoods along with coast rhododendron (*R. macrophyllum*), *R. occidentale* is the only Pacific Northwestern azalea. The typical flowers have a candy-cane quality in their dark pinkish red tubes, light pink petals with darker veins, and streaks and spots of yellow on the uppermost petal. The leaves are deep green, narrowly spoon-shaped, and come out with or after the flowers. Although it is deservedly popular in Europe, on this continent it does not thrive outside the Pacific Northwest. The blooms have a strong, musky sweet fragrance.

Rhododendron periclymenoides (nudiflorum)
Pinxterbloom Azalea

ZONES: 4–8; sun to light shade
SOIL: Moist, acid
NATIVE TO: Moist woods, stream sides; Massachusetts to New York and Ohio south to eastern Kentucky, northern Alabama, and northern Georgia
SIZE: Height 3–8 feet, width 3–5 feet
COLOR: Light to dark pink; blooms in spring

Pinxterbloom azalea grows abundantly in the woods of southern New England as well as on down the spine of the Appalachians, and I loved its little pink flowers even before I knew what an azalea was. The flower's typical color and shape are like those of Piedmont azalea, though the floral tube is shorter, and, as with Piedmont azalea, it is easy to find light as well as dark pink forms in the woods. It has a faint, honeysuckle fragrance; small, light green, oval, round-tipped leaves; and a spreading, stoloniferous habit when it's happy. Rose-shell azalea (*R. prinophyllum* [*R. roseum*]) is basically the northern extension of the species, overlapping pinxterbloom in the South, becoming more common as you move north,

Rhododendron cumberlandense. *Cumberland azalea is one of my personal favorites. It is a shrub of moderate stature with deep green, glossy leaves that are an ideal foil for the large, red-hot flowers that appear toward the very end of spring.*

and replacing it in central New England up into Quebec and northern Ohio. It has wider, slightly bluer leaves and darker pink flowers with a penetratingly sweet perfume—the strongest of any of the spring-blooming azaleas.

Rhododendron prunifolium
Plumleaf Azalea

ZONES: 5–9; sun to light shade

SOIL: Moist, acidic

NATIVE TO: Damp ravines and stream sides, southwestern Georgia and eastern Alabama

SIZE: Height 4–8 (15) feet, width 4–6 feet

COLOR: Light or dark orange red; blooms in late summer

Plumleaf azalea is native to Georgia and Alabama, but given its southern provenance, this wonderful species has proved fairly hardy and adaptable. Its chief claim to fame is a habit of holding its flower buds clear through spring and a good part of the summer before finally unfurling the hot-colored blooms (not fragrant) in the languid days of summer. The petals are smaller and less ruffled than the spring-blooming flame azaleas, and it is a spectacular thing to have come into flower in the shade garden during this overpoweringly green time of year. As with the other orange species, the stamens, too, are dyed this color. Leaves are oval, medium green; the habit is clumping and upright-rounded.

Rhododendron vaseyi
Pinkshell Azalea

ZONES: (4)5–8; sun to light shade

SOIL: Moist to moderately dry

Rhododendron prunifolium. *It is quite remarkable, in the dog days of summer, to be strolling through the shade garden and come across a blazing orange azalea in full regalia. Such is the magic of plumleaf azalea.*

NATIVE TO: Cliffs, balds, and forest gaps at high elevations in the Appalachians of North Carolina

SIZE: Height 4–8 (10) feet, width 4–7 feet

COLOR: Light pink, occasionally dark pink or white; blooms in early spring

Like the rhodora (*R. canadense*), this elegant azalea puts forth its shell pink blooms before the leaves in early spring and is the first of the azaleas to bloom at the Garden. The petals are not fully fused together into a trumpet, so each rounded petal tip rolls back (reflexes) to give the bloom a flatter, more asymmetrical profile. The foliage is long and lance-shaped, medium to dark green, and holds up very well to powdery mildew, which can partially defoliate many azaleas in a rainy summer. Thus the leaves survive to reliably develop a good red-maroon fall color. In habit it is a nonstoloniferous, wide-oval shrub. The rarity of this species has always perplexed me, because it is about the easiest and most vigorous one we grow, tolerating a good bit of drought and swampy muck and seeding itself around a bit too. *R. vaseyi* does not cross with other species, but it sets very good crops of seed for me every year.

Rhododendron viscosum
Swamp Azalea, Stickybud Azalea

ZONES: 4–9; sun to light shade

SOIL: Moist to wet

NATIVE TO: Wooded and open swamps, stream sides; Maine to Ohio south to southeastern Texas and Florida

SIZE: Height 4–10 (15) feet, width 3–5 feet

COLOR: White to pink; blooms in summer

When swamp azalea comes into bloom, its honeysuckle-clove fragrance drifts through humid air like an elixir. It is a small-leaved plant, with blades variously glaucous or glossy green and small flowers equipped with very long tubes seemingly out of proportion with the narrow corolla. I imagine moths must visit this plant at night, though bees certainly buzz it during the day. The anther filaments and style vary from white to a rich, purply red. Hammocksweet azalea (*R. serrulatum*) is a southeastern coastal plain species that has been separated from *R. viscosum* mainly because it blooms later—as late as early fall. It is hardy in Zones (6)7 to 9.

Evergreen Rhododendrons
Rhododendron catawbiense
Catawba Rhododendron

ZONES: (4)5–8; sun to shade

SOIL: Moist to moderately dry, acidic

NATIVE TO: Bluffs and balds in the southern Appalachians and rarely in the Piedmont; Virginia to Kentucky south to Alabama and Georgia

SIZE: Height 4–10 (18) feet, width 5–12 feet

COLOR: Violet pink; blooms in spring

Though in the wild this robust, bold-leaved rhododendron is restricted to rocky woods and summits, its progeny, and especially myriad hybrids like 'Roseum Elegans' and 'English Roseum', have been used extensively in landscape plantings elsewhere. It is a very tough and adaptable shrub in moderate climes, though it needs careful siting (a cool, moist but well-drained acid soil) at lower elevations in the Southeast and in the Midwest. Catawba rhododendron has revolute (rolled-under) leaf margins, making it very easy to distinguish it from *R. maximum,* which has flatter leaves. Like all evergreen rhododendrons, the leaves curl up like cinnamon sticks when the temperature drops below freezing because they lack guard cells on their leaves to close off the stomatal pores; rolling up the blade is the next best measure to limit water loss. Flowers are displayed in big puffy trusses just as the new leaves are starting to emerge, and a plant in full regalia is almost overwhelming in its purplishness. The leaves are tawny fading to deep satin green. Seeing this species in full bloom up on the rolling Appalachian balds is an experience everyone deserves to have at least once.

Rhododendron macrophyllum
Coast Rhododendron, Pacific Rhododendron

ZONES: 7–9; sun to light shade

SOIL: Moist, acidic

NATIVE TO: Coastal and middle-elevation wet forests; southwestern British Columbia south to northern California

SIZE: Height 6–12 feet, width 6–10 feet

COLOR: Light to very dark pink; blooms in spring

In the middle Cascades and along the coastal redwood belt, you can commonly see this rather stiff or stilted, upright shrub forming an impenetrable understory at the edge of the forest — it has that look of a nervous person with his shoulders all hunched up. It has long, thin leaves and big clusters of relatively small flowers coming with the tawny new growth. In the Pacific Northwest, where it can be grown well, enthusiasts have selected many color forms.

Rhododendron maximum
Rosebay, Great Laurel

ZONES: 4–8; sun to shade

SOIL: Moist to moderately dry

NATIVE TO: Mountain forests and swamps; eastern Maine and southern Ontario to Pennsylvania, Tennessee, and northern Georgia

SIZE: Height 6–10 (25) feet, width 4–15 (25) feet

COLOR: Pink; blooms in early summer

With its big, drooping donkey's-ear leaves and dainty pink flowers, rosebay is an unmistakable plant. It is the most cold-hardy of the bigleaf rhododendrons, but reaches true luxuriance in the southern Appalachians, where every hill is covered with an understory of rosebay. The stems tend to collapse under snow and falling debris, then layer in and start a new trunk so that in time you are presented with an impenetrable serpentine tangle, a "laurel hell" nearly impossible to get through. Rosebay has a taller, lanki-

(LEFT) Rhododendron catawbiense. *Combining a show-stopping floral display, adaptability, good evergreen foliage, and excellent winter hardiness, Catawba rhododendron and its hybrids have become a staple of the landscape industry.*

(RIGHT) Rhododendron maximum. *In many parts of the Northeast, overpopulation of whitetail deer is threatening stands of rosebay. Deer will eat rhododendrons only when their other food supplies are exhausted, which is inevitable when populations grow beyond the carrying capacity of the land. In winter, deer like to yard or herd in the sheltered swamps preferred by rosebay, which is within easy reach for a midnight snack.*

er habit than *R. catawbiense,* especially in shade, but it is a great plant for screening and for naturalizing and it can bloom in heavier shade than almost any other *Rhododendron* species.

Rhododendron minus

Piedmont Rhododendron, Carolina Rhododendron

ZONES: (4)5–8(9); sun to light shade
SOIL: Moist to moderately dry
NATIVE TO: Stream banks and moist slopes; North Carolina to Tennessee, south to Georgia and northwest Florida
SIZE: Height 3–8 feet, width 4–10 feet
COLOR: Rose-violet, occasionally white; blooms in spring to late spring (see text)

Until recently, there were three related lepidote rhododendrons in the Southeast, *R. carolinianum, R. chapmanii,* and *R. minus,* but these have now been combined as *R. minus.* All have leathery, dull green leaves oval in outline with pointed tips. They spread slowly but surely to form large colonies of individual stems. Carolina rhododendron (var. *carolinianum*) is the first to bloom, opening its small but dense, ruffled trusses in midspring. It is also the largest form, easily becoming a wide mound 8 to 10 feet high and half again as wide. Concurrently or soon after comes Chapman's rhododendron (var. *chapmanii*), a less winter-hardy variety from the Florida Panhandle that is usually lighter in color. Finally, as spring is beginning to wane, Piedmont rhododendron (var. *minus*) opens its little lilac blooms down among the new leaves, where they are harder to see. This is the smallest in stature, growing only 3 to 4 feet high in my experience.

Rhus typhina. *Staghorn sumac develops exceptional fall color. As in most leaves, the color develops first at the margins and proceeds gradually toward the center, which is closer to nourishing veins and thus lives longer.*

Rhus (ROOS)
Anacardiaceae
Sumac

Sumacs definitely have an image problem. Even though taxonomists have graciously removed the infamous poison oak, poison ivy, and poison sumac to their own dastardly genus, *Toxicodendron* (see box, p. 220), sumacs are still considered by most people to be roadside weeds of little horticultural value. (Interestingly, the father of modern taxonomy himself, Carolus Linnaeus, was given a twig of poison ivy and one of fragrant sumac, and mistook them for the same thing, which he labeled *Rhus toxicodendron*— a name that became nomenclaturally invalid for this reason.) So, the sumacs have hired me as an image consultant, and I will do my best. Borrowing from Ian Frasier ("Tomorrow's Bird," *DoubleTake,* Fall 2000), I

have come up with a slogan: "Rhus: We want to be your *only* shrub," and an acronym: SUMACS, for Sexy, Undemanding, Mellifluous, Appropriate, Colorful Shrubs.

Sexy? Most sumacs have fine, pinnate foliage that hangs palmlike and alluringly from thick, masculine branches jutting up like antlers ready for the rut, and cultivars like *R. typhina* 'Laciniata' display foliage as intricately cut and lacy as the finest lingerie. *Undemanding?* These are successional plants adapted for life in the worst possible conditions. They can survive drought, fire, and infertile soils while fending off diseases and insects with ease. While they do tend to wander (or, as we like to say at SUMACS, display a healthy curiosity about the surrounding landscape), this can work to your advantage in places where there is a lot of desperate ground to cover or vulnerable, bare soil to protect. *Mellifluous?* The sumacs suggested this one, and I'll admit I had to look it up —it means smooth or honeyed—but it works. Sumacs flower from the ends of the new growth after the leaves have matured a rich, glossy green. The flowers themselves are respectfully petite, 5-petaled affairs bunched in large, dense clusters. They are superlative nectar plants, providing bees as well as an assortment of other insects with a ready midsummer feast. *Appropriate? Rhus* species are important mem-

Rhus typhina

bers of the ecosystem, colonizing open ground and altruistically paving the way for trees to become established that will eventually overtop them and spell their end. They look much more appropriate and connected in a successional landscape or woodland edge than any of the invasive species — such as tree of heaven, multiflora rose, empress tree, or Scotch broom—that would try to displace them.

Color? Herein lies perhaps their greatest strength, for sumacs are wizards at fall color. On female plants, the nectar-rich flowers give way to hard, brilliant scarlet or crimson fruits displayed in fuzzy, grape-bunched clusters from the branch tips, and as if this were not enough advertisement, they also flag down birds with incredible displays of fiery orange, red, burgundy, and yellow turning leaves. I am continually impressed with the consistent and unbeatable fall color of these mounding, colonizing shrubs along roadsides, fencerows, and old fields from year to year.

CULTURE: Sumacs are easily established in moist or dry and inhospitable locations where little else survives, but they require at least 5 to 6 hours of summer sun — the more the better — to thrive and stay put. It is possible to dig out sections of stolon with an attached shoot in late winter to early spring, but it is more reliable to use established container plants. As with *Aralia* species and some other stoloniferous shrubs, if the trunks are healthy and growing unmolested, root suckering is kept to a minimum by apical dominance. Still, you can expect the colony to slowly expand from the roots, and you need to plan accordingly. I have seen the larger sumacs used effectively in island beds surrounded by mown lawn, and we have a nice stand developing in a bed surrounded by parking lots on three sides. They are also effective on banks or at the woodland edge, where shade will control their spread. In expectation of an inevitable flurry of root sprouting, I do like to cut all the stems back to the ground every 3 to 4 years during the winter to keep the clumps full and vigorous; the only disadvantage to this is that it curtails flowering (and fruiting, on females) quite a bit.

USES: Massing, reclamation, soil stabilization.

WILDLIFE: I have mentioned the sumacs' value as nectar plants as well as sources of fruits for overwintering birds. The fruits are not a bird's first choice, and many hang on, getting a bit threadbare over the winter until they are eventually eaten or fall off. Sumacs are the primary larval host for the red-banded hairstreak butterfly (*Calycopus cercrops*).

PROPAGATION: Moderately easy from root cuttings and seeds.

Rhus aromatica
Fragrant Sumac

ZONES: (3)4–9; sun to part sun
SOIL: Moist to dry, well-drained
NATIVE TO: Dunes, open, dry woods and banks; southwestern Quebec to Alberta and western Oregon south to California, Mexico, and Florida
SIZE: Height 3–6 feet, width 4–10 feet
COLOR: Pale yellow; blooms in spring

The euphemistically named *R. aromatica* has a decidedly skunky smell if you crush the leaves. It flowers in spring with the emerging leaves, not in summer like the others. The plants form tangled, quickly spreading colonies of thin, upright, or scandent branching shoots clothed quite liberally in leathery, 3-parted leaves (hence Linnaeus's confusion with poison ivy). Fragrant sumac is *not* poisonous, though, and it is a valuable shrub for bank stabilization and the like, able to survive and thrive in very hot, nutrient-poor soils. Fall color ranges from scarlet to burgundy, and female plants form small but showy clusters of fuzzy red fruits in late summer. *R. trilobata* (lemonade sumac, skunkbush) is a similar species widespread in the Rocky Mountains from Alberta south to Mexico. Its leaflets are a bit more deeply lobed (more like poison oak). As with all sumacs, the ripe berries can be steeped in boiling water for 20 to 30 minutes and then flavored with sugar to make a very refreshing red lemonade. I have made it before, using berries of staghorn sumac (*R. typhina*), and it is quite good.

Rhus copallinum (copallina)
Shining Sumac, Winged Sumac

ZONES: 4–9; sun, part sun
SOIL: Moist to dry, well-drained
NATIVE TO: Dry woods, clearings, fencerows, cliffs, and old fields; southern Maine to Indiana and Nebraska south to Texas and Florida
SIZE: Height 5–8 (15) feet, width 6–10 feet
COLOR: Pale yellow; blooms in summer

Shining sumac grows like a smaller version of smooth sumac (*R. glabra*), with stiffly forking, pithy stems supporting a canopy of finely pinnate, lustrous deep green leaves that color brilliant red in autumn. The leaves are composed of 3 to 7 pairs of 1¼-inch-long leaflets set along a winged central rachis. It does spread, but even so, smaller size and glossy foliage combine to make this a better choice for tighter landscape situations. In full sun, it is typically wider than tall, with a multitrunk rounded or mounded shape, depending on the prevalence of root suckers around the margins of the colony.

Rhus glabra
Smooth Sumac

ZONES: (3)4–9; sun, part sun
SOIL: Moist to dry
NATIVE TO: Old fields, woodland edge, roadsides, and other dry, open habitats; Maine and southern Quebec to Manitoba south to Texas and northern Florida, also disjunct populations in British Columbia and Washington
SIZE: Height 8–16 feet, width 12–20 feet
COLOR: Yellow-green; blooms in summer

In the field this species is distinguished from staghorn sumac (*R. typhina*) by the absence of scurfy hairs on the finger-thick twigs that grow from few-

✤ Poison Ivy, Poison Oak, and Poison Sumac ✤

Though I can't imagine many people growing and propagating these plants (though they are also great bird plants and are lovely in their fall splendor, and poison ivy has been cultivated in England for its attractive fall color since about 1640!), I will mention the poisonous species, which cause severe itchy rashes, as a point of interest. You can distinguish the poisonous genus *Toxicodendron* from the nonpoisonous genus *Rhus* because the flowers are borne in axillary, not terminal, inflorescences. Poison sumac *(Toxicodendron vernix)* is a rather handsome shrub or small tree in fall with pinnate leaves and white berries that grows in open swamps and along waterways throughout eastern North America. Eastern poison oak *(T. toxicaria [toxicarium]* or *T. pubescens)* is found along the coastal plain in sand barrens from New Jersey to Florida and inland from Virginia to Kansas, south to Texas. It has 3-parted leaves, like poison ivy, but they are scallop-lobed much like white oak's. Along the Pacific coast, there is a closely related species of poison oak *(T. diversilobum)*, which looks very similar. Poison ivy, the last and probably most feared of all, comes in two forms. The type that usually becomes a vine when a suitable support is located and sprouts a dense beard of aerial rootlets with which it attaches is the widespread eastern *T. radicans. T. rydbergii* doesn't form aerial rootlets and instead is a low shrub. It is more common westward but grows almost throughout northern North America.

In all of them, the poison is contained in resin ducts within the phloem, which ooze sap when broken (dried sap on the plant surface resulting from an earlier wound continues to be poisonous). The toxin is extremely decay resistant, and a sensitive person came down with a rash after handling a 200-year-old herbarium specimen! When you get some on your skin, the poison forms chemical complexes with the skin within several hours. Strong solvent-type soaps will remove the oil if you wash within a few hours; after that, no amount of scrubbing will take the problem away. The allergic reaction is related to the phenomenon of organ transplant rejection; once this foreign protein is bound to your skin, your body can't recognize its own skin and begins to fight it as if it were an infectious agent. (Some of the Native American words for the plants were also used to describe venereal disease.) Only humans and a few other primates are sensitive to the poison, and despite fears to the contrary, you can't spread it by breaking blisters. The oil is not volatile when burned, but you can inhale bits of it clinging to floating ash and develop a severe internal reaction — my grandfather had to be hospitalized once after burning some vines.

Toxicodendron radicans. *Poison ivy is a natural No Trespassing sign, keeping many casual human visitors away from its spot of repose. Curiously, though, we are the only ones affected by its poisons; deer eat it with impunity. It is a remarkably adaptable plant, one of the few that can survive in seaside dunes as well as dark, wooded swamps.*

forking branched trunks in fast-spreading colonies. Its pinnate leaves are similar in length to those of staghorn (16–20 inches long), but the individual leaflets are narrower and more finely toothed. Of all the *Rhus* species, this has been the hardest to contain in my experience, and is best reserved for wild areas. In the southern Appalachians there grows a closely related species, *R. michauxii* (Michaux's sumac), a very rare and genetically depauperate plant found in scattered locations on dry sandy soils in Virginia, North Carolina, and Georgia. When I worked at Niche Gardens in North Carolina, we were asked to grow up quantities of this sumac for The Nature Conservancy for use in restoration efforts in the western part of the state. Though I could raise it clonally through root cuttings, I tried everything I could imagine to germinate the seeds — fire, boiling, stratification, and scarification — and only managed to get a few seedlings to grow. Most of the seeds were empty, which I suppose you might expect in an inbred population that is probably relying on vegetative reproduction (clonal spread). It is also crossing with the sympatric *R. glabra*, which doesn't help things much.

Rhus typhina
Staghorn Sumac

ZONES: (3)4–8; sun, part sun

SOIL: Moist to dry

NATIVE TO: Open places, old fields, roadsides; Nova Scotia to southern Quebec and Minnesota south to Ohio, Virginia and in the mountains to northern Georgia

SIZE: Height 8–18 (25) feet, width 8–20 feet

COLOR: Yellow-green; blooms in summer

Staghorn sumac — named for the honey-colored bristly hair that coats year-old stems the way fuzz coats developing antlers — grows in expanding colonies that look much like trees buried up to the crown because the oldest, tallest branches cluster in the middle and young upstarts gather toward the edge. The long, pinnate leaves are composed of 15 to 29 lance-shaped, 2-to-3-inch leaflets paired up along a thin central rachis. Each sessile leaflet is roughly toothed along the margin, and they tend to droop a bit in a vaguely palm-frond way. The red berries on females are effective well into winter, but eventually the felt loses its luster to the cold. The thick hair on the stems is lovely when backlit by the low winter sun, and the cultivar 'Laciniata' is especially fine in leaf, with each leaflet deeply incised along the margin to appear doubly pinnate. This cultivar has orange fall color instead of the scarlet that is typical of the species.

Ribes odoratum

Ribes (RYE-bees)
Grossulariaceae
Currant, Gooseberry

Ribes odoratum. I can tell buffalo currant has come into bloom before I even see the plant, so penetratingly sweet is its fragrance. It unfurls these sulfur yellow blooms in early spring, when the nose is most in need of olfactory delights.

There are a number of native *Ribes* species in North America, though it is primarily the European species, like black currant and red currant (*R. nigrum* and *R. sativum*) and European gooseberry (*R. uva-crispa*) that are cultivated for their fruits. Cultivation of both native and imported strains reached its zenith around the late 1800s, but has now virtually ceased because of an introduced pathogen and an unfortunate relationship. In the Ural Mountains of central Russia, there is a white pine blister rust (*Cronartium ribicola*), that was accidentally introduced into Western Europe in the mid-ninth century. Europe's native white pines were resistant to the disease, but North American relatives, like eastern white pine (*Pinus strobus*), which had been imported to Europe as ornamentals, began succumbing to the rust. Around 1910, an American nurseryman imported thousands of infected white pine seedlings from France and Germany and used them in reforestation efforts throughout the northern part of North America, efficiently spreading the disease across most of the natural range of the 5-needled pines. Like most rusts, this species needs an alternate host. In this case the alternates are members of the genus *Ribes*, and native gooseberries and currants were unfortunately widely available and susceptible to infection. Thus, through a strange mix of events involving careless plant importation and exportation, yet another exotic disease became entrenched in a place where the indigenous species had little resistance.

The rust begins as orange blisters on the leaves of *Ribes* species which erupt during the summer to release spores that travel through the air if it is cool and rainy and enter pines through the needles. After several years, twig and branch dieback is evident where the fungus has girdled the conductive tissues. All the 5-needled pines (bristlecone, western, southwestern, and eastern white, sugar, limber, and whitebark pines) are susceptible to the rust, and it has proved most devastating to western white pine *(P. monticola)*, eventually killing over 90 percent of the wild populations throughout the West. To curtail the rust's spread, the government paid armies of people in the 1920s and '30s to go out and rip up both native and cultivated *Ribes* plants in New England, the Great Lakes, and the West and imposed a ban on importing or cultivating all currants that was not lifted until 1966. Now, after nearly 100 years of battling the disease, debate still rages among foresters and horticulturalists about the dangers of planting currants and gooseberries. Some states, including Massachusetts, still have laws against their cultivation, and I would ask your state agricultural extension agent about local laws before planting them.

This being said, native pines are developing resistance to the disease, and selective breeding and reintroduction of *P. monticola* and *P. lambertiana* have helped save these species. Also, many of the native *Ribes* species are resistant, too—certainly more so than the European black currant—and I will focus on a few of the more ornamental and less susceptible species. My personal opinion is that the disease is so well entrenched over most of the native range of white pines, and wild currants are so abundant, that planting a few in your garden will have little real impact. Whether or not to encourage wide-scale planting in pine-dominated areas is a question that is being hotly debated by researchers more knowledgeable than I.

All *Ribes* species have palmately veined leaves more or less divided into 3 to 5 lobes and toothed or incised along the margin. They are caney plants that are continually sprouting new shoots from the crown or woody base to replace the old, which grow up and begin blooming in their second year on short side branches. Flowers are typically small, 5-petaled, greenish yellow or white, and narrow to a slender tube attached to the immature fruit. Most *Ribes* species are not particularly ornamental in flower, but there are a few with incredibly fragrant or showy flowers that are well worth growing for this reason. The gooseberries' stems, petioles, and sometimes even leaf undersides and fruits are spiny or thorny, and they bloom in single or few-flowered clusters. Their fruits are translucent green, with a surface more or less reticulated with thin veins. Most currants lack thorns and flower in drooping racemes that develop from the leaf axils as the blades are expanding. They bear fruits that are black or bright red and ripen over an extended period in late summer and early fall.

CULTURE: *Ribes* plants are very adaptable and capable of growing in moist or dry locations, and many will bloom and fruit moderately even in light shade. In my experience, two or more individuals for cross pollination will give better fruit yields. Since the currants ripen successively, you need to plant more than you might think you will need to get a useable crop in one picking, but you can leave the rest for the birds. There is little you can do to prevent or treat blister rust, as the disease is systemic and once established will live on perennially in the plant's tissues. There are other diseases, like powdery mildew, that may partially defoliate the plants. The best defense is vigilance. Watch for signs of the orange blisters on *Ribes* leaves in summer and pull up and burn the affected plant(s).

USES: Specimen (some species), massing, fruit production.

WILDLIFE: Fruits are excellent summer forage for birds, and are primary larval host plants for the hoary comma, dark-gray comma, and green comma butterflies *(Polygonia gracilis, P. progne, and P. faunus)* and the tailed copper *(Lycaena arota)*.

PROPAGATION: Moderately easy from cuttings, easy from seed.

Ribes americanum
Eastern Black Currant

ZONES: 3–7; sun to light shade
SOIL: Moist to moderately dry
NATIVE TO: Moist woods and openings; Nova Scotia to Alberta south to Colorado, Indiana, and Delaware
SIZE: Height 3–5 feet, width 3–4 feet
COLOR: Creamy white; blooms in spring
A many-stemmed shrub with canes branching toward the tops; deciduous, 3-lobed leaves like red maple's that are medium green in color and dotted with honey-colored glands on the lower surface; and drooping clusters of insignificant flowers followed by ⅜-inch black edible berries with a long whisker-like projection coming from the end. Western black currant *(R. hudsonianum)* is a very close relative that is native to most of the northwestern quarter of North America. Both are good native substitutes for European black currant.

Ribes aureum
Golden Currant

ZONES: 4–8; sun, part sun
SOIL: Moist to moderately summer-dry

NATIVE TO: Stream banks and washes in sagebrush desert, openings in pine forest; South Dakota and Saskatchewan to British Columbia south to California and New Mexico

SIZE: Height 3–6 feet, width 3–4 feet

COLOR: Bright yellow; blooms in spring

Golden currant is a very tough ornamental species growing as a multistem shrub with fairly thick, woody bases; irregularly toothed and scalloped, 3-to-5-lobed leaves growing on short spur branches; and long-tubed, showy flowers in thick clusters in spring. The flowers release a powerful, sweet, clovelike fragrance that is just wonderful, and is one of the best ways of finding the plants in the wild. The orange fruits are sweet-tart and edible, ripening over 3 to 4 weeks toward the end of summer. This is closely related to the widespread western buffalo currant (*R. odoratum*, also listed as *R. aureum* var. *villosum*), which has gray-green leaves, brown, woody trunks of similar spread, and shorter flowers just as powerfully endowed with a penetrating, sweet-clove aroma. We had one at Garden in the Woods, and it never failed to draw comment from early-season visitors who wondered, "What is that incredible smell?" The plant fades into the background by summer, and tends to lose its leaves to various minor afflictions by the time the black fruits ripen later in the season. Leaves that survive turn yellow to burgundy before falling off in autumn.

Ribes hirtellum
American Gooseberry

ZONES: (3)4–7; sun, part sun

SOIL: Moist to dry

NATIVE TO: Open woods, cliffs, stream banks, thickets; Newfoundland and Quebec to Alberta south to Nebraska, Illinois, West Virginia, and Pennsylvania

SIZE: Height 2–3 feet, width 2–3 feet

COLOR: Greenish white sometimes tinged with pink; blooms in late spring

This is but one of a bewildering number of low, twiggy and thorny gooseberries with whitish flowers and ½-inch translucent green fruits flushed with pink or purple. The tart fruits of this particular plant lack spines or glands, and thus it is one of the best natives for fruit production (several cultivars and hybrids have been introduced). Whitestem gooseberry (*R. inerme*) is a less thorny species that is basically the West Coast extension of *R. hirtellum* found throughout the western mountains. It has fewer stipular thorns, but neither species is particularly spiny. Wild gooseberry (*R. missouriense*) has long, single spines at the nodes and fruits as good as *R. hirtellum*'s. It ranges farther east and south, to Arkansas and Tennessee.

Ribes sanguineum
Red-flowering Currant

ZONES: (5)6–8; part sun to light shade

SOIL: Moist to moderately dry

NATIVE TO: Wooded or open slopes and valleys; the Pacific Coast from British Columbia south to northern California

SIZE: Height 5–10 (15) feet, width 3–6 feet

COLOR: Pink to reddish pink, red, or white; blooms in late winter to early spring

Red-flowering currant is one of the showiest species in flower and it's widely grown for that purpose (the black fruits are unpalatable at best). It becomes an arching, caney shrub with small, almost rounded, gray-green, 3-lobed, deciduous leaves that emerge very early from little spur branches all along the stems along with upright racemes of beautiful hot pink flowers with a white center. It does well in the Pacific Northwest and in Western Europe, and there are a number of named cultivars. We have a few growing at the Garden, and they seem reasonably winter-hardy here, though we get some dieback in a bad year. This and our generally drier climate keep them shorter than plants I have studied out West, but they flower well anyway in early spring. Canyon currant (var. *glutinosum*) is a more drought-tolerant form from California with larger, drooping, pink-flowered racemes.

Ribes speciosum
Fuchsia-flowered Gooseberry

ZONES: 7–9; sun, part sun

SOIL: Moist to dry

NATIVE TO: Moist wooded or open slopes near the

Ribes sanguineum. *Red-flowering currant is handsome in bloom, and many cultivars are available from specialty nurseries on the West Coast.*

immediate coast of California

SIZE: Height 3–10 (14) feet, width 3–5 feet

COLOR: Dark pinkish red; blooms in late winter to early spring

This terribly spiny gooseberry is a remarkable sight in flower, the equal to any of the true fuchsias to be sure. It becomes a tall multistem shrub covered in small, leathery, and glossy semi-evergreen leaves borne on short spurs. Dangling pairs of 1-inch-long purply red tubular flowers with very long exerted stamens adorn the branches early in the season. Needs a cool, maritime climate.

Rosa arkansana

Rosa (RO-sa)
Rosaceae
Rose

What can I say about this most loved and scorned of all flowering shrubs? Indeed, a rose is a rose is a rose in a certain essential way, but a rose is also an eyesore when it stands prickly and leafless after a summer of disease. I love the flawless convolutions of the classic tea rose as much as anyone, but honestly, this is the only thing that these roses have going for them. Except in a perfect climate (like England's or northern California's), most garden roses are so prone to disease and winter injury that I fail to understand why people insist on devoting whole areas of their yards to a bare briar patch (a.k.a. rose garden). The native or wild roses are not perfect, either: they can get powdery mildew and black spot, and the single, 5-petaled flowers don't have the fluted luxuriousness of the tea rose, but on the whole they are basically carefree, drought-tolerant, winter-hardy shrubs with satin pink flowers set with a fringed doughnut of bright yellow anthers, just as you'd expect in a rose. Since the flowers are all completely fertile, they will set quantities of blood red or maroon hips loaded with vitamin C that are an important winter food for mockingbirds and others.

As a group the roses are low-spreading, stiff-caned shrubs armed more or less along the length of the canes with thorns and bristles. The thorns are described as infrastipular (at the base of the petiole), petiolar (on the petiole), or bristly (lining the stem between the leaf nodes). Leaves are deciduous or semi-evergreen, hanging on longest at the tips of the most vigorous canes, lustrous or leathery dark green and pinnately compound in typical rose fashion. The wild roses do flower profusely and lavishly, but the 2-inch blossoms are not the "knock your socks off at 200 feet" puffballs that adorn the semidouble and

double hybrids, and since they do set seed, flowering lasts only 2 to 4 weeks. Still, they are pretty in a wildflower way and have the familiar rosy perfume.

CULTURE: Although I do run into powdery mildew problems when roses in the nursery are irrigated, I have grown most of these native roses in the garden and they have clean foliage three years out of four, and I never spray anything on them. If you look

at wild roses as just that, and don't worry about a few blemished leaves, then you will not be disappointed. Japanese beetles are a problem where they are a problem, but as I have mentioned elsewhere, they are much less prevalent in many places than they used to be. Full sun and well-drained soil are best for most of the species covered here. They are, as a group, very drought tolerant and require little more than some fertilizer in spring. All but climbing prairie rose (*R. setigera*) will run at the roots (spread), though good culture seems to keep species like Virginia rose (*R. virginiana*) clumped and contained. It is not difficult to head back a wayward rose with a sharp spade in spring. Flowers are borne on the older canes, so do not prune the shrubs back hard in winter as you would a tea rose.

USES: Naturalizing, massing, shrub border.

WILDLIFE: Rose hips are a good winter food source for birds.

PROPAGATION: Moderately difficult from cuttings, moderately easy from seed.

Rosa arkansana
Arkansas Rose, Dwarf Prairie Rose

ZONES: 4–8; sun

SOIL: Moist to dry, well-drained

NATIVE TO: Prairies, fencerows, and clearings; New York to Alberta south to Colorado, Texas, Missouri, and Maryland

SIZE: Height 1–2 feet, width 4–8 feet

COLOR: Soft pink with darker veins; blooms in late spring to early summer

A rapidly spreading, low species (really a tall ground-

Rosa arkansana. Arkansas rose is more of a spreading groundcover than a bush rose. It is a good choice if you want to stabilize a dry bank or naturalize some roses in a wildflower meadow.

cover), with short, stiff canes and long, dark-green leaves composed of 9 to 11 finely toothed, oval leaflets. The flowers are large and luminous for the size of the plant, clustered and up-facing amid the upper leaves. Hips are deep red and ¾ inch across. Prickly wild rose (*R. acicularis*) is an equally bristly spreading species usually a foot taller on average that ranges clear across the northern third of North America and into Eurasia. It has leaves with only 5 to 7 leaflets and flowers tending toward dark rose pink. The spines are usually so thick on the slower-growing stems as to nearly obscure them. Hips are gray-purple and ½ inch in diameter.

Rosa blanda
Smooth Rose

ZONES: (3)4–7; sun, part sun

SOIL: Moist to dry

NATIVE TO: Dry woods, prairies, dunes, and outcrops; Quebec to Manitoba, south to Indiana, Missouri, New York, and Maine

SIZE: Height 2–6 feet, width 6–12 feet

COLOR: Light to dark rose pink; blooms in early to midsummer

This is another quickly spreading, colonizing rose, whose stems are a bit taller than those of *R. virginiana*. The plants form dense, leafy, impenetrable thickets in favorable situations. Leaves have 5 to 7 blue-green leaflets. The flowers come over a fairly long period, opening darker and fading lighter pink, but on the plants I have grown they are a bit droopy and irregular-looking. The stems are mostly spineless, except down low, but a vast population on Mt. St. Pierre in Quebec confused even the experts with its thorns—it turned out to be the very local var. *hispida*. Hips are red and ½ inch wide.

Rosa carolina
Carolina or Pasture Rose

ZONES: 4–9; sun, part sun

SOIL: Moist to dry

NATIVE TO: Upland woods, dunes, prairies, and fencerows; Maine to Minnesota south to Texas and Florida

SIZE: Height 2–3 feet, width 3–4 feet

COLOR: Light to dark pink; blooms in summer

Carolina rose is similar in many respects to Virginia rose (*R. virginiana*), but its leaflets are a bit narrower, glossy, dark green and pointed, and its stems are set with both back-curved infrastipular thorns just below the leaf base and bristly spines along the internodes. Flowers are held up singly or in pairs from the new growth, and like many other rose blooms, often open darker and fade over two to three days to light pink. The petioles, young stems, and shining hips are deep crimson. This is one of my favorites, as it is not too expansive in the garden and the leaves and stiff

stems are very attractive. In the wild it spreads to form loose, patchy colonies, but is much thicker and mounded in cultivation. It is one of the best species for the Southeast, and is fairly cold-hardy, though it may experience some dieback in Zone 4.

Rosa nutkana
Nootka Rose

ZONES: 5–8; sun, part sun

SOIL: Moist to moderately dry

NATIVE TO: Shorelines, thickets, clearings, and roadsides; British Columbia to Oregon

SIZE: Height 5–10 feet, width 3–5 feet

COLOR: Soft pink; blooms in early to midsummer

Nootka rose is usually a caney, rounded shrub spreading to form thickets. Flowers, borne singly atop the new twigs, are among the largest of any of the wild roses, up to 3 inches in diameter. A typical plant will be armed with a pair of stout, infrastipular thorns but not many bristles, except on young, vigorous twigs. I have grown this species several times, and though the foliage is thin and dull green, the large flowers are quite lovely.

Rosa palustris
Swamp Rose

ZONES: 4–9; sun

SOIL: Moist to wet

NATIVE TO: Swamps, bog margins, freshwater marshes, and damp shores; Nova Scotia to Minnesota south to Arkansas and Florida

SIZE: Height 3–5 feet, width 3–6 feet

COLOR: Rose pink; blooms in summer

In the wild, swamp rose is intermixed with wetland grasses and sedges as well as other shrubs, but if you give it a bit of room and damp soil, it becomes a dense rounded shrub bearing clusters of flowers over stiff little leaves composed of 3 to 5 leaflets. It sets

Rosa nitida. *Shining rose has just about the best foliage of any wild rose, in my opinion. Each leaf is composed of seven to nine narrow, serrated leaflets with a glossy, bright green patina. The canes and flower stems are liberally set with thorns and bristles that catch the sunlight.*

quantities of small, round, red-orange fruits late in summer that, while not as large as some other rose hips, have a good visual effect, and their size may make them easier for some birds to handle. *R. palustris* has only pairs of thick, back-curving infrastipular and petiolar thorns. Another, smaller wetland rose that I particularly like is shining rose or New England rose *(R. nitida)*, which lights up marsh and river shores through eastern Canada and New England with big pink flowers held over shiny, fine-textured foliage arrayed on bristly stems. I usually get to see it up close only when we are canoeing during the summer.

Rosa setigera
Climbing Prairie Rose

ZONES: 4–9; sun, part sun
SOIL: Moist
NATIVE TO: Thickets, hedgerows, swamp margins; southwestern Ontario to Iowa and Kansas south to Texas and Florida
SIZE: Height 4–8 feet, width 5–10 feet
COLOR: Light to dark pink; blooms in early to mid-summer

Rosa setigera is the closest we get to a native climbing rose. It sends out long, weak canes set with stout, back-curved thorns and large leaves with 3 oval leaflets (5 on lower leaves) grooved deeply along the veins. There are some thorns on the petioles as well. It holds its fairly large flowers in clusters of 3 to 7 from the tips of both primary and axillary canes. Since the flowers in each cluster open up over the course of a week, starting out dark pink and fading light, a shrub in full bloom has a striking multicolor appearance.

Rosa setigera. *Climbing prairie rose is a perfect cottage-garden subject, for the long canes can be trained on fences or trellises and its multicolored floral display is as pretty as a country quilt.*

The hips are small and ruddy green. Still, *R. setigera*'s habit and prolific flowering make it about the best wild substitute for the hybrid climbers.

Rosa virginiana
Virginia Rose

ZONES: 3–8; sun, part sun
SOIL: Moist to dry
NATIVE TO: Woodland gaps and margins, thickets, dunes, roadsides, and fencerows; Newfoundland south along the coast through New England to Pennsylvania and Virginia and occasionally inland to Missouri
SIZE: Height 2–4 (6) feet, width 3–6 feet
COLOR: Light medium pink; blooms in early to mid-summer

Probably the most common wild rose along much of the East Coast, Virginia rose is a disease-resistant, drought-tolerant colonizing plant with shiny, leathery leaves that turn deep red or maroon to match the young canes before they fall. Flowers are borne singly or in pairs on short axillary branches on the older canes, and these are followed by brilliant scarlet fruits that remain reasonably plump and visually effective for most of the winter. In a garden situation, *R. virginiana* will increase its diameter by 6 to 12 inches each year, becoming a mounded patch of stiff, upright canes set with stout, infrastipular thorns but no bristly spines. Flowers come in a flush in early summer, then sporadically a few at a time over the next 6 to 8 weeks.

Rosa woodsii
Desert Wild Rose

ZONES: 4–7; sun
SOIL: Moist to fairly dry
NATIVE TO: Sandy or rocky soils on slopes, woodland margins, washes, roadsides, and ravines; Minnesota to British Columbia south to Arizona, western Texas, and northern Mexico
SIZE: Height 2–4 feet, width 4–8 feet
COLOR: Pink; blooms in late spring to early summer

Desert wild rose grows throughout much of the arid West, but it prefers soils that are not extremely dry, especially in the Great Basin. It spreads to form dense thickets of intertwined canes set with long, thin spines, mostly below the nodes. The typical 2-inch-wide flowers are followed by bright red teardrop-shaped fruits. The leaves are divided into 7 to 9 rounded, pointed, or flat-tipped, dull gray leaflets of medium substance. This is certainly the best choice for the Great Basin and Rocky Mountains, and the dense colonies help stabilize soil and provide cover for wildlife.

Rubus odoratus

Rubus (ROO-bus)
Rosaceae
Raspberry, Blackberry, Bramble

Growing up in the cool, humid climate that blackberries relish, I spent as much time battling them back as I did enjoying their fruits. It's interesting that some of the most aggressive, impenetrable species were introduced and have naturalized, including the Himalayan blackberry (*R. discolor*), which grows like kudzu all over the Pacific Northwest, and wineberry (*R. phoenicolasius*), one of the best-tasting of the raspberries, though it is highly invasive and is spreading everywhere along the Atlantic coast. There are dozens of native *Rubus* species in our flora, and most are readily interfertile and promiscuous, creating a range of intermediate hybrids that make identification difficult (and affect fruit quality for good or for ill).

Blackberries and raspberries have a unique habit of growth that has produced its own terminology. Vigorous stems, called primocanes, come from the roots in spring, often growing quickly and to great length the first year but not flowering. The following spring the primocanes send out short, flowering side branches, called floricanes, which set fruit and die. Thus, any colony is an intertwined tangle of primocanes and floricanes, both dead and alive. The exceptions among the woody species are two of the most ornamental, *R. odoratus* and *R. parviflorus,* whose floricanes live for 3 to 4 seasons, branching more thickly and flowering each year. These two lack thorns, but most *Rubus* species are well armed along the stems, petioles, and even the undersides of the leaves with thin, sharp spines or prickles. There are also a number of herbaceous *Rubus* species that are beyond the scope of this book, such as the delectable apple-flavored cloudberry (*R. chamaemorus*), which grows in cold bogs throughout much of the North; you have to try this one at least once!

Rubus flowers are typically 5-petaled and are borne in branched panicles or terminal racemes, and polli-nated flowers melt away to reveal the delectable, dimpled fruit, which is really a cluster of small drupes. It helps to have more than one individual for good fruit set. The easiest way to tell raspberries from blackberries is by picking the fruit. Raspberries come away from a little greenish white core, so the picked fruit is hollow. Blackberries come away flush from the stem, so their centers are solid. Also, most blackberries have 5 palmate leaflets arranged like a big hand, whereas raspberries have either 3 or 5 to 7 pinnate leaflets. Purple-flowering raspberry and thimbleberry have very large 3-to-5-lobed but undivided leaves. All of the following *Rubus* species are deciduous without appreciable fall color.

CULTURE: Generally no culture is necessary if you live in a suitable climate and select local species. Most raspberries and blackberries are plants of disturbed or successional areas, seeding in by bird droppings, growing for a time, and eventually succumbing to competition as well as increasing viral loads, aphids, galls, leaf diseases, and the like. Commercial varieties should be screened for viruses, because once these are established in the plant they spread in fluids exchanged on pruning equipment or in the saliva of sucking insects like aphids and thrips. In field trials of a number of varieties, we found that in commercial production, 3 to 5 years of bearing fruit was all we could expect before viruses reduced yields below commercially viable levels. Of course, in a naturalized situation, kept clear of woody competition, the plants fend for themselves very well, needing only occasional pruning to remove dead canes; alternatively, you can mow the patch to the ground every 5 years and forgo fruits for a season. Best growth and fruiting is in moist, fertile soils, but many of the wild species are reasonably drought tolerant (in a dry year, fruit may be largely aborted). Fertilization in spring with a balanced, organic fertilizer or manure will increase yields.

USES: Naturalizing, fruit production.

WILDLIFE: Blackberries and raspberries are of obvious value to birds and many mammals, including bears, deer, and even foxes. You may have to net the plants to get a bumper harvest, but a healthy bramble patch will produce enough fruits for humans and other animals, too.

PROPAGATION: Easy from cuttings, layers, and seeds.

Rubus allegheniensis
Common Blackberry, Allegheny Blackberry

ZONES: (3)4–7; sun, part sun
SOIL: Moist
NATIVE TO: Disturbed habitats; Nova Scotia to Quebec and Minnesota south to Missouri, Virginia, and in the Appalachians to Tennessee and North Carolina

Rubus odoratus.
Though its fruits are less delectable than red raspberry's, purple-flowering raspberry has by far the showiest flowers in this genus. Do not remove the flowering canes until you are sure they are dead, for unlike most Rubus species, this one keeps its canes for three to five years.

SIZE: Height 3–6 (8) feet, width 4–8 feet
COLOR: White; blooms in late spring to summer
The common blackberry is just one of a number of tall blackberries with palmate leaves native to mostly the cooler, more humid parts of the continent. Of the dozens of named species in this group, many represent intergrades and hybrids, so my best advice is to find a plant you like, and grow it regardless of its exact identity. These are big, fast-growing, thicket-forming plants with arching primocanes and round or cylindrical fruits containing fairly large, crunchy seeds. Flowers and then ripe fruits appear over a 4-to-8-week period during the summer.

Rubus idaeus
Red Raspberry

ZONES: (3)4–8; sun, part sun
SOIL: Moist to moderately dry
NATIVE TO: Disturbed habitats; Newfoundland to Alaska, south to the mountains of Arizona, Iowa, and Pennsylvania
SIZE: Height 2–6 feet, width 3–5 feet
COLOR: White; blooms in late spring to early summer
Red raspberry is remarkably widespread and common here as well as throughout Eurasia, and most of the cultivated varieties come from selections made from it. The plants sprout bristly, thorny, lax primocanes covered with a glaucous bloom. They usually arch over and root again at the tips, in effect leapfrogging from place to place (you can prevent this by keeping the cane tips off the ground). The 3-to-5-lobed pinnate leaves are light green above and chalky white below and the flowers and fruits are arranged in small clusters from leaf axils and tips. The berry is typically bright red and very tasty, ripening over 4 to 6 weeks in summer.

Rubus occidentalis
Blackcap Raspberry

ZONES: 3–8; sun, part sun
SOIL: Moist to moderately dry
NATIVE TO: Thickets, clearings, disturbed areas; Quebec to North Dakota and eastern Colorado south to Arkansas and Georgia
SIZE: Height 3–6 feet, width 4–8 feet
COLOR: White; blooms in early summer
Blackcap raspberry has a similar growth habit to *R. idaeus,* with 3-to-5-parted pinnate leaves medium green above and white below (some leaves may be occasionally palmately lobed like blackberries, but the fruit comes away from the stem with a hollow center —hence the name blackcap). Its stems have down-curved thorns, not bristles. Hybrids between this and red raspberry are the purple raspberries of commerce (*R. × neglectus*), which have the same lax, sprawling habit and glaucous canes as the parents.

Rubus odoratus
Purple-flowering Raspberry

ZONES: (3)4–6; sun to light shade
SOIL: Moist
NATIVE TO: Damp woodlands, margins, stream sides, and thickets; Nova Scotia to Maine and west to Michigan; south mostly in the mountains to Tennessee and Georgia
SIZE: Height 3–6 feet, width 4–8 feet
COLOR: Deep rose purple; blooms in summer
Purple-flowering raspberry is certainly the showiest of all native species, with roselike flowers up to nearly 2 inches wide and possessed of a shimmering, satiny texture. The soft, light gray-green foliage is also attractive, kind of like a big 3-lobed maple leaf covered in fuzz. Flowers yield to salmon-colored, squat, hollow berries that are not as sweet as typical raspberries but good enough that I tend to eat more than I mean to each year from the stock plants and have too little seed to sow. The upright to arching canes lack spines or thorns, and live for a few years before fading out. It spreads, like the other *Rubus* species, by stolons to form mounded colonies. Thimbleberry (*R. parviflorus*), is similar in many ways, though its leaves are typically 5-lobed and the showy, pure white flowers are a bit smaller overall. It is a common woodland species in the western mountains, and grows also around the Great Lakes in Ontario, Michigan, and northern Minnesota.

Rubus spectabilis
Salmonberry

ZONES: 5–8; sun, part sun
SOIL: Moist
NATIVE TO: Clearings, moist woods, disturbed areas; Alaska south to northwest California
SIZE: Height 5–12 feet, width 6–15 feet
COLOR: Dark reddish pink; blooms in spring
Salmonberry has fruits colored like its namesake, though amber fruits are common, too. It is a nearly thornless, vigorously stoloniferous raspberry that blooms and sets fruits very early so that they ripen in late spring to early summer. They are a bit watery and mild, but certainly popular with many people. Their high water content makes shipping them nearly impossible, so you'll have to grow your own.

Salix (SAY-lix)
Salicaceae
Willow

Salix discolor

As a group, the willows are weak-wooded, fast-growing shrubs and trees of cool and cold climates. They bear long, thin leaves set densely on flexible stems that will keep growing as long as weather permits, so it is not uncommon to see whips that have gained 3 to 4 feet in a season. One of the most familiar species is the lovable pussy willow (*Salix discolor*), whose silken silver catkins (the male flower clusters) swell and fluff out as soon as there is a hint of warmth in early spring. The largest and most numerous catkins are formed on vigorous new growth, so if you are raising pussy willow for this purpose, hard pruning every few years (cut the crown back by a third before growth begins in spring) and good culture will ensure a marvelous display. You can force pussy willow twigs indoors any time after early February, as they require less winter chilling than most plants. All willows produce downy male catkins, though some are larger and more colorful than others, and in many cases the flowers open after the leaves have begun to expand, blocking the catkins from view. Female catkins have less down and are not quite as showy, being composed mostly of teardrop-shaped capsules that triple in size after pollination before bursting open to release clouds of cottony seeds to the winds. Most of the cut pussy willows sold by florists are European, especially florist's willow (*S. caprea*), and gray florist's willow (*S. cinerea*), or Asian, including the black willow (*S. melanostachys*), from Japan.

Willows, very adept at reclaiming ground at the edges of glaciers, underwent explosive evolution after the most recent ice ages. There are roughly 40 species native to North America, and many of these freely hybridize. As a result, willows are notoriously difficult to identify in the field, and this confusion has curtailed their wider use in gardens. On the other hand, one willow is often as good as the next for their intended role in life—stabilizing watercourses and colonizing disturbed, damp, open areas. Since willow seeds freely travel on the winds like their cousins the aspens, chances are if you have a place for one, it is already there, and if not, you can usually establish some by snipping a few shoots from a nearby stand in late winter and sticking the cut ends into damp earth.

The fine-colored foliage of species like the thin-leaved coyote willow (*S. exigua*) and woolly sage willow (*S. candida*), or the glossy green shining willow (*S. lucida*) can add interest and screening to gardens. Additionally, a number of dwarf, Arctic, and alpine willows offer possibilities in a rock garden or tundra simulation. Snowbed willow (*S. herbacea*) and the choice bearberry willow (*S. uva-ursi*) are two I have grown successfully in Massachusetts. All species are deciduous, and, with the exception of these dwarf species, fall color is typically an unspectacular mix of yellow and green.

CULTURE: With willows, moist or wet soils are the rule, as is at least half a day's sun. As I have mentioned, they are among the easiest plants to propagate; a cut dormant stem sunk into the ground will often take root, as will stems stuck in water. (Willows contain a natural rooting hormone that can be extracted and used to root cuttings—see p. 272.) Most shrubby species benefit from rejuvenation every 5 to 10 years, and you can even treat them as semiperennials, cutting the stems to the ground every other year to maintain a full, even crown. The commonly heard caveat about weeping willow (*S. babylonica,* an introduced species) is true of the natives as well. They have adventurous, water-seeking roots that can easily clog septic systems and storm drains within an area two to three times their dripline area. The dwarf willows need a cool, well-drained, but moist root run.

USES: Watercourse bank stabilization, screening, massing, (some) rock garden.

WILDLIFE: The succulent twigs of willows provide winter forage for small mammals. Many, many moth and butterfly larvae feed on the leaves of willows, often leaving the foliage a bit tattered by late summer. The list of moths includes the twin-spotted sphinx moth (*Smerinthus jamaicensis*), New England

Salix discolor. As cute as little stuffed animals and loved by all as harbingers of spring, the silver-haired pussy willow catkins are really designed to trap sunlight. Like a miniature greenhouse, the catkin's interior heats up well above the ambient air temperature, allowing it to grow in the cold of late winter.

buck moth (*Hemileuca lucina*), the bristly brown and gray caterpillar of the frosted dagger moth (*Acronicta hastulifera*), as well as the impressed dagger moth (*Acronicta impressa*), red-winged sallow moth (*Xystopeplus rufago*), false-sphinx moth (*Pheosia rimosa*), sigmoid prominent moth (*Clostera albosigma*), and the bizarre, dead-leaf mimic, the white furcula caterpillar (*Furcula borealis*). Some of the butterflies that feed on willows are the white admiral, western admiral, and orange-tip admiral (*Limenitis arthemis*, *L. weidemeyerii*, and *L. lorquini*), green comma (*Polygonia faunus*), comma tortoise shell and mourning cloak (*Nymphalis vau-album* and *N. antiopa*), and aspen dusky wing (*Erynnis icelus*).

PROPAGATION: Easy from cuttings, moderately easy from seed.

Salix candida
Sage Willow

ZONES: 2–6(7); sun, part sun
SOIL: Moist to wet, alkaline
NATIVE TO: Alkaline wetlands; Labrador to Alaska, south to Colorado, Illinois, and New Jersey
SIZE: Height 3–5 feet, width 3–5 feet
COLOR: Silvery yellow; blooms in early spring

Sage willow has an unmistakable ghostly gray aura and a blends-with-anything quality that makes it a useful background plant in the shrub border. In the wild it is restricted to limestone soils, but in the Garden, it does well in slightly acidic soils as well. The linear leaves are about ½ inch wide by 3 inches long. They are silvery green above and woolly white below. The white hairs coat the new twigs and give way on older branches to a red-brown bark.

Salix uva-ursi. You probably would not suspect that bearberry willow, a little alpine groundcover, was a willow except for its upright catkins, seen here frothing into seed.

Salix discolor
Pussy Willow

ZONES: 2–7; sun, part sun
SOIL: Moist to wet
NATIVE TO: Swamps and other wet, open ground; Newfoundland to Alberta south to Montana, South Dakota, Missouri, and Delaware
SIZE: Height 6–15 feet, width 4–8 feet
COLOR: Silvery yellow; blooms in late winter to early spring

The sight of silky catkins stretching out along pussy willow twigs is a sure sign that winter is on the wane. This is a common wetland shrub or occasionally a small, multitrunked tree with oval 2-inch-long dusty green leaves. Cut stems forced indoors will often root; these can be kept growing in a vase of water placed in a sunny window and then be planted outside once the danger of frost has passed.

Salix exigua
Coyote Willow, Sandbar Willow

ZONES: 3–9; sun
SOIL: Moist to wet
NATIVE TO: River and stream banks, gravel bars and islands; New Brunswick to British Columbia south to northern Mexico, Texas, and Virginia
SIZE: Height 4–10 feet, width 6–15 feet
COLOR: Yellow; blooms in spring

Almost any respectable stream or river throughout most of North America will have a complement of rounded, densely branched coyote willows lining its banks. The species is adept at surviving the vagaries of flood and ice, and a section of branch stripped away in a spring torrent may take root where it comes to rest on a shore downstream. Over its wide range, this species varies somewhat, but in general the gray-green leaves are long and thin, averaging less than ½ inch across and 3 to 6 inches in length. It readily hybridizes with other sympatric willows, and I have been frustrated on more than one occasion trying to sort out the true species from the hybrid swarm. Catkins open with the expanding leaves, rendering them virtually invisible from a distance.

Salix herbacea
Snowbed Willow, Herb-like Willow

ZONES: 1–6; sun, part sun
SOIL: Moist, cool, well drained
NATIVE TO: Tundra and alpine summits; Labrador to Alaska south in the mountains of the eastern United States to New York and Maine
SIZE: Height 1-6 inches, width 1–2 feet
COLOR: Dark silvery yellow; blooms in spring

Of all the low, creeping willows, this is the most reduced. In fact it is barely a woody plant, as the lignified stems act like rhizomes creeping through the moss and crevices in bare rock. Short side branches rise from the creeping stems. The catkins are relatively small, but they have a chestnut brown and silver color much like bearberry willow's that is cute up close. The nearly round ¾-inch leaves bunch like overlapping scales at the tips of the branches. *S. uva-ursi* (bearberry willow) grows sympatrically with snowbed willow but can be distinguished by its more congested growth habit; leathery, deep green leaves with prominent herringbone veins; and larger (about 1 inch long) dark silver catkins that fluff out as the new leaves unfurl. Given a cool, acidic soil and protection from hot, dry winds, it grows into a compact, 6-inch-high mat of twisted twigs and pretty leaves.

Salix lucida
Shining Willow

ZONES: 2–7; sun, part sun
SOIL: Moist to wet
NATIVE TO: Swamps, streamsides, and other wet ground; Labrador to Saskatchewan, south to Nebraska, West Virginia, and northwestern Virginia
SIZE: Height 6–20 feet, width 4–8 feet
COLOR: Yellow; blooms in spring

The glossy, bright green foliage of *Salix lucida* makes it one of the easier species to recognize at a glance. Each 2-to-4-inch-long leaf is narrowly oval in shape, with a long slender tip. Catkins are produced on leafy side branchlets just as the larger leaves begin to spring from the twig tips, so they are not especially ornamental. The plants can reach tree-like proportions, but it is more common to see the shimmering foliage covering rounded, many-stemmed shrubs extending 6 to 10 feet in all directions.

Sambucus racemosa
Sambucus (sam-BEW-kus)
Caprifoliaceae
Elderberry, Elder

Fruits are the raison d'être as far as elderberries are concerned. Small individually, the berries are produced in large flat or pyramidal bunches at the tips of the caney twigs. Birds quickly devour the sugary fruits, but if you can beat them to it, you can boil the pulp down and strain it to make a tangy wine or jelly.

Elderberries are remarkably fast-growing shrubs when their simple needs are met, producing pithy, weak-wooded canes clothed in paired, compound leaves. Older canes lose productivity after several seasons, but they are continually reinforced with vigorous suckers coming from the base and roots that

will eventually take their place. Occasionally, you may find wild plants with thick woody trunks and lower branches, but more often the clumps are composed of many thinner canes coming up from a central base as well as from nearby roots. Red elder blooms in spring on short branches or tips of the canes just as the new leaves are toughening up. Its pyramidal flower clusters are thus relatively smaller than those of common elderberry (*S. canadensis*) and more scattered through the leaves. Blue elderberry flowers a bit later than red elder, after the new growth has had time to expand. This extra growing time means larger flower clusters. On a vigorous *S. canadensis*, the flat-topped, white inflorescences can be as large as a Frisbee, with small, 5-petaled individual flowers, each one with 5 stamens surrounding a short style. The stamens add both frothiness and a touch of butter yellow to the picture, so that from a distance, the blooms have an ivory cast and a soft pile. The combination of these ivory Frisbees set over the large compound leaves is quite beautiful.

CULTURE: Common elderberry is the most adaptable of the lot, thriving anywhere the soil is not dry and where the plant's large leaves bathe in at least a few hours of sun. We grow red elder easily enough at the Garden, but it is not a plant for the hotter parts of

Sambucus racemosa ssp. pubens. The remarkable thing about scarlet elder is not just the brilliant color of the fruits but their ripening in midsummer, when green dominates the landscape. Amid shades of emerald, moss, jade, and olive, the clusters of scarlet berries practically leap to your eye.

the United States. I have not tried blue elder, though judging by its preferred habitat, it is certainly the most drought tolerant of the three. All elders benefit from hard winter pruning every few years to remove older or weaker canes and encourage vigorous, heavily flowered new shoots. Cut the canes back to the larger stubs or trunk near the ground. *S. canadensis* can almost be cut like a perennial and still bloom well in season, and this may be the best way to handle it in more formal situations. In my experience, isolated specimens set good quantities of fruits, so it appears they are self-compatible—they don't rely on cross-pollination. I have noticed consistent partial defoliation on plants both in the wild and in gardens that appears to be the work of a large caterpillar, though I have never actually found the culprit. In general, I consider these to be easy, informal shrubs.

USES: Mixed borders, naturalizing.

WILDLIFE: Flowers are good sources of nectar, and birds relish the early-ripening, sugary fruits.

PROPAGATION: Easy from cuttings, moderately easy from seeds.

Sambucus caerulea
Blue Elderberry

ZONES: (4)5–8; sun, part sun
SOIL: Moist to moderately dry
NATIVE TO: Woods, thickets, and meadows, stream sides; Idaho to British Columbia south through California to New Mexico
SIZE: Height 6–15 (25) feet, width 3–10 feet
COLOR: Creamy white; blooms in late spring to early summer

Blue elderberry is the western cousin of common elder. Its most notable feature is the waxy bloom that covers the fruit and twigs, lending the dark blue berries a lighter, blueberry blue cast. Its leaves and flowers are similar in size and arrangement to its eastern relative, but it tolerates drier locations than *S. canadensis*.

Sambucus canadensis
Common Elderberry

ZONES: (3)4–9; sun to light shade
SOIL: Moist to wet
NATIVE TO: Moist woods, fields, and roadsides; Nova Scotia to Manitoba south to Mexico and Florida
SIZE: Height 5–10 feet, width 3–8 feet
COLOR: Creamy white; blooms in early summer

Common elderberry is an agreeable informal shrub with pinnate leaves composed typically of three pairs of oval, pointed lateral leaflets and one terminal leaflet, all toothed enough to notice along the margins. They run up the canes in pairs, often separated by long internodes that quickly gain the canes altitude. In the sun, the rachis and petiole pick up some of the maroon pigment that infuses the flower pedicels and the berries themselves. Metallic-scented flowers and then sugary ⅛-inch berries are borne on large, flattened panicles that jut out from between the topmost pair of leaves on a cane. The fruits have a luminous quality when the sun hits them the right way—sort of a glistening deep reddish purple like a glass of Cabernet held up to the light. From a distance, or on a dark day, the fruits appear almost black, and hang from the stems so prolifically that they weigh them down. As with any wide-ranging species, try to locate plants from local genotypes for best performance in your area. I was startled to see common elder blooming in February down in the cypress swamps of south Florida. This subtropical race seems to never go completely dormant in winter.

Sambucus racemosa ssp. pubens
Red Elder, Scarlet Elder, Red-berried Elder

ZONES: 3–7; sun to light shade
SOIL: Moist
NATIVE TO: Woodland and woodland edge, wet thickets, stream sides, roadsides; Newfoundland to British Columbia south to California, Minnesota, Pennsylvania, and in the Appalachians to Tennessee and North Carolina
SIZE: Height 4–10 feet, width 3–8 feet
COLOR: Creamy white; blooms in spring

Red elder is a circumboreal species represented in North America by the subspecies *pubens*. It is a plant of the cold north that I see regularly in northern New England and Canada as well as in the western mountains and in the rainforests along the northern Pacific coast. When I first came to work for the New England Wild Flower Society, there was a plant of this species in the nursery with a remarkable zig and zag habit from one set of leaves to another and I thought I had found my first million-dollar baby. I promptly planted it in the stock beds, ready to begin propagating it in earnest the following spring. Unfortunately, heavy snows that winter broke it off at the ground, and to my dismay, when it sprouted back from the roots, it had typical, straight stems; it is now a big shrub with nary a sign of the lightning bolt upon it.

Red elder has pinnate leaves with an average of 5 leaflets (the others have 7), and these are more or less suffused with a light down, especially on the undersides. Pyramidal flower heads are followed by bright red fruits that ripen in early summer, a few weeks earlier than either *S. canadensis* or *S. caerulea*. The fruits are stunning, for they possess both vibrant color and a shiny, soft translucence like a ripe tomato. They need to be well cooked before they are consumed to destroy their sour aftertaste. Unfortunately, the flowers have a mildly rank odor as well. Black-fruited forms (*S. racemosa* ssp. *pubens* var. *melanocarpa*) are fairly common in the Pacific Northwest. Larger forms, to 30 feet, growing in the temperate rainforests of Oregon north along the Pacific Coast to British Columbia and Alaska are labeled var. *arborescens*.

Sassafras albidum

Sassafras albidum
(SAS-a-fras)
Lauraceae
Sassafras

ZONES: 4–9; sun, part sun

SOIL: Moist to moderately dry

NATIVE TO: Woodland margins, fencerows, old fields, rocky or sandy places; southern Maine to Michigan south to Missouri, eastern Texas, and Florida

SIZE: Height 30–60 (90) feet, width 12–25 feet

COLOR: Light yellow; blooms in spring

Sassafras is a likable sort of tree. It travels skyward in the up-and-out, up-and-out fashion of pines, with a strong central leader that shoots up a foot or two during the growing season and finishes off the year by setting a few short branches near the tip that will grow out horizontally as the leader continues vertically the following spring. Thus, a length of bare trunk separates whorls of branches and the crown develops a characteristic layered silhouette that is unmistakable against the gray winter sky. As the whorls of branches grow wider each year, they have a swooping, out and up pattern like that seen in dogwoods and azaleas, in which the twigs form a series of connected W's with foliage bunched at the outermost tips. Sassafras leaves are curious things (it's part of what I find likable about them). The most typical shape resembles a two-thumbed mitten about 4 inches long. Other leaves may only have one thumb or none at all, depending on the whims of the

particular tree. The first leaves on a twig tend to be unlobed, and larger, lobed leaves form as growth proceeds into early summer. The leaf blade is glaucous green on top and three shades lighter below, and droops conveniently so you can make out its shape.

Sassafras is one of the few large berry-producing trees in eastern forests, and like black gum, it advertises this with a spectacular conflagration of scarlet, orange, and yellow leaves to draw attention to bloomy blue-black fruits clustered among them on bright red pedicels. These fruits are the inevitable outcome of commingled pollen and stigmas brought together through the efforts of industrious bees. Sassafras is quite lovely and delicate in flower, all the more so because the 6-tepaled chartreuse flowers spring from enlarged terminal buds with a flush of new leaves, managing to flower quite nicely before the foliage obscures them from view. The inflorescences effect a skirted arrangement below the leaves much like fringetree's, though less dramatically. Sassafras are dioecious, so you'll need both male and female trees to see any fruit. From an aesthetic point of view, there is little difference between male and female flowers—both haze the crown with bright yellow-green for a week or so in spring.

As you might expect from a disturbance-adapted tree, sassafras readily colonizes if the opportunity presents itself. The trunks develop an orange-brown alligator-hide bark that is easy to recognize and highly ornamental. Along roadsides and fencerows, it is common to see not one but a grove of umbrella-like silhouettes leaning and twisting in competition with each other for space. What triggers this rush to root sprouts is a mystery to me: I have had some trees in my yard that grew contentedly as a single trunk, while others were readily thicket forming. It could be a genetic trait or a response to wounding or some environmental condition like poor soil or drought. At any rate, while you need to take a certain rambunctiousness into account with sassafras, in the right situation, like the boundary between lawn and field or field and forest, it is interesting in carriage, flower, and leaf, and I highly recommend it.

The laurel family is well known for the fragrant oils that many of its members contain. The European true laurel (*Laurus nobilis*) and our own redbay (*Persea borbonia*) have a pungent, oregano scent, while spicebush (*Lindera benzoin*) is more musky and clovelike. The bark and roots of sassafras have their own spicy smell, a sort of pleasantly sharp version of spicebush's scent, and the roots were so highly valued by Europeans that the search for them paved the way for eventual settlement of New England by English pilgrims in the early 1600s. The first British explorations of the area came about not in the interest of religious freedom, but rather to secure quantities of sassafras root from which to distill the valuable oil, touted as a restorative tonic.

Sassafras albidum. Spectacular fall color is but one of sassafras's charms. In the seventeenth century English explorers came to our Atlantic coast in search of sassafras roots. Boiled, the roots yielded a fragrant oil that was brewed into a restorative tonic.

CULTURE: Sassafras suffers from a difficult reputation regarding transplanting. When I was first working with native plants, everyone warned me not to bother with sassafras, as it is impossible to transplant. However, after doing a bit of experimenting and asking others what they had tried, I realized that many had simply dug up what appeared to be seedlings but which were actually root suckers with no real roots of their own and no chance of surviving when removed from life support. If you start with container-grown seedlings, sassafras is as easy to grow as anything else, and once established in a sunny spot, it can handle a fair bit of drought. Drought will keep it small (and encourage suckers), but a shrubby colony is attractive, too. On rich soils, sassafras may grow to 70 feet or more, with trunks over 3 feet in diameter, but in general, individual stems are not very long-lived. The primary reason is attack by the canker fungus *Nectria galligena*, which causes the familiar target-like lesions seen also on some birches and maples.

USES: Specimen, grouped or massed along boundaries.

WILDLIFE: Female sassafras trees, should they set a crop of oil-rich fruit, are much appreciated by migrating birds. Sassafras is a primary larval host plant for both the spicebush swallowtail and the laurel swallowtail butterflies (*Papilio troilus* and *P. palamedes*).

PROPAGATION: Moderately easy from seed.

Sequoiadendron giganteum. *Walking through a grove of ancient giant sequoias is one of the most humbling experiences I have ever had. It is hard to believe such massive things are even possible, and harder still to believe they're alive.*

Sequoiadendron giganteum

Sequoiadendron giganteum

(se-kwoi-a-DEN-dron)
Cupressaceae
Giant Sequoia, Big Tree

ZONES: 6–8; sun, part sun
SOIL: Moist, at least in spring
NATIVE TO: Mixed montane coniferous forests at 4,500–7,500 feet in the central California Sierras
SIZE: Height 40–120 (300) feet, width 20–40 (60) feet
COLOR: Yellow; blooms in spring

Big things are humbling — I'm not sure why, exactly. This is especially true when you are in the presence of very big *living* things, even if they are so inconceivably large as to seem as inanimate as a cliff or a building. After several millennia, giant sequoias attain a height and girth almost beyond comprehension — they are truly, truly mammoth and certainly the largest living things on earth. (Discounted are more nebulous contenders like the recently discovered, vast, mostly underground fungus colonies or clonal groves of quaking aspens, both of which stretch over many acres but appear individually much smaller). Today the big tree is restricted to a narrow belt of montane forest in the California Sierras roughly 260 miles long and meandering along the moister western slopes between 4,500 and 7,500 feet above sea level. The mountains to the east create a barrier to winter moisture coming off the Pacific, which thus falls as snow in the redwood belt. It can pile up 30 feet deep around the trunks during wet El Niño years. The snow slowly melts and recharges the groundwater to help the trees weather bone-dry summers. With summer drought come fires that scar the land and scorch the bark of old trees, clearing off less fire-tolerant competition and helping young, shade-hating sequoias to become established. The punky, rusty red bark of mature trees is incredibly thick, protecting the cambium from all but the most intense forest fires. Many old trees bear the scars of past conflagrations, or the spiral wounds created by

lightning tracing its way from the upper branches to the ground. Deeply fissured and channeled bark is really the thing you notice about the big tree, for in all but seedlings and saplings, most of the leaves hang far up in the canopy, out of sight and out of danger from the searing heat of ground fires. Sequoia foliage is scaly and lies forward against the ropelike twigs in a spiral pattern; this differs from the flattened arrangement of relatives like false cypress and western red-cedar. The foliage has an undeniably archaic character, in both shape and arrangement on the jointed, knobby branches. This primeval feeling carries through in the shape of the tree itself. Young trees—those less than 500 years old!—construct a rounded, soft green crown of swooping branches projecting thickly from a hulking trunk and buttressed base that seem out of scale with the fine canopy above. Small, oval cones set with diamond-shaped scales decorate the branch tips in vast numbers.

Fortunately for this monumental species, most of the surviving groves are located on protected public lands. Miners searching for gold during the 1849 gold rush first discovered the trees, and within a few years lumberjacks began felling them for their structurally weak but rot-resistant wood. However, their location high up in the inaccessible Sierras, their tendency to shatter and splinter when felled, not to mention the logistical problems related to cutting and moving trees of such huge size (a large tree may contain over 100,000 board feet of lumber in a trunk almost 30 feet wide at the base) made harvesting difficult. Roughly two-thirds of the original trees remain standing today.

The situation of the coast redwood (*Sequoia sempervirens*) is not as fortuitous. This is an equally large and remarkable tree that grows in a narrow band about 450 miles long within 35 miles of the northern California–southern Oregon coast, where it is within reach of the summer fogs that come in off the ocean most afternoons during the summer and condense on and replenish the needles. Coast redwood's form is similar to the giant sequoia's, but its needles are linear and arranged quill-feather fashion along the twigs, much like hemlock's. It has the ability, shared by few other conifers, to sprout from basal burls that grow along the stump, and this allows it to come back more easily after fire or logging. Its cinnamon heartwood is as remarkably rot-resistant as *Sequoiadendron*'s and is less brittle. Consequently, the accessible old-growth trees have been almost completely cut out. Only about 1 to 2 percent of the original old-growth coast redwoods now survive on protected lands.

CULTURE: Both species grow most satisfactorily in cool, maritime climates. Coast redwood was once a much more widespread tree; it is adapted to the cool temperate climate, with mild, wet winters and warm, humid summers, that is now found in the United States only along the central Pacific Coast. Coast redwood thrives in cultivation in the British Isles as well as north of its natural range to coastal British Columbia. Its performance in the eastern United States is less than spectacular. It will live in the Southeast and to a lesser extent in the warmer parts of the Northeast, but it never gains much size because twigs and leaders are killed by winter cold or by heat. Giant sequoia fares better, and fine garden specimens can be found in temperate parts of the Northeast, espe-

cially along the coast. The trees do not grow extremely tall (40–70 feet), but they do form beautiful, swollen trunks of a diameter pleasingly out of scale with their modest height. Transplant container-grown trees into soil that retains some moisture through the summer in a spot that receives at least 3 to 4 hours of sun. They are relatively shallow-rooted, so need some supplemental irrigation during drought for the first few years until established.

USES: Specimen.

PROPAGATION: Moderately easy from seed.

Sorbus sitchensis

Sorbus (SOR-bus)
Rosaceae
Mountain-ash

Sorbus sitchensis. *A mountain-ash hung with ripe fruits is a glorious sight indeed.*

The scarlet or orange fruits of the genus *Sorbus* are one of the true glories of the mountain landscape, getting your attention like traffic cones on the highway, even amid the brilliant autumn colors of maples and aspens. The fruits must be a bit starchy and unpalatable to birds at first, but after a few cycles of freeze and ferment in fall, they are eaten by robins, grosbeaks, waxwings, and friends—in fact, judging by the sluggish and fearless way the birds hang on the trees, the alcohol content of the fruits must provide quite a little nip to warm their weary wings. The native mountain-ashes have pinnate leaves composed of 11 to 17 narrow serrated leaflets spaced neatly in pairs along the central rachis. The leaves alternate up stout twigs that curve up from a short central trunk to form a rounded, dark green crown. The compound leaves droop down a bit toward the ground-bound viewer, giving the tree an agreeably jagged texture—a nice foil for flat-topped clusters of lace doily–white flowers crowning all the branch tips in late spring, just after the leaves have expanded. Flowers yield to clusters of fruits that ripen over the course of the summer. The berries show to good advantage for two months or more, at first backlit by the golden and apricot fall foliage, then hanging brightly on the bare, gray branches.

One note of caution: Even under the best conditions, *Sorbus* is prone to a gradual, inevitable defoliation that leaves them potentially threadbare by the time fruit is ripe. If you are an optimist by nature, you might say, "All the better to see the glorious fruit …" and you just may be right. Their tendency to lose lower leaves through the season is partly a response to the various leaf diseases they are subject to, and partly just a general tendency of the tribe. These are small trees or large shrubs at home in the colder parts of the Northern Hemisphere, where the growing season is naturally short and winters long. Consequently, I think that mountain-ashes accomplish their necessary yearly photosynthesis rather quickly, and they retain this efficiency even when grown at lower latitudes with longer summers. At the Garden, by August the trees have a "come *on*, already" look about them as though they are expecting winter is just around the corner, not on the other side of town.

CULTURE: I don't mean to disparage these beautiful trees, for in the northern reaches of North America they are one of the finest small lawn trees one could plant. I saw them being used quite liberally and to great effect in eastern Canada in just such a way. Farther south or at lower elevations, you need to temper their use with the knowledge that they will likely drop their leaves before autumn. Keep the trees healthy with a light application of fertilizer in spring, supplemental water during drought, and a spot with good air movement yet one that is not hot and dry. The mountain-ash sawfly (*Pristiphora geniculata*) can be a troubling pest in the East. Some years it will completely defoliate both American mountain-ash (*S. americana*) and showy mountain-ash (*S. decora*) in the Garden and in the wild, and the trees really don't leaf out much again that season. Fortunately, it does not seem to bother sitka mountain-ash (*S. sitchensis*).

USES: Specimen, lawn tree. They cast a fairly light shade so that grass survives below.

WILDLIFE: Food (and inebriant?) for birds.

PROPAGATION: Moderately easy from seed.

Sorbus americana
American Mountain-ash

ZONES: 2–5(6); sun, part sun
SOIL: Moist
NATIVE TO: Moist woodland, slopes, wet thickets, openings; Newfoundland to Minnesota south to Illinois, Pennsylvania, and in the Appalachians to northern Georgia
SIZE: Height 15–35 (50) feet, width 8–20 feet
COLOR: Creamy white; blooms in late spring

American mountain-ash is commonly a large, multi-trunk shrub or small tree with bark that is smooth and gray when young, rougher and sooty when old. The leaflets are fairly narrow and splay out stiffly from a red central stem. The ¼-inch fruits are an intense scarlet red and show to brilliant effect as the leaves color up in late summer to early autumn. Showy mountain-ash (*S. decora*) has an overlapping range and looks similar from a distance, but its leaflets are broader and a shade darker green. The fruits are larger (⅜ inch) and a shade closer to crimson. It blooms and fruits a week or two after *S. americana*. It is a beautiful tree, and I frankly prefer it to American mountain-ash for both foliar and fruit effect.

Sorbus sitchensis
Sitka Mountain-ash

ZONES: 3–6; sun, part sun
SOIL: Moist
NATIVE TO: Montane coniferous forest, gaps, thickets, and bog margins; Montana to Yukon and Alaska south to British Columbia, California, and Idaho
SIZE: Height 8–20 feet, width 6–10 feet
COLOR: Creamy white; blooms in late spring

Sitka mountain-ash has larger, broader leaves than the two preceding species; accordingly it has a stronger texture and presence in the garden. Its fruits

Sorbus sitchensis. *Big, saucer-sized flower clusters burst from the branch tips of our Sitka mountain-ash in mid-spring.*

are likewise about twice the size of *S. americana,* up to nearly ½ inch in diameter, and are borne in flat clusters up to 8 inches across and range in color from highway orange to bright scarlet. Though it tends to defoliate in our garden by late in the season, it doesn't suffer from sawfly damage like its eastern relatives. It is quite a spectacle in full fruit and probably is our best all-around ornamental *Sorbus.* Western mountain-ash *(S. scopulina)* is a similar, though finer foliaged species from the interior, mountainous areas of western North America.

Spiraea tomentosa

Spiraea (spy-REE-ah)
Rosaceae
Spirea, Meadowsweet

Spireas are woody plants that have the sort of robust growth and habit of blooming on new wood that make them comfortable in the company of either herbaceous perennials or other shrubs. When out of bloom, meadowsweet is a nondescript blob that sends out vigorous stems set with closely alternating, finely toothed leaves with a vaguely bluish cast to their upper surface and a lighter blush below. The leaves of most species set their most pronounced teeth toward the rounded tip of the blade, with a mere suggestion of dentition toward the base. This, coupled with their blue-green color and contrasting reddish brown, caney stems, gives all the *Spiraea* species a characteristic look.

Within the genus are two basic patterns: taller shrubs with arching canes and pointed flower panicles, and lower, mounding species with flat-topped blooms. Most are very pretty in flower, carrying their little 5-petaled white or pink blooms in dense, flattened or billowing spirelike heads from the tips of the new growth in the dog days of summer. Tufts of stamens protrude beyond the corolla of each flower, and the result is heads that have a decidedly frothy or foaming look. They produce a vaguely industrial

perfume like that of inexpensive beauty products, most likely designed to attract beetles. Beetles as well as bees and butterflies readily visit the flowers and lounge listlessly on the frothy heads.

CULTURE: As a whole, spireas are easy-to-grow shrubs tolerant of a range of soils and moisture levels. Larger clumps can be divided with a sharp spade and transplanted in spring or fall. Since they are fast growing and bloom on new wood, hard pruning every few years will not interrupt flowering if you accomplish it when the plants are dormant. In fact, spireas are one of the few woody species that can survive yearly mowing and still bloom regularly, and they really look their best in mixed, naturalized, or meadow situations where any late-summer foliar indecencies will be tactfully screened by other plants (mildews and other diseases may attack the leaves in hot, humid weather, partially defoliating them). These are mostly cool temperate species that thrive in the North but languish in the Deep South. In full sun and moist, fertile soil, the plants may luxuriate to the point of aggressiveness, but all in all they are tough, resilient, and reliably fast-growing shrubs providing us with intensely colorful flowers at a time when little else is in bloom.

USES: Mixed borders, massing, meadows, watersides.

WILDLIFE: Excellent nectar plants for bees, beetles, and butterflies.

PROPAGATION: Easy from cuttings or seed.

Spiraea alba
Meadowsweet

ZONES: 3–8; sun, part sun

SOIL: Wet to dry

NATIVE TO: Swamps, pond shores, old fields, meadows, dry, rocky woods; Newfoundland to Alberta south to South Dakota, Missouri, and North Carolina

SIZE: Height 2–5 feet, width 2–5 feet

COLOR: White, sometimes with a hint of pink; blooms in mid- to late summer

Meadowsweet lofts its familiar pyramidal panicles in a variety of habitats. There are two varieties, the more western variety, *S. alba* var. *alba,* which is more commonly a wetland plant with yellow-brown twigs, and var. *latifolia* (also listed as *S. latifolia*), with dark brown or burgundy stems and much greater ecological flexibility. As is the case with all the white species, the flower clusters tend to get a bit muddy after some of the flowers begin to fade. It is an adaptable plant, but for floral effect I prefer the sympatric *S. tomentosa.* Other white-flowered species include birchleaf spirea *(Spiraea betulifolia),* a low, spreading spirea from open woodlands, meadows, and slopes in both the Appalachians and Rocky Mountains, and Appalachian spirea *(S. virginiana),* which is restrict-

Spiraea tomentosa. The flowers of steeplebush are tightly packed together, providing a secure landing pad for pollinating beetles and bees. I like the way the clusters poke out aggressively from beneath the uppermost leaves.

ed to ravines and moist slopes in the Appalachians. Both have large, flat clusters of white flowers fading to brown and a rapidly colonizing disposition.

Spiraea douglasii (menziesii)
Douglas Spirea

ZONES: 4–8; sun, part sun
SOIL: Moist to wet
NATIVE TO: Pond shores, stream sides, wet meadows and swamps; Montana to British Columbia south to California, Idaho, and Colorado
SIZE: Height 3–7 feet, width 3–6 feet
COLOR: Vivid pink fading to light pink; blooms in summer

In a damp, sunny location, Douglas spirea is magnificent in flower, with pointed pyramidal clusters opening bubble-gum pink and fading to a smoky rose. The leaves are gray-green above and silvery white below, creating a nice contrast that adds visual interest to the floral display. It willingly spreads to form colonies—a fact that must be considered when you place it.

Spiraea splendens (densiflora)
Mountain Spirea

ZONES: 3–7; sun, part sun
SOIL: Moist, cool
NATIVE TO: Subalpine meadows, alpine slopes, and stream sides; Alberta to British Columbia south to California and Wyoming
SIZE: Height 1–2 feet, width 1–2 feet
COLOR: Vivid pink; blooms in summer

This low-growing mountain species rivals any of the Asian cultivars in the lavishness of its bloom. Fairly small, dark green leaves mound on slowly spreading stems that erect luminous pink flowers in cauliflower-shaped clusters at their tips. The flowers are especially lovely when set off by the reds of paintbrush (*Castilleja* spp.) and the purple of alpine asters and fleabanes in damp mountain meadows. The blooms open dark pink and fade two shades lighter, for a subtle two-toned effect. It requires a cool, moist location to thrive, but it is one of my favorite spireas and certainly worth giving a try.

Spiraea tomentosa
Steeplebush

ZONES: 3–8; sun, part sun
SOIL: Moist to moderately dry
NATIVE TO: Swamps, pond shores, and wet meadows
SIZE: Height 2–5 feet, width 2–5 feet
COLOR: Light to medium pink; blooms in mid- to late summer

Steeplebush gets its name from the narrow, pointed pink flower clusters that adorn the stiff or arching

Stewartia malacodendron. *An alluring combination of crinkly, pure white petals and midnight violet anthers lands silky stewartia among the ten most beautiful native shrubs and small trees. This photograph was taken at the North Carolina Botanical Garden in Chapel Hill. The staff maintains an excellent display of southeastern native plants, sampling the breadth of the region's remarkable flora in aesthetically sensitive and informative interpretive displays.*

canes in summer. As the first blooms become pollinated, smaller side shoots begin to bloom, fleshing out the panicle and keeping the plants colorful for at least a month. In the wild it is a plant of damp, open places, but it will tolerate less moisture under cultivation.

Stewartia malacodendron

Stewartia (stew-AR-tia)
Theaceae
Stewartia

In an evolutionary sense, stewartias are just a stone's throw from camellias—a fact readily apparent if you've seen them in bloom. Stewartia's huge flowers have the sensual ebullience of a single camellia or peony blossom: 5 wrinkled petals form a shallow saucer with a crinkly rim. The stamens that ring the center of the corolla are often a deep, blackish purple and are set off beautifully by the pure white cup of petals. Stewartias are certainly some of our most evocative and expressive flowering shrubs—more garden aristocrats than everyday things—that need to be sited where their blooms can be fully appreciated.

In habit, both mountain stewartia and silky stewartia are thin-twiggy shrubs that can be pruned into single-trunked small trees wider than tall or can be allowed to grow freely into a mounded, suckering shrub in the fashion of witch-hazels. The deeply veined foliage is medium green, deciduous, and set mostly on the circumference of the crown, so the plants have a light, dappled appearance in leaf. The flowers open among the leaves after they have expanded, which does obscure them somewhat. The bark is a uniform warm brown, without the sycamore-like mottling of their Asian cousins.

CULTURE: Site stewartias in moist, fertile, well-drained soil. Root rot can be a problem in the South, especially in clay. If clay soils can be avoided, stewartias are excellent flowering shrubs for southern gardens. These are understory plants in the wild, happiest where they receive some sun as well as protection from strong winds and the worst heat of the day. We have had a silky stewartia at the Garden now for 7 years, and though it is growing slowly and suffers some tip dieback in hard winters, it has weathered some pretty tough storms and droughts. Like many southern genera (*Franklinia, Elliottia*) it continues growing late into the season, so we protected it the first three years (see *Elliottia*, p. 116). Transplant from containers in spring. Take some time to shape the plant when it is young to encourage a strong, single trunk and even branching. Lightly fertilize yearly in spring. Stewartias take several years to settle in before they really begin to bloom heavily.

USES: Specimen.

PROPAGATION: Difficult from cuttings and seed.

Stewartia malacodendron
Silky Stewartia

ZONES: (6)7–9; part sun
SOIL: Moist, rich, slightly acidic
Native to: Moist woods and stream sides along the coastal plain from Virginia to Florida and Louisiana
SIZE: Height 6–15 feet, width 6–12 (20) feet
COLOR: Pure white; blooms in late spring

Considered by many to be the most beautiful of all stewartias in flower, *S. malacodendron* is usually a spreading, suckering shrub in the wet thickets it prefers in the wild. In cultivation, it can become an attractive small tree with a fine network of branches and twigs. The stamens on this species are a uniform dark purple-red with a gray-blue tip contributed by the pollen itself. They are truly magnificent in contrast within the 3-inch saucer of pure white petals. Its leaves are oval and cinched to a narrow base where the blade meets the petiole, and the leaf buds are covered with long gold-to-purplish silky hairs.

Stewartia ovata
Mountain Stewartia

ZONES: (5)6–8; part sun
SOIL: Moist, rich, slightly acidic
NATIVE TO: Damp mountain woods and thickets; in the Appalachians from eastern Kentucky to northern Virginia and northern Alabama
SIZE: Height 8–16 feet, width 6–14 feet
COLOR: White; blooms in late spring

Mountain stewartia is certainly more winter-hardy than silky stewartia; like its cousin it can be either a fine-twigged shrub or small tree. The flowers of the species have white stamens, but *S. ovata* var. *grandiflora* has larger flowers (up to nearly 4 inches across), with purple filaments like silky stewartia's, as well as a few extra petals. It's definitely the variety to seek out.

Styrax americanus

Styrax (STY-rax)
Styracaceae
Snowbell, Storax

Styrax americanus. A photograph can convey the pretty, dangling-earring floral display of a well-grown American snowbell, but it cannot hope to capture the rich, citrusy perfume that emanates from the blooms.

Snowbells are among the most ornamental and least appreciated of our flowering shrubs. They are close kin to the silverbells, sharing the habit of decorating every twig with dangling, 5-petaled flowers of a shade befitting their common name. The petals are reflexed, so the blooms are less bell than small, upside-down Easter lily blooms with a cluster of long, orange anthers dangling in the middle. The scent is penetratingly sweet-citrusy, and the heady aroma lofts out on the slightest breeze when the plants are in bloom. Flowers come from either the axils of the expanding leaves or the terminal racemes out beyond them, depending on the species. Partly because of the way the petals flare out and up, and partly because they hang beneath the leaves, the flowers do not stand out as boldly as say, a mock-orange's, or even a silverbell's. Even so, a flowering snowbell has a certain delicacy and grace that I find absolutely charming, and the fragrance is a welcome bonus.

In the wild, the genus prefers the dappled light along streams, where the upper tree canopy is less dense and the soil moist and fertile. They will send up new sprouts from near the base of the existing stems, slowly expanding to form colonies, especially in heavier shade. There are two species in the Southeast, one in California, and an additional species complex, sycamore-leaf snowbell (*S. platanifolius*), restricted to western and west-central Texas, especially the limestone-rich Edwards Plateau (one of the most botanically rich and interesting areas in the United States).

CULTURE: Site snowbells in moist, fertile soil and dappled shade or morning sun. *S. rediviva* is the exception, thriving in drier soils and full sun. In early spring, transplant container-grown plants or carefully dug rooted suckers taken from the edge of an established plant. You can often find good crops of seedlings coming up around a healthy, older shrub that are fairly easy to move as well. Only American snowbell is reliably hardy north of Zone 7, and though some dieback and snow breakage may occur in hard winters, this grows and blooms well for us at Garden in the Woods.

USES: Massing or understory shrub or small tree.
PROPAGATION: Moderately easy from seed.

Styrax americanus
American Snowbell

Symphoricarpos albus var. albus. The twigs of common snowberry are hung with large quantities of chalky fruits from late summer well into winter. Hard pruning of the older, less productive stems every three to five years will encourage vigorous new growth and bloom.

ZONES: 5–9; part sun to light shade
SOIL: Moist
NATIVE TO: Stream sides, low woods, and swamp margins; Virginia to Florida and Louisiana north along the Mississippi to southern Indiana, occasionally into Ohio and Pennsylvania
SIZE: Height 4–12 feet, width 4–15 feet
COLOR: White; blooms in late spring

With its medium green, oval leaves held in an upward slant along nearly horizontal twigs and ¾-inch-wide flowers dangling in a row below, American snowbell has a unique layer-cake look that I especially like. The flowers appear one to a leaf axil from the new growth, just as the latter is finished expanding. The leaves themselves have a ruffled, undulating margin, especially when they receive some sun. New sprouts come annually from the base of the plant, so with time it becomes a wide, rounded, many-stemmed clump. We are growing up seed from one of the most northerly populations in Indiana, which we hope will suffer less dieback during hard winters than more southern genotypes. Interestingly, this parent stand is also growing in drier, sunnier conditions, and so remains a compact 4-foot mound. Sycamore-leaf snowbell *(S. platanifolius)* is similar in overall habit and leaf shape, but its flowers are borne 2 or more per axil on short racemes. It is restricted to central Texas, where it lives along streams flowing through limestone canyons. Chapparal snowbell *(S. rediviva)*, with larger, glossier foliage, ranges throughout the western half of California.

Styrax grandifolius
Big-leaf Snowbell

ZONES: (6)7–9; part sun, light shade
SOIL: Moist to somewhat dry
NATIVE TO: Wooded slopes, floodplains, and stream banks; Virginia and southern Illinois south to Louisiana and Florida
SIZE: Height 8–25 feet, width 6–15 ft
COLOR: White; blooms in late spring

I planted big-leaf snowbell in my backyard in Durham, North Carolina, and it established well in the fairly dry shade under pines. The leaves are quite large, to 8 inches long and 5 inches wide, so although they attempt to hold themselves upward, they droop sleepily along the outer edges in an endearing fashion. It spreads relatively fast by root suckers to form dense colonies of thin, vertical trunks with the tallest toward the center, similar to large fothergilla *(Fothergilla major)*. Flowers are of the same shape and size as those of *S. americanus*, but they hang in sprays of 5 to 20 on arching racemes at the tips of the new growth where they are a bit easier to see. It is a mystery to me why this plant is not more common in woodland gardens.

Symphoricarpos albus var. albus

Symphoricarpos
(sim-for-i-KAR-pos)
Caprifoliaceae
Snowberry, Coralberry

The chief ornamental characteristic of this small genus are large (often ponderously large for the size of the plant), colorful fruits that appear in late summer and continue to hang on the ends of bare, arching canes well into winter. All snowberries send out vigorous new canes clothed in paired, oval to almost round leaves from the roots and bases of the larger branches. Usually these have a cool, blue-gray complexion that's distinctive and pretty, and they hold themselves out stiffly in the fashion of honeysuckles. From late spring on into early summer, clusters of small white flowers begin to appear; first at the tips of short side branches, then later at the terminus of the suckering new growth. The flowers, only about ¼ inch wide, consist of 5 flaring petals fused toward their bases to form a rounded bowl and tinged more or less with an infusion of pink. These quickly yield to the berries, which begin to take shape lower on the tight little cluster as the last of the flowers are still blooming just above. Most of the species have chalky white fruits filled nebulously with small seeds. Depending on how well a certain fruit was pollinated, it may be only ½ inch in diameter or swell to over an inch in a lumpy and bloated, comical way. The Latin name for the genus is a 10-dollar word meaning "tightly clustered fruits." Coralberry is the primary exception, for the berries are arranged in small axillary groups strung along the last 6 to 12 inches of the stem. They are brilliant purplish red.

Symphoricarpos species are closely related to honeysuckles, and they share a zest for living that is undaunted by poor soils and shade. Granted, the spreading, arching snowberry canes lack anything approaching a sophisticated architecture, but they are well worth planting in challenging sites where their fruit displays can be enjoyed by people and others, too.

CULTURE: Snowberries and coralberries are easily transplanted into a range of soils and moisture conditions, except for swamps. They are used chiefly in such spots as parking lot islands and dry, difficult-to-mow slopes. You can also treat them something like perennials and cut the stems back to within 6 inches of the ground every 4 years. This will encourage heavy fruit set, at least in the second and succeeding years, and keep the mound more even and presentable. The white species will tolerate light shade, but like honeysuckles, leaves can be badly affected by mildew under these conditions. (A vigorous plant can usually compensate with a continual supply of new leaves.)

USES: Massing in difficult sites, soil stabilization.

WILDLIFE: The fruits are slowly but eventually eaten by birds.

PROPAGATION: Easy from cuttings, moderately difficult (slow) from seed.

Symphoricarpos albus
Common Snowberry

ZONES: 3–7; sun to light shade
SOIL: Moist to dry
NATIVE TO: Dry, rocky woods, outcrops, old fields, woodland margins; Quebec to Alaska south to California, Minnesota, and Virginia
SIZE: Height 2–3 feet, width 3–4 feet
COLOR: White flushed with pink; blooms in late spring to early summer

Common snowberry is the most widespread of a group of related white-flowered species. It has oval to nearly rounded leathery leaves with a matte blue-gray patina lining arching stems in two flattened ranks. The eastern var. *albus* bears fruits up to ½ inch

wide, whereas the western var. *laevigatus* produces fruits twice this girth, and is the form most often sold in nurseries. Western snowberry (*S. occidentalis*) ranges over the western half of the United States and southern Canada. It is very similar to the common snowberry, although it is more freely suckering and prone to run at the roots. Mountain snowberry (*S. oreophilus*), a shrub of the western cordillera, has performed well for us in terms of fruit production and mildew resistance, and it's my pick of the three snowberries considered here.

Symphoricarpos orbiculatus
Coralberry

ZONES: 3–8; sun, part sun
SOIL: Moist, well-drained to dry
NATIVE TO: Dry, rocky outcrops, old fields, woodland margins; Connecticut to Michigan and Colorado south to Louisiana and North Carolina, naturalized elsewhere
SIZE: Height 3–4 feet, width 4–8 feet
COLOR: White flushed with pink; blooms in late spring

In the cultivated landscape, expect coralberry to become a dense mound of fine branches hung in fall with a tremendous load of ½-inch berries. The fruits remain on the naked canes for quite a while, but eventually birds will eat them and disperse the seeds. The plant is truly spectacular when loaded with coral red fruits in fall. Its leaves are small and oval in outline and closer to green than blue. Pink snowberry (*S. microphyllus*), from New Mexico, was crossed with coralberry to create × *chenaultii* (Chenault coralberry), a very pretty small-leaved shrub with white berries flushed rose pink where the sun hits them.

Taxodium distichum (tax-OH-dium)

Taxodium distichum var. *distichum*

Cupressaceae
Baldcypress, Pondcypress

ZONES: 4–10; sun, part sun

SOIL: Moist to wet or inundated

NATIVE TO: Rivers, lake shores, and swamps: Delaware south along the coast to Florida and Texas, and up the Mississippi to southern Illinois and Indiana

SIZE: Height 60–90 (165) feet, width 20–60 feet

COLOR: Pale yellow; blooms in late winter, early spring

Taxodium distichum var. distichum. *Few places are more magical than dripping wet cypress forests. These humid wetlands along the Gulf and southern Atlantic coasts are as close to subtropical jungle as you'll find in the continental United States, providing a home for epiphytic orchids, bromeliads, and ferns found nowhere else in the country.*

Think of bayous; think of tannin-black swamps swimming with alligators and dripping with moss; think of oppressive humidity and torporific heat, and you'll have pictured the place cypress calls home. Baldcypress and its cousin, pondcypress, are members of an ancient line of extremely long-lived, statuesque conifers related to the redwoods. Their thick, fluted and buttressed trunks are covered with a thin gray-brown, fibrous bark, which offers scant protection from the frequent fires that sweep through the Southeast in spring. So the cypresses have retreated to freshwater or brackish swamps and the floodplains of rivers, where fire can rarely find purchase. Cypress is one of the few temperate trees that is able to thrive in standing water, a feat it accomplishes with the aid of pneumatophores, or "knees"—cone-shaped outgrowths of the roots that form in shallow water and rise above the high-water mark. It is unclear whether these knees act like snorkels to actually provide oxygen to the submerged parts of the root system or just use the higher levels of oxygen locally for their own respiration and then send the products of this respiration elsewhere in the tree. Either way, these cypresses are able to withstand conditions that few other trees save tupelos and mangroves can tolerate, and accordingly you often find almost pure stands of cypress in flooded swamps and estuaries. Like the larches to the north, baldcypress goes bald during the winter and raises a new crop of needles each spring. Light floods through the leafless canopy all winter,

encouraging heavy loads of epiphytes on the trees, such as Spanish moss (*Tillandsia usneoides*) and other bromeliads, orchids, mosses, and ferns able to survive in the mild, subtropical winter. Old trees along the Gulf Coast may become so covered with these epiphytes that the large limbs become nearly obscured. Farther north, the deciduous leaves help cypresses weather severe winters in style, helping to explain their surprising cold hardiness.

When in leaf, baldcypress (*T. distichum* var. *distichum*) has a wonderfully soft, fresh green texture. The supple, half-inch-long distichous (meaning "arranged in two rows or ranks") needles splay out in bird-feather ranks along the new growth. The first and last needles to form on each twig are shorter than the others, adding to the feather-like appearance of the whole. Long, tasseled pollen cones adorn the trees in late winter or early spring before the leaves have emerged, and at this time they have a melancholy aspect straight out of a gothic southern novel. Young trees have a pyramidal form with a rounded top, but as they mature and shed lower branches, they lose apical dominance so that the higher side branches grow up equal to the center, and the tree takes on a characteristic flat-topped silhouette identifiable from a mile away. As winter approaches, the needles turn a striking coppery brown before dropping.

Pondcypress (*distichum* var. *imbricarium*—formerly *T. ascendens*) is notably different, with needles flattened against whipcord branchlets like a giant clubmoss (it is similar to the giant sequoia in this way). It is on the whole a smaller tree with a narrow, steeple-like shape in the landscape. In the wild, it favors pocosins and pond shores near the south Atlantic coast, but it intergrades with baldcypress to such a degree that the two have been combined as varieties of one species. Pondcypress is a very interesting, even primeval, tree, and although slightly less winter-hardy (Zones 5–10), it is equally adaptable regarding soil conditions. Its unconventional look works very well in formal or modern designs in addition to naturalized settings.

CULTURE: Given their wild preference for southern swamps, both *Taxodium* varieties are surprisingly winter-hardy, and will grow well away from the water if the soil is reasonably moist. (The trees will not develop the extreme buttressing or knees in drier soils.) Both can be grown throughout most of the eastern United States; baldcypress has become popular as a park or terrace tree where its welcome summer shade gives way to equally welcome winter sun. Containerized or smaller balled and burlaped saplings are relatively easy to transplant in spring or fall. It is more difficult to establish them directly in water, though the effect of the tree rising out of a still pond is stunning. The one potentially serious problem we have encountered with baldcypress is cypress leaf blight, caused by the native fungus *Cercospora sequoiae*. Our largest tree is infected with this disease, which causes defoliation of the crown in late spring and the death of all but the uppermost and outer twigs. The tree has lived with the disease for many years, but it looks pretty threadbare for the first half of the summer. I have not noticed this problem to such an extent on other plantings or on pondcypress, so it may be a function of siting or of this tree's genetic predisposition.

USES: Waterside, park or street tree, especially effective planted in linear formal plantings, as the crowns are very uniform in youth.

PROPAGATION: Moderately easy from seed.

Taxus canadensis

Taxus (TAX-us)
Taxaceae
Yew

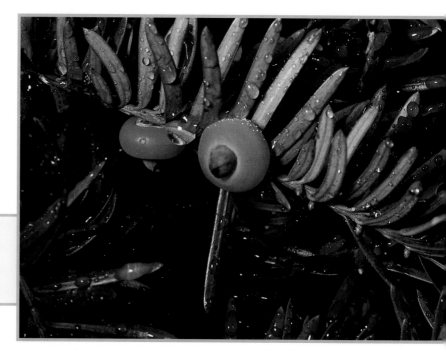

In the landscape trade there is no dearth of *Taxus*. These highly adaptable shrubs can be sheared into almost any shape and have thus been subjected to the most humiliating haircuts by the topiarilly challenged. (One of my friends and I even began taking photos of embarrassing yew haircuts for a yet-to-be-compiled album of shame.) The yews commonly sacrificed to foundation plantings and hedges are the Japanese yew (*T. cuspidata*), the English yew (*T. baccata*), and the hybrid offspring of the two, *T. × media* (called, imaginatively, the Anglojap yew). Both parents have the potential to become very large shrubs or even broad trees, so you have to keep after them if you don't want your house swallowed up. In North America we have three additional species. Pacific yew (*T. brevifolia*) is the giant of the group, capable of growing to 60 feet or more in the wet, Pacific coastal rainforests. Florida yew (*T. floridana*) is more modest in size, becoming a wide, rounded, irregularly branched shrub no taller than a ranch house. Finally there is Canada yew (*T. canadensis*), a sprawling groundcover usually less than waist-high. Though they are not generally used like the Eurasian species, they can serve a similar function, for they are evergreen shrubs that can be shaped into all manner of hedges and topiary or be allowed to grow naturally in a looser fashion.

Yew seeds and sometimes the foliage are notoriously poisonous, both to humans and livestock—all but *T. brevifolia* contain the alkaloid taxine. Despite popular wisdom, the fleshy red aril that surrounds the yew seed does not contain the poison; the seed itself does. Deer and moose have over time become immune to this chemical, though, and yews are one of their favorite winter foods. As deer populations have skyrocketed in the East, it is common to see foundation plantings picked clean of every accessible needle and twig. It's a pruning job even worse-looking than the most infamous human efforts. As the

deer herds grow, wild stands of Canada yew are becoming much less common and are restricted to inaccessible slopes over some of the species range. I mention this because where deer and moose are abundant, it is not worth planting yews. Otherwise, they are acceptable shade-tolerant, deep evergreen conifers for moist, acidic soils. All arrange their soft needles in flattened sprays, with new growth flushing out at angles from the tip. Old needles remain on the twigs for years, which helps to flesh out what would otherwise be a thin, bony canopy. Dormant axillary buds remain viable for many years along the trunk and branches, allowing the plant to resprout should its crown be cut back or eaten. The two larger species are dioecious, while the Canada yew bears both male and female cones.

CULTURE: Yews will grow in full sun, but they thrive in shade. Avoid waterlogged soils or sites subject to strong, drying winds. Container-grown or balled and burlaped yews can be transplanted readily in spring or fall, and they can be lightly pruned or shaped at any time during the growing season. Hard pruning (removing more than the outermost 3–6 inches of the crown) should be done in late winter to early spring, before new growth has commenced. Unlike many conifers, a healthy but overgrown old yew can be rejuvenated by being pruned back severely—even down to the main trunk or trunks, and it will still resprout again in season.

USES: Hedges, screens, groundcover (*T. canadensis*).

WILDLIFE: Birds devour the berries (arils) soon after they become ripe, and the evergreen branches provide good winter cover.

PROPAGATION: Moderately easy from cuttings, difficult from seed.

Taxus canadensis.
Bright red berries are easy to spot against the dark green boughs of a Canada yew, but coaxing the pointed seeds blanketed in their fleshy skin to germinate is a challenge that requires several years of propagatorial patience before they finally emerge.

Thuja plicata. *A thick, rich green canopy of flattened branches, pretty buff-colored bark, and a formal shape make western red cedar perfectly comfortable in the cultivated landscape. These trees are especially useful as a screen or as a dark backdrop for smaller plants. Thuja produces copious quantities of seed once it is mature, but few of the tiny offspring find just the right spot to germinate and grow.*

Taxus brevifolia
Pacific Yew

ZONES: (5)6–8; sun to shade
SOIL: Moist, acidic
NATIVE TO: Damp forests; western Montana to British Columbia and southeastern Alaska south to northern California and northern Idaho
SIZE: Height 10–40 (65) feet, width 8–18 feet
COLOR: Yellow; blooms in spring

The Pacific yew is a common understory plant of wet, Douglas fir/red cedar forests, preferring the high shade and breathing room of old-growth stands. Its ¾-inch needles are yellowish green on their upper surfaces, which detracts somewhat from its appearance, but it can grow into a nice, broad, diffusely branched pyramidal tree with lovely reddish purple flaking bark. This bark is a good source of taxol, a chemical that shows promise in anticancer therapy.

T. floridana (Florida yew) is smaller but similar in leaf arrangement and size, though its foliage is a dark, glossy green. It is restricted to the Apalachicola River system in northwestern Florida.

Taxus canadensis
Canada Yew

ZONES: 2–6; part sun to shade
SOIL: Moist, cool, acidic
NATIVE TO: Rich forests, bogs, ravines, and shaded slopes; Newfoundland to southeastern Manitoba south to northern Iowa and New York and in the mountains to Tennessee and Virginia
SIZE: Height 2–3 (6) feet, width 3–10 feet
COLOR: Yellow; blooms in spring

Canada yew is a very shade-tolerant evergreen shrub with a trailing habit and dark green inch-long needles. The upsweeping and flattened branches resemble the lower limbs of a hemlock or fir that have fallen to the ground and taken root. It has a fairly open, loose look to it, but we have employed it as a groundcover in shady sites. We lost many of our plants a few years ago when a herd of deer spent the winter in the Garden.

Thuja plicata

Thuja (THEW-ya)
Cupressaceae
Red Cedar, White Cedar, Arborvitae

Two *Thuja* **species** are native to North America, both stately evergreen conifers with scalelike needles, pyramidal habit, and peeling, red-gray bark concealing intoxicatingly aromatic, highly decay-resistant wood. Both have distributions centering on the 48th parallel, which forms the boundary between much of Canada and the United States. They grow in the company of spruce, fir, and larch in a climate that is cool to cold and moist to wet. They are among my favorite conifers, with their thick, flaring, shaggy trunks and narrow, rounded crowns of feathery green-black needles turning ruddy red during winter (there are cultivars of both species that hold their green color more tenaciously in winter).

In the wet forests of the Pacific Northwest lives the mighty western red cedar *(T. plicata)*, one of the largest and longest-lived of all the Pacific giants. In rich soils along rivers and streams, it may live for 800 years and reach a height of over 200 feet, carried to the sky on a strong central trunk up to 15 feet in diameter at its base. It is a superb landscape specimen, quickly becoming a formal, narrow pyramid of deepest green needles that droop in flattened sprays. The eastern species, arborvitae *(T. occidentalis)*, is but a stripling by comparison, but manages to reach a respectable girth in a sharply harsher climate — old trees may be 4 feet at the base yet only 40 feet tall. Both produce valuable wood, which has been harvested to such an extent that rare it is to find any extant specimens reaching the dimensions just described. Arborvitae has been planted extensively in the East, especially the pencil-thin or dwarf-globular cultivars, which bear little resemblance to the wild trees. The narrow forms like 'Nigra' are popular as shade- and cold-tolerant screening plants, yet their congested branches trap an inordinate amount of snow, causing older trees to bend like drunken sailors or even break off in winter storms. I was always puzzled as to why such a cold-climate tree would be so snow breakage–prone until I spent some time in northern Maine during the winter. Wild trees are much more diffusely branched and stocky, shedding most of the snow and preventing breakage. Sometimes natural and human selective pressures are completely at odds.

CULTURE: Both *Thuja* species prefer moist, cool, organic soils, though I have seen arborvitae thriving in less than ideal landscape situations. About 14 years ago, I found a seedling growing in a container plant received from a West Coast nursery; I potted it on and it turned out to be *T. plicata*. I planted it out on Cape Cod in pure sand, and it has done reasonably well ever since — it's now about 18 feet high. Certainly growth is markedly slower in poor soils, but I think that as long as you live in a fairly cool, humid climate, some liberties may be taken in placement. The trees are easily transplanted from containers or moved as balled specimens either in spring or fall.

USES: Specimen, screening, hedge, foundation plantings (some of the dwarf cultivars).

WILDLIFE: Nest sites and winter cover for birds.

PROPAGATION: Moderately difficult from cuttings, moderately easy from seed.

Thuja occidentalis

Arborvitae, Northern White Cedar

ZONES: 3–6(7); sun to light shade
SOIL: Moist to somewhat dry, moderately acidic to alkaline
NATIVE TO: Mostly limestone-enriched soils of swamps, low woods, and fens, cliffs and talus slopes; Nova Scotia to Manitoba south to northern Indiana, Michigan, and Connecticut (relict populations occur farther south to western North Carolina and Tennessee)
SIZE: Height 20–40 (60) feet, width 5–20 feet
COLOR: Yellow; blooms in spring

Deer like to winter-browse arborvitae, and the wild trees counter this by forming dense, spreading colonies of layering branches that sweep down from the trunk, then begin to establish their own apical dominance and grow vertically. Eventually the center leaders in the colony become inaccessible and grow up above the reach of the wood goats. It has the distinction of being the first tree sent to Europe — it was sent to France in 1536 or 1566 (sources differ) — and many of the cultivars are of European origin.

Thuja plicata

Western Red Cedar

ZONES: (4)5–7; sun to light shade
SOIL: Moist to moderately dry, acidic

NATIVE TO: Damp forests, typically on floodplains and along streams or swamp margins; Alaska south along the coast to northern California and also on the east side of the Rockies in southwestern Alberta, western Montana, and northern Idaho
SIZE: Height 40–60 (225) feet, width 10–18 (30) feet
COLOR: Yellow; blooms in spring

As Canadian hemlock succumbs to the woolly adelgid, the landscape industry is looking for a suitable shade-tolerant, fast-growing evergreen replacement, and I think red cedar comes the closest. Like hemlock, it casts a dense shade and may release allelopathic compounds that inhibit the growth of other plants, so it is difficult to grow anything under western red cedar's shade. It is a graceful and elegant tree, with a formal conical shape and impossibly deep green needles less prone to winter reddening than those of *T. occidentalis*. As the source of just about all the cedar used in construction, it is one of the most valuable lumber trees in the Pacific Northwest.

Tsuga canadensis

Tsuga (SOO-ga)
Pinaceae
Hemlock

Tsuga canadensis. Soft, lazy branches are the hallmark of most hemlocks. Even as the Canada hemlocks on my property are dying from the accumulated sucking of millions of woolly adelgids, I hold out hope that resistant strains will be discovered that will save this noble species from extinction.

I grew up among hemlocks. Every day when I looked out my bedroom window, I saw their dripping, drooping, impossibly green branches swaying animatedly just outside. Out the front door were young trunks I'd limbed up above my head to expose rusty gray, square-chunky bark, and in the backyard was an immense old patriarch with a hollow core accessed by two long vertical slits through its chunky, red rusty bark on the north and west sides. For two years in a row, a pair of pileated woodpeckers excavated a nest in its punky heartwood and we sat at the kitchen table and watched as they came and went with food for their young. Hemlocks have the ability to grow up in the shade cast by other trees, germinating on logs kept mossy and damp by the exclusion of wind and light caused by these other trees. Their branches set out nearly horizontally, bearing flattened needles aimed at catching the weak filtered sun coming through mature oaks, pines, or firs. One of the biggest challenges all saplings face as they plunge upward into the canopy of larger trees is the whipping and thrashing inflicted upon their branch tips as the wind smacks them against larger, rougher limbs. Most conifers have a dominant leader, which, if destroyed by this branch whipping, takes a season or two to reestablish. Not hemlocks: they can quickly shunt hormones to another branch tip, and up it goes higher into the canopy until it breaks into the sun and begins slowly to replace the other species that nurtured it as a seedling.

The pendulous quality of hemlock branches is a result of their pattern of growth. In spring, new twigs start off quickly and elongate faster than they can stiffen up, so they arch out and down under the accumulated weight of all those feathery, ¾-inch needles. As growth tapers off, the branch forms reaction wood on the upper side, which contracts and pulls the branch up to the vertical or horizontal, depending on whether it is destined to be a leader or branch. This explains why hemlocks are so quick to replace a damaged leader. Some trees are genetically unable to form reaction wood, and these become weeping (see the article by Peter Del Tredici, *Arnoldia* 40, no. 5). The magnificent weeping or prostrate cultivars like *T. canadensis* 'Sargentii' or 'Coles' are merely unable to right their branch tips later in the season.

Hemlocks are surely one of the most beautiful and adaptable conifers. They are completely evergreen, keeping their dark green color even in winter, they are very shade tolerant, and they are also reasonably drought tolerant once established. They can be clipped and pruned into hedges and topiary, and they are fairly fast growing and easy to transplant. So it is heartbreaking now for me to walk in the woods around my house and see all the eastern hemlocks dying or dead. An introduced pest, hemlock woolly adelgid *(Adelges tsugae)*, which is related to aphids, has spread slowly north from the Shenandoah Valley of Virginia over the last half century, leaving a trail of rotting hulks in its wake. The insect moves from stand to stand on birds, cars, the wind, or occasionally its own wings, quickly colonizing defenseless native hemlocks and slowly draining their life's blood. Frantic attempts to find natural predators for

the woolly adelgid have yielded a few promising leads, and a small black ladybug is being released in lightly infested areas around the Northeast. The overwintering adelgid eggs seem to be largely killed when temperatures drop below 0° F, so it has yet to be seen whether severe New England winters, isolated trees' natural resistance, or some combination of predators will keep the eastern hemlock from vanishing like the chestnut. (Interestingly, although the high mountains of North Carolina are full of both eastern hemlock and the equally susceptible Carolina hemlock, I have seen little sign of adelgid damage there, and those trees are practically next door to the original introduction site of the pest over the line in Virginia. Perhaps there is some control agent at work that has yet to be discovered.) Both western hemlocks have natural resistance to this insect and so remain relatively unaffected.

CULTURE: Ideally, site hemlocks in humusy, moist, acidic soils. Like many conifers, they prefer cool, humid climates as are found in the northeast United States, southern Canada, the western mountains, and the West Coast. They can be grown at lower elevations in the Southeast, but they really don't thrive unless you can provide a cool, damp microclimate. Other than the woolly adelgid, there are few other pests that badly trouble hemlock. In areas infested by the woolly adelgid, there is little point in planting either Canada hemlock or Carolina hemlock now, unless you are committed to yearly applications of insecticides. The western species will grow in the Northeast, but not with the vigor of the native ones. I can only hope that this pest will be checked soon, before we lose all of our trees.

USES: Specimen, screen, hedge (especially useful in the shade).

WILDLIFE: Nesting sites and winter cover for birds. Birds may also eat the seeds.

PROPAGATION: Moderately difficult from cuttings, moderately easy from seed.

Tsuga canadensis
Eastern Hemlock, Canada Hemlock

ZONES: 4–7; sun to shade

SOIL: Moist to moderately dry

NATIVE TO: Moist ravines, mixed forests, rocky hillsides; New Brunswick to southern Ontario south to Minnesota, southern Alabama, and the mountains of Georgia

SIZE: Height 60–80 (100) feet, width 25–40 feet

COLOR: Cones yellow and purple; blooms in spring

Eastern hemlock has distinctly flattened, two-ranked needles that are dark green above and mint green below (a third row of needles along the upper twig has shrunk down to be almost vestigial). It is capable of 2 to 3 feet of vertical gain in a season when young, and even old trees have a wonderful fluidity and softness about them. It casts a very dense shade, as all hemlocks do, and little else can survive underneath one. Western hemlock (*T. heterophylla*), from the maritime forests of the Pacific Northwest, is very similar in appearance. It is a very fast-growing tree; I have seen them add 4 to 5 feet in a season in regenerating stands in the Olympic National Forest. It has slightly smaller needles than eastern hemlock and they are a bit more gray-green in color. Seed from inland populations in British Columbia, Idaho, and Montana should theoretically do well in the Northeast, but in practice they need a good, moist soil and protection from winter winds.

Tsuga caroliniana
Carolina Hemlock

ZONES: 4–7; sun to shade
SOIL: Moist to moderately dry
NATIVE TO: Mountain slopes and ridges in the southern Appalachians; Virginia and Tennessee to northern Georgia and western South Carolina
SIZE: Height 40–60 (80) feet, width 20–25 feet
COLOR: Cones yellow; blooms in spring

Carolina hemlock grows in the misty Blue Ridge Mountains in the company of eastern hemlock, red spruce, and Fraser fir. Its dark green needles whorl around each twig instead of splaying out in two flattened ranks; a small difference that translates into a shaggier appearance to the tree overall. It tends to grow more slowly and narrowly than eastern hemlock, and, interestingly, it is more closely related to some of the Asian members of the genus than it is to the other native species. It no doubt has lived in these mountains for eons, since the days when the floras of North America and Eurasia were connected by land bridges long since submerged by the action of plate tectonics and erosion. Its seed cones are 1 inch long — twice as large as those of Canada hemlock — and flare out like a small architectural feature from the branch tips in autumn.

Tsuga mertensiana
Mountain Hemlock

ZONES: 4–7; sun, part sun
SOIL: Moist, cool
NATIVE TO: Damp forests and subalpine slopes; Montana to British Columbia south to California and northern Nevada
SIZE: Height 40–60 (120) feet, width 20–40 feet
COLOR: Yellow; blooms in spring

Mountain hemlock's needles whorl haphazardly around the twig much like those of Carolina hemlock. The stomatal bands that give a minty cast to the undersides of other hemlocks are here present on the upper sides as well, resulting in a uniform glaucous cast to the tree. Mountain hemlock has a stockier,

even shaggier look than Carolina hemlock, with a tall, narrow crown bred to shed heavy snow loads. It is the dominant tree in the subalpine forests of the Cascades, where its dark trunks are obscured by thick pelts of bearded lichens and moss. Unfortunately, it suffers in the heat and humidity of the eastern United States, but we have kept it alive at the Garden.

Tsuga mertensiana. *Compare the silhouette of mountain hemlock with that of Canada hemlock on page 245. This species is noticeably stiffer and more tufted looking.*

Ulmus americana

Ulmus (UL-mus)
Ulmaceae
Elm

The sad tale of the American elm and Dutch elm disease is a story almost everyone knows, because elms were until recently the street tree of choice in America. *U. americana* is one of the few trees that forms a high, arching canopy that lofts its branches neatly above trucks, houses, and utility lines. It is also relatively tolerant of urban conditions, and quickly grows into a magnificent, thick-trunked, V-shaped specimen. The Dutch elm fungus *Ceratocystis ulmi* was imported accidentally into Colorado in the 1930s and has since spread throughout the trees' natural range. It can be spread by bark beetles or move through the roots of an infected tree to those of an adjoining one, so whole elm-lined streets are usually laid bare very quickly. (The roots of trees of the same species growing in close proximity may fuse or "graft" together, and thus fluids, as well as diseases, are easily exchanged.) After the first wave of the disease swept through this country in the 1950s and '60s, resistant trees were identified, named, and cross-bred, which has resulted in moderately to highly resistant progeny like the cultivars 'Liberty', 'Princeton', 'Valley Forge', and 'New Harmony'. I question the logic of planting large numbers of these resistant cultivars, for as with all monocultures, some other problem will undoubtedly crop up to trouble them. In moderation, though, they may help

to bring back the Gothic-arched sylvan splendor that was Elm Street in the early twentieth century. Luckily, there is enough natural resistance in wild populations that young, breeding-sized elms are everywhere apparent, and this suggests that in time they will outwit the disease on their own and begin to live to a ripe old age again. Whether they will ever be the common street tree they were 50 years ago remains to be seen.

All native elms have oval, pointed leaves with a characteristic saw-toothed edge. In the wild, they are found primarily in the rich alluvial soils of floodplains. Young trees are capable of tremendous growth, and 2 to 4 feet in a season is possible in an ideal location. Even as saplings, the V-shaped habit is apparent as new growth heads up and out on a steep vertical angle. Besides American elm and slippery elm, there is a group of harder-wooded species called collectively the rock elm group *(U. alata, U. crassifolia,* and *U. thomasii)*. All the native species are more or less susceptible to Dutch elm disease and a host of other, less virulent diseases and pests.

CULTURE: Elms prefer moist, fertile soil and sun, which will also help to boost disease resistance. Elms transplant fairly easily when young and usually don't exhibit any signs of disease for the first 10 to 25 years. Resistant forms of the American elm are available from many nurseries and from the Elm Research Institute in Westmoreland, New Hampshire.

USES: Street and shade tree.

WILDLIFE: Primary food plant for the larvae of the question mark and comma angelwing butterflies *(Polygonia interrogationis* and *P. comma)*.

PROPAGATION: Moderately easy from seed.

Ulmus alata

Winged Elm

ZONES: (5)6–9; sun, part sun

SOIL: Moist to dry

NATIVE TO: Floodplains forests to dry woodlands, fencerows, and old fields; Virginia to Ohio and Missouri south to Texas and northwestern Florida

SIZE: Height 30–50 (80) feet, width 20–40 feet

COLOR: Yellow-red; blooms in late winter to early spring

Winged elm is a common successional tree in the South, tolerating drier soils in the wild than most others in the genus. Most trees develop amazing flattened corky wings down either side of the twigs. I have often wondered what possible benefit these wings provide the tree and can come up with nothing really satisfactory (fire resistance? water or gas absorption? photosynthesis?). Anyway, the wings look a bit weird but attractive, and the trees are commonly planted in the South as a street tree. They possess moderate resistance to Dutch elm disease and form wide-rounded crowns from a vase-shaped base. Leaves are about 4 to 7 inches long and 2 to 3 inches wide. Fall color is a muddy brown-yellow. September elm (*U. serotina*) and cedar elm (*U. crassifolia*) are two rarer winged elms from the Southeast. They are seldom cultivated because of both their rarity and their susceptibility to Dutch elm disease.

Ulmus americana

American Elm

ZONES: 3–9; sun to part sun
SOIL: Moist to moderately dry
NATIVE TO: Floodplains and swamp forests, old fields and fencerows; Nova Scotia to Saskatchewan south to eastern Nebraska, Texas, and central Florida
SIZE: Height 60–80 (100) feet, width 30–50 feet
COLOR: Yellow-red; blooms in late winter to early spring

American elm is certainly one of our most handsome large shade trees, and there is no real replacement for the arch-shaped allée formed by two rows of the trees planted down a suburban lane. I would suggest you plant one of the resistant cultivars (in moderation) if you want this effect, but look also to some of our other native trees for shade so we can avoid the problem of monocultures in the future. Slippery elm (*U. rubra*) is a smaller but similar relative that grows over practically the same range. Its common name comes from the mucilaginous inner bark that was used in medicinal preparations by Native Americans. It is rarely cultivated.

Ulmus thomasii

Rock Elm

ZONES: 4–8; sun, part sun
SOIL: Moist to dry, circumneutral
NATIVE TO: Rich woods, stream banks, rocky limestone slopes and outcrops; New Hampshire to Minnesota irregularly south to Iowa, Arkansas, and Virginia
SIZE: Height 40–60 (90) feet, width 20–40 feet
COLOR: Yellow-purple; blooms in spring

This member of the rock elm group has 3 to 5 corky wings that come and go up the twigs, creating a lunar landscape in miniature. The northern extension of winged elm, it bears similar papery seeds resembling fried eggs coated with fine hair and edged with bristly eyelashes. It's a good substitute for *U. alata* in the North, though it performs best in soils of neutral pH.

Vaccinium corymbosum

Vaccinium (vak-SIN-nium)
Ericaceae
Blueberry, Cranberry

Vaccinium corymbosum. *Highbush blueberries are one of the easiest home orchard crops. They require little care and reward you with lots of delicious fruit.*

No one who lives in a climate suitable for blueberries should be without some in their yard. Where else can you find plants that are so carefree, pretty in flower, leaf, fall color, and winter aspect—not to mention whose fruits are so good to eat! Even after chomping my way through what has been an excellent blueberry season, I still can't get enough of these versatile fruits. The genus divides into roughly three groups: the highbush blueberries, which are mostly clumping, deciduous shrubs in the range of 3 to 10 feet tall; lowbush blueberries, generally under 2 feet and often colonizing in habit; and the cranberries, which with one exception are prostrate, evergreen groundcovers with sour, deep red berries. There are only four cranberries in our flora, including *V. macrocarpon*, the commercial cranberry. Things are not as simple among the blueberries. There are quite a number of species, and many of these freely hybridize and intergrade. The lowbush group is especially frustrating to sort out, and I am still befuddled by a range of plants growing in my own back woods that appear to be hybrids between *V. angustifolium* and *V. pallidum*. Therefore, I don't think I need to cover every last species in detail, and will focus instead on the more distinctive players and leave the others to the steadfast blueberry botanists to sort out.

Before you can have fruits you need flowers, and blueberry flowers are on the whole all very similar. They are composed of five waxy petals sealed together to form an upside-down urn, opening only at the bottom where the petals roll back a bit; this lip gives bees a foothold as they hang upside down to forage inside with their tongues. Blueberries are moderately self-infertile, so plant more than one individual or cultivar in close proximity to ensure good fruit set. If all goes well, the pouched flower will fall away, revealing the beginnings of a round fruit swelling above the calyx. Though leaf shape and summer color are variable, just about every deciduous *Vaccinium* species develops beautiful fall color in shades of red, orange, purple, and burgundy. There is nothing prettier than a flaming sea of blueberries out on the heath. The evergreen types assume a maroon cast as winter nips the leaves, then green up again when warm weather returns in spring.

CULTURE: All *Vaccinium* species prefer acidic soils and a humid climate. Even so, there are plants for dry, shady situations and most sunny places as well as just about everywhere in between. There are heat-tolerant species native to the Southeast and cold-loving ones growing up to the Arctic Circle. They are fibrous-rooted and easy to transplant or, in the case of spreading species, to divide off sections before growth begins in spring. Feed lightly in spring with a balanced, organic fertilizer.

USES: Massing, specimen, fruit production.

WILDLIFE: *Vaccinium* is one of the best genera for wildlife. Flowers are copious nectar producers, berries are eaten by everything from birds to chipmunks and bears, and the leaves are foraged by a large number of butterfly larvae, including the pink-edged sulfur, arctic sulfur, and blueberry sulfur *(Colias interior, C. palaeno,* and *C. pelidne),* zigzag fritillary *(Boloria freija),* brown elfin *(Callophrys augustus),* cranberry bog copper *(Lycaena epixanthe),* and cranberry blue *(Plebejus optilete).*

PROPAGATION: Easy to difficult from cuttings, moderately easy from seed.

Vaccinium angustifolium
Lowbush Blueberry

ZONES: 3–7; sun to light shade
SOIL: Well-drained, moist to dry
NATIVE TO: Upland woods, rocky outcrops, and barrens; Labrador and Newfoundland to Manitoba south to Minnesota, Illinois, New Jersey, and in the mountains to North Carolina
SIZE: Height 8–24 inches, width 1–3 feet
COLOR: White tinged with pink; blooms in spring
This is the famous Maine blueberry, a common dry-site species in the East with narrow 1-inch leaves on twiggy zigzag stems that arise from a creeping rhizome to form colonies. It makes a fine low ground-cover and produces delectable, strong-flavored fruits in clusters on leafless side branchlets. Lowbush blueberry develops a brilliant orange-red fall color. Though it will grow in shade, it fruits heavily only in sun. Hillside blueberry *(V. pallidum)* is 50 percent larger than *V. angustifolium* with oval, glaucous blue-green leaves and it seems to fruit more heavily in shade. Other interchangeable species include small black blueberry *(V. tenellum),* a southeastern plant rarely over 10 inches tall, and velvetleaf blueberry *(V. myrtilloides),* nearly identical except for its downy leaf undersides and preference for moister soils. Cascade blueberry *(V. deliciosum)* is one of the West Coast equivalents.

Vaccinium arboreum
Farkleberry, Sparkleberry

ZONES: 6–9; sun to light shade
SOIL: Moist, well-drained to dry
NATIVE TO: Dry or rocky woods; Virginia to Kentucky and southern Indiana south to Texas and Florida
SIZE: Height 8–15 (30) feet, width 4–10 feet
COLOR: White; blooms in spring
V. arboreum is noteworthy for its size: farkleberry is the largest *Vaccinium* in our flora, capable of becoming a small tree with twisted trunks and thin bark mottled in purple, gray, and brown. The flowers are more bell- than urn-shaped, and they are lovely dangling from the axils of small, flowering shoots; the black fruits are dry and inedible. The leaves are glossy green above, paler below, turning pink or deep red and finally dropping late in the fall.

Vaccinium corymbosum
Highbush Blueberry

ZONES: 3–8; sun
SOIL: Wet to moderately dry
NATIVE TO: Open or wooded swamps and bogs, old fields and watersides; Nova Scotia and Maine to Michigan south to Texas and Florida
SIZE: Height 3–10 feet, width 3–10 feet
COLOR: White tinged with pink; blooms in spring
Highbush blueberry is most abundant in damp, open habitats, where it sets copious amounts of bloomy blue-black fruits with excellent sweet-tart flavor. The wild forms have fruits about ¼ inch in diameter, but years of breeding have led to the cultivars that produce the ½-inch fruits most of us are familiar with in the supermarket. These larger berries are generally sweeter and softer than the wild ones, but it is a matter of taste as to which you prefer overall. Culture of the cultivars is the same as for the wild species. Some selections have been made from *V. virgatum* (rabbit-eye blueberry), the Deep South extension of highbush blueberry that is preferable in Zones 8–9. Other cultivars have been developed for their cold or heat

tolerance, early or late ripening fruit, and self-compatibility, not to mention unique flavor. Ask your local nursery or extension agent for cultivars that perform well in your area. As with many species in this genus leaf color is highly variable in wild stands, ranging from glossy medium green to glaucous blue. Older plants are beautiful in winter, with craggy, contorted stems setting out from a central crown—it's worth growing them for this feature alone. Fall color ranges from burgundy to brilliant crimson and orange. Southern highbush blueberry (*V. elliottii*) is similar, though better adapted to drier soils and southern heat and humidity. Its range is south near the coast from Virginia to Florida. Common deerberry (*V. stamineum*) has a habit similar to the broad, domed, craggy look of highbush blueberry, with oval leaves that are occasionally a shockingly lovely blue-gray, and large, yellowish blue, insipid, inedible fruits. I am growing out seedlings from some particularly vivid blue plants and hope for the best.

Vaccinium crassifolium
Creeping Blueberry

ZONES: 6–9; sun to light shade
SOIL: Moist, well-drained to dry
NATIVE TO: Sandy pine barrens; southeastern Virginia to Georgia, near the coast
SIZE: Height 10–20 inches, width 2–3 feet
COLOR: White; blooms in spring

Creeping blueberry is an excellent substitute for the groundcover bearberry (*Arctostaphylos uva-ursi*) in the Southeast, where the latter performs poorly. It is a mat-forming evergreen with ½-inch leathery, elliptical leaves set closely along the trailing or weakly upright stems. The foliage turns dark burgundy in winter. It will grow reasonably well in high pine shade and dry, well-drained, acidic soils. The flowers are small, and I can't vouch for the fruits as I have only grown the cultivar 'Well's Delight', which hasn't set fruit. (It likely needs another cultivar for cross-pollination.)

Vaccinium macrocarpon
Cranberry

ZONES: 3–7; sun, part sun
SOIL: Moist to wet
NATIVE TO: Sphagnum bogs; Newfoundland to Manitoba south to Illinois, Ohio and Virginia and in the mountains to North Carolina
SIZE: Height 1–3 inches, width 18–28 inches
COLOR: Pink marked with red and white; blooms in early summer

It is remarkable that such a large fruit could come from such a tiny plant. Granted, the tart, ¾-inch berries have large air cavities inside, but when you consider that the cranberry plant is a ground-hugging mat of thread-thin stems lined with thin, leathery, ½-inch evergreen leaves, it is still an impressive feat. Though it will grow in any moist soil and makes a decent groundcover, in the wild it is found scrambling over moss in floating bogs. The flowers are interesting little things if you can get low enough to see them—5 reflexed petals with a cluster of stamens protruding like a beak. They flower heavily enough to create a pink cloud over our bog in early summer. The fruits slowly turn from green to glossy red above and white on parts kept from the sun. I could pick enough for a big batch of jelly every fall from our 6-by-6-foot patch. Small cranberry (*V. oxycoccos*) is an even tinier species from cold northern bogs. It is basically a half-scale version of *V. macrocarpon*—almost too small to see in the landscape but cute nonetheless.

Vaccinium parvifolium
Red Blueberry

ZONES: 6–8; sun to light shade
SOIL: Moist
NATIVE TO: Damp coniferous forests and clearings; British Columbia south to northern California
SIZE: Height 3–12 feet, width 3–6 feet
COLOR: White flushed with pink; blooms in spring

Red blueberry is a familiar sight in the Pacific Northwest's rainforests. Often they sprout out of tree stumps along with salal (*Gaultheria shallon*), where a bird evacuated the seeds. This is an attractive plant with wispy, light green, flattened branches and light, bright green leaves usually less than an inch long. The small but edible fruits are bright red, so they really stand out amid the foliage like holiday decorations.

The little cranberry bog copper butterfly (Lycaena epixanthe) *feeds on nectar produced by the cranberry's shooting-star flowers, and its caterpillars eat the leaves almost exclusively.*

Vaccinium vitis-idaea ssp. *minus*

Mountain Cranberry, Lingonberry

ZONES: 3–6; sun, part sun
SOIL: Moist, cool
NATIVE TO: Alpine ridges, foggy coastal headlands, bogs; Greenland and the Northwest Territories and Alaska south to British Columbia, Minnesota, and Maine
SIZE: Height 4–8 inches, width 1 foot
COLOR: Pink; blooms in late spring

Our reduced native form of the European lingonberry is a charming little evergreen, a tufted mound of glossy green, cupped foliage that turns burgundy in winter. The flowers are not reflexed like those of the common cranberry, but the ⅜-inch fruits have a similar flavor. Lingonberry is something for the specialist, but it is well worth growing if you have a suitable spot. We grow it in a damp, cool, mossy bed in the company of Labrador tea (*Ledum groenlandicum*) and alpine bearberry (*Arctostaphylos alpina*).

Viburnum dentatum.
The species name means "with teeth," a reference to the jagged margins of the arrowwood leaf. The jet black fruits are decorative for only a week or two because birds quickly consume them.

Viburnum dentatum

Viburnum (vye-BUR-num)
Caprifoliaceae
Viburnum

As I walked recently through one of my favorite berrylands in the Cape Cod National Seashore, the viburnums were stealing the show. I was struck again by the unbelievable color transmu-

tations their fruits go through on their way from green to ripe. Witherod (*V. nudum*) is my favorite; it begins with a whitish pink that becomes saturated closer to flamingo before switching to red, blue, and finally almost black by early fall. Today the witherods are all in the first blush of pink, a marked contrast to the green and blue arrowwood and the flushing crimson of cranberrybush. I can look forward to the burgundies and scarlet that will develop in the falling leaves later in the season as a cue to birds that the fruits have achieved full ripeness. Most viburnum fruits are more flamboyant than the flowers—flat-topped or domed clusters of small, frilly off-white blossoms conglomerated into a 3-to-6-inch wide lace-doily landing pad for bees. These appear at the tips of the crown when the new growth is fully expanded. Hobblebush and cranberrybush are the showiest in flower, as they ring this disk with a necklace of large, white bracts à la hydrangeas. Many of the species produce flowers that start out smelling faintly sweet but become mildly unpleasant as the flowers mature. I imagine this is an insurance policy aimed at attracting whatever bees, wasps, and beetles may be in the area. It is not strong enough to pose problems in the garden.

The nice thing about this genus is that its members are generally amenable, fast-growing shrubs equally at home in the cultivated and wild landscape. Viburnums in an open situation develop a rounded or mushroom shape as new sprouts come up from a narrow base, then arch and lean outward as successive bouts of maternity weigh the older branches down. The more shade-adapted, understory species like *V. acerifolium* and *V. lantanoides* are freer at the roots, spreading about in search of light and thus remaining open, smaller specimens. All the native species are deciduous; the leaves grow in pairs up caney stems.

CULTURE: Most viburnums are found in the wild in open wetlands and thickets, but they are more adaptable than this habitat preference might suggest. Any site that is not excessively dry will suffice, though hobblebush needs a moist, cool soil to perform well. There is a direct correlation between the amount of sun a plant receives and the amount and quality of its fruit displays. Full sun and moist soil will ensure heavy crops yearly, while partial shade and drought will curtail fruiting or force the plants to bear heavily only every 2 to 3 years. In a recent spring we had an unusually late freeze after a spell of hot weather, which burned off the developing flowers on viburnums as well as on hollies, chokeberries, and cherries (not to mention many of the nut trees). The result was a poor fall for humans and other animals around here. It is relatively easy to dig and move suckers from the extremity of a clump before they have leafed out in spring. Wait a year or two and cut the transplant off near the ground in late winter, which encourages newer and straighter stems. All viburnums benefit from — in fact, relish — occasional late-winter thinning or hard rejuvenative pruning to remove less productive older stems. They are easily transplanted from containers in spring or fall, and in summer, too, if irrigation can be provided.

Until recently, viburnums have been pest-free, aside from some powdery mildew and other minor afflictions. Since 1978, however, a new threat has been moving south from Montreal, where it was first imported from Europe. The viburnum leaf beetle (*Pyrrhalta viburni*), a ¼-inch-long, oval, black and brown beetle, has been working its way down the coast from Quebec, through the Maritime provinces and Maine, leaving a path of destruction in its wake. It favors arrowwood but also feeds on cranberrybush and mapleleaf viburnums. Larvae emerge in spring from eggs that overwinter under caps of excrement along the twigs and begin feeding on soft new leaves. Often the whole shrub is completely defoliated by the time the beetles mature into adults in summer. Just how much of a threat this insect poses remains to be seen. I don't know how it will deal with the heat farther south, or whether, after a few years of infestation, resistant individuals or some natural predator will help control them. We can all help slow the spread by not transporting any viburnums from affected areas and by learning to recognize the signs of infestation.

USES: Massing, screens, specimen.

WILDLIFE: Excellent-quality fruits for migrating songbirds.

PROPAGATION: Easy to difficult from cuttings, moderately difficult from seed.

Viburnum acerifolium
Mapleleaf Viburnum

ZONES: 3–9; sun to shade
SOIL: Moist to dry
NATIVE TO: Woods; New Brunswick to Quebec and Minnesota south to Louisiana and Florida
SIZE: Height 3–6 feet, width 3–6 feet
COLOR: Creamy white; blooms in late spring

On first glance this is a sparse, suckering shrub of little ornamental value, but it is one of the few shrubs that thrive in the understory of fairly dry upland woods — a habitat we have far too much of around here. Its leaves are shaped much like those of red maple, with 3 pointed lobes and leaf veins radiating out from a central point where blade meets petiole. In autumn, as the clusters of oval, flattened fruits are turning from green to deep blue-black, the foliage turns a pretty smoky burgundy on top and purple-gray below. In a cultivated situation, it remains a twiggy, spreading shrub with few stems larger than ½ inch in diameter. Squashberry (*V. edule*) is similar in form, preferring moist woods and thickets clear

across boreal North America. Its leaves are rounder, and the fruits ripen yellow, then deep red.

Viburnum dentatum
Arrowwood

ZONES: 4–9; sun to light shade
SOIL: Moist to dry
NATIVE TO: Swamps, thickets, upland and floodplain forests; Maine to Illinois south to Texas and Florida
SIZE: Height 6–12 (15) feet, width 4–10 feet
COLOR: Creamy white; blooms in late spring

Taxonomists have had a field day with arrowwood, splitting the poor thing into five species and at least eight varieties on the basis of slight differences in the shape and luster of the leaf, the hairiness of the petiole, and the dimensions of the seed. These include downy arrowwood (*V. rafinesquianum*), Missouri arrowwood (*V. molle*), bracted arrowwood (*V. bracteatum*), and smooth arrowwood (*V. recognitum*). I think Mike Dirr sums it up well when he says that if you "envision this group as a north–south, east–west continuum showing slight differences in leaf characteristics, pubescence, habit and size but possessing similar creamy white flowers and blue to blue-black fruits then [you] have grasped the essence of a confusing group of species" (*Manual of Woody Landscape Plants*, p. 1065). Arrowwood is typically a vase-shaped to rounded shrub producing a number of fast-growing sprouts from its narrow base that grow up and out and achieve a stem diameter of under 1 inch before they die out and are replaced. Straight, vigorous sprouts can be fashioned into light, durable arrows if you so desire. The thin leaves are oval to nearly round and strongly toothed along the margin. The blade folds slightly along the diagonal veins that set out from a strong midvein, giving the leaf a ridged-potato-chip appearance.

Viburnum lantanoides (alnifolium)
Hobblebush

ZONES: 4–6; shade
SOIL: Moist, cool
NATIVE TO: Damp woodlands; Nova Scotia to Ontario and Minnesota south to Pennsylvania and New York and in the Appalachians to North Carolina and Tennessee
SIZE: Height 3–10 feet, width 4–12 feet
COLOR: White; blooms in early spring

Hobblebush, a true shade-loving plant that scorches in sun and heat, is one of the stars of our garden. In early spring, the leafless branches are decorated with flattened disks of whitish flowers surrounded by a ring of 1-inch-wide, 5-parted flowerlike bracts. The leathery 4-to-6-inch oval leaves provide a bold background for woodland wildflowers, and they turn an incredible mix of mint green, pink, and burgundy in fall, just as the fruits have changed from red to dark burgundy, then black—their mature color. In winter, the picturesque horizontal branches are lovely silhouetted in the snow. In the wild, this species spreads via root suckers to form tangled colonies that can trip the unwary woodland walker. However, give it a favored place in the garden, and it is satisfied to remain a domed clump with nary an errant root sucker to be seen. Its winter buds lack scales, so you can clearly see the unexpanded leaves and flower buds awaiting the return of warm weather. As the leaves expand, they retain a puckered, folded shape that showcases a soft white underside.

Viburnum lentago

Nannyberry

ZONES: 3–7; sun to light shade
SOIL: Moist to dry
NATIVE TO: Woods, thickets, swamp margins, fencerows, and roadsides; Quebec to southern Saskatchewan south to Montana, Colorado, Missouri, and New Jersey
SIZE: Height 8–15 (25) feet, width 6–12 feet
COLOR: Creamy white; blooms in late spring
Nannyberry gets its name from the wet-goat odor of the flowers and ripe fruits. It produces domed clus-

ters of ½-inch-long olive-shaped berries that undergo a color metamorphosis from green to red to blue-black, like witherod's. It differs from witherod (*V. nudum*) in the character of its leaves, which have a thinner texture and more rounded shape. Nannyberry can get to be quite large in time, and I prefer witherod for foliage effect and more manageable size, but this is a tough and adaptable shrub that tolerates drier soils than its swamp-lovin' cousin.

Viburnum nudum

Witherod, Possum Haw

ZONES: 3–9; sun, to light shade
SOIL: Wet to moderately dry
NATIVE TO: Woods, swamps and thickets; Newfoundland to Manitoba south to Texas and Florida
SIZE: Height 6–12 feet, width 4–15 feet
COLOR: Creamy white; blooms in late spring
This is my favorite native viburnum. It has a wonderful fruit display: the fruits are rounded and can be nearly ½ inch in diameter and, because they ripen successively, the fruits in each cluster display a kaleidoscope of colors. The plants also have a well-behaved, rounded, multistem habit and leathery, narrowly oval pointed leaves often finished with a glossy sheen as though waxed. Fall color can also be outstanding—from deep red to brilliant scarlet. There are two varieties, the southern *V. nudum* var.

Viburnum opulus *var.* americanum. *Like most trees and shrubs, American cranberry bush sets far more fruit when it receives at least four hours of direct sun. Birds will eat the fruits and then roost in nearby trees as they digest, evacuating the seeds and skins on the forest floor. Viburnum seedlings that become established there can grow in the dimmer light, but they seldom fruit abundantly unless some disturbance removes part of the tree canopy that shades them.*

nudum (possum haw, smooth witherod), with glossier leaves, and the more northern *V. nudum* var. *cassinoides* (witherod, formerly a separate species, *V. cassinoides*), bearing smaller leaves with a matte gray-green finish.

Viburnum opulus var. *americanum (trilobum)*

American Cranberrybush

ZONES: 2–6(7); sun, part sun
SOIL: Moist to wet
NATIVE TO: Damp thickets, low woods, and swamps; Newfoundland to British Columbia south to Washington, Iowa, Ohio, and Pennsylvania
SIZE: Height 5–15 feet, width 4–10 feet
COLOR: White; blooms in late spring to early summer
Cranberrybush is a vase-shaped to mounded caney shrub with large, maple-shaped leaves and big dripping clusters of brilliant red, glistening fruits that develop in late summer. The fruits have a semitransparent outer skin, allowing light to refract from the dewy interior as it does in gooseberries and currants. The result is something that looks awfully good to eat, and—if you add enough sugar—the tart ½-inch berries are quite tasty in jellies and spreads. The leaves take their cue from the fruits, turning red, orange, and yellow before dropping in fall. A necklace of 5-parted sterile bracts surrounds the dome of fertile flowers and greatly enhances the floral display. This is a very fast-growing shrub, producing suckers from the base that zoom up 6 feet or more in a season and begin to branch and flower their second year. Accordingly, a hard pruning once a decade will not affect flowering for long. Confusion reigns in the nursery trade regarding the proper identity of this plant versus that of its wider, shorter Eurasian sibling, *V. opulus* var. *opulus*. The two are most easily distinguished by the shape of a pair of glands near the base of the petiole. The North American form has stalked glands that look like small mushrooms, whereas the Eurasian has stalkless glands like little nubs. Many of the plants labeled var. *americanum* (or *trilobum*) in the trade are in fact the Eurasian form.

Viburnum prunifolium

Black Haw

ZONES: (3)4–9; sun to light shade
SOIL: Moist to dry
NATIVE TO: Woods, thickets, and fencerows; Connecticut to Wisconsin and Iowa south to Kansas, Texas, and Georgia
SIZE: Height 8–15 (20) feet, width 6–15 feet
COLOR: Creamy white; blooms in early spring
Black haw forms a craggy, horizontal to broad oval canopy from a stubby trunk reinforced with vigorous suckers growing vertically from its nether

regions (close to a crabapple or hawthorn in shape). The relatively small and attractive leathery leaves, 2 inches long on average, appear on short, spurlike twigs (again like crabapples). Its flowers open as the leaves are still expanding, to good visual effect. I think it is the showiest-flowered of the group save the white-bracted species, hobblebush and cranberrybush. In the wild it spreads from the roots to form thickety colonies, but this can be curtailed with judicious pruning. While you are at it, remove some of the lower branches and balance out the crown, as a well-pruned black haw has a craggy shape that is quite beautiful as a specimen. The edible olive-shaped fruits make a very good jelly; they ripen from bluish pink to red to deep blue-black. Fall color is usually burgundy red. Southern black haw (*V. rufidulum*) is a more southeastern relative with a rusty-downy pubescence on the leaves and twigs.

Vitis labrusca. Wire has been strung along the top of this stone wall to train a young fox grape along its course. Once the main vines have grown to the diameter of a dime, the wire will be unnecessary, for the trunks will have become set in their ways.

Vitis labrusca

Vitis (VY-tis)
Vitaceae
Grape

The subtle yet important difference between wild and cultivated is not so subtle in the world of grapes. If your only experience has been with the bland, sugary grapes on the supermarket shelves, then you owe it to yourself to try the tongue-tickling, lip-smacking, flavor-saturated sensation of biting into a ripe wild grape along a sylvan path. In the wild, these high-climbing vines are capable of growing 100 feet up through the limbs of tall forest trees and into the sunlight. They are not very shade tolerant, so the presence of old, shaggy brown grape vines hanging from the canopy is a sign that some previous disturbance such as logging, land clearing, or storms knocked down some trees and allowed sunlight to penetrate to the forest floor, letting the vines get started. After that, they needed only to climb higher and higher each year to stay ahead of the tree branches closing behind. You often find wild grapes along the edge of the woods or along a river or stream—places where both light and support are freely at hand—or, more accurately, at tendril.

Grapes are descended from plants bearing opposite leaves, a fact made clear by the vestigial leaf scar that abuts many petioles. Other leaves are paired with a forking tendril that flails around as it lengthens, looking for something to hold on to. If it finds purchase (often another grape vine), this tendril curls around madly, securing the stem and helping to lift the whole plant higher. These tendrils are the main means of support holding the grape in the canopy, so they can survive for several seasons, becoming woodier as they age. Still other leaves are paired with racemes or panicles of small, greenish white flowers. Flowers are borne on the new growth, allowing the vines to be cut back hard during the late winter to control their spread. The best fruits come from growth originating from 1-year-old canes, so when pruning, try to cut back most but not all of the previous season's growth and leave 6-inch sections from which the new wood will spring.

CULTURE: Wild grapes are not greatly troubled by pests and diseases. They have more fungus resistance than cultivated grapes, and though Japanese beetles can be a problem, they don't require the frequent spraying necessary in many vineyards. If you are raising grapes for fruit, provide them with an arbor or trellis (in vineyards, two stout, horizontal wires set about 2 and 4 feet off the ground are preferable). You will need to tie the vines in place (old nylons work well) since you will be removing most of the tendrils during your winter pruning. Late frosts will nip the vines and destroy new growths carrying the undeveloped flower buds for that year. The good cold air drainage found on slopes will minimize this threat as well as the equally tragic possibility of an early fall cold snap that could ruin the fruit. Grapes are adaptable plants, but again, if fruit production is your goal, full sun and reasonably moist soil are preferable. Fertilize in spring with a balanced organic fertilizer.

PROPAGATION: Moderately easy from cuttings or seed.

Vitis labrusca
Fox Grape

ZONES: 4–8; sun, part sun
SOIL: Moist to moderately dry
NATIVE TO: Woodlands, fencerows, and thickets; Maine to southern Michigan south to Tennessee and South Carolina
SIZE: Height 4–75 feet (depending on support), width 4–8 (20) feet
COLOR: Greenish white; blooms in early summer

This common grape has 3-lobed, broad, 4-to-8-inch-wide leaves with a rusty gray cast to the lower surface. Many home-orchard catalogues carry selections of this species; it is the primary ancestor of the slipskin, Concord, or 'Labruscana' varieties, which are some of our most flavorful wild grapes. The fruits are round, roughly ½ inch wide on wild plants, and have a strong, sweet taste once you bite through the thick, bitter skin. This species and its varieties are well suited to culture in the northern half of the United States and southern Canada. There are a dozen or so other grapes in the flora, but most produce small fruits (less than ¼ inch) that are not worth the trouble to eat.

Vitis rotundifolia
Muscadine, Scuppernongs

ZONES: 6–9; sun, part sun
SOIL: Moist to moderately dry
NATIVE TO: Woods, thickets, roadsides; Delaware to Kentucky and Missouri south to Texas and Florida
SIZE: Height 8–100 feet (depending on support), width 6–15 (30) feet
COLOR: Greenish white; blooms in early summer

Whereas the fox grape and selections from it are adapted to the short, northern summer, muscadines relish the long, sultry season of the Deep South. Their leaves are small by grape standards, 2 to 4 inches in diameter, and are nearly round and noticeably toothed along the margin. They have a nice, dark green, glossy sheen above and a more yellow green tint below. Wild muscadines produce reddish purple fruits about ¾ inch in diameter on average, but cultivars have been developed with fruits nearly twice that size (scuppernongs are white-fruited cultivars). The sweet, tangy pulp is protected by a leather-thick skin that one has to unceremoniously spit out after rolling out the large seeds—not a fruit you can eat daintily. It is not as easily contained as fox grape, so plan to give it some room to ramble each summer.

Wisteria frutescens

Wisteria frutescens

(wis-TEE-ria)

Fabaceae

American Wisteria

ZONES: (4)5–9; sun, part sun

SOIL: Moist to wet

NATIVE TO: Alluvial forests, margins of damp woods and riverbanks; Virginia to Arkansas south to Texas and Florida

SIZE: Height 10–25 (60) feet, width 6–8 feet

COLOR: Violet-blue; blooms in late spring to early summer

The Asian wisterias have long been popular garden plants. They look so evocative and romantic clinging to the walls of one's country manor whilst the guests play cricket out on the lawn. In a cool, maritime climate like Britain's or the northern United States, they are moderately well behaved, especially if you have a staff of gardeners to pull them off the window screens and telephone wires. Plant them in the southern United States though, with its long, subtropical summers, and they become monsters. I waged war against Chinese wisteria (*W. sinensis*) when I lived in Durham, North Carolina. It had traveled by way of the swampy creek that ran below the house, and it sent long cablelike roots into the meager woods, which poked up exploratory suckers every few yards in search of a weakness in the canopy. Given a modicum of sunlight, up the vines went, snaking like a giant constricting serpent around pines and sweetgums and slowly strangling the life out of them. As trees died and fell, the vines sprung out with added verdure, turning the once woods into a low wisteria jungle. It is more insidious than kudzu, methinks, because in this fashion it can penetrate into closed-canopy forests. I present this as a counterpoint to our native species, which shares with its Asian cousins fine, pinnate leaves and charming flowers but lacks their overwhelming

aggressiveness. In fact, American wisteria is downright well behaved, growing as a twining 10-to-20-foot woody vine with twigs that are at first reddish brown, then age to warm gray as they gain diameter. The leaves are dark gray-green and are composed of 5 to 6 pairs of lateral leaflets and one terminal, all pointed ovals around 2 inches long. The leaflets droop down slightly along the central stem, exposing a softer green underside even when you view them from the side. The vines set out as long, thin whipcord stems with leaves developing 1 to 2 feet lower down once the stem has stiffened. Unlike the Asian species, American wisteria flowers after most of the first flush of leaves has expanded, holding its tight 3-to-4-inch cones of pealike blooms up stiffly above the leaves on 3-inch stems. The flowers with their inch-wide, rounded pea-style flags, come in several waves over the course of 2 to 4 weeks (compare this to the blink-and-you-miss-it flowering of *W. sinensis*). Their one drawback is that they lack the penetrating jasminelike perfume of the Asian forms.

Wisteria macrostachya (or *W. frutescens* var. *macrostachya*), the Kentucky wisteria, grows in floodplain forests, along rivers and swamps, up through the Mississippi river system from Kentucky and southern Indiana to Louisiana. Its most notable distinguishing feature is the size of the inflorescence —as much as a foot long. Dangling down from the leaves, the blooms evoke the same romantic feeling as the Asian types. Each raceme is composed of up to 90 individual violet flowers, each set with a flag petal

(LEFT) Wisteria frutescens. *American wisteria bunches its flowers together in short, dense racemes.*

(RIGHT) Wisteria macrostachya. *In contrast, Kentucky wisteria produces longer, dangling sprays more similar in effect to the Asian species.*

like *W. frutescens*'s. It is a bit more cold-hardy, and this, combined with its more lavish bloom, makes it the type to seek out and grow. There are several lovely white cultivars out there as well.

CULTURE: With wisteria you need to give a little thought to support. This vine doesn't get as large as the Asian types, but it really comes into its own once a thick, coiled trunk develops, so you want to provide a support that is both sturdy and will allow the trunks to show to advantage in winter. The stems will become hopelessly tangled in chain link and other fencing and be nearly impossible to remove. We have it trained up a wooden arbor that defines one of the entrances to the Garden. The plants continually send up shoots from the base that ramble off in bad-hair-day fashion, so these are routinely removed. The rich green foliage is then concentrated across the top of the arbor. Aside from light shaping in summer and some thinning in winter, it requires little care. Wisterias have fleshy, shallow roots that are hard to dig and transplant, so it is best to begin with plants grown in containers from cuttings; this gives earlier flowering than seed-grown plants.

USES: Arbors, trellises.

PROPAGATION: Moderately easy from cuttings, moderately difficult (slow to bloom) from seed.

Xanthorhiza simplicissima. *One of yellow-root's best features is its coppery yellow fall color, which develops best in sun.*

Xanthorhiza simplicissima

Xanthorhiza simplicissima

(zan-tho-RY-za)
Ranunculaceae
Yellowroot

ZONES: 3–9; sun to shade
SOIL: Moist to dry
NATIVE TO: Rich woods, mostly in the Appalachians; southeastern New York to Pennsylvania and Kentucky south to Alabama and the Florida Panhandle
SIZE: Height 12–18 inches, width 2–4 feet
COLOR: Purple-bronze; blooms in early spring

Yellowroot is one of the most adaptable, carefree plants we have in the Garden, yet it remains relatively anonymous in the world of horticulture. It sends up short, knobby stems from a sulfur yellow root system. These add a flush of leaves each year, gradually gaining height but never sending out any side branches. (The leaves are bunched toward the tip of each stem in palm fashion.) Foliage emerges early in spring, to take full advantage of the increased light levels on the forest floor at that time. The leaves are rich green pinnate arrangements with 3 to 5 leaflets, all deeply and irregularly toothed to impart a

rather fine texture to the foliage. Each woody stem is spaced about 6 inches from its neighbors, so the tuft of leaves has some breathing room. Along with the leaves come interesting sprays of starry, brownish purple flowers with a waxy substance that lends them a starched-shirt rigidity as they splay out on their wiry pedicels. The every-which-way effect of emerging leaves and purple panicles has a "Flower Arranging 101" look to it, but the blooms really blend in with the dead leaves on the forest floor, so it's hard to notice. As the flowers fade, the tuft of leaves continues to expand, becoming a solid cover of 6-to-8-inch lacy foliage for the rest of the summer and burnishing bronze-gold as they fade in autumn.

I admit there is nothing spectacular about this species—no cobalt blue flowers, mottled bark, or sinuous, silvery variegation in the leaves. Still, the plants form spreading colonies of downright weed-unfriendly foliage that keeps looking green and lush in shade and drought. We use it to cover large areas under rhododendrons, and it is even thriving in dry shade along the entrance road. Give it a bit more sun and moisture, and yellowroot really shines, becom-

ing a dense, rich green mound of moderately spreading stems.

CULTURE: Transplant in spring, either by digging up rooted sections or using container-grown material. Though it can tolerate poor, acidic soils and shade, at least a few hours of sun and a shot of fertilizer as the leaves are expanding will show off the foliage to its best weed-smothering advantage. Stems will keep growing a few inches a year, and after a decade or two the patch will appear leggy and unkempt, so it is a good idea to clip these older stems off near the ground occasionally. With time, yellowroot can cover large areas, so don't plant it next to your cherished little darlings. Wayward stems can be headed back with a spade and relocated.

USES: Tall groundcover, massing.

PROPAGATION: Easy from root cuttings and division, moderately easy from seed.

Zenobia pulverulenta

Zenobia pulverulenta
(ze-NOH-bia)

Ericaceae
Dusty Zenobia

ZONES: 5–9; sun, part sun
SOIL: Moist to wet, acidic
NATIVE TO: Wet woods, pocosins; along the coastal plain from Virginia to South Carolina
SIZE: Height 2–4 feet, width 3–4 feet
COLOR: Waxy white flushed with pink; blooms in late spring to early summer

Picture a large-leaved, boisterous blueberry colored a soft, startling silvery blue, and you can begin to imagine dusty zenobia at its finest. By nature it is a suckering, arching shrub of damp, peaty places, sending up fast-growing shoots from the lower sections of older stems that begin growing vertically, then curve and bend over toward the prevailing light. Stiff, 1½-to-3-inch reluctantly deciduous oval leaves arrange themselves thickly along the stems, and as the first flush of new foliage is well under way, beautiful, bell-shaped, licorice-scented flowers appear on long, straight stems. The flowers are ⅜ inch across—very large compared to those of blueberries, leatherleaf, or staggerbush, with which you might compare them—and they pack so thickly along the stems in perfect, stiff or dangling clusters that zenobia has my vote for loveliest of the bell-shaped heaths. The fused petals have the translucent quality of fine alabaster when backlit by the morning sun. Now, on to the silvery blue . . . in a wild population of zenobia, among the leathery green or green-tinged purple that is typical for their foliage, you may be lucky to find a plant with a heavy powdery bloom that is truly extraordinary. The emerging leaves bear a hint of purple, which mixes with the silvery blue of a Monet sunset and provides the perfect foil for the waxy white bellflowers, which form on side shoots springing from year-old wood.

Zenobia pulverulenta. *The flowers of dusty zenobia are large compared to those of relatives like blueberries, and they form spectacular bunches at the tips of small twigs. Zenobia is one of the last plants to develop fall color and shed its leaves in the garden. This year it still had quite a few red and orange leaves on display after Thanksgiving.*

Zenobia has a looser, more informal habit than an azalea or highbush blueberry. Since it continues growing late into the fall, it tends to suffer some tip dieback in cold, snowless winters. However, since the best foliage color develops on the vigorous growth, a bit of late-winter pruning will do no harm other than to possibly remove some of the flower buds. There are several named cultivars on the market, including 'Woodlander's Blue', but these are very difficult to root from cuttings and thus hard to find. Seedlings are easy to raise, but variable as to leaf coloration. We have an isolated blue-leaved plant that is self-fertile, and I find that 50 to 60 percent of its seedlings have blue foliage. The characteristic begins to develop in the first year, allowing me to cull the seedlings and select the best early in the plants' life. Alternatively, a mixed planting of green and blue-leaved seedlings is very pretty, and both develop fine purply red fall color.

CULTURE: Damp, acidic soil is necessary for good growth, and at least 4 hours of sun will encourage dense foliage and strong leaf coloration. In Zones 5–6, the cane stems will need some tidying up after a hard winter to remove dead tips and persistent withered foliage.

USES: Massing, damp borders, bogs.

PROPAGATION: Difficult from cuttings, moderately easy from seed.

Propagation

Growing plants from seeds or cuttings is a tremendous source of satisfaction for me—an opportunity to learn about a particular species and to grow many plants otherwise unavailable in the trade. It is also the best way to bring local plants into your own garden. Plants "want" to grow and reproduce, and have been doing so without my help for millions of years. What we do or don't do to aid them may help determine their eventual success, but the overwhelming desire for life burns as bright in the smallest seed as it does in us. There is something vaguely parental about plant propagation; nurturing a fragile new life into adulthood connects you to it far more profoundly than just buying a blooming specimen at the local garden center. I think of myself as a facilitator—providing optimal growing conditions for the plants under my care to vastly increase their relative success over what it would be in the wild. If an oak tree produced 100,000 acorns over ten years (a number I am pulling out of my hat), it would be doing well if one or two of those offspring reached adulthood. If I went out one fall and collected a few hundred nuts and grew them on and then planted the seedlings in a good sunny place, I would have increased the tree's success rate by more than a hundredfold.

My approach to teaching plant propagation, as in any other aspect of horticulture, is to try to demystify and simplify the process as much as possible. As with any craft, there are tricks and shortcuts, but there is no substitute for experience, observation, and patience. So do not be discouraged if your first few attempts fail—you can learn as much from failures as from successes.

In this chapter, I begin with an overview of seed propagation and the reasons I like to propagate from seed, followed by sections on seed collection, cleaning, and storage; seed sowing; and requirements for germination. Next comes an overview of asexual propagation techniques, focusing mostly on stem cuttings with short references to root cuttings, layering, and grafting.

About Seed

Most plants reproduce naturally by seed, and it is my propagation method of choice for several reasons. First, it is pretty straightforward, requiring little equipment or sophisticated chemicals to be successful. Second, seedlings retain a genetic diversity that is lost when one propagates clonally, allowing you to select plants that are especially well adapted to your particular conditions. Out of a batch of 500 seedlings, there are always a few that grow more vigorously, bloom more colorfully, or resist disease more completely than the others. By choosing them, you are performing a gardener's brand of natural selection that will over several generations yield plants more amenable to your particular locale and its blend of soil, climate, and exposure. Third, plants are subject to a variety of systemic, incurable diseases, including viruses, mycoplasma-like organisms (MLOs), and rusts, as well as internal parasites like

❧ Cloning ❧

The word "cloning" has become politically charged of late because of the advances in animal cloning and the implications for human reproduction, so this term warrants further discussion. Technically, a clone is an exact genetic copy of the original, and many plants reproduce clonally on their own, especially in conditions that are not favorable for seed germination and establishment. American beech is a case in point. Beeches now found in the northern part of the species' range in New England and southern Canada likely moved back north after the retreat of the glaciers, when conditions were not favorable for establishment of seedlings. (Possible reasons might include heavy rodent predation of the nuts, a period of droughty summers that killed off many seedlings, or soils that were too cold or infertile to allow seedlings to grow properly.) As a consequence, northern beeches spread abundantly from root sprouts, so that whole groves covering an acre or more are all really one clone descended from a single seedling that managed to get established. Natural selection favoring suckering individuals has led to a preponderance of clonal beech groves in the Northeast. The situation is different in the Southeast, where beeches are far less likely to root-sucker. Whatever the pressures that led to this form of reproduction in the North, they were obviously lacking in the unglaciated South. Consequently, southern beech stands are made up of many genetically distinct trees grown from a large number of seedlings.

Clonal (asexual) reproduction has certain advantages over seedling (sexual) reproduction. I have already mentioned its advantage under conditions not favorable for seedling recruitment (see the descriptions of *Populus tremuloides* and *Gaylussacia brachycera* for other examples). Clonal reproduction may evolve when pollination becomes unreliable (say when the plant's preferred pollinating insect has gone extinct or is rarely available). Blueberries growing in the forest understory are visited only erratically by bumblebees, which prefer the warmth of bright sunlight. Accordingly, shade-grown blueberries set little fruit and spread around on colonizing rhizomes. Given a place in the sun and some hungry bees, however, and these same plants will invest much more energy in fruit and seed production and less in colonization.

The major disadvantage of clonal propagation (whether in sheep or beech trees) is that the genetic diversity of a given population is necessarily reduced. Sexual recombination is the primary means by which genes are reshuffled over time, ensuring that a species retains a diverse gene pool that will allow it maximum flexibility in an uncertain future (mutations, which can occur in clonal populations, are much less reliable events). Should a grove of genetically identical beeches become infected with a deadly bark fungus, it is likely to kill all of the trees (a phenomenon that is occurring right now with beech bark disease). Contrast this with a stand of genetically distinct seedling beeches. Even if the disease kills one tree, others may be more resistant, and their seedlings will have the opportunity to colonize the land vacated by the death of the weaker trees. Genetic diversity is the fuel that drives natural selection.

In the nursery industry, clonal propagation (tissue culture, stem cuttings, division) is the rule rather than the exception. This allows for the selection and dissemination of superior cultivars with bigger flowers, more colorful bark, or resistance to a particular disease (but not all diseases). I see nothing wrong with clonal plant propagation from an ethical standpoint, but it does raise issues identical to those faced by a clonal stand of beeches. What happens when a specific disease or environmental problem like ozone pollution develops that preferentially kills or weakens particular widely planted clones like *Betula nigra* 'Heritage'? Further, since many plants are self-incompatible (meaning that a plant or a genetically identical stand cannot pollinate itself), clonal populations may be largely unable to set viable seed. Although this may be an advantage in a cultivated situation, it is a major problem in restoration/revegetation.

foliar nematodes, which build up in their tissues over time. These can spread rapidly in a nursery situation on unsterilized pruning equipment or by means of insect outbreaks; sucking insects like aphids and thrips are the mosquitoes of the plant world, spreading disease by exchanging fluids the way mosquitoes spread human illnesses. Most of these diseases are not passed from parent to seed, and thus seeds are a clean slate, so to speak. The difference in vigor between a virused cultivar and its virus-free offspring is truly dramatic. Disease-free plants are of obvious value in a garden situation, and they become even more important if one is undertaking a restoration project, planting out species into the wild.

A related subject is that of provenance and genotype. In the wild, plants are constantly undergoing natural selection. The seedlings that are the most fit —endowed with traits that help them compete most effectively in a certain place—will be more likely to survive and reproduce. A red maple that originates in central Florida has, over generations, accumulated genetic traits that allow it to thrive in the long, warm season and short winter of the Deep South, whereas one from southeastern Minnesota has evolved in a much cooler climate with a shorter growing season. I was amazed to see red maples blooming in south Florida in late January—a full three months before they do in Massachusetts. Who is to say whether a plant from the South would thrive in a northern climate, or vice versa? Certainly provenance, or place of origin, must be taken into account. Provenance is becoming more of an issue in the field of habitat restoration and conservation biology, but it is worth discussing in this context as well. The provenance of a particular plant is its family history—where it was born, where its parents lived, and so on. Information like this becomes important if you are trying to propagate plants that will be the most fit in your particular environment. Underlying this idea of provenance is the issue of genotype, an organism's genetic profile. Since it is very hard to map out the unique genetic identity of a particular plant, where that plant comes from is used to infer certain things about its genotype. We can infer that a red maple from Minnesota will have more inherent cold tolerance but less heat tolerance than a seedling from south Florida, though without exhaustive and expensive genetic testing, we cannot know for sure just how different these two individuals are. In effect we are creating a stereotype, with its advantages and its limitations. It may be that even though the two trees have very different provenances, genotypically they are quite similar—Florida was a great refuge for northern plants during the last ice age, and many species moved north again only fairly recently in geological terms. Thus the population as a whole is genetically similar over its range. On the other hand, the two could be quite different genotypes, and mixing them up could create a soup of intermediate offspring that might be better adapted to either place— or less well adapted. We don't know the answers, and until we do I think we should adopt the precautionary principle and try to grow plants from our own region whenever possible. It is one of the best reasons I can think of to get out there, collect seed in your own backyard, and start propagating!

Seed Collection

Gardens are often great sources of seed, because they are readily accessible and because, hopefully, the plants are growing vigorously and well, so the quality and quantity of seed are better than in the wild. However, in a garden where different species are mixed together, it is easy for hybridization to occur, and seed from cultivated plants often turns out to be different from the parent. Further, many plants are self-incompatible, meaning they cannot pollinate themselves and set viable seed. They need pollen from another plant of the same species (or sometimes of a closely related species). If you have only one plant of such a species, you may never get seed. I sometimes have had to borrow a plant for stud service so that I can obtain viable seed. Self-incompatibility actually exacerbates the problem of hybridization in gardens. Both lowbush blueberry and velvet-leaf blueberry are mostly self-incompatible. If you have just one of each, most of the viable seed that either produces will be of hybrid origin, and the resulting plants will have characteristics somewhere in between the parents (in this case not such a bad thing, as the hybrids can be superior garden plants). If you are planning to collect seed from garden plants with a reputation for promiscuity, collect from plants that are isolated from other related species (especially if they are wind-pollinated, like willows) or hand-pollinate the flowers to prevent unwanted hybridization. Even in the case of wind-pollinated species, if you overwhelm the stigmas with the correct pollen, pollen from other species will have a tough time settling on. Once the pollen grains germinate and begin growing pollen tubes, other pollen is excluded, either because the stigma is no longer receptive or because space on the stigma is limited.

Wild-collected seed is another option, and has the dual advantage of being more likely true to type as well as being from plants of local provenance. However, there are several disadvantages. Many seeds ripen within a very short time, and it is hard without experience to time your visits just right so you do not miss the seed. There is also an ethical question to be considered regarding wild-collected seed. Theoretically, harvesting seed from a wild population lessens the chances of that population's long-term success because it reduces its total genetic resource. In reality, it would be very hard in most cases to collect enough seed from a population to seriously threaten its survival. But as a precaution, never collect seed from rare plants and take only a few seeds from each plant when possible. There is a big difference between taking 1 percent of the available seed and 75 percent. Never collect seed without the landowner's permission, and remember that it is a crime to collect anything on state or federal land. Ideally, use wild-collected seed to establish cultivated stock that can be the source of future seed, *and never wild-collect the plants themselves.*

I remember a toy I was fascinated with as a child, a gelatin capsule that you dropped into a glass of water. As it dissolved, a sponge shaped like a giant animal cracker popped out. The little sponge animal lay patiently in its gelatin cocoon waiting for the waters to set it free. I think of seeds in a similar way. Although they don't spring up fully formed, they do emerge as little copies of their parents from something that hardly resembles a plant, little piles of beads or fluff transformed almost magically into delicate flowers or forest giants. A friend once gave me a seed as big as a chestnut with a coat like polished turquoise. He had plucked it from a leguminous vine that grew near his Peace Corps home in Brazil. It had journeyed around with him in pockets and boxes and writing-desk drawers through 10 years of winters and springs by the time he gave it to me. After admiring it for a while, I nicked the seed coat with a file and ceremoniously dropped it into a glass of water, where I left it overnight, then planted it. Sure enough, three days later two huge cotyledons sprang triumphantly from the soil and grew into something resembling a giant bean plant.

Of course most seeds would not have survived this sort of careless storage. A mature seed contains an embryonic plant, usually complete with a rudimentary leaf or leaves and root surrounded by food reserves in the form or fats, proteins, and starches. After fertilization, there is a period of maturation, during which the embryo develops to a certain size and the parent fills the seed with the food reserves necessary to allow the embryo to survive dormancy and then germinate and become established enough to begin to photosynthesize on its own. Seed that is collected prematurely is often insufficiently prepared and will never germinate. Fortunately, most seeds give clues to help us determine when they are ripe. The seed coats, the protective jacket that surrounds most seeds, typically turns from green or white to gold, brown, or black when ripe. If a seed is contained within a fleshy fruit as with cherries and viburnums, ripening of the fruit can be taken as a clue that the seeds inside are ready to harvest. Seeds that ripen in pods or capsules will be ready when their container begins to yellow, split, and dry. If you are unsure, pull open a fruit or pod and examine the seeds. Are some or all the seed coats darkened? (It helps to have some immature seeds for comparison.) It is usually a good idea to split open a few seeds to make sure they contain viable embryos, as sometimes a plant will produce empty seeds that otherwise appear viable but will never germinate. Split open one of the seeds with your fingernail or a knife. Is the inside white and plump, filling the shell and appearing firm, not milky? Then chances are the seeds are ripe and viable. Most ripened seed should be harvested and allowed to dry in the open air, though there are exceptions (see below). Drying does several things. First, it lowers the moisture content of the seed, making it harder for pathogens to attack it in storage. Drying also triggers physiological changes in the seed, slowing down its metabolism and readying it for dormancy; in fact, some seed will germinate well only after a period of dry storage (usually two to three months is sufficient).

Seed Cleaning and Storage

A seed is actually a living, functioning plant, which continues to burn energy in storage—energy it needs to germinate and grow. The faster you clean and store your seeds after harvest, the longer they will live. Slowing down the rate at which the seed metabolizes its energy reserves increases not only its life in storage but also its vigor and success when it is germinating. Immature seed still developing in the parent has a moisture content near 100 percent. As the seed ripens and the seed coat dries, a barrier, called an abscission layer, forms between the seed and the parent, cutting off water and drying the seed. Drying should continue after harvest to bring the seeds down to an ideal moisture content of between 3 and 10 percent. Because the relative humidity of a family house is rarely this low, desiccants such as silica gel (used to dry flowers and sold in hobby stores) are often employed by people who are serious about long-term storage of seed. However, if you plan on sowing the seed within a year or two, just letting it dry completely under household conditions will usually be sufficient. If the capsules (the fibrous covering of some seeds) or chaff appear crispy, then the seed is likely dry enough. The other way to slow down the aging process of seed is to refrigerate it. Metabolism involves chemical reactions that are greatly slowed as the temperature is lowered to near freezing, and air-dried seed stored in paper envelopes in the refrigerator will stay viable 5 to 10 times longer than seed kept at room temperature.

Most of the seed I harvest is allowed to dry at room temperature for a week or two, then cleaned to remove any chaff and leaf debris and also any insects that may be present. There are several tools that make the job easier. An old rolling pin works well to crush woody capsules, and as long as you roll gingerly, you will not damage the seed. Screens of several mesh sizes are very handy, and you can make them out of window screen or hardware cloth fastened onto a wooden frame. Kitchen stores are good sources of finer-mesh sieves as well. Round seeds can be effectively separated from chaff by gently shaking them on a tilted surface such as an open manila file folder. Let the seeds roll down, then fluff up the chaff to allow more to fall. It is sometimes difficult to distinguish the seed from the chaff. In the descriptions for each genus I have tried to give a brief description of the seed, but if you have difficulty with a particular species, sowing the whole lot, chaff and all, will probably do no harm.

CLEANING SEEDS OF PULPY FRUITS

Seed that develops in fleshy fruits such as sassafras, hawthorn, or blueberries must be extracted before drying or sowing. Many fruit pulps contain inhibitory chemicals that retard germination if not removed. These are usually flushed away as the fruits pass through the digestive system of animals that eat the fruits and disperse the seed in their droppings. Small amounts of seed can be mashed and washed in a strainer in the sink, but if you are planning to clean larger quantities, I would recommend that you invest in a hand-held milkshake blender that you use only for cleaning seeds. Choose one that comes with several blades, and test a small batch of seed to make sure it does not suffer in the blending. We use a Cuisinart Quick Prep with a disk blade that looks like a miniature cheese grater and is safe for most seed. Fill the blender cup half full with water and add some berries and blend for a minute or two. Pulp and dead seeds float and good seed sinks, so you can fill the cup all the way up after blending and gently pour off the floating debris. It may take several refillings and pourings to get all the pulp out, but you will be left with perfectly clean seed. This also helps to quickly scarify large batches of seeds as it cleans.

Another technique for cleaning away pulp involves soaking the fruits in a dish or pail of water for a week or two. This results in a stinking, fermenting mess that should be confined to the garage or porch, but after washing in a strainer under a jet of water, the seed is fairly clean. Actually, the fermentation process is particularly effective at destroying germination-inhibiting chemicals in the pulp. Once the seed is cleaned of pulp, it can be air-dried for storage or sown immediately.

Fruits that contain small seeds, such as *Vaccinium* species, some honeysuckles, and snowberries are hard to clean with either the blender or fermentation methods. Though some seed may settle out, often it stays suspended in the pulp or is washed through the strainer and down the drain. In this case I use either "smear and peel" or dehydration ("raisin") procedure. The first requires only a good-quality ab-

sorbent paper towel (one that stays together when wet). Simply squish the fruit on the towel with your thumb, then smear it across the surface. The towel will absorb most of the liquid, and if you let it dry for a day, the seeds can be easily peeled or flicked off the paper. These may not need any additional cleaning, but as a precaution, I usually rinse them in a glass of water and strain them out; very small seeds can be strained by pouring through a coffee filter. Air-dry the seeds before storage or sow them immediately.

The "raisin" procedure involves air-drying the fruits until they are shriveled but still pliable. They can then be opened with a fingernail and the seeds scooped out.

HYDROPHILIC SEEDS

Certain seeds are intolerant of drying out below a moisture content of 30 to 90 percent, needing instead to be sown immediately when ripe. The list of plants with so-called ephemeral (meaning short-lived or transitory) or recalcitrant (meaning hard to deal with) seeds includes firs, pawpaws, and many of the oily nut trees such as oaks, buckeyes, and walnuts. The term "ephemeral" is not entirely accurate, however, and I think it leads to misconceptions about handling the seeds correctly. Many of these species have seeds that are very long-lived if stored moist. I think a more accurate term would be *hydrophilic*, meaning it requires the presence of water. In general, hydrophilic seeds are associated with stable temperate-forest communities. I believe that these seeds have lost their ability to withstand drying out for the same reason cave animals have lost their sight: in a temperate climate, with even, reliable rainfall, there is no need to waste resources preparing for desiccation if it is not a threat. The seed of these

While an expensive set of brass cleaning screens certainly comes in handy, you can buy a good set of different-sized mesh sieves at your local kitchen supply store for far less money. We air-dry most seeds in manila envelopes or brown paper bags until we can clean them, and store the cleaned seed in plastic or paper bags in the refrigerator until needed.

plants simply ripens, falls, or is consumed by animals and eventually is dispersed among the leaf litter, never having to dry out. Many of the western equivalents of eastern woodland plants live in areas where summers are drier, and thus have seeds that can withstand desiccation more readily.

When you are working with species with hydrophilic seeds, it is important to never let them dry, ideally sowing them immediately after they are collected and cleaned. Alternatively, they can be stored in self-sealing plastic baggies or sealed glass or plastic containers in the refrigerator for up to a year or more and still remain viable. I usually err on the side of caution, and if I am unsure about a particular species, I store the seed in a sealed, waterproof container. As a rule, if the hydrophylic seed in question matures in a fleshy fruit or moist capsule, clean the seed as described above, then put it in a plastic bag and add a handful of dampened vermiculite before sealing, to ensure a very high moisture content. Remember, you are not trying to germinate these seeds, merely to keep them hydrated (think of a tobacco humidor). Add just enough water to the vermiculite to keep the environment barely damp. Too much water may lead to fungus problems. Species that have hydrophilic seeds are indicated in the Propagation Table (page 277) by an asterisk (*) in the Germination Conditions column.

Seed Sowing Materials

The actual process of seed sowing usually goes quite quickly if you have the materials prepared. It is important to consider several things before beginning: containers, potting mix, and a place to put the flats.

CONTAINERS

Theoretically, anything that will hold soil can work as a container. However, a container's shape and size greatly influence the way water drains through a soil mix. A flat, which is much wider than tall, will hold more water for a given volume of soil than a tall, narrow pot. You can see this for yourself using a kitchen sponge. Soak the sponge in water until it is saturated. Do not wring it out. Place it flat on a screen and let it drain until it stops dripping. In this position it is much like a low seed flat in shape. Now tip it up so that it stands on a narrow end and watch a lot more water drain out. This is what happens to soil in a tall, narrow container. Low seed flats are handy for seed sowing, but you must use a freely draining mix for adequate drainage. Tall, narrow pots, with a height at least twice their width, are better for moisture-sensitive alpine and dry-land species. Always use containers—new ones if possible—with large drainage holes in the bottom. If you do use secondhand containers, at least wash them with soap or, even better,

soak them overnight in a household bleach solution of 9 parts water to 1 part bleach, then thoroughly rinse them. This will kill pathogens and weed seeds.

One-quart paper milk containers make excellent deep pots for seedlings that have taproots. Open up the top completely, and for drainage, either completely cut off the bottom or snip half an inch off each of the four bottom corners. Removing the entire bottom is a bit messier, but it has the advantage that contact with the air will kill the root tips, in effect root-pruning the seedlings. Place the pots on a tray when you fill them and leave them on it for a few weeks, or at least until the mix is stabilized and well moistened.

SEED-STARTING MIXES

A good seed-starting mix is key. It is worth paying for a commercial bagged mix rather than trying to blend your own. I use a soilless, peat-based seed-starting mix that is about half peat and fine screened bark and half fine perlite and vermiculite. There are quite a few brands on the market that are all very similar. If you have trouble finding a suitable mix, go to a good nursery in the area and see if they will sell you a bag of the mix they use. Some mixes substitute ground coconut-husk fiber (coir) for some of the peat. Coir is expensive (much of it is imported from Indonesia), it ties up more nitrogen than peat-based mixes, so you need to use a higher-nitrogen fertilizer, and weeds such as liverworts seem to really love it. Avoid mixes that contain soil or compost; even when pasteurized they break down quickly and become sodden. A peat-perlite-vermiculite mix will work for 90 percent of the plants covered in this book. The standard mix holds too much water for many dryland/alpine species, so I blend in one part #1-filter sand, washed sand, fine gravel, or brown pumice stone for every two parts of potting mix.

Commercial mixes come with what is called a starter charge of fertilizer in them, but you will have to fertilize the germinated plants regularly with a liquid fertilizer once they are up and growing; use it at half strength and apply it every week or two from spring to midsummer.

PLACING FLATS

During the warmer parts of the year, seed flats can be set out on the open ground, but putting them on a table with a screen over them will keep away weeds, cats, and other furry diggers. If you live in an area where temperatures routinely fall below 20° F in winter, it is best to provide some protection for the seed flats. A cold frame with a floor set below grade and walls of concrete block or pressure-treated lumber is an excellent solution. This is not like the cold frame used to start vegetables, which are really minigreenhouses with transparent lids. You want something that will keep out the sun and keep the seeds

Seeds of umbrella magnolia (Magnolia tripetala). Magnolias have one of the most remarkable seed dispersal mechanisms of any plant in this book. The bright, red-coated seeds drop out of their follicles and dangle in the breeze on slender white threads. The movement and color of the seeds attract birds, who eat and disperse them. I pick the cones when the seeds are just beginning to fall out and let them dry for a week. After gently cleaning off the oily red coat, I sow the seeds in flats covered with wire cloth or keep them damp and refrigerated over the winter to prevent losses to mice and other rodents.

(and container plants, for that matter) consistently cold or frozen. You can site it in either sun or shade; shade is best if you are working with slow-growing woodland plants. Also, the cold frame will not heat up prematurely in late winter. In either case be sure to cover the frame at the beginning of winter with a reflective, insulating layer. For a small frame, pieces of rigid Styrofoam insulation, available in half-inch and one-inch-thick sheets, work well. You can get these at home-improvement centers. Cut the Styrofoam to size, set it over the top of the frame, and hold it down with ropes or bricks. Remove the cover as soon as you can in late winter to prevent heat buildup from the sun, which would cause premature germination.

Inevitably, any covered spot full of plants and seeds will attract mice and other rodents. You can enclose individual flats or even the whole frame in hardware cloth. I fashion covers out of 3-foot-wide, ½-inch-gauge hardware cloth notched and folded down at the corners. This will make a tight cover for a number of pots or trays (mine are usually about 3 feet square when completed). A second cover of the same size can be used underneath to totally protect the seeds from predation. Resorting to rodent traps and poison baits is not out of the question. Many growers use wax-impregnated bait blocks sold for rodent control that are placed in dispensers. A cheap dispenser can be fashioned out of a 10-inch section of PVC pipe capped on both ends. Drill a 1-inch hole through one cap to allow access. This will keep bait dry and prevent larger animals from gaining access.

To germinate many of the larger, nutritious seeds and nuts, such as those of magnolias, oaks, snowbells, and hickories, the safest thing is to chill them in the refrigerator and plant them outside in spring. Otherwise they will be the targets of marauders. In autumn, soak cleaned nuts/seeds in a pail of water for 24 hours. This allows the seed to absorb the water it needs to begin the germination process. Then strain the seeds and shake off all excess water (a salad spinner works well for this) and enclose them in a heavy-duty self-sealing freezer bag or plastic container and place them in the refrigerator (not the freezer) for at least three months. Check the seeds once a month and add a teaspoon or so of water if they seem dry or a handful of dry vermiculite, which acts like a sponge, if they seem too wet. Plant them out in spring. You will still have to screen against squirrels and other animals until the seedlings have germinated and begun growing, but this storage method gives far better control during the winter.

Sowing Seed

As a rule of thumb, you should sow seeds about as deep as they are thick. Fill a container with moistened mix and lightly tamp it down, then sprinkle on the seeds and dust a light coating of more mix over them. I cover all my seeds with an additional ⅛-inch layer of #1-filter sand (see Germination Code H, p. 270, for a discussion of sand). Fine gravel, usually called chicken or turkey grit, or washed builder's sand (not beach or sandbox sand) works well too. To wash sand, fill a 5-gallon bucket half full with sand, then stick a running garden hose into the bucket and poke it around in the sand. Water, carrying finer particles, will start to flow over the top of the bucket, leaving the larger, heavier sand particles behind in the bucket. It takes a little practice to get the water flow rate correct so as not to wash out too much of the sand. Sand or fine gravel not only helps protect small, surface-sown seeds, but also keeps rain and normal watering from floating off larger seeds and cuts down on the fungus disease called damping off.

After sowing the seeds, water the flats thoroughly and keep them well watered from that point on. Once you have wetted the seeds and begun the germination process, drying out will kill them or at least greatly set them back. For slow-to-germinate seeds (Germination Codes C and D), I recommend covering the flats with spun-bonded row cover — the white, permeable fabric used in vegetable gardens to promote germination and protect crops from insects — and placing them in the shade. It shades the flats and keeps out weeds. (It is not a substitute for winter insulation, though, as it provides only a few degrees of frost protection.) To prevent fungus problems, be sure to remove the fabric immediately when seedlings begin to germinate.

SEED BED OR GARDEN?

An alternative to growing seedlings in containers is to sow seeds directly in a prepared seed bed or open spot in the garden. A seed bed can be constructed like a raised bed used for vegetables; use concrete block or timber for the sides and fill it with good-quality topsoil. Sowing directly in the garden can be as simple as just scratching in seeds here and there. This is certainly a low-maintenance alternative, but expect more attrition and loss through predation. It works well for taprooted species like buckeyes and walnuts, whose roots are difficult to accommodate in most containers, as well as those like silverbells or hollies that take a few years to germinate. Seeds larger than ¼ inch in diameter can be mulched with an inch or two of rotted straw, leaves, or bark mulch to control weeds. Seeds smaller than this may not be able to push through the mulch and are generally harder to grow successfully this way.

Germination Codes

The process of seed germination begins when the ripened seed falls from the parent and culminates in the emergence of the seedling from below ground. You have likely grown tomatoes or marigolds from seed. In the case of such warm-season or tropical annuals, all that is needed to complete the process of germination is moisture and warmth. The seeds of most plants that grow in a temperate climate, where conditions are unfavorable for growth part of the year because of excessive cold, heat, or drought, have evolved mechanisms to prevent premature germination during periods unfavorable to growth — specifically, winter. Understanding these mechanisms and providing the conditions to overcome them is the critical skill that you must learn in order to grow native plants from seed. In the Propagation Table (p. 277) there is a column called Germination Conditions, and for each plant there is one or more lettered germination codes or seed treatments. For each genus I have listed the germination approach that has worked well for me and should provide good results if followed carefully. I will now explain these germination codes and any relevant information about seed biology that pertains to them. For the sake of convenience, I will refer to two temperatures, 70° F and 40° F, in these explanations. This does not mean you need to keep the seed at exactly those temperatures to get good results. Temperatures from 32° to 42° F are adequate for chilling, and temperatures from 60° to 80° F for warmth are fine. Think of the germination codes as recipes rather than as inviolable horticultural laws. You can often fudge here and there or substitute one thing for another and your seeds will still germinate. All the seed flats are placed in outdoor cold frames, kept well watered, and overwintered under insulation. The seedlings come up as they will.

GERMINATION CODE A: seed will germinate within 4 weeks if sown at 70° F.

This is a common pattern with tropical and annual plants, and a few hardy perennials fall into this category as well. Addition of water is the mechanism allowing the seed to germinate, so this pattern is most common with dryland and desert plants, which must be ready to grow when the rains come (technically this is referred to as non-deep physiological dormancy). Many A-type seeds need a period of 1 to 3 months of dry storage after ripening prior to planting in order to germinate. Thus, seed collected in fall and sown immediately will germinate poorly, whereas seed that has been cleaned and stored dry (in a paper envelope at 40° F) for three months will come up well.

Some plants will germinate with an A treatment, but emergence will be erratic and slow. In fact, some seed may require a year of dry storage to germinate well when sown warm. Interestingly, only 60 days of moist, cold storage, or cold stratification, will often yield the same results. Partly this is because the length of dry-storage or after-ripening time necessary to overcome dormancy is much longer than with cold stratification. A period of moist cold will generally have no ill effects, and it makes the process less complicated if you are handling many different seeds.

GERMINATION CODE B: seed will germinate upon being shifted to 70° F after 90–140 days of moist, cold stratification at 40° F.

This is by far the most common germination pattern among the temperate plants. Cold stratification means seed is kept cold and moist in the ground, in flats, or even in bags in the refrigerator. It is vital that the seed be sown and well moistened before being exposed to cold. Water "activates" hormone and enzyme systems in the seed that block germination and allow the embryo to measure the length of cold that it has received. Dry, cold storage will not usually substitute for moist stratification if the seeds are truly type-B germinators. The easiest way to germinate seeds of this type is to sow them outdoors in the fall, either directly in the garden or in prepared beds or pots kept in a cold frame or crawl space that does not get too cold (below 15° F). Time your sowing so that the seeds will have at least one to two weeks above freezing to absorb moisture before cold sets in. Sowing the seeds too early in the fall, when temperatures still average above 55° F, may spur some to germinate prematurely. Natural temperature changes are often much more effective than those you might achieve by placing the flats in a refrigerator, and some species need very long "winters" to germinate. However, if you receive your seeds late in the winter, or live in an area where winter temperatures do not stay regularly below 50° F, or do not have a place to keep them outdoors, you can sow them in pots and place them inside a plastic bag in the refrigerator (not freezer) section of your fridge. A method that takes even less space is to mix the seed with some damp vermiculite in a self-seal baggie and put this in the refrigerator. Keep the seeds in the refrigerator for at least three months and then sow the lot in a container or outdoors just as you would any seed. If the seeds still don't germinate, you may have to place the container back in the refrigerator for another 30 to 60 days. If possible, I like to remove the seeds from cold storage in late winter and put them out in the cold frame, so that they will benefit from the cool, fluctuating temperatures there.

GERMINATION CODE C: seed germinates only after multiple cycles of warm and cold, typically 40°–70°–40°–70° F.

Multicycle germination is common in the lily family and woodland forbs, but it is, thankfully, rarer among woody species. The C treatment is a slow process that discourages many beginning propagators, but it is really not too difficult. Long germination times are necessary for several reasons. First, some seeds are two-stage germinators: after their first cold period they germinate underground to form a rudimentary root system, but they must be exposed to another cycle of cold and warmth to send up the cotyledon(s). Second, some plants, like *Halesia* species, have embryos that are not fully developed when the seed is ripe, and they need a full growing season to mature the embryo and prepare for germination. Others, like some hollies, have extremely hard seed coats that need time to weather away so that water can permeate. In all cases where the seed is both hydrophilic (noted in the table by an asterisk) and a C-type germinator, germination may be enhanced by collecting the seed when it is immature and sowing it immediately outdoors. This means collecting the seed about three to four weeks early, but you may have to experiment with a particular genus to get the timing right. Seed should be plump and full-size, but still green or white without a hardened or darkened seed coat. If, as with hobblebush viburnum (*Viburnum lantanoides*), the seed ripens in a fleshy fruit, harvest when the fruit is beginning to color up—when it has lost most of its green color and is turning red, blue, yellow, or whatever its ripe color is. Most C germinators need exposure to the natural cycling or fluctuating temperatures and long warm and cold seasons (four to six months) that you find outdoors, and germination under artificial conditions of refrigeration and greenhouse is hit or miss. Seed sown in beds or cold frames and kept watered and allowed to go through the natural seasons will give the best results.

GERMINATION CODE D: seed needs a period of warm, moist stratification followed by cold stratification and will germinate after being shifted back to warm, for example, 70°–40°–70° F.

This is a common cycle with early-ripening species, such as leatherwood and many dogwoods, that naturally experience this pattern when their seeds fall to the ground in early summer. It is also common in plants (such as hornbeam and fringetree) with immature embryos that need a period of warm, moist temperatures to continue development to the point where the seedling is physiologically mature enough to accept a period of cold stratification. In some of these germination is further hindered by a hard seed coat that must first be worn through to start the process. If the seed ripens early enough in the season so it can be cleaned and sown when there are still two to three months of temperatures averaging above 50° F, seedlings will come up the following spring without problem. However, when we sell seed of plants like fothergilla that has been stored at 40° F

Staggerbush (Lyonia mariana) *seedlings. Like all members of the heath family, including blueberries and huckleberries, staggerbush seeds are what I term moss germinators — meaning that they require warmth, high humidity, and light to germinate well. I provide this by surface-sowing the seeds and sealing the flat in a plastic bag placed in a warm, bright location, preferably under fluorescent lights set to be on for sixteen hours and off for eight.*

since collection, it will not germinate until it receives three to four months of warm, then three to four months of cold temperatures, so typically will not emerge until the second spring if sown outdoors in February or March. This is also true in the case of *Stewartia* species, whose seeds ripen too late in the fall to receive an adequate warm period for maturation, even if sown immediately upon collection. I usually sow the seed in flats or in damp vermiculite in a plastic bag and place them in a warm spot such as on top of the refrigerator or near a radiator — anywhere above 65° F will suffice — and leave them for at least three months before moving them to a cold frame or the refrigerator for three to four months more. In this way they come up well the following spring instead of waiting an additional year.

Finally, it is possible to collect the seeds of some plants, such as viburnums and ashes, before the seed is completely mature. The embryo/endosperm should completely fill the seed cavity, but the seed coat should still be fairly green — it takes some practice to gauge the stage with the ashes, but with viburnums and many others, the partially ripened berry is a good clue. If this seed is sown immediately — either because the seed coat has not fully hardened and so permits water flow, or the embryo has a longer warm period in which to mature — the seed will begin germinating in the fall or at least more consistently the following spring.

GERMINATION CODE G: seed will not germinate in the presence of chemical inhibitors.

Many, if not most, seeds that ripen in fleshy fruits must be well washed to eliminate all pulp to remove germination-inhibiting chemicals in the fruit. See Cleaning Seeds of Pulpy Fruits, page 264.

GERMINATION CODE H: seed requires light to germinate.

Small seeds that lack the resources to germinate deep underground are sensitive to light and will germinate only when a certain minimum intensity of light hits the seed coat. This is a cue that they should be positioned at or near the soil surface. As a rule of thumb, I treat any seed smaller than a grain of salt as a type H, because they need to be sown shallowly anyway, whether light is important or not. A few large-seeded species require light, but these are rare. The easiest way to handle H seeds outdoors is to sow them over the surface of a tamped and dampened seed mix and cover them with a ⅛-inch layer of washed, coarse quartz sand. Like glass, quartz sand transmits some light, yet it provides some protection from drying and weather. I use #1-filter-washed sand, because it is uniform and coarse. It is available at swimming-pool supply stores, but you can make your own by washing builder's sand in a bucket (see page 267). The washed sand will have a few large pebbles, which can be picked out; otherwise it is a good size, really a fine gravel. Alternatively, you can sow the seed on the surface of a moistened flat of seed-starting mix and enclose the flat in a large, self-sealing bag (see Moss Germination, page 271). The drawback to this system is that the seeds of non-moss-adapted species are vulnerable to damping off when raised in a very humid environment, and must be watched carefully. Some people have good results placing an uncovered flat in a tray of water; the water wicks up through the drainage holes in the flat to keep the medium moist. Remove the flat from the tray or the plastic bag as soon as the seedlings germinate to prevent disease.

GERMINATION CODE I: seed requires scarification because of an impermeable seed coat.

Many plants in the bean, rose, bayberry, and buckthorn families have hard outer seed coats that will not let water in to reach the embryo unless they are partially removed or scarified. Scarification means the splitting, abrading, or softening of a water-impermeable seed coat to allow imbibition (absorption of water) and thus speed germination. Many legumes, which otherwise would take a year or more to germinate, will germinate almost immediately after scarification. I have used several methods. Placing a pile of seeds between two pieces of fine sandpaper and grinding the top piece back and forth quickly with your palm is easy and effective. It is not necessary to remove much of the seed coat, and typically 15 to 30 seconds of grinding is sufficient.

Heat may also be used to break the seed coat. Some people swear by the hot-water method, where near-boiling water is poured over a pot of seeds, which are then allowed to cool and soak overnight before planting. The soaking allows the seeds to imbibe all the water they need and may wash away inhibitors coating the seed. I have had mixed results with this treatment. It works well with *Ceanothus,* in particular.

A dramatic way of providing heat is by burning combustible materials over the seed. Place the seeds on a metal trash-can lid or in a large metal can and then place a big handful of dry pine needles or leaves over the seeds (dried sagebrush is popular in the West) and set it ablaze. The heat of the fire will phys-ically scarify the seeds the way hot water does — sometimes to the point of killing them, if you overdo it — and the smoke leaves chemical residues on the seed that recently have been found to stimulate ger-mination. Most of the research in this type of germi-nation has been done in Australia and South Africa, where a large percentage of species will not readily germinate without smoke. This treatment holds promise with certain fire-adapted chaparral and rangeland species here as well. To guarantee that the seed is well smoked, get the fire started as described, then place a jar or cover over the fire and seeds, putting the fire out and trapping the smoke for an hour to allow its absorption by the seed. "Smoked water" is a cleaner and equally effective method. Ready-to-use smoked water is available from special-ty suppliers, or you can make your own by bubbling smoke through water for 20 minutes. Soak the seeds overnight in the solution, sow them, and water them with it. Research on smoke treatment is just begin-ning in this country, so it is hard to know how many species would benefit from the treatment. My guess is that within a few years, soaking chaparral, sage-grassland, and some fire-adapted forest-tree seeds in smoked water before sowing them will be standard procedure.

The hand-held blender method of cleaning seeds (see Cleaning Seeds of Pulpy Fruits, page 264) also helps scarify them, and is an easy way to treat seeds like hawthorns as you clean off the pulp. Sowing the seed outdoors in fall also means that the seed coat will be weathered by spring, and for many legumes, a combination of sandpaper scarification and cold stratification in a cold frame gives me consistently good results.

GERMINATION CODE *: seed is hydrophilic, intolerant of dry storage (see Hydrophilic Seeds, page 265).

This category includes all seeds that do not take des-iccation very well. Freshly collected seed should be sown immediately or alternatively stored for future use in sealed plastic bags or containers at 40° F with-out first drying it after harvest. Species whose seeds ripen in capsules, such as stewartias, can be partially dried to facilitate removal, but the capsules and debris should not be allowed to get completely dry before the seeds are cleaned. Seed may be stored with a handful of slightly damp vermiculite mixed in, as this maintains a consistent saturated atmosphere. With most woody species this is unnecessary, as long as the container is very tightly sealed to prevent water loss through evaporation. I prefer to seal the seeds in a zipper-type baggie and place this inside a tightly lidded glass or plastic jar. Hydrophilic seeds stored in this fashion can remain viable for a year or more, depending on the species.

MOSS GERMINATION: seed germinates best in the presence of both light and high atmospheric moisture, as would be found on a damp, mossy substrate in the wild.

It has become increasingly clear to me that a large number of small-seeded species, especially the rhododendrons, germinate more robustly and are less troubled by desiccation if they are sown indoors on a moist surface and are kept in a warm (65° to 75° F), well-lighted location. These species have evolved to germinate naturally on the surface of damp beds of moss, which provides even moisture, freedom from competition, and the light necessary for estab-lishment, but is usually relatively sterile and acidic. Accordingly, I sprinkle seeds over the surface of a well-dampened, fairly lightweight but often acidic substrate, either a mixture of equal parts peat and perlite or a blend of 1 part peat, 1 part perlite, and 2 parts of a commercial seed-starting mix. I mist the seeds lightly to assure good seed-soil contact and enclose the flat in a large, self-sealing plastic bag. This is placed under a two-tube, 4-foot-long fluores-cent shop light or high-pressure sodium lights, set on a timer to provide 16-hour days and 8-hour nights. The high humidity, light, and warmth promote rapid germination. I usually leave the flat in the sealed bag until the seedlings have produced a few true leaves, then I take them out, fertilize them with one-quar-ter-strength liquid fertilizer, let the flat drain, and place it back in the bag, this time leaving the bag open a crack at the top. Watch the seedlings carefully, and remove them at any sign of molding or damping off. The peat-perlite recipe is more acidic and is used for species especially prone to damping off, as the fungi are suppressed at low pH. Tap water may con-tain high levels of dissolved salts that can be harmful to sensitive species. Our tap water is very alkaline, so I have resorted to collecting rainwater and even to shoveling and melting snow in a big trash can inside the greenhouse. When the snow is fully melted and warmed, I use it for watering. The effects on salt-sen-sitive, moss-germinating species like members of the heath family (Ericaceae) has been fantastic and well worth the effort. If you have a small number of plants, distilled water is an easier option.

A variation on this procedure that is an excellent way to start small-seeded, acid-loving genera like *Kalmia* is moss-sowing. If you have a damp spot in the yard where moss grows well and stays fairly damp through the growing season, you can shake the seeds into the moss carpet and carefully water them in. You may have to supplement watering to keep the moss damp. Alternatively, you can establish a moss carpet in a container by transplanting some tufts of moss. The tight-growing, carpeting types like fern-leaf moss are easiest to get going. A mix of equal parts peat and sand is good for acid-loving mosses, but others grow well on the surface of regular potting mixes, as anyone who grows plants in containers can attest. Sphagnum works well, and certainly use it if you have some growing wild because it usually stays evenly moist. You can grow it by burying some of the long strands almost to their tips in a partially submerged container of equal parts peat and sand; it will need a season to become thick and established. All mosses are best watered with rainwater or distilled water.

Cuttings

Stem Cuttings

Every seed that germinates is a small miracle of sorts, but the formation of roots on a stem cutting is to me an event even more miraculous. Stem cuttings are sections of stem, usually with attached leaves, that are forced to initiate roots and become new plants. Many woody plants are very easy to root from stem cuttings, even without fancy equipment, if you follow some basic rules. The basic principle involved in this bit of horticultural wizardry is cell plasticity. All developing cells, be they human or carrot, have a certain potential to be anything the organism needs them to be. Undifferentiated cells in the growing tip of a plant are "told" by specific hormones that they should become leaves, flowers, roots, and so on. These undifferentiated cells can also be found in wound tissue that forms after cells have been damaged. One hormone messenger responsible for initiating these cells to become root cells (among other things) is indole-3-acetic acid (IAA) or its less expensive synthetic equivalent, indole-3-butyric acid (IBA), which is a component of many commercial rooting powders and liquids. When you expose a stem cutting to IBA, the hormone persuades cells either in the dormant bud within each leaf axil or in the wound tissue (callus tissue) that begins to form over the cut surface to become roots.

Cuttings offer certain advantages over seed, namely speed and the ability to produce an exact duplicate—a clone—of a special plant. Some plants, such as bearberry, are much easier to produce from cuttings than from seed. Obviously, by cloning plants you are not getting the genetic diversity you would from seed, and you need a little more equipment and practice to root cuttings well. Stem cuttings, the most common type of vegetative or clonal propagation, follow the same principles as those used in tissue culture. (In tissue or cell culture, undifferentiated cells or small cuttings are isolated in a sterile environment, then exposed to various hormones as well as nutrients and carbohydrates for energy to promote rapid cell growth or proliferation.)

In the Propagation Table (page 277), I refer to IBA talc, KIBA, and Dip 'N Grow, or liquid IBA. These all contain the same hormone(s), often at different concentrations, but the carrier—the way the hormone is delivered—varies in some important ways. Talc is simply hormone mixed with talcum powder, which clings to the wet surfaces of the cutting. It is easy to use and readily available at most garden centers and nurseries. Talc preparations come at premixed concentrations, usually about 1,000 to 8,000 parts per million, or ppm, which makes them less flexible than other products. Also the talc formula is not readily soluble, so uptake of the hormone into the wounded tissues is often incomplete. To get around insolubility problems, some formulations, like Dip 'N Grow, use alcohol as a solvent and carrier. These usually come as a standard 1 percent concentrate (10,000 ppm), which is diluted with water to achieve the desired concentration. Alcohol-based IBA is very soluble, and because the cutting is dipped in the liquid for anywhere from 5 seconds (what I call in the text "guide-dip") to 24 hours, more is absorbed into the tissues. The drawback is that the alcohol can burn sensitive stem tissue, especially when used with softwood cuttings. In an attempt to circumvent this, as well as to avoid using other toxic solvents like methanol and antifreeze, a potassium salt formulation called KIBA was developed that is soluble in water. KIBA is dissolved in water in a concentrated form, then diluted and used in the same manner as the alcohol-based formulations. Though it is not quite as readily taken up as alcohol, the water-based solution can be used at higher concentrations without burning.

Willow bark extract contains willow rooting substance (WRS), a natural auxin (a hormone that affects the growth activity of cells) produced in the inner bark of most willows. The extract is a handy, cheap, and often effective substitute for commercial synthetics. To make it, take about ten 2-to-3 foot willow branches, cutting the current year's growth after the leaves have fallen in the autumn. Cut the branches into 2-inch lengths, then pour a gallon of warm water over them and let them steep for 24 to 48 hours. The resulting liquid can be used as a replacement for 200 ppm KIBA soak, and the strength can be adjusted by varying the ratio of stems to water.

This works best with softwood cuttings. Prepare cuttings and then place them with their butt ends in the liquid for 24 hours, remove them, and handle them like other cuttings. Store the unused liquid in a sealed container in the refrigerator (be sure to label it!), and it will remain effective for several years.

You may wonder why I bother with all the information about parts per million in the Propagation Tables. If 1,000 ppm is good, wouldn't 10,000 be better? Not really. Auxin at the right levels will promote rooting, whereas a stronger dose may lead to mad cell division and callusing without any rooting.

Remember that when you sever a growing stem from its root system, you are not only cutting off its water supply, you are severely hampering its ability to manufacture energy and absorb nutrients. It becomes a race against time to get the cutting to root before its meager nutrient and energy reserves are exhausted. Always take cuttings from healthy, vigorous plants, as these will have proportionately more reserves. Avoid drought-stressed or nutrient-deficient specimens. Plants shunt reserves to the growing tips, and the cells in rapidly growing tissue are more plastic, so always take tip cuttings (from the top 3 to 6 inches of new growth) that are actively growing or have just finished and show no sign of flowering. Related to this is the idea of juvenility. Propagators discovered long ago that it is easier to root a cutting from a rapidly growing seedling or stump sprout than from a mature or senescent shrub or tree. Therefore plants used for cuttings are kept—either in containers or in beds—well fertilized and watered, and are routinely cut back to promote rapidly growing "young" wood. Often, if you can get an older plant to root, the rooted cutting will have more juvenility than the original and will make a better source of cutting wood.

There are three basic classifications of stem cuttings mentioned in this book: softwood, semihardwood, and hardwood. Softwood cuttings are made from soft, actively expanding growth taken mostly in late spring to early summer (and later if the tips continue growing rapidly late in the season). Usually these are tip cuttings taken from the top 3 to 6 inches of the most vigorous terminal growths. The cut stem should still be green and flexible—able to bend 30 degrees without creasing or breaking. They are called softwood because they have less lignin (the main stiffening component of wood), than semihardwood and hardwood cuttings. Most perennials and many easy-to-root woody plants such as snowberry and blackberry are done from softwood cuttings, as are more difficult plants, like birches, maples, and serviceberry. Softwood cuttings usually have a higher level of hormones in their tissues than harder wood, and since their cells are still young and rapidly differentiating, they require a less-concentrated rooting hormone. Easy-to-root species should be treated with 1,000 to 1,500 ppm IBA, while hard-to-root species, like maples, may need 8,000 ppm or higher. The main disadvantage with softwood cuttings is that they are easily dehydrated and need a very humid environment coupled with fairly high light, because they don't have the carbohydrate reserves of older cuttings. Rooting the cuttings in a polytent and using grow lights will work on a small scale, but a mist or fog room is preferable for large numbers of cuttings. Hardwood cuttings are made from fully lignified, mature wood and are usually taken when the plants are dormant, after the first hard freezes. These cuttings are slower to root and generally need more hormone (7,000 to 10,000 ppm IBA) than softwoods, but they are much tougher and don't need the humid atmosphere and high level of light that softwoods require. Semihardwood cuttings, taken from mid- to late summer as the twigs are turning from green to brown and after the leaves have expanded, are intermediate between softwood and hardwood cuttings in their hormone and humidity requirements.

Many conifers and broad-leaved evergreens like rhododendrons will root effectively from hardwood cuttings. Hardwood cuttings benefit from wounding, which can be done by using a knife or pruners to slice off a strip of bark on one or two sides. Take cuttings from the current year's growth, usually between October and February; I find with most plants that November–December is best, as the cuttings are fully dormant but still have fairly high carbohydrate reserves. Place them in a shaded cold-frame that is deep and well insulated enough so that the soil does not freeze. The cover should be clear to allow light through. Cuttings will root slowly over the winter and spring, and should be watered enough to maintain a damp medium. If you have a cool greenhouse (40 to 50° F), bottom heat of 65° F may speed rooting.

It is best to take all cuttings on a cloudy, humid day and prepare them immediately. If you cannot prepare them and plant them immediately, keep the material in sealed plastic bags in a refrigerator or ice chest to slow degradation. Stem cuttings should have at least two leaf nodes separated by a section of stem. Unless I am really short on material or the stems are very long, I try to leave three to six nodes on each cutting. I let softwood cuttings soak in a shallow bin of water while I work, to prevent desiccation. Strip or cut off the leaf or leaves from the lowest node, wound the cutting if necessary, and dip this freshly cut lower end into rooting hormone. If using talc, simply dip the bottom in it, withdraw it, and place the cut end an inch or two deep into the rooting medium. If using strong liquid formulations, dip the bottom half inch of the cutting into the solution for 5 to 10 seconds, then place the cutting in the rooting medium. For a rooting medium, I usually use a mix of two parts commercial peat-lite seed-starting potting mix and one part coarse perlite. Acid-loving plants and many others root well in a 1:1 mix of peat moss and coarse perlite or a 1:1:1 mix of peat moss, aged pine bark, and sand (good for hardwood cuttings). For rot-prone softwood cuttings, straight perlite that has been well compacted and wetted works well. You can use any sort of growing container to root cuttings, but the larger the pot or flat, the coarser the mix needs to be. I prefer 16-by-16-inch flats that are 3 inches deep, unless I am rooting under mist in a greenhouse, in which case I prefer "plug" trays—trays with separate small cells for each plant—with 50 or more plugs.

Sterility and sanitation are important. Always use clean trays (for sterilizing used trays, see page 266) and fresh, unused rooting medium. To lower the risk of disease transmission, soak cutting tools for 20 minutes in a 10 percent bleach solution before taking cuttings from a new plant. (Flaming the tools with a propane torch also works.)

The key to success is keeping the cuttings in a humid environment to cut down or eliminate water loss. The stem can absorb some water, just as a rose in a vase can, so if the air is saturated, even a softwood cutting can still grow and manufacture energy at a much reduced rate. Rooting is a race against time, and repeated moisture stress will usually lead to failure. Light is also important. Hardwood cuttings can be rooted successfully without much light, but most cuttings take better in strong light. Commercial propagators typically use greenhouses equipped with mist or fog systems that keep cuttings bathed in moisture and strong light. If the air temperature falls below 65° F, heat mats or circulating warm water are used to keep the root zone warm. The home propagator can approximate these conditions by placing cuttings and container in a sealed plastic bag or by creating a small "polytent" from thin plastic dry-cleaner bags stretched over a wire or wooden frame constructed against a window that receives morning sun or under grow lights set for 16-hour days. Commercial propagators often use a mist system consisting of fine water nozzles set to turn on when humidity drops below a predetermined level. The mist settles on the cuttings, preventing dehydration. The drawback to mist is that constantly wet leaves are susceptible to fungal diseases. Fog systems are similar, but they use a much finer nozzle to put moisture into the air without actually wetting the leaves. You can construct a homemade fog system using a larger polytent made from 2-mil plastic drop-cloths (available in the paint section of any hardware store) draped over a frame. Set up an ultrasonic humidifier under the tent next to the cuttings and adjust it to run just enough to keep them from wilting. Set this up outdoors in a lightly shaded spot during the summer or under grow lights at other times of the year. Alternatively, slow-to-root shade plants like rhododendrons and many conifers can be stuck in flats and covered with a breathable, spun-bonded polyester row cover such as Reemay (sold at garden centers) and placed in a shady cold frame that is regularly watered.

Check softwood cuttings after 2 to 3 weeks by gently tugging on them. If you feel resistance, take them out of the bag or row cover and give them a light fertilizing. Transplant them to larger pots once leaf growth recommences and the root systems are well developed. Hardwood cuttings may take 2 to 3 months to root.

Some woody plants, such as stewartias and fothergillas, are particularly resentful of disturbance the first year; they should be left alone in the rooting flat, overwintered, then potted up once new growth begins in spring.

Root Cuttings

Fleshy-rooted or colonial trees and shrubs like sumac and sweet shrub can be propagated from root cuttings, which are basically the opposite of stem cuttings: stem buds are induced to form from root cells. Since root systems store energy for the plant in winter and shunt it to the aboveground parts in spring, the best time to take these cuttings is before growth begins in late winter to early spring, when root reserves are high. There is not a hormone preparation readily available that promotes the induction of shoots from roots, so this procedure works only on species that have the natural ability to regenerate from the root system. Typically, 1-to-3 inch sections of the largest roots are removed and stuck either vertically or at a 45-degree angle in a coarse, sterile medium like builders' sand or vermiculite. When you cut the roots, try to keep track of the upper and lower ends and then orient them in the tray in the same direction. Keep the flat watered and warm, and new shoots should emerge within 6 to 8 weeks. *Calycanthus* and *Diervilla* will root more easily if you use only sections of root with an attached shoot or the beginning of a shoot. An even easier method that often works is to dig down around a healthy plant in early spring and sever some of the larger roots from the crown. Leave them in place, then relocate the resulting plants in fall.

Layering

One of the easiest methods of vegetative propagation is layering. Some plants, including raspberries, bearberries, cranberries, and willows, will form stem (adventitious) roots on their own, without the addition of hormones. Layering is a straightforward, if slow, procedure. Simply bend down a stem without severing it from the parent, place a rock over it to hold it against the ground, then cover the rock and section of stem with soil and/or organic mulch. Come back in a year and cut the rooted stem free below the layered section and replant it. Fast-growing, cane-forming, sprawling, or ground-covering species are better candidates for layering than slower-growing trees or shrubs.

Grafting

Of all the propagation methods, grafting is the most vaguely Frankensteinian, not to mention costly and labor-intensive. One study found grafting to be on average 14 times more costly than seed production! (See Conner, "Propagation of Upright Junipers.") It involves inserting tissue, in the form of a bud, or scion (twig), from one individual into the tissue of another, the rootstock. In many cases, different species within the same genus are combined in this way. The tissues form a wound callus that fuses together, eventually melding into uninterrupted conductive tissue connecting rootstock and scion. Grafting is an ancient art that was used extensively in the days before rooting hormones and tissue culture to multiply difficult-to-root cultivars such as apples and pears. It is a fascinating skill, but one beyond the scope of this text to describe adequately. Because of its relative cost as well as the problems of incompatibility between scion and rootstock (the plant equivalent of transplant rejection), grafting is best reserved for only the most stubborn, impossible-to-root cultivars.

Potting On

Getting the seeds to germinate or the cuttings to root is only half the battle, but I think it is the tougher half. Once you have a flat of healthy seedlings or well-rooted cuttings, keeping them healthy is pretty straightforward. Seedlings (and to some extent cuttings) have more plasticity than adults—that is, they are often more tolerant of transplanting damage and, if conditions are right, will continue growing and getting larger much more quickly than they would in the wild. For example, maple seedlings are easy to transplant from the seed flat to small individual 2-to-3-inch pots after their cotyledons are fully expanded. In the wild, first-year seedlings rarely put up more than 1 or 2 leaves or grow more than 2 to 3 inches before fall. However, in pots, with adequate fertilizer and water, they will continue to put out new leaves and after a season will be 8 to 16 inches tall, large enough to move into a 2-gallon container or nursery bed the following spring. Timely repotting, fertilization, and watering allow growth at 3 to 4 times the rate a wild seedling can usually muster. (I usually fer-tilize transplants every two weeks with liquid fertilizer mixed as directed on the label.)

Propagating plants in pots has a number of advantages over garden beds: faster growth, portability, sanitation, and ease of transplanting regardless of season. More and more woody plants are being raised in containers instead of in the ground. For a small nursery or home garden, I recommend growing in containers for the first year or two, if not longer, though it is much easier to move seedlings or cuttings into a growing bed or field once they are large enough to fend for themselves. I use two sorts of small containers for young seedlings or cuttings, depending on the particular species' rate of growth. Liner pots—so named because they were developed as a way to grow transplants to a size where they could be "lined out," or transplanted into field rows—are typically 2 to 4 inches wide and 3 to 10 inches deep. These deep pots accommodate long roots without taking up a lot of bench space. You can make perfectly good liner pots out of 1-quart milk cartons with their four bottom corners snipped off to allow water to drain. For fast-growing material that will be moved ("stepped up") into larger containers, I prefer plug trays. These take up less space, but have too little soil volume to hold the plants for more than a few months. I always try to transplant seedlings at the cotyledon stage or just after the first few true leaves have emerged, because their root systems are small and less easily damaged.

We use the same mix for plugs and small pots as we do for starting seeds. To bring plugs up to salable or plantable size, transfer them to 4-to-8-inch containers in early to midsummer; if you wait longer, they will not have time to get established before winter. Use a coarser mix for the larger pots to provide the necessary drainage. Do not add garden soil to your container mix and add compost only with caution. Water should pass quickly through the finished blend, not pool on top even for a few seconds. Adding rotted pine bark or perlite to the seed-starting mix will accomplish this, or you can blend your own. I have developed a blend that works well for most plants we grow.

1. Prepare bark mixture. Combine:
   3 parts aged, dark brown-black pine bark (it should have the consistency of pine bark mulch)
   1 part baled peat moss
   1 part coarse perlite

2. Prepare amendment. For each cubic foot of bark, blend:
   ¾ cup of powdered dolomite lime
   ⅓ cup wetting agent (optional but helpful)
   1 cup coated, balanced, time-release fertilizer

3. Blend amendment with bark mixture.

Wetting agents, available from greenhouse supply companies, are surfactants used to quickly wet organic mixes that otherwise repel water when dry. Time-release fertilizers, also called controlled-release fertilizers, or CRFs, such as Osmocote and Nutricote, release nutrients into the pot slowly as plants require them. Select a balanced (even-numbered, for example 13-13-13) type. One drawback to this mix is that it can lead to soil interface incompatibilities (see page 24). If you plan on raising woody plants in anything larger than a 6-inch pot, I would recommend substituting sand for at least part of the perlite and/or bark. This will also make the pots heavier and less likely to tip over when the plants become larger.

An even better method, if you have the space and are comfortable digging, balling, and burlaping your plants later, is to transplant them from the liner pots directly into field rows in early spring. They can be planted out directly into the wild or in the garden, but a few years in the more controlled environment of a nursery bed will dramatically improve your plants' survival while giving you time to stake, shape, and evaluate your stock. I usually prepare a nursery bed as I would any garden bed, tilling under weeds, adding compost to loosen and improve the soil, and fencing against deer and rodents. Space the transplants far enough apart to allow for growth (2-to-3-foot spacing will usually be sufficient for a few years), and mulch them with bark, hardwood chips, sawdust, or weed fabric to suppress the inevitable weeds. Some people swear by black weed fabric, and I have seen great results with it, but I find it very hot and sterile-looking. Fertilize after you set the transplants out, then again each spring to keep them growing vigorously. Despite the necessity of weeding the rows, this is a far less labor-intensive way to raise plants on a small scale. Overwintering is more straightforward, and you can go away for a few days without worrying that your plants will dry out or blow over, as they might in containers.

Overwintering

To overwinter containers, whether they be seed flats, liners, or 7-gallon pots, you need to keep in mind that roots are generally far less hardy than trunks and branches. Trees like white oak, which can survive −30° F in the wild, can be killed outright if their roots are exposed to temperatures below 15 to 25° F for even a day or two. If you live in a place where winter temperatures may drop into this range, you can overwinter a small number of containers by heeling them into the ground to protect the roots. Sink the pot so that the lip is just above grade. Water it before the ground freezes and after it thaws. Smaller pots and seed flats are best overwintered in a cold-frame, a box made of concrete blocks or pressure-treated wood that is buried partially belowground. Leave the pots uncovered until temperatures drop into the 30s and uncover again once temperatures are staying above 25° F. When temperatures fall, cover the frame with opaque insulation such as rigid Styrofoam held in place with rocks, ropes, or some such contrivance. Insulating blankets are another option; we use a flexible foam product called Microfoam that is designed for overwintering container plants. We lay the foam over the pots and then put a layer of white polyethylene sheeting over that. This is weighted down with boards or stapled to a wooden frame.

Taller woody plants in pots can be tipped on their sides so that they can be covered. A hoop or Quonset-style greenhouse is also ideal for these larger plants. Depending on the severity of your climate, a single layer of white plastic greenhouse film may be all that is required. In Zone 5 and below, two-layer inflated coverings or supplemental heaters may be needed to keep temperatures above 24° F. I have a friend who overwinters quite a few shrubs by packing them into the crawl space under his house in December and removing them as soon as it begins to thaw.

It is very important that you take the time to prune and shape young woody plants in the nursery. You can't teach an old dog new tricks, and it's hard to prune an old plant that was poorly shaped in its youth. A specimen that begins life with a straight trunk and solid, well-spaced, balanced limbs will be less likely to develop structural problems later on. I routinely stake trees and larger shrubs in the nursery with bamboo or tomato stakes, depending on the size, so that they develop a straight lower trunk. Old nylon stockings or plastic flagging tape are good, flexible materials to use as ties. Leave the stakes in place only for as long as is necessary to develop a trunk that can stand alone, and be careful to move the ties every year to avoid bark rot, which is basically the same thing that happens if you leave an adhesive bandage on your finger too long. Multitrunked shrubs will benefit from pruning and shaping to develop a few equal, well-spaced stems.

Abies   Fir p. 31   **FALL**   **B***

SEEDS: The large, cocoon-like female cones grow vertically from the upper sides of the highest branches, making it difficult to get at them. They shatter when ripe, and the little winged seeds helicopter off on the breeze. Try to pick a few cones in fall when they have gone from purple or green to brown, and let them air-dry indoors until they begin to split apart. Then separate the seeds from the interlocking scales. If they don't open, soak them overnight in warm water to loosen the resin, then put them in the freezer for a day or two while still wet, then let them air-dry again. If you learn what to look for, you can usually find sections of shattered cones under mature trees with some seeds still stuck inside. Or lay out a tarp on a windless fall day and shake the seed down. Seed germinates best in cool temperatures, so fall sowing outdoors with germination in spring is the best method. The little seedlings emerge with a whorl of 4–7 cotyledons, and that's about all the growing they'll do the first year.

CUTTINGS/DIVISIONS: Cuttings are difficult. Cultivars are usually side-grafted, with *A. balsamea* the preferred understock.

Acer   Maple p. 34   **LATE SPRING TO FALL, DEPENDING ON SPECIES**   **A or B***

SEEDS: Maple seeds ripen at different times. *A. rubrum* and *A. saccharinum* seed ripens quickly, falls to the ground in late spring, and sprouts immediately to take advantage of what is left of spring moisture. The other species ripen in late summer to autumn. Collect seed as it falls from the tree and sow. I don't bother removing the wings. Viability of seed varies from plant to plant and from year to year, possibly due to poor cross-pollination, drought, or some sort of predator avoidance. I use a pair of locking pliers to pop open some of the seeds and check for embryos before collecting from a particular tree. Set the pliers to clamp shut just enough to open the hull but not crush the embryo. Often whole crops of seedlings appear under mature trees, and a few of these can be dug and moved where you want them. With good culture, seedlings will put out a few sets of leaves the first year and take off after that.

CUTTINGS/DIVISIONS: Cuttings are difficult at best, but some of the cultivars are being produced this way. Bud grafting is the traditional method for vegetative production, using seedling understock of the same species.

Aesculus   Buckeye p. 38   **LATE SUMMER TO FALL**   **B***

SEEDS: Buckeye seeds are among the largest of any of our native plants. Female or perfect flowers are clustered at the base of the raceme, and usually only 1 to 2 flowers per spike set seed. The seed is enclosed in a lumpy, three-sectioned husk, in some species armed with a few half-hearted spines. Since squirrels will scavenge every available seed, I usually pick the ones I can reach when the husks have begun to yellow in late summer but before the seams open up. Let them dry only long enough for the husk to crack and then plant the seeds. Seed production, especially on bottlebrush buckeye, is very inconsistent. I once foolishly tried fall sowing in a cold frame outdoors, but the rodents dug up every seed during the winter. Now I collect the seeds and put them in damp vermiculite in the refrigerator for the winter. By spring some have sent out root radicals, and the lot are transplanted individually into deep, 6-inch-wide containers. The seedlings emerge quickly. Germination is hypogeal, with 1 to 2 sets of leaves emerging the first year. Be sure to protect the germinated seedlings, because the fat underground cotyledons remain for the first few months and squirrels will destroy young plants to get at them. The large taproot can be trimmed before transplanting; I have removed as much as 30 percent without apparent harm to the seedling.

CUTTINGS/DIVISIONS: Seed is the easiest method, but the running species can be propagated by root cuttings taken in winter before or after the ground has thawed. Stick 3-to-4-inch sections of the horizontal suckering roots vertically in 1:1 peat-sand mix and place in a cold frame to produce new shoots in spring. Or just dig up a few of the suckering growths with their attached section of root and pot them up.

Agarista   Florida leucothoe p. 158   **FALL**   **A, H (moss)**
   See Leucothoe.

Alnus   Alder p. 40   **FALL**   **B**

SEEDS: Collect seed when the female catkins (strobules) begin to darken and spilt. They break open much like a pine cone, with scales separating to reveal round, winged seeds inside. Many species will germinate immediately if the fresh seed is sown in a greenhouse. Dry seed will need 2 to 3 months of cold stratification. Fall sowing outdoors is easiest; seedlings will emerge in spring, first as a pair of cotyledons, then with alternating true leaves. Put into liners when the first true leaf has expanded and they will grow rapidly, ready for transplant to larger containers or the field the following spring. See also *Alnus* entry, Culture, p. 41, for notes on inoculation with nitrogen-fixing bacteria.

Amelanchier   Serviceberry p. 43   **EARLY TO MIDSUMMER**   **B, G, I***

SEEDS: Harvest the small, comma-shaped brown seeds when fruits just begin to turn from red to purple for easier extraction—and you are less likely to lose seed to the birds. Mash-wash or blender-clean the pulp off and either sow immediately or store in

A: seed will germinate within 4 weeks if sown at 70° F. **B**: seed will germinate upon being shifted to 70° F after 90–140 days of moist, cold stratification at 40° F.
C: seed germinates only after multiple cycles of warm and cold, typically 40°–70°–40°–70° F. **D**: seed needs a period of warm, moist stratification followed by cold stratification and will germinate after being shifted back to warm, for example, 70°–40°–70° F. **G**: seed will not germinate in presence of chemical inhibitors. **H**: seed requires light to germinate. **I**: seed requires scarification because of an impermeable seed coat. *****: seed is hydrophilic, intolerant of dry storage (see Hydrophilic Seeds, p. 265). Moss Germination: seed germinates best in the presence of both light and high atmospheric moisture, as would be found on a damp, mossy substrate in the wild.

plastic and sow outdoors in fall. Either way, seed germinates well after 3 months' cold stratification. Seeds harvested from fully ripe fruits benefit from light scarification before sowing. Seedlings emerge with a pair of cotyledons and then the first leaf. Transplant to liners at the cotyledon stage and larger pots the following spring.

CUTTINGS/DIVISIONS: Seed is the easiest method, but cuttings of many species root reasonably well. I have had the best luck with vigorous growth from younger sprouts and stems. Take cuttings two weeks after flowers fade in spring; leaves should be expanded but still not fully stiffened. Treat with 2,000–4,000 ppm KIBA. When subsequently potted, cuttings taken from the colonial species will often send up new stems from near the callus as well as more from the cutting. Stoloniferous species can be dug and divided in spring before buds swell. Take smaller stems near the edge of the colony with a length of stolon attached. Several cultivars, especially *A. × grandiflora* selections, are being propagated in quantity through tissue culture, and this has certainly helped to increase both availability and interest in the genus.

Andromeda   Bog rosemary p. 45   LATE SUMMER   A or B, H (moss)

SEEDS: Collect the round seed capsules when they turn dark brown and begin to crack, and shake or crush out the tiny seeds. Germinate as for *Rhododendron*. If no seedlings are evident after 3 weeks, put the flat in a plastic bag and place in the refrigerator for 60 days, then try again.

CUTTINGS/DIVISIONS: Take winter cuttings from the top 2 to 3 inches of previous years' growth. Wound it, treat it with 3,000 ppm IBA, then cover with Reemay and place in a cool greenhouse or pit cold frame. These should root very well by spring. Propagation from seed is not difficult, but cuttings will gain you about a year of growth.

Aralia   Hercules club p. 46   FALL   B, G (I)

SEEDS: Collect fruits as they turn deep purple — watch carefully: I have lost many to birds who were more attentive than I. Avoid collecting the green unripe clusters as their seed will not be viable. Ferment or clean in blender. Seeds are flattened, about 1/16 inch long, and hard. Fall sowing outdoors has produced consistent germination for me the following spring, and young plants grow quickly. Transplant to plugs, then to 1-gallon containers in early summer and the seedlings will be ready for the garden by fall. If you ferment rather than blend (blending scarifies as it cleans) scarification with light sandpaper may improve germination.

Arbutus   Madrone p. 47   FALL   B, G, H

SEEDS: Harvest the berries when they have turned red, and blender-clean. There are 4 to 5 fairly small, hard seeds in each fruit. Sow shallowly, as some light is necessary for good germination.

Arctostaphylos   Manzanita p. 48   LATE SUMMER TO FALL   B, G, I

SEEDS: Collect fruits when they are fully ripened — red or maroon-brown. Pollination or fruit development can be sporadic, with some plants laden with fruit while others nearby have only scattered berries. The crescent-shaped seeds fuse together into a clump in the center of the fruit as though fossilized, and like fossils they are very hard and thus difficult to germinate. The seeds have a plug of tissue that guards a water channel into the seed, which must be removed by either burning or acid scarification. Failed attempts at mechanical scarring led me to try the frightening procedure of soaking the seeds in a 50 percent solution of sulfuric acid for 10 to 30 minutes and then sowing seeds outdoors in fall. Germination is sporadic and never high. Probably either slow weathering or fire is the means by which the seeds are scarified in the wild, and some success has been reported after burning seeds in a small pile of pine needles. Seedlings are relatively large for the heath family, and are best transferred to deep liner pots filled with coarse, peaty mix for a season and lightly fertilized with a balanced liquid. Pinch once or twice to encourage branching.

CUTTINGS/DIVISIONS: Cuttings are my preferred method, as seed germination is slow and requires intensive scarification. My first attempts using semihardened, current-season wood taken in midsummer produced about 45 percent rooting, but since then, only about 10 percent. Fall or late-winter cuttings taken after the new wood is dormant are far easier, and result in 50 to 90 percent success depending on the individual used (7,000-10,000 KIBA quick dip). Use 4-to-6-inch vigorous current-year twigs and place treated cuttings in a cool, bright spot. Rooting takes 1 to 3 months. Rooted cuttings should be handled like seedlings.

Aristolochia   Pipevine p. 51   FALL   B

SEEDS: The flattened, more or less heart-shaped seeds fall from fluted capsules that peel open to release them, and the seeds float down with the aid of a banner-like wing that clings to their top. You have to search around under the leaves for the capsules, as they are green like the foliage; look in the axils near the beginning of the current year's growth. Some seeds may still be stuck in the inner sections of the capsule even after they have split and the skin is peeled back. Seedlings send up a pair of cotyledons followed by a series of leaves that immediately begin to twine. If transplanted from the seed flat early, before they become entangled with their neighbors, and given some support, they grow quickly and are ready for planting out after one season.

A: seed will germinate within 4 weeks if sown at 70° F. **B:** seed will germinate upon being shifted to 70° F after 90–140 days of moist, cold stratification at 40° F. **C:** seed germinates only after multiple cycles of warm and cold, typically 40°–70°–40°–70° F. **D:** seed needs a period of warm, moist stratification followed by cold stratification and will germinate after being shifted back to warm, for example, 70°–40°–70° F. **G:** seed will not germinate in presence of chemical inhibitors. **H:** seed requires light to germinate. **I:** seed requires scarification because of an impermeable seed coat. ***:** seed is hydrophilic, intolerant of dry storage (see Hydrophilic Seeds, p. 265). Moss Germination: seed germinates best in the presence of both light and high atmospheric moisture, as would be found on a damp, mossy substrate in the wild.

CUTTINGS/DIVISIONS: Cuttings taken from semi-hard new growth and treated with 2,000 ppm IBA will root, but I find the large leaves and twisting stems frustrating to work with; I resort to cuttings only when seed isn't available. I tried spur cuttings from expanding side shoots, but this failed completely. Carefully select 2 to 3 node cuttings with short internodes and trim the leaf by half before sticking them.

| *Aronia* | Chokeberry p. 53 | FALL | **B, G** |

SEEDS: Harvest the fruits in fall when they have ripened and mash and clean the seeds. Alternatively, you can wait until winter, when the fruits have shriveled and peel the seeds free from the raisin-like skin. I think they partially stratify within the fruits, because seeds collected in winter need less chilling than fall-harvested ones do. Seeds are small, dark brown, and comma-shaped. Seedlings and cuttings should be put into individual 2½-to-3-inch liner pots after germination, tip-pruned once, and grown for a season before potting on.

CUTTINGS/DIVISIONS: Conventional cuttings taken in early summer and treated with a moderate 4,000 ppm KIBA quick dip root well under mist.

| *Artemisia* | Sagebrush p. 54 | LATE FALL TO EARLY WINTER | **A, H** |

SEEDS: Seeds are very small and ripen late in the season. Harvest the flower heads whole and dry them in a paper bag or hang over newspaper. Seeds will shake out of the bracts as they dry. Seeds need a period of dry storage to after-ripen, so keep them in a paper envelope in the refrigerator until spring, then surface-sow them when temperatures have warmed into the 70s. Seedlings should be carefully moved into plugs as soon as they are big enough to handle, then potted into a coarse mix or held over and planted out directly in the ground the following spring.

CUTTINGS/DIVISIONS: Cuttings will root, but stems and leaves are prone to rotting under mist or in heavy media. About 50 percent of semihardwood cuttings of *A. tridentata* treated with 1,000 ppm IBA talc and placed in pure perlite under a Reemay tent rooted.

| *Asimina* | Pawpaw p. 56 | LATE SUMMER TO FALL | **B, G*** |

SEEDS: Collect the fruits when they begin to turn from green to yellow-green; the seed coats should be light brown inside. You can pick them a few weeks early and let them ripen indoors in a paper bag—just don't forget about them, or the whole place will start to smell like overripe fruit and your family will lambaste you. The seeds are about the size and shape of a lima bean with a warm brown seed coat, and there are 3 to 8 per fruit. A sort of pulpy skin surrounds the seeds, which you can remove with your teeth or by soaking for a week in a bucket of water. Seeds germinate hypogeally after 1 to 3 months of cold stratification, but mice and voles love them, so I would recommend stratifying them in a plastic bag in the refrigerator and sowing them in spring. First-year seedlings are sensitive to ultraviolet light, and thus need some shade during the heat of the day, but after that, full sun will produce better plants.

CUTTINGS/DIVISIONS: Selected cultivars of pawpaw are grafted onto seedling understock. Seed is the preferred method of propagation.

| *Befaria* | Tar-flower p. 116 | FALL | **B, H** |
| | *See Elliottia.* | | |

| *Betula* | Birch p. 58 | FALL TO WINTER | **(A) B, H** |

SEEDS: Collect the female cones (strobules) when they lose the last of their green color. Most species will hold some cones well into winter. Pick them carefully, as they disintegrate very easily and the seed will blow away (*B. nigra* seeds ripen in spring). The fine, reddish brown, papery seed is hard to separate from the 3-pointed bract-scales once you crush the dry cones, but winnowing or just the right size of screen will separate most of them. Birches are very light-dependent for proper germination. Surface-sow and cover with a light layer of coarse sand, then place outside for the winter to stratify. (Only *B. nigra* will germinate without winter stratification.) Seedlings will send up a pair of cotyledons and 1 to 3 true leaves (sometimes more) the first year. Birch seedlings and cuttings will grow indeterminately if given regular fertilizer until day length drops below about 14 hours.

CUTTINGS/DIVISIONS: Seeds are easy enough to start unless you want to propagate cultivars. Timing is critical, and you want to harvest fairly long (6-to-8-inch) shoots with a basal spur or heel attached (where it connects to the previous year's growth). In early to midsummer, look for shoots that are still actively growing but are becoming semihard toward the base of the cutting. Prune off the softest, undeveloped tips and stick the rest. Wounding and 2,000 ppm IBA talc usually give good results.

| *Bignonia* | Cross-vine p. 61 | LATE SUMMER | **A** |

SEEDS: The papery seed ripens in abundance within long constricted pods and sprouts within a few weeks of planting. When seedlings are 6 to 8 inches tall, pinch them back regularly to keep them from entangling each other. Seed is the easier propaga-

---

A: seed will germinate within 4 weeks if sown at 70° F. **B:** seed will germinate upon being shifted to 70° F after 90–140 days of moist, cold stratification at 40° F. **C:** seed germinates only after multiple cycles of warm and cold, typically 40°–70°–40°–70° F. **D:** seed needs a period of warm, moist stratification followed by cold stratification and will germinate after being shifted back to warm, for example, 70°–40°–70° F. **G:** seed will not germinate in presence of chemical inhibitors. **H:** seed requires light to germinate. **I:** seed requires scarification because of an impermeable seed coat. ***:** seed is hydrophilic, intolerant of dry storage (see Hydrophilic Seeds, p. 265). **Moss Germination:** seed germinates best in the presence of both light and high atmospheric moisture, as would be found on a damp, mossy substrate in the wild.

tion method, but you have no guarantee that the offspring will have the same color as the parent.

CUTTINGS/DIVISIONS: Cuttings taken from vigorous growth in early summer and treated with 1,000 to 2,000 ppm IBA root pretty well, albeit slowly. I stuck many cuttings of this species when I was in North Carolina, but I didn't produce enough to sell in quantity. I did find some differences in rootability between cultivars. Rooted cuttings will continue growing, and an additional season in the nursery will produce huskier plants.

Callicarpa   American beautyberry p. 62   **FALL TO WINTER**   **A or B, G**

SEEDS: Harvest berries when they turn magenta. Each contains 3 to 4 small seeds that can be squeezed or mashed from the fruits and either sown in fall and left outdoors or sown in spring (germination will take longer in spring).

CUTTINGS/DIVISIONS: Take softwood cuttings with 2–3 nodes each from just below the growing tips in summer. These root very easily. Treat with 1,000 ppm IBA talc and place under mist or in a polytent.

Calocedrus   California incense-cedar p. 63   **FALL**   **B***

SEEDS: The winged seeds are ready to harvest when the cones begin to turn brown. The cones look like rosebuds when closed and flare open to release seeds. Individual trees do not set heavy crops each year, so it is feast or famine from year to year. The seeds are hydrophilic; let the cones dry only enough to extract seeds and sow them immediately. Place the flat outdoors, and expect germination in spring. Seedlings emerge with a pair of cotyledons first sandwiched inside the seed coat, then springing free as a tuft of needles quickly develops between them. As the shoots lengthen, the longer needles give way gradually to scale-like ones. Transfer to 2½-inch pots the first year, 6-inch or larger the second. Seedlings grow moderately fast and require little shaping or pruning.

Calycanthus   Sweetshrub p. 64   **FALL TO WINTER**   **A or B**

SEEDS: Sweetshrub seed is one of the easiest and most fun to collect. The very large, mahogany brown seeds are about the size of a dry kidney bean. They ripen in large, misshapen pods that hang from the twigs like deflated balloons. The pods stay on the plant all winter, so you can pick them after the leaves fall. The seeds are easy to shake free from cracked pods. Fall sowing out doors results in very good germination, each seedling emerging with massive rolled cotyledons that unravel quickly and begin to send up pairs of leaves. There is no endosperm in the seeds—they are all cotyledon, and it's worth germinating them just to see the seedlings emerge. Dirr reports that seeds collected in fall before the seed coat darkens germinate within three weeks. The problem then is what to do with them for the winter.

CUTTINGS/DIVISIONS: I haven't had much luck with stem cuttings. The leaves seem to drop off at the slightest provocation. Root cutting works better. The plants sucker heavily from the roots when grown in a luxurious soil. You can lift the shallow, fleshy roots in summer, when the sprouts are visible. Cut the root into lengths, each with a shoot attached. Pot and treat them like cuttings for a few weeks. Usually, additional shoots will pop up from the root cuttings within 6 weeks.

Campsis   Trumpet vine p. 65   **FALL**   **B**

SEEDS: The papery seed is packed in tremendous quantities within each 4-to-6-inch-long cigar-shaped pod. Harvest the pods when the first ones start to crack open and let them dry until all have disgorged their contents. I usually sow the seeds in fall and stratify them outdoors. The seedlings sprout with abandon in spring. The cotyledons have a distinctive two-lobed outline, and the little fellas will grow like the dickens if you put them into plugs, then gallon pots. Frequent tip pruning is necessary during the first year to keep the vines from entangling and rooting into each other or their neighbors.

CUTTINGS/DIVISIONS: Cuttings are not really necessary unless you want to multiply a cultivar. Two-node cuttings taken in early summer from fairly soft wood root easily enough in about 3 weeks. I usually trim back the leaves to three pairs of leaflets on each side and give the cut end a big dip in 1,000 ppm IBA talc.

Carpentaria   Tree anemone p. 66   **LATE SUMMER TO FALL**   **A, H**

SEEDS: Pick the five-chambered capsules (shaped like a Turkish dome) when they turn brown. Crush or allow to crack and shake the tiny seeds free. The seedlings will germinate immediately if surface-sown, but they are very susceptible to damping off, so use a well-drained seed mix, cover with sand, and put them in a well-ventilated spot. Seedlings grow well once they are past the critical postemergence period, and can be moved when they are big enough to handle.

CUTTINGS/DIVISIONS: Semihardwood cuttings root well, especially if taken off vigorous sucker wood and treated with 2,000 ppm IBA. Suckers that have formed away from the center can be dug and moved in spring.

Carpinus   American hornbeam p. 67   **FALL TO EARLY WINTER**   **D**

SEEDS: The ridged, pointed seed is quite thoroughly attached at the base of the lobed involucral bract. You can strip the bracts off or not—I have sown seeds without first laboriously hand-stripping the seeds. You can harvest them when the bracts first begin to turn brown in fall. Either pick them or wait a few weeks until the leaves are shed, spread a tarp underneath the tree,

A: seed will germinate within 4 weeks if sown at 70° F. **B**: seed will germinate upon being shifted to 70° F after 90–140 days of moist, cold stratification at 40° F.
C: seed germinates only after multiple cycles of warm and cold, typically 40°–70°–40°–70° F. **D**: seed needs a period of warm, moist stratification followed by cold stratification and will germinate after being shifted back to warm, for example, 70°–40°–70° F. **G**: seed will not germinate in presence of chemical inhibitors. **H**: seed requires light to germinate. **I**: seed requires scarification because of an impermeable seed coat. *****: seed is hydrophilic, intolerant of dry storage (see Hydrophilic Seeds, p. 265). Moss Germination: seed germinates best in the presence of both light and high atmospheric moisture, as would be found on a damp, mossy substrate in the wild.

then give it a good shake. Sow immediately and keep seeds in a warm location for a few months to complete after-ripening before placing them outside in a cold frame. Many will germinate the first spring, and more the next.

Carya   Hickory p. 68   FALL   **B**

SEEDS: Hickories are not difficult to grow from seed, provided you protect them from rodents. Collect them from the ground in fall. Squirrels will dislodge some earlier, still tightly enclosed in a hard green husk, and these may not be large enough yet to be viable. Look for good-sized nuts whose husks are turning dark brown and beginning to crack along the seams and pull away. Certain species crack out of their skin more easily than others. Let the husks dry indoors until they become brittle, and you should be able to persuade them with your fingers and a rolling pin. Handle the husked nuts like acorns. Seed will germinate hypogeally when taken out of cold storage in spring, first sending out a long, thick taproot and then a stem and a few pinnate leaves. The best method is to sow the seeds where you want the trees after you remove them from the fridge, but very deep (at least 12 inches), narrow pots will work for a year to get them started. After that, set them into the garden or woods; if you wait longer, the taproot may be damaged when you transplant it.

Cassiope   Mountain heather p. 71   SUMMER   **A, H (moss)**

SEEDS: The very fine seed germinates easily if handled like that of *Rhododendron*. I sow the seed in fall and keep it under lights in the greenhouse over winter. Since the greenhouse runs rather cool at this time of year, the seedlings grow well, especially if left enclosed in a bag. By spring, 1-inch-high seedlings are ready to be planted out. It is better to establish them directly in the garden, even though they are small, rather than attempting to get them through the summer in the warmer soil of pots (as I have tried in vain to do).

CUTTINGS/DIVISIONS: Take cuttings from the new growth in late summer, treat with 2,000 ppm IBA, and stick them in a 5:2:3 bark-peat-sand mix. Keep them under Reemay in a shaded spot and they will usually root by fall. Keep the flat in a cold frame until spring.

Castanea   Chestnut p. 72   FALL   **B***

SEEDS: Chestnut seeds are protected by a formidable coat of sharp spines that puts sea urchins to shame. When you find a fruiting tree, look for the husk-covered nuts on the ground in early fall. The husks begin to dry either on the tree or on the ground if they have been knocked off, peeling back from the tip like snarling lips to expose one or two or even three brown nuts packed together to form a globe, with their flat sides pressed together. Sacrifice one and cut it open to make sure it is filled. I have been able to get viable nuts only at the Connecticut Agricultural Experiment Station in Hamden, where chestnut blight–resistant individuals have been planted. The trees are self-sterile, and it is rare to find two trees flowering in any proximity in the wild. The precious nuts should be stored in lightly dampened vermiculite in a plastic bag in the refrigerator over the winter. Nuts are hydrophilic, but rot in the bag if moisture is too high. Aim for pleasantly damp, not soaking wet. Plant them in individual deep pots in spring. Protect these from rodents even after germination. Germination is hypogeal, and seedlings grow fairly quickly. One of the reasons that *Castanea* was so competitive before the blight is its ability to either grow indeterminately or send out two to three flushes of determinate growth under favorable conditions. Blight can infect the seed coats of seeds obtained from infected parents, but not the embryo itself. Therefore, be very careful not to transport seeds from infected areas to parts of the country, like the Pacific Northwest, where blight is not established.

Catalpa   Catalpa p. 74   LATE FALL TO WINTER   **A, H**

SEEDS: The flattened seed, a papery wing surrounding an immature embryo in the center, looks a bit like a fried egg. The embryo has a pair of two-lobed cotyledons spread and ready to go inside the seed coat, and forces itself out the center of the flattened husk when moisture and warmth infuse it. Collect the pods at some point during the winter and crack them open to shake out the seeds (or you can just leave the pods intact inside your refrigerator until ready to plant the seeds). Sprinkle the seeds over the surface of your mix in spring and cover only with a light layer of sand. Germination will begin in a few weeks. The seedlings can be moved to liners after the first true leaves expand.

Ceanothus   Wild lilac p. 76   LATE SUMMER TO FALL   **B, I**

SEEDS: Ripe seed is violently ejected from the three-part capsules, so to get some you have to watch the inflorescences carefully, and when you see a few dry empty capsules, pick others that are beginning to turn brown. Dry capsules in a sealed paper sack until popping has stopped. The seeds are fairly small and hard, and smoke and fire stimulate the germination of some species, so that seedlings can quickly grow and colonize even forested areas from long-dormant seed. Hot water or sandpaper scarification should suffice for most, though some Californian species have been found to germinate well only with smoke treatment. Three months of cold stratification after scarification gives the best results. I have had mixed results with *Ceanothus* seed. Only 10 percent of unscarified, lightly covered seed left outside over winter germinated. Sandpaper scarification and stratification

---

A: seed will germinate within 4 weeks if sown at 70° F. **B**: seed will germinate upon being shifted to 70° F after 90–140 days of moist, cold stratification at 40° F. **C**: seed germinates only after multiple cycles of warm and cold, typically 40°–70°–40°–70° F. **D**: seed needs a period of warm, moist stratification followed by cold stratification and will germinate after being shifted back to warm, for example, 70°–40°–70° F. **G**: seed will not germinate in presence of chemical inhibitors. **H**: seed requires light to germinate. **I**: seed requires scarification because of an impermeable seed coat. *: seed is hydrophilic, intolerant of dry storage (see Hydrophilic Seeds, p. 265). Moss Germination: seed germinates best in the presence of both light and high atmospheric moisture, as would be found on a damp, mossy substrate in the wild.

gives better results, but hot water soaking and fall sowing has been the best. Pour lightly boiling water into the container of seeds and allow the water to cool overnight. Strain the seeds and sow them immediately and place them outside for the winter. When seed germinates, a pair of cotyledons appear with a set of true leaves between them. Transfer the seedlings to individual liner pots for a season before planting them in larger containers. Inoculate container plants with *Frankia* bacteria by mixing a cup of soil taken from around wild plants with a gallon of water and watering the pots with the slurry. Pot seedlings in a well-drained mix. Growth the second year is rapid, and seedlings will bloom in 2 to 3 years.

CUTTINGS/DIVISIONS: Softwood cuttings root fairly well with most of the species, and cultivars can be produced this way. Take cuttings from vigorous new growth in early summer, treat with 1,000 ppm IBA, and stick in a 1:3 peat-perlite mix.

Celastrus   American bittersweet p. 79   **FALL TO WINTER**   **B, G***

SEEDS: Collect seeds when the capsules split open in fall. Many seeds will hang on for much of the winter unless eaten, but as the fleshy aril dries, it is more difficult to remove. Seeds are about ⅛ inch long and narrow, dark brown, with a pointed tip and large abscission layer. Soak the seeds in water or run them through the blender to remove the red aril (though judging by the swarm of seedlings that can appear underneath female plants, removal of the aril may not be necessary for germination). Sow outdoors in the fall. Seedlings emerge with a pair of large, rounded cotyledons and grow quickly to maturity, blooming in 2 years.

CUTTINGS/DIVISIONS: Softwood cuttings taken from expanding growth any time during the season will root fairly easily (1,000 ppm IBA), and this is the best way to assure that you get the true species and the proper mix of male and female plants. Rooted cuttings will continue to grow rapidly, and the tendril-like growths need to be regularly tip-pruned to keep the crop from becoming a mass of twisted vines. Even, so, some snarling will occur, so you can cut the containers back hard when the vines are dormant in winter

Celtis   Hackberry p. 80   **FALL TO WINTER**   **B, G (I)**

SEEDS: Collect the leathery fruits at any time after they have colored; they are easier to see after leaf drop. Clean off the pulp in the blender or soak them for a week and mash them and rinse them in a strainer. The nut is a round, very hard-shelled affair fluted over its surface with a netting of ridges. With such hard nuts, I imagine some scarification helps germination, so I clean them in the blender. Fall sowing outdoors will usually produce good germination after the weather has warmed in late spring. The pair of cotyledons are notched at the tip; move the plants into individual liner pots as soon as these have expanded. Hackberries do grow an initial taproot as well as a network of fibrous roots, so use a fairly deep (6 to 7 inch) container.

Cephalanthus   Buttonbush p. 82   **FALL TO WINTER**   **A, H**

SEEDS: The thick balls left after the flowers fall in summer turn from dark green to brown in the fall. Some shatter quickly, but others, usually the ones that ripen last, hang on well after the leaves fall, and these are easier to find. The pointed, scale-like, tawny seeds can be separated from the bracts that intersperse them by breaking up the balls with your thumb and forefinger and running the lot through screens. Seed will germinate immediately if handled like *Rhododendron*.

CUTTINGS/DIVISIONS: Roots often form adventitiously on submerged stems, so it is not surprising that this species roots readily from cuttings. Semihardwood cuttings taken in summer and dipped in 1,000 ppm IBA talc will root in water or a peat-perlite mix. Alternatively, you can snip off naturally rooted stems growing in water during the summer and pot them up like rooted cuttings with fairly good success.

Cercis   Redbud p. 83   **FALL TO EARLY WINTER**   **(A) B, I**

SEEDS: Collect the pods as they begin to dry and blacken, or wait until leaf drop, when they are easier to see. In the Southeast, pods left on the trees may become infested with insects, so collect seeds early, as the fruits turn brown-black. Insects are not a problem in the Northeast. Lightly crush the flat pods and shuck them like peas. The flat, olive brown seeds have a hard seed coat that needs to be abraded before sowing. I have had good results with sandpaper, and hot-water soaking also works. Sow seeds outdoors in a cold frame. After a winter outdoors, two huge cotyledons spring up, followed closely by the first heart-shaped leaf. Transfer seedlings to liners and continue to fertilize them. They will grow quickly and bloom within 4 to 5 years. *C. occidentalis* needs little if any cold stratification, and will begin to germinate within a few weeks after scarification and sowing.

Cercocarpus   Mountain mahogany p. 85   **LATE SUMMER TO FALL**   **B**

SEEDS: My limited experience has involved fall sowing (outdoors) of dry seed with styles removed. After germination in the spring, the seedlings poke along in the container. Collect seeds when the tails begin to fluff out, and wear protective gloves when plucking and handling, to avoid the irritating hairs. After two or three true leaves have formed, transplant into 3-inch pots filled with a well-drained mix.

A: seed will germinate within 4 weeks if sown at 70° F. **B:** seed will germinate upon being shifted to 70° F after 90–140 days of moist, cold stratification at 40° F. **C:** seed germinates only after multiple cycles of warm and cold, typically 40°–70°–40°–70° F. **D:** seed needs a period of warm, moist stratification followed by cold stratification and will germinate after being shifted back to warm, for example, 70°–40°–70° F. **G:** seed will not germinate in presence of chemical inhibitors. **H:** seed requires scarification because of an impermeable seed coat. **I:** seed requires scarification because of an impermeable seed coat. *: seed is hydrophilic, intolerant of dry storage (see Hydrophilic Seeds, p. 265). Moss Germination: seed germinates best in the presence of both light and high atmospheric moisture, as would be found on a damp, mossy substrate in the wild.

Chamaecyparis   False cypress p. 87   FALL   **B, H* (moss)**

SEEDS: Collect cones when they begin to brown and crack open in fall. Dry them indoors for a week or so, then shake them on a screen to dislodge the small seeds, which are pointed ovals with two wings shaped like eyelids. Viability of seed can be low, and they are hydrophilic, so sow them as soon as you get them out of the cones for best germination or refrigerate them in sealed plastic containers. Sow them in a flat with only a light sand cover and leave outside in a cold frame for the winter. They can also be handled like *Vaccinium*. Despite low seed viability you should get a good crop of little false cypresses that can be stepped up after 6 weeks.

CUTTINGS/DIVISIONS: Treat winter cuttings with 8,000 to 10,000 ppm KIBA and keep them cool and damp. Place them on bottom heat in a cool or cold greenhouse or cold frame if possible.

Chamaedaphne   Leatherleaf p. 89   FALL   **A, H (moss)**

SEEDS: Collect capsules as they dry and let them continue to dry indoors for 7 to 10 days, until the seed can be shaken out. Light pressure with a rolling pin will help to crack stubborn capsules. The small seed is a moss germinator, so it can be sown like *Rhododendron*.

CUTTINGS/DIVISIONS: Semihardwood cuttings can be rooted in midsummer with 2,000 ppm IBA. An easier method for small quantities is to sever rooted layers under the sod and carefully lift them so as not to tear the threadlike roots. Do this in early spring. Treat these like rooted cuttings until new growth commences in earnest.

Chilopsis   Desert Willow p. 90   FALL   **A, H**

SEEDS: Collect ripe pods when they have turned from green to brown, crack them open, and strip out the seed, which is 2-lobed and covered with a long, white beard on either end. Surface-sow under warm temperatures (70°F).

Chionanthus   Fringetree p. 91   EARLY FALL   **D, G**

SEEDS: The seed is ripe when the fruit begins to turn dark blue. The seed coat is hard but brittle. The oily flesh can be removed by rubbing the fruits over a screen or fermenting them for 1 to 2 weeks. Germination is hypogeal; either sow in fall and wait two years or give them warm, then cold, as described for *Stewartia*. Seedlings emerge with vigor, usually with a pair of true leaves, and will grow a second or third pair supported by a stout little stem if potted on early. Female trees often have an abundance of seedlings coming up around their feet, and I have dug and potted many self-sown, 1-to-2-year-old seedlings.

Chrysolepis   Golden chinkapin p. 74   FALL   **B**

SEEDS: Seeds can be collected as for chestnut (*Castanea*). The seeds are not hydrophilic, but can be handled the same way, perhaps with a shorter period of cold stratification. Seedlings are difficult to keep in containers and preferably should be sown *in situ* in spring.

Chrysothamnus   Rubber rabbitbrush p. 92   FALL   **A or B, H**

SEEDS: Seed can be collected after the pappus dries and the heads turn tan. Some seed hangs on the plants late into the winter, but try to get it just as it ripens to avoid losing too much to the wind. I have had good germination with surface sowing in the greenhouse as well as fall sowing outdoors. Seedlings grow rapidly with light, regular fertilization. Interestingly, the pappus helps orient the seed so that the radical can emerge correctly. Removing it retards establishment.

CUTTINGS/DIVISIONS: Softwood tip cuttings, taken from new shoots well before flower buds appear, will root easily (1,000 ppm IBA talc).

Cladrastis   American yellowwood p. 93   LATE SUMMER TO EARLY FALL   **B, I**

SEEDS: Collect and clean seed as for *Cercis*. The seeds have an impermeable seed coat, which can be worn down with sandpaper. Fall-sown scarified seed germinates well in spring. Seedlings should be moved to liners quickly for their first season. Yellowwood is undeniably gangly in youth, even with careful pruning and shaping.

Clethra   Summersweet p. 94   FALL   **A, H (moss)**

SEEDS: Seed is tiny and rusty red. Collect the capsules as they brown and begin to crack. Seed is not shed quickly, and I have collected good amounts of seed as late as December in Boston. Sow as for *Rhododendron* but remove the seeds from the bag as soon as they germinate. Avoid overwatering, as they are prone to damping off. The seedlings grow quickly and bloom within 2 to 3 years.

CUTTINGS/DIVISIONS: Softwood cuttings with 2 to 6 nodes taken in late spring to early summer root extremely easily, using 1,000 ppm IBA talc, under mist or a polytent.

Cliftonia   Buckwheat Bush p. 108   LATE SUMMER TO FALL   **B, H**

SEEDS: There are 3 to 5 small seeds per capsule, which can be picked after they turn completely brown. Plant the seed, capsule and all, as the embryo is difficult to remove from the capsule without damaging it.

A: seed will germinate within 4 weeks if sown at 70° F. **B:** seed will germinate upon being shifted to 70° F after 90–140 days of moist, cold stratification at 40° F. **C:** seed germinates only after multiple cycles of warm and cold, typically 40°–70°–40°–70° F. **D:** seed needs a period of warm, moist stratification followed by cold stratification and will germinate after being shifted back to warm, for example, 70°–40°–70° F. **G:** seed will not germinate in presence of chemical inhibitors. **H:** seed requires light to germinate. **I:** seed requires scarification because of an impermeable seed coat. ***:** seed is hydrophilic, intolerant of dry storage (see Hydrophilic Seeds, p. 265). Moss Germination: seed germinates best in the presence of both light and high atmospheric moisture, as would be found on a damp, mossy substrate in the wild.

Corema   Broom crowberry p. 95   **EARLY SUMMER**   **B (I?)**

SEEDS: There are 1 to 2 seeds in each of the little, hard fruits, which cluster in balls at the base of the current whorl of growth. Roll the fruits free with your thumb and forefinger and catch them in the palm of your other hand. It is nearly impossible to remove the seeds from fruit completely, so I just sow the whole fruit outdoors in fall after scarifying it a bit with sandpaper. Germination takes place the following spring: leave the seedlings undisturbed the first season and transfer to liners the next.

CUTTINGS/DIVISIONS: Cuttings are my preferred propagation method. Take them in midsummer, when the new growths are still actively expanding near their tips but after their bases have become woody and brown. Treat 2-to-3-inch cuttings of this current wood with 2,000 ppm IBA and stick them in a rooting flat in a bark-peat-perlite mix. Keep them in light shade under Reemay. About 50 to 60 percent will root. The percentage is better under mist. Leave cuttings undisturbed until spring, then pot them into liners. Lightly shear the potted, growing cuttings once or twice to encourage branching.

Cornus   Dogwood p. 97   **SUMMER TO FALL, DEPENDING ON SPECIES**   **B or D, G**

SEEDS: The challenge here is getting the seed before the birds do. I have been thwarted several times, with *C. alternifolia* and *C. racemosa*, especially. You can pick the seeds once a few of the outer ones in the cyme begin to color. In general, the summer-ripening species like *C. racemosa*, *C. alternifolia*, *C. amomum* should be cleaned and sown immediately so they can after-ripen while it is still warm. These have juicy fruits containing a few small, brown seeds. You can blend them and then use the smear-and-peel technique to clean them. Sow later-maturing, red-fruited species like *C. florida* and *C. nuttallii* in fall; they require only a cold period. Each contains one ⅛-inch-long nutlike seed best cleaned of pulp in the blender. The bigger seed means a bigger seedling come spring.

CUTTINGS/DIVISIONS: Softwood tip cuttings taken in early to midsummer from vigorous twigs and treated with 1,000 to 2,000 ppm IBA will root readily under mist. Leave them in the rooting flat through the winter and pot them on in spring. Propagate red osier and other suckering, shrubby dogwoods from hardwood whips, as described for *Populus*.

Corylus   Hazelnut p. 100   **LATE SUMMER TO FALL**   **B***

SEEDS: To increase your odds of getting some nuts before the squirrels do, pick a few late in summer before the husks have yellowed and scrape the bracts away to check for ripening of the seed coat. The nut husks are the same color as the leaves, so lift up a branch and look underneath. If the seed coat is beginning to brown and separates easily from the bracts (husks), pick all the nuts you can and let them air-dry for a week indoors. Be sure to wear heavy gloves for this, as the bracts are prickly. After a week, they should loosen enough that you can extract the seed. Seal the seeds in a plastic bag with some moist sand or vermiculite and put them in the refrigerator until spring. Germination is hypogeal. Sow the stratified nuts in deep liner pots 1 to 2 seeds per pot in spring.

CUTTINGS/DIVISIONS: It is often difficult to find even a few nuts on wild plants, so I don't rely on seed propagation. Instead, in the spring I slice off one of the smaller suckers that spring up 6 inches beyond the main clump of stems on an established plant. Do this before flowering in spring and trim back a third of the twig before replanting it.

Cotinus   American smoketree p. 101   **SUMMER**   **B, I**

SEEDS: The seed ripens fairly early in the season but hangs on the panicles for about a month, so collecting it is not too difficult. Most trees set only scattered fruit, which are about ⅛ inch long, flattened and somewhat kidney-shaped, and stand out on the fluffy pedicels. Store them dry in the refrigerator until fall, then scarify them with sandpaper to remove the dried husk and sow in an outdoor cold-frame. After the seedlings germinate in spring, transfer them quickly to liners.

CUTTINGS/DIVISIONS: I have failed miserably with cuttings. Softwood cuttings (10,000 ppm KIBA quick dip) taken in early summer will root under mist, though most will just drop their leaves. The next hurdle is to get the rooted cuttings to leaf out the following spring. Leave them undisturbed in the flats until growth recommences the following year. I wish you the best of luck.

Crataegus   Hawthorn p. 102   **FALL OR EARLY WINTER**   **D, G, I**

SEEDS: Collect the fruits as they ripen and clean the seeds by mashing and fermenting or cleaning in the blender. Many have extremely thick seed coats; grind them down with a few minutes of sandpapering. A few weeks of warm stratification before cold will allow water to permeate the seed coat and hasten germination. Allow two years for germination before you give up on them, and transfer germinated seedlings into 4-inch pots to give roots room to spread.

Croton   Alabama croton p. 105   **LATE SUMMER TO FALL**   **B**

SEEDS: Collect capsules as they dry and begin to split and lightly crush them to dislodge the seeds. The 3-sided capsules contain up to 3 oval, ¼-inch seeds. Sow them and cover them lightly. Seedlings may also be dug from under a parent plant.

CUTTINGS/DIVISIONS: Dirr reports that hardwood cuttings taken in late fall and treated with 3,000 ppm IBA rooted fairly well.

A: seed will germinate within 4 weeks if sown at 70° F. **B**: seed will germinate upon being shifted to 70° F after 90–140 days of moist, cold stratification at 40° F. **C**: seed germinates only after multiple cycles of warm and cold, typically 40°–70°–40°–70° F. **D**: seed needs a period of warm, moist stratification followed by cold stratification and will germinate after being shifted back to warm, for example, 70°–40°–70° F. **G**: seed will not germinate in presence of chemical inhibitors. **H**: seed requires light to germinate. **I**: seed requires scarification because of an impermeable seed coat. *****: seed is hydrophilic, intolerant of dry storage (see Hydrophilic Seeds, p. 265). **Moss Germination**: seed germinates best in the presence of both light and high atmospheric moisture, as would be found on a damp, mossy substrate in the wild.

Cupressus   Cypress p. 106 — FALL TO WINTER — **B, H**

SEEDS: Cones take two years to ripen, so look on previous growth for cones that have gone from green to brown. Cones of most *Cupressus* species are wholly or partially serotinous, so even older cones can be collected if they have not cracked open. They don't detach very easily, so use a pair of shears. Drop cones into a pan of boiling water for 1 minute to loosen up the resin that holds them shut, and let the cones air-dry until they open. Screen out the chunky little seeds, surface-sow them with a light sand cover, and give them a 1-to-3-month period of cold stratification. Full sun and a well-drained mix is necessary to prevent seedlings from rotting.

CUTTINGS/DIVISIONS: I have rooted a few cuttings of Arizona cypress cultivars using late-winter hardwood material from vigorous trees, 10,000 ppm IBA dip, and bottom heat. The best I have done is about 25 percent rooting.

Cyrilla   Titi p. 107 — FALL — **A, H (moss)**

SEEDS: Collect the capsules as they begin to turn brown and the lowest in the raceme are cracking open. The small seed can be shaken out through a screen and treated as for *Rhododendron* with good results.

CUTTINGS/DIVISIONS: Cuttings taken in summer from semihardwood using 2,000 ppm IBA talc root readily under mist.

Decumaria   Wood vamp p. 108 — FALL — **A, H (moss)**

SEEDS: Collect the capsules as they dry and brown, then screen out the tiny seeds. Germinate as for *Rhododendrons*—easy.

CUTTINGS/DIVISIONS: This species tends to layer and form adventitious roots on its own. The easiest method is to dig self-layered stems and pot them up separately. I have also rooted 3-inch semihardwood tip cuttings taken in summer as roots began to appear on their own, and also hardwood cuttings taken in late fall after leaf drop. These last I treat like *Juniperus*.

Diervilla   Bush-honeysuckle p. 109 — LATE SUMMER TO FALL — **A or B, H**

SEEDS: The capsules remind me of *Sesame Street*'s Ernie—thinly egg-shaped with a tuft of hair (the persistent calyx) on top. The capsules ripen late in the growing season, going from green or burgundy to brown. Crack open a few and look for seeds that have begun to blacken, pick some, and allow them to dry indoors. The seeds look remarkably like poppy seeds, round, gray-black, and covered with a whitish bloom. They germinate easily if handled as for *Rhododendron,* or sow in fall; cover with a bit of sand, and leave outdoors for winter.

CUTTINGS/DIVISIONS: Softwood cuttings taken from nonflowering vigorous tips in summer root readily (with 1,000 ppm IBA talc, under mist or a polytent). Most plants are produced by cuttings commercially. Cuttings will flower more quickly than seedlings in containers. It is also easy to dig the often abundant root suckers at any time during the season and pot them up or plant them separately.

Diospyros   Persimmon p. 110 — FALL TO EARLY WINTER — **B, G, I**

SEEDS: The large, roughened, warm brown seeds are easy to collect by mashing them from ripe fruits. Seedlings germinate readily after 3 months of cold stratification. Germination is epigeal. Transfer the black-rooted seedlings to deep liner pots when the cotyledons have expanded. Light scarification can partially replace stratification or be used in conjunction with it. Persimmons are fast growing when young, and flowering begins in 5 to 7 years from seed.

Dirca   Leatherwood p. 112 — LATE SPRING TO EARLY SUMMER — **D***

SEEDS: *D. palustris* hides its ⅜-inch, olive-shaped fruits among the leaves, and they quickly fall after changing from leaf green to yellow green. *D. occidentalis* fruits are reddish and easier to see. Seed set is much higher when there are at least two plants for cross pollination. Collect fruits and sow immediately. The seeds germinate better *without* cleaning off the fruit pulp first. Seedlings germinate hypogeally after a summer and winter. Step them into liners after cotyledons have expanded, then into larger pots a year later. Alternatively, let seeds drop below the parent and dig seedlings as needed. This is a fairly slow-growing genus (6 inches a year), and it takes 3 to 4 years before they begin to bulk up.

Dryas   Mountain avens p. 113 — EARLY SUMMER — **B***

SEEDS: The long-tailed seeds are easy to see and collect as they ripen and the tails fluff out. I have germinated dry seed, but I think that the genus is moderately hydrophilic, so harvest the seed, make sure it is dry, and store in a sealed bag in the refrigerator until you are ready to sow it in fall. Sow in a well-drained mix and leave the seedlings undisturbed until the second spring, when they can be teased apart and potted separately. Germination percentages are fairly low in my experience. The seedlings are slow growing at first, forming just a little leathery rosette the first summer. Cuttings are faster, if you have material to work with (it doesn't take long to strip a plant of cuttings).

CUTTINGS/DIVISIONS: Semihardwood cuttings taken in late summer root reasonably well. Snip the whorl of leaves and attached 1-inch stem, dip in 2,000 ppm IBA talc, and stick the cuttings horizontally if necessary, so the leaves are facing upward.

A: seed will germinate within 4 weeks if sown at 70° F. **B**: seed will germinate upon being shifted to 70° F after 90–140 days of moist, cold stratification at 40° F. **C**: seed germinates only after multiple cycles of warm and cold, typically 40°–70°–40°–70° F. **D**: seed needs a period of warm, moist stratification followed by cold stratification and will germinate after being shifted back to warm, for example, 70°–40°–70° F. **G**: seed will not germinate in presence of chemical inhibitors. **H**: seed requires light to germinate. **I**: seed requires scarification because of an impermeable seed coat. *****: seed is hydrophilic, intolerant of dry storage (see Hydrophilic Seeds, p. 265). **Moss Germination**: seed germinates best in the presence of both light and high atmospheric moisture, as would be found on a damp, mossy substrate in the wild.

Elaeagnus Silverberry p. 114 **SUMMER TO FALL** **B, G**

SEEDS: Fruits ripen sequentially and can be plucked as they begin to turn from orange to red. There is an inhibitor in the pulp, so thoroughly blender-clean or macerate and let them ferment for a week. Seedlings come up fairly easily after outdoor cold stratification and can be stepped up immediately into liners.

Elliottia Georgia plume p. 115 **LATE FALL** **B or D, H (moss)**

SEEDS: Seeds ripen in woody capsules, but seed is not often set and viability is notoriously low, possibly as a result of low genetic diversity. Seed collected in mid- to late fall should look plump and brown with well-developed wings under magnification (not shriveled). Best germination occurs if the seed is surface sown and refrigerated for a few weeks, then handled as for *Rhododendron*. Seedlings produced at the Arnold Arboretum have not grown vigorously, again possibly due to inbreeding depression.

CUTTINGS/DIVISIONS: Al Fordham (the former propagator at the Arnold Arboretum) took root cuttings in late winter while the plant was dormant. Take ¼-to-½-inch diameter shallow horizontal roots and cut them into 4-inch lengths. Lightly cover with sand and place them on bottom heat. Vegetative shoots begin to appear in spring. These shoots have enough juvenility that you can take hardwood cuttings in late summer and root them using 3,000–8,000 ppm IBA talc, under mist or a polytent.

Empetrum Crowberry p. 96 **FALL** **B, G, H (moss)**

SEEDS: Collect fruits when they turn black or red and use the smear-and-peel technique to clean off pulp. Sow as for *Vaccinium*.
CUTTINGS/DIVISIONS: See *Corema*.

Ephedra Jointfir p. 116 **MIDSUMMER TO FALL** **A or B, G**

SEEDS: Seeds germinate easily without pretreatment, but they can be also sown in fall and left out over the winter. Collect when seed coats have turned brown. The seeds are easily visible, developing singly or in pairs amid a nest of papery cone scales on female plants. The first year a single thin stem emerges from a pair of narrow cotyledons and grows to 2 to 4 inches in several jointed flushes. Leave these in the seed flat until the second spring (light fertilization will flush a few more segments). Seedlings will grow slowly but surely if potted in a well-drained mix.

CUTTINGS/DIVISIONS: Cuttings taken from current season's growth in late summer are said to root easily, but I have not tried this myself.

Fagus American beech p. 118 **FALL** **B***

SEEDS: The nuts are relished by squirrels, but many of the prickly husks fall or are knocked down with the faceted nutlets still inside. Remove the husks, then handle the nuts as described for oaks. It is a good idea to drop the cleaned nuts in water and discard any floating (nonviable) ones before proceeding. The seedlings are epigeal, emerging with a pair of distinctively ruffled, fan-shaped cotyledons that quickly send up a taller stem with a set of true leaves.

Fallugia Apache plume p. 119 **SUMMER** **A**

SEEDS: Harvest when the style has gone from pink to white and the hairs have fluffed out (it will be easy to dislodge seeds once ripe). Air-dry seeds for at least 2 to 3 months and store them in a paper envelope in the refrigerator until needed. They germinate quickly when sown under warm conditions. Transplant at the cotyledon stage into a sharply drained mix, and the seedlings will begin to put out the distinctive bird's-foot leaves. *Fallugia* is pretty easy to germinate, but careful attention to watering and full sun is needed to prevent damping off and other diseases.

CUTTINGS/DIVISIONS: Supposedly straightforward from softwood cuttings taken from nonflowering stems, but I have not tried it.

Fothergilla Fothergilla p. 120 **MID- TO LATE SUMMER** **D***

SEEDS: Seeds need a very long period of warm temperatures followed by cold to germinate. Collect the capsules as they turn from green to greenish yellow in summer. If you are not sure, cut one open with pruners to see if the seed coat has darkened to a warm brown. Put the capsules in a big paper bag, staple it shut, and let dry for a week or two until the popping sound of ejected seeds has died down. Mature capsules will eject the oval, pointed, shiny chestnut brown seeds, which can be picked out. If they are not ejected, you will have to pry them out using a nut pick—not an easy task. Sow the seed in a flat immediately and leave outdoors until temperatures begin to cool. Then bring it into a warm greenhouse or home for 2 more months before putting outside for the winter. Seeds need 4–5 months of warmth for adequate after-ripening. Seedlings should come up in spring, but if not, give them another year before discarding the flat. Cuttings are easier if you are set up for them.

CUTTINGS/DIVISIONS: I have rooted fothergilla very easily from softwood cuttings taken from vigorous container stock, but have had poor results when I take them from our established garden specimens, even if I stick cuttings taken from the rapidly growing sprouts. It would seem that juvenility is important. Treat wounded 3-inch cuttings with 2,000 ppm IBA and place under

A: seed will germinate within 4 weeks if sown at 70° F. **B**: seed will germinate upon being shifted to 70° F after 90–140 days of moist, cold stratification at 40° F. **C**: seed germinates only after multiple cycles of warm and cold, typically 40°–70°–40°–70° F. **D**: seed needs a period of warm, moist stratification followed by cold stratification and will germinate after being shifted back to warm, for example, 70°–40°–70° F. **G**: seed will not germinate in presence of chemical inhibitors. **H**: seed requires light to germinate. **I**: seed requires scarification because of an impermeable seed coat. *****: seed is hydrophilic, intolerant of dry storage (see Hydrophilic Seeds, p. 265). Moss Germination: seed germinates best in the presence of both light and high atmospheric moisture, as would be found on a damp, mossy substrate in the wild.

mist or a polytent. Leave the rooted cuttings undisturbed until they begin to push out new leaves, which may not happen until the following spring. If you try to pot them sooner, they will not make it through the winter.

Franklinia   Franklinia p. 121 — LATE FALL — **B**

SEEDS: Look for ripening capsules at the base of the current season's growth just as flowering ends in late fall. Ripe capsules will start to yellow and open up in a strange zigzag way. Sow the ⅛-inch round seeds as soon as collected and leave them out in the cold frame for the winter. Germination will occur in spring. Seedlings grow very quickly once they get going.

CUTTINGS/DIVISIONS: Softwood or semihardwood cuttings taken from juvenile material root easily with 1,000 ppm talc under mist or a polytent, but overwintering can be a problem.

Fraxinus   Ash p. 122 — LATE SUMMER TO FALL — **D**

SEEDS: The canoe-paddle samaras are easy enough to pick off the ground under female trees as they fall late in the growing season. Most of the species appear to need a few months of warm stratification for after-ripening of the embryo, followed by 3 months of cold stratification. Otherwise, germination will take two years. Ash seedlings have large cotyledons like maples that usually only produce one set of undivided true leaves the first season.

Fremontodendron   Flannelbush p. 125 — LATE SUMMER TO FALL — **B, I**

SEEDS: The seeds ripen in bristly capsules that crack open and slowly release their shiny brown captives. Look for capsules that have recently cracked to assure ripeness (wear gloves). Crush the capsules with a rolling pin and extract the seeds. Soak them in warm water overnight before sowing outdoors for winter stratification.

CUTTINGS/DIVISIONS: Softwood tip cuttings treated with 1,000 ppm IBA and placed in a polytent root easily.

Gaultheria   Salal p. 126 — LATE SUMMER TO FALL — **A, H, G (moss)**

SEEDS: Remove the small seeds from the ripe blue-black berries, either by smearing the fruits on a towel with your thumb and flicking out and rinsing the seeds or by drying the fruits until they crumble to dust between your fingers and the seed can be picked out. Germinate as for *Rhododendron*. If started indoors in late fall and stepped into larger containers in spring, the seedlings will be large enough to sell or plant out by the following fall (1 year after sowing).

CUTTINGS/DIVISIONS: Take semihardwood or hardwood cuttings from August to October. They will root slowly if treated with 2,000 to 3,000 ppm IBA. I think you get a much more balanced, well-branched, vigorous result from seed.

Gaylussacia   Huckleberry p. 127 — MID- TO LATE SUMMER — **B, H (moss)**

SEEDS: Collect fruits and clean and sow seeds as for *Vaccinium*.

Gelsemium   Carolina jessamine p. 128 — LATE SUMMER TO FALL — **(A?) B, H**

SEEDS: Seeds ripen in oval capsules. Collect them when they begin to brown and crush them lightly to break them open along the seams so the small, papery seeds can be shaken free. Though cuttings are the common method of propagation, seedlings germinate easily and grow quickly.

CUTTINGS/DIVISIONS: Take 2-to-4-node cuttings from semihard new growth and treat it with 1,000 ppm IBA. They will root quickly and easily in 2 to 3 weeks. Take cuttings early enough in summer that they can flush out and grow for 6 weeks before the onset of cold weather.

Gleditsia   Honeylocust p. 129 — FALL TO EARLY WINTER — **A, I**

SEEDS: Collect the pods once they have turned leather brown. They usually fall from the trees in great numbers, making collection easy. Crack or crush them open and scrape out the hard, oval, ¼-inch seeds from the pulp. Store cleaned, dry seed in an envelope in the refrigerator over the winter, then treat it and sow it in spring. The very hard seed coat must be well scarified, using sandpaper, a file, or hot water. Check the efficacy of your treatment by leaving some scarified seeds in a glass of water overnight to see if they swell up. Scarified seed germinates within a week if sown under warm temperatures. Plant soaked, swollen seed directly in liner pots, 1 to 2 seeds per pot. The seedlings come up with cotyledons and their first pinnate leaf and proceed quickly. Step seedlings into larger containers the following spring.

Gordonia   Loblolly bay p. 122 — FALL — **A***

SEEDS: Collect the capsules when they turn brown and begin to split and shake the seeds free. Sow immediately indoors and grow under lights over the winter. Or store them until spring in a sealed plastic bag in the refrigerator and surface-sow them in flats outdoors.

CUTTINGS/DIVISIONS: Summer cuttings treated with 2,000 to 3,000 ppm IBA root easily and will continue growing vigorously.

Gymnocladus   Kentucky coffeetree p. 130 — FALL TO EARLY WINTER — **A, I**

SEEDS: The stumpy 3-to-4-inch-long pods fall from the female trees over the course of a few months late in the season, so search

A: seed will germinate within 4 weeks if sown at 70° F. **B**: seed will germinate upon being shifted to 70° F after 90–140 days of moist, cold stratification at 40° F. **C**: seed germinates only after multiple cycles of warm and cold, typically 40°–70°–40°–70° F. **D**: seed needs a period of warm, moist stratification followed by cold stratification and will germinate after being shifted back to warm, for example, 70°–40°–70° F. **G**: seed will not germinate in presence of chemical inhibitors. **H**: seed requires light to germinate. **I**: seed requires scarification because of an impermeable seed coat. *****: seed is hydrophilic, intolerant of dry storage (see Hydrophilic Seeds, p. 265). Moss Germination: seed germinates best in the presence of both light and high atmospheric moisture, as would be found on a damp, mossy substrate in the wild.

the ground underneath. The seed coat is even harder than honeylocust's. For a small quantity, try nicking off a little chunk with a pair of bypass-style pruners and soak seeds overnight. Sow directly into 3-inch liner pots and step up to 6-to-8-inch pots the following spring. The first few years the seedlings put out short flushes of growth from the main stem, with little side branching, so they are easily accommodated in containers.

Halesia   Silverbell p. 131 — **FALL TO EARLY WINTER** — **C**

SEEDS: The winged capsules are very easy to collect, as they hang on all winter after leaves are long gone. Put the whole lot (wings need not be removed) in a bucket or freezer bag, fill it with warm water and let the capsules soak overnight. Dump and squeeze out the excess water and put them in a sealed freezer bag in the refrigerator for the winter. The following spring, sow the seeds in flats or beds outside. Husky seedlings will emerge a year later.

CUTTINGS/DIVISIONS: Take softwood cuttings from late spring to early summer from vigorous young growth. Treat it with 3,000 ppm IBA quick dip and place under mist. Transplant rooted cuttings quickly into liner pots and grow them on for a year before stepping up. Cuttings are fairly easy to do and certainly are faster than seed.

Hamamelis   Witch-hazel p. 133 — **FALL** — **B or D**

SEEDS: The capsules give little outward sign that they are about to crack and launch their seeds—I seem to miss them as many years as I hit it right. Check your plants for open capsules, and collect all others once the first few crack (the seed stays in there for a day or so after the capsule splits). Dry the seed in a well-closed shopping bag until popping stops. Good seed is about ⅜ inch long, shiny dark brown, and pointed at both ends. Many seeds of either *H. virginiana* or *H. vernalis* may be weevil infested. To eliminate bugs, drop the seeds in a glass of water overnight, discard floaters, and sow the rest. *H. virginiana* needs 2 months warm and 3 cold, so if you get the seed early enough, sow it immediately or leave in a warm place for a while before transferring to the cold. *H. vernalis* germinates with just a cold period.

CUTTINGS/DIVISIONS: Cuttings are difficult but possible if handled as for *Fothergilla*.

Hudsonia   False heather p. 135 — **SUMMER** — **B, I**

SEEDS: The seeds are about the size and color of a gray sand crystal. They ripen in little chaffy capsules along the stem in midsummer (just about greenhead fly season, so I inevitably get a few large welts to remember the occasion by). Inevitably some sand gets mixed in when I collect seed, but it is unnecessary to separate it out. Scarify with sandpaper and sow outdoors in fall; germination takes place in spring. Seedlings develop a slender stem clothed in small leaves that eventually branches. It is hard to get a bushy plant from cuttings or seed, but light tip pruning will help, as will careful fertilization with a mild liquid solution every 2 weeks in summer.

CUTTINGS/DIVISIONS: Take 2-inch or longer, semihardwood tip cuttings in mid- to late summer. Treat with 1,000 to 2,000 ppm IBA and stick in a 1:1 peat-sand mix. These root readily if I place them under mist, a polytent, or Reemay. Overwinter these in the tray and pot into liners in spring, using a well-drained, sandy mix. One light shearing in midsummer will provide more cutting material and promote branching.

Hydrangea   Hydrangea p. 136 — **FALL TO WINTER** — **A or B, H**

SEEDS: The seeds are among the smallest I handle, and it is tough to get completely clean seed, or even to know whether you have gotten seed at all, without the aid of a microscope. The seed tends to drop in fall–winter for *H. quercifolia* and winter–spring for *H. arborescens,* but you can collect either when the capsules go from light green to dark brown. Dry capsules for 2 weeks, then gingerly crush with a rolling pin, and screen the seed and associated chaff. Seed germinates easily if surface-sown as for *Hypericum,* with the same cautions regarding damping off.

CUTTINGS/DIVISIONS: Two-to-three-node softwood tip cuttings with each leaf trimmed in half root very easily — in fact, *H. quercifolia* is one of the plants I like to have students try because it is so reliable. Treat cuttings with 1,000 to 2,000 ppm IBA and place under mist or in a polytent (I have also used Reemay and natural shade).

Hypericum   St. John's wort p. 137 — **FALL** — **A or B, H**

SEEDS: Collect capsules as they brown late in the season, dry and crush them, and sieve out the small red-brown seeds. They will germinate within a few weeks if surface-sown. I usually sow them in late fall with a light sand cover and leave outdoors, transferring the seedlings when they are large enough to handle into plug trays, then pots. Seedlings actually catch up to stem cuttings if grown this way. One or two light shearings during the season will give bushier plants.

CUTTINGS/DIVISIONS: Soft or semihardwood tip cuttings taken in early to midsummer root readily. Use 2,000 ppm IBA, and place in mist. They have the annoying habit of trying to come into bloom in the rooting trays, even if I pinch off the flowers. I haven't figured a way around this problem yet, so I rely on seed.

A: seed will germinate within 4 weeks if sown at 70° F. **B:** seed will germinate upon being shifted to 70° F after 90–140 days of moist, cold stratification at 40° F. **C:** seed germinates only after multiple cycles of warm and cold, typically 40°–70°–40°–70° F. **D:** seed needs a period of warm, moist stratification followed by cold stratification and will germinate after being shifted back to warm, for example, 70°–40°–70° F. **G:** seed will not germinate in presence of chemical inhibitors. **H:** seed requires light to germinate. **I:** seed requires scarification because of an impermeable seed coat. ***:** seed is hydrophilic, intolerant of dry storage (see Hydrophilic Seeds, p. 265). Moss Germination: seed germinates best in the presence of both light and high atmospheric moisture, as would be found on a damp, mossy substrate in the wild.

Ilex   Holly p. 139 — FALL — **C or D***

SEEDS: Holly seed is easy to collect, as the red or black berries stand out in fall. Hard, tan seeds are embedded in the mealy pulp, and these are best mashed over a screen and rinsed with running water until all the pulp has been removed. Holly seeds have both impermeable seed coats and immature embryos, so 60 to 120 days of warm stratification prior to cold is necessary. In general, more southern species need longer warm stratification and shorter cold than the more northern ones, like winterberry. Place the seeds in damp vermiculite in a plastic bag and keep in a warm spot indoors, then refrigerate for 3 to 4 months. Or you can just clean the seeds and sow in flats. Leave them outdoors under Reemay until the seed germinates: this can take anywhere from 1 to 3 years. Seed is not difficult, but it does take patience. Seedlings should be potted up individually and fertilized regularly to encourage more stem growth.

CUTTINGS/DIVISIONS: Most hollies are produced vegetatively using semihardwood or hardwood tip cuttings taken from the most vigorous new growth in early summer (deciduous species) or late fall to early winter (evergreen species). For summer cuttings, use 1,000 to 2,000 ppm IBA and place in mist. For winter cuttings, use 3,000 to 8,000 ppm KIBA and place in a polytent or cold frame with bottom heat.

Illicium   Anise p. 142 — LATE SUMMER TO FALL — **B**

SEEDS: Collect the interesting star-shaped fruits from late summer to fall as they begin to brown and split, and extract the ¼-inch, glossy brown seeds. Sow outdoors. Large seedlings will emerge the following spring.

CUTTINGS/DIVISIONS: Semihardwood tip cuttings root well when treated with 2,000 ppm KIBA quick dip and placed under mist.

Itea   Virginia sweetspire p. 144 — FALL TO EARLY WINTER — **A, H (moss)**

SEEDS: Collect as for *Leucothoe*; sow as for *Rhododendron*.

CUTTINGS/DIVISIONS: Hardwood cuttings taken in late summer to fall (before fall color develops) root very easily. Use 3-to-5-node cuttings and treat them with 3,000 ppm IBA.

Juglans   Walnut p. 145 — FALL — **B***

SEEDS: Collect the large, yellow fruits as they drop in fall and crack open the husk by placing the fruit between two boards and putting your weight on them. Some people lay out the seeds in their driveway and run over them a few times with the car. Wear gloves, as the husks will stain your skin brown or yellow. The corky nut should come free if the husk is still soft and green. Put the seeds in a big freezer bag, fill it with water, and soak overnight. Drain off all excess water, seal the bag, and put it in the refrigerator for the winter. Plant the seeds in growing beds in spring. This is safer than fall sowing, which puts the nuts at the mercy of ravenous rodents. Germination is hypogeal, and a husky seedling shoots out of the ground with a few sets of leaves in spring. Seedlings are fairly easy to move when they are 1 to 3 years old.

Juniperus   Juniper p. 147 — FALL — **B or D, G, I**

SEEDS: Juniper berries (cones) are blue-black when mature. Different species ripen at different rates: *J. virginiana* and *J. ashei* fruits ripen the first year, *J. occidentalis*, *J. deppeana*, and *J. scopulorum* ripen the second, and *J. communis* ripens the third year. Collect the ripe berries and run them through the blender to remove the waxy, resinous fruit (a few drops of dishwashing liquid added to the water before blending will help separate the pulp and seed). It is best to sow the seeds immediately in flats outdoors and let them go through the rest of the summer, fall, and winter; most should germinate the following spring, but it may take a few years for all the seeds to sprout. Collecting the berries just as they begin to color, thoroughly cleaning/scarifying them in the blender, then sowing immediately will usually give the best results.

CUTTINGS/DIVISIONS: Junipers are one of the most widely grown container plants, and most of the material is vegetatively produced. However, with the exception of the ground-covering species like *J. horizontalis* and *J. communis*, they are generally difficult to root. After Thanksgiving but before Valentine's Day, take cuttings from the current season's wood with a heel of older wood attached. Vigorous, juvenile-needled growths are best—grasp the twig near the base and peel it off the older wood to get a heel cutting. Treat cuttings with 3,000 to 4,000 ppm, either Dip 'N Grow or KIBA quick dip, and place them on bottom heat in a cool or cold greenhouse or cold frame. If they are going to root, they will have produced several white, fleshy roots by spring.

Kalmia   Laurel p. 150 — LATE SUMMER TO FALL — **A, H (moss)**

SEEDS: Moss germinators. Collect the capsules, dry and crack them, and shake out the tiny reddish seed. Sow as for *Rhododendron*.

CUTTINGS/DIVISIONS: Cuttings are very difficult, though rooted layers can be lifted from the spreading species. Cultivars are mostly produced through tissue culture.

A: seed will germinate within 4 weeks if sown at 70° F. **B**: seed will germinate upon being shifted to 70° F after 90–140 days of moist, cold stratification at 40° F. **C**: seed germinates only after multiple cycles of warm and cold, typically 40°–70°–40°–70° F. **D**: seed needs a period of warm, moist stratification followed by cold stratification and will germinate after being shifted back to warm, for example, 70°–40°–70° F. **G**: seed will not germinate in presence of chemical inhibitors. **H**: seed requires light to germinate. **I**: seed requires scarification because of an impermeable seed coat. *: seed is hydrophilic, intolerant of dry storage (see Hydrophilic Seeds, p. 265). Moss Germination: seed germinates best in the presence of both light and high atmospheric moisture, as would be found on a damp, mossy substrate in the wild.

Larix Larch p. 153

A or B, H

SEEDS: The erect cones ripen in the autumn of their first year and remain on the plant for several years after they have shed their seed, so about the time of needle drop, search the cones on the current season's twigs. Later in winter you can usually scavenge a few seeds that got stuck in the scales. Seed weevils prey on larch, so check seed—especially seed stuck in open cones—for telltale exit holes. If cones are not fully open, soak them in hot water and let dry, then shake or screen out the seeds. I usually surface sow seed outdoors, and the little whorl of cotyledons emerges in spring. Winter stratification may not be necessary, but it is easy enough. With good culture, you can persuade these to begin growing a shoot and more needles the first season.

Ledum Labrador tea p. 154

FALL

A, H (moss)

SEEDS: Collect and sow as for *Rhododendron*. It is not particularly difficult if you have grow lights set up to keep the seedlings growing all winter, and the fuzzy little leaves are sooo cute!!

CUTTINGS/DIVISIONS: Dirr recommends taking cuttings from late fall to early winter from the current whorl of growth. Treat with 4,000 to 8,000 ppm IBA and place in a polytent with bottom heat. I raise this species from seed.

Leiophyllum Sand myrtle p. 155

LATE SUMMER TO EARLY FALL

A, H (moss)

SEEDS: Collect the tiny, clustered capsules as they turn from red-green to brown, and dry, crush, and sieve the dusty rusty seeds. This species germinates very well when handled as for *Rhododendron,* but seedlings are very tiny and slow. I usually sow them under grow lights in fall, grow them all winter and spring, and transfer them to plugs in summer. I continue growing them outdoors, overwinter them, and pot them up into 2-quart pots the following spring. Cuttings are unquestionably faster, but I use seed as a backup should they fail.

CUTTINGS/DIVISIONS: I have had decent though not spectacular success with semihardwood cuttings taken in midsummer from the still actively growing stems. Take 3-to-4-inch cuttings, treat with 2,000 ppm IBA Dip 'N Grow and place under Reemay outdoors or under mist indoors. Use a very porous medium to prevent stem rot. About 45 percent will root. Dirr reports that fall cuttings placed under a polytent rooted well, and this may be the best season to take them.

Leucothoe Dog hobble p. 156

FALL

A, H (moss)

SEEDS: As for *Rhododendron*. The seeds are tiny, but they germinate quickly if sown indoors under lights. Not all plants produce capsules, and fruit production varies on individual plants from year to year. Last fall I searched dozens of clumps before finding one loaded with chains of spherical capsules right outside the greenhouse door.

CUTTINGS/DIVISIONS: Hardwood cuttings taken in early winter from the evergreen species are very easy to root and certainly faster than seed if you have a cool greenhouse and bottom heat. Take 3-inch 4-to-6-node cuttings from the top 1 foot of current growth. Treat with 3,000 to 5,000 ppm KIBA or Dip 'N Grow.

Lindera Spicebush p. 158

FALL

B, G*

SEEDS: Collect the fruits just as they begin to turn yellow-orange to prevent loss to birds. The seed coat is soft, so gently macerate the seeds by hand and rinse them under running water in a sieve. Or ferment for a week and clean them in a sieve. Seedlings germinate hypogeally after a winter outdoors and grow on well enough in containers. Protect seeds from rodents.

Liquidambar Sweetgum p. 160

FALL

B, H

SEEDS: Collect the prickly dangling capsules as they turn from green to brown in fall. Usually, open-grown trees will have some within reach at the ends of the branches. Dry them indoors until the capsules split and then shake out the ¼-inch winged seed (you can put the dried capsules in a paper bag and shake). The seed germinates best with 30 to 60 days of moist, cold stratification. Seedlings germinate epigeally. First cotyledons appear, then a little triangular leaf. Transplant early on into liners.

CUTTINGS/DIVISIONS: The survival of cuttings is chancy. Some cultivars are now being produced by tissue culture.

Liriodendron Tulip poplar p. 161

FALL

B

SEEDS: Squirrels and chipmunks relish the seeds, and unless you have access to an open-grown, low-flowering tree or you're a particularly good shot, you will have to be content with the rodents' castoffs. They gnaw off and drop the missile-like seed heads before the winged seeds have taken flight. Look for heads with seeds that are turning tan and beginning to peel off. Whatever pollinates the flowers does a pitiful job, because only about 10 to 20 percent of the seed is viable. Good seed will look plump and swollen at the base of the wing; cut a few open with a pair of pruners to see if the endosperm is full and white. You can handle the seed as for *Quercus:* chill for 3 months in a plastic bag with dampened vermiculite. Or sow it in flats outdoors and take your chances with rodents. Seedlings germinate epigeally in spring, with 2 cotyledons and a heart-shaped, dusky green leaf on a long slender petiole. Seedlings should be planted out or potted up individually and watered and fertilized regularly to keep them growing all season—6 to 12 inches or more is possible the first year.

A: seed will germinate within 4 weeks if sown at 70° F. **B**: seed will germinate upon being shifted to 70° F after 90–140 days of moist, cold stratification at 40° F. **C**: seed germinates only after multiple cycles of warm and cold, typically 40°–70°–40°–70° F. **D**: seed needs a period of warm, moist stratification followed by cold stratification and will germinate after being shifted back to warm, for example, 70°–40°–70° F. **G**: seed will not germinate in presence of chemical inhibitors. **H**: seed requires light to germinate. **I**: seed requires scarification because of an impermeable seed coat. *: seed is hydrophilic, intolerant of dry storage (see Hydrophilic Seeds, p. 265). Moss Germination: seed germinates best in the presence of both light and high atmospheric moisture, as would be found on a damp, mossy substrate in the wild.

Lonicera Honeysuckle p. 163 — SUMMER TO FALL — **B or D, G (or possibly protracted A)**

SEEDS: Collect the berries as they ripen. The fruit of longer-blooming species ripens over an extended period, and not all ripe fruit contains viable seed. The vining species have flattened but plump seeds, usually with a crease down the middle like a coffee bean. The shrubby types have smaller seeds, but more per fruit. To check viability, cut one or two seeds open and look for plump, white endosperm that fills the seed. We have poor seed set on shade-grown _L. hirsuta_ and _L. sempervirens,_ partly because of low pollinator visitation, but partial self-incompatibility may be a factor. Seed collected from a mixed-species planting may contain a large percentage of hybrids. Clean either by the smear-and-peel method or by letting the berries get raisinlike and then extracting the seeds. Cleaned, viable seed germinates best after a period of cold stratification, though the early-ripening _L. hirsuta_ and _L. oblongifolia_ need warm, then cold. Sow these immediately after collection and cleaning. Be patient —_Lonicera_ seed may not begin germinating until midsummer following a winter outdoors. On the other hand, _L. involucrata_ germinated after 4 weeks at warm temperatures, suggesting it is a protracted A type.

CUTTINGS/DIVISIONS: I struggled with cuttings from vining types of honeysuckle until I started taking them later in the season, using straight perlite for a rooting medium, and after we installed a fog system in the greenhouse. Cuttings taken too early tend to rot in the growing medium, and mist encourages botrytis and mildew on the leaves. Nonflowering, 2-to-3-node vigorous tip cuttings taken in mid-July to mid-August, treated with 2,000 ppm KIBA dip, and placed in pure perlite under fog will root about 75 to 90 percent and start growing as soon as the roots begin to show.

Maclura Osage orange p. 165 — FALL — **B, G**

SEEDS: Collect the big fruits from the ground in fall, put them in a bucket, and leave them where they will be exposed to freeze and thaw come winter, as in a garage. In late winter or early spring, mash the softened fruits between your fingers and feel out the ¼-inch-long, hard purplish seeds. Finish cleaning them by rinsing under water in a sieve. Sow outdoors in flats. Seedlings will germinate when the weather warms. This is much, much easier (though it is a bit repulsive) than trying to get the seeds out of the hard, fresh fruits.

Magnolia Magnolia p. 166 — LATE SUMMER TO FALL — **B, G***

SEEDS: The seeds are easiest to collect when they are just starting to pop out of the cones. I use a pole pruner to lop off cones high in the canopy (wear a helmet!). Unopened but red-flushed cones should be air-dried indoors until the seeds pop out. Or you can wait for the seeds to drop out of the cones onto the ground (they are fairly easy to see), though rodents quickly carry most of them off after a few days. The seed coat is thin and I have chopped the poor, watermelon-like seeds to bits when I have tried to blender-clean them. Instead, ferment them in water for a week and rub off the oily flesh (aril) with your fingers and rinse them in a sieve under running water. To prevent mice from stealing seeds, I keep them in sealed plastic bags with damp vermiculite in the refrigerator for the winter and sow outside in earliest spring. They germinate fairly late in spring, but the seedlings grow reasonably fast (3 to 6 inches the first year). Move germinated seedlings to 2-to-3-inch liners for the first season.

Mahonia Mahonia p. 169 — LATE SUMMER TO FALL — **D, G**

SEEDS: Mahonia fruits ripen slowly; be sure to wait for the skin to become dark blue (not greenish blue or teal). Collect the seed early enough in the season to allow a month or two of warm temperatures (above 50° F, on average) once they are sown. Blender-clean and sow the seeds immediately outdoors. Germination commences the following spring. If you collect the seed too late, put the cleaned seed into a bag of moistened vermiculite and keep it warm for 3 months. Then put it in the refrigerator for 2 to 3 months and sow outdoors as soon as you can in early spring.

Malus Crabapple p. 171 — FALL — **B, G**

SEEDS: Collect the fruits when they turn yellow or red and blender-clean. The small, comma-shaped seeds will germinate after outdoor or refrigerator cold stratification. Seedlings are easy to transplant and grow.

Menziesia Minnie-bush p. 172 — FALL — **A, H (moss)**

SEEDS: I have never been able to collect viable seed from our one plant of _M. pilosa._ This could be a problem of self-infertility or the dryness of the location. Wild stands set good quantities of small woody capsules. Pick, crush, and shake these to remove the seed. Sow as for _Rhododendron._

CUTTINGS/DIVISIONS: Softwood cuttings treated with 3,000 ppm KIBA and handled like azaleas failed to root after 2 months in the fog room.

Myrica Bayberry p. 173 — LATE SUMMER TO FALL — **B and C, G, I**

SEEDS: Collect the berries when they turn dark gray in fall. I have had good success cleaning off the wax in a blender, but you can

---

A: seed will germinate within 4 weeks if sown at 70° F. **B**: seed will germinate upon being shifted to 70° F after 90–140 days of moist, cold stratification at 40° F. **C**: seed germinates only after multiple cycles of warm and cold, typically 40°–70°–40°–70° F. **D**: seed needs a period of warm, moist stratification followed by cold stratification and will germinate after being shifted back to warm, for example, 70°–40°–70° F. **G**: seed will not germinate in presence of chemical inhibitors. **H**: seed requires light to germinate. **I**: seed requires scarification because of an impermeable seed coat. *****: seed is hydrophilic, intolerant of dry storage (see Hydrophilic Seeds, p. 265). Moss Germination: seed germinates best in the presence of both light and high atmospheric moisture, as would be found on a damp, mossy substrate in the wild.

also grind the fruit over a screen under running water with some dish detergent. Scarify and sow outdoors. Some germination will occur in spring, more the following spring. (I have probably been inconsistent in scarifying.) *Myrica gale* can be surface-sown without cleaning; a bit of sand or gravel will help prevent seeds from floating to the sides of the container when watered. Seedlings grow indeterminately if kept fertilized and watered, and a few light tip-pinches will yield a nicely branched little transplant.

CUTTINGS/DIVISIONS: Sections of root with the associated shoot can be easily teased up in early spring and transplanted. This is the best way to propagate known females.

Nemopanthus Mountain holly p. 175 **SUMMER** **D, G**

SEEDS: Collect the fruits and blender-clean or macerate and ferment. Seeds need a long warm period followed by cold, so they may not germinate until the second spring, even if you sow immediately after collecting them. Alternatively, put the cleaned seed in a plastic bag with some damp vermiculite and completely forget about it for 8 months as it gathers dust on your desk. Rediscover it during your annual February office cleaning, sow outdoors, and have a good crop of seedlings emerge when it warms (true story).

CUTTINGS/DIVISIONS: Cuttings will root if handled like the deciduous *Ilex* species. (Nurseries are producing sexed material this way.)

Nyssa Tupelo p. 176 **FALL** **B, G**

SEEDS: Collecting the fruits can be difficult in the forest. Use binoculars to spot a female tree, spread out a tarp, climb up the trunk on a ladder, grasp a side branch, and shake like the dickens. Blender-clean the fruit (this unfortunately wears away the beautiful ridges on the seed coat of the larger species—a floatation aid?—but doesn't harm the embryo itself). Sow the seed in a cold-frame secured against rodents. Germination will take place the following spring. Transfer newly emerged seedlings to individual 6-to-8-inch containers. Growth is rapid in containers; 3 feet or more is possible after two seasons.

Oplopanax Devil's club p. 178 **SUMMER** **D***

SEEDS: The fruits are easy to see when they turn bright red but are hard to collect, as the pedicels are very spiny. Put on thick gloves and gingerly clip off a cluster of fruits. Blender cleaning works well. Sow the tan, flattened seeds (about the size of a hulled sunflower seed) at once and leave them in the cold frame for the winter. The large cotyledons will emerge in the spring. Seedlings will produce several true leaves and a short thorny stem the first year. I have had terrible trouble with slugs, who seem to relish the foliage, so place the flat out of their reach on a table.

Osmanthus Wild olive p. 179 **FALL** **C, I**

SEEDS: Fruits ripen in clusters along previous season's wood. Collect the seeds when the fruits turn from light green to bloomy black. The blender will damage the brittle seed, so hand-clean by rubbing over a screen. Each berry contains 1 large oval seed. Sow the seed immediately and place outdoors in a cold frame screened against rodents. Germination should begin in the second spring, with some more the following year.

CUTTINGS/DIVISIONS: *Osmanthus* is hard to root, and even when I have succeeded, the cuttings go right to flowering and thus hardly grow.

Ostrya Hop hornbeam p. 180 **FALL TO EARLY WINTER** **D**

SEEDS: I usually wait until the leaves have fallen to collect the seed. Spread a tarp under a well-laden tree and give it a good shake. The hard, ¼-inch, light brown seeds can be shucked out of the bladder-like bract by hand or by rubbing over a screen. Sow outside. Germination will take place the second spring. To get seed to germinate in one season, give it a period of warm stratification prior to cold. You can do this by harvesting the seed in late summer and cleaning and sowing immediately. Or sow fall-collected seed indoors and give it 2 months of warm followed by 3 to 4 months of cold in the refrigerator.

Oxydendrum Sourwood p. 181 **FALL** **A, H (moss)**

SEEDS: Collect the capsules when they turn brown in autumn, then dry and crush/shake them to remove the seeds. Sow as for *Rhododendron*. This is easy from seed. There are several sourwoods growing around the edge of the nursery at Niche Gardens, and at first I didn't recognize that the fast-growing woody weeds in my seed flats were indeed *Oxydendrum* that had filtered down from the neighboring trees. With fertilizer and water, the seedlings will continue growing dangerously late into summer, but except for a bit of tip dieback, they will cruise through the winter without harm from an early fall freeze.

Parthenocissus Virginia creeper p. 182 **EARLY FALL** **B, G**

SEEDS: This is an easy plant to collect seeds from because the bright red foliage signals when the seeds are black and ripe. Mash and clean them over a screen. Sow them in fall and leave out in the cold frame for the winter. Expect germination in spring.

A: seed will germinate within 4 weeks if sown at 70° F. **B**: seed will germinate upon being shifted to 70° F after 90–140 days of moist, cold stratification at 40° F. **C**: seed germinates only after multiple cycles of warm and cold, typically 40°–70°–40°–70° F. **D**: seed needs a period of warm, moist stratification followed by cold stratification and will germinate after being shifted back to warm, for example, 70°–40°–70° F. **G**: seed will not germinate in presence of chemical inhibitors. **H**: seed requires light to germinate. **I**: seed requires scarification because of an impermeable seed coat. *****: seed is hydrophilic, intolerant of dry storage (see Hydrophilic Seeds, p. 265). Moss Germination: seed germinates best in the presence of both light and high atmospheric moisture, as would be found on a damp, mossy substrate in the wild.

Seedlings grow rapidly and begin to vine almost immediately, so transfer to individual pots and keep lightly pinched to avoid an impossible tangle.

CUTTINGS/DIVISIONS: Take 3-node cuttings from the upper top 12 inches of vigorous stems. Use 3,000 ppm Dip 'N Grow or KIBA and mist.

Paxistima Cliff green p. 183   LATE SUMMER   **B, H***

SEEDS: The tiny peapod capsules turn yellow or burgundy as they ripen. Pick whole clusters and let them dry for a week or so, then crush them over a screen. The seeds have a fringed aril attached, but you need a microscope to see this. Surface-sow immediately, cover with a thin layer of sand, and place outdoors for the winter.

CUTTINGS/DIVISIONS: Tip cuttings are much easier and faster than seed. Collect 2-to-3-inch sections from current growth in midsummer and treat with 2,000 to 3,000 ppm IBA talc or liquid. I usually leave them outdoors in the shade under Reemay, though placing them under fog works very well, too. Keep rooted cuttings in the flat until the following spring. Overwintered cuttings potted up in spring keep growing and branching all summer and become beautiful, deep green 4-by-6-inch mounds by fall. Light tip pruning early in the season promotes even branching.

Philadelphus Mock-orange p. 184   SUMMER   **(A) B, H**

SEEDS: The small seeds can be collected from capsules after they dry. Even if you are a bit late and the capsules are already open, there should be some seed still inside. *P. lewisii* has germinated for me without pretreatment, but it and the eastern complex come up more readily if they are chilled for at least 60 days after sowing. Sow in fall, cover with light sand, and set the flat outdoors for the winter. This always works splendidly. Seedlings grow 6 to 8 inches the first year (pinch to force a few side branches) and bloom in 2 to 3 years from seed.

CUTTINGS/DIVISIONS: I have had mixed results with softwood cuttings, which is surprising because other authors report them to be easy. The cuttings root easily, but I have had trouble with stem rot in the medium. The stems are pithy when mature, so use tip cuttings and stick these in straight perlite after treatment with 1,000 ppm IBA.

Phyllodoce p. 71   LATE SUMMER   **A, H (moss)**

SEEDS: As for *Cassiope*.

CUTTINGS/DIVISIONS: As for *Cassiope*.

Physocarpus Ninebark p. 185   LATE SUMMER   **A or B, H**

SEEDS: Seeds ripen in a small cluster of podlike follicles. Pick these clusters as they turn yellow and brown, dry them, and run them over a screen to free the small seeds. You can either keep seeds dry in a refrigerated paper envelope for the winter and sow in spring, or sow them in fall (sand cover only) and leave them out to stratify for the winter as for *Philadelphus*.

CUTTINGS/DIVISIONS: Take 3-to-4-node softwood cuttings from near the tips of vigorous sucker wood in early summer, treat it with 1,000 ppm IBA talc, and place under mist. These root easily, but move them out of the mist quickly after rooting to prevent mildew and other fungus problems. Cuttings are the preferred propagation method.

Picea Spruce p. 187   FALL   **A or B, H**

SEEDS: Cones ripen in fall, and the small seeds, which look exactly like little maple samaras, spin off in the wind. Collect when cones begin to crack, though even cones that have fully opened for a while still contain some seeds. (You can also shake the trees and catch the falling seeds in a butterfly net—a good test of hand-eye coordination.) When cones are dry, run your finger over the scales from tip to base while shaking to free the seeds. I prefer to sow the seeds in late fall and overwinter them outdoors. The first whorl of soft cotyledons will pop up the following spring. Careful, light fertilization and attention to watering in a controlled greenhouse situation will spur seedlings to grow somewhat indeterminately, putting on 3 to 6 times the stem growth they would in the wild. Otherwise, the seedlings grow slowly for the first few years, building food reserves and a root system, before sending up a surge of new tip growth in years 3 or 4 and beyond.

Pieris Fetterbush p. 189   FALL   **A, H (moss)**

SEEDS: Collect and sow as for *Rhododendron*. I have found fetterbush particularly easy to raise from seed over the winter in a cool room or greenhouse equipped with supplemental lights, but the seedlings are somewhat lax until they are about 2 inches tall. Keep the medium (I use 1:1 peat-perlite) strongly acidic to discourage root disease.

Pinckneya Fever tree p. 190   FALL TO WINTER   **A, H**

SEEDS: Clusters of oval capsules begin turning brown in late summer, and many hang stubbornly on the twigs well into winter. Pick these before they crack in half, and lightly crush, shake, and sieve them to remove the small, winged, light brown seeds. Germinate and handle as for *Cephalanthus*.

A: seed will germinate within 4 weeks if sown at 70° F. **B**: seed will germinate upon being shifted to 70° F after 90–140 days of moist, cold stratification at 40° F.
C: seed germinates only after multiple cycles of warm and cold, typically 40°–70°–40°–70° F. **D**: seed needs a period of warm, moist stratification followed by cold stratification and will germinate after being shifted back to warm, for example, 70°–40°–70° F. **G**: seed will not germinate in presence of chemical inhibitors. **H**: seed requires light to germinate. **I**: seed requires scarification because of an impermeable seed coat. *: seed is hydrophilic, intolerant of dry storage (see Hydrophilic Seeds, p. 265). Moss Germination: seed germinates best in the presence of both light and high atmospheric moisture, as would be found on a damp, mossy substrate in the wild.

NAME	SEED RIPENS	GERMINATION CONDITIONS

Pinus Pine p. 191 **FALL** **(A) B (I)**

SEEDS: Many pines produce cones every few years (comparable to oaks' mast years), and cones take 2 years to fully develop. Often one can find a number of still unopened ripe cones under trees, knocked down by rodents. I know of one grower who shoots down cones with a .22 rifle — he's a better shot than I am. Even opened cones usually contain a few seeds stuck in resin. Be careful with these seeds, however, as they may not be viable. Collect unopened cones and let them dry indoors for a few weeks. If they still haven't popped open, put them in a warm oven (under 120° F) for an hour or two. This helps soften the resin, especially with the serotinous species (a 30-second dip in boiling water does the same thing). Most pine seeds are wind-dispersed, and so have little wings; these needn't be removed before sowing. The bird- and mammal-dispersed pinyon species and others without wings should be lightly scarified before sowing. All the pines I have tried in the cold frame germinated after a winter, though some of the western species may germinate without a cold period if the seed is sown fresh. I have also handled them as described for *Quercus,* as scavenging mice can be a problem in the cold frame. The seedlings emerge with a whorl of cotyledons. Once these are fully expanded, transfer them to liner pots for a year or two.

Platanus Sycamore p. 196 **FALL TO WINTER** **A or B, H**

SEEDS: Sycamore balls are resilient things, hanging on the branches well into winter. Often you can find some fresh or partially disintegrated ones underneath the trees or on a fallen or low branch. Bring the balls indoors and let them dry a few weeks so they can be easily crushed and broken apart. The thin, pointed nuts, about ¼ inch long, radiate from the center intermixed with fine hairs. Rub the seeds over a screen to free them from as many hairs as possible. Surface-sow fresh seed in late fall in flats and leave them outdoors, or sow dry stored seed in early spring. Seedlings grow very quickly with fertilization, so after germination transfer them to plugs for 4 to 6 weeks, then pot on in larger containers or in the ground in early summer. It is very satisfying to watch the leaves grow larger with each passing week.

Populus Poplar p. 197 **LATE SPRING TO EARLY SUMMER** **A, H***

SEEDS: Poplar seeds erupt in frothy, webbed masses from the chains of small pods. The seeds are wrapped inside silky hairs that allow them to travel on the wind. Pick the chains when you see the first few begin to split open or you see cotton floating around near the grove, and let them dry in a bag for a few days until all have spit. Comb out the seed and attached silk (do this outdoors, as the down gets everywhere). The silk also helps cement the seed to the soil surface, so merely spread the cottony mass about ¼ inch thick over a dampened flat of seed mix and mist it with a hose until the silk is wetted and seeds have flattened against the soil surface. Keep the flat damp. Small seedlings—at first bearing little resemblance to the parent—will begin popping up in a matter of weeks. These can be transplanted to individual containers when 2 inches high, and they will continue growing for the rest of the summer. It is reasonable to expect 16-to-24-inch seedlings in one season. This procedure also works with willows.

CUTTINGS/DIVISIONS: Most poplars (except for aspens) and willows can be rooted from year-old whips. Cut 16-to-24-inch sections of the previous season's wood in late winter, before catkins have expanded on the tree, and stick the butt end 6 to 8 inches into moist soil or a glass of water. These will root and leaf out in spring. This method is useful in restoration projects, as stands can be quickly established in erosion-prone areas. It is also fun to do with kids to get them interested in plant propagation—you can't start too early.

Potentilla Shrubby cinquefoil p. 199 **LATE SUMMER** **A or B**

SEEDS: For reasons explained in the descriptive section, isolated individuals of the North American variety rarely set seed. Mixed plantings or wild stands usually have a good crop, but because they bloom sequentially, only a portion will be ripe at any one time. The seeds are like little eggs in a nest formed by the cup at the base of the flower. The fuzzy seeds can be flicked or crushed out of the cap. Store these and sow outdoors in late fall or early spring; seedlings will come on quickly when the weather warms.

CUTTINGS/DIVISIONS: Treat 3-inch softwood cuttings with 1,000 ppm IBA talc and stick in pure perlite under mist or a polytent. Cuttings root readily and can be potted on into 6-inch containers, which they will fill by autumn.

Prunus Plum, cherry p. 201 **LATE SUMMER TO FALL** **B, G**

SEEDS: Collect the ripe fruits and ferment and soak or blender-clean to remove the pulp (this cleaning may not be truly necessary; as black cherries that fall from the parent into nursery containers germinate in droves the following spring). Sow in flats and leave them outdoors for the winter. Most will germinate robustly in spring. Transplant these into individual liners as soon as the cotyledons have expanded. Seedlings will continue growing if fertilizer and love are provided unconditionally.

Pseudotsuga Douglas fir p. 204 **LATE SUMMER** **B***

SEEDS: When cones turn brown and begin opening, they can be picked and brought indoors. Shake out the seeds and store them dry in sealed plastic bags in the refrigerator until late fall, then sow and leave them outdoors for the winter. Or place the seeds

A: seed will germinate within 4 weeks if sown at 70° F. **B**: seed will germinate upon being shifted to 70° F after 90–140 days of moist, cold stratification at 40° F. **C**: seed germinates only after multiple cycles of warm and cold, typically 40°–70°–40°–70° F. **D**: seed needs a period of warm, moist stratification followed by cold stratification and will germinate after being shifted back to warm, for example, 70°–40°–70° F. **G**: seed will not germinate in presence of chemical inhibitors. **H**: seed requires light to germinate. **I**: seed requires scarification because of an impermeable seed coat. *****: seed is hydrophilic, intolerant of dry storage (see Hydrophilic Seeds, p. 265). Moss Germination: seed germinates best in the presence of both light and high atmospheric moisture, as would be found on a damp, mossy substrate in the wild.

in damp vermiculite and chill for 2 to 3 months in the refrigerator, then plant them out in spring. Handle seedlings as described for *Pinus*.

CUTTINGS/DIVISIONS: Take cuttings in late winter and treat them with 6,000 to 8,000 ppm IBA liquid. They will root well when handled as for *Juniperus*.

Quercus   Oak p. 205   FALL   **B***

SEEDS: Oaks are fun to raise from seed and are a good example to use with children because they are so large and dramatic in their emergence. So many things feed on acorns that it is sometimes difficult to collect reasonable numbers. Mast years, when all the oaks in a woodland produce bumper crops of acorns, usually occur every 2 to 4 years. I have found that one or two years after a good, rainy spring and summer will often be a banner year. (In 2001, late frosts destroyed the oak catkins, so the following two falls are likely to be poor for acorns.) In good mast years we are troubled far less by rodents in the winter, presumably because they have enough to eat. Collect acorns from the ground beneath the tree, looking for large, heavy nuts with a cap that is missing or readily falls away between your fingers. Weevils bore into and destroy a large proportion of nuts, especially in a lean year, so look for tiny round entrance holes in the shell and discard any nuts so afflicted. Unfortunately, not all affected nuts are possible to spot, so collect 2 to 3 times as many as you think you'll need. I collect half a bucket of acorns, fill it with water, and remove the floating (dead or damaged) nuts. Let the rest soak for a day or two, until the shells look saturated. Strain out the acorns and transfer them to plastic freezer bags partially filled with dampened vermiculite and store them over the winter in the refrigerator. Since the white oaks send out a root in fall, these will sprout in the bags, but the roots are usually okay if there is enough vermiculite to pad them. Plant out the nuts in spring. With red oaks, I like to take the bag out of the refrigerator and leave it somewhere warm for a few weeks, so I can pull out the healthy nuts as they split and discard the rest. Plant each prechilled, germinating acorn in a 3-to-4-inch-deep container or directly in the field. Germination is hypogeal, with one flush of leaves or possibly two the first season.

Rhododendron   Rhododendron, azalea p. 212   FALL   **A, H (moss)**

SEEDS: With the azaleas, especially, hand pollination is the best guarantee of getting plants true from seed. Pollen from the same plant will work, but I have better seed set if I cross two individuals of the same species. Comb the sticky pollen out of the anthers with a small paintbrush and transfer to another plant's stigma, which juts out beyond the stamens. Once a stigma has received pollen, it is less likely to "take" other pollen, but just to be sure, some people net the flowers with cheesecloth to keep bees away. Collect seed in fall as the capsules turn from green to brown and begin to split at the seams, after the first frosts. The waferlike rusty seed is held in the folds of each section of capsule; if it does not shake out easily, crack or lightly crush the capsules to free the seed. Try to get as little chaff as possible, as this encourages rot. Good seed should be swollen in the middle and surrounded by a stubby papery wing. Sow seed immediately on well-wetted pure peat, 1:1 peat and perlite, or 1:1:2 peat, perlite, and commercial seed mix. Your choice depends on how much water you plan to give them. Put the sown flat in a plastic bag and place under grow lights—4-foot, 2-tube fluorescent shop fixtures are cheap and effective. Set lights to be on for 16-hour days and off for 8-hour nights. (Most heath family members will continue to grow as long as day length is above a certain minimum. In this way, seedlings can be forced to grow much more rapidly and over a longer season than they would in the wild.) You can also sow the seeds in spring, when days are getting longer anyway, or use the moss-sowing method detailed on p. 271. Once seeds sprout, crack open the bag. After a few weeks give them a light dose of fertilizer and thoroughly drain off excess water before placing the flat back in the bag. Our water is hard (high in calcium and magnesium), so I have to use melted snow or rainwater to water the seedlings until they can be moved outdoors in spring. Results have been fantastic since I switched to rainwater. Seedlings can be weaned out of the flat and stepped up to individual plugs or liner pots when 1 inch tall, then potted on again in spring. They begin blooming in 4 to 5 years from seed, versus 1 to 2 years from cuttings.

CUTTINGS/DIVISIONS: Cuttings are reasonably easy for the evergreen species if taken in late summer. Cut the current seasons' whorl near the base, above where it emerged from the bud, treat it with 3,000 ppm IBA, and stick it in a bark or peat-perlite medium under mist or a polytent. It's a good idea to reduce leaf area by 30 percent by clipping off leaf tips of the large-leaved species. Cuttings are slow but will root in 2 to 4 months in a greenhouse or under lights with bottom heat. Azaleas are are more difficult; take cuttings from vigorous shoots in early summer before the stems have become woody and brown. Use 1,500 ppm KIBA and mist or a polytent. If the cuttings root, try to force out a new flush of growth to assure they make it through the winter with light fertilizing and supplemental lights.

Rhus   Sumac p. 218   EARLY FALL TO EARLY WINTER   **A or B, I**

SEEDS: Collect clusters of berries from females in fall or early winter. Dry for a week, then scarify the berries with sandpaper; some or all of the red fruit will flake off, and you don't have to remove the rest before sowing. Soak the scarified seed overnight

---

A: seed will germinate within 4 weeks if sown at 70° F. **B:** seed will germinate upon being shifted to 70° F after 90–140 days of moist, cold stratification at 40° F.
C: seed germinates only after multiple cycles of warm and cold, typically 40°–70°–40°–70° F. **D:** seed needs a period of warm, moist stratification followed by cold stratification and will germinate after being shifted back to warm, for example, 70°–40°–70° F. **G:** seed will not germinate in presence of chemical inhibitors. **H:** seed requires light to germinate. **I:** seed requires scarification because of an impermeable seed coat. ***:** seed is hydrophilic, intolerant of dry storage (see Hydrophilic Seeds, p. 265). **Moss Germination:** seed germinates best in the presence of both light and high atmospheric moisture, as would be found on a damp, mossy substrate in the wild.

in warm water, then sow outdoors for the winter. Germination takes place in spring. Ideally, sow them early enough so they will receive 2 to 3 months of cold stratification, though the large pinnate-leaved species can be collected and sown toward the end of winter with good result.

CUTTINGS/DIVISIONS: The best way to produce cultivars or known females is by means of root cuttings taken in late winter. Dig shallow ¼-to-½-inch-diameter roots as soon as the ground thaws—look for them 3 to 4 feet out from the trunk—and cut them into 2-to-3-inch sections. Lay them flat or at a 45-degree angle in a tray half filled with sand, then cover them with more sand. Place on bottom heat (65° F). Callusing followed by rooting, then shoot formation, will be evident by late spring. Transfer to individual 6-to-8-inch containers once shoots are partially expanded.

Ribes Currant p. 221 SUMMER B, G

SEEDS: The various species ripen at different times, but generally the fruits begin to color 8 to 10 weeks after pollination. Currants are easy, as the fruits turn from green to red or black, but gooseberries' color is more subtle. Watch the fruits and try to gauge when they have stopped expanding. Color will usually shift from green to a more translucent yellow-green. Also, look for the small, dark brown seeds suspended in the pulp. The seeds of *Ribes* species are best extracted using the smear-and-peel technique. Sow outdoors in fall and the seedlings will emerge in spring. I pot these into plugs after the cotyledons have expanded, then move them to large containers 4 to 6 weeks later.

CUTTINGS/DIVISIONS: Softwood cuttings of *R. odoratum* taken in early summer, treated with 1,000 ppm IBA talc, and placed in fog will root nearly 100 percent, but the potted cuttings tend to be lanky and less presentable than seedlings. In the days before rooting hormones and mist systems, *Ribes* cultivars were rooted like roses, by taking 4-inch sections of the current year's growth after the leaves have fallen, storing these in barely damp peat in the refrigerator, then sticking them in sand beds in a cool greenhouse in early spring.

Rosa Rose p. 224 LATE SUMMER TO WINTER B, G, I*

SEEDS: Collect the hips when they have turned fully red or orange, slice open, and spoon out the seeds. Often there are as many shriveled, unfilled seeds in a hip as good ones, so look for plump seeds about ⅛ inch long. It is also a good idea to cut a few open to check for endosperm, as well as to float the seeds (discard any that float). I have had excellent germination using fresh seed collected in fall, scarifying it with sandpaper, and sowing it outdoors. I had less success if I waited until winter to collect and treat the seeds. Seedlings emerge in spring. Transfer them to plugs and, 4 weeks later, to 6-inch containers. Grow roses in a sunny, breezy spot and try not to water them late in the day. Powdery mildew is usually not a severe problem in the garden and in the wild, but it can get pretty bad under irrigation in the nursery. Cut the crop back to 3 inches after leaves drop in fall. Seedlings bloom in 2 to 3 years.

CUTTINGS/DIVISIONS: The traditional method for producing garden roses is to cut 3-to-4-inch sections off the current season's canes in late fall to early winter, store these in barely damp peat in the refrigerator or root cellar, then stick them vertically in sand beds in late winter. I have tried this with *Rosa virginiana* and *R. carolina*, without success. Softwood cuttings taken in early summer, treated with 2,000 ppm KIBA quick dip, and placed under fog will root more easily, though in my experience, seed is still far more satisfactory with the wild roses. Cuttings are lanky and easily snapped off the first year, while seedlings come out well branched and stocky. Our isolated white form of *R. virginiana* comes 100 percent true from seed. The running types like *R. arkansana* are easily dug and divided.

Rubus Raspberry p. 227 SUMMER B, G

SEEDS: Collect and clean as for *Ribes*. For the drier-fruited species (*R. odoratus* and *R. parviflorus*), I collect the ripe fruits and air-dry them until they are hard, then grind them apart with my fingers and sow the seeds uncleaned outdoors in fall. Germination occurs in spring. All others have too high a water content, and the berries begin to mold instead of drying. The smear-and-peel technique is thus preferable for blackberries and red raspberries.

CUTTINGS/DIVISIONS: Cultivars are traditionally produced as for roses, though virus transmission is a potential problem. Layering, whether natural or encouraged, is another easy propagation method.

Salix Willow p. 229 LATE SPRING TO EARLY SUMMER A, H*

SEEDS: As for *Populus*.

CUTTINGS/DIVISIONS: As for *Populus*.

Sambucus Elderberry p. 231 MID- TO LATE SUMMER B, G

SEEDS: Collect and clean using smear-and-peel technique as for *Ribes*. Seed is easily germinated after a winter outdoors, and seedlings come along very quickly. I made the mistake of mixing up some elderberry and *Aralia* fruits when collecting, and the elderberry quickly overtook the fast-growing *Aralia* in the seed flat.

CUTTINGS/DIVISIONS: It is very easy to root 2-node softwood cuttings taken from vigorous tips in early to midsummer. Trim each

---

A: seed will germinate within 4 weeks if sown at 70° F. **B**: seed will germinate upon being shifted to 70° F after 90–140 days of moist, cold stratification at 40° F. **C**: seed germinates only after multiple cycles of warm and cold, typically 40°–70°–40°–70° F. **D**: seed needs a period of warm, moist stratification followed by cold stratification and will germinate after being shifted back to warm, for example, 70°–40°–70° F. **G**: seed will not germinate in presence of chemical inhibitors. **H**: seed requires light to germinate. **I**: seed requires scarification because of an impermeable seed coat. *****: seed is hydrophilic, intolerant of dry storage (see Hydrophilic Seeds, p. 265). **Moss Germination**: seed germinates best in the presence of both light and high atmospheric moisture, as would be found on a damp, mossy substrate in the wild.

leaf in half—the cuttings are big. Treat with 1,000 ppm IBA, and place in mist or a polytent. If you have sufficient stock, this is the easiest method, though seeds are also simple.

Sassafras Sassafras p. 233 — FALL — **B, G***

SEEDS: Blazing sassafras leaves or birds in a feeding frenzy are your cue to start searching for fruit. Use binoculars to spot a female tree ripe with seed, then spread out a tarp and shake down the ripe, deep blue, olive-shaped berries; each is about ¼ inch long and stuck in the cupping end of a bright red pedicel. To beat the birds to them, pick fruits when the pedicel turns red but before the skin darkens. The seed coats are fairly soft, so fermentation, mashing, and straining are the best way to clean off the pulp. Sow seeds immediately in flats placed outdoors or in prepared seed beds. Seedlings germinate strongly in spring, and despite superstitions to the contrary, are easily transplanted, even bareroot, until they are 3 to 4 years old.

Sequoiadendron Giant sequoia p. 234 — EARLY FALL — **A or B, H**

SEEDS: *Sequoiadendron* cones take a few years to mature, so search for ripening cones on 2-to-3-year-old wood. The cones continue to add growth rings around their base as they grow, so look for cones with 3 distinct rings. After the cones turn from green to yellow as they are about to shed seed, harvest them and dry indoors until they open. Shake out and screen the small, papery brown seed (old brown cones may still contain some viable seed as well). Sow as for *Vaccinium*, but open the bag and remove seedlings as soon as they begin to germinate to prevent damping off. Seedlings will continue to grow under lights set for 16-hour days with light fertilization. They will be ready for larger containers as weather warms in spring.

Sequoia produces small, oval cones that ripen in one season, so look for them at the base of the current season's growth (old seedless cones remain on the tree from previous seasons). Cones collected as they yellow should open after air drying. If they prove stubborn, heat them in a warm oven (see the technique under *Pinus*). Unlike giant sequoia's, redwood seeds need no chilling and can be handled as for *Rhododendron*. Seed viability is usually low, so collect and sow 3 times the necessary seed.

Sorbus Mountain-ash p. 235 — LATE SUMMER — **B or D, G, I**

SEEDS: Collect the fruits as soon as they are ripe and blender-clean them to remove pulp; this also lightly scarifies the seed, which may improve germination. Sow immediately outdoors; germination takes place the following spring. This warm-cold treatment has worked well with *S. americana*, *S. sitchensis*, and *S. racemosa*, though Dirr and Hauser report that all but the first will germinate after only a period of cold stratification.

Spiraea Spirea p. 237 — LATE SUMMER TO FALL — **A or B, H**

SEEDS: The tiny seeds ripen in small, clustered, podlike capsules that turn from green to yellow-brown when ripe. Dry these indoors for several weeks and sieve out the dustlike seed. Seed can be sown as for *Hypericum*. A first-year seedling will fill a gallon container by the end of the season, and will grow more compactly than vegetatively propagated plants this first year, with small leaves and a nice, tight-branching habit.

CUTTINGS/DIVISIONS: Softwood cuttings taken from the 6 inches of strong young growth are easy to root (use 1,000 to 2,000 ppm IBA).

Stewartia Stewartia p. 238 — EARLY FALL — **D***

SEEDS: Look for ripening capsules among the foliage, and pick them before they split. Dry indoors until they crack open and the seeds can be teased out. Seed of *S. ovata* is slightly winged, like a pine nut, and the capsules crack open at the tips. *S. malacodendron* seed is unwinged, shiny dark brown, and the capsules open along the sides, making extraction a bit more difficult. Sow cleaned seed immediately. If you sow outdoors in either flats or beds, germination will occur the second spring. Alternatively, pack seeds in moist vermiculite in a plastic bag and keep it in a warm place for 3 months (make sure the vermiculite stays moist), then refrigerate the bag for 3 months. Sow the seeds in flats and place them outdoors. Grow seedlings in liners for a year before potting on.

CUTTINGS/DIVISIONS: Take semihardwood 3-inch tip cuttings in early summer, when the twigs snap if bent but are still green. If treated with high hormone levels (6,000 to 8,000 ppm KIBA), cuttings will root fairly readily under mist. Leave them undisturbed in the rooting tray until the following spring. Cuttings usually do not send out more top growth until the next year, and disturbing them too early will lead to nearly complete winter losses. Overwinter rooted flats in a cold frame or, ideally, a minimally heated greenhouse.

Styrax Snowbell p. 239 — FALL — **B* (moderately hydrophilic)**

SEEDS: The North American species are easier to germinate than the Asian. I have excellent luck when I collect the seeds in the fall as the leaves yellow. Crack open the husk and pull out the olive pit–sized seed. Sowing outdoors for winter stratification is dangerous, as rodents will eat seed. Better yet, put the seeds in a bag of dampened vermiculite and leave in the refrigerator until

---

A: seed will germinate within 4 weeks if sown at 70° F. **B**: seed will germinate upon being shifted to 70° F after 90–140 days of moist, cold stratification at 40° F. **C**: seed germinates only after multiple cycles of warm and cold, typically 40°–70°–40°–70° F. **D**: seed needs a period of warm, moist stratification followed by cold stratification and will germinate after being shifted back to warm, for example, 70°–40°–70° F. **G**: seed will not germinate in presence of chemical inhibitors. **H**: seed requires light to germinate. **I**: seed requires scarification because of an impermeable seed coat. *****: seed is hydrophilic, intolerant of dry storage (see Hydrophilic Seeds, p. 265). Moss Germination: seed germinates best in the presence of both light and high atmospheric moisture, as would be found on a damp, mossy substrate in the wild.

early spring, then plant them outside in flats. Seedlings come up with big cotyledons and are fast growing. Prick out the seedlings once cotyledons are expanded and pot into 3-inch liners. With fertilization, they will continue to grow through the season, topping out at around 6 to 8 inches their first year. The trees begin blooming when only 3 to 4 years old.

Symphoricarpos   Snowberry p. 240   FALL   **D**

SEEDS: Seeds need to be mashed or blender-cleaned from the ripe fruits. Sow as for *Stewartia*. The seed is slow to germinate but not difficult, though cuttings are the easier method.

CUTTINGS/DIVISIONS: Softwood to semihardwood cuttings taken in early to midsummer and treated with 1,000 ppm IBA talc will root readily after a few weeks. Pot these on and they'll continue to grow. If you need only a few, layering will also work.

Taxodium   Baldcypress p. 242   FALL   **B, H**

SEEDS: Triangular seeds ripen inside cones that are green turning purplish. The cones disintegrate when dry, so it is difficult to separate the seeds and chaff, but sowing the lot seems to do no harm. Sow crushed seed and cone scales and cover with sand, then leave outdoors for the winter. Germination takes place in spring. Seedlings will continue growing through the summer with regular light fertilization and can be transferred to liners or 6-inch pots when 2 to 3 inches tall.

Taxus   Yew p. 243   LATE SUMMER TO FALL   **D or C***

SEEDS: The single seed is encircled by a fleshy cone scale, or aril, that is open at the apex. Seeds ripen sequentially over 3 weeks, so unless you have access to a large planting, it is difficult to collect many at one time. Squeeze out the seeds and rinse them in a sieve, then sow them immediately and leave them outdoors. Seedlings emerge in the first or second spring after sowing. Hybrids may result from mixed garden plantings, so try to collect from isolated or wild stands.

CUTTINGS/DIVISIONS: Since seeds are often hard to collect in any quantity and are slow to germinate and grow, I usually propagate yews by hardwood cuttings. Take 3-inch sections of current year's growth in November or December. Handle as for *Juniperus*. Cuttings root readily and can be potted on in spring.

Thuja   Red cedar p. 244   FALL   **B, H***

SEEDS: Harvest cones when they turn yellow in fall. Extract seeds, surface-sow immediately, and leave the flats outdoors. Seedlings will appear in spring and should be left in the seed flat until 2 inches tall, then transferred to liners.

CUTTINGS/DIVISIONS: Hardwood cuttings taken in winter root reasonably well if handled like *Juniperus*.

Tsuga   Hemlock p. 245   FALL   **B, H**

SEEDS: Cones ripen in fall. Collect as they begin to turn brown and dry indoors—this is especially important with *T. carolina*, which quickly drops its seeds. The seeds are winged, but the papery wings are so fragile (they look like diaphanous insect wings) that they disintegrate upon handling, so not to worry. The seed is a thin, irregular shape, pointed at both ends, about ⅛ inch long, and tawny brown. Surface-sow and leave in the cold frame for the winter. Seedlings put out a few needly cotyledons the first year and can be encouraged to do more with light fertilizing.

CUTTINGS/DIVISIONS: Hardwood cuttings root reasonably well if handled as for *Juniperus*.

Ulmus   Elm p. 248   EARLY TO MIDSUMMER   **A or B**

SEEDS: Collect the papery seeds from under trees after they fall, or pick the clusters as they begin to brown on the twigs in early summer. If sown right away, the seed may germinate within a few weeks, or it may need to go through a period of winter stratification. I recommend collecting the seed, storing it dry in a plastic bag in the refrigerator until fall, and sowing it outdoors for the winter.

Vaccinium   Blueberry p. 249   MID- TO LATE SUMMER OR FALL   **A or B, H (moss)**

SEEDS: Blueberries are best cleaned using the smear-and-peel technique where you mash the fruit on a paper towel and smear it out in a 1-inch streak. Let the pulp dry for a few days and peel or flake off the tiny brown seeds. Shake the seeds on a manila envelope to separate them from any remaining bits of skin, which can cause fungus problems if not removed before sowing. With some species I have worked with, if I sow seeds as for *Rhododendron* and keep the bagged flat in a warm location, the seedlings are slow to emerge and have the half-expanded look indicating insufficient levels of GA3. Consequently, I place the sealed bag of surface-sown seeds (same mixes as for *Rhododendron*) in the refrigerator for 60 days, then remove it and grow it under lights for the rest of the winter. Chilled seedlings will outstrip their unchilled siblings by the beginning of spring, and can be stepped into plugs at this time and into 6-to-8-inch containers in early summer.

CUTTINGS/DIVISIONS: The creeping cranberries freely layer on their own, and these layered stems can be cut off and potted separately. They will also root readily as summer cuttings (treat with 1,000 ppm IBA, though it may not be necessary). Creeping colonizing species like *V. angustifolium* and *V. crassifolium* may be treated like root cuttings by cutting off the small (3-to-8-inch) shoots and their attached section of rhizome from the outskirts of the colony before they leaf out in spring. Cultivars of high-

---

A: seed will germinate within 4 weeks if sown at 70° F. **B**: seed will germinate upon being shifted to 70° F after 90–140 days of moist, cold stratification at 40° F. **C**: seed germinates only after multiple cycles of warm and cold, typically 40°–70°–40°–70° F. **D**: seed needs a period of warm, moist stratification followed by cold stratification and will germinate after being shifted back to warm, for example, 70°–40°–70° F. **G**: seed will not germinate in presence of chemical inhibitors. **H**: seed requires light to germinate. **I**: seed requires scarification because of an impermeable seed coat. *****: seed is hydrophilic, intolerant of dry storage (see Hydrophilic Seeds, p. 265). Moss Germination: seed germinates best in the presence of both light and high atmospheric moisture, as would be found on a damp, mossy substrate in the wild.

bush blueberry are produced mostly from early-summer softwood cuttings taken from nonfruiting sucker shoots. Treat them with high levels of hormone (6,000 to 8,000 ppm IBA) and place under mist. Leaf drop and stem rot are problems. As a rooting mix use 1:2 peat-perlite. Water carefully.

Viburnum   Viburnum p. 252   **LATE SUMMER**   **D**

SEEDS: Seeds mature one to a berry late in the summer. Viburnums require a period of warm stratification before cold, which is difficult to accommodate if you have to wait until the seed is fully ripe and summer is on the wane. In this case, germination will take 2 years on average. What has worked well for me is to collect the seeds just as they begin to flush with color; they turn from green to pink or red usually in early August in Massachusetts. Put them in a bucket and run the prep blender through them to break the skins a bit, then let them ferment and soak for 1 to 2 weeks. Run the blender again to remove the now softened flesh, and sow the seeds immediately outdoors in a warm spot. The flattened seeds (rather like coffee beans) will often send out a root in fall, and cotyledons will emerge after winter stratification. I am not sure whether early collection of seed works because the seed coat is not fully hardened or because the embryo needs less after-ripening or has more time to mature before the onset of cold, but it has worked with species like *V. lantanoides,* which have proved stubborn otherwise. In spring, pot seedlings into liners and step up again the following year. Hobblebush is a slow grower, needing cool shade and time, but the others come on very quickly after the first year.

CUTTINGS/DIVISIONS: With the exception of *V. lantanoides,* all the viburnums are pretty easy to root. Use nonflowering sucker growths; these often have long internodes, but as long as there is one node below the rooting mix and one above, the cutting should root and grow well. Treat with 1,000 to 2,000 ppm IBA talc or 2,000 to 3,000 ppm KIBA quick dip. Cuttings taken in early summer should continue to grow, so these can be potted into large containers or liner pots.

Vitis   Grape p. 255   **LATE SUMMER TO EARLY FALL**   **B, G**

SEEDS: Just about everyone has cleaned grape seeds, and it is certainly one of the most enjoyable crops to process. Pop a few grapes in your mouth, spit out the seeds into a towel, and they are ready to sow. You can use a blender or fermentation if you don't like grapes. Seedlings grow quickly after winter stratification; pot them up singly and give them a bamboo stake to climb.

CUTTINGS/DIVISIONS: Selected cultivars are propagated by cuttings. Three-node summer cuttings treated with 1,000 ppm IBA will root easily. Trim the leaves in half to make the cuttings less unwieldy.

Wisteria   Wisteria p. 257   **LATE SUMMER TO FALL**   **A, I**

SEEDS: The hard, flattened seeds mature in a two-sided pod that splits open like a peapod, then each half corkscrews so that the dried pod looks like the antlers of some African ungulate. As pods begin to yellow, allow them to dry and extract the seeds. Like the Asian species, this is slow to bloom from seed, and with only one cultivar, seed production is spotty. I prefer to root it from cuttings.

CUTTINGS/DIVISIONS: Collect cuttings from vigorous new growth, but discard the soft tip section with its undeveloped leaves. Cut tings taken in summer and treated with 1,000 ppm IBA talc root very well. I lose many over the winter if I try to pot them up, so I recommend leaving the cuttings in the rooting tray and fertilizing them a few times to flush new growth. Let them overwinter in a protected frame or cold greenhouse and pot on the following spring. The potted vines are difficult to keep contained, so I let them grow at will during the summer and untangle and cut them back after leaf drop in late fall.

Xanthorhiza   Yellowroot p. 258   **LATE SUMMER TO EARLY FALL**   **B, H***

SEEDS: The seeds ripen in small, papery comma-shaped pods or capsules set in clusters of 1 to 5 on thin peduncles. These will turn from green to gold to brown when ripe, and should be picked when the gold is just beginning to turn brown. Dry the capsules indoors. Separate the small football-shaped seeds from the dry, open capsules with a sieve. Surface-sow them, cover with sand, and leave the flats out in the cold frames for the winter. Transfer seedlings to plugs when large enough to handle, in early summer, then move them to liners to overwinter. Pot them on or plant them out the following spring.

CUTTINGS/DIVISIONS: The traditional method is to take root cuttings (with a stem attached) before growth begins in late winter, though seed yields a fuller, better-looking container plant in my opinion.

Zenobia   Dusty zenobia p. 259   **FALL**   **A, H (moss)**

SEEDS: Collect the pods as they brown and shake out the rusty seed. Sow and handle as for *Rhododendron.* Seed from blue-leaved plants will come partially true.

CUTTINGS/DIVISIONS: Cuttings are very difficult, which makes production of good, blue selections a problem. I have rooted a few late-summer tip cuttings taken from vigorous suckers. They are touchy when placed under mist. It is much easier to collect seed from an isolated blue individual (plants will self-pollinate) and segregate the bluer seedlings once they are a few inches tall.

A: seed will germinate within 4 weeks if sown at 70° F. **B**: seed will germinate upon being shifted to 70° F after 90–140 days of moist, cold stratification at 40° F. **C**: seed germinates only after multiple cycles of warm and cold, typically 40°–70°–40°–70° F. **D**: seed needs a period of warm, moist stratification followed by cold stratification and will germinate after being shifted back to warm, for example, 70°–40°–70° F. **G**: seed will not germinate in presence of chemical inhibitors. **H**: seed requires light to germinate. **I**: seed requires scarification because of an impermeable seed coat. *****: seed is hydrophilic, intolerant of dry storage (see Hydrophilic Seeds, p. 265). Moss Germination: seed germinates best in the presence of both light and high atmospheric moisture, as would be found on a damp, mossy substrate in the wild.

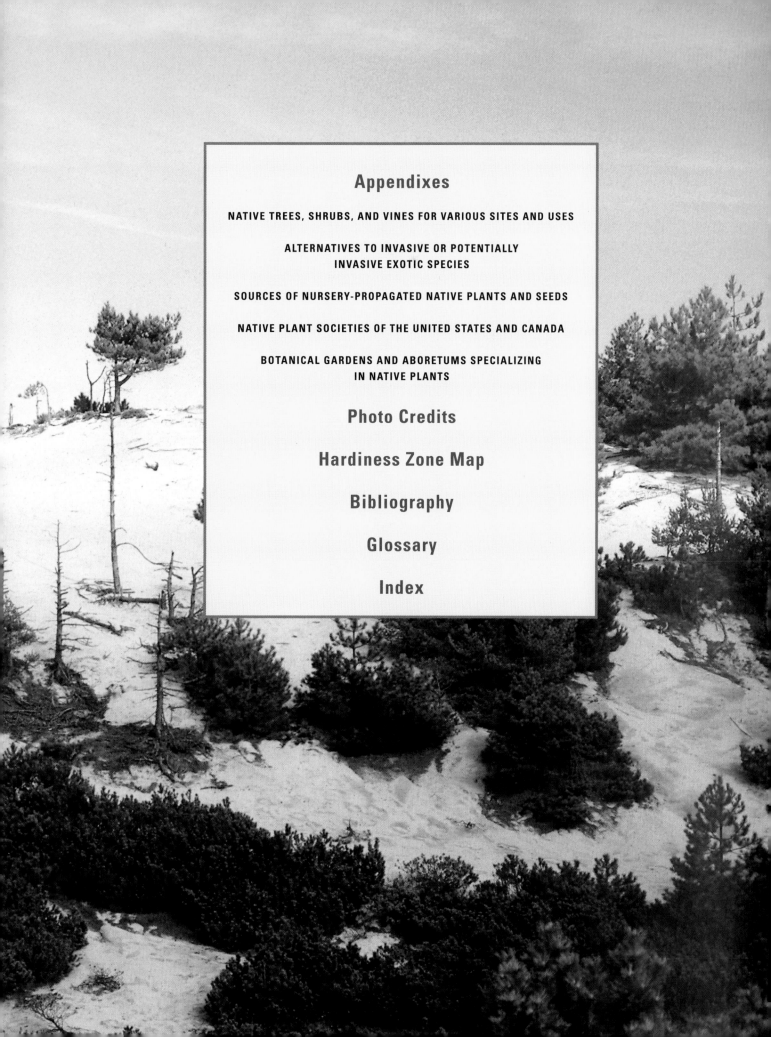

NATIVE TREES, SHRUBS, AND VINES FOR VARIOUS SITES AND USES

Plants for Dry, Sunny Locations

TREES

Acer negundo (box elder)
Amelanchier arborea (downy serviceberry)
A. laevis (Allegheny serviceberry)
Arbutus spp. (madrone)
Betula populifolia (gray birch)
Carya glabra (pignut hickory)
C. pallida (sand hickory)
C. texana (black hickory)
C. tomentosa (mockernut hickory)
Celtis spp. (hackberry)
Crataegus spp. (hawthorn)
Cupressus spp. (cypress)
Diospyros spp. (persimmon)
Gleditsia triacanthos (honeylocust)
Gymnocladus dioicus (Kentucky coffeetree)
Liquidambar styraciflua (sweetgum)
Maclura pomifera (Osage orange)
Pinus banksiana (jack pine)
P. contorta (lodgepole pine)
P. edulus (pinyon pine)
P. monophylla (singleleaf pinyon)
P. rigida (pitch pine)
Populus tremuloides (quaking aspen)
Prunus pensylvanica (pin cherry)
Quercus alba (white oak)
Q. coccinea (scarlet oak)
Q. falcata (southern red oak)
Q. garryana (Oregon white oak)
Q. margaretta (sand post oak)
Q. marilandica (blackjack oak)
Q. montana (*prinus*) (chestnut oak)
Q. stellata (post oak)
Sassafras albidum (sassafras)
× *Cupressocyparis leylandii* (Leyland cypress)

SHRUBS AND VINES

Aesculus californica (California buckeye)
A. parviflora (bottlebrush buckeye)
A. pavia (red buckeye)
Amelanchier alnifolia (saskatoon, western service-berry)
A. nantucketensis (Nantucket serviceberry)
A. pumila (dwarf serviceberry)
A. stolonifera (running serviceberry)
Arctostaphylos spp. (manzanita, bearberry)
Aronia arbutifolia (red chokeberry)
Artemisia spp. (sagebrush)
Carpentaria californica (carpentaria)
Ceanothus spp. (New Jersey tea, California lilac)
Cercis occidentalis (western redbud)
Cercocarpus spp. (mountain mahogany)
Chilopsis linearis (desert willow)
Chrysothamnus spp. (rabbitbrush)
Corema conradii (broom crowberry)
Cornus racemosa (gray dogwood)
Diervilla spp. (bush-honeysuckle)
Elaeagnus commutatus (silverberry)
Ephedra spp. (jointfir)
Fallugia paradoxa (Apache plume)
Fremontodendron californicum (flannelbush)
Gaylussacia spp. (huckleberry)
Hudsonia spp. (false heather)
Hypericum prolificum (shrubby St. John's wort)
Ilex glabra (inkberry holly, gallberry)
I. vomitoria (yaupon)
Itea virginiana (sweetspire)
Juniperus spp. (juniper)
Kalmia angustifolia (sheep laurel)
Lonicera caerulea (waterberry)
L. canadensis (fly-honeysuckle)

Red alder (Alnus rubra).

Plants for Wet, Sunny Locations

TREES

Acer rubrum (red maple)
Carya aquatica (water hickory)
Chamaecyparis thyoides (Atlantic white cedar)
Fraxinus nigra (black ash)
F. pensylvanica (green ash)
Larix laricina (tamarack)
Magnolia grandiflora (southern magnolia)
M. virginiana (sweetbay magnolia)
Nyssa spp. (tupelo)
Picea mariana (black spruce)
Pinus elliottii (slash pine)
P. palustris (longleaf pine)
Platanus spp. (sycamore)
Quercus bicolor (swamp white oak)
Q. palustris (pin oak)
Taxodium distichum (baldcypress)
Thuja occidentalis (northern white cedar, arborvitae)

SMALL TREES

Carpinus caroliniana (American hornbeam)
Fothergilla major (large fothergilla)

SHRUBS

Alnus spp. (alder)
Andromeda polifolia (bog rosemary)
Aronia arbutifolia (red chokeberry)
Betula glandulosa (dwarf birch, swamp birch)
B. pumila (bog birch)
Cephalanthus occidentalis (buttonbush)
Chamaedaphne calyculata (leatherleaf)
Clethra alnifolia (summersweet)
Cornus amomum (silky dogwood)
C. sericea (*stolonifera*) (red osier dogwood)
C. stricta (southern swamp dogwood)
Cyrilla racemiflora (titi)
Hamamelis virginiana (common witch-hazel)
Ilex coriacea (sweet gallberry)
I. decidua (possum-haw)
I. glabra (inkberry holly, gallberry)
I. laevigata (smooth winterberry)
I. verticillata (winterberry)
Itea virginiana (sweetspire)
Kalmia cuneata (white wicky)
K. hirsuta (hairy wicky)
K. polifolia (bog laurel)
Ledum groenlandicum (Labrador tea)
Lindera benzoin (spicebush)
Litsea aestivalis (pond spice)
Myrica gale (sweet gale)
M. heterophylla (swamp candleberry)
M. pensylvanica (northern bayberry)
Nemopanthus mucronatus (mountain holly)
Pinckneya bracteata (fever tree)
Potentilla fruticosa (shrubby cinquefoil)

L. utahensis (Utah honeysuckle)
Myrica spp. (except *M. gale*) (bayberry)
Paxistima spp. (cliff green)
Physocarpus spp. (ninebark)
Pinus aristata (Rocky Mountain bristlecone pine)
Potentilla fruticosa (shrubby cinquefoil)
Prunus americana (wild plum)
P. andersonii (desert peach)
P. angustifolia (chickasaw plum)
P. caroliniana (cherry laurel)
P. maritima (beach plum)
P. mexicana (bigtree plum)
P. monsoniana (wildgoose plum)
Quercus ilicifolia (bear oak)
Q. minima (dwarf live oak)
Q. prinoides (dwarf chinkapin oak)
Rhododendron vaseyi (pinkshell azalea)
Rhus spp. (sumac)
Ribes aureum (golden currant)
R. odoratum (buffalo currant)
Rosa acicularis (prickly wild rose)
R. arkansana (Arkansas rose)
R. carolina (Carolina rose)
R. virginiana (Virginia rose)
R. woodsii (desert wild rose)
Spiraea alba (meadowsweet)
S. betulifolia (birchleaf spirea)
Symphoricarpos orbiculatus (coralberry)
Vaccinium crassifolium (creeping blueberry)
Viburnum prunifolium (black haw)
Xanthorhiza simplicissima (yellowroot)

VINES

Gelsemium sempervirens (Carolina jessamine)
Parthenocissus quinquefolia (Virginia creeper)

Rhododendron arborescens (smooth azalea)
R. atlanticum (coast azalea)
R. canadense (rhodora)
R. serrulatum (hammock-sweet azalea)
R. viscosum (swamp azalea)
Rosa nitida (shining rose)
R. palustris (swamp rose)
Salix spp. (willow)
Sambucus canadensis (elderberry)
Vaccinium corymbosum (highbush blueberry)
V. elliottii (southern highbush blueberry)
V. macrocarpon (cranberry)
V. uliginosum (bog bilberry)
V. virgatum (rabbiteye blueberry)
Viburnum dentatum (arrowwood)
V. lentago (nannyberry)
V. nudum var. *cassinoides* (witherod)
V. opulus var. *americanum* (American cranberry bush)
Zenobia pulverulenta (dusty zenobia)

Plants for Dry, Shady Areas

TREES

Acer negundo (box elder)
A. rubrum (red maple)
Betula lenta (black birch)
Halesia tetraptera (Carolina silverbell)
Ostrya virginiana (hop hornbeam)
Tsuga canadensis (Canada hemlock)
T. caroliniana (Carolina hemlock)

SMALL TREES

Amelanchier arborea (downy serviceberry)
A. laevis (Allegheny serviceberry)
Cotinus obovatus (American smoketree)
Ilex opaca (American holly)
Oxydendrum arboreum (sourwood)

SHRUBS

Corylus americana (American hazelnut)
C. cornuta (beaked hazelnut)
Croton alabamensis (Alabama croton)
Gaultheria shallon (salal)
Gaylussacia baccata (black huckleberry)
Hydrangea arborescens (wild hydrangea)
Illicium floridanum (anise)
Kalmia angustifolia (sheep laurel)
K. latifolia (mountain laurel)
Leucothoe axillaris (coast leucothoe)
L. fontanesiana (dog-hobble)
Mahonia repens (creeping mahonia)
Myrica heterophylla (swamp candleberry)
M. pensylvanica (northern bayberry)
Rhododendron maximum (rosebay)
R. minus var. *carolinianum* (Carolina rhododendron)
Symphoricarpos albus var. *albus* (common snowberry)

S. occidentalis (western snowberry)
Vaccinium angustifolium (lowbush blueberry)
V. crassifolium (creeping blueberry)
V. pallidum (hillside blueberry)
Viburnum acerifolium (mapleleaf viburnum)
V. dentatum (arrowwood)
V. nudum var. *cassinoides* (witherod)
Xanthorhiza simplicissima (yellowroot)

VINES

Decumaria barbara (wood vamp, climbing hydrangea)
Parthenocissus quinquefolia (Virginia creeper)

Plants for Hedging and Screening

TREES

Abies spp. (fir)
Arbutus spp. (madrone)
Chamaecyparis lawsoniana (Port Orford cedar)
Cupressus spp. (cypress)
Fagus grandifolia (American beech)
Gordonia lasianthus (loblolly bay)
Liquidambar styraciflua (sweetgum)
Magnolia grandiflora (southern magnolia)
M. virginiana (sweetbay magnolia)
Picea spp. (spruce)
Pinus spp. (most pines)
Thuja spp. (white cedar, red cedar)
Tsuga spp. (hemlock)
× *Cupressocyparis leylandii* (Leyland cypress)

SMALL TREES

Amelanchier canadensis (Canada serviceberry, shadbush)
Cercocarpus ledifolius (curl-leaf mountain mahogany)
Crataegus spp. (hawthorn)
Ilex cassine (dahoon)
I. opaca (American holly)
Maclura pomifera (Osage orange)
Taxus brevifolia (Pacific yew)

SHRUBS

Acer glabrum (Rocky Mountain maple)
Amelanchier alnifolia (saskatoon, western serviceberry)
Arctostaphylos canescens (hoary manzanita)
A. manzanita (common manzanita)
A. patula (greenleaf manzanita)
Aronia arbutifolia (red chokeberry)
Artemisia tridentata (big sagebrush)
Ceanothus impressus (Santa Barbara ceanothus)
C. purpureus (hollyleaf ceanothus)
C. sanguineus (red-stem ceanothus)
Cercocarpus intricatus (littleleaf mountain mahogany)
Chilopsis linearis (desert willow)
Clethra spp. (clethra)

Common witch-hazel (Hamamelis virginiana).

I. vomitoria (yaupon)
Illicium floridanum (anise)
Itea virginiana (sweetspire)
Juniperus communis (common juniper)
Kalmia latifolia (mountain laurel)
Leucothoe fontanesiana (dog-hobble)
Myrica spp. (bayberry)
Osmanthus americanus (wild olive, devilwood)
Prunus caroliniana (cherry laurel)
Rhododendron catawbiense (catawba rhododendron)
R. macrophyllum (coast rhododendron)
R. maximum (rosebay)
R. minus var. *carolinianum* (Carolina rhododendron)
Rhus coppalinum (winged sumac)
Salix candida (sage willow)
Spiraea alba var. *alba* (meadowsweet)
S. douglasii (Douglas spirea)
S. tomentosa (steeplebush)
Viburnum dentatum (arrowwood)
V. lentago (nannyberry)
V. nudum var. *cassinoides* (witherod)
V. opulus var. *americanum* (American cranberry bush)
V. prunifolium (black haw)

Ground Covers

SHRUBS

Arctostaphylos alpina (alpine bearberry)
A. nevadensis (pinemat)
A. uva-ursi (bearberry)
Cassiope spp. (mountain heather)
Ceanothus diversifolius (pinemat)
Corema conradii (broom crowberry)
Diervilla lonicera (dwarf bush-honeysuckle)
Dryas drummondii (yellow avens)
Empetrum nigrum (black crowberry)
Gaultheria shallon (salal)
Gaylussacia baccata (black huckleberry)
G. brachycera (box huckleberry)
G. dumosa (dwarf huckleberry)
Hudsonia ericoides (false heather)
H. tomentosa (beach heather)
Hypericum buckleyi (Blue Ridge St. John's wort)
H. suffruticosum (trailing St. John's wort)
Juniperus communis (common juniper)
J. horizontalis (creeping juniper)
Leiophyllum buxifolium (sand myrtle)
Mahonia nervosa (longleaf mahonia)
M. repens (creeping mahonia)
Paxistima spp. (cliff green)
Phyllodoce spp. (mountain heath)
Potentilla fruticosa (shrubby cinquefoil)
Prunus pumila (sand cherry)
Rosa arkansana (Arkansas rose)
Salix herbacea (snowbed willow)

Cornus racemosa (gray dogwood)
C. sericea (red osier dogwood)
Cyrilla racemiflora (titi)
Diervilla sessilifolia (southern bush-honeysuckle)
Fothergilla gardenii (dwarf fothergilla)
Hypericum densiflorum (dense St. John's wort)
H. frondosum (golden St. John's wort)
H. kalmianum (Kalm's St. John's wort)
Ilex coriacea (sweet gallberry)
I. glabra (inkberry holly, gallberry)

S. lanata (limestone willow)
S. uva-ursi (bearberry willow)
Spiraea betulifolia (birchleaf spirea)
S. splendens (mountain spirea)
Taxus canadensis (Canada yew)
Vaccinium angustifolium (lowbush blueberry)
V. crassifolium (creeping blueberry)
V. deliciosum (cascade blueberry)
V. macrocarpon (cranberry)
V. myrtilloides (velvetleaf blueberry)
V. tenellum (small black blueberry)
V. uliginosum (bog bilberry)
V. vitis-idaea var. *minus* (mountain cranberry, lingonberry)
Xanthorhiza simplicissima (yellowroot)

VINES

Bignonia capreolata (cross-vine)
Campsis radicans (trumpet vine)
Decumaria barbara (wood vamp, climbing hydrangea)
Gelsemium rankinii (swamp jessamine)
Parthenocissus quinquefolia (Virginia creeper)
Vitis labrusca (fox grape)

Evergreens

TREES

Abies spp. (fir)
Arbutus spp. (mandrone)
Calocedrus decurrens (California incense-cedar)
Chamaecyparis spp. (false cypress)
Chrysolepis spp. (golden chinkapin)
Cupressus spp. (cypress)
Gordonia lasianthus (loblolly bay)
Magnolia grandiflora (southern magnolia)
M. virginiana (sweetbay magnolia)
Picea spp. (spruce)
Pinus spp. (pine)
Pseudotsuga menziesii (Douglas fir)
Quercus agrifolia (coast live oak)
Q. chrysolepis (canyon live oak)
Q. geminata (sand live oak)
Q. virginiana (southern live oak)
Sequoia sempervirens (coast redwood)
Sequoiadendron giganteum (giant sequoia, big tree)
Thuja spp. (red cedar, white cedar)
Tsuga spp. (hemlock)
× *Cupressocyparis leylandii* (Leyland cypress)

SMALL TREES

Ilex cassine (dahoon)
I. opaca (American holly)
Juniperus spp. (juniper)
Taxus brevifolia (Pacific yew)
Torreya spp. (torreya)

SHRUBS

Agarista populifolia (Florida leucothoe)
Andromeda polifolia (bog rosemary)
Arctostaphylos spp. (manzanita, bearberry)
Carpentaria californica (carpentaria)
Cassiope spp. (mountain heather)
Ceanothus cuneatus (buckbrush ceanothus)
C. diversifolius (pinemat, trailing ceanothus)
C. gloriosus (Point Reyes creeper)
C. impressus (Santa Barbara ceanothus)
C. jepsonii (muskbrush)
C. prostratus (mahala mat)
C. purpureus (hollyleaf ceanothus)
C. velutinus (sticky laurel)
Cliftonia monophylla (buckwheat bush, black titi)
Corema conradii (broom crowberry)
Dryas spp. (avens)
Empetrum spp. (crowberry)
Ephedra spp. (jointfir)
Fremontodendron spp. (flannelbush)
Gaultheria shallon (salal)
Gaylussacia brachycera (box huckleberry)
Hypericum tetrapetalum (four-petaled St. John's wort)
Ilex coriacea (sweet gallberry)
I. glabra (inkberry holly, gallberry)
I. vomitoria (yaupon)
Illicium spp. (anise)
Kalmia spp. (laurel)
Leiophyllum buxifolium (sand myrtle)
Leucothoe axillaris (coast leucothoe)
L. davisae (Sierra laurel)
L. fontanesiana (dog-hobble)
Mahonia spp. (Oregon grape)
Myrica californica (California bayberry)
M. cerifera (waxmyrtle)
M. heterophylla (swamp candleberry)
M. inodora (odorless waxmyrtle)
Osmanthus americanus (wild olive, devilwood)
Paxistima spp. (cliff green)
Phyllodoce spp. (mountain heath)
Pieris spp. (fetterbush)
Prunus caroliniana (cherry laurel)
Rhododendron catawbiense (catawba rhododendron)
R. macrophyllum (coast rhododendron)
R. maximum (rosebay)
R. minus (Carolina rhododendron)
Ribes speciosum (fuchsia-flowered gooseberry)
Vaccinium crassifolium (creeping blueberry)
V. macrocarpon (cranberry)
V. oxycoccos (small cranberry)
V. parvifolium (red blueberry)
V. vitis-idaea var. *minus* (mountain cranberry, lingonberry)

VINES

Bignonia capreolata (cross-vine)
Gelsemium rankinii (swamp jessamine)

Plants with Interesting Bark

TREES
Acer pensylvanicum (striped maple, moosewood)
Amelanchier arborea (downy serviceberry)
Arbutus arizonica (Arizona madrone)
A. menziesii (Pacific madrone)
Betula allegheniensis (yellow birch)
B. cordifolia (heartleaf birch)
B. nigra (river birch)
B. papyrifera (paper birch)
Calocedrus decurrens (California incense-cedar)
Carya laciniosa (shellbark hickory)
C. ovata (shagbark hickory)
Celtis spp. (hackberry)
Chamaecyparis spp. (falsecypress)
Diospyros spp. (persimmon)
Fagus grandifolia (American beech)
Ostrya virginiana (hop hornbeam)
Pinus albicaulis (whitebark pine)
P. jeffreyi (Jeffrey pine)
P. ponderosa (ponderosa pine)
Platanus occidentalis (sycamore)
Populus tremuloides (quaking aspen)
Quercus alba (white oak)
Q. macrocarpa (bur oak)
Q. montana (chestnut oak)
Sassafras albidum (sassafras)
Sequoia sempervirens (coast redwood)
Sequoiadendron giganteum (giant sequoia, big tree)
Taxodium distichum (baldcypress)
Thuja plicata (western red cedar)
Tsuga mertensiana (mountain hemlock)
Ulmus alata (winged elm)

SMALL TREES
Amelanchier canadensis (Canada serviceberry, shadbush)
Carpinus caroliniana (American hornbeam)
Cercocarpus spp. (mountain mahogany)
Cornus florida (flowering dogwood)
Cotinus obovatus (American smoketree)
Diospyros texana (Texas persimmon)
Franklinia alatamaha (franklinia)
Juniperus deppeana (alligator juniper)
Prunus pensylvanica (pin cherry)

SHRUBS
Arctostaphylos spp. (manzanita, bearberry)
Clethra acuminata (cinnamon clethra)
Cornus sericea (red osier dogwood)
Hypericum frondosum (golden St. John's wort)
Vaccinium corymbosum (highbush blueberry)
V. elliottii (southern highbush blueberry)
V. virgatum (rabbiteye blueberry)

VINES
Aristolochia spp. (pipevine)
Campsis radicans (trumpet vine)
Vitis spp. (grape)

Plants with Outstanding Fall Color

TREES
Acer spp. (maple)
Betula spp. (birch)
Carya spp. (hickory)
Cladrastis kentukea (American yellowwood)
Fagus grandifolia (American beech)
Fraxinus spp. (ash)
Larix spp. (larch)
Liquidambar styraciflua (sweetgum)
Liriodendron tulipifera (tulip poplar)
Magnolia macrophylla (bigleaf magnolia)
Nyssa spp. (tupelo)
Ostrya virginiana (hop hornbeam)
Populus spp. (poplar)
Prunus serotina (black cherry)
Quercus spp. (oak)
Sassafras albidum (sassafras)
Taxodium distichum (baldcypress)

SMALL TREES
Acer circinatum (vine maple)
A. pensylvanicum (moosewood)
Carpinus caroliniana (American hornbeam)
Cornus alternifolia (pagoda dogwood)
C. florida (flowering dogwood)
C. nuttallii (western dogwood)
Cotinus obovatus (American smoketree)
Crataegus spp. (hawthorn)
Diospyros spp. (persimmon)
Fothergilla major (large fothergilla)
Franklinia alatamaha (franklinia)
Magnolia ashei (Ashe's big-leaf magnolia)
Oxydendrum arboreum (sourwood)
Prunus pensylvanica (pin cherry)
Sorbus spp. (mountain ash)

SHRUBS
Acer spp. (maple)
Amelanchier spp. (serviceberry)
Aronia spp. (chokeberry)
Dirca spp. (leatherwood)
Fallugia paradoxa (Apache plume)
Gaylussacia spp. (huckleberry)
Hamamelis spp. (witch-hazel)
Hydrangea quercifolia (oak-leaved hydrangea)
Itea virginiana (sweetspire)
Lindera benzoin (spicebush)
Prunus spp. (wild plum, cherry)
Rhododendron vaseyi (pinkshell azalea)
R. viscosum (swamp zzalea)
Rhus spp. (sumac)
Rosa virginiana (Virginia wild rose)
Toxicodendron spp. (poison ivy)

Vaccinium spp. (blueberry)
Viburnum spp. (viburnum)
Xanthorhiza simplicissima (yellowroot)

VINES
Parthenocissus quinquefolia (Virginia creeper)

Plants That Provide Food (Nuts or Berries) and Cover for Birds and Mammals

Abies spp. (fir)
Acer spp. (maple)
Aesculus spp. (buckeye)
Amelanchier spp. (serviceberry)
Aralia spinosa (devil's walking stick)
Arbutus spp. (madrone)
Arctostaphylos spp. (manzanita, bearberry)
Aronia spp. (chokeberry)
Asimina spp. (pawpaw)
Carpinus caroliniana (American hornbeam)
Carya spp. (hickory)
Castanea spp. (chestnut)
Celtis spp. (hackberry)
Chamaecyparis spp. (cedar, false cypress)
Chionanthus spp. (fringetree)
Chrysothamnus spp. (rabbitbrush)
Cornus spp. (dogwood)
Corylus spp. (hazelnut)
Crataegus spp. (hawthorn)
Cupressus spp. (cypress)
Diospyros spp. (persimmon)
Elaeagnus commutatus (silverberry)
Empetrum spp. (crowberry)
Fagus grandifolia (American beech)
Gaylussacia spp. (huckleberry)
Ilex spp. (holly)
Juglans spp. (walnut)
Juniperus spp. (juniper)
Larix spp. (larch, tamarack)
Lindera spp. (spicebush)
Lonicera spp. (honeysuckle)
Magnolia spp. (magnolia)
Mahonia spp. (mahonia, Oregon grape)
Myrica spp. (bayberry)
Nemopanthus mucronatus (mountain holly)
Nyssa spp. (tupelo)
Oplopanax horridus (devil's club)
Ostrya virginiana (hop hornbeam)
Parthenocissus spp. (Virginia creeper)
Picea spp. (spruce)
Pinus spp. (pine)
Prunus spp. (plum, cherry)
Pseudotsuga menziesii (Douglas fir)
Quercus spp. (oak)
Rhus spp. (sumac)
Ribes spp. (gooseberry, currant)
Rosa spp. (rose)
Rubus spp. (blackberry, raspberry)

Sambucus spp. (elderberry)
Sassafras albidum (sassafras)
Sorbus spp. (mountain ash)
Symphoricarpos spp. (coralberry, snowberry)
Taxus spp. (yew)
Thuja spp. (red cedar, white cedar)
Tilia americana (basswood)
Toxicodendron spp. (poison ivy, oak, sumac)
Tsuga spp. (hemlock)

Mountain laurel cultivars (Kalmia latifolia).

Vaccinium spp. (blueberry)
Viburnum spp. (viburnum)
Vitis spp. (grape)

Good Nectar Sources for Butterflies and Bees

TREES

Aesculus spp. (buckeye)
Arbutus spp. (madrone)
Castanea spp. (chestnut)
Gleditsia triacanthos (honeylocust)
Gordonia lasianthus (loblolly bay)
Gymnocladus dioicus (Kentucky coffeetree)
Halesia spp. (silverbell)
Nyssa spp. (tupelo)
Sassafras albidum (sassafras)
Ulmus spp. (elm)

SMALL TREES

Aesculus pavia (red buckeye)
Crataegus spp. (hawthorn)
Diospyros spp. (persimmon)
Halesia diptera (two-winged silverbell)
Malus spp. (crabapple)
Sorbus spp. (mountain ash)
Stewartia spp. (stewartia)

SHRUBS

Aesculus parviflora (bottlebrush buckeye)
Arctostaphylos spp. (bearberry)
Callicarpa americana (American beautyberry)
Carpentaria californica (carpentaria)
Ceanothus spp. (ceanothus)
Cephalanthus occidentalis (buttonbush)
Chilopsis linearis (desert willow)
Chrysothamnus spp. (rabbitbrush)
Clethra spp. (clethra)
Cliftonia monophylla (buckwheat bush, black titi)
Cornus spp. (dogwood)
Cyrilla spp. (titi)
Diervilla spp. (bush-honeysuckle)
Dryas spp. (mountain avens)
Elaeagnus commutatus (silverberry)
Elliottia racemosa (Georgia plume)
Fothergilla spp. (fothergilla)
Fremontodendron californicum (flannelbush)
Gaultheria shallon (salal)
Hamamelis spp. (witch-hazel)
Hudsonia spp. (beach heather)
Hydrangea spp. (wild hydrangea)
Hypericum spp. (St. John's wort)
Ilex spp. (holly)
Itea virginiana (sweetspire)
Kalmia spp. (laurel)
Ledum spp. (Labrador tea)
Leiophyllum buxifolium (sand myrtle)
Leucothoe spp. (leucothoe)

Lindera benzoin (spicebush)
Lonicera spp. (honeysuckle)
Mahonia spp. (mahonia)
Nemopanthus mucronatus (mountain holly)
Oplopanax horridus (devil's club)
Osmanthus americanus (wild olive, devilwood)
Philadelphus spp. (mock-orange)
Phyllodoce spp. (mountain heath)
Physocarpus spp. (ninebark)
Pieris spp. (andromeda)
Potentilla fruticosa (shrubby cinquefoil)
Prunus spp. (cherry, plum)
Rhododendron spp. (azalea)
Rhus spp. (sumac)
Rosa spp. (wild rose)
Rubus spp. (raspberry, blackberry)
Sambucus spp. (elderberry)
Spiraea spp. (spirea)
Styrax spp. (snowbell)
Symphoricarpos spp. (snowberry)
Vaccinium spp. (blueberry)
Viburnum spp. (viburnum)
Zenobia pulverulenta (dusty zenobia)

VINES

Bignonia capreolata (cross-vine)
Gelsemium sempervirens (Carolina jessamine)
Wisteria spp. (wisteria)

Important Larval Hosts for Butterfly and Moth Caterpillars

TREES

Betula spp. (birch)
Carya spp. (hickory)
Castanea spp. (chestnut)
Celtis spp. (hackberry)
Fagus grandifolia (American beech)
Fraxinus spp. (ash)
Juglans spp. (walnut)
Pinus spp. (pine)
Populus spp. (poplar)
Quercus spp. (oak)
Sassafras albidum (sassafras)
Ulmus spp. (elm)

SMALL TREES

Amelanchier spp. (serviceberry)
Asimina spp. (pawpaw)
Carpinus caroliniana (American hornbeam)
Crataegus spp. (hawthorn)
Juniperus spp. (juniper)
Malus spp. (crabapple)

SHRUBS

Amelanchier spp. (serviceberry)
Arctostaphylos spp. (manzanita, bearberry)
Asimina spp. (pawpaw)

Cassiope spp. (mountain heather)
Ceanothus spp. (ceanothus)
Cercocarpus spp. (mountain mahogany)
Chamaedaphne calyculata (leatherleaf)
Chrysothamnus spp. (rabbitbrush)
Lindera spp. (spicebush)
Myrica spp. (bayberry)
Potentilla fruticosa (shrubby cinquefoil)
Prunus spp. (cherry, plum)
Rhus spp. (sumac)
Ribes spp. (gooseberry, currant)
Salix spp. (willow)
Sambucus spp. (elderberry)
Vaccinium spp. (blueberry)
Viburnum spp. (viburnum)

VINES
Aristolochia spp. (pipevine)

Trees, Shrubs, and Vines Less Favored by Deer and Other Herbivores

TREES
Abies spp. (fir)
Acer spp. (maple)
Aesculus spp. (buckeye)
Betula spp. (birch)
Castanea spp. (chestnut)
Catalpa spp. (catalpa)
Chamaecyparis spp. (false cypress)
Fagus grandifolia (American beech)
Fraxinus spp. (ash)
Gleditsia triacanthos (honeylocust)
Gordonia lasianthus (loblolly bay)
Larix spp. (larch)
Liquidambar styraciflua (sweetgum)
Liriodendron tulipifera (tulip poplar)
Magnolia spp. (magnolia)
Ostrya virginiana (hop hornbeam)
Picea spp. (spruce)
Pinus spp. (pine)
Platanus spp. (sycamore)
Pseudotsuga menziesii (Douglas fir)
Quercus spp. (oak)
Taxodium distichum (bald cypress)
Tsuga spp. (hemlock)
× *Cupressocyparis leylandii* (Leyland cypress)

SMALL TREES
Cercis canadensis (eastern redbud)
Cornus alternifolia (pagoda dogwood)
Cornus florida (flowering dogwood)
Cotinus obovatus (American smoketree)
Crataegus spp. (hawthorn)
Magnolia spp. (magnolia)
Oxydendrum arboreum (sourwood)
Salix spp. (coyote willow)

SHRUBS
Arctostaphylos spp. (manzanita, bearberry)
Artemisia spp. (sagebrush)
Calycanthus floridus (Carolina allspice)
Ceanothus spp. (ceanothus)
Corema conradii (broom crowberry)
Elaeagnus commutatus (silverberry)
Gaultheria shallon (salal)
Hamamelis spp. (witch-hazel)
Ilex glabra (inkberry holly)
I. vomitoria (yaupon)
Illicium spp. (anise)
Juniperus spp. (juniper)
Leucothoe spp. (leucothoe)
Lindera benzoin (spicebush)
Mahonia spp. (mahonia)
Myrica spp. (bayberry)
Paxistima spp. (cliff green)
Pieris floribunda (fetterbush)
Potentilla fruticosa (shrubby cinquefoil)
Prunus spp. (cherry, plum)
Rhus spp. (sumac)
Spiraea spp. (spirea)
Symphoricarpos spp. (snowberry)
Vaccinium spp. (blueberry)
Viburnum spp. (viburnum)

VINES
Lonicera spp. (honeysuckle)
Parthenocissus quinquefolia (Virginia creeper)
Vitis spp. (grape)
Wisteria spp. (wisteria)

ALTERNATIVES TO INVASIVE OR POTENTIALLY INVASIVE EXOTIC SPECIES

In the last 300 years, North America has seen a tremendous influx of nonnative plant species as a result of human activities. For example, of the 2,814 species of plants growing wild in Massachusetts, fully 45 percent (1,276 species) have been introduced, either on purpose or by accident, from other parts of the globe (Sorrie and Somers, *The Vascular Plants of Massachusetts: A County Checklist*, p. xiii). Many of these plants are agricultural weeds that began arriving in shipments of grain or ships' ballast soon after European colonists came here in the early 1600s. Others were introduced by horticulturists or the federal government for use in gardens or for soil stabilization, reforestation, and the like.

It is impossible to know what effect this monumental immigration has had on native plants and animals continent-wide. Certainly, of the many thousands of plants introduced in the United States and Canada from abroad, only a small number (estimates range from 3 to 7 percent) are thought to pose a serious threat to native ecosystems. These problem few are quite a big problem, however. "Invasive exotics" have few if any natural predators to keep them in check, instead running rampant and displacing entire communities of native plants as well as the insects, fungi, birds, mammals, reptiles, and bacteria that depend on them. Be it kudzu in the South, eucalyptus in California, Brazilian pepper in Florida, Oriental bittersweet in the Northeast, or Himalayan blackberry in the Northwest, invasive species have the potential to completely alter habitats, disrupt natural cycles of disturbance and succession, and, most important, greatly decrease overall biodiversity, pushing rare species and then even less rare species to the brink of extinction. Invasive species may even represent the greatest future threat to native plant and animal species worldwide—greater even than human population growth, land development, climate change, and pollution.

It is high time that we horticulturists recognize our responsibility to cease the importation and introduction of new and potentially invasive exotic plants *and* to stop growing and planting known or suspected invasives — *regardless* of their ornamental value or consumer demand. I believe that we need to adopt the precautionary principle as far as plant introductions are concerned, and assume that a species and all of its cultivars are invasive until proven otherwise. We must discontinue the current approach of "innocent until proven destructive." At least let's not make this situation any worse.

Toward this end, I here provide a list of invasive or potentially invasive woody exotics, compiled on the basis of information from the Plant Conservation Alliance's Alien Plant Working Group, and suggest possible native alternatives. I have tried to find substitutes that offer similar ornamental features and adaptability, but lack invasive tendencies. Please bear in mind that the freedom from pests and diseases, and thus ease of culture, that makes some "grow-anywhere" exotic species so popular in the landscape industry is the same resiliency that allows them to escape and run rampant. Very few native plants are as problem-free as some of the worst invaders, and this is the very reason these native plants are not invasive. But be aware, too, that a few native species, such as black locust and some of the junipers and cypresses, have the potential to become moderately invasive if planted far outside their native range. So, instead of searching for a few foolproof species that will grow anywhere, we as gardeners and landscape professionals need to broaden our horizons quite a bit. We have an amazing native flora here, which can fill our gardens and wild lands with beauty, diversity, and life if we just take the time to notice and learn.

INVASIVE OR POTENTIALLY INVASIVE EXOTIC	POSSIBLE NATIVE SUBSTITUTES
Acer platanoides (Norway maple), *A. pseudoplatanus* (Sycamore maple)	*Acer leucoderme* (chalk maple) *A. macrophyllum* (bigleaf maple) *A. rubrum* (red maple) *Aesculus flava* (yellow buckeye) *Betula allegh'eniensis* (yellow birch) *B. nigra* (river birch) *Celtis laevigata* (sugarberry) *Cladrastis kentukea* (yellowwood) *Fagus grandifolia* (American beech) *Fraxinus pensylvanica* (green ash) *Gymnocladus dioicus* (Kentucky coffeetree) *Liquidambar styraciflua* (sweetgum) *Liriodendron tulipifera* (tulip poplar) *Quercus bicolor* (swamp white oak) *Q. palustris* (pin oak)
Ailanthus altissima (tree of heaven)	*Acer negundo* (box elder) *Amelanchier arborea* (downy serviceberry) *A. laevis* (Allegheny serviceberry) *Aralia spinosa* (Hercules club) *Carya illinoiensis* (pecan) *Diospyros virginiana* (persimmon) *Gymnocladus dioicus* (Kentucky coffeetree) *Juglans nigra* (black walnut) *J. microcarpa* (little walnut) *Maclura pomifera* (Osage orange) *Ostrya virginiana* (hop hornbeam) *Rhus typhina* (staghorn sumac) *Sassafras albidum* (sassafras)
Akebia quinata (akebia)	*Bignonia capreolata* (cross-vine) *Gelsemium* spp. (jessamine) *Wisteria frutescens* (American wisteria)
Albizia julibrissin (silktree)	*Cercis canadensis* vars. (redbud) *Gleditsia triacanthos* (honeylocust) *Gymnocladus dioicus* (Kentucky coffeetree)
Alnus glutinosa (European alder)	*Alnus incana* (speckled alder) *A. serrulata* (smooth alder) *Fothergilla major* (large fothergilla)
Ampelopsis brevipedunculata (porcelainberry)	*Aristolochia tomentosa* (pipevine) *Gelsemium sempervirens* (Carolina jessamine) *Lonicera sempervirens* (trumpet honeysuckle) *Parthenocissus quinquefolia* (Virginia creeper)
Berberis thunbergii (Japanese barberry), *B. vulgaris* (European barberry)	*Callicarpa americana* (beautyberry) *Cercocarpus* spp. (mountain mahogany) *Elaeagnus commutatus* (silverberry) *Itea virginica* (sweetspire) *Myrica* spp. (bayberry) *Rhododendron vaseyi* (roseshell azalea) *Symphoricarpos orbiculatus* (coralberry) *S. × chenaultii* (Chenault snowberry)

INVASIVE OR POTENTIALLY INVASIVE EXOTICS	POSSIBLE NATIVE SUBSTITUTES
	Vaccinium angustifolium (lowbush blueberry)
	V. myrtilloides (velvetleaf blueberry)
Betula pendula (European white birch)	*Betula nigra* (river birch)
	B. papyrifera (paper birch)
Buddleia davidii (butterfly bush),	*Aesculus parviflora* (bottlebrush buckeye)
B. alternifolia (alternate-leaved butterfly bush)	*Callicarpa americana* (American beautyberry)
	Ceanothus spp. (California lilac)
	Clethra alnifolia (summersweet)
	Cyrilla racemiflora (titi)
	Diervilla spp. (bush-honeysuckle)
	Hydrangea arborescens (wild hydrangea)
	Hypericum spp. (St. John's wort)
	Itea virginiana (sweetspire)
	Oxydendrum arboreum (sourwood)
	Rhododendron spp. (azalea)
	Sambucus spp. (elderberry)
	Spiraea spp. (meadowsweet)
	Symphoricarpos spp. (snowberry)
	Viburnum spp. (viburnum)
Celastrus orbiculatus (Oriental bittersweet)	*Celastrus scandens* (American bittersweet)
	Parthenocissus quinquefolia (Virginia creeper)
Crataegus monogyna (English hawthorn)	*Crataegus phaenopyrum* (Washington hawthorn)
	C. viridis (green hawthorn)
Cytisus scoparius (Scotch broom)	*Ceanothus* spp. (California lilac)
	Ephedra spp. (Mormon tea)
	Myrica spp. (bayberry)
	Prunus maritima (beach plum)
Elaeagnus angustifolia (Russian olive),	*Ceanothus* spp. (ceanothus)
E. pungens (thorny elaeagnus),	*Cercocarpus* spp. (mountain mahogany)
E. umbellata (autumn olive)	*Chionanthus virginicus* (fringetree)
	Elaeagnus commutatus (silverberry)
	Myrica spp. (bayberry)
	Osmanthus americanus (wild olive)
	Prunus americana (wild plum)
	P. maritima (beach plum)
	P. monsoniana (wildgoose plum)
	Quercus ilicifolia (scrub oak)
	Shepherdia canadensis and *argentea* (silverberry)
	Styrax americanus (American snowbell)
	Styrax platanifolius (sycamore-leaf snowbell)
	Viburnum prunifolium (possum haw)
Eucalyptus globulus (Tasmanian blue gum)	*Arbutus menziesii* (Pacific madrone)
	Calocedrus decurrens (incense cedar)
	Quercus lobata (valley oak)
	Sequoiadendron giganteum (giant sequoia)
Euonymus alatus (burning bush)	*Amelanchier bartramii* (mountain serviceberry)
	Aronia spp. (chokeberry)
	Clethra alnifolia (summersweet)
	Cornus spp. (dogwood)

	Cotinus obovatus (American smoketree) *Itea virginica* (sweetspire) *Ilex glabra* (inkberry holly) *I. vomitoria* (yaupon) *Lindera benzoin* (spicebush) *Vaccinium corymbosum* (highbush blueberry) *V. elliottii* (southern highbush blueberry) *Viburnum nudum* (witherod) *V. prunifolium* (possum haw)
Euonymus fortunei (wintercreeper)	See suggestions under *Hedera helix*
Frangula alnus (*Rhamnus frangula*) (glossy buckthorn), *Rhamnus cathartica* (common buckthorn)	*Amelanchier canadensis* (shadbush) *Aronia* spp. (chokeberry) *Crateagus* spp. (hawthorn) *Cornus spp.* (dogwood) *Hamamelis* spp. (witch-hazel) *Ilex* spp. (holly) *Lindera benzoin* (spicebush) *Maclura pomifera* (Osage orange) *Nemopanthus mucronatus* (mountain holly) *Vaccinium corymbosum* (highbush blueberry) *Viburnum dentatum* (arrowwood) *V. lentago* (nannyberry) *V. nudum* (witherod)
Hedera helix (English ivy)	*Arctostaphylos uva-ursi* (bearberry) *A. nevadensis* (pinemat) *Decumaria barbara* (wood vamp) *Gaultheria shallon* (salal) *Gelsemium sempervirens* (Carolina jessamine) *Leucothoe axillaris* (coast leucothoe) *L. davisae* (Sierra laurel) *Mahonia nervosa* (longleaf mahonia) *M. repens* (creeping mahonia) *Parthenocissus quinquefolia* (Virginia creeper) *Paxistima* spp. (cliff green) *Vaccinium crassifolium* (creeping blueberry) *Xanthorhiza simplicissima* (yellowroot)
Ilex aquifolium (English holly)	*Arbutus menziesii* (Pacific madrone) *Ilex cassine* (dahoon) *I. opaca* (American holly)
Ligustrum spp. (privet)	*Agarista populifolia* (Florida leucothoe) *Ilex cassine* (dahoon) *I. glabra* (inkberry holly) *I. vomitoria* (yaupon) *Illicium floridanum* (anise) *Myrica* spp. (bayberry) *Osmanthus americanus* (wild olive) *Prunus caroliniana* (cherry laurel) *Rhododendron minus* vars. (Carolina rhododendron)
Lonicera japonica (Japanese honeysuckle)	*Lonicera ciliosa* (orange honeysuckle) *L. dioica* (limber honeysuckle)

INVASIVE OR POTENTIALLY INVASIVE EXOTICS	POSSIBLE NATIVE SUBSTITUTES
	L. flava (yellow honeysuckle)
	L. sempervirens (trumpet honeysuckle)
Lonicera maackii (Amur honeysuckle),	*Aesculus parvifolia* (bottlebrush buckeye)
L. morrowii (Morrow's honeysuckle),	*A. sylvatica* (painted buckeye)
L. tatarica (Tatarian honeysuckle),	*Amelanchier* spp. (serviceberry)
L. × bella (*morrowii × tatarica*) (hybrid honeysuckle)	*Diervilla sessilifolia* (southern bush honeysuckle)
	Dirca palustris (leatherwood)
	Ilex glabra (inkberry holly)
	I. vomitoria (yaupon)
	Lonicera involucrata (twinberry)
	Nemopanthus mucronatus (mountain holly)
	Viburnum spp. (viburnum)
Paulownia tomentosa (empress tree)	*Asimina triloba* (pawpaw)
	Catalpa spp. (catalpa)
	Chionanthus virginicus (fringetree)
	Magnolia acuminata (cucumbertree magnolia)
	M. macrophylla (bigleaf magnolia)
Populus alba (white poplar)	*Populus tremuloides* (quaking aspen)
Rosa multiflora (multiflora rose)	*Rosa setigera* (climbing prairie rose)
Rosa rugosa (rugosa rose)	*Rosa carolina* (Carolina rose)
	R. virginiana (Virginia rose)
	R. acicularis (prickly wild rose)
Rubus discolor (Himalayan blackberry),	*Rubus allegheniensis* (Allegheny blackberry)
R. phoenicolasius (wineberry)	*R. odoratus* (flowering raspberry)
	R. occidentalis (blackcap raspberry)
	R. parviflorus (thimbleberry)
	R. spectabilis (salmonberry)
Spiraea japonica (Japanese spirea)	*Ceanothus americanus* (New Jersey tea)
	Leiophyllum buxifolium (sand myrtle)
	Spiraea douglasii (Douglas spirea)
	S. splendens (mountain spirea)
	S. tomentosa (steeplebush)
	Vaccinium uliginosum (bog bilberry)
Tamarix spp. (tamarisk)	*Chilopsis linearis* (desert willow)
	Fallugia paradoxa (Apache plume)
Ulex europaeus (gorse)	*Ceanothus* spp. (California lilac)
	Philadelphus lewisii (western mock-orange)
	Vaccinium parvifolium (red blueberry)
Ulmus pumila (Siberian elm)	*Ulmus alata* (winged elm)
	U. thomasii (rock elm)
Wisteria floribunda (Japanese wisteria),	*Campsis radicans* (trumpet creeper)
W. sinensis (Chinese wisteria)	*Wisteria frutescens* (American wisteria)
	W. macrostachya (Kentucky wisteria)

SOURCES OF NURSERY-PROPAGATED
NATIVE PLANTS AND SEEDS

Not all of the plants covered in this book are readily available, but there is a growing network of specialty mail-order nurseries, and you can find almost anything with a little searching. The power of the Internet is bound to improve access both to information and plants in the coming years.

The following list of nurseries was compiled by staff and volunteers of the New England Wildflower Society with additional information from the Lady Bird Johnson Wildflower Center in Texas. This list emphasizes sources for nursery-propagated native plants, and much of the information is based on responses to a written questionnaire. It is by no means complete but does offer a wide cross-section of firms whose inventory is at least 25 percent native North American plants. We have listed only nurseries claiming that they do not sell wild-collected plants and that they do wild-harvest

seed responsibly or buy from reputable collectors. However, we cannot guarantee the truth of those claims or the accuracy of information reported by suppliers. The catalogue prices are those for 2001 and are subject to change. Please note that some of the nurseries are wholesale only; we include them as a service to those in the trade.

Several good source listings are available, including *Gardening by Mail*, by Barbara Barton (Houghton Mifflin, 1997) and *The Anderson Horticultural Library's Source List of Plants and Seeds* (Minnesota Landscape Arboretum, 3675 Arboretum Dr., Box 39, Chanhassen, MN 55317-0039). The Lady Bird Johnson Wildflower Center has compiled an extensive searchable source list called Native Plants Online, accessed through the Web site www.wildflower.org.

Allendan Seeds

1966 175th Ln.
Winterset, IA 50273
515-462-1241; fax 515-462-4084
RETAIL/WHOLESALE MAIL ORDER
SEEDS ONLY
98 percent native; specializes in native grasses and wildflowers, particularly Midwest ecotypes.

Alpine Hollow Tree Farm

P.O. Box 464
Sandy, OR 97055
503-669-5245
WHOLESALE/RETAIL/MAIL ORDER
PLANTS ONLY
75 percent native; trees and shrubs.

Arrowwood Nurseries, Inc.

870 W. Malaga Rd.
Williamstown, NJ 08094
856-697-6045
njplants@aol.com
WHOLESALE/MAIL ORDER
PLANTS AND SEEDS
100 percent native; 75 percent nursery-propagated, and 25 percent seeds from other nursery source. Specializes in grasses, sedges, rushes, and woody plants of the New Jersey coastal plain. Will contract-grow. Mail order for seeds only; may ship small plant orders. Catalogue free.

Bitterroot Restoration, Inc.

445 Quast Ln.
Corvallis, MT 59828
406-961-4991
sales@revegetation.com
www.revegetation.com
WHOLESALE/MAIL ORDER
PLANTS ONLY
100 percent native; 100 percent grown from wild-collected seed. Specializes in restoration and revegetation of large disturbed sites. Offers a range of services: consultation, native plants, project implementation. Catalogue free with minimum order.

Beauty Beyond Belief

3307 S. College Ave. Suite #104
Fort Collins, CO 80525
970-204-0596; fax 970-204-0821

WHOLESALE

SEEDS ONLY

80 percent native; shrubs, wildflowers, and native grasses. Catalogue free to licensed dealers.

Bluebird Nursery

P.O. Box 460
519 Bryan Street
Clarkson, NE 68629
1-800-356-9164; fax 1-402-892-3738
sales@bluebirdnursery.com

WHOLESALE/MAIL ORDER

PLANTS ONLY

Bluebird Nursery

8320 Freeman Rd.
Boonville, NY 13309

RETAIL/MAIL ORDER

PLANTS ONLY

75 percent native; specializes in eastern woodland species.

Bluestem Nursery

4101 Curry Rd.
Arlington, TX 76001
817-478-6202
grassman@bluestemnursery.com
www.bluestemnursery.com

WHOLESALE

PLANTS ONLY

95 percent native; 70 percent propagated from stock, 10 percent wild-collected seed, and 20 percent seed and liners from other nursery source. Specializes in plants for central South and native ornamental prairie grasses, sod- or container-grown. Minimum order required for sod-grown. Cost varies for custom CD with color pictures. Paper catalogue free.

Bluestem Prairie Nursery

13197 E. 13th Rd.
Hillsboro, IL 62049
217-532-6344
bluestemnursery@yahoo.com (e-mail for information only, no orders)

RETAIL/MAIL ORDER

PLANTS AND SEEDS

100 percent native; 100 percent propagated from stock. Special interest in tall-grass prairie restoration with an extensive selection of plant species native to the Illinois prairie. Custom-blended seed mixes. Catalogue free.

Bluestone Perennials, Inc.

7211 Middle Ridge Rd.
Madison, OH 44057
800-852-5243
bluestone@bluestoneperennials.com
www.bluestoneperennials.com

WHOLESALE/RETAIL/MAIL ORDER

PLANTS ONLY

50 percent native woody plants; 98 percent propagated from stock and 2 percent from other nursery sources. Specializes in perennials and ornamental shrubs. Container-grown plants. Free shipping for large orders. Catalogue free.

Bobtown Nursery

16212 Country Club Rd.
Melfa, VA 23410
757-787-8484; fax 757-787-8611
bobtown@visi.net

WHOLESALE/MAIL ORDER/PICK UP/TRUCKING

PLANTS ONLY

75 percent native; majority nursery-propagated. Specializes in native shrubs and wetlands plants. Offers liners, rooted cuttings, seedlings, bareroot transplants, balled and burlaped plants, and 1-to-10-gallon containers. Catalogue free.

Broken Arrow Nursery

13 Broken Arrow Rd.
Hamden, CT 06518
203-288-1026
brokenarrow@snet.net
www.brokenarrownursery.com

WHOLESALE/RETAIL/MAIL ORDER

PLANTS ONLY

30 percent native; 85 percent propagated from stock, and 15 percent from other nursery source. Specializes in *Kalmia* cultivars and many unusual ornamental shrub cultivars. Landscaping consultation provided. Catalogue $2.

Clyde Robin Seed Co., Inc.

P.O. Box 2366
Castro Valley, CA 94546
510-705-0425; fax 510-785-6463
sales@clyderobin.com
www.clyderobin.com

RETAIL/MAIL ORDER

SEEDS

70 percent native; trees, shrubs, and wildflowers. Catalogue free.

Colvos Creek Nursery

P.O. Box 1512
Vashon Island, WA 98070
206-749-9508
colvoscreek@juno.com

WHOLESALE/RETAIL/MAIL ORDER

PLANTS ONLY

40 percent native; 100 percent propagated from stock. Majority of plants are Northwest natives. Container grown and shipped with rootballs enclosed in plastic bags. Catalogue $3.

Comstock Seeds

8520 W. Fourth St.
Reno, NV 89523
775-746-3681; fax 775-746-1701
ed@comstockseed.com
www.comstockseed.com

RETAIL/MAIL ORDER

SEEDS

45 percent native; shrubs, wildflowers. Specializes in native collections and drought-tolerant species.

Cultured Natives

36170 County 14 Blvd.
Cannon Falls, MN 55009-5239

RETAIL/MAIL ORDER

PLANTS ONLY

100 percent native; 100 percent propagated from stock. Specializes in field-grown native Minnesota flora. Shipped dormant and bareroot. Catalogue free.

Desertland Nursery

11306 Gateway East
El Paso, TX 79927
915-858-1130; fax 915-858-1560
desertland@worldnet.att.net

WHOLESALE/RETAIL/MAIL ORDER

PLANTS AND SEEDS

50 percent native; trees, shrubs, cacti, and succulents. Catalogue $1.

Doyle Farm Nursery

158 Norris Rd.
Delta, PA 17314
717-862-3134

WHOLESALE/RETAIL/MAIL ORDER

PLANTS ONLY

80 percent native; 80 percent propagated from stock and 20 percent from other nursery sources. Specializes in native and unusual perennials and grasses. Plant list free.

Environmental Concern, Inc.

201 Boundry Ln.
P.O. Box P
St. Michaels, MD 21663
410-745-9620
info@wetland.org
www.wetland.org

WHOLESALE/MAIL ORDER

PLANTS AND SEEDS

99 percent native; grasses, wildflowers, trees, and shrubs, 85 percent grown from seed (wild-collected and from seed stock), 15 percent from cuttings or division. Specializes in wetland species. Catalogue free.

El Nativo Growers, Inc.

200 S. Peckhaw Rd. (mailing address only)
Azusa, CA 91702
626-969-8449; fax 626-969-7299
sales@elnativogrowers.com
www.elnativogrowers.com

WHOLESALE/RETAIL (IN FUTURE)/MAIL ORDER

PLANTS AND SEEDS

30 percent native; trees, shrubs, wildflowers, and grasses. California natives and other drought-tolerant plants.

Ernst Conservation Seeds

9006 Mercer Pike
Meadville, PA 16335
800-873-3321; fax 814-336-5191
ernstsales@ernstseed.com
www.ernstseed.com

WHOLESALE/MAIL ORDER

SEEDS ONLY

75 percent native; trees, shrubs, and wildflowers. Reclamation seed and mixes.

F. W. Schumacher Co., Inc

P.O. Box 1023
Sandwich, MA 02563
508-888-0659
treeseed@capecod.net
treeshrubseeds.com

WHOLESALE/RETAIL/MAIL ORDER

SEEDS ONLY

50 percent native; 80 to 90 percent wild-collected seed. Specializes in bulk sales of tree and shrub seeds for nurserymen and foresters. Catalogue free.

Fairweather Gardens

P.O. Box 330
Greenwich, NJ 08323
856-451-6261; fax 856-451-0303
www.fairweathergardens.com

RETAIL/MAIL ORDER

PLANTS ONLY

30 percent native; trees, shrubs, perennials. Catalogue $4. No shipments west of Rockies.

Flagstaff Native Plant and Seeds

400 E. Butler Ave.
Flagstaff, AZ 86001
928-773-9406; fax 928-773-0107
www.nativeplantandseed.com
nativeplants@flaglink.com

WHOLESALE/RETAIL/MAIL ORDER

PLANTS AND SEEDS

80 percent native; trees, shrubs, wildflowers. Catalogue $3.50.

Forest Farm

990 Tetherow Rd.
Williams, OR 97544-9599
541-846-7269
forestfarm@rvi.net
www.forestfarm.com

RETAIL/MAIL ORDER

PLANTS ONLY

30 percent native; 100 percent propagated from stock. Specializes in ornamental and useful plants from around the world. Extensive offerings. Catalogue $5.

Freshwater Farms

5851 Myrtle Ave.
Eureka, CA 95503
800-200-8969; fax 707-442-2490
info@freshwaterfarms.com
www.freshwaterfarms.com

WHOLESALE/RETAIL/MAIL ORDER

PLANTS AND SEEDS

95 percent native; trees, shrubs, and wildflowers. Medium-sized wetland and riparian plant material and redwood understory shrubs and forbs. Also performs site-specific seed collection for contract growing and restoration projects. Home of the North Coast Seed Bank. Catalogue free.

Gardens North

5984 3rd Line Rd. N.
North Gower, Ontario
Canada K0A 2T0
613-489-0065
garnorth@istar.ca
www.gardensnorth.com

WHOLESALE/RETAIL/MAIL ORDER

SEEDS ONLY

50 percent native; 100 percent propagated from stock. Specializes in production and sale of hardy perennial seed for northern gardens. Includes many woodland seeds. Organic growing methods. Catalogue $4.

Heritage Seedlings, Inc.

4199 75th Ave. SE
Salem, OR 97301
503-585-9835
sales@heritageseedlings.com
www.heritageseedlings.com

WHOLESALE/MAIL ORDER

PLANTS ONLY

35 to 40 percent native; 100 percent propagated from stock. Specializes in unusual deciduous trees and shrubs from seed of North American and European/Asiatic origin. Greenhouse- and field-grown. Catalogue free.

Heronswood Nursery, Ltd.

7530 NE 288th St.
Kingston, WI 98346
360-297-4172; fax 360-297-8321
www.heronswood.com

RETAIL/MAIL ORDER

PLANTS ONLY

25 percent native; 90 percent propagated from stock, 10 percent from other nursery source. Has a "no resale of wild-collected plants" policy. Extensive selection of rare and unusual native and exotic plants. Catalogue $5.

Inside Passage Seeds & Native Plant Services

P.O. Box 639
Port Townsend, WA 98368
800-361-9657; fax 360-385-5760
inspass@whidbey.net
www.insidepassageseeds.com

WHOLESALE (PRIMARILY)/RETAIL/MAIL ORDER

SEEDS ONLY

95 percent native; trees, shrubs, wildflowers. Specializing in seed of maritime Northwest species.

Ion Exchange

1878 Old Mission Dr.
Harpers Ferry, IA 52146-7533
800-291-2143; fax 563-535-7362
hbright@acegroup.cc
www.ionxchange.com

WHOLESALE/RETAIL/MAIL ORDER

PLANTS AND SEEDS

100 percent native; majority propagated from stock, some seed wild-collected. Specializes in native wildflowers and grasses for praires, woodlands, and wetlands. Offers consulting and contract growing services. Catalogue free.

Jane's Native Seeds

1860 Kays Branch Rd.
Ouenton, KY 40359
502-484-2044

WHOLESALE/RETAIL/MAIL ORDER

SEEDS ONLY

95 percent native; trees, shrubs, wildflowers.

Joseph Brown Native Seeds

7327 Hoefork Lane
Gloucester Point, VA 23062
804-642-0736

RETAIL/MAIL ORDER

SEEDS ONLY

95 percent native; 95 percent from stock, 5 percent other nursery source, some seed wild-collected. Uncommon selection of eastern U.S. native species. Catalogue $1.

Lamtree Farm

2323 Copeland Rd.
Warrensville, NC 28693
336-385-6144
bushy@skybest.com

WHOLESALE/RETAIL/MAIL ORDER

PLANTS AND SEEDS

98 percent native; specializes in native rhododendrons. Field-grown stock. Catalogue $2.

Larner Seeds

P.O. Box 407
Bolinas, CA 94924
415-868-9407; fax 415-868-2592
info@larnerseeds.com
www.larnerseeds.com

WHOLESALE/RETAIL/MAIL ORDER

PLANTS AND SEEDS

100 percent native; 100 percent propagated from stock. Specializes in California natives, with demonstration garden of all coastal native plants. Mail order seeds only; plants shipped within California. Catalogue $2.50.

Lazy K Nursery, Inc.

705 Wright Rd.
Pine Mountain, GA 31822
706-663-4991
info@lazyknursery.com
www.lazyknursery.com

WHOLESALE/RETAIL/MAIL ORDER

PLANTS ONLY

90 percent native; 100 percent propagated from stock. Specializes in native rhododendrons. Container-grown. Catalogue $1.

Little Valley Farm

5693 Snead Creek Rd.
Spring Green, WI 53588
608-935-3324

RETAIL/MAIL ORDER

PLANTS AND SEEDS

100 percent native; 90 percent propagated from stock, 10 percent from other nursery source. Specializes in woodland and prairie wildflowers, shrubs, and prairie grasses. Catalogue free.

Lower Marlboro Nursery

P.O. Box 1013
Dunkirk, MD 20754
301-812-0808
mssds@erols.com

RETAIL/MAIL ORDER

PLANTS ONLY

80 percent native; wildflowers, some trees and shrubs. 100 percent propagated from stock. Specializes in eastern U.S. natives with special interest in genetically diverse species. Catalogue $2.

Mary's Plant Farm

2410 Lanes Mill Rd.
Hamilton, OH 45013
513-894-0022
marysplantfarm@voyager.net
www.marysplantfarm.com

RETAIL/MAIL ORDER

PLANTS AND SEEDS

50 percent native; 100 percent propagated from stock. Specializes in ordinary and unusual selections, including shade-loving perennials and flowering shrubs, understory trees, and shade trees. Catalogue $1 (refundable).

Native Gardens

Rt. 1, P.O. Box 464
5737 Fischer Ln.
Greenback, TN 37742
865-856-0220
meredith@native-gardens.com
www.native-gardens.com

WHOLESALE/RETAIL/MAIL ORDER

PLANTS AND SEEDS

99 percent native; 97 percent propagated from stock, 3 percent from other nursery source. Specializes in native North American species. Catalogue free.

Native Seeds, Inc.

14590 Triadelphia Mill Rd.
Dayton, MD 21036
301-596-9818

WHOLESALE/RETAIL/MAIL ORDER

SEEDS ONLY

90 percent native; 40 percent propagated from stock, 60 percent from other nursery source. Specializes in native North American meadow wildflowers. Offers regional seed mixes. Catalogue free.

Native Sons Nursery

1123 East Redbud Road
Knoxville, TN 37920-3655
865-577-2624; fax 865-577-2624
Info@native-sons-nursery.com
www.native-sons-nursery.com

WHOLESALE/RETAIL/MAIL ORDER

PLANTS AND SEEDS

100 percent native; wildflowers. All plants either nursery-propagated or rescued. Specializes in orchids and trilliums. Catalogue free.

Needlefast Evergreen, Inc.

4075 W. Hansen Rd.
Ludington, MI 49431
231-843-8524; fax 231-843-1887
nickel@needlefastevergreens.com
www. needlefastevergreens.com

WHOLESALE/RETAIL/MAIL ORDER

PLANTS ONLY

70 percent native; trees and shrubs. Seedlings for reforestation. Catalogue free.

New England Wild Flower Society

180 Hemenway Rd.
Framingham MA 01701-2699
508-877-9348
newfs@newfs.org
www.newfs.org

RETAIL/MAIL ORDER (SEED ONLY)

PLANTS AND SEEDS

95 percent native; 90 percent propagated from stock, 10 percent from other nursery source. Specializes in northeastern woodland wildflowers. Mail order seed only. Catalogue $2.75 (free with membership).

Niche Gardens

1111 Dawson Rd.
Chapel Hill, NC 27516
919-967-0078
mail@nichegardens.com
www.nichegardens.com

RETAIL/MAIL ORDER

PLANTS ONLY

60 percent native; 95 percent propagated from stock, 5 percent from other nursery source. Sends large, healthy plants. Garden consultation and design services available. Catalogue $3.

North Creek Nurseries, Inc.

388 North Creek Rd.
Landenberg, PA 19350
610-255-0100
ecoplug@earthlink.net
www.northcreeknurseries.com

WHOLESALE/MAIL ORDER

PLANTS ONLY

70 percent native; 100 percent propagated from stock. Specializes in perennials, grasses, and some shrubs, in cell packs or plugs. Offers 90 varieties in 5-inch-deep "landscape plugs" for quick meadow establishment. Custom-grown orders taken with adequate notice. Catalogue free.

Northwest Native Seed

17595 Vierra Canyon Rd., Suite #172
Prunedale, CA 93907
oreonana@juno.com

RETAIL/MAIL ORDER

SEEDS ONLY

100 percent native; 100 percent wild-collected seed. Specializes in seed collected from western U.S., from the coast to alpines. Catalogue $2.

Orchid Gardens

2232 139th Ave. NW
Andover, MN 55304

RETAIL/MAIL ORDER

PLANTS ONLY

95 percent native; 100 percent propagated from stock. Uncommon selection of northern woodland natives. Field-grown in northern Minnesota. Bareroot mail order. Catalogue $1.

Pierson Nurseries, Inc.

24 Buzzell Rd.
Biddeford, ME 04005
207-499-2994; fax 207-499-2912
piersonnurseries@lamere.net
piersonnurseries.com

WHOLESALE/RETAIL/MAIL ORDER

PLANTS AND SEEDS

95 percent native; trees, shrubs, wildflowers. Specializes in herbaceous and woody wetland plants.

Plant Delights Nursery

9241 Sauls Rd.
Raleigh, NC 27603
919-772-4794
office@plantdel.com
www.plantdel.com

RETAIL/MAIL ORDER

PLANTS ONLY

25 percent native; 95 percent propagated from stock, 5 percent from other nursery source. Specializes in breeding hostas, U.S. natives, and new, strange perennials. Catalogue: 10 stamps or box of chocolates.

Plants of the Wild

P.O. Box 866
123 Stateline Rd.
Tekoa, WA 99033
509-284-2848
kathy@plantsofthewild.com
www.plantsofthewild.com

WHOLESALE/RETAIL/MAIL ORDER

PLANTS AND SEEDS

99 percent native; 99 percent propagated from stock, 1 percent from wild-collected seed. Specializes in natives, including woody plants, wildflowers, grasses, and wetland species. Container-grown. Will contract-grow species not listed. Catalogue $1.

Prairie Moon Nursery

Rte. 3, Box 163
Winona, MN 55987
507-452-1362
pmnrsy@luminet.net
www.prairiemoonnursery.com

RETAIL/MAIL ORDER

PLANTS AND SEEDS

100 percent native; 95 percent propagated from stock, 5 percent other nursery source. Natives for wetland, prairie, savanna, and woodland. Organic methods. Plants shipped bareroot. Custom seed mixes available. Catalogue free.

Prairie Nursery

P.O. Box 306
Westfield, WI 53964
800-476-9453; fax 608-296-2741
cs@prairienursery.com
www.prairienursery.com

WHOLESALE/RETAIL/MAIL ORDER

PLANTS AND SEEDS

100 percent native; majority propagated from stock. Specializes in prairie wildflowers, grasses, and sedges. Offers an extensive selection of seed mixes as well as customized mixes. Consultation and other services available. Catalogue free.

Prairie Ridge Nursery

9738 Overland Rd.
Mt. Horeb, WI 53572
608-437-5245
crmeco@chorus.net
www.prairieridgenursery.com

WHOLESALE/RETAIL/MAIL ORDER

PLANTS AND SEEDS

100 percent native; 90 percent propagated from stock, 10 percent from other nursery source. Specializes in native restorations. Offers wildflowers, grasses, sedges, and rushes. Consultation services available. Catalogue free; restoration guide $5.

Prairie Seed Source

P.O. Box 83
North Lake, WI 53064

RETAIL/MAIL ORDER

SEEDS ONLY

100 percent native; 100 percent propagated from stock. Dedicated to the preservation and proliferation of southeastern Wisconsin prairie genotype and related ecosystem members. Catalogue $1.

The Primrose Path

921 Scottdale-Dawson Rd.
Scottsdale, PA 15683
724-887-6756
primrose@a1usa.net
www.theprimrosepath.com

WHOLESALE/RETAIL/MAIL ORDER

PLANTS ONLY

25 to 30 percent native; 100 percent propagated from stock with the exception of *Trillium sessile,* which was rescued. Specializes in shade-tolerant plants including unique selections of *Asarum.* Catalogue $2.

Shooting Star Nursery

444 Bates Rd.
Frankfort, KY 40601
502-223-1679; fax 502-227-5700
ShootingStarNursery@msn.com
www.shootingstarnursery.com

RETAIL/MAIL ORDER

PLANTS AND SEEDS

100 percent native; 95 percent propagated from stock, 5 percent from other source. Specializes in eastern U.S. natives of forest, prairie, and wetland. Container- and garden-grown. Design consultation. Catalogue free (refundable).

Siskiyou Rare Plant Nursery

2825 Cummings Rd.
Medford, OR 97501
541-772-6846; fax 541-772-4917
catalog@wave.net
www.siskiyourareplantnursery.com

RETAIL/MAIL ORDER

PLANTS ONLY

30 percent native; 100 percent propagated from stock. Grows hard-to-find hardy perennials, shrubs, and smaller conifers, and alpine and rock garden plants. Container- and garden-grown. Catalogue $3.

Smith Nursery Co.

P.O. Box 515
Charles City, IA 50616
515-228-3239

WHOLESALE/RETAIL/MAIL ORDER

SEEDS ONLY

70 percent native; 50 percent propagated from stock, 5 percent wild-collected, and 45 percent from other nursery source. Specializes in trees and shrubs including shade trees, fruit bearing, and ornamental. Catalogue free.

Sunlight Gardens

174 Golden Ln.
Andersonville, TN 37705
800-272-7396
sungardens@aol.com
www.sunlightgardens.com

WHOLESALE/RETAIL/MAIL ORDER

PLANTS ONLY

80 percent native; 75 percent propagated from stock and 25 percent from other nursery source. Specializes in eastern natives for retail through mail order only. Shipped in 3½-inch pots. Catalogue free.

Sylva Native Nursery & Seed Co.

1683 Sieling Farm Rd.
New Freedom, PA 17349
717-227-0486
plants@sylvanative.com
www.sylvanative.com

WHOLESALE/MAIL ORDER

PLANTS AND SEEDS

100 percent native; 70 percent wild-collected seed, 30 percent from other nursery source. Offers wetland, riparian, upland forest, and meadow plant species, including trees. Catalogue free.

Virginia Natives

P.O. Box D
Hume, VA 22639-0903
540-364-1665
vanatus@erols.com

WHOLESALE/RETAIL/MAIL ORDER

PLANTS ONLY

70 percent native; 75 percent propagated from stock, 25 percent from other nursery source. Specializes in regional wildflowers, ferns, grasses, shrubs, and trees native to eastern U.S. Catalogue $1.25.

WE-DU Nurseries

2055 Polly Spout Rd.
Marion, NC 28752
828-738-8300
wedu@wnclink.com
www.we-du.com

PLANTS ONLY

50 percent native; 95 percent propagated from stock, including trillium and orchid, 5 percent from other nursery sources. Specializes in natives and rare perennials, woody plants, and ferns. Catalogue $2.

Wetlands Nursery

P.O. Box 14553
Saginaw, MI 48601
989-752-3492; fax 989-752-3096
jewelr@aol.com

WHOLESALE/RETAIL/MAIL ORDER (SEED ONLY)

PLANTS AND SEEDS

100 percent native; 100 percent propagated from stock. Specializes in wetland plant species native to Michigan. On-site project consulting services on wetland ecology. Catalogue free.

Wildlands Restoration / Coronado Heights Nursery

2944 N. Castro
Tucson, AZ 85705
520-882-0969
grtamdsrt@aol.com

WHOLESALE/RETAIL/MAIL ORDER

PLANTS AND SEEDS

99 percent native; trees, shrubs, wildflowers. Seeds of the interior West.

Wild Earth Native Plant Nursery

P.O. Box 7258
Freehold, NJ 07728
732-308-9777
wildearthnpn@compuserve.com

WHOLESALE/RETAIL/MAIL ORDER

PLANTS ONLY

98 percent native; 100 percent propagated from stock. Specializes in flora of eastern U.S. Uses seed-propagated plant material whenever possible to maintain genetic diversity. Catalogue $2.

Wildseed Farms

P.O. Box 3000
425 Wildflower Hills
Fredericksburg, TX 78624-3000
800-848-0078; fax 830-990-8090
wsf@fbg.net
www.wildseedfarms.com

WHOLESALE/RETAIL/MAIL ORDER (SEED ONLY)

PLANTS AND SEEDS

75 percent native; wildflowers. Catalogue free.

Wind River Seeds

3075 Lane 51 1/2
Manderson, WY 82432
307-568-3361; fax 307-568-3364
wrstaff@windriverseed.com
www.windriverseed.com

RETAIL/MAIL ORDER

SEED ONLY

95 percent native; trees, shrubs, grasses, wildflowers. Specializes in reclamation seed for western U.S. Catalogue free.

Woodlanders, Inc

1128 Colleton Ave.
Aiken, SC 29801
803-648-7522
woodlanders@triplet.net
www.woodlanders.net

RETAIL/MAIL ORDER

PLANTS ONLY

70 percent native; 85 percent propagated from stock, 15 percent from other nursery source. Specializes in southeastern U.S. natives, including trees, yuccas, palms, grasses, ferns, bulbs, tubers, and nursery-propagated endangered plants. Catalogue $2.

NATIVE PLANT SOCIETIES OF
THE UNITED STATES AND CANADA

ALABAMA

Alabama Wildflower Society
c/o Caroline R. Dean
606 India Rd.
Opelika, AL 36801
334-745-2494
www.auburn.edu/~deancar/

ALASKA

Alaska Native Plant Society
P.O. Box 141613
Anchorage, AK 99514-1613
907-333-8212

ARIZONA

Arizona Native Plant Society
P.O. Box 41206
Sun Station
Tucson, AZ 85717-1206
http://aznps.org/

ARKANSAS

Arkansas Native Plant Society
P.O. Box 250250
Little Rock, AR 72225
501-279-4705
www.anps.org

CALIFORNIA

California Botanical Society
Jepson Herbarium
1001 VLSB #2465
University of California
Berkeley, CA 94720
www.csupomona.edu/~calbotsoc/

California Native Plant Society
Allen Barnes, executive director
1722 J St., Suite 17
Sacramento, CA 95814-2931
916-447-2677
www.cnps.org

Southern California Botanists
Department of Biology
California State University
Fullerton, CA 92834
714-278-7034
www.socalbot.org

Theodore Payne Foundation
10459 Tuxford St.
Sun Valley, CA 91352-2126
818-768-1802
www.thodorepayne.org

COLORADO

Colorado Native Plant Society
P.O. Box 200
Fort Collins, CO 80522-0200
http://carbon.cudenver.edu/~shill/conps.html

CONNECTICUT

Connecticut Botanical Society
Casper J. Ultee, president
55 Harvest Ln.
Glastonbury, CT 06033
860-633-7557
www.vfr.com/cbs/

Connecticut Chapter
New England Wild Flower Society
www.newfs.org/chapters.html

DISTRICT OF COLUMBIA
Botanical Society of Washington
Department of Botany, NHB 166
Smithsonian Institution
Washington, D.C. 20560
www.fred.net/kathy/bsw.html

FLORIDA
Florida Native Plant Society
P.O. Box 690278
Vero Beach, FL 32969-0278
561-462-0000
www.fnps.org

GEORGIA
Georgia Botanical Society
Teresa Ware, membership chairman
2 Idlewood Court NW
Rome, GA 30165-1210
706-232-3435
http://science.kennesaw.edu/org/gabotsoc

Georgia Native Plant Society
P.O. Box 422085
Atlanta, GA 30342-2085
770-343-6000
www.gnps.org

HAWAII
Native Hawaiian Plant Society
P.O. Box 5021
Kahului, HI 96733-5021
www.philipt.com/nhps/

IDAHO
Idaho Native Plant Society
P.O. Box 9451
Boise, ID 83707-3451
www.idahonativeplants.org

ILLINOIS
Illinois Native Plant Society
Forest Glen Preserve
20301 E. 900 North Rd.
Westville, IL 61883
www.inhs.uiuc.edu/inps/
217-662-2142

INDIANA
Indiana Native Plant & Wildflower Society
Katrina Vollmer, membership chairman
3134 Greenbriar Lane
Nashville, IN 47448-8279
812-988-0063
www.inpaws.org

IOWA
Iowa Prairie Network
www.iowaprairienetwork.org

KANSAS
Kansas Wildflower Society
c/o R. L. McGregor Herbarium
University of Kansas
2045 Constant Ave.
Lawrence, KS 66047-3729

KENTUCKY
Kentucky Native Plant Society
c/o Department of Biological Science
Eastern Kentucky University
521 Lancaster Ave.
Richmond, KY 40475-3102
www.knps.org

LOUISIANA
Louisiana Native Plant Society
216 Caroline Dormon Rd.
Saline, LA 71070

MAINE
Josselyn Botanical Society
Rick Speer, corresponding secretary
566 N. Auburn Road
Auburn, ME 04210

Maine Chapter
New England Wild Flower Society
www.newfs.org/chapters.html

MARYLAND
Maryland Native Plant Society
P.O. Box 4877
Silver Spring, MD 20914
http://mdflora.org/

MASSACHUSETTS
New England Botanical Club
22 Divinity Ave.
Cambridge, MA 02138
617-308-3656 (Ray Angelo)
www.huh.harvard.edu/nebc

New England Wild Flower Society
180 Hemenway Rd.
Framingham, MA 01701-2699
508-877-7630
www.newfs.org

Cape Cod Chapter
New England Wild Flower Society
www.newfs.org/chapters.html

MICHIGAN

Michigan Botanical Club
University of Michigan Herbarium
North University Building
1205 N. University
Ann Arbor, MI 48109-1057
www.michbotclub.org

Wildflower Association of Michigan
c/o Marji Fuller
3853 Farrell Rd.
Hastings, MI 49058
616-948-2496
www.wildflowersmich.org

MINNESOTA

Minnesota Native Plant Society
220 Biological Services Center
University of Minnesota
1445 Gortner Ave.
St. Paul, MN 55108-1020
www.stolaf.edu/depts/biology/mnps/

MISSISSIPPI

Mississippi Native Plant Society
Ron Wieland
Mississippi Museum of Natural Science
111 N. Jefferson Street
Jackson, MS 39202
601-354-7303

MISSOURI

Missouri Native Plant Society
P.O Box 20073
St. Louis, MO 63144-0073
314-577-9522
http://web.missouri.edu/~umo_herb/monps/index.html

MONTANA

Montana Native Plant Society
P.O. Box 8783
Missoula, MT 59807-8783

NEVADA

Northern Nevada Native Plant Society
P.O. Box 8965
Reno, NV 89507-8965
www.state.nv.us/nvnhp/nnnps.htm

NEW HAMPSHIRE

New Hampshire Chapter
New England Wild Flower Society
www.newfs.org/chapters.html

NEW JERSEY

The Native Plant Society of New Jersey
Office of Continuing Professional Education
Cook College
102 Ryders Ln.
New Brunswick, NJ 08901-8519
www.npsnj.org

NEW MEXICO

Native Plant Society of New Mexico
P.O. Box 5917
Santa Fe, NM 87502-5917
http://npsnm.unm.edu/

NEW YORK

Long Island Botanical Society
Eric Lamont, president
Biology Department
Riverhead High School
Riverhead, NY 11901
www.molins.sunysb.edu/libs/LIBS.HTML

New York Flora Association
New York State Museum
3132 CEC
Albany, NY 12230

Niagara Frontier Botanical Society
Buffalo Museum of Science
1020 Humboldt Pkwy.
Buffalo, NY 14211
www.acsu.buffalo.edu/~insrisg/botany/

The Finger Lakes Native Plant Society of Ithaca
Cornell Cooperative Extension
532 Cayuga Heights Rd.
Ithaca, NY 14850
607-257-4853

NORTH CAROLINA

North Carolina Wildflower Preservation Society
North Carolina Botanical Garden
P. O. Box 3375, Totten Center
University of North Carolina
Chapel Hill, NC 27599-3375
www.ncwildflower.org

Western Carolina Botanical Club
c/o Bonnie Arbuckle
P.O. Box 1049
Flat Rock, NC 28731
828-696-2077

OHIO

Central Ohio Native Plant Society
Jim Davidson, President
644 Teteridge Rd.
Columbus, OH 43214
614-451-3009

Cincinnati Wildflower Preservation Society
c/o Victor G. Soukup
338 Compton Rd.
Wyoming, OH 45215-4113
513-761-2568

Native Plant Society of Northeastern Ohio
c/o Jean Roche
640 Cherry Park Oval
Aurora, OH 44202
330-562-4053
http://community.cleveland.com/cc/nativeplants

Ohio Native Plant Society
6 Louise Dr.
Chagrin Falls, OH 44022

OKLAHOMA

Oklahoma Native Plant Society
c/o Tulsa Garden Center
2435 S. Peoria
Tulsa, OK 74114
918-747-0735
www.usao.edu/~onps/

OREGON

Native Plant Society of Oregon
P.O. Box 902
Eugene, OR 97440
www.npsoregon.org

PENNSYLVANIA

Botanical Society of Western Pennsylvania
Loree Speedy
5837 Nicholson St.
Pittsburgh, PA 15217
412-521-9425
http://home.kiski.net/~speedy/b1.html

Delaware Valley Fern and Wildflower Society
Dana Cartwright
263 Hillcrest Rd.
Wayne, PA 19087
610-687-0918

Muhlenberg Botanical Society
c/o The North Museum
P.O. Box 3003
Lancaster, PA 17604-3003

Pennsylvania Native Plant Society
1001 East College Avenue
State College, PA 16801
www.pawildflower.org

RHODE ISLAND

Rhode Island Wild Plant Society
P.O. Box 114
Peace Dale, RI 02883-0114
401-783-5895
www.riwps.org

SOUTH CAROLINA

South Carolina Native Plant Society
Rick Huffman, president
P.O. Box 759
Pickens, SC 29671
864-868-7798
http://cufp.clemson.edu/scnativeplants/

Southern Appalachian Botanical Society
Charles N. Horn, secretary-treasurer
Biology Department, Newberry College
2100 College St.
Newberry, SC 29108
803-321-5257

Wildflower Alliance of South Carolina
P.O. Box 12181
Columbia, SC 29211
803-799-6889

SOUTH DAKOTA

Great Plains Native Plant Society
P.O. Box 461
Hot Springs, SD 57747-0461

TENNESSEE

American Association of Field Botanists
P.O. Box 23542
Chattanooga, TN 37422

Tennessee Native Plant Society
P.O. Box 159274
Nashville, TN 37215

TEXAS

El Paso Native Plant Society
c/o Wynn Anderson, Botanical Curator
Chihuahua Desert Gardens
University of Texas, El Paso
El Paso, TX 79968
915-747-5565

Lady Bird Johnson Wildflower Center
4801 La Crosse Ave.
Austin, TX 78739-1702
512-292-4200
www.wildflower.org

Native Plant Society of Texas
Dana Tucker, Coordinator
P.O. Box 891
Georgetown, TX 78627-0891
512-868-8799
www.npsot.org

UTAH

Utah Native Plant Society
P.O. Box 520041
Salt Lake City, UT 84152-0041
www.unps.org

VERMONT

Vermont Botanical and Bird Clubs
Deborah Benjamin, secretary
959 Warren Rd.
Eden, VT 05652
802-635-7794

Vermont Chapter
New England Wild Flower Society
www.newfs.org/chapters.html

VIRGINIA

Virginia Native Plant Society
Blandy Experimental Farm
400 Blandy Farm Ln., Unit 2
Boyce, VA 22620
540-837-1600
www.vnps.org

WASHINGTON

Washington Native Plant Society
7400 Sand Point Way NE
Seattle, WA 98115
206-527-3210
www.wnps.org

WEST VIRGINIA

West Virginia Native Plant Society
P.O. Box 75403
Charleston, WV 25375-0403

Eastern Panhandle Native Plant Society
P.O. Box 1268
Shepherdstown, WV 25443
www.epnps.org

WISCONSIN

Botanical Club of Wisconsin
Wisconsin Academy of Arts, Sciences, and Letters
1922 University Ave.
Madison, WI 53705
www.wisc.edu/botany/herbarium/BCWindex.html

WYOMING

Wyoming Native Plant Society
1604 Grand Avenue
Laramie, WY 82070
www.rmh.uwyo.edu/wnps.html/

CANADA

North American Native Plant Society
P.O. Box 84, Station D
Etobicoke, ON M9A 4X1
Canada
416-680-6280
www.nanps.org

Alberta Native Plant Council
Box 52099, Garneau Postal Outlet
Edmonton, AB T6G 2T5
Canada
www.anpc.ab.ca

Field Botanists of Ontario,
c/o W. D. McIlveen, RR. 1
Acton, ON L7J 2L7
Canada
www.trentu.ca/fbo/

Native Plant Society of British Columbia
2012 William St.
Vancouver, BC V5L 2X6
Canada
604-255-5719

The Wildflower Society of Newfoundland and Labrador
c/o Botanical Garden
Memorial University of Newfoundland
306 Mt. Scio Rd.
St. John's, NF A1C 5S7
Canada
www.ucs.mun.ca/~hclase/wf/

Nova Scotia Wild Flora Society
c/o Nova Scotia Museum of Natural History
1747 Summer St.
Halifax, NS B3H 3A6
Canada
www.navnet.net/~csensen/

Flora Quebeca
83 rue Chenier
Saint-Eustache, PQ J7R 1W9
Canada

Native Plant Society of Saskatchewan
P.O. Box 21099
Saskatchewan, SK S7H 5N9
Canada
306-668-3940
www.npss.sk.ca

Thames Valley Wildflower Society
1 Windsor Crescent
London, ON N6C 1V6
Canada

Toronto Wildflower Society
43 Anaconda Avenue
Scarborough, ON M1L 4M1
Canada

Waterloo-Wellington Wildflower Society
c/o Botany Department
University of Guelph
Guelph, ON N1G 2W1
Canada
www.uoguelph.ca/~botcal

BOTANICAL GARDENS AND ARBORETUMS
SPECIALIZING IN NATIVE PLANTS

ARIZONA

The Arboretum at Flagstaff
4001 Woody Mountain Rd.
Flagstaff, AZ 86001-8775
928-774-1442
www.thearb.com

Arizona-Sonoran Desert Museum
2021 N. Kinney Rd.
Tucson, AZ 85743-8918
520-883-1380
www.desertmuseum.org

Desert Botanical Garden
1201 North Galvin Pkwy.
Phoenix, AZ 85008
480-941-1225
www.dbg.org

CALIFORNIA

Davis Arboretum
University of California
One Shields Ave.
Davis, CA 95616-8526
530-752-4880
http://arboretum.ucdavis.edu/

Quail Botanical Gardens
230 Quail Gardens Dr.
Encinitas, CA
760-436-3036
www.qbgardens.com

Rancho Santa Ana Botanic Garden
1500 North College Ave.
Claremont, CA 91711-3157
909-625-8767
www.rsabg.org

Santa Barbara Botanic Garden
1212 Mission Canyon Rd.
Santa Barbara, CA 93105
805-682-4726
www.sbbg.org

Strybing Arboretum and Botanical Gardens
Ninth Avenue & Lincoln Way
San Francisco, CA 94122
415-661-1316
www.strybing.org

University of California Botanical Garden
200 Centennial Dr. #5045
Berkeley, CA 94720-5045
510-642-0849
www.mip.berkeley.edu/garden/

COLORADO

Denver Botanic Gardens
909 York St.
Denver, CO 80206
720-865-3500
www.botanicgardens.org

CONNECTICUT

Connecticut College Arboretum
5625 Connecticut College
270 Mohegan Ave.
New London, CT 06320
http://camel2.conncoll.edu/ccrec/greennet/arbo/

DELAWARE

Mt. Cuba Center for the Study of the Piedmont Flora
P.O. Box 3570
Greenville, DE 19807-0570
302-239-4244
(Visitors by appointment)

DISTRICT OF COLUMBIA

U.S. National Arboretum
3501 New York Ave., NE
Washington, DC 20002-1958
202-245-2726
www.ars-grin.gov/na

FLORIDA

Bok Tower Gardens
1151 Tower Blvd.
Lake Wales, FL 33853-3412
863-676-1408
www.boktower.org

Fairchild Tropical Garden
10901 Old Cutler Rd.
Coral Gables, FL 33156-4299
305-667-1651
www.ftg.org

GEORGIA

State Botanical Garden of Georgia
University of Georgia
2450 S. Milledge Ave.
Athens, GA 30605
706-542-1244
www.uga.edu/~botgarden

HAWAII

Harold L. Lyon Arboretum
University of Hawaii
3860 Manoa Rd.
Honolulu, HI 96822
808-988-0456
www.hawaii.edu/lyonarboretum/

National Tropical Botanical Garden
3530 Papalina Rd.
Kalaheo, HI 96741
808-332-7324
www.ntbg.org

Waimea Arboretum and Botanical Gardens
Waimea Arboretum Foundation
59-864 Kamehameha Highway
Haleiwa, Hawaii 96712
808-638-8655
www.hereinhawaii.com/WAF.htm

ILLINOIS

Chicago Botanic Garden
1000 Lake Cook Rd.
Glencoe, IL 60022
847-835-5440
www.chicago-botanic.org

Morton Arboretum
4100 Illinois Rte. 53
Lisle, IL 60532-1293
630-968-0074
www.mortonarb.org

MASSACHUSETTS

Arnold Arboretum
Harvard University
125 Arborway
Jamaica Plain, MA 02130-3500
617-524-1718
www.arboretum.harvard.edu

New England Wild Flower Society
Garden in the Woods
180 Hemenway Rd.
Framingham, MA 01701-2699
508-877-7630
www.newfs.org

MINNESOTA

Minnesota Landscape Arboretum
University of Minnesota
3675 Arboretum Dr., P.O. Box 39
Chanhassen, MN 55317-0039
952-443-1400
www.arboretum.umn.edu

MISSOURI

Crosby Arboretum
P.O. Box 1639
Picayune, MS 39466
601-799-2311
http://msstate.edu/dept/crec/camain.html

Missouri Botanical Garden
PO Box 299
Saint Louis, MO 63166-0299
314-577-5100
www.mobot.org

NEBRASKA

Nebraska Statewide Arboretum
P.O. Box 830715
University of Nebraska
Lincoln, NE 68583-0715
402-472-2971
http://arboretum.unl.edu/

NEW JERSEY

The Rutgers Gardens
Cook College, Rutgers University
112 Ryders Ln.
New Brunswick, NJ 08901
732-932-8451
http://aesop.rutgers.edu/~rugardens/

NEW YORK

Brooklyn Botanic Garden
1000 Washington Ave.
Brooklyn, NY 11225-1099
718-623-7200
www.bbg.org

New York Botanical Garden
200 St. and Kazimiroff Blvd.
Bronx, NY 01458-5126
718-817-8700
www.nybg.org

NORTH CAROLINA

J.C. Raulston Arboretum
North Carolina State University
Horticultural Field Laboratory
4301 Beryl Rd.
Raleigh, NC 27695-7609
919-515-3132
www.ncsu.edu/jcraulstonarboretum/

North Carolina Botanical Garden
CB 3375, Totten Center
University of North Carolina
Chapel Hill, NC 27599-3375
919-962-0522
www.unc.edu/depts/ncbg

North Carolina Arboretum
100 Frederick Law Olmsted Way
Asheville, NC 28806-9315
828-665-2492
www.ncarboretum.org

OHIO

Holden Arboretum
9500 Sperry Rd.
Kirtland, OH 44094-5172
440-946-4400
www.holdenarb.org

OREGON

Berry Botanic Garden
11505 SW Summerville Ave.
Portland, OR 97219-8309
503-636-4112
www.berrybot.org

PENNSYLVANIA

Bowman's Hill Wildflower Preserve
P.O. Box 685
New Hope, PA 18938-0685
215-862-2924
www.bhwp.org

Morris Arboretum of the University of Pennsylvania
100 Northwestern Ave.
Philadelphia, PA 19118
215-247-5777
http://www.upenn.edu/morris/

TEXAS

Mercer Arboretum and Botanic Gardens
22306 Aldine-Westfield Rd.
Humble, TX 77338-1071
281-443-8731
www.cp4.hctx.net/mercer

San Antonio Botanical Gardens
555 Funston Pl.
San Antonio, TX 78209
210-207-3250
www.sabot.org

UTAH

Red Butte Garden and Arboretum
300 Wakara Way
Salt Lake City, UT 84108
801-581-4747
www.redbuttegarden.org

VIRGINIA

Norfolk Botanical Garden
6700 Azalea Garden Rd.
Norfolk, VA 23518-5337
757-441-5830
www.virginiagarden.org

WASHINGTON

Bellevue Botanical Garden
12001 Main St.
Bellevue, WA 98005
425-452-2750
www.bellevuebotanical.org

WISCONSIN

University of Wisconsin Arboretum
1207 Seminole Highway
Madison, WI 53711-3726
608-263-7888
http://wiscinfo.doit.wisc.edu/arboretum/

CANADA

Memorial University of Newfoundland Botanical Garden
306 Mt. Scio Rd.
St John's, NF A1C 5S7
709-737-8590
www.mun.ca/botgarden

Montreal Botanical Garden
4101 Sherbrooke E
Montreal, PQ H1X 2B2
514-872-1400
www.ville.montreal.qc.ca/jardin/en

Royal Botanical Gardens
P.O. Box 399
Hamilton, ON L8N 3H8
905-527-1158
www.rbg.ca

University of Alberta Devonian Botanic Garden
Edmonton, AB T6G 2E1
780-987-3054
www.discoveredmonton.com

University of British Columbia Botanical Garden
6804 SW Marine Dr.
Vancouver, BC V6T 1Z4
604-822-3928
www.hedgerows.com/UBCBotGdn

VanDusen Botanical Garden
5251 Oak St.
Vancouver, BC V6M 4H1
604-257-8666
www.vandusengarden.org

Related Organizations

American Association of Botanic Gardens and Arboreta
351 Longwood Rd.
Kennett Square, PA 19348
610-925-2500
www.aabga.org

American Chestnut Foundation
469 Main Street, P.O. Box 4044
Bennington, VT 05201-4044
802-447-0110
http://chestnut.acf.org/

American Conifer Society
John Martin
P.O. Box 3422
Crofton, MD 21114-0422
410-721-6611
http://www.conifersociety.org/

American Horticultural Society
7931 East Boulevard Dr.
Alexandria, VA 22308
703-768-5700
www.ahs.org

American Rhododendron Society
11 Pinecrest Dr.
Fortuna, CA 95540
707-725-3043
www.rhododendron.org

Canadian Botanical Conservation Network
P.O. Box 399
Hamilton, ON L8N 3H8, Canada
905-527-1158 x309
www.rbg.ca/cbcn

Center for Plant Conservation
Missouri Botanical Garden
P.O. Box 299
St. Louis, MO 63166-0299
314-577-9450
www.mobot.org/CPC

Elm Research Institute
Elm Street
Westmoreland, NH 03467
800-367-3567
www.libertyelm.com

Garden Club of America
14 E. 60th St.
New York, NY 10022
212-753-8287
www.gcamerica.org

International Oak Society
Richard Jensen, membership chair
Department of Biology, Saint Mary's College
Notre Dame, IN 46556
219-284-4674
www.saintmarys.edu/~rjensen/ios.html

International Plant Propagators Society, Inc.
c/o Washington Park Arboretum
2300 Arboretum Drive E
Seattle, WA 98112
206-543-8602
www.ipps.org

Lady Bird Johnson Wildflower Center
4801 La Crosse Blvd.
Austin, TX 78739-1702
512-292-4200
www.wildflower.org

Magnolia Society
c/o Roberta Hagen
6616 81st St.
Cabin John, MD 20818
www.tallahassee.net/~magnolia/

National Garden Clubs
4401 Magnolia Ave.
St. Louis, MO 63110
314-776-7574
www.gardenclub.org

Native Plants Journal
University of Idaho Press
P.O. Box 441107
Moscow, ID 83844-1107
800-847-7377
nativeplants@uidaho.edu

Perennial Plant Association
3383 Schirtzinger Rd
Hilliard, OH 43026
614-771-8431
www.perennialplant.org

Plant Conservation Alliance
Bureau of Land Management
1849 C St., NW, LSB-204
Washington, DC 20240
202-452-0392
www.nps.gov/plants

Society for Ecological Restoration
1955 W. Grant Rd., #150
Tucson, AZ 85745
520-622-5485
www.ser.org

Wild Ones Natural Landscapers
P.O. Box 1274
Appleton, WI 54912-1274
877-394-9453
www.for-wild.org

Wildflower — North America's Magazine of Wild Flora
P.O. Box 335
Postal Station F
Toronto, ON M4Y 2L7
Canada
fax 416-466-6428
www.wildflowermag.com

PHOTO CREDITS

Jean Baxter: 9
Frank Bramley/NEWFS: 37, 97, 191, 227, 230, 231, 243
Albert Bussewitz/Massachusetts Audubon Society: iv-v, ix third from top, 1 fourth from top, 53, 56, 67, 74, 79, 100, 107, 109, 121, 156, 158, 161, 165, 166, 171, 187, 207 top, 207 bottom, 221, 240, 252, 258, 259, 261 third from top
William Cullina: vii third from top, ix second from top, ix fourth from top, 2 left, 4 right, 5, 6, 10, 11 top, 13 left, 14 second from left, 14 third from left, 15 third from top, 24, 25, 28 left, 30 inset, 30, 31, 45, 51, 64, 83, 89, 91, 94, 95, 114, 131, 137, 141, 142, 147, 153, 163, 172, 175, 178 left, 178 right, 183, 184, 188, 204 right, 214 left, 215, 216, 217 left, 224, 237, 238, 239, 245, 255, 261 second from top, 261 fourth from top, 265, 266, 270, 309
William Cullina/NEWFS: 15 top right, 33, 101, 112, 136, 144, 182, 189, 203, 226, 233, 236
R. Todd Davis: 15 second from top, 65
Ken Druse: xi second from top, 1 top center, 1 top right, 8 top, 43, 128, 173, 257 right
Derek Fell: vi, x, xi top right, xi third from top, xi fourth from top, 26, 29, 46, 105 left, 110, 118, 122, 125, 129, 161, 176, 210, 242
Heffron: 251
Hal Horwitz/NEWFS: 21, 212

Dorothy S. Long/NEWFS: ii-iii, 14 fourth from left, 96, 152, 155, 214 right, 229
John A. Lynch: vii top right, 1 third from top, 13 right, 18, 27, 36, 99, 135, 160, 169, 194, 209, 217 right, 218, 220, 249, 300-301
John A. Lynch/NEWFS: 68, 70, 82, 120, 139, 149, 204 left, 205, 306, 314
Charles Mann: viii, 11 bottom, 14 top left, 15 top center, 16, 47, 48, 54, 61, 80, 84, 85, 90, 92, 116, 119, 193, 197, 260, 261 top center
Dr. Larry Mellichamp: 58, 105 right, 108, 115, 180, 190,
NEWFS: ix top right, 50
Jerry Pavia: vii second from top, 1 second from top, 3, 4 left, 12, 15 fourth from top, 20, 34, 38, 76, 93, 126, 127, 130, 185, 195, 199, 223, 234, 235, 244, 247, 257 left, 261 top right, 304
Joanne Pavia: vii fourth from top, 17, 40, 71, 102, 113, 145, 196
Walt & Louiseann Pietrowicz/NEWFS: 7
Adelaide M. Pratt/NEWFS: 2 right, 8 bottom, 133, 150, 201, 254
Susan A. Roth: 23 right, 62, 63, 106
Willa Schmidt/NEWFS: 225
Edward Steffek: 179
Michael S. Thompson: 23 left, 28 right, 66, 87, 154, 176
Mary M. Walker/NEWFS: 72

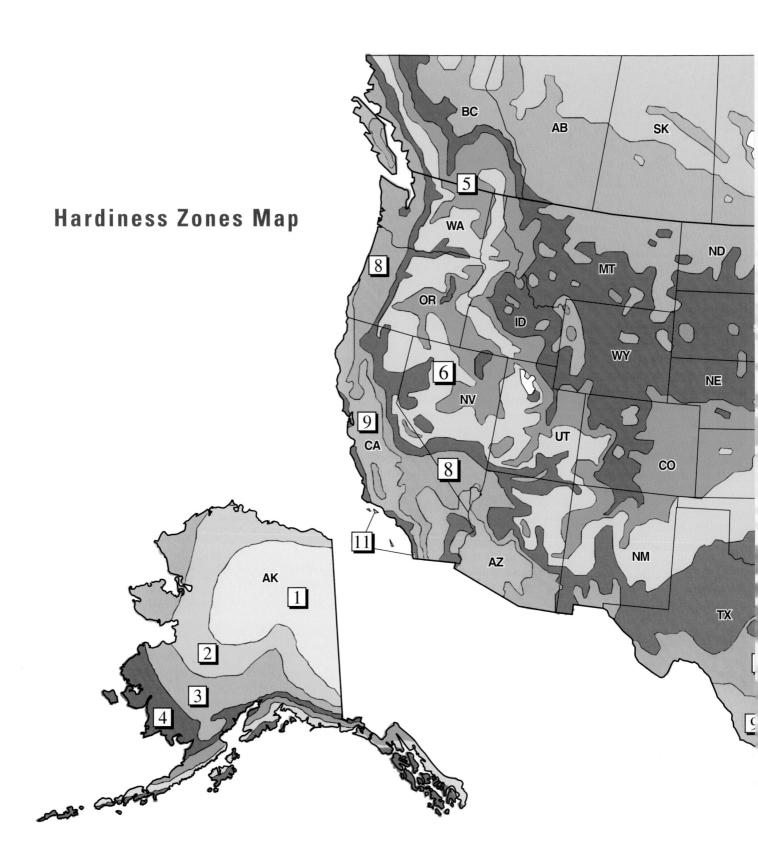

Hardiness Zones Map

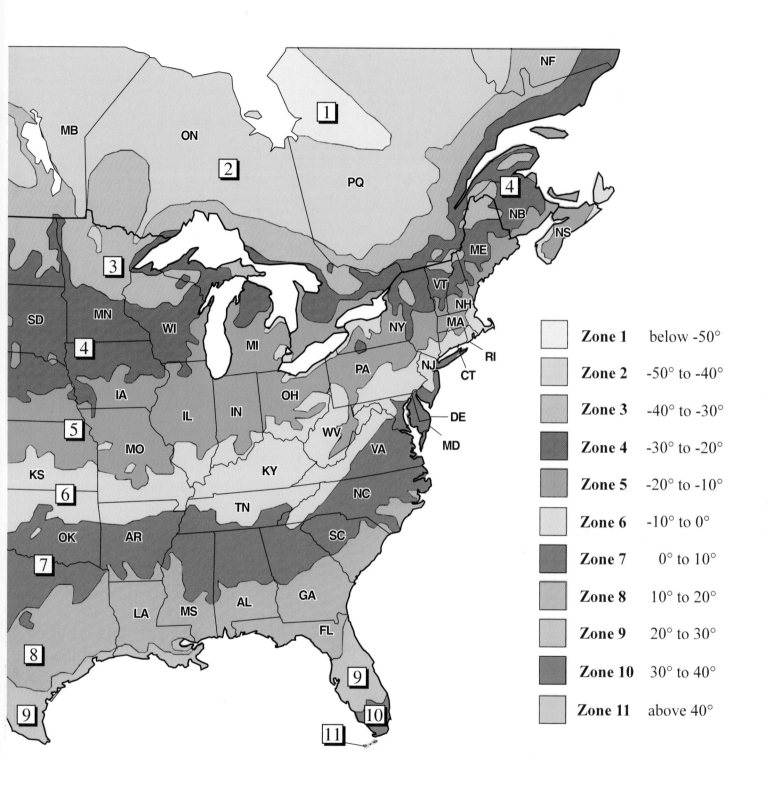

Zone 1 — below -50°
Zone 2 — -50° to -40°
Zone 3 — -40° to -30°
Zone 4 — -30° to -20°
Zone 5 — -20° to -10°
Zone 6 — -10° to 0°
Zone 7 — 0° to 10°
Zone 8 — 10° to 20°
Zone 9 — 20° to 30°
Zone 10 — 30° to 40°
Zone 11 — above 40°

BIBLIOGRAPHY

Bailey, Robert G. *Description of the Ecoregions of the United States.* Miscellaneous Publication 1391. 2nd ed. Washington, D.C.: U.S. Department of Agriculture, Forest Service, 1995.

Barbour, Michael G., and William D. Billings. *North American Terrestrial Vegetation.* Cambridge, England: Cambridge University Press, 1988.

Baskin, Carol C. and Jerry M. Baskin. *Seeds: Ecology, Biogeography, and Evolution of Dormancy and Germination.* San Diego, Calif.: Academic Press, 1998.

Barkley, T. M., et al., eds. *Flora of the Great Plains.* Lawrence, Kans.: University Press of Kansas, 1986.

Benvie, Sam. *The Encyclopedia of North American Trees.* Buffalo, N.Y.: Firefly Books, 2000.

Bir, Richard E. *Growing and Propagating Showy Native Woody Plants.* Chapel Hill, N.C.: University of North Carolina Press, 1992.

Brown, Claud L., and L. Katherine Kirkman. *Trees of Georgia and Adjacent States.* Portland, Ore.: Timber Press, 1990.

Conner, D. A. "Propagation of Upright Junipers." *Combined Proceedings of the International Propagation Society* 35:719–21.

Correll, Donovan S., and Marshall C. Johnston. *Manual of the Vascular Plants of Texas.* Richardson, Texas: University of Texas, 1979.

Cronquist, Arthur, et al. *Intermountain Flora: Vascular Plants of the Intermountain West, U.S.A.* Vols. 1–5. New York: New York Botanical Garden, 1994.

Cullina, William. *The New England Wild Flower Society Guide to Growing and Propagating Wildflowers of the United States and Canada.* Boston: Houghton Mifflin, 2000.

Deno, Norman C. *Seed Germination Theory and Practice.* 2nd ed. State College, Pa.: Norman C. Deno, 1994.

Dirr, Michael A. *Dirr's Hardy Trees and Shrubs: An Illustrated Encyclopedia.* Portland, Ore.: Timber Press, 1997.

———. *Manual of Woody Landscape Plants.* Champaign, Ill.: Stipes, 1998.

Dirr, Michael A., and Charles W. Heuser. *The Reference Manual of Woody Plant Propagation: From Seed to Tissue Culture.* Athens, Ga.: Varsity Press, 1987.

Druse, Ken. *The Natural Habitat Garden.* New York: Clarkson Potter, 1994.

———. *Making More Plants: The Science, Art, and Joy of Propagation.* New York: Clarkson Potter, 2000.

Foote, Leonard E., and Samuel B. Jones. *Native Shrubs and Woody Vines of the Southeast: Landscaping Uses and Identification.* Portland, Ore.: Timber Press, 1989.

Foster, H. Lincoln. *Rock Gardening.* Portland, Ore.: Timber Press, 1982.

Gleason, Henry A., and Arthur Cronquist. *Manual of Vascular Plants of the Northeastern United States and Adjacent Canada.* 2nd ed. New York: New York Botanical Garden, 1991.

Godfrey, Robert K. *Trees, Shrubs, and Woody Vines of Northern Florida and Adjacent Georgia and Alabama.* Athens, Ga.: University of Georgia Press, 1988.

Harlow, William M., et al. *Textbook of Dendrology.* 8th ed. New York: McGraw-Hill, 1996.

Harper, John L. *Population Biology of Plants.* London: Academic Press, 1977.

Hartman, John R., et al. *Pirone's Tree Maintenance.* 7th ed. London: Oxford University Press, 2000.

Hartmann, Hudson T., et al. *Plant Propagation: Principles and Practices.* 6th ed. Upper Saddle River, N.J.: Prentice-Hall, 1997.

Hightshoe, Gary L. *Native Trees, Shrubs, and Vines for Urban and Rural North America.* New York: Van Nostrand Reinhold, 1988.

Hitchcock, C. Leo, and Arthur Cronquist. *Flora of the Pacific Northwest.* Seattle: University of Washington Press, 1987.

Holmgren, Noel H. *The Illustrated Companion to Gleason and Cronquist's Manual.* New York: New York Botanic Garden, 1998.

Johnson, Warren T., and Howard H. Lyon. *Insects that Feed on Trees and Shrubs.* 2nd ed. Ithaca, N.Y.: Cornell University Press, 1988.

Kartesz, John T. *A Synonymized Checklist of the Vascular Flora of the United States, Canada, and Greenland.* 2nd ed. Volume 2: Thesaurus. Portland, Ore.: Timber Press, 1994.

Kramer, Paul J. and Theodore T. Kozlowski. *Physiology of Woody Plants.* Orlando, Fl.: Academic Press, 1979.

Lanner, Ronald M. *Trees of the Great Basin: A Natural History.* Reno, Nev.: University of Nevada Press, 1984.

Lembke, Janet. *Shake Them 'Simmons Down.* New York: Lyons & Bradford, 1996.

Liberty Hyde Bailey Hortorium, Cornell University. *Hortus Third: A Concise Dictionary of Plants Cultivated in the United States and Canada.* New York: Macmillan, 1976.

Martin, W. C., and C. R. Hutchins. *A Flora of New Mexico.* Hirschberg, Germany: J. Cramer, 1980.

McMinn, Howard E. *An Illustrated Manual of California Shrubs.* Berkeley, Calif.: University of California Press, 1951.

Millspaugh, Charles F. *American Medicinal Plants.* New York: Dover Publications, 1974.

Morin, Nancy R., et al., eds. *Flora of North America.* Volumes 2 and 3. Oxford, England: Oxford University Press, 1997.

Mozingo, Hugh N. *Shrubs of the Great Basin: A Natural History.* Reno, Nev.: University of Nevada Press, 1987.

Munz, Philip A. *A California Flora.* Berkeley, Calif.: University of California Press, 1968.

Nelson, Gil. *The Shrubs and Woody Vines of Florida: A Reference and Field Guide.* Sarasota, Fl.: Pineapple Press, 1996.

———. *The Trees of Florida: A Reference and Field Guide.* Sarasota, Fl.: Pineapple Press, 1994.

Pammel, L. H. *A Manual of Poisonous Plants.* Cedar Rapids, Iowa: Torch Press, 1911.

Peattie, Donald C. *A Natural History of Trees of Eastern and Central North America.* Boston: Houghton Mifflin, 1966.

———. *A Natural History of Western Trees.* New York: Bonanza Books, 1952.

Polar, Jim, Andy MacKinnon, et al. *Plants of Coastal British Columbia Including Washington, Oregon, and Alaska.* Vancouver, B.C.: Lone Pine Publishing, 1994.

Radford, Albert E., et al. *Manual of the Vascular Flora of the Carolinas.* Chapel Hill, N.C.: University of North Carolina Press, 1978.

Schwintzer, Christa R., and John D. Tjepkema, eds. *The Biology of Frankia and Actinorhizal Plants.* San Diego, Calif.: Academic Press, 1990.

Scott, James A. *The Butterflies of North America: A Natural History and Field Guide.* Stanford, Calif.: Stanford University Press, 1986.

Simpson, Benny J. *A Field Guide to Texas Trees.* Austin, Texas: Texas Monthly Press, 1988.

Sinclair, Wayne A., Howard H. Lyon, and Warren T. Johnson. *Diseases of Trees and Shrubs.* Ithaca, N.Y.: Cornell University Press, 1987.

Soper, James H., and Margaret L. Heimburger. *Shrubs of Ontario.* Toronto, Ontario: Royal Ontario Museum, 1982.

Sorrie, Bruce A., and Paul Somers. *The Vascular Plants of Massachusetts: A County Checklist.* Westborough, Mass: Massachusetts Division of Fisheries and Wildlife, Natural Heritage and Endangered Species Program, 1999.

Stephens, H. A. *Woody Plants of the North Central Plains.* Lawrence, Kans.: University Press of Kansas, 1973.

Steyermark, Julian A. *Flora of Missouri.* Ames, Iowa: Iowa State University Press, 1975.

Voss, Edward G. *Michigan Flora.* Ann Arbor, Mich.: University of Michigan, 1985.

Welsh, Stanley L. *A Utah Flora.* Provo, Utah: Brigham Young University, 1993.

Wyman, Donald. *Trees for American Gardens.* 3rd ed. New York: Macmillan, 1990.

Young, James A. and Cheryl G. *Seeds of Woody Plants in North America.* Rev. ed. Portland, Ore.: Dioscorides Press, 1992.

GLOSSARY

abscission layer. A zone of specialized tissue separating two plant parts, such as leaf and stem.

acidic. Having a pH below 7.0, generally found in soils in high rainfall regions not derived from limestone.

actinorhizal. Forming a symbiotic association with bacteria in the genus *Frankia*. The bacteria infect specialized roots of the plant and extract (fix) atmospheric nitrogen and convert it into a form the plant can use.

adventitious. Coming from an unusual or atypical place.

after-ripening. A process of embryo maturation, necessary for germination, which continues after a seed has been removed from the parent and which requires a certain set of environmental conditions, usually warmth and moisture.

alkaline. Having a pH above 7.0, generally found in soils of low-rainfall or limestone regions.

alkaloid. A large group of nitrogen-based compounds produced by plants. Many are poisonous or otherwise pharmacologically active.

allelopathy. The release by a plant of chemical(s) (mostly into the soil) that retard or prevent the growth of other plants.

alpine. Technically, growing above the tree line. In horticulture, used more broadly to refer to mountain plants with low, cushion-forming, or otherwise compact habits that are useful for the rock garden.

alternate. Having flowers and leaves attached one per node, not paired.

anther. The pollen-bearing tip of the male part of the flower (stamen).

appressed. Lying flat against the stem, not spreading.

aril. A fleshy outgrowth or swelling of the seed coat.

axil. The point or angle where a stem connects to a leaf.

axillary. Arising from an axil.

bald. A rocky summit characterized by thin soils and subject to high winds and fire. Balds typically are found at latitudes or elevations too warm for true alpine vegetation to succeed. They are dominated by grasses, wildflowers, and shrubs.

balsam. A volatile terpene, B-pinene, with a recognizable odor.

biennial. Living only two seasons and typically forming a low rosette of leaves the first year and a tall flowering stem the next.

bleeding. Excessive exudation of sap after wounding of the cambium, a problem for susceptible species when a branch or section of bark is damaged or removed in late winter or spring when sap is moving up from the roots.

boreal. Northern, typically referring to the cold temperate coniferous forests of northern North America and Eurasia.

bract. A modified leaf associated with but not part of a flower or inflorescence, often brightly colored and acting in lieu of petals to attract pollinators.

caespitose. Densely tufted or tightly clumped.

callus. Thickened tissue, often associated with wound healing.

calyx. The sepals of a flower taken as a group.

cambium. A lateral meristem that produces phloem tissues externally and xylem tissues internally.

carpel. The modified, fertile leaf that surrounds the seeds.

caudex. A swollen, perennial woody stem or base at or below ground level.

cauline. Having leaves attached to an aboveground stem, rather than the base of a plant.

cellulose. A complex sugar (polysaccharide) that provides strength and resistance to decay.

chlorotic, chlorosis. Having abnormally yellow tissue as a result of insufficient chlorophyll, caused by nutrient deficiency or attack by a pathogen.

circumboreal. Literally, "around the north," meaning distributed in northern North America and northern Eurasia.

cleistogamous. Having flowers that are self-pollinating and never open.

clonal. Describing a group of stems or individual plants that originated from the same fertilized ovule (seed) and are thus genetically identical.

clumping. A habit of growth characterized by tightly spaced stems and/or rhizomes.

cold frame. A box or frame designed to protect potted plants or seeds from temperature extremes during winter. The frame is usually set partially below soil grade so as to be insulated by the earth. An insulating, waterproof covering — sash windows, plastic sheeting, rigid or flexible foam insulation — is laid on top before extreme cold (below 20°F) sets in.

colonial. Forming spreading patches or loose clumps connected by underground rhizomes or roots.

compound. Composed of two or more leaflets.

conifer. Any needle- and cone-bearing plant in the families Pinaceae, Cupressaceae, or Taxaceae.

connate. Grown together or fused.

cordate. Heart-shaped, typically referring to a leaf base.

corolla. The petals of a flower taken as a group.

cotyledon. The first or embryonic leaf or leaves of a seedling.

cross; to cross. A hybrid between two species (or genera); to create such a hybrid with controlled pollination. Represented by an × between the genus name and species name.

crown. Either the enlarged junction of the stem and roots (important in herbaceous plants as the source of new stem buds) or the canopy of a tree or large shrub.

cyme. A flat-topped flower cluster with flowers opening in the center first.

deciduous. Losing leaves at the end of the growing season.

determinate. Terminating in a preformed bud and therefore able to expand or grow to only a predetermined length.

dicot, dicotyledon. The class of angiosperms characterized as having two cotyledons, net-veined leaves, and flower parts typically in fours and fives.

dioecious. Bearing male and female flowers on separate individuals.

diploid. Having a normal double set of chromosomes in each cell.

drupe. A fleshy fruit containing a hard shell (endocarp) surrounding, typically, a single seed.

dry-land. Originating in or adapted to environments receiving an average of 10 inches of rain or less yearly.

ecotype. A subpopulation of a species adapted to a specific habitat or habitat type.

endemic. Having a small native range encompassing a particular geographical region.

endosperm. The tissue surrounding a seedling embryo, designed for food storage.

epigeal. Having cotyledons that emerge aboveground and begin to photosynthesize.

filiform. Slender, threadlike.

frass. The fecal matter of insects.

fruit. A ripened ovary and any affiliated tissue containing the seeds.

GA3. Gibberellic acid, an important plant growth hormone that induces stem elongation, flowering, and seed germination. It is used to overcome dormancy in seeds requiring a period of cold stratification.

genotype. A group of individuals within a species sharing a very similar genetic constitution.

genus (plural is genera). A group of closely related plants. The first word, capitalized, of the binomial Latin name.

glabrous. Smooth, hairless.

glaucous. Having a waxy bloom that covers leaves or stems and imparts a bluish cast.

gyno-dioecious. A species in which some individuals have female flowers and others have perfect flowers.

hardwood. In forestry, an angiosperm (that is, not a conifer) with relatively hard wood. In propagation, a stem cutting that has matured to the point of becoming woody (lignified).

head. A dense cluster of flowers.

herbaceous. Lacking woody stems, usually indicating that the plant dies back to the ground in the dormant season.

hirsute. Covered in coarse, stiff hairs.

hybrid. A plant with parents of different species or even different genera.

hydrophilic. Water-loving; referring to seeds that are intolerant of dry storage.

hypogeal. Having cotyledons that remain underground, with the first true leaf or leaves emerging aboveground. The opposite of epigeal. Many hypogeal germinators require more than one season to emerge aboveground.

indeterminate. Not terminating in a bud or leaf and thus theoretically able to keep growing indefinitely.

inflorescence. A cluster of flowers.

internode. The section of stem between leaf nodes.

involucre. In angiosperms, a set of bracts surrounding the base of an inflorescence.

lanceolate. Lance-shaped; long and narrow and widest below the middle.

legumes. A family of plants (Fabiaceae) characterized in part by the presence of nitrogen-fixing bacteria in special nodules on the roots

lignin. A large complex polymer that is highly hydrophobic (water-repelling) and decay-resistant. It is mechanically strong and gives wood most of its tensile strength.

linear. Long and narrow with nearly parallel edges.

lobed. Deeply indented but not divided into separate leaflets.

mallet cutting. A softwood cutting with an attached heel of older wood or rhizome.

meristem. An area of undifferentiated cells where new plant parts originate.

monocot, monocotyledon. The class of angiosperms characterized as having a single cotyledon, parallel venation, and flower parts typically in threes.

monoculture. Widespread cultivation of a particular species, cultivar, or clone, which may encourage the spread of debilitating diseases and pests.

monoecious. Bearing both male and female flowers or perfect flowers on a single plant.

morphological. Regarding form and structure.

mycorrhizal roots. Modified roots containing mycorrhizal fungi.

mycorrhiza (plural is mycorrhizae). A symbiotic association between certain fungi (mycorrhizal fungi) and the roots of higher plants.

nitrogen-fixing. Of bacteria in the genera *Rhizobium, Frankia,* and *Bradyrhizobium* capable of converting gaseous nitrogen into the fixed or reduced form ammonium, which can be used in biological processes.

node. Place on a stem where a leaf or leaves attach.

oblong. Rectangular with rounded corners.

obovate. Generally egg-shaped but wider toward the tip.

open-pollinated. Pollinated from any available source. The opposite of hand-pollinated. In gardens, open pollination can lead to hybridization between related species that are typically separated in the wild.

opposite. Having two flowers or leaves attached at the same node—paired.

ovary. The structure that contains the ovule and/or seeds.

ovate. Egg-shaped.

ovipositor. An extension of the abdomen of certain female insects through which eggs are deposited.

palmate. Radially lobed or divided, with all segments originating from a central point, like the fingers of a hand.

panicle. A branched inflorescence.

pappus. The modified calyx found in Asteraceae flowers that forms bristles, wings, or parachutes on a seed to aid dispersal.

pedicel. The stalk of a single flower in a cluster.

peduncle. The primary stalk attaching a flower or inflorescence to the stem.

pedunculate. Borne on a peduncle.

perennial. A plant with a life span of two years or more.

perfect flower. A flower that has functional male and female parts.

perfoliate. Having a leaf or pair of leaves fused along the margins and wrapping around the stem so that the stem appears to pierce the leaf.

perianth. A flower's sepals and petals collectively.

petal. A modified leaf surrounding the sexual parts of a flower that is variously colored, shaped, and patterned to attract pollinators.

petiole. A leaf stalk.

phytophthora. *Phytophthora cinnamoni*, a fungus that causes root disease and subsequent wilt symptoms and dieback of the crown.

pilose. Covered with sparse, long, straight hairs.

pinnate. Compound with leaflets arranged along either side of a central stalk (rachis).

pistil. The female parts of a flower — the stigma, style, and ovary — as a unit.

pocosin. A swamp or marsh, typically used of wetlands along the southeastern coastal plain.

pollen. The male gametophytes, or haploid cells, that fertilize the female ovule.

polyploid. Aberrant cells (or organisms) having more than the standard two sets of chromosomes.

prostrate. Growing low or flat on the ground.

provenance. A plant's place of origin.

pubescence. Short, soft hair.

quick-dip. A method of applying rooting hormone by holding a stem cutting in a liquid containing the hormone for 3 to 10 seconds.

raceme. An unbranched inflorescence of pedunculate flowers that is typically long and thin.

rachis. A central stalk, typically of a pinnately compound leaf.

radical. The primary root that develops from a germinating seed.

ray flower. A modified (and often sterile) outer flower, typical of an Asteraceae inflorescence, in which the corolla has been fused into one strap-like super-petal.

reflexed. Bent backward (more extreme than recurved).

rhizome. An underground stem, typically prostrate and producing roots below and shoots or leaves above.

rosette. A flattened, circular cluster of leaves, usually arising directly from the crown.

running. Spreading quickly to form a colony by means of long rhizomes, stolons, or stems sprouting directly from the roots.

scandent. Climbing, vining.

scape. A leafless flower stem growing directly from the crown.

scree. Soil substrate composed of various sizes of rock and grit with very little fine material or organic matter. Found in rock-fall areas. For use in the garden, scree soils can be blended, using one part topsoil, two parts leaf compost, and eight parts grit and pea gravel.

sepal. One of a set of modified outer floral leaves, typically green, but often, as in many lilies, the same color as the petals and nearly indistinguishable from them.

seral. Pertaining to a sere, or series of ecological stages (succession). For example, a short-lived (early-seral) species appears early in the ecological succession and gives way to longer-lived (late-seral) species.

serotinous. Pertaining to a seed cone or capsule that remains unopened on the plant for a long time, usually years but occasionally decades. In some fire-adapted pines, the cones are covered in a thick resin that must be heated or burned off, allowing the cone to spring open and release the seed.

serpentine. A type of mineral (rock) containing high levels of magnesium and heavy metals, especially nickel, which make soils derived from it toxic to most plants. Specialized, serpentine-tolerant plant communities often develop on this mineral.

serrate. Sharply toothed along the margin.

sessile. Lacking a peduncle or petiole, attached directly to the base without a stalk.

shrub. A woody plant smaller than a tree (in this book, less than 15 feet tall), usually with several stems originating from a single base or spreading stem.

sinus. A cleft between two lobes of a leaf.

softwood. In the context of this book, plant stem tissue that has not fully matured or hardened. Also, coniferous trees.

stamen. The male portion of a flower, consisting of the anther and filament (stalk).

stigma. The section of the pistil (typically the tip) that is receptive to pollen.

stratification. Originally, placing seed between layers of earth (sowing). In popular usage, cold stratification means sowing seeds and chilling them at temperatures below 45°F for the length of time necessary to overcome dormancy. Warm stratification means sowing and placing seeds in a warm location (70–80°F) for a period of time to overcome dormancy or allow after-ripening.

stolon. A long, creeping, aboveground stem. Also a slender rhizome that grows near the surface.

stoloniferous. Producing stolons.

stomata. Small pores in the epidermis of a leaf that allow gas exchange between the leaf interior and the outside environment. In most species the size of the opening is controlled by special guard cells that dilate or constrict as necessary. This is an important function, as water is lost through evaporation when the stomata are open. Some conifers organize the pores into stomatal bands, which are visible because they are lighter in color than the surrounding leaf tissue.

style. The stalk that connects the stigma to the ovary.

subalpine. Growing in the zone just below the tree line in the mountains.

subtended. Set below.

symbiosis. The relationship between two organisms that form a close and mutually beneficial association.

sympatric. Occupying the same place; growing together.

sympodial. Growing in a series, as in a rhizome or branch in which each segment arises from the previous one, like feet set heel to toe, heel to toe.

tepals. A set of sepals and petals that are indistinguishable from each other.

tetraploid. Having four sets of chromosomes per cell; a plant with four sets of chromosomes.

tree. A large woody plant (in this book more than 15 feet tall), typically with one stem or trunk originating from the roots.

tomentose. Covered in dense, woolly hair.

tuber. A thickened rhizome used for food storage. Tubers can also form on roots (tuberous roots).

vernalize. To chill a plant or seed for the period of time necessary for it to overcome dormancy and begin to grow.

vine. Any plant with a stem too weak to support itself and thus relying on other plants or structures for support.

whorled. Having three or more flowers or leaves attached to each node.

woody plant. Plant with at least some perennial stems composed of a hard, fibrous blend of cellulose and lignin.

xeric. Dry.

xeriscaping. Landscaping with drought-tolerant plants for water conservation.

INDEX

Numbers in *italics* refer to pages on which photographs appear.